THE
KINGDOM
OF
CANADA

W. L. MORTON

THE KINGDOM OF CANADA

A GENERAL HISTORY FROM EARLIEST TIMES

McClelland and Stewart

DESIGN: FRANK NEWFELD

The Canadian Publishers

McClelland and Stewart Limited

25 Hollinger Road, Toronto

Corrections and minor revisions have been made throughout, and particularly in the latter part of Chapter 19. The bibliography and some of the reading lists have been expanded.

An additional chapter brings the narration down to the general election of 1968. No claim is made that the account here given of events and personalities from 1960 to 1968 is historical. It is a summary of the best published accounts of and comments on those years, as shaped by the writer's reflections on a period he has himself observed.

I owe thanks to Jan Kupp, Fernand Ouellet, and Lovell Clark for the substance of some of the revisions in the text; to Peter Newman for his *Renegade in Power* and his columns, to John Saywell for his invaluable volumes of the *Canadian Annual Review*, 1960 to 1966, to Ramsay Cook and Richard Jones for their writings on French Canada; to the public men and publicists of Canada for the lively debate of the years of frustration. For what I have made of it all, in statement and opinion, I myself am responsible.

W.L.M.

Trent University,
July 1968.

This book attempts to explain the existence and nature of present-day Canada in terms that take account of all the factors of its development, the French as well as the English, the British as well as the American, and to infuse the economic and political story with a strain of the social and intellectual.

It presents the record of experiences common to Canadians of whatever origin, and of whatever part of the country, as they strove to build their settlements and colonies and eventually their nationhood on the economy of northern lands. Out of those common experiences came the unity of Canada, a unity made political by the action of French and English in the Confederation of 1867. Each nationality chose union as the best means to preserve its own character, the English accepting the cultural duality of Canada, the French entering a partnership which ended the subordination imposed by the conquest of 1760. From that compact came the country of today, still seeking to be united and independent, at once a member of the Commonwealth and a good neighbour in America.

I offer lively thanks to colleagues who read and criticized certain portions of the book: W. J. Eccles; Guy Frégault; Hilda Neatby; Marcel Trudel; T. S. Webster. It is a pleasure to acknowledge the good fortune that made the services of C. C. J. Bond available for the preparation of maps that enhance the text. My obligation to Miss Dorothy Newman for typing the manuscript is past reckoning, as is that to the editorial staff of McClelland and Stewart Limited. I am also once again indebted to my own university for financial and other aid in the preparation of this book and related studies. All this help so generously given of course leaves me solely responsible for the form and content of what follows.

W. L. MORTON

University of Manitoba,
January 1963.

CONTENTS

MAPS

FOR D. R.

Normandy
1944

BOOK ONE

THE COLONIAL
PERIOD

THE NORTHERN ROUTE
AND MARITIME FRONTIER
[860-1536]

On a map of the northern hemisphere, centred on the Pole, America runs like a peninsula southward from Asia. The great bulk of the continent may also be seen as the last of the straggle of islands that lies across the North Atlantic. It was by the ice and water of the narrow Bering Strait that the prehistoric peoples of America, the Indians and the Eskimoes, crossed from Asia. The people of historic times first came from Europe island by island across the broad Atlantic.

The first to come from Europe were Norse voyagers who had followed the islands across the sea, seeking new fisheries, new farmsteads, new hunting grounds. They were pushing forward a maritime frontier, the westward fringe of that Viking empire which eastward ran along the rivers of Russia to the Black Sea. They were helped in their westward ventures by the fitful easterly winds which in spring and early summer play along the northern edge of the prevailing westerlies in the North Atlantic. It was this chance to voyage westward which enabled the Norse frontier of fish, fur, and farm to extend from Norway to Greenland by the tenth century and opened a northern sea route to America.

In consequence, the history of the Canadian lands and their peoples begins, not with the assured voyage of Columbus in 1492 by the southern route of the trade winds, but with the doubtful Norse ventures of the tenth century. It begins in the spread of the maritime frontier of the Norse people across the North Atlantic.

The connection so formed, though always slight, was never broken. When the Scandinavian empire was shaken in the fourteenth century by the rise of the Hanseatic League of North Germany, the seamen of Bristol began to move into its North Atlantic reaches by way of the Icelandic fisheries. They too began to quest westward, in 1480; it is probable that John Cabot, the Italian navigator, and King Henry VII came late to the aid of a venture of some years' trial. The commercial friends of the Bristol men, the Azoreans, shared the quest, and it was watched by their rivals of Normandy and Brittany. English and French fishermen and merchants renewed in the early sixteenth century the northern route of the Norse and carried forward in North America the old maritime frontier of fish, fur, and farm from which Canada was to spring.

CHAPTER 1

The Northern Voyages and Settlements

860-1536

The first touch between Europe and Canada was that of the Viking voyagers of the tenth century. Those Norse voyagers are best known as pirates and raiders, looters of monasteries and spoilers of towns. As such indeed they appeared around the coasts and along the rivers of western Europe in the eighth and ninth centuries. No one could guard effectively against the sudden descent of the dragon ships and the swift attack of the horsed raiders.

The Norse Vikings, however, were a highly civilized and versatile people, not merely the barbarous pirates and warriors they seemed. The raiders were followed by shrewd and honest traders who with their swift ships built a commercial empire ranging eastward from the Baltic to the Black Sea, and from the Baltic westward to the Hebrides. After the warriors in the Viking ships came the fishermen of the Norwegian coastal waters who followed the herring across the North Sea; and after the fishermen, settlers with their families seeking new homesteads. And the seamen-warriors who took their trim, light ships through the English Channel to Biscay and the Straits of Gibraltar were kinsmen of the first oceanic voyagers of the Western World.

They became the first of seamen because their ships were fit, superbly fit, for sailing the summer seas. (The storms of winter no ship was able to endure until much later.) The Viking long-ship, a war vessel primarily, was built with a light and supple strength which made it swift and seaworthy. When its single mast was stepped and the square sail raised it would run before a fair wind at six to seven knots. The merchant ship, the *kaupskip*, was a *hafskip* or ocean-going vessel, shorter and broader and with a higher freeboard than the long-ship. But it shared the same shapely mould and clinker build. The type which later plied to Iceland and Greenland was the *knörr*, a sturdy vessel partly decked in stem and stern. It could bear a considerable cargo amidships. When it carried a colony out, the livestock was shipped in the waist and the men and their families occupied tents raised on the decks in bow and stern. The masters of these craft steered by the stars, by sight of land and flight of birds, and above all, by some

directional sense as wonderful as that of the plains Indian of the America the
Viking prows were to raise. The results of all these skills were reduced to sailing
directions which can be read in the sagas to this day.

As raiders, traders, colonizers, the Norsemen in their slim, swift ships not
only conquered the Danelaw in England and Normandy in France. They also
opened a transmarine route to the Orkney Islands, colonized them and passed
on to Scotland, the Western Isles, and Ireland. Following Irish hermits beyond
the Orkneys, they discovered the Faroes. And then about 860, again preceded
by Irish hermits, they discovered the land they called Iceland. The Norse
frontier was bounding over the seas to embrace the westward islands.

Discovery was followed in all cases by settlement, as the conquest of settled
countries had been. For the great outburst of Norse energy in the ninth and
tenth centuries was caused by over-population at home as well as by the quest
for trade abroad. In Sweden and Denmark the best lands had been accumulated
in few hands. The poor freeman had to clear forest and drain swamp, or seek
land afar. In mountainous Norway, land was even more scarce.

There indeed a way of life prevailed that was perfectly adapted for transmission
to the islands that fringed the Arctic Ocean. The Norseman won his living by
extensive use of scant resources. He hunted, and this brought him into touch
with the Lapps and Finns of the interior and the north, and added a non-Nordic
strain to Norse blood, as was to happen in Greenland. He fished, and became a
seaman. He farmed the narrow lands on the shelves of the fjords and mountain
valleys. He ran his stock on the hillsides and on mountain pastures, wintering
them on hay won in the valleys during the brief northern summer. As farmer and
herdsman he became an explorer, watching for new valleys and pastures. Norway
was, in short, an arctic frontier, a frontier of fish, fur, and farm, all combined in
one precarious economy.

The narrow farm, however, was the base for this many-sided economy, and
the limits of arable land were soon reached along the fjords of Norway. As a
result, the discoveries of the western islands were soon followed by the movement
of settlers. The process is described and recorded in the great *Landnáma* saga of
Iceland, the history of the 'land-taking.'

The migration to Iceland began about the year 874. It went forward swiftly
and by 900 most of the island's coast was occupied. The best lands were taken
up, the flocks of sheep were grazing among the hills, the fishing-boats were
riding in the harbours. In the houses of stone and turf the Norse women, reserved
as goddesses and oftentimes as authoritative, spun and wove and baked in a
resolute housewifery that matched the toil of the husbandman on sea and meadow.
Already the fierce independence of the Norse had produced its local patriotism;
the sense of freedom, and the respect for law freely assented to, made Iceland
a republic and produced its *Althing*, or assembly of the people. And this way
of life, with the folk culture of tale and ballad which was its sentiment and spirit,

was sustained by a regular commerce with the old and new lands of the oceanic realm of the Vikings.

The impulse which had sent them overseas was not yet spent. Bold and restless men might yet move after the fashion of the Norse maritime frontier to lands still farther on. In 981, Eric the Red, an unbending man and perhaps a quarrelsome one, whose family had come to Iceland because of manslaughter, left its shores because of trouble with his neighbours to search out land reported to the westward. (On a clear day, indeed, mountains could be seen from the mountains of western Iceland.) He found the land and named it Greenland, on the principle that a good name would attract settlers.

Eric thus proved himself a worthy predecessor of that line of real-estate promoters who were to settle North America. In 985 he led back a fleet of twenty-five ships to the west shore of the vast, ice-covered island. Of these only fourteen reached the colony, with perhaps three hundred and fifty persons, their household goods and livestock on board. In settlements soon to be called Eastern and Western Settlements, at the heads and along the sides of the fjords which angled far inland, they built their farmsteads and set their stock to run. And soon the young men were going down the inlets of the fjords to fish and to collect the driftwood which was Greenland's sole source of timber. Before many years, it may be presumed, they went to the "north parts" to hunt the seal and the walrus, as their kinsfolk did in northern Norway. There at some time they were to meet the *Skraelings*, a primitive and dwarfish folk who lived much as did the Eskimoes of historic times, and who were presumably Eskimoes.

Before the Greenlanders were long in their new homes, however, the impetus of Norse expansion, if the sagas are to be believed, was to carry their ships farther yet on the northern route to the west. Again it was the restless following of Red Eric that was to furnish the leaders. First, one Bjarni Herjúlfsson missed Greenland on a voyage from Iceland, and three times sighted unknown land to the west before he put back and reached Greenland. He had discovered America, but no one sought out the new lands he had sighted. Then Eric's son, Leif, was in the Western Isles and Norway in 999. On his voyage home he sailed direct from Norway, passing below Iceland. He missed the sighting of Hvarf, the present Cape Farewell, which would have warned him to bear north-west, and failed to make the change of course. In consequence he drove on towards the unknown coast of America. It was probably the rugged coast and towering cliffs of Labrador that made him sure he was off course and sent him back north-eastward to the Greenland colonies.

There Leif, the saga tells us, himself settled down. But there was much talk of the land Herjúlfsson and Ericsson had sighted to the westward, and some two or three years after Leif's return it was decided to explore and perhaps to settle the unknown land. Under Thorfinn Karlsefni a party of a hundred and

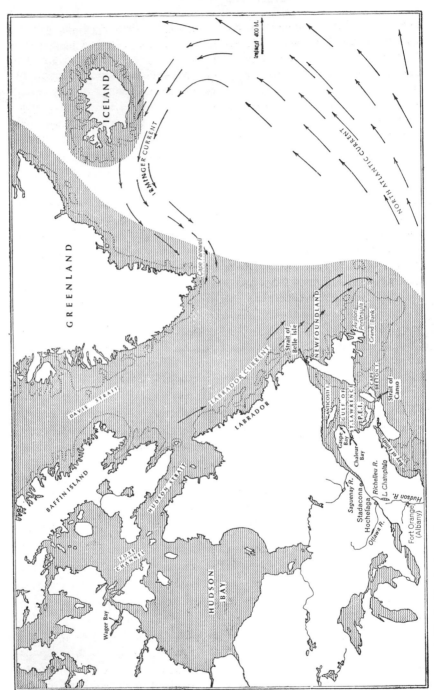

ICELAND

IRMINGER CURRENT

NORTH ATLANTIC CURRENT

GREENLAND

Cape Farewell

DAVIS STRAIT

LABRADOR CURRENT

Strait of Belle Isle

NEWFOUNDLAND

Avalon Peninsula

Grand Bank

BAFFIN ISLAND

HUDSON STRAIT

LABRADOR

ANTICOSTI

GULF OF ST. LAWRENCE

Gaspé

Chaleur Bay

P.E.I.

CAPE BRETON

Strait of Canso

FOXE CHANNEL

Saguenay R.

Stadacona

Hochelaga

Ottawa R.

Richelieu R.

L. Champlain

Hudson R.

Fort Orange (Albany)

Wager Bay

HUDSON BAY

Ireland 400 M.

I *The North Atlantic Approaches*

sixty in three ships sailed north-west and then south, to what they named Helluland, the land of flat stones. This was probably southern Baffin Island. Sailing southward still they came to what was, in their eyes at least, a wooded coast. This they called Markland (land of woods); it was probably some forested part of the Labrador coast. They now followed the coast south for many days until they reached a country they called Vinland (a fabulous name signifying abundance). Its location is uncertain, but it seems probable that it was farther south than Newfoundland, in Nova Scotia or even in New England.

Wherever its location, the settlement failed to take root. From the sagas it is evident that attacks by the natives – called Skraelings, here as in Greenland – were the cause of the withdrawal of Karlsefni's colonists. To settle the verge of a peopled continent was a greatly different task from that of taking up the vacant lands of Iceland or the empty fjords of Greenland. And there were too few of the warriors, whose ancestors had broken the English kingdoms of Northumbria and Mercia and wrested the lower Seine from France, to make head with battle-axe and spear against the arrows and darts, the ambushes and the onslaughts of the natives. Three years after setting out, the surviving colonists were back in Greenland, and with them was the boy Snorri, the first child born of European parents in America.

The Norse voyagers and colonizers had thrown a wide-meshed net of empire across the North Atlantic. But this maritime frontier of fisher-farmer folk had neither the weight nor the numbers to bridge the ocean and grasp a continent. No proof exists of further attempts at exploration or colonization in Markland or Vinland. The forests of the American coast, however, were visited by Greenland ships for cargoes of timber to use at home or to sell in Iceland. Thus for three centuries the commerce of the Norse sea-realm extended to the coasts of America, and America contributed somewhat to the flow of trade that held this widespread community together.

The Icelanders and Greenlanders received from Europe metals, manufactured goods, and cereals, the last in Greenland at least. In return they sent walrus hides, arctic ivory (walrus tusks and narwhal horns), the down of the eider duck, the white falcon of Greenland, highly prized by royal and noble hawkers of Europe, and the occasional polar bear, for diplomatic gifts of state and for royal display. The Arctic, like the tropics, had its exotic commodities.

This North Atlantic trade flourished until the beginning of the fourteenth century. Then a decline began. It was to be aggravated by the Black Death of the mid century. In the main, however, it is to be ascribed to the rise and competition of the great trading towns of the German Hanseatic League, and to the imposition by the kings of Denmark of a royal monopoly on the traffic. (The second may well have been a response to the first.) Greenland then, its position in some ways comparable to that of the Red River colony later, became dependent for its better cloth and tools, and even for grain, on the annual ships of the Danish monopoly. In time the ships ceased to be annual and sailed ever more uncertainly at ever greater intervals. The last licensed ship seems to have sailed from Greenland in 1410, but that is not to say that unlicensed ones did not reach it throughout the rest of the century. It seems most likely, for example, that English ships did, for there are records of raids. But regular and legitimate contacts dwindled until even the bishops of Gardar in Greenland, duly appointed though they were until the Reformation, ceased to travel to their distant see. The ties, commercial, ecclesiastical and social, were frayed away one by one. The Greenlanders were left to come to terms with the harsh environment of their island. They seem to have slowly abandoned their ancestral culture and Christian faith to mingle with the Skraelings, from which union the modern Greenland Eskimoes descend.

This loss of the remotest colony of the Norse Atlantic realm did not mean, however, that the northern route to America which the Norsemen had established was lost from the knowledge and minds of European men. The sagas preserved the history of the discovery of Markland and Vinland, while the sailing directions of the Norse mariners were also preserved in the sagas and, no doubt, in the oral maritime tradition of the north. Danish seamen, moreover, voyaged once at least to Greenland between 1471 and 1480. The King of Portugal, pursuing the Portuguese exploration of the Atlantic, approached the King of Denmark, and the two organized the expedition. Two Norwegian skippers, Pining and Pothurst, commanded a mixed Danish and Azorean force, the Azoreans under one João Corte-Real. The details and the purpose of this voyage are obscure, and our knowledge of it is largely conjectural. How far they sailed is not known; certainly to the east coast of Greenland and perhaps even to Labrador and Newfoundland, or Land of the Baccalos (Codfish), where the Corte-Reals of the next generation were to explore. But the expedition is not to be regarded only as the last use of the northern route by Scandinavian seamen. It was rather the first use of the old Norse sea-route by seamen who sought, like their Norse predecessors, new fisheries and new sources of trade. Among these the merchants and seamen of the fifteenth century in the Iceland fisheries were foremost and chief. And on their prosaic tacking along the old route a Venetian navigator and adventurer – John Cabot, as the English called him – was to impose his theory of the practicability of a voyage in northern latitudes to the coasts of Asia and the spiceries of the Far East. Columbus had, it is thought, visited Iceland but decided against the use of the northern route.

Between the voyage of Pining and Pothurst and those which inaugurated the age of world oceanic discovery there was, in the words of Vilhjalmur Stefansson, "no gap." And with the Scandinavian seamen the next explorers of the North Atlantic had ancient and intimate connections. These were the seamen and merchants of Bristol.

Between the voyages of exploration of the Bristol men and the last Greenland voyages there was also no gap. During the fifteenth century Bristol fishermen had developed the English Icelandic fishery, the source of "stock fish." Traders from Bristol, and also from east-coast towns like Bishop's Lynn, voyaged to Iceland and probably to Greenland. Bristol seamen raided Icelandic settlements and carried off the people. In short, the English were taking over the commercial empire of Scandinavia in the North Atlantic as the Hanse towns of Germany had done in the North Sea.

Of this development little is known except that it happened. Nor is it known why a merchant trading with both Portugal and Iceland, one John Jay of Bristol, should have sent a ship westward in 1480 under an expert ship-master, John Lloyd, "to traverse the seas" in search of the long-fabled island of Brazil. Lloyd found no island, but it is almost certain that his voyage was the first of a number by which the North Atlantic was combed between 1480 and 1490 for islands to westward.

Among the promoters of voyages were two other Bristol merchants, Robert Thorne and Hugh Eliot. It may be that one of their expeditions found some unknown land to the westward, for there is an authoritative notation to the effect that Thorne and Eliot discovered Newfoundland "Circa an. 1494." It is even argued that their navigator from 1491 was John Cabot and that a landfall was made by him on Cape Breton Island in 1494. Again, what is known permits of no certainty beyond this, that the Bristol men, working on the basis of their own experience in trading with Iceland (and perhaps Greenland also) and with the Azores, were seeking before 1491 to add to the number of islands and coasts their ships might visit. There is no evidence that they were seeking to do more than extend that part of the old Norse empire to which they had fallen heir.

Upon this plodding and practical development of the old Norse maritime frontier the Italian navigators, Columbus and John Cabot, imposed their concept of a direct voyage to Asia across the Atlantic Ocean. Columbus had already discovered and colonized the islands he called the Indies in 1492, when John Cabot was still sailing from Bristol to find the land of the Great Khan written of by Marco Polo. Whatever earlier voyages Cabot may have made, in a quick deft voyage of reconnaissance in 1497 he crossed to "the New Found Land" and coasted it far enough to establish the south-westward trend of the shore, probably along Nova Scotia and New England. He was convinced that he had reached the lands of the Great Khan; that is, the continent of Asia.

Cabot was now hailed as a great discoverer and rewarded by Henry VII, not with the famous £10 alone. He was authorized by the grant of a charter, the first in English imperial history, to lead an expedition to occupy the new lands, to annex them, and to govern them for the Crown of England. In this, however, he must have been acting for the hard-headed Bristol traders who had for years, after all, put up the money to discover the new lands and now saw some hope of returns commensurate with their risks and losses. The extent of their hopes is indicated by the dispatch in 1498 of an expedition of six ships, of which one had to put back to Ireland under stress of weather. The remainder sailed by way of Iceland, around Greenland, and up to 63 degrees north latitude. They apparently traded in Labrador and then stood down the coast, perhaps as far south as Chesapeake Bay. Though there is no positive evidence, it is believed that some at least of the ships returned. But John Cabot is heard of no more, and the belief that the new-found lands were part of Asia was no longer taken for granted. Cabot had failed to outreach Columbus, and like Columbus had been baffled by a continent undreamt of in his cosmography.

Despite Cabot's failure, the Bristol traders were to persist in their attempts to find new lands to trade in, and they were now joined by their old friends, the Portuguese. It may be that with Cabot in 1498 there had sailed one João Fernandez, the Labrador (roughly translated, farmer or squire) of the Azores who gave his name first to Greenland, then to Labrador. Reports of Cabot's second voyage, perhaps made by Fernandez himself, led the King of Portugal to commission Fernandez in 1499 to seek new islands within the Portuguese sphere as established by the Demarcation Line of 1494. Of any islands he might discover, Fernandez was to be governor.

There is no record that the Labrador made another voyage under the Portuguese flag. In 1500, however, the King gave a commission to explore to Gaspar Corte-Real, son of the João Corte-Real of the voyage of 1472. Gaspar sailed from Lisbon to Greenland, rounded Cape Farewell to the west coast, and then returned. It would seem that he was searching for a sea route to Asia. In 1501 he sailed again to Greenland, crossed Davis Strait, and sailed down the coast of Labrador to Newfoundland. From there he sent two ships home, only to vanish without trace in the third while following the coast farther south. His brother Miguel in the following year sailed to Newfoundland, but also perished in unknown waters. Another Portuguese expedition followed in 1503, and with it the Portuguese ceased to search for a north-west passage to Asia. From the date of these voyages, however, Portuguese fishing vessels sailed to the Newfoundland Banks and Portuguese governors claimed authority over Newfoundland, a shadowy sovereignty almost forgotten in Canadian history.

Meantime, the men of Bristol had recovered from the disappointment of Cabot's voyage of 1498, and if João Fernandez did not sail under his Portuguese commission he remained convinced that something was to be made of the lands encountered in the north-west Atlantic. In 1501 he, with two other Azoreans, joined with three Bristol merchants to obtain a patent from Henry VII empowering them to discover, annex and govern lands theretofore "and at present unknown to all Christians." Two voyages followed, in 1501 and 1502. Some success is indicated by the issue of a new patent in 1502 to "the Company of Adventurers to the New Found Lands." There is evidence that the Company sent out expeditions annually from 1503 to 1505, but what was sought, what trade was found, is unknown. It is possible that the Bristol men still sought a seaway to Asia; it is certain that the English Newfoundland fishing, like the Portuguese, dates from this time and these voyages.

It is also possible that John Cabot was concerned with these voyages until 1505. It is a matter of record that his son Sebastian was resident and employed in Bristol in that year, for he was then given an annuity of £10 by Henry VII. Four years later, in 1509, Sebastian sailed with two ships on a voyage of discovery to the north-west, the known details of which are obscure and confused. Probably the simplest, as it is the boldest, interpretation of the evidence is the best. It is certainly the most attractive. This view holds that Cabot coasted along Labrador, entered Hudson Strait, and passed into Foxe Channel and Basin up to latitude 67° 30′ N. The unconfined waters he saw to the west he believed to be the sea which led to Asia. His crews, however, had had enough of ice and rock-bound coasts, and Cabot was compelled to turn back, with a secret belief he kept to himself for most of a long life of mystery and intrigue. His disappointment was less bitter, his fate kinder, than that of Hudson who was to perish in the ice at the bottom of the bay a century later.

The great voyage of Sebastian Cabot, if such indeed was its climax, was the last recorded effort of Bristol to become the English emporium of the North Atlantic and Asiatic trade. Only the Newfoundland fishing remained, and Bristol and the other west-country ports from Dorset to Cornwall were to resort more and more to the shores of the new-found land.

There they and the Portuguese were speedily joined by French fishermen – Normans, Picards, and Bretons. There was too much cross-channel traffic for the new fishery to be kept a secret. Indeed, the searcher of the records of the west ports of France, as of England, is often left wondering if in fact the fishery had not been known to fishermen for years before the explorers and the merchants came probing the waters off Newfoundland. However that may be, the French fishermen easily and naturally took the northern route to the Grand Banks. It is only another illustration of the fact that the maritime development of northern Europe was a single process, and one in which the French ports were not at all backward. The French as well as the English were grasping at the spoils of the sea empires of the Norse and the Hansa, and it was only fitting that Normans and Bretons should follow the northern seaway first traced by Celtic monks and Norse seamen.

Certain it is that the fishermen of northern France were on the banks of Newfoundland in the first years of the sixteenth century, perhaps as early as the Portuguese and perhaps earlier than the English. It is said that Breton fishermen first fished there in 1504, Normans almost as soon. Basque fishermen of both France and Spain were perhaps as early as they. Apart from the visits of fishermen, the first French voyages to compare with those of the Cabots and the Corte-Reals were made by Jean Denys of Honfleur and Thomas Aubert of

Dieppe to Newfoundland in 1506 and 1508 respectively. Denys explored the north-east coast of the island to the Strait of Belle Isle. Aubert's voyage seems to have been one of some magnitude. Besides exploring the east coast thoroughly down to Cape Race, he took seven Indians (Beothuks) back to France. A vivid description of them dates from 1512. It may well be that some of the laudation that has been spent on others as the discoverers of Canada should be accorded to this little-known Dieppois whose voyage did so much to bring the dim shores and strange people of the new-found land into focus.

The main outcome of the French ventures in the North Atlantic, however, was that they won for French fishermen a share in the international fishery of the Newfoundland Banks. That great addition to Europe's supply of fish was needed for the hundred and forty-three days of fast and abstinence of the Church's calendar. By 1510, Newfoundland fish was being sold in the fish market of Rouen; by 1514, tithes in Brittany were being paid in part by the produce of the overseas fishery. Sea route to Asia or not, precious metals or not, Europe had found on the Newfoundland Banks a vast new supply of a staple food. Between the old continent and the new, the northern sailing route followed by the fishing-boats in April-May of each returning year formed a tie which has lasted from that time to this.

The international fishery was not only the earliest link between Canada and Europe. Its development was to be the prime mover in the establishment of still other ties. These were the fur trade and colonization. Had the fishermen remained fishermen only, this would not have happened. But from early times the fishery developed in two modes, that of the wet fishery and that of the dry. The former was carried on from ships on the Banks, where the fish were taken, cleaned and heavily salted on board. In this "wet" or ship or banks fishery, there was little resort to the shores of Newfoundland. In the dry fishing, the fish were dried on platforms called flakes before being lightly salted and shipped, and this of course required landing, and a brief season's residence on shore. Out of these contacts with the shore the fur trade took its early, casual beginnings. The natives, still living in the Stone Age, hungered for the metals and the textiles of the Europeans, and the latter sought the bargains the eager savages proffered in furs for which there was good demand in Europe.

The French showed in time a preference for the wet fishery, because they had an abundance of cheap and excellent salt from the Bay of Biscay. So also did the Portuguese. The English, coming from a climate which forbade the solar extraction of salt, inclined to the dry fishery, which was sparing in the use of that article. Their lightly salted fish was to sell at a premium when the Protestant Reformation, by diminishing the demand for fish in northern Europe, made the markets of the Mediterranean more competitive.

There are indications that the fishermen explored the intricate coastline of Newfoundland in search of good beaches, new banks, and fresh sources of bait.

There can be little doubt that they knew the Strait of Belle Isle, the west coast of the island, and the gulf beyond. But of formal exploration there was little for some years after the voyages of Aubert in 1508 and Sebastian Cabot in 1509. Little is known of the expedition of the Englishman, John Hare, in 1512; it seems to have been a light-hearted adventure that ended in starvation for most of the party on the Newfoundland coast. It was the Portuguese who resumed the quest for further knowledge of the Atlantic shoreline. In 1521 the explorer João Alvares Fagundes was made governor of the Portuguese Demarcation lands south of those already awarded the Corte-Reals. He had traced in 1520 the west coast of Cape Breton Island through the Strait of Canso, and crossed to and followed eastward the south coast of Newfoundland. On a later voyage he explored the Bay of Fundy and named it Deep River (Rio Fundo). Between 1521 and 1525 he even founded a colony, or fishing station, on Cape Breton, probably in Spanish Bay.

Fagundes was exploring the lands given him to govern. But if he and the fishermen were content with what they found in the north-west Atlantic, the kings and scholars of Europe were not. It was not yet clear what the new-found lands in the north-west were; whether, as was supposed by some, a great archipelago, or, as by others, a projection of Tartary. The return of Magellan's *Victoria* in 1522 from the circumnavigation of the globe raised the question anew. Francis I of France, in collaboration with merchants of Dieppe and Italian bankers of Rouen, chose an Italian navigator, Giovanni Verrazano, to explore the uncertainly mapped coast between Florida and Newfoundland in search of an opening.

Driven back on the northern route, as it would seem, in 1523, Verrazano sailed again early in 1524 by a southern course to the vicinity of Cape Fear in North Carolina. With him there perhaps went a sailor of St. Malo who had been on the Grand Banks before, one Jacques Cartier. Verrazano coasted first south, then north until he had passed Nova Scotia, Cape Breton, and Newfoundland to the Strait of Belle Isle. From there he returned without having discovered a strait leading to Asia. He did, however, link the coastline traced by the Spaniards in the south with that traced by the Portuguese and the English in the north. Moreover, Verrazano recognized definitely, as perhaps Sebastian Cabot had done, that North America was not an archipelago but a continent. As he said boldly, it was a new world which Aristotle had not known. And he had laid the geographic foundation for the voyages of Jacques Cartier, voyages Verrazano himself might have made had he not been lost on a third and private voyage in 1527.

Beside these voyages, the expeditions of Estevan Gomez, a Portuguese in Spanish service, and of John Rut, an Englishman, in 1525 and 1527 respectively, are of little significance. Both were in quest of the North-West Passage. The term North-West Passage, however, had now assumed the meaning it was henceforth to bear, of a way around or through the continent of North America. And the quest of that passage was to be the modern form of the maritime frontier of the Norse world. In Canada it was not to lead to tropic riches or temperate plenty; it was to perpetuate the fish, fur, and farm economy of the north.

It was Jacques Cartier who was to seek a passage from France through the continent Verrazano had defined. In this he was carrying on the work of the man who had perhaps been his master. Before the Breton captain could be commissioned to sail, however, the way had to be prepared. When the Portuguese and the Spaniards, following mediaeval usage, had claimed a monopoly of the routes their seamen had found to the Indies, their claims had become not only, as was intended, patents for a private way, but also, as it proved, title to two new continents. Other monarchs, particularly those of England and France, had been careful not to admit the full claims of the Iberian kingdoms. But the Spanish and Portuguese pretensions were substantial enough to lead to endless bickering and to cloud darkly any other claim. If France, therefore, were to have some share in this newly discovered heritage of Adam, it must be through some concession, if not from Spain, at least from the papacy which had sanctioned the claims of Spain and Portugal by the Bull of 1493. Francis I, who had always chafed at Spain's pretensions in the New World, in 1533 entrusted the task of winning a modification of the papal sanctions to Cardinal Le Veneur, a Norman prelate deeply interested in overseas discovery. The Cardinal succeeded in persuading Pope Clement VII to agree that the Papal Bull had sanctioned the Spanish title to lands discovered by Spaniards but not to those that others might yet discover beyond the Demarcation Line. Such an exegesis greatly modified the Spanish position. On this basis any good Catholic, not least the King of France, could proceed to appropriate lands in the New World, provided they were beyond the coasts traced by Gomez in 1525. To discover such lands, with a passage to Asia, was the task set Cartier, the successor to Verrazano.

Cartier was not only the continuer of Verrazano's work, he was the protégé of Cardinal Le Veneur. Now that the Cardinal had cleared the way for French enterprise among the dimly known shorelines of the new-found land, he put Cartier forward as the captain to lead an expedition. Cartier was not ill-equipped for his commission. He had followed the sea as seaman and master mariner since boyhood, and was about forty-three in 1534. Besides his possible voyage with Verrazano, he had sailed with the fishermen to Newfoundland and had perhaps voyaged to Portugal and even Brazil. Now he was ordered to make for the opening of Belle Isle Strait and enter to search for lands containing precious metals and for a passage-way to Asia. In this first voyage supported by the French Crown, Francis I was seeking to match in the north the riches of New Spain and its access to the South Sea.

The expedition, consisting of two ships, sailed on April 20, 1534, and was quickly in the Strait of Belle Isle, taking up where Verrazano had left off. After surveying Labrador – "the land that God gave Cain," he said, in wonder at its roughness – Cartier followed the west coast of Newfoundland. It is necessary to remember that, to him, it might have been the Pacific coast of a slender America and the quaint, particular narrative which records the voyage breathes all the excitement of this wonderful journey into waters with unknown shores. He apparently failed to detect Cabot Strait, and continued by the Magdalen Islands and Prince Edward Island to the south shore of the Gulf of St. Lawrence.

Here he met the land mass of the continent and the heat of midsummer. And as his ships pass into the Bay he called "des Chaleurs," the reader is conscious that the grey-black seas, the fog-bound headlands and faint blue shores of the North Atlantic coast have been left behind for the sun-bright streams and the light-drenched forests of the inland main. Cartier's journal is a seaman's idyll written after the passage of stormy seas.

From Chaleur Bay, Cartier passed on to Gaspé Bay. There he raised a thirty-foot cross and took possession of the land in the name of Francis I. Thus he consummated the diplomacy of his patron, Le Veneur. And by doing so he began New France. For France, first of the European nations, had pushed beyond the ancient maritime frontiers of the Vikings' northern route, the frontier of the fisheries and casual commerce, to claim title to the new land for the exploitation of its soil and for passage by its waters to Asia.

As he lay in the sweltering Chaleur Bay, Cartier had met Indians of Micmac-Algonkian stock and had friendly exchanges with them, but apparently learned nothing. Later on at Gaspé he met Iroquoian Indians from up the St. Lawrence. Two of these he persuaded to accompany him back to France, and it was by information gained from them that his second voyage was to be guided.

From the Bay, Cartier ran by Gaspé head, mistook the channel of the St. Lawrence River south of Anticosti Isle, and went on to the north shore of the Gulf. Then he perceived the westward opening of the great river to the north of Anticosti. The season, however, was late, his provisions were low, and Cartier sailed home by way of the Strait of Belle Isle.

During the winter he and his patrons learned from the two Indians news of a "kingdom of Saguenay" inland to the north-west, which was to be reached by ascending a great river. On this river were two countries, Canada and Hochelaga. The kingdom itself was the place where red copper came from, and it was rich in minerals of all kinds. (This was perhaps an account of copper taken from the deposits of free copper on the south shore of Lake Superior and brought to the Gulf in trade by way of the Saguenay River.) Here, at least, was some basis for the hopes which had inspired the first voyage. Francis I and Cardinal Le Veneur were pleased indeed to send Cartier with three ships in 1535 on the most famous voyage in Canadian history, to discover the Kingdom of Saguenay.

The second voyage was to lack, however, the brisk expeditiousness, if it was to exceed the accomplishment, of the first. The departure was late, the arrival off Anticosti later. And Cartier did not ascend the St. Lawrence at once, but sought for a passage – was it the mouth of the Saguenay? – along the north shore. August 10 he spent in a bay which he named for the feast of St. Laurent, a saint popular in Brittany; and the name was to extend to the gulf and the river. When at last he ascended the St. Lawrence he found no passage to the northwest, for he missed the Saguenay.

In his narrative there lingers something of the awe which that tremendous river inspired then and still inspires. Finally on September 14 the ships threaded their way by the Isle of Orleans and their leaders and crew saw before them the narrowing of the river beneath Cape Diamond. This was Quebec, the strait of the river of Canada. On the slope of the cape was the Iroquoian village of Stadacona, with whose startled and apprehensive chief, Donnacona, Cartier was soon in talk by means of his interpreters from Gaspé. Near the mouth of a small river, now the St. Charles, he decided to winter, but first he meant to seek the route to Saguenay. With his smallest ship, the *Emerillon*, Cartier ascended the river to Hochelaga, which he reached on October 2. All along the river the autumn woods flared and smouldered in smoky glory; the vines hung heavy by the waterside; the meadows were thick with grass and tinted by the late asters. Again, as at Chaleur, the seamen were overwhelmed by the warmth and richness of a continent outwardly so chill and so forbidding.

Hochelaga was only another Iroquoian village, its long-houses of bark enclosed in a stockade at the foot of the mount that Cartier named Mont Royal. From its summit he learned that the Kingdom of Saguenay, rich in copper, silver, and gold, lay beyond the nearby rapids he could not pass, and up a distant river, the later Ottawa, which also opposed three rapids between him and the mysterious kingdom.

He had to turn back to make ready for the winter, perhaps meaning to ascend the river beyond Hochelaga in the spring. But Canadian cold and winter scurvy, despite a native remedy which saved many of his crews, left his force decimated, and in 1536 he returned to a France once more at war, a France with no thought or energy to spare for the quest of the Kingdom of Saguenay. Nevertheless, Cartier had begun New France; not as a colony, it is true, but as a concept. Thereafter there was the land known as Canada, and to it France would maintain its claim. The northern route had at last led beyond the fogs of Newfoundland and the iron coast of Labrador to the warm and rich interior, the river and country of Canada.

ADDITIONAL READING

BRØGGER, A. W. *The Viking Ships: Their Ancestry and Evolution.*
JULIEN, C. A. *Les Voyages de découverte et les premiers établissements.*
LEWIS, A. R. *The Northern Seas: Shipping and Commerce in Northern Europe.*
STEFANSSON, V. "Introduction," *The Three Voyages of Martin Frobisher,* Vol. I.
WILLIAMS, MARY W. *Social Scandinavia in the Viking Age.*

THE COLONIZATION
OF NEW FRANCE
[1537-1701]

When Jacques Cartier returned to St. Malo in the spring of 1536, the era of maritime exploration in the north-west Atlantic was over. The east coast of a continent stood firm from Florida to Hudson Strait. Cartier had penetrated the gulf and river of St. Lawrence and under his royal commission had claimed their lands for France. The next step was to colonize those lands and create a New France overseas.

Many things impeded French colonization of the St. Lawrence, among them the struggle with the Hapsburgs in Europe and the religious conflict within France itself. But the chief obstacle was lack of money for colonization. The kings of France had none to spare from their building and their wars; and those making money in the New World, the fishermen and the fur traders, had no interest in settling the lands they visited only in the summers. They had, indeed, every reason to fear competition from colonists.

Another French interest that did not wholly lend itself to the work of colonization was the conversion of the natives to Christianity. The first French missions were at bottom opponents of both colonization and commerce. They feared the possible ill example of colonists, the possible corruption of the natives by commerce. From these fears came the imposition of religious uniformity on New France, and a tendency in the religious orders to divorce themselves from colonization and even from the inescapable fur trade.

Thus the needs of commerce, colonization, and conversion were at variance. When Henry IV had ended the religious wars, however, he attempted to bring the three to work together by imposing a monopoly on the fur trade and making colonization, and to a degree conversion, a charge on the profits of the commerce in furs. This policy, which underlay the development of New France from 1599 to 1661, explains the want of success in Champlain's heroic labours. It explains also the domination of colonization by the fur trade and the rise of a fur-trade bourgeoisie before 1661.

In that year two new elements entered the development of New France; royal authority, and royal finance. The King assumed the task hitherto laid on the fur trade, and exerted a control that was modified but not diminished by the grant of a

KC—B

commercial monopoly in New France to the French West India Company. The native genius of France now asserted itself in rational authority and centralized power, by which commerce, colonization, and conversion were brought into alignment. Under royal direction, New France received in the decade after 1663 its essential population, the stock from which the French-Canadian nation sprang.

The royal policy did not everywhere prevail. The fur-trade bourgeoisie *evaded the King's control by means of the* coureurs de bois *and created an inland commercial empire against his wishes and explicit orders after 1672. But when Louis XIV in 1701 accepted the Spanish Succession for his grandson, the outlaw empire of the fur trade suddenly became necessary to the House of Bourbon. New France had received colonists for the farm lands of the St. Lawrence but the fur trade of the up country had helped ensure that the overseas empire of France should rest not so much on colonization as on commerce and sea power.*

CHAPTER 2

The Origins of New France
1537-1632

Cartier had returned to find France once more at war with Spain and the Empire. Francis I for the moment had no thought for Canada or the Kingdom of Saguenay. By 1538 the struggle was ended and Cartier was able to put forward plans for a third voyage and a second attempt to reach the fabled riches of Saguenay. The Indian chief, Donnacona, a fluent and plausible romancer, whom he had brought back with him, succeeded in convincing Francis of the wealth of Saguenay, and Cartier was soon assured of support for his new attempt.

A change came over the King's plans, however, before the expedition was ready to sail. Francis I had decided to challenge the Spanish monopoly of the New World. Possession, not discovery alone, he had informed Spain and Portugal, gave title to new lands. Now he would possess what Cartier had discovered. The result of his decision was to make the expedition one to take possession of the two lands of Canada and Hochelaga and to found a French colony in them. Such an expedition required as head not a master mariner but a soldier and gentleman who could command and defend a colony. Accordingly the new expedition was placed under the direction of Jean François de la Rocque, Sieur de Roberval – a Protestant gentleman, a soldier, and a favourite of the King. His appointment indicated the changed character of the undertaking. It was no longer a voyage in quest of precious metals; it was a major expedition designed to achieve permanent occupation of Canada and put the French claim beyond question. The precious metals of Saguenay were not to be disregarded, but the quest for them was now part of the new and larger scheme.

It may be that the old and new plans were not fully integrated. At any rate, Cartier sailed alone in May 1541. He established his headquarters not on the St. Charles but at the Cap Rouge River, nine miles above Quebec. Here an establishment was built, protected by two forts, which was named Charlesbourg-Royal. When Roberval failed to overtake him, Cartier sent back two ships to report. While the forts and buildings were being erected Cartier went up once more to Hochelaga, viewed the Lachine rapids and was told that there was only one more rapid above, but that the Ottawa was not navigable as far as Saguenay. He was also told that the copper of the kingdom was to be obtained not by the Ottawa but by the Saguenay River. With this somewhat discouraging news he returned to Charlesbourg-Royal.

There a kind of mining fever had seized on his people even before he had left, and they had, they fancied, since found minerals enough to compensate for the elusive riches of Saguenay. Gold dust, iron ore, and diamonds had been discovered, and were put up in barrels for transport to France.

Roberval, for his part, had been delayed by his inability to raise enough money to sail. In consequence, he had resorted to piracy off the coasts of Brittany, a not unusual means of raising money in those days. When even his piracies did not yield him enough ready money, the complaints of his victims did at last move the King to meet the greater part of his expenses. Meantime Cartier's two ships had arrived and their favourable reports spurred on the expedition.

Roberval sailed in April 1542, only to meet Cartier at Newfoundland. Cartier had had a difficult winter and had abandoned the colony. He now evaded his chief and quietly continued on his way home, to sail to Canada no more. Roberval went on without him. He rebuilt Charlesbourg-Royal, and in the fall ascended to Hochelaga, without result. He kept his motley company of gentlemen, sailors, and convict colonists in good order during the winter, but scurvy ravaged them. In the following summer, Roberval once more ascended the St. Lawrence to Hochelaga and perhaps entered the Ottawa. But apparently he judged the journey up the river to be too dangerous and another winter unendurable. He could not in any case have stayed, for Francis I was on the verge of another war and sent to recall him. The colony returned to France to find that the gold dust sent back was not gold, and that "not worth a Canadian diamond" had become a byword. The first great speculation in Canada had failed.

France had also failed to plant the first colony of any kind that had been attempted in New France. The remote blue shorelines, the flashing waters of Newfoundland, the Gulf and the Saguenay were once more left to the fishermen and the fur traders.

From the end of Roberval's attempt at colonization to the end of the century, little is known, except by inference, of the connection between France and the lands claimed as New France. There can be no doubt that there were continuous and developing connections, but they were not the public and recorded connections of enterprises with royal backing or missionary purpose. They were private, commercial, and undocumented. They were, in short, the economic ties of the cod fishery and the fur trade, and it was in that development, particularly in the last two decades of the century, that the destiny of New France was determined for the following hundred years. By the expansion of the fur trade from the casual contacts of fishermen with Indians along-shore to regular trading voyages to the rendezvous at Tadoussac at the mouth of the Saguenay,

French traders committed themselves to New France. They committed themselves to the exploitation of the Canadian (or Laurentian) Shield, the ancient rock plateau which lay north of the St. Lawrence, and to a commercial – which meant also a military – alliance with the Indians who hunted over the Shield.

This alliance was the beginning of the "Laurentian coalition" of Algonkians, Hurons, and French that was to dominate the history of New France until 1701. The Algonkians extended over the Shield and south-eastward into the forest country of the Appalachian system of New England and Acadia. Between those of the Shield and those of Acadia a wedge had been driven down the St. Lawrence valley by Iroquoian Indians of a semi-agricultural way of life. It was these Iroquoian people whom Cartier had met as summer visitors at Gaspé and had found established at Quebec.

The French traders, however, in roving along-shore and in trading at assembly points such as the Strait of Canso, Roche Percée off Gaspé, and Tadoussac, dealt only with Algonkians – principally the Micmacs of Acadia, the Malecites of Gaspé, and the Montagnais, as the French called the nomads of the Shield north of the St. Lawrence. To these primitive people with their Stone Age culture they brought the marvels of metal tools and woven fabrics. The Indians at once exhibited a reckless lust to possess these utilitarian wonders. When they found that furs, a principal product of their hunting economy, would obtain the goods they desired, they began to hunt a surplus beyond their personal needs.

The results were far-reaching. The Indians began in many areas to press upon the numbers of fur-bearing animals. They attempted to extend their hunting grounds by travel or by war. Furs were also sought in barter, and to inter-tribal war was added inter-tribal trade. It soon reached far inland to the headwaters of the St. Maurice and the Ottawa. On the north the Montagnais and the tribe known as Algonkins, on the south the Micmacs and Malecites, superior in the strength of their iron hatchets and knives, began to press back the Iroquois from Gaspé and the banks of the St Lawrence valley. By the beginning of the seventeenth century the Algonkian tribes had cleared the land of Canada, and much of Hochelaga, of the agricultural tribes. They themselves then claimed but did not fully occupy these lands.

Yet already there had appeared that long-neglected aspect of the fur trade, its dependence on a minimum of agriculture. What the Algonkians desired was the cornfields of Stadacona and Hochelaga, to stabilize the seasonal uncertainty of the hunter's food supply. Inland this stability was won not by war but by trading furs for corn with the Indians of Iroquoian stock whom the French later nicknamed Huron (from *huré*, bristly) because of the boar-like hair left in a ridge down the centre line of their shaven heads. These people, long hostile to their relatives, the Iroquois of the Five Nations, had settled in the vicinity of Georgian Bay. It was their commerce with the neighbouring Algonkin bands that brought them into the Laurentian coalition – the first example of that union

II   *Fur Trade Routes and Portages of Eastern America*

of southern agricultural lands with the Shield which was to be the economic
basis of Canada.

In the 1580's, it would seem, these developments were greatly quickened by
the increased use of the fine wool of the beaver by Parisian hatters for felt-
making. Now the hunt became specialized. The "beaver frontier" formed and
then retreated; the trade spread rapidly inland; the Indians' catches mounted,
and the flow of European goods was quickened. Records remain of a voyage
of merchants from St. Malo up the St. Lawrence in 1581 in search of new trading
sites. In 1588 two nephews of Cartier, Etienne Chaton and Jacques Nouel,
sought and obtained a monopoly of the trade in fur and copper for twelve years,
with permission to take out sixty convicts a year to work the copper mines. (The
monopoly was reduced to one of copper only after a fierce outcry by the Estates
of Brittany.) The result of such developments as these was that the French fur

trade became committed on the north shore of the St. Lawrence to the exploitation of the Shield and the alliance with the Laurentian coalition in the
sixteenth century, not the seventeenth as is generally believed. It was then determined that New France would be primarily a northern colony, devoted to the
fur trade and the development of a northern economy. It was also determined,
twenty-odd years before Champlain ascended the St. Lawrence to war on the
Iroquois, that New France would continue the ancient war of the Algonkian
nomads with the semi-sedentary tribes of the great river, the Mohawks and their
confederates of the Five Nations of the Iroquois league.

In this period of quickened growth of the fur trade there began, it seems
correct to infer, two developments which characterized the trade with the
Indians for two centuries thereafter. One was the recognition by the European
traders of "captains" or chiefs among the bands. To these men special honour
was shown, in order that they might exert themselves to bring their countrymen
to trade with plenty of furs. This usage may have powerfully affected the modes
of Indian tribal custom. The second was the beginning of the practice of leaving
young men to winter among the Indians, to learn the language and become
interpreters and men of influence with the natives. These were the first of the
hivernants, the winterers, some of whom were to leave names famous in the
trade and exploration of America.

If the fur trade had committed France to the exploitation of the Canadian
Shield, the French fisheries were committing that country to the colonization
of Acadia also. The development of the international fishery, carried on by the
Portuguese, English, Spanish, and French on the Banks of Newfoundland, was
accompanied by the development of French fisheries within the Gulf of St.
Lawrence. But whereas the French fishery on the Banks was a "wet" or ship
fishery to a greater degree than that of the English, for example, the fisheries at
Cape Breton and Gaspé were dry fisheries. The whale fishery pursued by the
Basques along the north shore of the Gulf also led to frequent contacts with the
shore. Thus the shores of the Gulf were becoming French territory, as Cartier's
taking possession of the western shore had implied. Yet all the French activities
off Newfoundland and in the Gulf were private. There was not one officer bearing a commission from the King of France, not one fortress to assert or even to
symbolize the title of France to the New France of Verrazano and Cartier.

Meanwhile, the English fishermen were steadily extending their dry fishery
on the shores of Newfoundland. And by the third quarter of the century England
was once more reviving the oceanic tradition her seamen had begun under the
Cabots. It had re-emerged with Willoughby and Chancellor's voyage to the
White Sea in 1555 and John Hawkins's voyage to Guinea in 1562. Richard
Hakluyt and John Dee were about to begin that work of propaganda which was
both to inspire and immortalize the great Elizabethan voyages. In 1576, Martin
Frobisher made the first of three successive annual voyages in search of a passage

to Asia by the north-west. He became involved in a quest of precious minerals, and his discovery of the south-east coast of Baffin Island and of the entrance to Hudson Strait probably revealed little the Greenlanders had not seen over five centuries before.

The Frobisher expeditions, themselves so fruitless, were the prelude to a more ambitious effort. In 1583 a group of London and West of England adventurers sent Sir Humphrey Gilbert to colonize Newfoundland as a base from which the search for the North-West Passage might be prosecuted. Thus the old claim arising from the Cabotian voyage was imposed on the seasonal occupation of the shoreline by the dry fishermen. This assertion of the English claim was not disputed by Philip II of Spain, who in 1580 had added Portugal and its empire to his domains. No more is heard of the shadowy Portuguese title to Newfoundland. The English even contemplated a settlement within the Gulf of St. Lawrence. But Gilbert's colony in the Avalon Peninsula was no more lasting. He himself perished at sea in 1584 and the long Newfoundland coast was left to the flakes of the fishermen and the huts of the growing number of "residents," the inhabitants of a colony which was not a colony.

The revival of English enterprise in the north-west Atlantic, thus inaugurated, was continued by the Arctic voyages of John Davis in 1585-88, and was to yield great geographic results under Hudson and Baffin in the next century. What the enterprise of the English did at the time was to reveal how France, if her kings did not assert their title by that actual occupation which Francis I had urged against the claims of Spain and Portugal, would lose New France to more ambitious "claimants," however numerous French fishermen and traders might be.

This danger, signalized by Frobisher's voyages, had prompted the grant of the governorship of New France (as given to Roberval) to the Marquis de la Roche in 1578. Not until 1584 did the Marquis dispatch an expedition, and then only to suffer the loss of its largest vessel with one hundred colonists on the French coast. The religious wars of France subsequently occupied him until 1597. In that year he organized a second expedition. He was named lieutenant for the King in Canada, Hochelaga, Saguenay, Labrador, Newfoundland, Acadia, Norumbega and Sable Island. As no colonists volunteered, La Roche contracted with Newfoundland fishermen to carry some convicts to his dominion. A mutiny among them led to their being put ashore on Sable Island. The survivors, who managed to live on the descendants of cattle left by the Portuguese years before, were taken off in 1603.

A grotesque ineptness seemed to characterize the efforts of the Marquis, who was in fact a creature of ill-timed impulses and constant misfortune. His failure left the French claims open to foreign intrusion just as Spain was about to yield tacitly her claim to the lordship of all the lands beyond the Demarcation

Line. But the task of colonization was beyond unaided private resources. Colonization and government depended upon the economic exploitation of the new lands, and the heavy overhead of the long Atlantic voyages, together with all the risks of missing the natives at the rendezvous, or of coming too late to get the furs, operated to make a monopoly desirable. These facts had been grasped as early as 1588, when the two nephews of Jacques Cartier had been granted their monopoly. Now in 1600, following La Roche's failure, a monopoly of the fur trade was requested by Pierre Chauvin. A Huguenot soldier from Dieppe, Chauvin had become a fur trader at Honfleur in 1594. He was granted a monopoly of the fur trade of the St. Lawrence for ten years, but Henry IV imposed a condition designed to make good the claims of France in North America. It was that Chauvin should transport fifty colonists a year to New France. In virtue of his monopoly Chauvin acted as the King's lieutenant, though he was not commissioned as such.

Associated with him was an experienced and sagacious fur-trader, François Gravé, Sieur Du Pont, commonly known as Pontgravé. With them on the first voyage in 1600 sailed Pierre du Guast, Sieur de Monts, and fifty colonists. Because Chauvin insisted on landing these at Tadoussac, the inclement trading station at the mouth of the Saguenay, the first effort at settlement ended miserably. Only sixteen persons remained to winter at Tadoussac. These survived only by taking refuge with the Indians, and it is doubtful whether they had successors.

It was not this failure to carry out the colonization of New France, however, that was to deprive Chauvin of his monopoly. The private traders, working through the *parlement* of Rouen and the Estates of Brittany, and also through friends at court, forced the admission of some merchants to the privileges of the monopoly. Chauvin died at this point, late in 1602, but was succeeded by the Sieur de Chaste. Two ships, one from St. Malo and one from Rouen, were to sail with those of the monopolist, and fifty colonists were to be taken out. To reconnoitre a suitable place for the settlement of the colonists, Pontgravé was sent out early in the spring of 1603. With him sailed a friend of de Chaste, Samuel de Champlain.

Champlain, a native of Brouage (near La Rochelle) and a captain in the wars of religion, was a man whose eagerness to explore combined the intellectual curiosity of the scholar with the intuitive eye of the scientist. It now led him to take up the abandoned quest of Cartier for the interior secrets of the lands beyond Hochelaga. Thus Champlain proposed to add the costs of exploration to those of colonization. In consequence the need for monopoly was increased, and there was to be no more persistent advocate of the fur-trade monopoly than Champlain.

The man who thus proposed to take up the work of Cartier had probably visited the Spanish Indies and was a skilful observer of new countries, as his own writings of this time still bear witness. A certain modesty and reserve,

KC-B*

however, a capacity to forget himself in his work, render him still a somewhat elusive personality. Few men can have written so much of their own achievement, and have said so little of themselves. A man of no extravagance or eccentricity of character, Champlain is marked only by the brilliance of his geographical intuition and the fortitude with which he pursued his aims. This fortitude he drew in part from his religious faith, but it rested primarily on an inherent steadiness and balance of character, the rare quality of equanimity. Only a man at rest within himself could have hoped as steadfastly as Champlain did. Only a hopeful man could have undertaken to plant a colony in Acadia or in Canada. Only a much enduring man could have succeeded. And Champlain was to succeed, and to become in history the father of New France.

In 1603 Champlain was still only an explorer and an observer, as de Monts had been in 1600. He was sent with Pontgravé to find a suitable place for the establishment of the colonists to be sent out in 1604. The two men ascended the St. Lawrence to the rapids at Lachine, then returned to explore the south shores of the Gulf and the region of Gaspé, where they were impressed by the reports of the Indians that the winters of this land were warmer than those of Canada. They therefore decided to recommend that the colonists be directed southward to the Bay of Fundy and the land of Acadia.

When Pontgravé and Champlain returned to France, it was to discover that de Chaste was dead. Chauvin's monopoly now ended. A new one was granted to de Monts, like Chauvin a Huguenot and old follower of Henry IV. His charter covered both the St. Lawrence and Acadia, and was open to merchants who might care to join. One hundred colonists a year for ten years were to be taken out, but this was later reduced to sixty a year. The proprietor and the company were also to assist the conversion of the savages to the Catholic faith, despite the Protestant faith of de Monts.

The organization of the new combination was complete by the spring of 1604. It was decided by de Monts, on the advice of Champlain and Pontgravé, to settle the colonists in the Bay of Fundy while trading in the Gulf of St. Lawrence. The purpose was to avoid the killing winters of Canada. A settlement was made on an island (Dochet Island) in the St. Croix River. Unfortunately the winter of 1604-5 was one of exceptional severity and there was much suffering and loss. In the following summer the colony was moved across the bay to Port Royal, where it was established successfully. Henceforth there was to be, somewhere in New France, a French settlement summer and winter.

From this base Champlain was able to proceed in the summers of 1605 and 1606 to his work of exploration. He surveyed and mapped the New France (New England) coast south as far as Rhode Island Sound. With his uncanny knack of geographical divination, he sensed the relation of the Hudson River, seen by Verrazano but yet unexplored, to the St. Lawrence. But short supplies and Indian skirmishes drove him back from Long Island Sound, and so the site which was to become New Amsterdam (New York) failed to become a new Rouen or a new La Rochelle.

Meanwhile, it had been demonstrated that while a colony might be established in Acadia, a monopoly could not be maintained there and in the Gulf of St. Lawrence. On that long coastline there was no point of control, and there were countless harbours for secret and illicit trading. Despite some captures and confiscations, free traders continued to haunt the coasts and keep up the prices the Indians demanded for their furs. And in France the attack on the monopoly was continued, with the addition of criticism at court of the monopoly being held by one of de Monts's faith.

As a result his monopoly was ended in 1607. The work of colonization and trading in Acadia was continued by the Sieur de Poutrincourt, one of the participating merchants, and his son, Biencourt. There Biencourt pursued the fur trade, while his father struggled to maintain and recruit the tiny colony at Port Royal. There, also, began the first missionary work in New France. Aided by the Marquise de Guercheville, who had made the colony her special care, Fathers Pierre Biard and Ennemond Massé of the Society of Jesus were sent out and began their mission in 1611. Acadia, despite de Monts's loss of the monopoly, thus continued its peculiar and checkered history from the beginning it had made under his aegis.

On Champlain's advice, de Monts decided to continue in the fur trade but to resort only to the St. Lawrence. Champlain had come to see that great river as a means of enforcing a monopoly of the trade and as the avenue to the sedentary tribes (the Hurons) of the interior and to the exploration of the west. At some key point on the river its passage could be controlled, and in company with the trading Indians Champlain might advance into the unknown west. The scheme was approved by Henry IV, and a one-year monopoly of the trade of the river was granted without the condition of taking out colonists.

Champlain now began without further distraction his great work of revealing the continental hinterland of New France and of ensuring that it remain French. While Pontgravé conducted the fur trade at the old base of Tadoussac, Champlain ascended the river and founded Quebec at the narrows of the St. Lawrence. This was the key to the fur trade, as it would be the key to Canada, provided the St. Lawrence were cleared of Iroquois raiders.

Champlain had learned in 1603 that, although the Iroquois had been driven back to their historic position on the Mohawk River and Finger Lakes of northern New York state, they still raided the St. Lawrence. They did so to intercept the Algonkins of the Ottawa and the Hurons of Georgian Bay when they came down the St. Lawrence to trade at Tadoussac. It was desirable therefore to check these raids, and to advance to Hochelaga to meet the Algonkins and Hurons. For this purpose Champlain in 1609 joined a war party of Montagnais and Algonkins. With them he ascended the "river of the Iroquois" (the Richelieu), explored the lake that bears his name, and sighted Lac St. Sacrement (Lake George). On the west bank of Lake Champlain an Iroquois war party was met and defeated, largely owing to the surprise and losses caused by Champlain's fire-arms. In 1610 Champlain renewed his aid to the tribes of the coalition by fighting the Iroquois again, this time at the mouth of the Richelieu, where he and his allies captured an Iroquois fortified camp. Champlain thus cemented his ties with the Laurentian coalition, cleared the St. Lawrence between Trois Rivières and Hochelaga of the Iroquois raiders, and opened the way for the Algonkins of the Ottawa and the Hurons of Georgian Bay to come down to trade.

The next step was to found a trading post at Hochelaga, and to unravel the watercourses of the country beyond Mont Royal. But the fur trade had been thrown open again in 1609, and Champlain had in effect opened the St. Lawrence to Hochelaga for his rivals more than for himself. Champlain and Pontgravé had therefore to maintain their factory at Quebec and endeavour to obtain a renewal of the monopoly. The years 1610 to 1613 saw a very rapid increase in the trade of New France, as the furs of the Great Lakes region began to flow out by Hochelaga. In 1613, however, Champlain succeeded, after a year of negotiation, in obtaining a new grant of monopoly on the St. Lawrence, under the patronage first of the Comte de Soissons and, on his death, of the Prince de Condé. The patron was, of course, to defend the monopoly against attack at court.

Thus reinforced, Champlain returned to the St. Lawrence in 1613, and when no Indians were found at Hochelaga, ascended the Ottawa to bring them down and to investigate the report of one Nicolas Vignau, an *hivernant* left to winter with the Indians, that he had seen an English ship wrecked on the shore of a great sea to the north. Vignau proved to be a liar and his trip a fiction, but his tale may have revealed some knowledge of the voyages of the English navigators, Henry Hudson and Thomas Button, in 1610 and 1612. They also were seeking a route to Asia and failed in the vast dead end of Hudson Bay. The failure of 1613 was, however, a prelude to Champlain's voyage of 1615 to the Huron country on Georgian Bay. That trip really crowned Champlain's work as a geographer. Even if the attack launched by Champlain and his Huron allies against the Iroquois villages proved a failure, Champlain had seen the continental dimensions of North America mirrored in the great "Freshwater Sea" of Lake Huron. That sight perhaps spelled out to him the immensity of the task of revelation that lay before the explorers of New France. Henceforth Champlain explored no more for "the western sea," but endeavoured to colonize Quebec and to convert the savages.

Hitherto he had urged colonization as a means of growing food and of manning the fortification at Quebec. Those objects he never lost sight of, though he was never to see them realized. Increasingly, however, he saw New France as a country led by European colonists but peopled by natives converted to Christianity and mingling their blood with that of their civilizers. As Spain had Hispanicized, France would Francize. The conversion of the natives had been a proclaimed policy of the French Crown since Roberval's expedition, but nothing had in fact been done before 1610. Champlain had invited the Society of Jesus to send missionaries to Quebec in 1608, but his invitation had been declined at that time. Now the victory of Catholicism in France and the still rising tide of the Catholic Reformation in Europe ensured that something would be done in Canada as in Acadia.

After the settlement of the monopoly in 1613, the work of evangelization could at last be undertaken. Three Recollect fathers of the Franciscan order, Fathers Denis Jamet, Jean Dolbeau and Joseph Le Caron, and one lay brother, Pacifique Du Plessis, came to Quebec in 1615, and with the support of Condé and Champlain addressed themselves to the conversion of the nearby Montagnais and the distant Hurons. Dolbeau attempted the conversion of the wandering Montagnais and Le Caron began the Huron mission in the fall of 1615. But the long journey to the Huron country, described by lay brother Gabriel Sagard in a famous account, the poverty of the Recollects, and the indifference of the fur traders, made it difficult to maintain the distant mission. The aid of the Society of Jesus was sought, and in 1625 Fathers Charles Lalemant, Jean de Brébeuf, and Ennemond Massé joined the Recollects at Quebec and in Huronia, and other fathers followed them. With the Jesuit missions began their *Relations*, the annual accounts of their endeavours.

The mission work and colonization in Acadia, however, had been brought to an abrupt end in 1613 when Samuel Argall of Virginia removed the colony of Port Royal and shipped its people back to France on the ground that the colony lay within the northern limits of Virginia. The raid was more a freebooter's foray than an act of state policy, and had no effect on the title to the region. This intervention was not to end either French enterprise or French colonization in Acadia, but it did mark the beginning of the bickering of private traders and clash of claim and counter-claim which were to constitute the history of Acadia for the next half century.

Moreover, Argall's raid on Port Royal foreshadowed an even more serious attack on Quebec. From 1615 to 1627 Champlain toiled with varying success to maintain a monopoly of the fur trade as a means of taxing the commerce of the country. He was thwarted by the free traders in New France and by intrigues at court. He wished to tax the fur trade in order to bring out colonists, to build fortifications at Quebec, to open a trading fort at Hochelaga. In none of these things did he achieve more than the maintenance of his purpose. In 1620, Condé gave way to the Duc de Montmorency, who continued Champlain as his lieutenant but gave the monopoly of the trade to the Huguenot brothers, Emery and Guillaume de Caën. These changes stabilized Champlain's position but yielded no additional revenue for the strengthening of the fortress at Quebec or for further exploration of the interior.

Champlain struggled on, to build up the colony and to promote the fur trade by which alone, it seemed, the colony could be nourished. The number of inhabitants at Quebec fluctuated around fifty; most were *engagés*, working out their three-year term of service and free at its end to return to France, as many did. Of true colonists there were few; chief among them was Louis Hébert, an apothecary turned farmer who had already tried the life of a colonist in Acadia. There was also Abraham Martin, the sea pilot who gave his name to the Heights on which he made his farm. The fur trade was kept flowing by *hivernants* like Etienne Brulé, who "was paid a hundred pistoles a year to incite the savages to come down and trade," as Champlain noted. Champlain himself approved, if he did not initiate, the peace treaty made in 1624 with the Iroquois after two years of Dutch absence, as it would help the missions and perhaps the trade. But the traders themselves opposed it, lest the Indians of the Laurentian coalition trade with the new Dutch post of Fort Orange on the Hudson River. The Iroquois for their part probably wanted peace in order to deal with the Mohicans, with whom they were warring on the Hudson.

However that might be, the colony, it was certain, could thrive only if the fur trade were regulated and colonists brought out steadily. In 1627 the firm hand of the great Richelieu, who was reorganizing the government of France, set the affairs of New France in order by combining the commercial interests of the North Atlantic trade in the Company of New France, or the Hundred Associates. In this corporation the Norman and Breton traders were swamped by the personality of the great Cardinal and the numbers of courtiers and officials he appointed as shareholders. Former traders such as the de Caëns were pushed aside and nursed a dangerous resentment. On the powerful company was placed the obligation, in return for a monopoly of fifteen years' term, to bring out three hundred colonists annually. This was the firmest effort yet made to combine commerce and colonization in New France. It was also decided, in view of the difficulties caused by religious differences in the binding of commerce and colonization together, and for the sake of unity in missionary work, that all colonists were to be of the Catholic faith.

The foundation of the Company made two things clear. One was that French private enterprise in New France, though abundant, was not to colonize New France, as Virginia and New England to the south were being colonized. French commerce, in Canada being only the fur trade, was incompatible with colonization, because every colonist was a charge on the profits of the trade and also a potential free-trader. The first lines were being written of what was to become an old story in New France and later in Red River. The second was that religious toleration in New France was impossible, because the Huguenot appeared only as a trader and therefore as an enemy to colonization. If New France was to be settled and the Indians assimilated, it must be by the agency of Catholic missionaries.

The Company's beginning was marred, however, by the outbreak of war in 1627 between England and France. At once Sir William Alexander, to whom James VI had granted Acadia from the Scottish Crown under the name of Nova Scotia, dispatched a body of Scottish colonists to Port Royal in 1627. And some English traders, of whom one, Jarvis Kirke, had connections with French traders and perhaps with the ousted de Caëns, moved to capture the fur trade of New France. One of Kirke's half-French sons, David Kirke, sailed to Quebec in 1628 with three ships and summoned it to surrender. Champlain refused, but Kirke captured a fleet of eighteen vessels sent by the Hundred Associates with colonists and supplies. The English traders and Alexander then formed the "Company of Adventurers to Canada" to exploit the fur trade. In 1629 the three Kirke brothers, David, Lewis, and Thomas, forced Champlain to surrender Quebec and took him to England, only to learn that the war had been ended by the Treaty of Susa on the basis of restoration of conquests.

But nothing was done until, under the Treaty of St. Germain-en-Laye, England surrendered Quebec in 1632. Meantime the Canada Company used it as a trading post and continued the fur trade of New France. In 1629, Alexander began the colonization of Cape Breton and was joined in the exploitation of the Acadia fur trade by Claude de La Tour, one of the French seigneurs of Acadia, whom Alexander had captured at sea and who changed his allegiance for a grant of land. Thus began a tangled thread of Acadian history in the first instance of the many changes of allegiance Acadia was to know. And while the Kirkes still held Quebec in 1631 the English renewed their quest for a route to Asia by Hudson Bay, Luke Foxe and Thomas James leading two expeditions into the great inland sea and thereby strengthening the claims Hudson and Button had made for the Crown of England in that region.

The English had thus infringed in Acadia and Hudson Bay the title to the lands Champlain sought to make French, and had blocked the development of New France for three costly years.

ADDITIONAL READING

BIGGAR, H. P.   *Early Trading Companies of New France.*
BISHOP, M. G.   *Champlain: The Life of Fortitude.*
BREBNER, J. B.   *The Explorers of North America.*
INNIS, H. A.   *The Cod Fisheries.*
JULIEN, C. A.   *Les Français en Amérique pendant la première moitié du XVIᵉ siècle.*
LANCTÔT, G.   "Cartier's First Voyage to Canada," *Canadian Historical Review*, September, 1944.
WILLIAMSON, J. A.   *The Voyages of the Cabots and the English Exploration of North America under Henry VII and Henry VIII*

CHAPTER 3

The Fur Trade and Mission of Huronia

1632-1661

In midsummer, 1632, a French ship once more worked its way up the St. Lawrence, passed the Isle of Orleans, and swung to anchor below the rock of Quebec. It was a trading-ship of Guillaume de Caën. A ship of the Canada Company's was already there, and the fort and warehouses of Quebec were still in English possession. They vacated without protest and de Caën's men took over. De Caën had been given permission to conduct the trade of Canada for the season of 1632 to compensate him for the termination of his grant by the charter of the Hundred Associates. Accordingly, his men now turned to trading with the Algonkins and the Hurons who had come down to Quebec. The Indians were pleased to find that their French friends had returned. They had not, they said, liked the English. Now the fur trade could once more flow unchecked to France although the Canada Company kept up a trade as interlopers in the Gulf for another year.

After the traders came the missionaries. In July 1632, Fathers Paul Le Jeune and Anne de Noüe landed and viewed with dismay their desolate chapel and the slovenly aspect of Quebec which the heretics had made only a fur post. But the dreary scene was cheered by the joyful welcome of the Hébert family. Once more the faith had returned to Quebec, and the fathers busied themselves with the restoration of worship, the renewed instruction of the Indians, and plans for new missions to the Algonkins and the Hurons in 1633. Richelieu had in fact made the Jesuits the sole missionary order to serve in New France; the Recollects were prohibited from returning.

The Jesuit fathers were aided as before by Champlain, who came back as governor of New France to supervise both the colony and the fur trade. The five years of absence had aged him but had not changed the nature of his task. That was still to induce the fur trade to yield the means of solidifying the French claim to New France with fortress, church, and settlement, and to bring the Indians to be "one people" with the French in the faith. Champlain at once joined the fathers in rebuilding the chapel, which was dedicated to Notre Dame de la Recouvrance.

It was not only Quebec that had been recovered by the Treaty of St. Germain-en-Laye, for Charles I of England had yielded up not only the claims of the Canada Company to Quebec but also those of Sir William Alexander and the Scottish Crown to Nova Scotia, or Acadia. Restored Acadia, however, was not to be governed from Quebec; in 1632 the Company of the Hundred Associates made Isaac de Razilly governor and Charles de Menou, Seigneur d'Aulnay de Charnisay, his lieutenant.

The grant of Acadia to Razilly was also an indication that Richelieu's great enterprise of 1627 had suffered in the attack of the Kirkes a blow from which it was never completely to recover. To the loss of three years of trade was added de Caën's licence to trade during 1632. That further loss was increased by damages won in the lawsuit de Caën launched to gain compensation for the cancellation of his grant in 1627. It is not surprising therefore that something of the enthusiasm of 1627 was dissipated by 1633. The Associates had little choice but to limit their enterprise and whittle down their obligations. Not only did they turn Acadia over to de Razilly, they turned the trade of Canada over to a trading association which paid them for its licence. By these means they hoped to recover from the set-back of 1628-32. In the meantime they could not fulfil the obligation to bring out three hundred settlers a year. And in 1635 Richelieu at last led France into the Thirty Years' War, and gave to victory in Germany the resources of which a part might have set struggling Canada on its feet.

The prosperity of the Associates and the colonization of Canada depended, of course, on the resumption of the fur trade. That, in fact, had never ceased; the Algonkins and the Hurons had brought down their furs to the English at Quebec as they had to the French. But a new pull was at work on the sensitive flow of the trade, the pull of Dutch Fort Orange established on the Hudson in 1624. There beaver trapped or pillaged by the Mohawks made its way; there it was possible for Algonkins and Hurons to send their furs, by trade with the Mohawks. Quebec was no longer an irresistible magnet, and it was now necessary to extend the reach of the French trade up the St. Lawrence. In the summer of 1634 accordingly, the traders and the missionaries, advancing hand in hand, began a post and mission at Trois Rivières. At that point the Algonkian Atikamegs came down the St. Maurice River, and the Huron flotillas were glad to stop. The French by this advance had planted their first step beyond tidewater and the reach of sea-going ships. The inland fur trade, as distinguished from the sea-coast trade, had begun in Canada. In the New France of the "recouvrance," the French were all unwittingly at the threshold of continental empire.

This first step of empire Champlain had guided. To him Trois Rivières, the St. Lawrence beyond, and the "river of the meadows," as men called the entrance to the Ottawa, were familiar waters. But now he could scarcely hope to ascend to Huronia and behold again the vast shimmer of the Freshwater Sea. The empire of France and the Faith in the heart of America was threatened by the persistent, stinging attacks of the Iroquois whose lands he had raided in his years of exploration, and who had now repudiated the peace of 1624. Champlain had scotched, not killed, the Iroquois menace. And now, he concluded, it must be dealt with anew, not by the provocation of a mere Indian raid but by the decisive attack of European infantry. One hundred and twenty light infantry with Indian auxiliaries, he wrote the King, would rout the Iroquois and make the French absolute masters of the country. And the English and Dutch, if deprived of the trade of the Iroquois, would be forced to give up the fur trade entirely. This, then, in the judgement of the veteran governor, was the force needed to give the French free access to the Huron country, which might mean control of the continent. One company of French infantry would serve to realize Champlain's dream of a French and Huron condominium by the Freshwater Sea, and of a passage to Cathay.

No such company was to be sent the old governor, and, had Richelieu sent them, Champlain could not have set himself at their head. In December, 1635, he died and was buried in the chapel on Cape Diamond, overlooking the basin of Quebec. His burial place, the land he had put before all else, was French again, but French no more securely than before. Champlain had led a crusade without crusaders, and New France still lay as he had found it, empty, vast, and barbarous.

The crusade, however, was to continue. That the masters of New France, the Hundred Associates, saw the preservation of the colony in that light was witnessed by the character of the man they had already chosen to succeed the aging Champlain. Charles Jacques Huault de Montmagny was a Knight of Malta and warrior against the infidel. He was the first of those French veterans of the Turkish wars who, like John Smith of Virginia, turned from fighting the Turk to Indian fighting and saw it all as one war. The Company appointed him as a commander who could garrison the river posts while the fur trade and the missions went inland. They were justified, for complete harmony prevailed between the new governor, the fur trade and the missions for the next twelve years.

Father Le Jeune had already gone back to the Montagnais and their smoke-filled wigwams, to resume in 1632 the mission and repeat the sufferings and the failure of Father Jean Dolbeau of the Recollects. But this mission, with its heroic misery, seems to have been a gesture, necessary but despairing. The main hope of the Jesuit fathers lay in the mission to the Hurons. On the conversion of this remarkable tribe they had, like Champlain and Richelieu, based their hope of building New France in part on a Franco-Indian community with its two people one in the faith.

There were excellent and even decisive reasons for this election of the Hurons as the chosen vessels of the faith. Their native intelligence was not inferior to that of the Iroquois or the Algonkian Indians, and in their trials of wit with the French they were quick and adroit. They were also systematic and assiduous traders. Spring after spring they traded the corn of their fields to the tribes of the upper Ottawa and of the Shield, and to those of the north coast of Lake Huron, for the furs of their winter catch. From this commerce came the bales of furs that the Huron flotilla brought down to Trois Rivières and Quebec. And from the sale of their furs they obtained European goods to barter, along with corn, for the next year's cargoes of beaver and marten. The effect of this middleman commerce of the Hurons was to make Huronia on Georgian Bay the centre of the fur trade from the Straits of Mackinac to the headwaters of the St. Maurice. Only the trade of the Saguenay moved independently down to Tadoussac. To bring the Hurons to the faith, to make them "one people" with the French, as Champlain had dreamed, would be to advance New France to the shores of the Freshwater Sea and incorporate the Indian fur trade into the trading system of the colony.

Nothing of course could better illustrate the developing relationship between the fur trade and the missions than this common interest in the commercial supremacy of Huronia. The quest for converts to the faith led to Huronia; it was in Huronia that the fur trade centred. If the Hurons were converted, the faith would radiate from Huronia along the lines of commerce as it had first spread along the roads of Rome. If the Hurons were converted, they would be bound by religion, as well as induced by commerce, to trade with their French and Catholic brethren. This was an alliance of trade and mission that was to outlast even the destruction of Huronia. Well might a missionary write that the trade was "necessary for the maintenance of the Faith in all these regions, for the good of the French colonies, and for the support of New France."

Thus it was that Fathers Brébeuf, Daniel, and Charles Lalemant embarked for Huronia in the returning canoes of the trading flotilla of 1634; the fur trade was to carry the missionary, as the missionary was to win the Indian trader to lasting alliance with the French. The Hurons were reluctant to oblige them. They had refused to take the fathers in 1633, and in 1634 they made them feel they were unwanted guests and resented burdens. This situation the fathers sought to remedy by being unobtrusive, by sharing the toil of paddling and carrying, and by accepting patiently the hardships of the journey and the rudeness of their hosts.

When they arrived in Huronia and began to establish their mission, the fathers had to suffer not merely the discomfort of Indian lodges and the strangeness of the Indian food, but also a concerted resistance to their mission by the acute and sophisticated savages. Smoke, filth, vermin, noise, the utter want of privacy – these were the commonplaces of Indian life, whether Algonkian or Huron. But the Hurons knew, from the first mission of 1625 and from their trips to Quebec, what the missionaries intended and what the effects on their life might be. They sensed that if the "Black Robes" came bearing on their lips the promise of eternal life, the way of life they preached spelled in fact the end of the Indian way. They also connected with the advent of the new-comers the new diseases that ravaged them. Why, they questioned, had so many died in the plague of 1634? Was it to ensure that there should be more French and fewer Indians? Was it the result of magic, the magic of the Black Robes' writing, against which, they said, the free-trader Basques had warned them? And what of the dreams that they had had, that those who had become Christians would become sedentary, and trade and hunt no more?

The fathers protested earnestly that the plague was a common affliction, that there was no magic in their writing. And they proceeded patiently and persistently in their ministrations. But Indian and missionary were alike confused and puzzled as they struggled in the conflict of a primitive and a civilized culture, a conflict in which one culture must prevail, and in which the Indian had no ally of disease or pestilence to pit against the swarming viruses of the city-dwelling European.

Thus it was that Huron medicine men could find fearful listeners when they declared that it was the Black Robes' magic that brought plague on the Hurons, or dried up their crops, or drove the fish from their nets. And when the plague raged again, as it did in 1637 and 1638, and the fathers urgently and gratefully baptized the dying, the medicine men were quick to point out how rapidly death followed the holy water. Then the lodges were shut against the missionaries, and lowering glances marked their progress through the villages.

But their hosts never turned completely against them. The Indian obligation to grant hospitality to all come thers, extraordinary tolerance of Indian society, preserved the missionaries from attack and left them to pursue their devoted work in the isolation of mid America. So isolated were they that flour to make the Host had to be hoarded and the sacramental wine used drop by drop. As they ministered to the sick, their medicines were soon exhausted, and they used sweetened water, or a few raisins, to comfort those they could not heal. So alone were they, that the Indians might have killed them like flies, without a murmur rising for many months. Yet they were spared, and in the smoke-filled lodges, through the heavy snows of the forests, the fathers pursued the work of salvation among the Hurons and their dependent tribes, the Tobacco and the Neutral Indians to the south of Lake Huron. Gradually to the task of baptizing infants *in extremis* was added the slow, uncertain toil of converting the adults. And if some of these were all too obviously "tobacco Christians," some few, the first seed of the harvest, were genuine converts who put off the old way to remain steadfast in the new.

The isolation of the mission to Huronia was intensified by the increasing pressure of the Iroquois on the canoe route to Quebec. Summer after summer, bands of Mohawks lay in ambush at the portages to surprise the trading parties, snatch a few scalps, and carry off the furs to Fort Orange. The Mohawks had exhausted their own beaver streams. Desperate for means to buy the kettles and hatchets of the Dutch traders, they were overrunning the hunting grounds of the Algonkins and plundering the trading flotillas of the Hurons.

Already by 1639 there were rumours that their raids might carry beyond the portages of the Ottawa and the middle reaches of the St. Lawrence, and strike Huronia itself. The villages of Huronia were protected, it is true, by the triple palisades of Iroquoian fortification. In spring, however, the young men were far away trading, and the women working in the fields were defenceless. An Iroquois war party would have spread devastation unrestricted. But the rumours were never more than rumours, and the word soon ran that the old men had spread them to keep the young men at home against the possibility of attack.

Thus the mission to Huronia went on amid resentments and alarms. Back on the St. Lawrence, the base from which the mission operated was being solidified. Quebec then was much like the trading or mining posts beyond the Arctic Circle today. There were warehouses and dwellings for the European trade and traders. There were chapels, schools, and hospitals for the service of the native people. Only the fort, perched on the brow of Cape Diamond, was a different, a seventeenth-century silhouette.

From this centre of their remote frontier, the Jesuit fathers reported annually to their superiors in the Province of France. By an inspiration, it became the practice to publish these *Relations*, and their accounts of toil and suffering for the faith matched the prevailing fervour of the more intense souls of the age. A gust of compassion for the heathen of Canada swept through the seminaries and convents of France. Funds flowed and volunteers, cleric and lay, came forward. As a result the Jesuits were able to open a seminary at Quebec in 1635 to educate Indian children, and were soon deep in the problems, domestic and psychological rather than pedagogical, of training the lads raised in the freedom of the wigwam and the camp to the discipline, the heat and the confinement of the school. Provision was made for their even shyer sisters in 1639 when Marie de l'Incarnation and the Ursuline nuns sent by Madame de La Peltrie arrived to begin their convent. They were accompanied by the three Augustinian nuns sent by Richelieu's niece, the Duchesse d'Aiguillon. The sisters opened a hospital, the Hôtel-Dieu, where for the first time on the St. Lawrence the ill and the dying could know the mercy of cleanliness and care.

Nor did the missionary zeal which sustained the fathers, and which had sent out the sisters, end with the foundation of the Seminary and the Hôtel-Dieu at Quebec. In 1639 the number of actual and prospective converts justified the beginning at Sillery, above Quebec, of a Christian Indian village. After some initial difficulties, it became firmly established and at once the pride of its people and the pledge of the incorporation of the Indians into the Christian community, the one people, of New France.

The other, the French element in the one people, was still lacking. The Hundred Associates, plagued by the expenses arising from de Caën's successful lawsuit, and hard put to it to find capital for the annual voyage, had not succeeded in sending more than a handful of colonists to New France. They did not lack will, perhaps, but they definitely did lack capital, and the returns from the fur trade gave no ready surplus for the expensive business of planting people overseas. Canada as yet was peopled only by missionaries, traders, and a few keen enthusiasts such as the physician Dr. Robert Giffard who made their life in the new land a hobby. Only down in Acadia did a handful of French peasants, perhaps two score in 1636, begin to have a stake in the lands of the Annapolis valley and along the sea marshes of Minas. They were survivors of the first settlement of de Monts and Poutrincourt, and new colonists brought by de Razilly. These families were the source from which the Acadian people was to spring.

Acadia was formally parcelled out in three great feudal grants or seigniories, held by Razilly, La Tour, and Nicolas Denys, but the boundaries were indefinite and the lordships in dispute. Razilly had died in 1636, and his lieutenant, d'Aulnay-Charnisay, succeeded him at Port Royal. D'Aulnay-Charnisay and Charles de La Tour began a long and tortuous struggle as rival lords and fur traders. Nicolas Denys, in his holding on the north shore of Acadia, kept aloof from this fray, as did the Acadian peasants of Port Royal. The feud raged with varying fortune and picturesque detail until d'Aulnay-Charnisay's death in 1650. Its chief importance was that it gave the New Englanders a chance to intervene in Acadia.

In Canada the Hundred Associates, if they sent out few colonists, did begin the granting of seigniories. Their purpose was to transfer to the new seigneurs the cost and effort of colonization. As early as 1634 the great seigniory of Beauport below Quebec was granted to Dr. Giffard, the genial physician from Perche who had chosen to practise in Quebec. In that year also, the lordship of Trois Rivières was granted to the Society of Jesus in addition to Notre Dame des Anges at Quebec, granted in 1626. More than a dozen other grants to lay and clerical seigneurs followed between 1636 and 1639.

The seigniory was the ancient feudal lordship of old France, much modified by time and varied by local custom. It was now transmitted entire to New France, except that a jealous and stronger Crown sometimes reserved to itself jurisdiction over "high" and "middle" justice; that is, over major offences and suits at law. But minor offences and petty litigation were usually left to the seigneur's court. The lord's economic rights, as embodied with local variations in the Coutume de Paris, the customary law of northern France, were transplanted with little change. They consisted in the main of the right to *lods et ventes*, a charge on transfers; the right of *banalité*, the exaction of a charge for services, such as milling; the customary rent of *cens et rentes*, a fixed payment for tenure. The seigneur also had social rights such as the pride of place in saints' day processions and in the parish church. It was the hope that the establishment of the old feudal complex, by which old France had been held and tilled, might prove an effective design for settling and clearing the new lands of Canada. The seigneurs, it was intended, would procure settlers to give their seigniories value.

The hope was only slowly and partly realized. The seigniories of Canada, like the patroonships of New Amsterdam, began as, and for the most part remained, great speculative holdings in wild lands. A few active seigneurs, led by the religious orders and by laymen like Giffard, did bring out settlers to start the actual peopling of Quebec. But it was only as settlement spread with the growth of population that the seigniorial system began to function. Of itself it did little at first to foster settlement.

Thus Canada continued to be a fur-trade colony and a mission. There were perhaps two hundred French people in Canada in 1642, not all of whom were settlers, or *habitants*. The Company of the Hundred Associates had failed, for want of capital rather than want of will, to fulfil the colonizing terms of its charter. The fur trade could not support the cost of peopling a colony. And the seigneurs too lacked capital and had had too little time.

Nor had the indefinite but daring concept of "one people" made progress. Too few Frenchmen had come; too few Indians had been converted to Christianity and a settled life. In fact, the intermarriage of French and Indian was to be the result not of policy but of the fur-trade practice of wintering. Men sent to winter with the hunting bands, to ensure that they brought their furs to the winterers' employer, formed unions with Indian women. But as long as the Hurons brought the furs of the interior down, there was no need for winterers, and Vignau and Brulé had no immediate successors.

The Huron trade in 1641 faced a more formidable threat than any it had yet known. In the spring of that year the guerrilla raids of the Iroquois on the trade route of the Ottawa and the St. Lawrence developed a new and increasing weight. Raiding was replaced by the campaigning of full-scale war. The bands of up to five hundred warriors were now partly armed with arquebuses, the fire-arm of the day. The French had refrained from trading guns to the Algonkians and Hurons, as the Netherlanders of Fort Orange had refrained from trading them to the Iroquois. In consequence, the Iroquois had none, or few, until 1641, and the Algonkians and the Hurons had none at that date. They still relied on the iron hatchets and arrowheads, the steel knives, and the body armour of woven twigs they had used when they drove the Iroquois from the banks of the St. Lawrence. Now, however, that superiority was ended by the Iroquois' obtaining the white man's most formidable weapon, the arquebus. They had got it, it is to be presumed, from New England or Netherlander free traders, for the government of New Netherland had not changed its policy and was not happy at the development.

Nor was the possession of fire-arms and the new weight of the attack merely the result of a fortunate change in trading. The Iroquois, and especially the Mohawks, were desperate for beaver. Their own beaver streams were seriously depleted, if not exhausted. They could not trade corn for furs like the Hurons, for they lacked water carriage for the grain their village fields produced in abundance. The only recourse was to intensify their raiding of the beaver streams of the Algonkian tribes to the east and north and to strengthen the pillaging raids on the Huron flotillas at the carrying-places of the Ottawa and the St. Lawrence. The fire-arms were a fortunate means to this end, but it was commercial desperation that drove the Iroquois on. The war now raging was in fact a commercial war fought to divert the fur trade of the St. Lawrence to the Dutch traders on the Hudson River. The savagery was incidental; the commercial motive was all-compelling.

The raids of 1641 and of 1642 made it plain to the French that new means must be found to cope with the menace of the Iroquois. The Iroquois had offered peace to them in 1641, but had excluded their Indian allies. Montmagny, faithful to that "Laurentian coalition" ratified by Champlain years before, had refused. Now the French must fight. They sent to France for help and more soldiers. The habitants of Trois Rivières and even of Quebec were called by Montmagny for service when the Iroquois threat mounted, and a naval patrol was organized for the St. Lawrence from Trois Rivières to the mouth of the Ottawa. In 1642, in an effort to block the Richelieu River route by which the Mohawks descended on the St. Lawrence and Trois Rivières, a fort was built at the mouth of the river with money sent by Cardinal Richelieu himself. The fort was raised in the face of daring Iroquois attack. But it was like attempting to block the passage of a swarm of bees.

A year before, Champlain's plan for a post on the Island of Montreal had been revived. It would be natural to assume that this, like the fort on the Richelieu, was a strategic response to the Iroquois raids. The island, if sufficiently garrisoned, was the key to entry of the Ottawa. But the project of building a fort and founding a colony there was in fact not a cool-headed piece of strategy but a new surge of the religious response to the *Relations* and the challenge of the Canadian mission.

Jérôme Le Royer de La Dauversière, a layman of great piety and philanthropy, had read of the advantages of soil and site the island possessed. He decided to found on it a colony consecrated to the Virgin Mary. He organized a society of Notre-Dame de Montréal for the purpose, with the help of the Abbé Jean Jacques Olier de Verneuil, who was soon to found the Seminary of St. Sulpice. Jean de Lauzon, the holder of the island, was persuaded to grant it to the society. Paul de Chomedey, Sieur de Maisonneuve, a direct and simple soldier, was engaged to plant the colony. He arrived at Quebec with a band of colonists in the late summer of 1641 along with Mademoiselle Jeanne Mance, who was to establish a hospital in the new colony. Maisonneuve proceeded at once, despite warnings of the Iroquois danger, to reconnoitre the site. After wintering at Quebec, he led his colonists to the south shore of the island and began the settlement which was to be Ville Marie de Montréal.

A more deliberate challenge to the Iroquois, a less prudent undertaking, it would have been difficult to devise. Only religious enthusiasm can explain, and perhaps justify, so rash a venture. Few settlements have begun among such perils. Fortunately, it was the fur trade, not the French settlements, that was under attack. Montreal survived as in 1642, 1643, and 1644 the Iroquois struck at the St. Lawrence and Ottawa trade route with persistent and baffling savagery. The Hurons grew fearful of the perils of the trade route; the volume of furs dwindled. The Hundred Associates wearied of the task of finding capital for the unrewarding trade of Canada.

Thus it was that in 1645 the Company of the Hundred Associates was prepared to turn the fur trade of Canada over to a new subsidiary company in return for the maintenance and peopling of the colony. This time, however, it was to a company formed in Canada and made up of Canadians. Its formation was the first public enterprise in Canada. It was also an indication of the extent to which the leading inhabitants were interested in the all-absorbing fur trade. The new association therefore assumed the appropriate name of the Communauté des Habitants, but it was seigneurs like Giffard and de Lauzon who were the leaders in this colonial undertaking. A Canadian *bourgeoisie* was in embryo. The company prepared to take over the trade in the season of 1646.

Inspired by concern for the fur trade, the French at the same time took the initiative in negotiating peace with the Mohawks. The peace was so much desired that the treaty contained secret clauses by which the French abandoned their Algonkian allies of the Laurentian coalition. Between the latter and the Mohawks there was only a truce. With the other Iroquois tribes no peace was made. The most eager traders, the French of the new company and the arrogant Mohawks, went through the slow ceremonial and deliberate rhetoric of an Indian council to make a peace which, however, still left them competitors for the trade of Huronia.

In 1646, as a result of the cessation of hostilities, the Huron trading parties again went out freely, leaving their undefended villages without worry. And in midsummer a great flotilla of canoes came down, to fill the warehouses of Quebec with bales of beaver. The Compagnie des Habitants had had an amazing first season and had obtained not only the furs of that year but the many which had been held back for fear of the Iroquois. A profit of 320,000 livres fell to the lucky speculators.

The profits of 1646 were, however, a windfall of the peace rather than a commercial return on goods exchanged. Yet the peace was incomplete, because the western Iroquois were not parties to it. And the Mohawks interpreted the fact that the Hurons took all the great shipment of furs in 1646 to the French as a violation of the treaty. They had therefore decided on war again when Father Isaac Jogues set out on a mission to the savages who had captured him in 1642 and from whom he had escaped to New Amsterdam in 1643, mutilated and near to death. He returned now with a calm daring aimed at success or martyrdom.

As a result of the ending of the peace, the suspicious and vengeful Mohawks abused, tortured, and killed him. But after his capture he had written to Quebec to say that he had learned the purpose of the Iroquois in breaking the peace. It was to make war on the Hurons, to kill their chief men and many of their people, and to "form with the remainder a single people and a single country." It was the planned extermination of the Huron nation, a genocide, which was the aim of the Iroquois in renewing the war. The result would be, they calculated, to place the whole trade of the interior in their hands.

The new attack began, as that of 1641 had done, with raids on the Ottawa portages and the reaches of the St. Lawrence from Montreal to Trois Rivières by bands of pillagers even more heavily armed with arquebuses. The Hurons were also armed with fire-arms now, but not so extensively. And they had failed to evolve tactics by which a flotilla of canoes and their loads could be passed over a portage in face of ambush or attack in war canoes. The flying squadrons of militia which were now organized by the French did something to hold the St. Lawrence open, but the Ottawa was beyond their reach. Few furs came to Quebec in 1647 in consequence, and the Compagnie des Habitants learned how hazardous was the great trade of Canada.

The bold men who had taken over the fur trade were, however, still pressing forward. With control of the trade they asked for a government more representative than the rule of Montmagny at Quebec and of lieutenant-governors at Trois Rivières and Montreal. In 1647 their request was granted in that a council was set up by royal decree, to consist of the governor, the Jesuit Superior and the lieutenant-governor of Montreal. The administration of the colony was thus made less autocratic, and syndics, or representatives, of the people of Quebec and Montreal were allowed to appear before the council on the business of their electors. This considerable political advance was quietly developed year by year thereafter, and it was accompanied by a similar economic measure, the opening of the fur trade to all habitants.

In the next year Montmagny, after a term of office rivalling Champlain's in duration and constancy, turned over to Louis d'Ailleboust, governor of Montreal in Maisonneuve's absence, the task of governing and of dealing with the Iroquois in peace and war.

The Iroquois, however, as Jogues's message had foretold, were no longer to be content with raiding and pillage in 1648. The entire confederacy was engaged. They were striking for control of the whole trade, and this meant the destruction of the Huron mission and the whole concept of French and Indian made one people in the faith. As a result of this new character of the war, there came in the summer of 1648 the long-rumoured attack on Huronia itself. It came when the fur flotilla, which had not gone down in 1647, was absent on the voyage to Montreal. On July 4, Fathers Jean de Brébeuf and Gabriel Lalemant, nephew of Charles, saw from the mission of St. Louis a column of smoke build up over the

III   *Huronia, as depicted on Du Creux's Map of 1660*

horizon in the direction of the outlying village and mission of St. Joseph, which was served at that time by Father Antoine Daniel. Soon the fugitives and the news came. A large Seneca war party had struck from the woods. They had broken through the palisades and begun the massacre of old and young. Father Daniel they had shot down as he baptized the dying, and had flung his body into the blazing ruins of his chapel. They had then departed, fearing the Huron rally, and left the first ruined village of Huronia, the first chapel desecrated, the first martyr slain.

The raid of 1648 was the knell of doom. Neither distance nor fortification had saved a Huron village from the reach of the Iroquois. Nor was it only Huronia that was menaced. The Iroquois bands at the portages prowled, empty-handed and daring, around Montreal and Trois Rivières. It is probable that the French had never heretofore been in peril from Iroquois attack other than petty raids for theft or scalps. But now the danger was mortal, for the pillage of the forts alone might have tempted the Mohawks, if left without furs to trade for goods and ammunition, to risk a heavy attack and to press it home. And there was little hope of reinforcement, for as the France of Richelieu emerged victorious in 1648 from the Thirty Years' War, the France of Mazarin in 1649 plunged into the civil war of the Fronde. New France in its mortal peril could not count on an old France so troubled.

The Canadians received no help from home in 1649, and in the same year they lost their Huron allies. In March, a powerful Iroquois expeditionary force of Mohawks and Senecas settled into position around the mission of St. Ignace. When the gates of the palisades were opened at dawn, they struck down the guards and rushed into the village, which woke in terror. The Huron warriors rallied and ferocious fighting set in. But the Iroquois prevailed, and St. Ignace was given over to flame and massacre. The Iroquois now took the trail to St. Louis, where Fathers Brébeuf and Gabriel Lalemant had rallied and encouraged their people. It was impossible to withstand the shock of the attack, or to match the musketry of the Iroquois. The fathers were captured and carried in triumph to St. Ignace. That night the Iroquois inflicted on Brébeuf and Lalemant those tortures of flame and red-hot iron by which they sought to assure themselves of victory in war and which were to win for their victims martyrdom and canonization.

The destruction of St. Ignace and St. Louis was the result of the greatest of the raids which had begun in 1641. But it meant more than that. If the Iroquois could deliver such blows in two years running, clearly they could destroy all Huronia. The Hurons, decimated by years of plague and wars, could not stand up to their numbers and their arms; the arquebuses of the Iroquois outmatched the few the Hurons had obtained from the French. Huronia was doomed.

Such was the instant conviction of the Hurons, a conviction born of fears which went back to the beginning of the mission and were now realized. The Huron villages, wealthy as no ordinary Indian village could be and often left ungarrisoned, had been a tempting prey, sure to draw attack. Now the conclusive blow had fallen, and all, both young and old, heathen and Christian, determined to flee the land on which calamity lay. In the summer of 1649 they straggled out from the villages, left standing empty beside their cornfields, and paddled across the waters of Matchedash Bay to the island now known as Christian Island. But the numbers were unmanageable, and no adequate stores of food could be found. Neither the nuts of the forests nor the waters of the bay made good the shortage, and the summer massacre was followed by a winter of starvation, disease, and cannibalism. There was, in short, no refuge for the people of Huronia, some eight to ten thousand as they were, because such a population had depended on the cornfields and on trade. When both were gone, only dispersion could save the surviving Hurons. And thus they scattered further in the following summer, some to Manitoulin Island, some to the west shore of the Freshwater Sea. A band of Christians led by the fathers made their way down to Quebec, where they settled first on the Isle of Orleans and eventually at Lorette.

Meanwhile, the Iroquois pursued their remorseless campaign, striking down in late 1649 and in 1650 the dependent neighbours of the Hurons, the Tobacco and Neutral nations. And from them, as from Huronia, the bands of prisoners, mainly women and children, but also many warriors, streamed into the lands of the Five Nations, to swell their numbers and make one people with them. The Iroquois was the victor not only in war but also in policy. It was he, it seemed in 1650, who was the uniter of peoples and the master of commerce.

The loss of the Hurons as allies in the Laurentian coalition was accompanied by failure to gain an ally in New England. The rapidly growing colonies of that region were becoming conscious of the fact that their fur trade was limited to westward by the converging trades of Canada and New Amsterdam and could never be part of the great fur trade of the continental hinterland. In 1647 they had sent an invitation to the government of Canada to enter into a commercial alliance. This was the first of many attempts by Boston to break through the barriers to the westward. Some correspondence followed, but the council of the New England Confederation was disposed only to enter a treaty of commerce, and not at all a defensive and offensive pact against the Iroquois. New England wanted entry to the great trade by which Canada lived, and Canada wanted help to subdue the Iroquois in order that it might enjoy the trade again.

It was a desire that was long to be thwarted. The years that followed 1651 were years of disorientation in the fur trade and mission of Canada. The great focus, the vital artery, Huronia, was gone. In its place was a wilderness, marked by the ashes of the villages and the weeds of the abandoned cornfields. And the Nipissing Indians, Algonkians who had traded fish for corn to trade for furs, were wiped out by the Iroquois in 1651. Nowhere north of lakes Ontario and Erie, or east of Huron, did they leave a commercial rival. They had destroyed utterly the great collecting agency of the fur trade, the Huron middlemen. And having broken the middlemen of the north-west, they proceeded to beat down their neighbours to the west, the Cat nation and the Eries. As a result, the survivors of all the tribes of what is now western Ontario and Michigan withdrew beyond Lake Michigan to the Wisconsin country.

There followed a disruption of the Canadian fur trade so thorough that in 1653 no furs came down to Quebec from the Ottawa. The Iroquois victory seemed to be complete.

Yet it was in fact a barren victory. The Iroquois had destroyed the Hurons, but they did not take their place. They could not, for the Iroquois were not traders to compare with the Hurons, nor could they move the corn of their inland villages to the north shore of Lake Huron for barter with the tribes of the Shield. Neither could they live on fish and berries as could the Ojibwa, nor were they canoe-builders to rival that tribe. Thus they were forced to continue their wars of conquest and pillage because they could not take over the peaceful commerce of the Hurons.

That commerce was something the tribes who had retreated to the Wisconsin country would not give up, as it was something Canada could not do without. It was not surprising, then, that in 1654 a flotilla of fur-laden canoes once more came down to revive and restore the trade of the colony. This was the first flotilla in many years that was not mainly a Huron fleet. The paddlers were for the most part Algonkians. Many of them belonged to that band of the Ojibwa tribe called the Ottawas, who were now to give their name to the Rivière des Prairies. Eager pupils of the Hurons as middlemen, the Ottawas were only partial substitutes for them, as they lacked the corn, the trading skill and the numbers to replace the Huron commercial empire. They were collectors and transporters of furs rather than true middlemen.

The flotilla of 1654, however, was in fact a portent that the stabilized fur trade of 1615–50, in which the Indians brought their furs down for sale on the St. Lawrence, was quite disrupted. Now, as in Champlain's day, young men had to winter with the Indians to ensure that the winter's catch came down to the French warehouses on the St. Lawrence and not to those of the Dutch on the Hudson. Thus the *coureur de bois*, foreshadowed in the career of Etienne Brulé and now matched by the Dutch *bosch-lopers*, came into being as the great Huron trade system was smashed. The French could no longer trade comfortably at the riverside in Montreal or Trois Rivières, but had to go far inland to bring their customers down. Soon indeed they would have to take goods inland as the trade in the *pays d'en haut*, the up country, became fiercely competitive. As a result, Governor Jean de Lauzon, who had succeeded d'Ailleboust in 1651, began in 1654 to allow only licensed traders to go out from the colony to trade.

This change in the conduct of the fur trade perhaps explains why it is in the early fifties that the missionaries begin to complain of the use of brandy as an article of trade. Liquor was the inevitable accompaniment of competition in the fur trade. It had always been used freely in Acadia and the Gulf. With the freedom of the habitants to trade it began to appear, along with the *coureur de bois*, in the trade above Quebec. It was the magnet used to draw the far tribes and to keep them from the Dutch, now that the Hurons were gone.

If 1653 had been a year of desolation, however, it had also been marked by overtures for peace by the western Iroquois. These tribes were engaged in the conquest of the Eries and other tribes of the south-west and wished to end the contest with the French and the remnants of the Laurentian coalition. Peace was concluded in the end with all the Five Nations, including even the intractable Mohawks. The peace opened up a new prospect, a prospect not only of reviving the mission of Jogues to the Iroquois but also of finding in the western Iroquois a check on the Mohawks and a replacement for the Hurons. For the Mohawks had been accustomed to exploit their middleman position even against their own confederates. But these could be supplied with goods, and send out their furs, by the direct route of the St. Lawrence as well as by tortuous waterways and land carriages of the Iroquois country. By such a stroke the disaster of 1649 might be recouped – and the conquerors of 1650 led captive.

With these high hopes Father Simon Le Moyne went to negotiate an understanding with the western Iroquois. He succeeded, and in 1655 a French mission settlement was begun in the land of the Onondagas. The French were welcomed by the hundreds of Huron captives, many still Christian, and for two years the mission prospered. But it was based on the illusory hope that the Iroquois would find the French better suppliers and more attractive allies than the Dutch, and that Jesuit diplomacy could permanently pacify the confederacy. The hope was quickly disappointed. By 1658 the Mohawks had openly broken the peace of 1653 and the western Iroquois were once more growing hostile. The mission was in mortal danger, from which it escaped only by a well-contrived flight.

The failure of the Onondaga mission was only one indication of the ending of the period of the fur trade and mission. In 1655 the Compagnie des Habitants, struggling in debt, had obtained a royal moratorium for five years, and in effect passed the fur trade back to the Hundred Associates. It had not been able to survive the blow of the destruction of the Huron trade and the cost of knitting new connections with the far west. The moribund Company of the Hundred Associates was unable to restore the French trade with new capital and a more vigorous management. The trade kept going as best it could, because the colony was organized for it and nearly all its energy given to it. But the rebuilding of the trading system after the destruction of the Huron commercial empire required that a major reorganization be carried out. How to do it was still obscure.

There was as yet no practical alternative to the fur trade. Agriculture was indeed progressing. In spite of the Iroquois raids, the granting of seigniories had continued, and the distribution of land to habitants. Along the great river's north bank from the Isle of Orleans to Quebec, at Trois Rivières and at Montreal, scattered clusters of farmsteads stood between the water and the forest. In the little villages some hardy families won their own subsistence from the soil. At Quebec, Trois Rivières, and Montreal the habitants were also supplying the needs of the townsmen, the religious communities, the crews of the annual ships, and the traders and hunters in from the forest.

The great need of pioneer agriculture was labour, and Canada was always short of it. Little of what population it had came from natural increase, because its French population was preponderantly male. In 1654 a party of young women was sent to Quebec from France, and the girls were speedily married off among the bachelors of Canada. A multiplication of French families, comparable with that proceeding in Acadia, now began.

Immigration was to remain for some time the main source of growth. For all the difficulties and dangers of the Iroquois wars, the two hundred people of 1642 had increased to an estimated six or seven hundred in 1653, and these were to increase to twenty-five hundred by 1663. It is somewhat difficult to explain how this immigration was brought about, as neither the Hundred Associates nor the Compagnie des Habitants met to any degree their obligations to bring out settlers. One source was the soldiery sent out to defend Quebec and Trois Rivières and the mission at Montreal. Some of these men became settlers. The growing number of seigneurs also brought out some colonists and *engagés*, mostly from Normandy, Picardy, Maine. and other provinces of northern and western France. Among the *donnés*, the lay helpers of the Jesuits, were some who became settlers. But most of the colonists seem to have come as labourers under contract for three years, as *engagés*, a system which had its counterpart in the indenture system of the English colonies. Many must have remained in Canada after their engagements were completed. There were also special efforts made, such as the great party of 1653 which brought over a hundred colonists to reinforce Montreal, and with them the devoted sister and teacher, Marguerite Bourgeoys. In 1659 another party of more than a hundred arrived. But, in the main, Canada was peopled before 1663 by driblets and handfuls.

There was not even such a trickle of people to Acadia. There the growth of population was solely by natural increase, as the children and grandchildren of the few settlers brought out before 1636, who had at that date about a score of married couples among them, spread along the shores of Annapolis Basin and to the Basin of Minas. By 1671 they numbered almost four hundred.

The slender but quickening growth of population was matched by growth in both church and state. For some years there had been talk of the need for a bishop in New France. The Archbishop of Rouen had indeed exercised some jurisdiction over New France and its clergy, but his claims were subject to dispute. The establishment of the Sulpicians in Montreal after 1642 also gave rise to some rivalry with the Jesuits as to whether a bishop when appointed would be a candidate of one order or the other. As the Sulpicians chose to recognize the jurisdiction of Rouen, with the power of the French episcopacy and the King behind it, their cause became identified with gallicanism, while the Jesuits, as was inevitable for members of the Society of Jesus, champions of papal power, looked to Rome and the ultramontane claims of the church. A polite round of ecclesiastical rivalry followed before the candidate of the Jesuits, a scion of the great house of Montmorency and a secular priest, François de Laval, was made Bishop of Petrea *in partibus infidelium* and Vicar Apostolic of New France in 1659. (He was to become Bishop of Quebec in 1674.) Outwardly reserved, Laval seemed to be rather a prince of the church than a father of his flock. But his aristocratic authority and unbending defence of his order made him a significant champion of the independence of the church and its missions at a time when the royal authority which upheld gallicanism at home was about to assert itself in New France.

The church in New France, as a result, was to remain an ultramontane and missionary church for the rest of the century, as it was long to keep the austere and puritanical strain the Jansenists left to the church which disowned them. But it had, with the growth of settlement, to found a sedentary church concerned more with the round of daily Christian life than with the baptism of dying infants and struggles with Indian medicine-men. The question of the trading of brandy for furs had already driven a wedge between missions and fur trade. In 1658 the clergy ruled that it was a mortal sin to sell brandy to Indians. Laval, after a bitter struggle, was to risk the old alliance of mission and fur trade by prohibiting the sale of brandy to the Indians. Thus began a long and indecisive quarrel which weakened that partnership with the fur trade which had lasted since 1615.

In secular government, the governor and council of 1647 continued with little change until 1657. As noted above, de Lauzon had succeeded d'Ailleboust in 1651, and in 1657 Pierre de Voyer, Vicomte d'Argenson, was to succeed de Lauzon. These men were popular governors, on easy terms with the seigneurs and traders who were the chief men of the colony. The council continued to function, and as the two to three syndics or representatives on it were the same seigneurs and traders who formed the Compagnie des Habitants, the government of the colony was very much influenced by this new, small, but powerful *bourgeoisie*. It was a natural development. A semi-popular government, combining political authority with the direction of the fur trade, best inspired the energies and disposed of the resources of Canada. The partial breakdown of charter government, the long distraction of the royal government, the tremendous concentration of zeal of the Jesuit missions – these had combined to let French settlement grow in an easy, natural way, governed by the ups and downs of the fur trade, to which a semi-popular government was a fitting climax. But this development on natural and popular lines was not to be permitted much longer.

In Acadia the feud between d'Aulnay-Charnisay and La Tour, interrupted by the death of the former in 1650, was resumed by his principal creditor, the merchant Emmanuel Le Borgne, whose pressure on La Tour drove the latter to turn to New England for aid. As a result in 1654, with aid from Cromwell's England, Acadia was captured by the New Englanders. There followed, however, not English settlement, for the Acadians were left to multiply on their farms, but the diversion of the produce of the fisheries and fur trade to New England until France reclaimed Acadia by the Treaty of Breda in 1667. The Acadians, a few of whom had twice lived through a change of allegiance, were beginning to become indifferent to external claims on their loyalty.

In Canada the great task was still the reorganization of the fur trade. The Ottawas had not filled the place of the Hurons. In 1656, a former *donné* turned trader, Médard Chouart, Sieur des Groseilliers, of Trois Rivières, came down from Lake Superior by the Ottawa with a great flotilla of fifty canoes. That was one way to restore the fur trade. But there was another. In May of that year, Jean Bourdon sailed for Hudson Bay. He was back in August, having had a fight with "*les sauvages*" and having failed to enter the Bay. Had he succeeded, he might have given a heavy if not a mortal blow to the fur trade of the Ottawa, by developing the trade of the new beaver country through Hudson Bay. When Groseilliers and his nephew, Pierre Radisson, came down again from the up country in 1660, the idea of reaching the beaver frontier west of Lake Superior by some less laborious and costly route was urgent in their minds. A fine for trading without a licence, together with the payment of the heavy tax of one quarter on furs, only sharpened their desire, and they set themselves to find support for an approach to the north-west by the Hudson River or by Hudson Bay.

How serious the need to reorganize was, and how hard-put Canada was for furs, was demonstrated that year by the heroic fight of Adam Dollard and his small band of companions at the Long Sault rapids of the Ottawa. There, imitating the Iroquois pillagers of the past, they ambushed an Iroquois band which had been trapping and trading on the upper Ottawa. They proposed to surprise them at the foot of the portage and despoil them of their furs, but all except eighteen of their Huron and Algonkian allies deserted and the desperate Iroquois fought savagely to force the passage. After three days of siege in a primitive Indian fort, the French were overwhelmed and slaughtered when Iroquois reinforcements arrived. The flotilla of Groseilliers and Radisson saw their remains as they came down from the far west. Dollard and his men had fought for furs, but it was a fight as heroic and necessary as legend has made it, for without furs New France could not live.

The struggle by the Long Sault illustrated the pass to which Canada had come. To live, to preserve the slow, seasonal life of annual ship and canoe flotilla, of eel fishing and the moose hunt, the slow, sloven life of fur post and northern mission, New France had to reach out into the far interior of the continent after the beaver which was the staple that alone could be sold overseas. But to keep up the trade a firmer base was needed – more population than Canada had yet attracted, more capital than the Hundred Associates had been able to secure, more support than old France had yet given. The colony of the fur trade and the mission must find some new centre of strength to replace Huronia, and it might find it in itself, in the Canadian *bourgeois* and the Canadian *coureur de bois*. So at least Pierre Boucher of Trois Rivières stoutly told the young King Louis XIV in 1661. But the King and his great minister, Jean-Baptiste Colbert, had decided that New France could be made part of a French mercantile empire to surpass those of the Netherlands and of England. Their decision was to impose a new character on the fur-trade colony.

ADDITIONAL READING

ADAIR, E. R. "Dollard des Ormeaux and the Fight at the Long Sault: a Reinterpretation of Dollard's Exploit," *Canadian Historical Review*, June, 1932.

BIGGAR, H. P. (ed.) *Works of Samuel de Champlain*, Vols. I-VI.

COLE, C. W. *Colbert and a Century of French Mercantilism.*

DESROSIERS, L. P. *Iroquoisie*, Vol. I.

HUNT, G. T. *The Wars of the Iroquois.*

INNIS, H. A. *The Fur Trade in Canada.*

Jesuit Relations (R. G. Thwaites' edition.)

LANCTOT, GUSTAVE *A History of Canada*, Vol. I: *From its Origins to the Royal Régime, 1663.*

ROCHEMONTEIX, C. *Les Jésuites et la Nouvelle-France*, Vols. I-II.

CHAPTER 4

The Emergence of the Canadian Bourgeoisie
1662-1685

It was not by chance that Pierre Boucher was visiting France in 1661. He had been sent there on a mission. The mission was part of a design of the new governor, Pierre Dubois, Baron d'Avaugour, who had decided that unless the power of the Iroquois were broken, New France could not survive. This also was the opinion of the chief men of the colony, and they with the Governor chose one of their own kind to approach the King. The Canadian *bourgeoisie* thus first stepped forward in history.

Boucher was admirably fitted for his task. Seigneur of Millevaches and St. Michel, commandant of Trois Rivières, he was also colonizer, land speculator, fur trader, soldier, and law officer. He was, in short, a leading member of that small group of Frenchmen of capacity and capital who had become Canadian and had proceeded to develop the land and exploit the fur trade. They were the originals of the *bourgeoisie* of New France, of that "beaver aristocracy" who were the actual strength of New France and the real directors of its fortunes. This fact had already been recognized in Boucher's case by the responsibilities placed on him as commandant of Trois Rivières and was emphasized by his ennoblement in 1661. Thus it was New France itself that spoke to Louis XIV when Boucher was received by the King.

Boucher's mission was to seek the military aid which would enable New France to subdue the Iroquois and open the Ottawa River to the fur trade. He asked in effect that the King exert his authority to supply New France with people for its development and soldiers for its defence. He convinced the King that New France possessed resources which, once immigration had been set flowing and the Iroquois were reduced to submission, could be developed so as to enrich and strengthen France itself. It was an argument that fitted well with the designs which were taking shape in the mind of Louis and of Colbert, who had become his Minister of Marine – minister, that is to say, of naval and colonial affairs.

Those designs were conceived on a grand scale. In 1659 Spain had signed the Treaty of the Pyrenees, the effect of which was to acknowledge that France had replaced Spain as the first power in Europe. But beyond that achievement was to arise the prospect that the line of the Spanish Hapsburgs might end with the death of the son of Philip IV, the sickly Charles. When that occurred, Louis, in right of his Spanish queen, might claim some part of the Spanish domains, either in the Old World or the New. From 1666, when Philip IV of Spain died, down to 1713, New France was to be affected by the struggles arising from the Spanish Succession and the French hegemony in Europe. By this new situation Louis XIV was moved in 1661 to lend to the defence and colonization of New France the support of his personal authority and to give the development of the colony an impetus that it had not received before.

To realize the dazzling prospects before France in 1661, two things were necessary. One was to prepare a settlement of the Spanish Succession in due course. The other, much more urgent, was the development of the colonies and commerce of France to offset the rivalry of the two maritime powers of the north, England and the Netherlands. France must have a navy if it was to have colonies; it must have colonies if it was to share in that commerce with the Americas and the Indies which had created the extraordinary wealth of England and the Netherlands. Colbert had already stimulated the development of the native industries and internal commerce of France. Now he was ready to turn to colonial development and seek, by imitating Dutch methods, to rival Dutch profits and power.

Louis therefore listened with attention to the plain discourse and factual arguments of Boucher, and promised that royal aid, including troops, would be sent to New France. Boucher himself returned there in 1662 full of hope and with a hundred colonists he had recruited. His coming sent a surge of hope through the colony. The troops, it is true, did not come with him, as they were diverted to help resist the advance of the Turks in Hungary, but there were other indications that the royal favour had been won and that at last the King of France was determined to make New France worthy of its name.

The reorganization of the government, for example, was taken in hand at once. The derelict Company of the Hundred Associates surrendered its charter in 1663. The old government by governor and council was remodelled by decree to conform with one form of French provincial government. That was the *pays d'élection* which, in contrast with the *pays d'état*, had no Estates, or representative assembly. At the same time, the government of the colony was consolidated by making the separate governments of Trois Rivières and Montreal subordinate to the royal officers at Quebec. The governor, as representative of the king, remained titular head of the province, and with him as head of society was associated the bishop. The position of the bishop, however, was to be altered, delicately and with some friction, from the independent position of leader of a missionary and ultramontane church to the independent but secondary role of supervisor of a church pervaded by the Gallican spirit of the French monarchy and episcopacy. This change, and a limitation henceforth of the governor's powers was caused by the institution of a third great officer, the *intendant*.

The addition of the intendant to the great executive officers of the province indeed constituted the most significant change made in 1663. The governor might represent the royal person; the intendant was the agent of the royal will. Historically, he was the instrument Richelieu had used to sap the aristocracy and to draw the control of local government from noble to royal hands. Justice, police, and finance were his special and even prime concern. Nothing therefore could have indicated with greater force the determination of Louis at once to strengthen and to control the government of his province of New France than the institution of this office. Moreover, the traditional responsibility of the intendant for financial and economic affairs in the province meant that henceforth the King was committed to the development of the economy, as well as to the defence, of the colony. Governor and intendant were absolutely dependent on the king; the bishop was in a measure dependent on the king's goodwill. These great officers of church and state were not meant to check each other in the performance of their offices, but in fact they often did. Much of the history of the colony was affected by the resultant friction. But neither the King nor his Minister of Marine desired it; the conflicts indeed only added to their difficulty in attempting to govern New France by annual dispatches across the Atlantic.

The bishop, particularly when a Laval, was especially likely to encounter difficulties with his official colleagues. The growth of population meant that the work of the clergy now consisted not only in the conversion of the Indians but also in ministration to the members of the church resident in New France. For this work secular priests rather than regular clergy were needed. To help supply them, Bishop Laval in 1663 founded his Great Seminary at Quebec. It was to train young men to be clerics, but still more, after the use of the early church and of some contemporary French dioceses, it was to be a collegiate centre for secular priests who would go out from it to minister to the laity and return for refreshment and instruction. The Seminary was an organization well fitted to the ecclesiastical needs of the colony, even when parishes were first created in 1678 and 1683. It also enabled the bishop to send his clergy where they were most needed from time to time. It was necessary that he should be able to do so, as the supply of clergy was simply not sufficient to allow a priest for every parish and mission; the general rule of old France that the *curé*, once appointed, could not be removed from his living, was impracticable in New France. The effect was to maintain the authority of the bishop and to prolong the missionary spirit and vigour of the church. Another result was perhaps to keep the church more independent of local ties and royal influence, more ultramontane and less Gallican. The King and his ministers disliked the policy and opposed it, but Laval stiffly held his position, as did his successor, Bishop Saint-Vallier. Only a few of the secular clergy of colonial New France ever became life tenants of their parishes during the remainder of the century.

Governor, bishop, and intendant, then, were the great officers who governed a French province. The circumstances of New France were not, however, actually those of a province of old France. Distance alone meant that its rulers were required to act without direction in a way their equivalents in France seldom were. The Council was therefore kept in being, although it had few counterparts in the provinces of France, and was given the weighty designation of Sovereign Council. (Its designation was changed in 1702 to "Superior Council," as the king became suspicious of its pretensions.) The governor and bishop were members, and the intendant joined them in 1665. The number of Canadian members was increased to five from the three of 1648. At first the governor and bishop nominated them annually, but in 1675 the king assumed this power. In the same year it was established that the intendant, not the governor, should preside at all meetings of the Council. With an attorney to handle its legal business and a clerk to keep its records in order, the Council was now constituted as it was to remain, except for some increase in membership and addition of legal officers in 1675, 1703 and 1742.

It must be said that it was a useful body. Even as a "representative" element in the government of New France, it was not without merit in the seventeenth century. While the practice of summoning representatives appointed by the syndics of the towns was discouraged after 1663, the king had little choice but to appoint some of the leaders of the Canadian *bourgeoisie* to membership on the Council. As an advisory body it served a useful purpose in acquainting new governors and intendants with the actual conditions of the colony. It sometimes managed, as did its successors in the British colonial period after 1763, to make those officers the agents of the *bourgeoisie* and colonial interests rather than of the royal will.

The Council's chief and most lasting work, however, was as a superior court, a court of appeal for the province subject only to appeal to the *conseil privé* of the King himself. By royal decree of 1663 the Coutume de Paris, the common law of northern France, was established as the law of New France. From this basis, the decisions of the Sovereign Council began the shaping of a body of Canadian precedents which was to become a customary law of Canada fitted to the peculiar needs and circumstances of the colony. By the eighteenth century the Council had become a law court and nothing more; in short, a French *parlement*.

By 1663, then, it may be said in summary, New France had acquired its essential institutions.

The remodelling of the government was accompanied by the retirement of Governor d'Avaugour. He was succeeded by Saffray de Mézy, a hot-tempered man who became involved in a quarrel with Laval over the composition of the Sovereign Council. His short and troubled career was terminated by his death in office two years later. Robert Louis, the first intendant appointed, seems not to have come to Canada at all. As a result, the new government and new policy did not really come into operation until 1665. In that year Daniel Rémy, Sieur de Courcelles, came out as the new governor and Jean Talon as the new intendant. Their arrival was overshadowed by the landing of the famous regiment of Carignan, sent as promised after the Turkish danger had been repelled. Commanded by Colonel de Salières, it numbered in all over twelve hundred men. With them came Alexandre de Prouville, Marquis de Tracy, a veteran of the Spanish-German wars, who was the King's lieutenant-general in America and possessed an overruling authority as governor and commander throughout New France and the French West Indies. His first exercise of this authority was to retire Maisonneuve, the veteran governor of Montreal, to France, by way of reducing the semi-independent colony of the Messieurs de Saint-Sulpice, as its proprietors were called, to obedience under the new order.

Tracy's prime mission, however, was to end the Iroquois danger. He attempted to do this by three campaigns against the Mohawks, who with the Oneidas did not hasten to make peace and promise not to molest the Ottawa allies of the French, as did the three other tribes of the Confederacy when the news of the coming of the troops reached them. A winter campaign led by de Courcelles failed; an expedition under Captain Pierre de Sorel to free prisoners succeeded without fighting. Then, as the Mohawks were still defiant, the grizzled and gouty Tracy led his troops through Mohawk villages abandoned by their warriors and womenfolk, and left in ashes the palisades, long-houses, and winter stores of corn. After thirty years the appeals of Champlain had been answered, and the might of France had humbled the Mohawks; the Confederacy as a whole was engaged in a bitter war with the Andastes to the south and was therefore anxious to avoid attack by the French or their allies. The result of Tracy's victory and the war with the Andastes was a peace which was unbroken for ten years.

This was a resounding success which confirmed the colony in its struggle for existence and gave it time to consolidate. Yet in a very real sense it was too late. In French eyes Tracy was chastising rebellious subjects, for the Iroquois had been considered to be such, and their territories part of New France, since Champlain's explorations and the treaty of 1624. But the Iroquois thought themselves independent, and had found in the Dutch of New Amsterdam supporters and allies who denied the French claims. After New Amsterdam had become New York, in 1664, the Iroquois found the English as willing to support them as the Dutch had been. Tracy's victory, if it surprised the English and cowed the Iroquois for the time being, only revealed that behind the Indian confederacy lay a menace to New France even more deadly than the Mohawks and their confederates. The thoughtful people of New France knew this was so, and Marie de l'Incarnation with her sober wisdom, and Jean Talon in his business-like way, talked of buying New York from the English or even of taking it from them by conquest. But no one at the court, not even Colbert, was prepared to deal so radically with the English menace behind the Iroquois danger.

The soldiers, at any rate, had done their work for the moment and cleared the way for the men of peace. Talon, the chief of these, was a complete contrast to the heavy old nobleman whose troops had secured New France. The Intendant was young, dapper, suave, *bourgeois* – the rising bureaucrat as against the veteran soldier. Moreover, he was a protégé of the great Colbert, who was in turn his exemplar and inspiration.

Talon's appointment was a second phase of the development of the royal policy touched off by Boucher's mission of 1661. The problem, as Colbert had seen then, was not merely one of succouring New France and its fur trade. It was one of creating a French colonial system which would match those of the English and the Dutch. Colbert had therefore in 1664 organized the East India Company and the West India Company on the model of those of the Netherlands and England. They were to lay the commercial foundations of a French mercantile empire in the East and the West. The West India Company was to combine the slave trade of West Africa with the plantation economy of the French West Indian Islands and so to develop the most profitable of colonial enterprises, the production of sugar and other semi-tropical products for the European market. The West Indies needed not only slaves but also cheap foodstuffs, such as salt fish and flour, and also lumber and barrel staves for building and shipping. These Canada and Acadia might supply, and therefore the West India Company was given a monopoly of the trade of New France as of the other French possessions in America.

The grant of Acadia was, in fact, a doubtful one, the title being clouded by events which had taken place in that troubled region. When in 1654 an English expedition sent to take New Netherland was turned by the New Englanders against Acadia on the news that peace had been made with the Netherlands, La Tour simply invoked the fealty he had once sworn to Sir William Alexander. Thus Acadia returned to the estate of Alexander whose heir was now an Englishman, Sir Thomas Temple. This loss did not, of course, extinguish the French claim, as England and France were at peace in 1654, and Colbert's grant to the West India Company was based on it. French diplomacy was able to make the grant good when in 1667 England surrendered Acadia by the Treaty of Breda and France once more took possession in 1670.

With the monopoly granted to the West India Company went full rights to the lands and resources of New France and full authority to govern the colony. As in fact, however, the Company left the appointment of the chief officers of government to the King, and soon relinquished the right to grant lands, the creation of the Company was not a return to Richelieu's policy of 1627. The important implication of the Company's control of New France was the assumption that the colony might be brought to produce other commodities than furs. The creation of a diversified economy was the responsibility of the new intendant, and he set himself to discharge it with zeal and ability.

KC-C*

The first need of Canada was people. The population in 1663 had risen to 2,500. Even if this number was surprising in view of the smallness of immigration since 1632, it still meant that there were too few hands to man the fur trade and to clear the soil. It meant also that those on whom the task of attracting people had been placed by the Hundred Associates had failed to discharge it adequately. These were the seigneurs. A few of these, like Giffard and Boucher, had tried to populate their seigniories. Most of them had simply waited for the growth of population to give value to the wild lands they held; that is, like thousands after them, they speculated in the growth of land values in America. But the attractions of Canada were not such as to draw many people from France unless their movement was actually stimulated and organized.

Talon found that the King had already taken measures to quicken the recruiting of immigrants by the seigneurs. In 1663 most of the undeveloped seigniories had been taken back by the Crown. Thus the Intendant had much scope in making new grants, both of lands once granted and of new lands around Montreal and on the Richelieu. From these lands the Iroquois menace had been lifted in 1666. Most of the new seigniories were military ones, granted to officers of the regiment of Carignan-Salières. The regiment, at Talon's plea, was disbanded in New France in 1668, and its officers and men were for the most part persuaded to settle on the banks of the Richelieu.

While Talon was thus creating new cadres for colonization, new settlements ni which *engagés* might work at clearing the forests and new habitants settle, he urged on Colbert the adoption of a policy of royal aid for a special kind of immigrant. Men in considerable numbers could be brought to Canada as labour; the problem was to induce them to remain. The best hope of peopling Canada lay in the natural increase sprung from a population in which the sexes were balanced. Both to induce men to stay, and to begin a native population, an inflow of marriageable women was necessary. But women had not come in sufficient numbers, and it was of course all but impossible in that age for unmarried young women to come without their families. The King was therefore induced to organize and finance the dispatch to Canada of respectable women from orphanages and poor families for whom there was the prospect of a husband and a home in Canada. Some hundreds of these "*filles du roi*" were sent out, and almost without exception were quickly and, so far as history knows, happily married.

The result of Talon's stimulus to immigration and a balanced population was that by 1676, ten years after his work began, the population had increased to an estimated 8,515. And not only had it more than doubled. It was now, for a colony, a population fairly well balanced between the sexes. From this two results followed. One was the beginning of that rapid natural increase which is one of the great facts of Canadian history as of Acadian, although no more so than of New England history. The other was that in settled New France there was practically no intermarriage with the Indians, and New France was spared that mixture of blood which led to so many complications in Spanish America. The Christian Hurons of Lorette and, when the mission to the Iroquois was renewed, the Christian Iroquois of Caughnawaga in the 1670's near Montreal, remained separate from the French.

It was accordingly rather ironic that Louis and Colbert, anxious to push their population policy to the limit, should have revived the "one people" concept and even forced it for a while on the reluctant authorities of the church. That concept, once so strong before the destruction of Huronia, had been discarded both by the missionaries and by the secular authorities. Now, after renewed but sceptical attempts at Sillery and Lorette, it was to be quietly dropped once more and for good.

The stimulation of the growth of population implied, of course, that the colony was to cease to be a mere depot of the fur trade and become an agricultural and industrial community. To the bringing about of this change Talon had also set his hand, and was at work in many directions. He saw, for example, that the pattern of settlement which had developed, the ranging of houses along the river banks, caused a dispersion which not only made defence against Indian raids more difficult, but also prevented the concentration of population that was necessary for industry. For this reason Talon set himself to create model circular villages near Quebec, which were laid out in sectors with the houses grouped on the inner points of the sectors. It was a neat, geometrical adaptation of the nucleus village of Europe, and little more artificial than the townships of New England. But it was not imitated, for the habitant could not resist the advantages the river front gave – the water, the fishing, the easy movement both summer and winter.

Talon's other efforts to stimulate industry were similarly to be brought to little or nothing by intangible but powerful factors in the life of the colony. He used his authority, and both royal and personal funds, to begin new industries by bounties and loans. The intent was to diversify the economy and the exports of Canada. Potash was made; the culture of hemp was begun; the cutting and shipping of lumber was undertaken; shipbuilding was initiated; a brewery was set up; flour mills were multiplied. Here, under the sharp eye and firm will of the Intendant, were the shipping and the goods which would enable Canada to export to France and the West Indies and take its part in the growth of the commercial empire of Colbert's dreams. It cannot be said that the efforts were wholly wasted, sustained as they were through both periods of Talon's work in Canada, from 1665 to 1668 and from 1670 to 1672. Some Canadian agriculture, some Canadian shipping, some Canadian industry, there was to be thereafter. But the shortage of capital and, above all, the high wages of the New World, checked any extensive development outside the fur trade. Only in the fur trade could capital earn an enticing profit; only the fur trade could pay the wages the free labourer could command in Canada.

For the same reasons, however, another aspect of Talon's work was brilliantly successful. That aspect went with and not against the current of the fur trade. To diversify further the economy of the colony, Talon sought to tie the little settlements along the St. Lawrence to the exploitation of the resources of the interior. One obvious way to do so was to explore more intensively than the fur traders had done, and for other resources. With this in mind, Talon in 1668 sent Jean Péré, followed by Louis Jolliet in 1669, in quest of the copper mines of Lake Superior from which Father Claude Allouez had brought an ingot in 1667.

Later he pushed the explorations he inspired beyond particular quests to large-scale exploration of the kind Champlain had prosecuted in his advance to the Freshwater Sea. He sent Simon François Daumont de Saint-Lusson in 1671 to the Sault Ste. Marie, long known to the *coureurs de bois* and the missionaries, and the great nodal point of the Lakes. There Saint-Lusson took possession in the King's name of all the lands that spread out from the Sault along its converging waters. Finally, in 1672, it was Talon again who chose Louis Jolliet, a Canadian, an educated man and a trader, to discover whether the river already known as the Mississippi flowed into the Gulf of California, or into the Gulf of Mexico. The hope was that it flowed into the Pacific by way of the former gulf, and that by the Lakes and the Mississippi the long-sought waterway to China might be found. When Jolliet and Father Jacques Marquette, who accompanied him, had descended far enough to be sure that the great river flowed into the Gulf of Mexico, Jolliet returned to report. He found that Talon had retired and not been replaced, and that he had to present himself to a new governor, Louis de Buade, Comte de Frontenac.

That Jolliet should have given the account of his voyage to Frontenac was in a way symbolic. Talon, in encouraging exploration, had launched New France towards the Mississippi Valley and possession of an inland empire; he had also stimulated the fur trade of Canada, leading it into new regions and making contacts with new tribes. In so doing he had distorted Colbert's policy. Colbert had wished the fur trade to prosper, but he had intended Canada to become a compact colony of settlement. Its agriculture and industries were to be part of a maritime and mercantile empire. Above all, Colbert was opposed to carrying on the fur trade by means of posts inland from Montreal; the Indians must be induced again to bring their furs down to Montreal. Not only had Talon distorted this policy; he had done so to his own profit, for his explorations were also trading expeditions. But in the hands of the new governor to whom Jolliet reported, the distortion was to be exaggerated to the great injury of New France.

Moreover, by 1672 the policy of Louis and Colbert had begun to waver on its course. As early as 1667, when the War of Devolution began in Europe, the sudden projection of the new French colonial policy had begun to yield to other considerations. War on the continent of Europe had at once caused a contraction of French colonial designs, whereas continental wars were opportunities for both the Netherlands and England to add to their colonies. This difference in consequence arose because the Netherlands and England put their naval power first. France by tradition and necessity had to put its army first, and thus the attempt to build up a navy which could win and defend a colonial empire was always likely to be sacrificed to the need to maintain the army. And the colonies themselves were sure to be made a poor third to navy and army. By 1668 Colbert was warning Talon not to count on help from France, and the warning became a refrain as the War of Devolution was followed by the Dutch War of 1672-78. Louis had chosen to try to anticipate the Spanish Succession by overrunning the Spanish and the independent Netherlands, and as a result provoked the first of those European alliances which were eventually to defeat him. In such circumstances it was highly dangerous for New France, against the policy and intention of Louis and Colbert, to be drawn into continental expansion by the fur trade. Such an expansion could be upheld only by the full energy of France, whereas the wars in Europe would leave its maintenance largely to the efforts of the Canadians, who in 1679 numbered only 9,400 people. Thus what seemed a planned advance to the Mississippi and control of the continent was actually an uncontrolled development of the Canadian fur trade, which continued without effective check until the end of the century.

The fur trade of itself had also entered a new stage after 1666. Three things governed its development for the next decade: the peace with the Iroquois, the controversy over the brandy traffic, and the ending of the monopoly of the West India Company in 1674.

The first factor, the peace with the Iroquois, meant that the Ottawas were now free to bring down their flotillas from the up country, much as the Hurons had done before 1648. This they did, although the retreat of the beaver frontier had led energetic *coureurs de bois* like Groseilliers to range beyond Lake Superior and the northern height-of-land in search of new beaver country. The Iroquois could offer less opposition to the French trade than at any time since 1640. They had subdued the Eries and the Cats on their western border but had themselves come under heavy attack by the Andastes and the Mohicans to the south and east. This war made it impossible to resist a French advance along the St. Lawrence and the Great Lakes into the empty peninsula of Michigan and the lands of the Illinois, both regarded as their hunting grounds by the Iroquois. But the Iroquois might and did attempt to lure the Ottawas and other western tribes to sell their furs to the Iroquois for re-sale to Albany rather than take them to Montreal. In this they had the aid of New York fur traders and the advantage of cheap English West Indian rum and cheaper and usually superior English goods.

From the commercial competition between the French and English trade arose the importance of the brandy question. Liquor was a great inducement to the Indians to trade with those who offered it. The pleasures of intoxication many Indians found irresistible, and once intoxicated they gave themselves up to orgies of lust and violence which sometimes ended in mutilation and death. On moral grounds, liquor had therefore to be denied them, or sold under rigid limitation. But in the woods, in the hands of French *coureurs de bois* and Dutch *bosch-lopers* engaged in keen competition for a winter's furs, limitations were scarcely to be imposed or observed. Thus although the clergy and many laymen were firmly opposed to the sale of liquor to the Indians, many of the traders held that the sale was a commercial necessity if the Indians and their furs were to be kept coming to Montreal.

The church's prohibition of 1659 had led to resentment and outright defiance among these traders, and Talon and Frontenac supported them. The ban also aggravated the delicate problem of working out a new relationship between church and state in the colony and aroused some feeling against the Jesuits, the chief advocates of prohibition. Their critics made confession to other clergy, such as the Recollects who had returned in 1670 with Talon's support, and did so with relief when the controversy was at its height. The upshot was a compromise in 1669 (renewed by royal decree in 1679 after the "Brandy Parliament" of 1678), when it was agreed to prohibit the taking of liquor into the woods but to permit its use in Montreal and other settlements, including trading posts in the up country, provided the Indians were not allowed enough to lead to excess. The controversy was resolved in this way, but the enforcement of the prohibition necessitated the regulation of the trade up-country. Hence the regulation of the liquor trade re-enforced a practice begun by Governor Lauzon in 1654, the issuing of licences to control the fur trade above Montreal.

In 1674 the West India Company surrendered its rights in New France. The "farm" of the fur trade of Canada, the obligation to buy the annual yield of the trade in return for the monopoly of the export, was thereafter leased to individual merchants or partnerships. The withdrawal of the Company threw the fur trade open to all Frenchmen, and this further increased the necessity of controlling the trade if the sale of brandy and the conduct of the trade were to be regulated. The governors began to use licences more and more to control the trade up-country.

The power to license, however, was the power to discriminate, to favour one man and deny another. Those denied might seek to pursue the fur trade through other channels. Already Iroquois traders, aided by *coureurs de bois*, were drawing furs to Albany on Hudson River, and the tribes of the north-west were going down to English posts on Hudson Bay. The English were in Hudson Bay because Groseilliers and his brother-in-law, Pierre Radisson, had sought support outside New France for their idea of trading with the far north-west through Hudson Bay. They tried to obtain support in France in 1661, and then in New England in 1662, and were there referred to a body of enterprising men of old England interested in colonial ventures. The result was a trial voyage of 1668 which brought the English trading-ship, the *Wivenhoe*, into James Bay. The *Eaglet*, which was to have taken Radisson to the mouth of the Nelson River, had been driven back to England. The venture in James Bay paid so well that in 1670 the Hudson's Bay Company was formed to make good the English claim to Hudson Bay and to conduct a fur trade from the great inland sea whose tributary rivers drained the greater part of the northern forests and the Precambrian Shield. Thence came the heaviest beaver and the glossiest furs.

Thus English competition was cutting into the French fur trade from north as well as south; and the only answer, as Louis and Colbert failed to grasp, and the justification in a measure of Talon's and Frontenac's evasion of the royal orders, was keener competition and further expansion. If the English trade was not checked by French competition and inland expansion, then the wars of tribal commerce would become the trade wars of the French and English in America. Expansion and competition up-country could only be the work of the *coureurs de bois*, and these men came into their own in the decade after 1670. Their numbers had risen to at least five hundred men by 1681, a major part of the young manpower of the colony.

The *coureur de bois* is commonly depicted as a type, and a type he was, as distinguished from the habitant. (It is doubtless true that the roles were often interchangeable.) The *coureur* was usually a young man; often he could range the woods in the winter and tend his farm in the summer. But the long voyages to the up country of course tended to make him a professional, and addiction to the life of the woods tended to make it impossible for him to settle down on the farm while the hardships of the woods could still be endured.

But among the *coureurs de bois* there were distinctions to be made. In the first place, it must be realized that they were the first manifestation of a recurrent necessity of Canadian agricultural life, the need of the young men to go out to work for wages if the family was to be supported and the young men themselves were to make a start in life. This was as necessary for young Canadians as it was for young Scots, Irish, or Swiss to hire themselves out as mercenaries. It was first the fur trade, then the timber trade, then the canal and railway construction that gave them seasonal employment and cash wages. Nor could the young men be kept content subsisting on the farm; labour was free in New France. For the majority of the young men, the life of the *coureurs de bois* meant no more than this, and they engaged themselves, as perhaps their fathers had done to come from France, to serve in the up country for a term. From these men the *voyageurs* of later fame derived.

Other *coureurs*, however, obviously did not work for wages but were themselves employers. These might perhaps be called master *coureurs de bois*. They were the equivalent of the *bourgeois*, the wintering partners of the later North West Company. Of this type the most outstanding in the seventeenth century were Louis Jolliet, Robert Cavelier, Sieur de La Salle, Nicolas Perrot, Daniel Greysolon, Sieur du Lhut, and Antoine de Lamothe-Cadillac. These men were really inland traders, who were financed by the merchants of Montreal to go up-country to bring down furs under licence, or, if need be, without licence. In Acadia their equivalent was the *capitaine de sauvages*. They were the managers of that mixture of exploration, peddling, Indian intrigue and tribal warfare called the fur trade.

The above description of the *engagé* and the *bourgeois* as two types of *coureurs de bois* does not, however, by any means exhaust the significance of the term. The *coureur de bois* of the records was usually an unlicensed trader; that is, a free trader, one who defied authority in trading and who perhaps took, or threatened to take, his furs to Albany. When he did come down to Montreal, wild, exuberant, perhaps defiant, he drank and rioted, spending his profits on women and finery. Often for good reason he did not return to his parish to rejoin his family and make confession, but remained in the woods, living the life of the Indians and mingling his blood with theirs to begin the race of the métis. As such, he was a threat to the prosperity of New France and a danger to its morals. What wonder that devout governors fumed at him, and that the ecclesiastics censured him, as the police and clergy were later to fret when the lumberjacks came out of the woods or the harvester expeditions came to town? But to prosper, New France had to contain this brood of her wild and lawless children; chide as she might, she dare not disown them. And the expansion of the fur trade alone could hold them, for it gave them occupation and the life they loved.

When, therefore, in 1672, the diplomatic but firm Courcelles returned to France, to be succeeded by Frontenac, New France was prepared by the explorations set on foot by Talon and the advance of the fur frontier beyond the Great Lakes for a period of rapid expansion. The Iroquois, subdued if not broken by Tracy, were still occupied by their wars with their neighbours and commercial rivals to the south. When in 1670 they had proposed to make war on the Ottawas, Courcelles had firmly told them that this would mean a French invasion of their lands. The Iroquois desisted at once. It is doubtful whether the attacks of the Mohicans and the Andastes would in any case have permitted them to win against the Ottawas. But an end to the war with the Andastes would free the Iroquois to bid again for the diversion of the trade of the Lakes to Albany.

This latent danger hung over New France, and the dispersion of effort which expansion of the fur trade would involve might leave the colony exposed to it. A strict confinement of the trade to that with the Ottawas, combined with a strenuous effort to remove the yet scarcely established English from Hudson Bay, would have been the most prudent policy for Canada. But such a policy did not commend itself to the new governor, nor did it fit with his personal interests and imperative needs.

Frontenac was a soldier and courtier whose life had been varied and stormy when in 1672 he was appointed Governor General of New France by the King. In his career he had acquired a body of debts and a skill in putting off creditors exceptional even in a nobleman of seventeenth-century France. These faults were both exaggerated and offset by strong traits of character, great bravado and a furious temper, disobedience to instructions and loyalty to subordinates, soldierly force and official vanity. The appointment as governor was one for which he had every reason to be grateful, for by it he was not only removed beyond the reach of his creditors and given an income; he was also afforded opportunity for gain by participation in the fur trade. Frontenac is not, of course, to be condemned on standards other than those of his own day. It had long been the tradition in France, as elsewhere, that men in public office might benefit financially by their offices. But there were degrees of rapacity permitted and he who exceeded them, like Fouquet, the notorious finance minister of Louis XIV, might expect to be exposed and punished. And Frontenac, by his soldierly bearing, his aristocratic *panache* and, above all, his classic prose, long screened from historians his desperate plight, his excessive rapacity, and the polished prevarication with which he concealed them.

In short, during his first term the Governor was to sacrifice the interests of the colony to the needs of his own desperate career. He was to disobey the clear and explicit orders of the King in 1674 and 1676 that the expansion of the colony was to be checked and the granting of licences limited. Frontenac chose to develop his own connection with the expanding fur trade and to create his own following among the *coureurs de bois* rather than obey his instructions. He thus strengthened the expansive tendencies the King sought to curb. He did so when French aid in troops and money had been limited by the war with the Netherlands. He in consequence exposed the colony to the danger latent in the rivalry with the Iroquois for the trade of the up country.

Frontenac, it must be said, was in many respects the heir of Talon. Not only did his term of office begin when Talon's ended, not only did he govern for three years before Talon's successor, Jacques Duchesneau, was appointed; Frontenac explicitly approved and took up two of Talon's policies, those of westward expansion and the diminution of Jesuit influence. That of the economic development of the colony he ignored. But he exaggerated every aspect of those policies and acerbated every issue by the violence of his temper and the extent of his greed.

The sober and cautious Talon, for example, perfect bureaucrat that he was, had endeavoured to reduce the influence of the Jesuits for the sake of the royal authority. In this there was nothing exceptional; every Catholic court in Europe was attempting the same. But Frontenac at once transformed the bureaucratic pressure into a direct assault. The Jesuit missions ran in a chain westward through the country of the Ottawas. They were at the focal points of the Ottawas' trading system, and no doubt the fathers were influential among these commercial clients of the French. Certainly they would know anything that went on in the Ottawas' country. Moreover, being desirous of sheltering their flocks, they opposed the use of brandy in the fur trade, which Frontenac defended. Frontenac at once took up the gossip that the Jesuits were more interested in the conversion of beaver than of souls. The Jesuits did engage by local barter in the fur trade to maintain their missions, but Frontenac chose to see them only as commercial rivals. Thus began that bitter strife with the order which ran over into his quarrels with Laval concerning the brandy trade. The truth is that Frontenac already saw the Jesuits as opponents of his design to enrich himself by the fur trade, and converted Talon's discreet gallicanism into a bitter feud motivated by personal interest.

The Sulpicians as well as the Jesuits were to incur the Governor's wrath. But the motivation was wholly profit in the fur trade, not at all a rancour against the order. The Sulpicians had appointed François-Marie Perrot, a nephew of Talon's, as governor of Montreal. When the merchants of Montreal began to suffer from the Governor's competition in the fur trade and protested, Perrot intervened on their behalf. The furious Frontenac arrested and imprisoned him. When the Abbé François Fénelon of Montreal defended Perrot in a sermon, Frontenac ordered them both sent to France.

These are instances of the spirit which governed Frontenac's building of the fort named after him at Cataraqui on Lake Ontario. Talon had recommended the construction of two posts, one on the north shore of Lake Ontario to control the Rideau and Trent River routes to the Ottawa and Georgian Bay, and one on the south shore to threaten the Iroquois country itself. Frontenac abandoned the idea of the latter but at once built the fort at Cataraqui, not merely to close the war-paths to the Ottawa River but to begin a fur trade. There came the scattered bands wandering in the former Huron country; there also came Iroquois from across Lake Ontario to trap and trade. The building of Fort Frontenac was the first step in the creation of a line of fur posts running south of the Ottawa route, a south-west trade which Frontenac would support, and from which he would profit. He also summoned the Iroquois to council at Cataraqui, but the result of his diplomacy and his commercial interests was that peace and trade with the Iroquois became the cornerstone of his policy, a peace he could not afford to break and a trade he was reluctant to lose.

To command the post and control this trade Frontenac supported Robert Cavelier, Sieur de La Salle, a Norman gentleman who had connections with Canada and a brother among the Sulpicians. La Salle had come to Canada in 1666, and from the seigniory he had obtained at Lachine above Montreal had entered the fur trade with a journey to Lake Erie in 1669. A brooding, ambitious man, who became a client of Frontenac, La Salle transcended the designs of his patron and aimed at control of the fur trade of the central continent. He became a master *coureur de bois* of the quality and daring of Groseilliers.

The way was now prepared for an advance into the south-west. In 1676 Frontenac built a post at Niagara and La Salle obtained from Colbert himself a licence to explore for the mouth of the Mississippi, to build a line of posts to that river, and to engage in the fur trade, provided he did not trade with the Ottawas.

In 1678 La Salle, with the egregious and garrulous Father Louis Hennepin, a Recollect, advanced by Niagara to Detroit and Michilimackinac. From there he proceeded, despite the loss of his vessel, the *Griffon*, by Lake Michigan and the Illinois River to the Mississippi. Here was the new beaver country, to which the Mississippi would serve as outlet. La Salle descended the Mississippi to its mouth in 1681.

While La Salle was thus exploring the lower Mississippi in 1678 another of the master *coureurs*, Du Lhut, an army officer suffering from the ennui of garrison life, had advanced in 1678 beyond Lake Superior through the Sioux country to the upper Mississippi. During these years the canny and able Nicolas Perrot was active in Wisconsin. The advance of these protégés and supporters of Frontenac had thus carried the fur frontier quite out of the St. Lawrence basin, as had Groseilliers and Radisson. They had therefore to seek a new outlet, as La Salle did in descending the Mississippi to avoid the long haul by the Great Lakes and the Ottawa. The reckless expansion of the fur trade was causing New France to break up into continental sections.

That expansion had also a second effect, and one of immediate consequence to New France. The line of posts by Fort Frontenac and the Great Lakes to the Illinois country and the Mississippi trenched upon the trading area of the Iroquois, to whom the tribes of the Lakes and especially the Miami and Illinois Indians had been tributary. The situation was not helped by the fact that the Illinois in 1678 had repulsed an attack by the Senecas. The Iroquois now felt that the threat to their control of their commercial dependants was too great. Freed from the fear of attack from the south since the defeat of the Andastes by the Virginians in 1676, and of French retaliation by the withdrawal or disbandment of all regular troops but four companies, the Iroquois could deal with the threat they saw in La Salle's advance into the Illinois country. In 1680 the Senecas and Onondagas marched into the Illinois country. The attack marks the beginning of the fourth Iroquois war, which was to bring New France once more into mortal peril.

The outbreak of war caused many and unanimous complaints against Frontenac; they came from Sulpicians and Recollects as well as Jesuits, from Duchesneau as well as Laval. Moreover, not only had the Iroquois menace revived; the colony was in no condition to resist. The riverside settlements, the *côtes*, were scattered and had no forts or places of refuge. The militia had not been trained. The responsibility was Frontenac's, and in the administration of the colony and in the Council he was at odds with all his colleagues. His temper, his pride, his absorption in his own interests and his preoccupation with his own dignity had gravely impaired the administration of the colony. His failure to curb the Iroquois and protect the Illinois and the Ottawas completed the dissatisfaction of the clergy and the traders. Convinced by the unanimity of the Governor's critics, Louis in 1682 summarily recalled him.

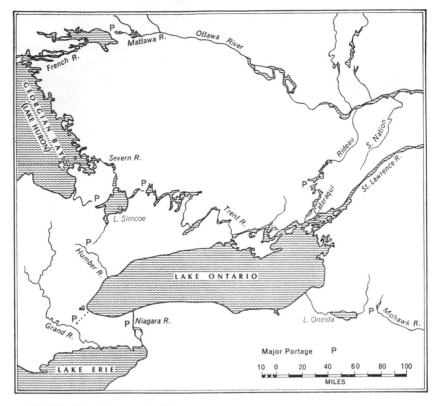

IV   *The Water Routes to the West*

Frontenac had ended his term in disgrace, but two important consequences flowed from his conduct in office. One was the considerable freeing of the government of New France from the missionary and clerical influence which had continued since the last days of Champlain. From his time on, the atmosphere of New France was more secular. The other was that the Canadian *bourgeoisie* had been provoked to assert itself. Frontenac's favouring of certain traders was the last step between the ending the monopoly of the West India Company and the taking over of the fur trade by the "beaver aristocracy" of Canada. This was the final answer to the question raised by the destruction of Huronia: how could the economic life of the colony be organized without a great Indian middleman tribe? Henceforth the Canadian trade was to be handled by the traders of Montreal, under varying degrees of control by governors and intendants.

Meantime, the colony was left to deal with the accumulated results of Colbert's mercantile experiment, Talon's failing industries, and Frontenac's rapacity. The colony was in fact better fitted to deal with the situation than might seem possible, for the events of the decade from 1672 to 1682 had strengthened the Canadian *bourgeoisie*. And the man chosen to lead the colony in the new circumstances was Joseph Antoine Lefebvre de La Barre, a member of the *noblesse de robe* – not an aristocrat or a soldier, but an administrator whom service under Colbert had brought to this unexpected eminence.

La Barre, however, showed himself a pompous, weak and vacillating man in New France. He began his governorship by placing himself in the hands of the *bourgeoisie* and in particular those of Charles Aubert de la Chesnaye, a bold and ambitious trader of Quebec. La Chesnaye wished New France to fight boldly for the control of the fur trade, both of the south-west and of the north-west, in order that the aim of the beaver aristocracy might be realized and Canada made the centre of the North American fur trade. The fur traders were not bent on war, but they were convinced the Iroquois must be curbed because weakness would mean that the Iroquois and the English would infiltrate the Canadian fur trade. And this was not merely fur-trade policy; the colony, clergy and laity alike, supported the policy in an assembly of notables held by La Barre in the fall of 1682. That policy meant the maintenance of the Illinois and the Miamis and the defeat of the Iroquois. It meant resistance to the Iroquois penetration of the country of the Illinois and still more of the Ottawas. It meant also the elimination of the English from their posts on Hudson Bay. The mercantilism of Colbert and Talon had wilted as French ambitions concentrated on the struggle in Europe, but in Canada it was being transmuted by the expansion of the fur trade and the new boldness of the beaver aristocracy into a Canadian commercial imperialism of continental proportions.

La Barre felt compelled to adopt the policy of the beaver aristocracy completely and at once. Indeed he gave them their head, freely issued licences to trade, and stimulated an outburst of trading such as New France had never known before. The *coureurs de bois* multiplied and the colonial economy became wholly one-sided once more. The policy of the *bourgeoisie* involved three measures. One was the putting of the trade on a war footing in the up country and conducting it from new or strengthened posts at Michilimackinac, Detroit, Kaministiquia, St. Joseph on the St. Clair River, St. Louis in the Illinois country. Thus the French traders sought to confirm their advance into the up country since 1672, and to seal off the line of the Lakes to the Iroquois and the English. At the same time, they in effect by-passed the Ottawas as middlemen, and so committed themselves to the conduct of the inland trade by French flotillas and from French posts. After 1681 the fur fair at Montreal ceased. Henceforth the French trade was to be conducted by war and diplomacy as much as by commercial methods, an inevitable reply to the superior quality and cheapness of English trade goods.

The second measure was the organization of the Compagnie du Nord to push the English out of Hudson Bay. This company La Chesnaye organized in 1682, and that year its first ship sailed from Quebec for the Nelson River. Under the command of Pierre Radisson, who had rejoined his countrymen and was a member of the new company, it was successful in capturing a Hudson's Bay Company ship and a New England interloper, and seizing their furs. But Radisson deserted to the English again in 1684 and returned to the Bay to capture the Fort Bourbon of the Canadian company, just built on the Ste. Thérèse (or Hayes) River.

The third step was an expedition against the Iroquois to punish them for pillaging French canoes and to force them to desist from the Illinois war. The organization of the necessary force was La Barre's concern, and he approached it with a mixture of ardour and apprehension which betrayed his anxiety. He proposed, he informed Louis XIV, to destroy the Iroquois power in North America. For this purpose he obtained in 1683 the dispatch of new regular troops, the Troupes de la Marine, detachments of which were henceforth to garrison New France. In 1684 the Governor led a combined force of about eight hundred Canadian militia and Troupes de la Marine to the east end of Lake Ontario. Morel de la Durantaye brought a hundred and fifty *coureurs de bois* and over five hundred Indians down to Niagara from the north-west, but before they joined La Barre the campaign was over. A shortage of supplies and an outbreak of influenza had halted his march, and he was obliged to temporize to save his force. Father Jean de Lamberville, who had renewed the Jesuit mission to the Onondagas and had tried to maintain the peace, came to La Barre's aid. A peace was patched up with the openly contemptuous Iroquois, and they and their stout supporter, Governor Thomas Dongan of New York, were the real victors of the campaign. The astute and forceful Dongan, who was developing a forward policy the Albany traders did not like, had asserted that the English possessions ran north to the St. Lawrence and the Great Lakes, and that the Iroquois were under the protection of the English. La Barre had done nothing to refute this claim. He retired to Montreal, his great effort frustrated.

Moreover, the Illinois were sacrificed by the peace and the Governor was doubly disgraced in the eyes of the Canadians. They had always regarded the Iroquois as being under French suzerainty, and the lands around the Lakes as French territory, and they resented the failure of the Governor to rebuke Dongan's pretensions. La Barre's failure in the field and the storm of protest from the colony led to his recall in 1685. But he was recalled, it is to be observed, because he had failed to serve the new masters of Canada. His failure did not cause them to cease that aggressive policy of expansion which would maintain the war with the Iroquois and their English patrons for supremacy in the fur trade.

ADDITIONAL READING

DELANGLEZ, J. *Frontenac and the Jesuits.*

ECCLES, W. J. *Frontenac: The Courtier Governor.*

FRÉGAULT, GUY *Frontenac.*

GROULX, LIONEL *Histoire du Canada français,* Vol. I.

HUNT, G. T. *The Wars of the Iroquois.*

NUTE, GRACE LEE *Caesars of the Wilderness.*

RICH, E. E. *Hudson's Bay Company,* Vol. I: 1670-1763.

CHAPTER 5

The Climax of the Fur Trade of New France

1686-1701

La Barre, the appointee of Colbert, had even more than Frontenac undone Colbert's policy of concentration and mercantile development. But his support had been given to the Montreal traders and the commerce with the Ottawas, not to Frontenac's connections in the south-west trade with the Iroquois territory. He had been able therefore, unlike Frontenac, to attempt to curb the Iroquois. In this La Barre's failure had been so complete, however, that Louis and his Minister of Marine did not have to be moved by the clamour against him in Canada; they knew at once that he must be recalled.

Changes which had taken place in France may have affected the choice of his successor. The great Colbert had died in 1683. His son, the Marquis de Seignelay, had succeeded to his father's office but not to his father's influence or power. That had been steadily passing to Colbert's rival, the Marquis de Louvois, who was interested more in war and diplomacy than in commerce, more in ascendancy in Europe than in empire in America. The King himself had not only been inclining to the policy of Louvois but also coming under the influence of Madame de Maintenon. Her influence had been confirmed when in 1684 the widowed king secretly married this conventional little middle-class woman, who made the court no less magnificent but certainly more respectable. The outlook of the *dévots*, especially that of Louis's confessor, Father la Chaise, was now in the ascendant at court.

Jacques René de Brisay, Sieur de Denonville, a religious man, was a candidate for the governorship of New France such as the new influence at court could readily approve. But he was a good candidate on other grounds. A soldier, a man of fair ability and some discernment, he was honest even by the best standards of his day, conscientious, and exceptionally able to work with both equals and subordinates. Moreover, he took his duties as the King's governor very seriously, and came to Canada solely to discharge his duties to the King, not to fill his pockets as well, as his immediate predecessors had done. Perhaps a telling earnest of Denonville's concept of his duty was that he brought his wife and daughters with him. In this he followed the good example of La Barre, and their wives were the only governors' ladies at Quebec since the pathetic Hélène de Champlain. Quebec became less a camp and more a court.

This sincere and conscientious man began his term of office with a survey of the situation left by the unchecked expansion of the fur trade under Frontenac and La Barre, and by their failure to curb the Iroquois and protect the Illinois. As a soldier he was horrified by the way in which the straggling riverside settlements of Canada were exposed to Indian attack. This seemed to him of a piece with the dispersion of the trading posts among the western Indians. He urged on the minister, therefore, the concentration of settlement for defence in the colony, though he despaired of seeing it done, and the limitation of the colony to the banks of the St. Lawrence. His urgings were not without effect, as they led to the beginning of the fortification of Montreal and Trois Rivières, and the building of blockhouses in the settlements for shelter during Iroquois raids.

In the matter of the limitation of the colony, however, Denonville found himself caught on the horns of a dilemma, for while the missionaries might deplore and oppose the development of the fur trade by the *coureurs de bois* and the use of brandy, the French missions and French influence in America were inextricably bound up with the French fur trade. To put it another way, the Iroquois were not only the enemies of the French fur trade, they were a deadly menace to the French missions. It followed, as Denonville wrote, that the propagation of the faith among the Indians depended "absolutely upon the humiliation of the Iroquois." Moreover, the Iroquois and their English supporters from New York would have to be stopped from entering the country of the French fur trade and missions, and from wooing the western tribes from the counters of the Canadian traders and the chapels of French missionaries.

Two things were therefore necessary. One was first to check and then to convert the Iroquois. The other was to build posts at what Denonville called "the passes" into the up country – Niagara, Detroit, "Toronto" – and use them to prevent the Iroquois trading with the tribes of the Lakes. The policy was a sober and realistic one, in that its aim was to defend French expansion beyond the settlements on the St. Lawrence and to limit it to the established posts and missions at Michilimackinac and to St. Louis and St. Joseph in the country of the Illinois and the Miamis. Denonville was to fail to carry it out, but substantially it was the policy that was in the long run to prevail.

The Governor's survey, however, was not confined to the Iroquois danger and the western posts. He saw clearly that the Iroquois were a threat because they were supported, if not incited, by the English of New York. The dangers to which New France was exposed, he declared, could be dissipated by the purchase of New York. Perhaps its proprietor, the new King of England, James II – a Roman Catholic, a friend and almost a client of the King of France – might be persuaded to sell it. If not, the English would continue to be a menace in the west, as they were also in Acadia and in Hudson Bay.

Acadia, indeed, though recovered in 1670, had not received either colonists or other support from old France. It was an outlying dependency of New France, a convenient shore for the fisheries at Ile Percée and the Straits of Canso. But Acadia with its Indians was only too likely to be lost to New England. The New England fishermen had the run of its bays. Acadian furs, such as were still obtained, were sold to Boston, not La Rochelle. And the Abenakis of the mainland, though loyal to their French traders and missionaries, were often sorely tempted by the cheapness and good quality of New England goods and ammunition. In short, Acadia could easily be lost by absorption into New England, yet it was apparent that Acadia was one of the bastions of the St. Lawrence gulf and river, and an important element in the defence of Quebec. French influence must be restored in Acadia if French sovereignty was to be maintained there.

In Hudson Bay the prospects for the French fur trade were even worse. Not only had the Hudson's Bay Company established itself in James Bay and at Fort Nelson, as the Canadian Company of the North had failed to do because of Radisson's treachery. The English company was also drawing down to its posts the bulk of the furs, and particularly the *castor gras*, the greasy beaver, on which the fur trade so largely depended. As Denonville wrote, "[the English] are cutting off our trade at the North – all the best of the Beaver Trade, both as to quality and as to quantity."

The English and Iroquois success in the up country, in Acadia, and in the Bay had one conclusive explanation, as the Canadians and their governors recognized and insisted. The English offered cheaper or better goods – in some things, such as scarlet blankets, both cheaper and better – to the Indians. Their goods were cheaper by as much as fifty or even a hundred per cent. Commercially, the French fur trade was outclassed. Its only possible recourse was to wood-running to outrange the English, to Indian diplomacy, and to war. For the Indian fur trade, as practised in the up country, on one side verged on friendship – the exchange of presents, or Indian giving – and on the other merged into war. Commercial inferiority was now to drive the Canadians to Indianize their trade and make it, as the *coureurs de bois* were well able to do, a trade war of raid, ambush and plunder.

Some difficulties stood in the way of recourse to a frank Indianization of the trade in 1686. Not only were France and England not at war; their kings were more than ordinarily friendly and out of that friendship might come the restoration of the Roman Catholic faith in England. Trouble in the American woods must not be allowed to stand in the way of a consummation so devoutly to be wished. In November 1686, the two kingdoms entered into a treaty of neutrality by which they undertook to refer their respective claims in North America to a commission for settlement. Between the sovereigns of England and France and their dependencies, all was amity.

Fortunately for the Canadian fur trade the Iroquois were dependants of New

France, so the French claimed, and the quarrel in Hudson Bay was a private quarrel between two commercial corporations. Thus while his minister in England was still negotiating the treaty of neutrality, Louis could approve Denonville's purpose to make war on the Iroquois, and Denonville could dispatch a party to Hudson Bay to retaliate on the Hudson's Bay Company for its seizure of Fort Bourbon in 1685. The party consisted of thirty men of the Troupes de la Marine and seventy Canadian volunteers, and the command was given to the Chevalier Pierre de Troyes, a veteran officer of the Carignan-Salières. A brave officer and stiff disciplinarian, he lacked the touch for leading the self-willed and mettlesome Canadians. The leadership of the expedition thus in fact fell on the leaders of the Canadians. These were three sons of Charles Le Moyne, Sieur de Longueuil. Le Moyne was a Norman immigrant who by faithful service to the settlement of Montreal, an unusual ability to influence the Iroquois, and all a Norman's hard-headedness in business, had become a wealthy trader and seigneur. His nine Canadian sons, reared in the fur trade and the Iroquois wars and some of them trained in the royal service of the Troupes de la Marine, were in the next decade to make the name of Le Moyne famous by land and sea. The three who led the Canadians under de Troyes were known by the names of their seigniories as Iberville, Sainte-Hélène and Maricourt. It is the first of these whom history remembers as Canada's foremost man-at-arms in his age, a commander who rarely fought save against odds and never fought but he was victorious.

The expedition set out on March 30, 1686, and tramped northwards on snowshoes by way of the Ottawa River and Lake Abitibi. The English posts at Moose and Rupert were surprised and overwhelmed, and in the course of the summer and winter the remaining posts on James Bay were captured. When Iberville returned to Canada in 1687, only Fort Nelson (or York Factory) was in the hands of the Hudson's Bay Company. As this had been recaptured by ships of the Company of the North in 1684, and its recovery by the English in 1685 was not known in 1687, the Company of the North was to refuse to be bound by the treaty of neutrality of that year to respect the English possession of Fort Nelson. Here lay the germ of future conflict in the Bay.

Denonville had meanwhile been studying how to carry out his instructions to protect the Illinois and defend the colony. He watched the growing boldness of the Iroquois in passing their raiding and trading parties into the country of the Upper Lakes. English instigation and support were evident behind their boldness. And the western tribes, disillusioned by La Barre's failure to use them to crush the Iroquois in 1684, had cause to wonder if it were not in their interest to abandon the French and trade with the Iroquois. Denonville finally decided that war, a preventive war, with the Iroquois was inevitable. He so reported and in March, 1687, Louis agreed and wrote that he had ordered the dispatch of the necessary troops. He added that his galleys as usual wanted rowers and that

Iroquois captives would serve, and should be sent to France, an instruction that was to have serious consequence.

Denonville had followed up his dispatch proposing war by sending orders to Du Lhut to fortify Detroit and to La Durantaye to fortify Toronto. These passes by which the Iroquois went to Michilimackinac were now to be closed and the up country sealed off by a line of forts. How necessary such measures were for the Canadian trade had been revealed in 1686 when a party of English traders from Albany had penetrated to Michilimackinac and traded on the strength of Dongan's claim that English territory extended to the lakes and that the trade with the north-west tribes was open to the English. In 1687 a second party of sixty English traders bound for Michilimackinac was deliberately ambushed and captured at Denonville's command. This entry of the English into the trade was a new and serious competition, although in the long run a competition as fatal to the Iroquois as to the French. In consequence, the master *coureurs de bois* of the up-country posts, such as Du Lhut and Perrot, worked assiduously in 1686 and early 1687 to hold the western tribes loyal to the French and to move them to assemble at Niagara, as in 1684, to crush the Senecas. It was only by the ceaseless exertion of the skill in Indian diplomacy their years in the woods had given them that they were able to persuade the reluctant and doubtful Hurons, Ottawas, and Potawatomis to take the war-path once more in midsummer, 1687.

In the colony Denonville and the new intendant, Jean Bochart de Champigny, toiled to organize, supply and equip the militia. They worked harmoniously, as Denonville's repeated "the Intendant and I" signified. By July a force of over 800 Troupes de la Marine and over 900 militia was on foot. Four hundred mission Indians accompanied them. Champigny proceeded to Cataraqui to make sure the supplies which had been forwarded were in order. Finding Iroquois camped in the vicinity, he captured them, lest they warn the Seneca villages. It was a necessary precaution, but these and other Iroquois prisoners were then sent to France for the galleys as the King had commanded.

Denonville advanced up the St. Lawrence in August. The movement was efficiently carried out, as was that from Cataraqui across the lake to the Iroquois borders. The *coureurs de bois* and western Indians joined Denonville from Niagara and the advance inland began. The Governor, a first-rate regimental officer, marched doggedly beside his men in the summer heat and the sweltering forest glades. The Senecas attempted an ambush which failed to trap the column; they were repulsed and made no further resistance. The French advanced into the heart of the home country of the most formidable of the Five Nations. For the first time the Seneca villages were burnt and the green corn was hacked down in the fields. Denonville then went on to the Niagara River, proclaimed French possession and built a fort at its mouth, in which he left a garrison under de Troyes. With Toronto already occupied, the routes to the up country were now blocked.

The Iroquois had not, however, been broken, much less annihilated. Denonville knew this, but he was powerless to strike again. An outbreak of measles and smallpox in the colony made a second expedition impossible that year. In 1688 both men and money were lacking, and the Governor's policy began to crumble. Fort Niagara ran out of provisions, and de Troyes and most of his men perished there. Denonville was not able to re-occupy the post. He ordered it to be demolished, and had indeed to contemplate withdrawal from Cataraqui. To abandon these checks on the Iroquois was, of course, to invite them to re-enter the fur trade of the up country and even to attack Montreal. Unless more troops were sent, the war could not be resumed.

When the Governor learned that only three hundred could be spared, a number insufficient to replace the wastage of war and disease, he decided he must negotiate. The Oneidas, Onondagas and Cayugas, influenced by Father de Lamberville of the Onondaga mission, began the tortuous processes of Iroquois diplomacy in June, 1688, and promised, in return for the restoration of the Iroquois prisoners in Canada and France, to undertake to persuade the Senecas and Mohawks to accept the treaty. It seemed that Denonville might yet come out of his difficulties with a good peace with the Five Nations. He wrote urgently requesting that the Iroquois galley-slaves be sent back to New France. In the up country, however, the tribes viewed the negotiations and the Governor's uncertainty with the suspicion which any improvement in relations between the French and the Iroquois always aroused in them. The ablest, wisest, and most sophisticated of their chiefs, the Huron Kondiaronk, the Rat, acted quietly; with a war band he fell on the deputies of the three Iroquois tribes as they returned to Montreal, killed one of them, and led the others to believe Denonville had ordered the ambush. His attempt to block the peace was thwarted, however, and an Iroquois envoy who had escaped was persuaded by the French that Denonville had nothing to do with Kondiaronk's attack.

The conclusion the defeated and bewildered governor drew, as he groped to grasp control of events again, was that French Indian policy could not succeed until New York was wrested from the English. The colonies that lived by the fur trade had to control the whole fur trade; for an economy so primitive there could be only one empire in America. He therefore urged again that New York be purchased or captured, but at a time when France hoped for English friendship, or at least neutrality in Europe, it was impossible to entertain the latter proposal. While the hope of keeping England neutral remained, France would not attempt to obtain New York to assure the security of New France. Nor did the English Revolution in October 1688 alter the situation at once, because James II sought refuge in France and Louis could hardly attack or even offer to purchase the possessions of his guest. The Huron attempt to prevent a peace being made had hardly been thwarted when the new governor of New York, Sir Edmund Andros, appointed by James, also began working on the Five Nations and called their envoys to Albany. The Governor accordingly sent Louis Hector de Callières to France to obtain reinforcements for Canada and to urge an attack on New York. Callières, the governor of Montreal, who had distinguished himself in the campaign of 1687, was convinced that the conquest of New York was necessary to the security and prosperity of New France, and he urged its capture on the Court with earnestness and ability. But the outbreak of war in Europe now began to govern the disposition of the men and resources of France. Denonville was recalled, with warm words of commendation for his services in New France, to a post at the French court.

Callières at once sought the post of governor for himself, but his suit was not successful. Instead, Frontenac, who had been recalled under a cloud in 1682, was once more sent to govern New France. Since his return he had worked tirelessly to regain favour. His wife and friends at court had aided him. Their joint efforts and seven busy years had had their effect. And at a time when the war demanded the services of the King's ablest men in Europe, Frontenac with his ten years' experience and considerable ability no doubt seemed the best available candidate for New France.

Whatever the reasons for restoring the once discredited governor, the policy the King adopted for Canada when the war with England began was bold and decisive. A naval expedition was to be sent to capture New York, with the aid of an attack from Canada. Frontenac was to impose peace on the Iroquois, to leave Niagara abandoned and withdraw if necessary from Cataraqui, to aid the Company of the North, and to recover Pentagoët in Acadia. The policy, in short, was to check the Iroquois immediately, and to render them powerless in the long run by the elimination of English support. It was a good strategic plan, but only two ships of war and no troops were assigned to its execution. Success depended upon Callières getting to Montreal early to arrange the expedition up the Richelieu for the capture of Albany and New York. Before Frontenac sailed he had learned that this necessary condition had not been met and that there would be no attack on New York.

There was, however, to be an attack on Canada. When the Iroquois learned that England and France were at war, they dropped all thought of peace and resolved to attack New France with all their force. They were confident the English of New York would help them. Thus when Frontenac arrived at Quebec in the dusk of an autumn evening on October 12, he learned that on August 5 the Iroquois had struck at the Island of Montreal and overwhelmed the settlement of Lachine.

The suddenness and brutality of the blow at Lachine horrified New France. But the attack on that settlement, successful as it was, really marked the failure of the Iroquois campaign. The attack of August 1689 was no ordinary Indian raid. It was an attack in force, and its aim was the isolation of the Island of Montreal and the destruction of French settlement there as Huronia had been destroyed. But the militia and the new blockhouses beat off the first attack at the east end of the island, and the Iroquois victors of Lachine were kept from doing further execution by the militia under Philippe de Rigaud, Marquis de Vaudreuil. The island was held, although other raiding parties burned and ravaged along the Richelieu and the St. Lawrence.

Even though the major object of the Iroquois campaign was foiled, however, its repercussions in New France were strong. The construction of blockhouses and fortifications was hastened. New France went on the defensive; the policy of limitation now fully prevailed. Still in command until Frontenac arrived, Denonville ordered Fort Frontenac to be blown up and abandoned. The colony was in danger of being driven back on the bounds it had had in the year of Dollard's defence of the Long Sault.

Such was the situation when Frontenac landed at Quebec. He proceeded at once to Montreal and from there dispatched reinforcements for the garrison at Fort Frontenac. They were too late, and met the garrison coming down the river. The cornerstone of Frontenac's former policy had been abandoned. Frontenac's next concern was to make a truce with the Iroquois. Three prisoners were sent back to the cantons, to request that delegates be sent to talk peace. But the Iroquois began a second series of heavy raids, in one of which they ravaged Ile Jésus north of Montreal. Thus a pattern was set which was to last for six years, Frontenac seeking peace with the Iroquois while they, crafty and ruthless as always, yet increasingly worried by the weakness and confusion of their English allies, struck, and watched, and struck again.

Frontenac's personal strategy was not yet wholly revealed, however; the project of an attack on New York, or at least on Albany, was kept alive by Callières and by the intendant Champigny, and Frontenac could not openly oppose it. But his own aims were different. He turned to *la petite guerre*, the guerrilla warfare of the Indian, and launched three raids in January 1690 on the New York and New England border. The justification was that they were in retaliation for the Iroquois raids, inspired, the Canadians were sure, by the English colonists. And it must be said that this kind of warfare was in accord with the resources of New France and the military ability of Canadians. From Montreal two hundred men, Canadians and Indians, fell on Schenectady in February. Later, François Hertel of Trois Rivières led a raid on Salmon Falls. From Quebec an expedition made contact with the Abenakis, led by their French chief, the Baron de Saint-Castin, and captured Fort Loyal in Maine. Through the snows and forest passes the haggard parties retreated from the smoking ruins with the plunder of New England kitchens, the floundering women, the fair-haired scalps. The purpose of the raids was to hold Anglo-American troops on the frontier, to plunder, and above all to keep the Indians loyal to New France by active and successful war. Frontenac's strategy seemed actually to be sanctioned by instructions from Louis in July 1690 to maintain "a strong and vigorous defence," as no reinforcements could be sent. There was no more planning for the capture of New York. Yet Frontenac was undoubtedly in error when he turned to border raiding. The same men and the same daring might have destroyed Albany and cut the supply line of the Iroquois.

Frontenac's campaigning was not left wholly to his own decision, however; there were other parties to the war. These were the New Englanders and New Yorkers. Stung to fury by the winter raids, they had come to feel – like Denonville and Callières and the beaver aristocracy – that a decision must be reached and the rivalry of French and English brought to an end. New England wanted to secure the fisheries and the fur trade of Acadia and to end the irritation of the Abenaki raids. But the backstop of Acadia was Quebec, and Quebec must therefore be captured. And the New York traders were anxious to take over the country of the Lakes. The French control of the west country turned on Montreal; therefore Montreal must be taken. The road to Quebec was by sea; that to Montreal lay up the Hudson and down the Richelieu. The basic plan of campaign was therefore simple, and was to become classic, a sea-borne expedition against Quebec combined with a land march on Montreal. The forces of New France could thus be divided, and Canada conquered at a blow.

In the late summer of 1690, accordingly, the English militia slowly gathered in camp at Albany. But this counter-blow to the raid on Schenectady never came; the New Yorkers were ravaged by smallpox and their army did not march. If, however, Montreal was spared attack, it was alarmed along with Frontenac when word arrived that a fleet of warships and transports was approaching Quebec. The ascent of an expedition had not been thought likely, so hazardous was the navigation of the St. Lawrence; Quebec lay imperfectly fortified and with few defenders. But the New England colonies had called out their militia, gathered a fleet from their shipping, captured Port Royal in Acadia, and penetrated the gulf and river.

Frontenac had to hurry down the river, while the regulars and militia followed from Montreal and the riverside seigniories. His men were working hard on entrenchments when the New England fleet commanded by Sir William Phips filed around the point of the Isle of Orleans. When summoned to surrender, Frontenac, with his unfailing flair for the baroque phrase and dramatic gesture, uttered his famous reply: "I will answer your general only with the mouths of my cannon and the shots of my muskets, that he may learn that a man like me is not to be summoned in this fashion."

It was a heroic front to assume before the weak defences of Quebec. But, if the Canadians were surprised and unready, the "Bastonnais" were not without their difficulties. A landing on a defended foreshore was not an easy undertaking for slightly trained and untried troops. Their commanders, Phips and Major John Walley, were inexperienced in large-scale manoeuvres. The smallpox was dragging down man after man in the crowded ships as it had done in the camp at

Albany. And it was mid October; the nights were already lengthening, and ice was forming at the water's edge.

While Phips bombarded the lower town of Quebec, the New England militia threw in their attack on the Beauport Flats below Quebec. They made their landing but were held by the tidal fords of the St. Charles River between them and Quebec, and harassed by a small force of Canadians led by Le Moyne de Longueuil and Le Moyne de Sainte-Hélène. Frontenac stood on the defensive behind the St. Charles, and wisely left the initiative to the isolated and starving enemy. After four days of misery in the mud, the New Englanders withdrew, in a disorderly re-embarkation during which they were not harassed by the Canadians. On October 19 the bombardment had ceased; the baffled force now returned to New England.

Disease and the difficulties and inexperience of the enemy had saved Quebec in 1690, and the formal credit belonged to Frontenac. For a year the return of the New Englanders was feared, and the Canadians strove to strengthen the defences of Canada. But, as the crisis passed, Frontenac could turn to his main interests, the imposition of a peace on the Iroquois and the stimulation of the western fur trade. The fur trade had, of course, years before precipitated a local war of its own in Hudson Bay. That war had in fact continued with the explicit permission of the King, despite the treaty of neutrality; the English were to be cleared from the Bay and the Company of the North reinstalled there. And since 1686 all the English posts but Forts Nelson and Severn had been held by the Canadian company. Nelson was, however, the richest prize of all, and the determination to regain it after its capture by the English in 1685 had kept the war alive in the Bay. But Nelson had to be captured by sea, and a naval expedition into the Bay was difficult to organize. In 1690 Iberville, as daring a seaman as he was a soldier, entered the Bay by sea, but finding himself too weak to take the main prize, Fort Nelson, had to be content with the capture and burning of Fort Severn, a minor post.

The Canadian attacks drove the English company to seek fur lands beyond their reach. In 1688 the English built a post at the mouth of the Churchill River. A young man, Henry Kelsey, who had sailed out with Radisson in 1684, was sent inland to persuade the Chipewyan Indians to come to the post. He failed, but became a devoted *coureur de bois*. In 1690 and 1691 he went inland from Fort Nelson to the Saskatchewan River and the prairies beyond to compose middle-man quarrels and persuade the plains Indians to come down to trade. These efforts were carried out under the threat of the loss of the southern posts to the Canadians.

For three successive years after 1690, Iberville was commissioned to lead a squadron to capture Fort Nelson. But late departures from France, the need to call at Quebec, the necessity of sailing in time to come out of the Bay before the Strait froze, each time thwarted Iberville. In 1694 he tried once more. It is known

KC-D

how this expedition was organized. Iberville undertook it as an entrepreneur acting for the state, and was to have a monopoly of the trade of Hudson Bay to July, 1697. His Canadians were free to trade on their own and were to have in addition a share in prizes and the trade. Thus did these Canadian mosstroopers make war pay: "they traded even in war parties." All went well, this time, and Fort Nelson became Fort Bourbon once more. But the Bay was still not all Canadian, for the English had collected their strength the year before and retaken Ste. Anne (Albany) and in 1695 they were to recapture Fort Nelson.

Elsewhere during these years the war smouldered. In Canada, near famine had prevailed in 1690, 1691, 1692 and 1693. The Iroquois kept the sower and the harvester from the fields; militia duty took men away from the farms at all seasons. The issue of card money, first begun in 1685 by the intendant, Jacques de Meulles, to meet a shortage of currency, became an annual issue during these years. The expedient was successful in creating a local currency that did not drain from the colony or into hoards, but it did cause inflation, contributing to the cost of living and the social misery. The loss of manpower in the war was heavy, estimated at five hundred men for 1690 and 1691 alone. Yet there was unemployment and beggary as people flocked from the river fronts into the towns for safety.

In Acadia, Joseph Robineau, Sieur de Villebon, recaptured Port Royal, and with the Abenakis harassed the New England frontier. In Newfoundland in 1690 the English suddenly captured Placentia, the seat of the French sedentary fishery on that island. This attack was an indication of the growing importance of the fisheries to the naval powers as a source of seamen. On the New York border, raids were made in 1692, but it soon became apparent that that colony could not organize another expedition against Canada.

The time had therefore come to deal with the Iroquois. Frontenac's object was to assure the continuance of the booming fur trade of the up country and with it the loyalty of the western tribes. To accomplish those ends, peace must be imposed on the Iroquois and it must be a peace between the Iroquois and the western tribes as well. To bring them to negotiate, raids were planned on the villages in 1692, but the raiding parties were not ready in time and the raids were postponed. Then in January, 1693, a large and telling raid was made on the Mohawks. After the destruction of the villages an attack was made on the English settlements, but it was decided to return to Montreal. Under pressure from the French, and not supported as much as they desired by the New Yorkers, the Iroquois began a series of negotiations which were prolonged for two years. Frontenac persisted in keeping these negotiations going, against the opposition of Callières and Champigny and despite the danger they created of the western tribes' making a separate peace with the Iroquois. He hoped to pacify the Iroquois without further fighting, while Callières and the Intendant thought the Iroquois were merely restoring their strength and pursuing the fur trade. They also suspected, and rightly, that Frontenac was using the lull to push his own interests in the fur trade once more, with the help of favourites among the *coureurs de bois*.

These were now ranging the up country again as far as the lands of the Sioux, as they had done during Frontenac's first term as governor. The numbers of the fur flotillas of 1693 and 1695, swollen by the stoppage of the Ottawa owing to fear of the Iroquois, were increased also by the return of *coureurs de bois* who had pushed beyond the middleman tribes into new territory among the Sioux and the Assiniboines. As a result the western tribes, disturbed by this undermining of their position and already fearful that they would be sacrificed in the nego-tiations with the Iroquois, became restless and began to fall away from the Canadian alliance.

In 1695, however, the Iroquois, having recovered from the French raids, and hopeful of winning the western tribes, began to raid the colony once more. The fortifications had been going steadily forward, and the blockhouses gave the settlements the means to ward off the raids, as Madeleine de Verchères had done in 1692. But the raids produced no response from Frontenac; in 1695 he re-stored Fort Frontenac in the face of positive orders from the Minister of Marine not to do so. In 1696 he had at last to strike hard in order to make the Iroquois submit and to restore the alliance of the western tribes who were on the verge of concluding peace with them. The Governor led a large expedition against the Onondagas. Even on this occasion, he used a pause at Cataraqui to strengthen Fort Frontenac. When the advance was resumed, the Canadians, with scarcely a loss, ravaged the villages of the Onondagas and the Oneidas. The blow was hard, but not conclusive. Yet it made the Iroquois, certain now they would get no effective help from the English, begin to seek peace in earnest. It also led the western tribes to rally to the French and begin to harry the Iroquois. No peace was to be made for four years, but the Iroquois, their manpower wasted while that of New France had grown in spite of all losses, were at last defeated and had to have peace.

The year of the Iroquois defeat, 1696, also marked the climax of the far-ranging fur trade of New France. And the Governor's game of enriching himself by playing favourites with the *coureurs de bois* was now at an end. The beaver market in Europe was glutted. The farmers of the revenue, required to take the beaver from Canada, which now included that from Hudson Bay, were crying for mercy. The attempt to control the trade and to limit the output by licences had failed. The licences had been multiplied by Frontenac, and the need for them ignored by the outfitting merchants and the *coureurs de bois* alike. The lease of the farm of the fur trade would expire in 1697, and unless drastic action were taken to check the flood of beaver it would be impossible to lease it again and the revenue of New France would be ruined. In 1696 the Minister of Marine, Louis Phélypeaux de Pontchartrain, ordered that all the western posts but one were to be evacuated and razed, and no more licences issued. The up-country trade of

Canada was to be stopped and the fair of Montreal made once more the rendez-vous to which the Indians were to bring down their furs themselves.

The trade could not be stopped at once, and could it indeed be stopped completely? The western Indians had come to rely on the posts and would resent their sudden destruction. Callières and Champigny endeavoured to have the instructions applied step by step, as the only way actually to limit output and bring the trade under control. But Frontenac in 1697 at first proposed to apply the instructions peremptorily and at once; his hope was to provoke a protest which would afford an excuse for having the instructions revoked, or at least an excuse for ignoring them. He came round only reluctantly to a more moderate course in order to allow the *voyageurs*, as he termed them, to evacuate. The grim old man, now seventy-five years of age, could not easily believe that he had received orders that must be obeyed, or that the uncurbed expansion of the beaver trade had at last brought its nemesis.

If it had met with a decisive check in the interior, however, the fur trade of Canada had made a new advance in Hudson Bay. The victory over the Iroquois in 1696 was followed by other victories in that year. They were victories of the irresistible Iberville, then in his penultimate year of glory. His first success was in Acadia. The French court was determined to hold that support of the fishery and glacis of Quebec, and viewed with increasing concern the effect of the New England post of Pemaquid, situated near the Kennebec River, on the fortunes and loyalty of the Abenakis. These, under Saint-Castin and the *capitaines de sauvages*, had destroyed Pemaquid in 1689, but the New Englanders had rebuilt it after Phips took Port Royal. Now, by its pressure and its goods, it was winning the Abenakis away from the French. Iberville was ordered to destroy it and sailed from France with two ships in March. On August 15, Pemaquid surrendered to Iberville's seamen and Saint-Castin's Indians and the fortunes of New France were restored in Acadia.

Iberville then struck at the English settlements in Newfoundland. The strategic importance of that great island for command of the Gulf of St. Lawrence, the necessity of maintaining the French fishery for the recruitment of seamen for the royal navy, the financial returns from the sale of dried cod, all these factors became more evident as in this war English and French realized the nature of their rivalry in America. Moreover, Iberville saw an opportunity to add the wealth of the fisheries to his monopoly of the fur trade of the Bay. The English settlements, protected by a squadron of the navy in summer, in winter lay exposed to attack by land, attack by such a winter's expedition as Canadians had learned to make under Iberville on James Bay and in the guerrilla raids on the New England frontier. He sought and obtained from the French court a monopoly of the English cod fishery of Newfoundland. Then, as he had done for service in Hudson Bay in 1694, he raised a band of Canadians for a campaign in Newfoundland.

Pontchartrain had commissioned Iberville to conduct the campaign in conjunction with Saint-Ovide de Brouillan, the governor of Placentia. Much trouble resulted, for the governor naturally resented Iberville's invasion of his jurisdiction. But Iberville, by his extraordinary patience and his ability to concentrate all his effort on the stroke against the enemy, avoided the conflict of authority which might have arisen. He let nothing delay the swift campaign in the winter of 1696–97 which La Potherie, a participant and its historian, so graphically describes. Striking up from Placentia, the Canadians captured St. John's and then picked off one by one the isolated settlements along the coast. The houses, flakes and boats went up in flame; the hapless captives were huddled in St. John's and on Red Island in Placentia Bay. Only Carbonear and Bonavista on their distant bays still defied the Canadian Cid.

Before the reinforcements necessary for their capture arrived, a squadron of three vessels, of which the *Pélican* was flagship, arrived at Placentia with orders for Iberville to recapture Fort Nelson. He took his ships through Hudson Strait, where the *Pélican* became separated from her consorts. When Iberville sighted the mouth of the Hayes, where Fort Nelson stood, it was only to see behind him the sails of three English ships, one of them H.M.S. *Hampshire*, a warship more heavily gunned than the *Pélican*. Iberville engaged at once, for he could not afford to have Fort Nelson reinforced. After a heavy fight in which all the vessels joined, *Pélican* and *Hampshire* shook themselves free and lunged at one another like fencers. *Pélican's* broadside, delivered by a superb stroke of seamanship as she came up on her opponent's windward quarter, shattered her water-line, and *Hampshire* drove under within three ship-lengths.

The other English ships then fled, and the battered victor was left in the rising wind and the surging breakers off the shoal shores o the Hayes estuary. There was no escape. *Pélican* drove ashore, and eighteen of her crew perished. But Iberville survived, and when his other ships came up, Fort Nelson was besieged and compelled to surrender. Except for Fort Albany, the Canadians were once more masters of the Bay.

It was well for Iberville, with his monopoly, and for New France, with its dependence on the fur trade, that this was so, for in 1697 commissioners had met at Ryswick in the Netherlands to end the wars. The peace treaty fully confirmed the amazing victories of Iberville and his Canadians. New France and the Canadian fur trade had reached the apex of their growth. The posts on the Bay were held; Acadia was held; the French fisheries were undisturbed, although the English settlements in Newfoundland, which had been recaptured, were left in English hands. New France had lost nothing held in 1688, and had gained, except for Albany, control of Hudson Bay.

In a larger view, of course, the peace was not so favourable. If France had lost nothing, it had gained little. The peace was merely a truce, soon to be threatened by the question of the Spanish Succession with its possibility that Spain and its empire might some day be united with France. And England, whose colonies menaced the fur trade and the fisheries, had grown in strength; the House of Commons thanked William III for the Peace of Ryswick by which, they said, he had "given England the balance of Europe." That ability to balance the powers of Europe could in the end destroy the balance of 1697 in America.

That it was a balance that had been struck in America was slowly revealed as the Iroquois reacted to the new situation. The peace did not include them; it confirmed neither New France nor New York in their claims to suzerainty over he Five Nations. The Iroquois, if reluctant to make peace with Canada, were resentful of the English withdrawal from the war and increasingly suspicious of English entry into the western trade and of English claims to suzerainty over themselves. These things, reflecting as they did the rising power of the English in America, gave the diplomats of the Five Nations much to ponder and debate.

Meantime, the peace found Canada struggling to adapt itself to the difficulties of the western fur trade. The colony was suffering from inflation; the issues of card money mounted year by year. Agriculture and industry had lagged during the war; there was continual beggary in the towns and the population grew but slowly. Then had come the cutting off of the licences and the withdrawal of the posts in 1697. The market for beaver was glutted; the warehouses in France were jammed; the western Indians were in distress and resentful. The *coureurs de bois* did not come in as ordered; many stayed in the up country by their settlements with their Indian wives and métis children, waiting to see what would happen. Even the Company of the North, established as it was in Hudson Bay, was unhappy, for its beaver too came into a glutted market and, in any case, Iberville had held a monopoly until July 1697 and taken the profits.

The truth was that even French possession of the Bay could be a blow to the fur trade of Canada. Groseilliers and Radisson had first raised this menace, and Iberville had revived it temporarily. The furs of the interior need not come down the St. Lawrence.

How very true this was the next undertaking of Iberville was to demonstrate. This Canadian had become too big for the little colony on the St. Lawrence. His exploits in the Bay and the Gulf turned his thoughts – as did perhaps the cancelling of the licences in 1696 – to the mouth of the Mississippi. Iberville now aspired to the inheritance of La Salle. He called Pontchartrain's attention to the consequences of France failing to control the mouth of the Mississippi, and in 1698 was dispatched to discover and occupy it for France. He did so, and founded Biloxi in 1699. This was the beginning of Louisiana, the greatest of the extensions of New France. But the immediate consequence was to induce a party of *coureurs de bois* in the up country, who had been warned by the Le Moynes of Montreal, to send their furs down the Mississippi to Iberville.

In Canada, Frontenac had died in November 1698 and had been succeeded by the able and honest Callières. Callières, struggling to deal with the situation created by Frontenac's encouragement of the trade and the abrupt stopping of the licences in 1696, protested sharply at the draining off of furs by the Mississippi when Canada stood in such need of the trade its merchants had built up, and when outlet was denied through Canada. The hinterland of New France was feeling the first pangs of sectionalism. Pontchartrain replied by forbidding the export of beaver or fine furs by the Mississippi, but it was clear that the situation in the up country must be dealt with carefully and cautiously if Canada, victor in war, was not to be ruined by peace.

The first need was to end the long war with the Iroquois. At this Callières, Champigny and Le Moyne de Maricourt worked patiently and persistently. Callières really wanted peace, and, unlike Frontenac, knew how to get it and was entangled in no private interest in the fur trade. And the Iroquois also wanted peace, and not peace only, but neutrality. The wars of the Iroquois were over; the Five Nations would no longer tilt the balance of America. Only the Mohawks were ever again to take the war-path against Canada. In 1700 the deputies came down to Montreal, grave, haughty, as unbending as ever. The presents were laid out; the belts passed to and fro; the proud gestures cut the air, the grave speeches waxed and ended. But the burden was peace; the manner was earnest, the old craftiness laid aside.

All turned then on what the western tribes would do. Kondiaronk, who had watched and pondered events, had made up his mind for peace. During the great council held at Montreal in 1701, while the old chief lay dying, he advised the chiefs of the western tribes to follow the French lead and make peace with the Iroquois. The Indian wars of the fur trade were ended on the St. Lawrence and the Lakes. The Iroquois, since 1641 the inveterate foes of the fur trade of Canada with the western tribes, swift foes who could be neither held nor hit, now withdrew from the contest. They raised the hatchet no more; they were neutral. But they were not neutral only, for they stood proudly in their own lands still, a barrier between the English and the French for another half century. And the Laurentian coalition, extended to the tribes of the Wisconsin country since 1670, tattered and attenuated as it had become, had fought the Iroquois to a standstill in the shifting strife of battle, treaty, and traffic which had marked the course of the great trade of Canada.

The treaty of 1701 was the crowning victory of New France as it reached what was to prove to be its apex of growth and achievement in trade and war. All along the river fronts the rejoicings ran. The horrors of the Indian wars were over. The habitants could widen their fields and watch their children play in peace, sure there would be no sudden shot from the forest. But there was little time for relaxation. New France had to turn at once to the new problems of the fur trade and the wars of the Spanish Succession. The Canadian *bourgeoisie*, who had fitted out the *coureurs de bois* and learned to trade through the inland posts, were still growing in numbers and wealth. They, with Frontenac's private trading and all the abuses of the lawless years between 1672 and 1697, had defeated Colbert's plan of a compact colony in a maritime and mercantile empire. They, with Frontenac and La Salle and the *coureurs de bois*, had built the wide empire of the fur trade, endlessly expansive and fragile as a spider's web.

And overnight they were to be justified. For when Louis XIV accepted the Spanish inheritance for his grandson Philip, then the trade of the interior with its need of outlets in Hudson Bay or by the Mississippi, which La Salle and Iberville had grasped so clearly, suddenly fitted in with the needs of the new Franco-Spanish imperial system. It was necessary to occupy the mouth of the Mississippi to check the advance of English colonists towards the Spanish dominion in Mexico. Thus Iberville, that hybrid of d'Artagnan and Pierre Radisson, was suddenly made the founder of Louisiana – a Canadian *bourgeois* who in seeking to control all the entrances to America for his own profit in the fur trade found himself, like another Champlain, laying a cornerstone of the continental empire of France in North America. It was the apotheosis of the Canadian *bourgeois* and the Canadian *coureur de bois*.

ADDITIONAL READING

ECCLES, W. J.   *Frontenac: The Courtier Governor.*
FRÉGAULT, GUY   *Iberville le conquérant.*
INNIS, H. A.   *The Fur Trade in Canada.*
KELLOGG, LOUISE P.   *The French Régime in Wisconsin and the Northwest.*
STANLEY, G. F. G.   *Canada's Soldiers* (1604-1960).

THE STRUGGLE FOR SUPREMACY IN AMERICA [1702-1760]

By 1701 New France had become, as part of the French Empire in America, part also of the European balance of power. For the next sixty years old France was to struggle to maintain its position in Europe and to preserve its colonial empire in America from conquest by England and the English colonies. England, for its part, sought to hold and wear down France in Europe and to make conquests in the colonies, a strategy perfected by the elder Pitt.

The task facing the rulers of New France after 1702, then, was to defend the extended empire in North America until France won a victory or a stalemate in Europe. The defence of New France depended upon holding certain strong points and keeping the Indian tribes true to the French alliance. After 1713 the strong points were Louisbourg on Isle Royale (Cape Breton), Quebec on the St. Lawrence, and Fort St. Frédéric (Crown Point) on Lake Champlain. By 1732 all were fortified. The alliance with the western tribes rested on the peace of 1701 which had ended the Iroquois wars. Thereafter the western tribes were loyal in their remote, inconstant manner, except for the Foxes of the Wisconsin country and the Natchez and the Chickasaws of Louisiana. Among these tribes English traders were influential, and from that fact came the Fox and Chickasaw wars between 1714 and 1742.

The Indian alliance would hold, however, only so long as the French fur trade was vigorous. After 1714 it faced the growing competition of English traders both from Hudson Bay and from the Atlantic colonies. To maintain the French trade, it was necessary to open new fur country, and in 1731 La Vérendrye carried the French fur trade into the north-west beyond Lake Superior. The new north-west repaired the depletion of the old, but of course it did not end the English penetration of the trans-Allegheny lands.

High prices caused by the War of the Austrian Succession drew the English traders to the Ohio. By this magnet they and western Indians were drawn together in the upper Ohio Valley. Their junction menaced the junction of the provinces of Canada and Louisiana in New France, and in 1749 New France met the challenge by laying formal claim to the Ohio Valley.

KC-D*

That valley was at issue, however, not merely for its furs; the land speculators and frontier squatters of the Anglo-American colonies were resolved to take up its lands. The fighting which began in 1754 was a conflict between the French fur-trade empire, with its Indian allies, and the planters and farmers of the English colonies. When England, led by William Pitt, the voice of the great London trading houses, brought its regular troops and naval power to the aid of the colonists, New France was in mortal peril. The Anglo-American aim was supremacy in America founded on the destruction of New France. When after six years of resistance New France capitulated, it was to the superior numbers which English sea power and the English colonies had brought to bear on the strong points of Louisbourg, St. Frédéric, and Quebec. When these fell, the fragile Indian empire of the fur trade vanished like the gossamer web it was, leaving only the habitants *of Canada as the residue of French empire in America.*

CHAPTER 6

The Spanish Succession and the Survival of New France

1702-1731

The peace between the colonies of France and England was shattered by the outbreak of war in Europe. When Charles II of Spain died at last in 1700 he willed Spain with all its dominions undivided to Philip, Duke of Anjou, grandson of Louis XIV. This act opened before Europe the prospect of that union of France with Spain and the Indies which had hung over the continent since the marriage of Louis forty years before. When Louis accepted the bequest for his grandson, the War of the Spanish Succession began.

In Europe it was to prove a long and costly struggle. The great coalition William III had forged, and which the Duke of Marlborough now led, outweighed but could not crush the firm and centrally placed power of France. The Whig government of England chose to make it a continental war, fought in Europe by great armies. The tremendous sequence of Marlborough's bloody victories began with Blenheim in 1704 and led on to Malplaquet in 1709. That battle was the beginning of a heroic and stubborn defence of France's northern frontier which transformed the war into a struggle for national survival and stayed the course of the victorious coalition.

The European character of the war meant that in America there was no immediate or general outbreak of hostilities. The colonies were war-weary; the metropolitan powers were seeking a decision elsewhere. Except in Acadia, colonial America was quiet. The Iroquois, true to their new policy, did not take up the hatchet, and the neutrality the warriors of the Confederacy had adopted seemed to commend itself as well to New York, New England, and New France. There were indeed even to be active and prolonged negotiations for a formal truce between the colonies.

It was well for New France that the great war in Europe did not bring about a return to the ravages of 1689 to 1697. At the end of 1701 New France stood at a height of fortune it had not reached before, and to which it was not to attain again. The Iroquois had made peace. The New Englanders and the New Yorkers had been repulsed. The country of the Lakes was French, its tribes won to fresh alliance with New France. Three of the four great entries to North America – the St. Lawrence, Hudson Bay, the mouth of the Mississippi – were in French hands. The policy of the Canadian *bourgeoisie* seemed to have achieved all its goals and to have earned most handsome dividends.

Yet in fact, if New France stood at the apex of that development of the fur trade which had begun in Frontenac's first term of office, the Canadian fur trade itself had broken down, its organization shattered. Not only had the enterprise of Groseilliers and Radisson created competition from Hudson Bay, competition whether from English or French; the work of La Salle, taken up by Iberville, had also brought a second competitive area into being with the colonization of Louisiana. Not only had this expansion of the area of the trade set up new rivals; the stopping of the issuance of licences by royal order in 1696 had jarred the operation of the trade and disrupted the flow of furs from the interior to Montreal.

More serious than all the above was the fact that a change in fashion in men's hats had combined with the glut produced by fixed prices and new beaver country to produce a fall in price so great that the French farmers of the trade had begged for relief. When this was granted, one Louis Guigues had attempted to combine the farm of the fur trade with a new sales policy, but failed. In 1700 he too was released from his engagement.

The failure of Guigues meant that the French capitalists despaired of handling the output of the fur trade in the existing conditions of the European market. Was the Canadian trade then to collapse? The triumphant but yet nascent *bourgeoisie* could not allow it to do so. In February, 1700, they took over the privileges of Guigues and formed a Company of the Colony. It was in effect the old Company of Habitants. Three members of the Superior Council sat on its board of directors, a sign that the whole colony had rallied to maintain the trade. But the new company had to face the old difficulties, and these were combined with the outbreak of war in 1702. By the end of 1704 it was bankrupt and the colony was threatened with ruin. So grave was the financial crisis that the Governor and Intendant had to begin once more the issue of card money. This recourse to inflation tided New France over its immediate difficulties, but it did not put the fur trade on a firm footing. That had to await on other events.

While New France floundered in this economic crisis, the war continued to be remote except in the Abenaki country of Acadia. There the Indians were under the pressure of the steady New England advance from river mouth to river mouth. River by river they had been cut off from the sea. Step by step they had been made dependent for trade goods on the traders from Boston. But the Abenakis knew what had happened to the Indians of New England; they knew ıt the Boston men had spared none. Their affections ran to their French chief, the Baron de Saint-Castin, to the French priests, and the French traders who wanted only their furs and left their woods in peace. They had therefore resisted the New Englanders with ambush and foray. When the war broke out, Governor Joseph Dudley of Massachusetts, aiming at the conquest of Acadia and, beyond it, of Canada, increased the pressure on the Abenakis. Governor Callières, an Indian fighter of the school of Frontenac, acted on orders from Pontchartrain in encouraging the Abenakis to raid down the rivers of Maine, in order to bind them to the French cause and to discourage a Bostonian assault on Acadia. There, and there only, did he waken the war in America, and then only through his Indian allies, even if these were led, as in 1702 in the raid on Deerfield, by a Canadian commander, Jean-Baptiste Hertel de Rouville.

The *petite guerre* in New England, however, did not necessarily mean, as it had not meant from 1689 to 1696, any war in the west. There the problem was to work out a policy to replace the vacuum which the cancellation of the licences had created in 1696. Callières was an honest man, but he was a realist who, while he recognized the excesses and abuses which accompanied the fur trade, held that its prosecution and the maintenance of ties with the western tribes was indispensable to the property and even to the survival of New France. He therefore sought, with the help of Vaudreuil, his successor as governor of Montreal, to replace the sudden and ill-administered policy of evacuation with one of Indian concentration at selected strategic sites – the "policy of posts."

It was a Canadian plan in the *bourgeois* tradition, because it sought to prevent the western Indians going to the Iroquois and the English by occupying the passages at Niagara, Detroit, and Michilimackinac. It also sought to hold them by inducing them to settle around these posts, as Cadillac persuaded a band of Foxes from the Wisconsin to settle at Detroit after 1704. At the same time the plan embodied a compromise the missionaries could approve. The Indians settled at the posts would be much more accessible to the fathers, and trade at the posts might also be conducted under regulations which would diminish its worst abuses. Here indeed was the outline of a policy for the conduct of the Indian trade which was to become a standard pattern for the remainder of the French régime. Three of the posts, Tadoussac, Frontenac, and Niagara, were to become royal posts, and all were to be under royal licence.

To persuade the court at Versailles to adopt this policy – so obviously one which men of the school of Frontenac could abuse – required time, and its implementation even more time. The first step was the preparation in 1703 and the dispatch in 1704 of an amnesty to the *coureurs de bois* who had remained in the up country since the cancellation of the licences. These men had lived as outlaws in the west for five years. The debts they owed to the merchants of Montreal had remained unpaid. Their furs had gone to Louisiana or, it may be assumed, to Albany. They had married Indian wives; their huts were filled with half-breed children. If, indeed, the end of the *coureurs de bois* and the beginning of the métis people of the west are to be given a date, it must be that of the cancellation of the licences in 1696. But the refusal of the *coureurs* to come to Montreal had brought the fur trade of Montreal to a halt. The furs were going to the Iroquois, which helps explain the peacefulness of those warrior traders during these years; and the Ottawas were serving the Iroquois middlemen. If the fur trade of Montreal was to be revived, the *coureurs de bois* must be persuaded to bring the fur flotillas down once more.

They were glad to receive the amnesty in 1704, and those who had collected their advances of "debt" to the Indians came down to the colony once more. The others said they would come next year. But many of them had in fact formed ties in the up country which would keep them from ever settling again on the banks of the St. Lawrence. The French colonies of the west, so largely of mixed blood, had begun, and the *coureur de bois*, restless and lawless, was to give way to the voyageur, an *engagé* who toiled at the paddle and the portage but did not winter with the Indians or collect furs.

The resumption of trade, however, was not accompanied by the revival of war between the Iroquois and the Ottawas and the other western tribes. War was not to feed trade as in the previous conflict. The peace with the Iroquois had been followed by the settlement of Canadian agents, ambassadors, it might almost be said, among the western Iroquois. First Le Moyne de Maricourt, then de Longueuil, lived among the Onondagas. When the Senecas proved themselves friendly, and indeed the tribe most attached to the French, Father Vaillant and Louis Thomas, Sieur de Joncaire, were sent among them. These resident agents of the Canadian government kept the western Iroquois well disposed to the French.

Their presence, and the policy they represented, meant that the French could not allow the western tribes to make war on the Iroquois who were now exploiting the middleman's position they had so long desired. When the Ottawas of Michilimackinac wanted to war on the Iroquois in 1704, Vaudreuil, acting in place of Callières who had died in 1703, remarked that they must not be allowed to do so as "the neutrality of the Indians must be maintained in the west." When a party of Ottawas attacked Iroquois at Fort Frontenac the same year, they were punished for the offence at Detroit. The French, that is, were trying to obtain furs through the old *coureurs de bois*, and by interception and persuasion at "the passages," but they were not endeavouring to stop the trading of furs to Albany by war. Until the policy of posts was fully applied, only half measures and a policy of peace were possible.

What the Court feared in the policy is sharply revealed by the rebuke administered by Pontchartrain to Vaudreuil in 1706 for not knowing, or affecting not to know, that Laporte de Louvigny, one Vincennes, and one Arnauld were engaged or reputed to be engaged in contraband trade. Even more pointed was his professed refusal to believe that the Governor himself had sold eight licences to trade. The Court of course feared the revival of the trading practices of Frontenac's day.

None the less, Pontchartrain dispatched Clérambault d'Aigremont in the same year to inspect the posts of Fort Frontenac, Niagara, Detroit and Michilimackinac, as the King was prepared to maintain these. D'Aigremont reported two years later that Niagara and perhaps Frontenac should be kept up but would have to be provisioned by the development of a settlement at La Galette (Prescott) on the St. Lawrence above the rapids. Niagara should be made a fort instead of the warehouse it had been. Detroit and Michilimackinac must also, he advised, be maintained. Pontchartrain replied in 1709 that La Galette might be established in the future. Niagara was not to be fortified, however, and the troops were to be withdrawn from Detroit, as the post had failed to keep the English out of the up country. Michilimackinac he agreed must be maintained. In short, the exposed posts of Niagara and Detroit, where Joncaire and Cadillac were suspected of trade with the Iroquois and the English, were not to be supported by the government, but the older posts of Michilimackinac and Frontenac were to have support.

At the same time, the minister declared that licences were not to be renewed, and reprimanded Vaudreuil for having issued them. The brandy trade was prohibited, as was the selling of beaver to the English. But amnesty was to be extended to the *coureurs de bois* who had remained at Michilimackinac.

Thus after five years of inquiry a fur-trade policy was worked out and applied. It was a system of trade and trade control from strategic sites, but of trade carried on under the limitations which royal policy and the missionaries sought to apply to the fur trade. But the application of this policy in 1709 and 1710 was accompanied by the awakening of the war on the New York border. The peace had spared New France; it had been profitable to New York, but now those profits were threatened by the new Canadian policy.

The habitants of New France had meanwhile benefited from the peace as had the fur traders of New France and New York. The long truce during the war and the depression of the fur trade had allowed the habitants of the Montreal district to cultivate their fields in peace, and the lower settlements around Trois Rivières and Quebec were relieved of the strain of militia service. The young men no longer went off in such numbers as *coureurs de bois* or guerrilla raiders, but married and settled down to burning the forest, breaking the land, and harvesting the heavy crops yielded by the virgin soil. And in the cottages by the river front the children multiplied as the daughters of the *filles du roi* in their turn had children and the balance of the sexes righted itself in the colony.

The picture ought not to be made too bright. If Indian raids and militia service practically ceased between 1704 and 1709, there were other afflictions. Smallpox ravaged the population, both white and Indian, in 1703. In 1705 the crops failed and there was famine. The bankruptcy of the Company of the Colony, and the inflation which followed, raised prices still further and increased the general distress. None perhaps suffered more than the Canadian *noblesse* and the seigniorial officer class. Many of these were old soldiers, accustomed to dependence on government; many were simply unable to master the skills and habits necessary to make their seigniories profitable. Accordingly they sought commissions in the Troupes de la Marine, government positions in the colony or as commandants of the new fur posts, pensions or other gratuities from the Court. This proud but dependent class was a principal element of Canadian society, and it embodied an attitude towards government which can be seen among French Canadians today.

In spite of these afflictions, the population of New France grew. In 1706 there were 8,552 males and 7,865 females in the colony; in 1719 the numbers were 11,279 and 11,251 respectively, a total increase of 6,113. Most of this gain was by natural increase. Practically the only immigrants since the days of Talon had been disbanded soldiers, of whom some hundreds had been settled in the district of Montreal.

The increase in population brought about a change in the operation of the seigniorial system. Settlement of the land had of course been the obligation imposed on seigneurs in New France. But even after the great resumption of 1663, many had continued simply to hold their lands undeveloped. The growth of population after 1700 began to force a rise in land values and enabled seigneurs, of whom some eighteen by 1712 were hard-fisted habitants, to exact a price for a grant of land to a *censitaire*. This was contrary to royal policy, and in 1707 the intendant, Jacques Raudot, proposed reforms that would prevent this and other abuses.

The result was the issue in 1711 of the two *arrêts*, or decrees, of Marly. By the first, lands had to be granted without payment to intending settlers, and at dues customary in the region. Failure to grant would lead to action by the claimant, and failure to settle a seigniory to forfeiture. The effect was to make the seigneur not a true landlord, but really a land agent of the king.

The second decree provided for forfeiture by the *censitaire* of a grant left uncultivated.

The same growth of population was of course accompanied by the development of agriculture. More mouths to feed and more hands for labour made possible the steady clearing of the river fronts and the gradual deepening of the fields back from the river. Between 1698 and 1706 the acreage under cultivation increased from 32,524 to 43,671 *arpents*. After 1705 the harvests improved and the shipment of wheat and flour to the fisheries and the West Indies became a more regular although still an occasional commerce. New France was at last producing, in good years, an agricultural surplus.

Production other than agricultural was as yet slight. Sawmills were becoming numerous, but they produced largely for local consumption. Some timber was shipped to France for the shipyards, and some sawn lumber exported to the Indies. But even with the competition of the fur trade for labour diminished, there was not yet the capital or the skill in management to make the timber industry really competitive in European and West Indian markets, or indeed even to organize a regular supply.

Other industries either failed or remained small and local. Shipbuilding, with the support of the royal government, began to flourish at Quebec in 1705, and the shipyard in the St. Charles River was steadily at work thereafter. Ships of increasing tonnage were built for the royal navy, and fishing vessels for the fisheries and the new seal fisheries on the Gulf were produced. With shipbuilding went the production of pitch and of hemp. The cultivation of the latter had continued from Talon's day and was well established. But as yet, despite the efforts of devoted people like Madame de Repentigny, who organized a weaving shop in Montreal with the aid of a subsidy, there was no other considerable industry in New France by 1710.

The growth of the Canadian economy was accompanied by the development of Canadian government, but in the latter as in the former there was no fundamental change. The one development that must be noted is the increasing reliance of the intendant, in civil as well as military matters, on the captain of militia in each seigniory or parish. Not only did the constant warfare of these years make the captain an active leader of his *côte*; the duties of the intendant in provisioning the garrisons and war parties, and the extensive regulation of industrial and agricultural affairs, made the captain equally important in civil matters. He became the chief agent, as the intendant was the mainspring, of government in New France.

The seigniory, the *côte* or river front, and the parish were normally although by no means always the same area, comprising the same people. Along the St. Lawrence the organization of parishes was well advanced and the church was well on its way in the transition from a missionary to a parochial church. In 1721 the parishes of 1683 were reorganized and in 1724 numbered seventy-seven. Much of the church's missionary past remained embedded in its institutions as the work of the missions went on in new settlements and among the Indians. But with the resignation of Bishop Laval in 1688 and his death in 1708, the heroic days in New France came to an end. His successor, Bishop Saint-Vallier, was a hot-tempered and difficult ecclesiastic who left no mark as Laval had done. During his long episcopate from 1688 to 1727, however, church and state assumed that position of mutual respect and independent co-operation which characterized their relations to 1760.

The year of Laval's death saw the war become active in America just as it began to languish in Europe. The fall of the Whigs in England and the rise of the Tories to power in 1709 had replaced the strategy of fighting the war in Europe with one of seeking cheaper victories at sea and in America. At the same time the implementation of the policy of maintaining posts in the west had helped arouse New York, and brought the long truce to an end.

The truce in the west had not at first been accompanied by any truce in Acadia and New England. The Abenaki raids of 1703, as noted above, were followed by others in 1704 and 1706. Acadian privateers attacked New England shipping. In 1704 the New Englanders struck back at Port Royal, but failed to take it. In 1705 Daniel d'Auger de Subercase, governor of Acadia and defender of Port Royal, attacked the English in Newfoundland, and Saint-Ovide, governor of Placentia, captured St. John's in Newfoundland, destroyed its forts, and left the town defenceless. Saint-Ovide's was a blow à la Iberville. But one of the curious features of this luke-warm war was the lack of any exploit by that incomparable corsair of the earlier war. Having planned a descent on New England which was never organized, Iberville died in Havana, probably of yellow fever, after fighting in the West Indies in 1706. Thus this most brilliant of Canadian soldiers, the representative of the militant *bourgeois* of the fur trade of New France, was not available when at last the war came to Canada.

The autumn of the year of Saint-Ovide's destruction of St. John's saw indeed the drafting of a proposed treaty of neutrality between New France and New England. The model of 1649 was followed and the two colonies proposed to enter into a diplomatic agreement. The French court approved, provided the terms of the treaty were not harmful to French prestige and that they did not permit trade between the French and English colonies. There is some suggestion that Vaudreuil, who had succeeded Callières as governor in 1705, was keener than his opposite number, Governor Joseph Dudley of Massachusetts. When the latter seemed to be playing for time in 1706, war parties were loosed on the New England frontier to quicken his deliberations. Colonel Peter Schuyler, Indian Commissioner of New York, was interested in the possibility of neutrality during these years; the Iroquois were interested, and spoke for Schuyler. In both 1707 and 1708 the French minister repeated that he was ready to approve a treaty of neutrality, provided it included all the French possessions.

Nothing came of the proposal, however, and already in 1707 the possibility of any truce being arranged was diminished by a second New England attack on Port Royal. Once more Subercase beat off the New Englanders, who retired after a siege which ended in mismanagement and some appearance of cowardice.

By the next year all possibility of concluding a treaty of neutrality was ended. The New Englanders were determined to destroy the privateers' nest of Port Royal. In New York the government and traders felt that the truce had served its purpose and could now only allow the French to strengthen their intercepting posts on the Lakes. A force of New York militia therefore advanced against Montreal in 1709 under Colonel Francis Nicholson. It failed to make contact with the Canadians, but in the following year the war against New France, now resolved on, was taken up in earnest on both the Acadian and the New York fronts. The increasingly Tory government of the United Kingdom, urged on by Samuel Vetch a New Englander who was convinced Quebec must be destroyed if New England was to be safe, had agreed in 1709 to support an attack on Quebec after the manner and on the scale of Phips' expedition of 1690. But the needs of the war in Europe intervened, and in 1710 the size of the expedition was cut down and its sailing delayed until the season was too late for an attack on Quebec. Nicholson, who was to have commanded against Quebec, then led the third expedition of the war against Port Royal as an objective secondary to Quebec. He captured the fortress from Subercase in September, 1710. Thereafter it remained in English hands as Annapolis Royal. But a second land expedition against Montreal was thwarted by disease.

Nicholson thereupon set out for England accompanied by four Mohawk chiefs to urge that in 1711 a second and full-scale expedition should be launched against Quebec. His urgings, with those of Samuel Vetch, the presence of the Mohawk chieftains, and the now completely Tory character of the administration, combined to procure the dispatch of an expedition in 1711. The naval commander was a not too competent seaman, Sir Hovenden Walker; the military leader for whom Nicholson was set aside, Brigadier-General John Hill, was a political favourite but a not too incompetent soldier. After delay in England, and even more serious delay victualling in Boston, the expedition was guided up the Gulf of St. Lawrence by Vetch. But Walker disagreed with Vetch about the course, miscalculated the currents, and had seven of his transports and one store-ship pounded to pieces on the ledges of Egg Island. A council of war decided that the expedition must withdraw. And in Quebec, where every effort had been frantically made to repel the attack, a cry of joy went up at the deliverance and the Church of Notre Dame de la Victoire (of 1690) became Notre Dame des Victoires. But the truth was that only a failure of seamanship had checked the blow that sea power had brought so near and that Quebec almost certainly could not have resisted.

The English disaster in the Gulf ended the flare-up of war in Acadia and on the St. Lawrence. Elsewhere little had occurred. Nicolas d'Ailleboust de Manthet had failed in an attempt in 1711 to capture Fort Ste. Anne (Albany) on Hudson Bay. All the other posts but one had remained unmolested in French hands; especially strong was Fort Bourbon (Fort Nelson, or York Factory), where Nicolas Jérémie held the command for twenty years from 1694 to 1714. In Canada, Vaudreuil had built a stone fort at Chambly to close the Richelieu route to the New Yorkers. The Indians were quiet except for a clash in 1712 between the French and the band of Foxes at Detroit, which resulted in the extermination of the band. It was the first and typical conflict between the French and that sullenly independent tribe. Apart from these small affairs, the war was dying down everywhere to a desultory end.

The conflict with the United Kingdom finally ended with the Treaty of Utrecht in 1713. Despite the desultory course and inconclusive outcome of the war in America, the terms of the treaty were to prove disastrous for New France.

There had been no English conquest in America, except that of Port Royal, and to offset that the French still held Hudson Bay. The treaty was made by the peace party in England – for this the Tories were, despite their readiness for a colonial campaign. The French negotiators showed their customary skill and pertinacity in contesting every clause of the draft treaty. Yet in the end the peace involved tremendous losses for New France, and only by stiff negotiations were the remaining strong points necessary for survival retained. In short, from 1713 New France was to live at the mercy of English sea power and under a menace that nothing short of French domination of Europe, if that, could remove.

The territorial losses suffered may be briefly stated. All posts in Hudson Bay were to be restored to the Hudson's Bay Company. The limits of the Company's territories and of New France were to be settled by a joint commission. Newfoundland was recognized as a possession of the British Crown subject only to the right of French fishermen – acknowledged after hard bargaining – to use the shore for obtaining fuel and bait, and for drying fish, from Cape Bonavista around by the Strait of Belle Isle to Pointe Riche on the west coast. All Acadia "with its ancient limits" was surrendered to the English; its inhabitants were given a year in which to withdraw to French territory if they chose not to become British subjects. After much negotiation, Isle Royale (Cape Breton) was retained by France as the guardian of the Gulf, and Isle St. Jean (Prince Edward Island) to provision the fortress.

Nor did the terms of the treaty end with territorial cessions. British sovereignty over the Iroquois was acknowledged. By Article XV all Indians were to be free to trade with either French or English, which meant that in effect the country of the Lakes was to be jointly occupied by the traders of Canada and of the English colonies.

In the matter of the Spanish Succession itself, the result of the war had been a draw. Spain and the Indies passed to Philip V, but the Netherlands were ceded to Austria, and the union of the French and Spanish crowns was prohibited. Thus the menace of a Franco-Spanish world empire was finally removed, although its shadow was later to disturb the eighteenth century as the Bourbon Family Compact.

The real significance of the war was that by virtue of sea power and of colonial population England was potentially, indeed virtually, dominant in North America after 1713. But France was still the first power of Europe, and in America held still the St. Lawrence and the Mississippi. The United Kingdom, for all its triumphs, was war-weary and wanted time to consolidate and prosper. The *détente* between France and the United Kingdom which followed the peace settlement was a reflection of the instinct of both countries that the time was not right for pushing the issue of colonial empire to a conclusion. During this *détente* New France might strengthen its position and hope for a reversal of the strategic balance in Europe and on the Atlantic. The essentials, it might seem, had been saved. The fisheries had been preserved, from which the manpower for the navy was recruited. Isle Royale had been held, and the Gulf kept open. It remained only to fortify the points of strength on which the security of Canada rested.

Thus it was that while in 1714 the French colours came down over Fort Bourbon (York Factory) and Placentia, while the Acadians on Annapolis and Minas basins discussed whether they should leave their farmlands and sea-meadows, Pontchartrain at Versailles pondered a memoir from Vaudreuil on what it was necessary to do to hold New France. It was a very Canadian document, penned by an officer who had in fact become Canadian and who was to found a Canadian family.

First, wrote Vaudreuil, the Troupes de la Marine must be brought up to strength. New France ought not again to run the risks it had miraculously escaped in 1711. Next, it would be necessary to reintroduce the use of trading licences, if the Indians were to be kept from trading with the English. The attempt to do without licences, this pupil of the school of Frontenac still stubbornly held, had been a failure which had played into the hands of the English and the Iroquois. Third, brandy must be used at Frontenac, Detroit, Michilimackinac and such other posts as might be established, to hold the Indians from going to the English. The emphasis in the memoir is that of the realists and the traders, who held that royal policy and the influence of the missionaries had ruined the trade and all but destroyed the colony for an ideal impossible of even partial fulfilment. It is almost as though Vaudreuil sensed that the era of the *dévots* and of the missionary fervour of the Jesuit saints had faded into the prosaic rationalism of the eighteenth century. Fourthly, he went on, the Abenakis must be held in firm friendship with the French if the loss of Acadia was to be minimized and the south-eastern approaches to Quebec guarded. And finally, Isle Royale must be fortified. The memoir was in fact the program of French policy in the next fifteen years.

The main preoccupation of Vaudreuil was with the west. His concern was only in part with the fur trade. In that matter his advice was followed, and the issue of licences was resumed in 1715, when fifteen were issued, and in 1716, when the original number of twenty-five was restored. In the management of the trade in the colony, the bankrupt Company of the Colony had sold its rights in 1706 to Messrs. Aubert, Neret and Gayot of France for twelve years. It was to remain in their hands until 1718 when they merged with the Company of the West, to which a monopoly was given that lasted until 1742. These steps did much to rehabilitate the trade, but they also revealed that the nascent Canadian *bourgeoisie* had failed to develop the strength to handle the great trade of Canada; the traders of Montreal had not become, and did not become, a native and self-sufficient business class.

It was an Indian war, however, rather than the trade, which occupied Vaud-reuil. When the general Indian peace was made in 1702, the Foxes at the termination of the council had doggedly announced that they were still at war with the Sioux. The announcement meant that they intended to maintain their place as the middlemen through whom the Sioux obtained their trade goods. In the announcement was the germ of the two Fox wars which this primitive and stubborn people waged to prevent the French trading directly with the Sioux. Few in number, repeatedly "exterminated," the Foxes always revived and opposed their barrier to the French advance, with the result that French control and exploitation of the west were seriously weakened.

The first Fox war, partly provoked by the massacre of the Detroit Foxes in 1712, began in the Wisconsin country in 1714 and lasted two years. A Canadian war party was defeated in 1715, when young Ramezay, son of Claude de Ramezay of Montreal, and Le Moyne, son of Longueuil, were killed. An expedition to the Wisconsin under Louvigny defeated the Foxes in their fortified encampment at Butte des Morts in 1716, but not decisively. It was possible to carry the French posts forward to Green Bay, Chequamegon and Kaministiquia in 1717 and 1718, but the Foxes were still defiant and attacked the Illinois Indians in 1718.

In doing so, they were deliberately fomenting trouble for the French. In that year – a memorable one for Louisiana and Canada, for in it Bienville, brother of Iberville, founded New Orleans as governor of Louisiana – the Illinois country was annexed to Louisiana. The cession was resented in Canada, where Louisiana was always feared as an economic rival. The loss of the Illinois seemed all too tangible a realization of this fear, and the country was actually in dispute between the traders and even the officials of the two colonies. Louisiana, necessary as it was to the French empire in America, none the less weakened Canada by attracting population and draining off trade. The French empire in America had to be as big as it was, but it was too big for its population and means of communication. This situation the Foxes were cleverly exploiting as they continued, as no other tribe of the north-west did, their dogged and pathetic opposition to Canadian trade and Canadian arms.

By this time the preparations required to begin the fortification of Isle Royale had been made. In 1720 a site was chosen at English Harbour (Havre à l'Anglois), the town of Louisbourg founded, and the fortification of the town and harbour begun. It was an ice-free harbour, adjacent to the fisheries and the gulf it was to protect. In the harbour a fleet could lie secure. Slowly the impressive stone walls, bastions, and batteries began to rise to constitute the Dunkirk of America. But the administration of the work was corrupt, the masonry faulty, the planning faultier still. Louisbourg was not in fact the bastion of New France it was meant to be.

The work at Louisbourg had repercussions throughout Acadia. Some Acadians removed there, and some to Isle St. Jean, to grow food for the garrison. The

French now began to reveal that by the ancient limits of Acadia they intended the peninsula of Nova Scotia, which ended at the Isthmus of Chignecto. The Acadians who remained in the peninsula had evaded taking the oath of allegiance and showed themselves increasingly reluctant to do so. They had begun to talk of a wish to remain neutral, a perpetuation of the weariness which had greeted the war of the Spanish Succession. But their neutrality would never have stood in the way of reunion with those of their own language and faith.

More definite was the effect on the Abenakis. That tribe had suffered serious losses by the peace settlement. After 1714 they continued to be pressed by the advance of the New Englanders colonizing along the river mouths. In 1722 the resentful Indians struck out at their unwelcome neighbours and the Abenaki war began. Vaudreuil, with the approval of the French court, secretly aided the Indians in the four years of the war. His aid not only kept the Abenakis true to the French alliance but also had the effect of limiting English jurisdiction to the peninsula of Nova Scotia. The Abenakis were the principal buttress of this policy of limitation and constriction, which New France was to pursue down to 1755. It was a policy of resisting by intrigue and Indian alliance the consequences of the peace settlement of 1713.

The warfare which smouldered and flared on the borders of Acadia and New England had no counterpart on the New York frontier. There the Iroquois were quiet, were indeed acquiring the habit of peace. But the competition of the traders of Albany in the fur trade of the west was a threat to the life of the colony. By Niagara and Detroit the New York and Iroquois trading parties passed to the up country. The western tribes came down to them through the very neighbourhood of Montreal. Albany men had their agents there diverting furs to the Hudson. In 1726 the English traders had actually to be limited to a two-day stay in Montreal itself. It seemed that New France was helpless once more before the commercial superiority of the English. Now Article XV of the Treaty of Utrecht, providing for free commerce by both English and French with the Indians, made it more difficult than in the past to intervene by other than commercial means in the trade of the western tribes with Albany.

Where the New York fur traders moved with their pack-horse trains and their boats, however, military forces might also move. This fact gave Vaudreuil an opportunity to intervene with military means. The frontiers of New France might legitimately be safeguarded and military measures thus used to strengthen the position of the French traders. Chambly on the Richelieu was already fortified and could be used to check trade between Montreal and Albany. Other such posts might be set up at similar points to supplement Fort Frontenac and Detroit.

The tentative beginnings of such a development of the policy of posts were rudely disrupted by the English establishment of Oswego on the south shore of Lake Ontario in 1726. In 1719 Joncaire, the Canadian agent among the Senecas, had built a picketed house for trade at Niagara, and the post was strengthened subsequently. Governor William Burnet of New York protested in 1721 that this was a violation of Article XV of the Treaty of Utrecht and of English sovereignty over the lands of the Iroquois. No agreement was reached and in 1725 the New Yorkers decided to build Oswego. The Canadian reaction was strong; the Montrealers wanted to raze it at once, and the Marquis de Beauharnois, Vaudreuil's successor as governor, called out the militia of the district.

But calmer counsels prevailed. Canadian reprisals took the old form of the restoration of the licences, which since 1716 had been once more abused and suppressed, and of the use of brandy; and the completion of the fortification of Niagara, to balance Oswego, was carried out in 1727. From these two fortified posts both New Yorkers and Canadians then proceeded to bid for the trade of the fortunate Indians. The French, with their inferior goods and superior transport, would seem, by and large, to have had to content themselves with the heavy, less valuable furs, while the light and high-priced went to the English, with their cheap goods and costly transport.

The line of French posts now ran from Chambly by Frontenac and Niagara to Detroit and Michilimackinac, with an offshoot to hold an important passage to Louisiana, St. Joseph's of the Miamis west of Detroit towards Lake Michigan. It was on this line that New France was to stand until 1749. But one earlier advance was made in a vital area. The New York attacks of 1709 and 1710 had been mounted by way of lakes St. Sacrement and Champlain. It was important to "spoil" any such attack in the future, and in 1731 this was attempted in the building of Fort St. Frédéric at what the New Yorkers called Crown Point. New York protested, but the fort was held and the defence of the Richelieu corridor doubled in depth. Attempts to colonize the southern lakes followed.

It was not only from the south, however, that the Anglo-American pressure was felt. In Hudson Bay the Company had resumed its trade at all the posts from Rupert's River to York Factory. It is true that the trade was still conducted at the mouths of the rivers; the English did not generally go inland after Henry Kelsey's journeys of 1688–91. Only in the north, in the new country of the Churchill, did the Company send inland to draw the Indians down to the restored fort at Churchill. William Stewart in 1715 travelled as far as Great Slave Lake to do this. Moreover, his superior, Governor James Knight, sailed north in 1719 to find the copper mines the Indians had reported, only to perish. From James Bay the Company's goods drew the Indians away from Montreal, and from Albany and York they tapped the rich beaverlands of the Assiniboines, who would otherwise have gone to Kaministiquia on Lake Superior.

This pressure on the country of the Lakes from both New York and James Bay had the effect of making the Montreal fur trade more than ever dependent on the trade of the Wisconsin and on the exploitation of new fur districts. The competition from Louisiana, and from Pennsylvania and the southern colonies, made the Ohio and Illinois country relatively unattractive. The Canadian traders had therefore to look to the north-west.

There were two lines of advance in that country. One was through the Wisconsin country to the lands of the Sioux on the upper Mississippi. But between the French posts and the Sioux hovered the still unsubdued Foxes. In 1727 they began to harry the advancing French and the second Fox war began. Fort Beauharnois was founded in the Sioux country in 1728, but a military expedition against the Foxes of four hundred Canadians and eight or nine hundred Indians under Francois Marchant de Ligneris was a failure. Thus the borders of the Sioux country were closed by the ambushes and forays of a prolonged and indecisive war. Neither a massacre of a Fox band in 1730 nor a second battle at Butte des Morts in 1733 was to cow the Foxes or prevent the Canadians from suffering fresh defeats.

The portages to the Sioux, then, were closed. A second line of advance remained open. That was by way of Kaministiquia and Rainy River to the country of the Assiniboines. There could be found in abundance the thick northern pelts and the "greasy beaver" which were the premium furs of the trade. There could be found new territory with resources which might help New France to redress the continental balance in America which had turned against it so seriously in the war of the Spanish Succession. For the first time, as on the later occasion of Confederation, Canada on the St. Lawrence was to seek in the far north-west the means to maintain itself against the pressure of the Hudson River and the Atlantic seaboard, the superior numbers, resources, and industry of the Anglo-Americans. If the central continent could not be held for Canada, Canada might yet endure as the country of the northern route and the primitive northern economy.

ADDITIONAL READING

BREBNER, J. B.   *New England's Outpost.*
FRÉGAULT, GUY   *La Civilisation de la Nouvelle-France.*
HAMMANG, F. H.   *The Marquis of Vaudreuil.*
KELLOGG, LOUISE P.   *The French Régime in Wisconsin and the Northwest.*

CHAPTER 7

The Balance of Empire in America
1732-1748

By 1732, New France had consolidated its position after the heavy losses of the Peace of Utrecht. Louisbourg was built; the Abenakis had been preserved; the New York frontier was fortified at St. Frédéric and at Niagara. But the line was breached at Oswego, and under the terms of the treaty the English fur trade went on, unchecked except by competition, across the line of the Lakes and even in the environs of Montreal. The wealth of the up country, still New France's principal source of income, was seeping down to New York and to Pennyslvania. The brittle strength of the fortified frontier was being sapped by English trade. And the reserves of French territory beyond the reach of the Anglo-American traders were narrowed down by the long reach of the streams flowing into Hudson Bay, down which the Crees regularly carried their pelts to Rupert and Albany. How, then, was New France, its defences breached, its trade diverted, to preserve its existence and to gather strength for the time when it would once more have to stand off Anglo-American attack until the military power of France achieved victory in Europe?

The question was a hard one, and none of those who lived with it from 1714 to 1744 – Vaudreuil and then Charles de la Boische, Marquis de Beauharnois, as governors, and Jacques Raudot, Claude Thomas Dupuy, and Gilles Hocquart as intendants – can have failed to feel from time to time that it was impossible to answer in terms that would ensure a Canadian victory over Anglo-American competition and attack. Yet the elements of a successful answer may be discerned in the circumstances of Canada, and all these were appreciated by the men who ruled New France and sought to defend it.

The first possibility of countering the Anglo-American pressure lay in adding new fur regions to those already exploited. Beyond the Wisconsin country lay the lands of the Sioux, already visited by Radisson and Du Lhut. Beyond Lake Superior lay the land of the Northern Sioux, the Assiniboines, already visited by Jacques de Noyon in 1688 and probably by others thereafter. These came to Kaministiquia on Lake Superior when they did not go to York Factory on the

Bay. The Canadian canoe-builders had for some years been turning out craft which could move goods to the Lakes in considerable bulk, and the voyageurs had acquired the skill as canoemen that was yet to carry the fur trade to the Pacific. If the lands of either the Sioux or the Assiniboines could be opened to trade, the French might exploit them far from rivalry by the plodding English with their pack-trains and heavy boats. And entry into the far north-west would not only avoid the competition of the Anglo-Americans and bring down to Montreal the bales of the rich beaver country of the upper Mississippi and of the Winnipeg Basin. It might also serve to offset the competition of the Hudson's Bay Company, and even to push back that enemy entrenched in the Canadian hinterland by depriving them of the best furs of their richest preserves.

To restore the fur trade at Montreal, however, was only part of the strategy of economic recovery necessary to give New France the strength to survive the next Anglo-American attack. The ability of France to succour New France depended on the maintenance of French naval forces which could at least pass the Atlantic and run convoys into Louisbourg and the Gulf. The manning of naval forces of that strength in the Atlantic depended in great part on the experienced seamen of the Newfoundland and Gulf fisheries, and the development of the French fishery was therefore a necessary part of the strengthening of New France.

Finally, as has already been noted, the Abenakis and Micmacs of the New England and Acadian frontiers had to be kept loyal and in good heart. The war roads from the Atlantic coast to the south shore of the St. Lawrence were now well enough known to make their possession by allies of Canada necessary to its defence. And in lost Acadia the Acadians remained, French and Catholic, whose recovery was not to be despaired of, and with whom contact must be maintained, if only by the bonds of the faith.

Of all these measures, the one that was new, untried, and of a magnitude sufficient to be decisive was the exploration and exploitation of the north-west. The fur trade of the north-west and its as yet undelimited lands might redress the commercial, and with the commercial the military, balance of empire in America. As was to be definitely and decisively the case a hundred and thirty-five years later, the north-west might in 1732 give Canada the margin of reserve by which to survive the weight of its southern neighbour, until the balance of power in Europe could once more redress the balance in America.

The man who was to throw the beaver of the Winnipeg Basin into the balance of empire in America was a Canadian veteran of the war of the Spanish Succession. Pierre Gaultier de Varennes, Sieur de La Vérendrye, a native of Trois Rivières, had served in the French army in the war of the Spanish Succession. Wounded at Malplaquet and invalided out of the army, he had returned to his homeland and married. By carrying on a fur trade at a family establishment on the upper St. Maurice and by means of the pay of his commission as lieutenant in the Troupes de la Marine, he began the rearing of his family. But the income so gained was too small for his necessities or his ambition, and in 1725 he obtained the licence to conduct the trade of the *postes du nord* situated on Lake Nipigon and at Kaministiquia.

While at the Nipigon post, La Vérendrye heard of the Winnipeg Basin and of a water route to it from Lake Nipigon, the tortuous canoe route over the height of land and by the Albany to the interlocking headwaters of the English River, a tributary of the Winnipeg. And two years later he learned from Father Nicolas Gonor, just back from Fort Beauharnois, of the difficulty, not to say impossibility, of carrying on the western fur trade against the sullen opposition of the Foxes and the suspicious independence of the Sioux.

The sum of what he had learned convinced La Vérendrye that a most profitable fur trade could be carried on in the Winnipeg Basin, and that the way to it lay by neither the Albany – English River route nor by the Wisconsin portages and the upper Mississippi, but west from Kaministiquia. Yet to make such an advance through four hundred miles of tangled waterways, and of portages both wooded and swampy, would involve heavy charges and slow returns. One would need a monopoly to succeed. How was that to be obtained?

La Vérendrye had recourse to the device, as old as New France, and indeed older, of acquiring a monopoly by assuming an obligation at best only incidental to the main purpose. As the monopolists of the first days of New France had undertaken to colonize in return for a monopoly of the fur trade, so La Vérendrye undertook, in return for a monopoly of the trade beyond Kaministiquia, to seek to discover the Western Sea.

The idea may have been suggested to him by the Indians at Nipigon telling of the "stinking" waters of a sea to the west. It may have been suggested to him by Beauharnois, who was to be his loyal patron. Or he may have learned from Father Gonor, or known by common report, of the interest the *savants* of the Regent's court had taken in this now somewhat academic subject, and how Father Pierre François-Xavier Charlevoix had been sent to America in 1720–21 to report on what route might best lead to the discovery of the Western Sea. This being then envisaged as a great inlet from the Pacific, as Hudson Bay was from the Atlantic, it was not thought to be as distant as the Pacific actually is. Father Charlevoix had correctly reported that the two most likely ways lay through the country of the Sioux and the country of the Assiniboines. It was by the latter that La Vérendrye undertook in 1731 to seek the Western Sea in return for a monopoly of the trade beyond Kaministiquia.

In that year La Vérendrye came up from Montreal to Kaministiquia to advance beyond the height of land into the headwaters of the Winnipeg River system. His men refused to make the arduous portage of the Pigeon River route over the watershed, but his nephew, Christophe Dufrost, Sieur de la Jemeraye, went on to Rainy Lake where he built Fort St. Pierre. The rest of the year was spent in trading and in improving the portages. In 1732 La Vérendrye went right

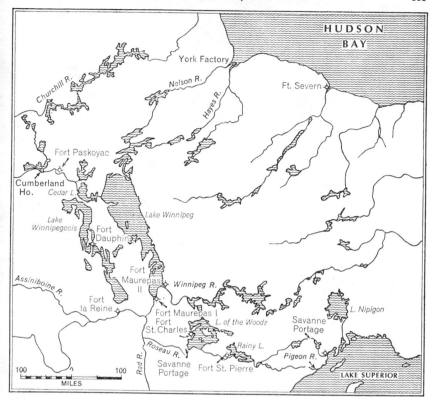

V *The Water Entries to the North-West*

through to the Lake of the Woods. There, on an island off the south shore of the inlet later to be known as the north-west angle, he built Fort St. Charles. It was a major post, with warehouses, dwellings, stockades and gardens. It was a good assembly point for the multitudinous waterways of the Lake of the Woods, and from it access was easy to two lines of advance into the Winnipeg Basin. One was by the Savanne portage to the Roseau River and Red River, the other by the Winnipeg River to Lake Winnipeg.

Here the advance paused for four years. It is true that La Jemeraye and one of La Vérendrye's sons went on in the fall of 1734 to Red River, on which they built the first Fort Maurepas, discreetly named after Jean Frédéric Phélipeaux, Comte de Maurepas, the French Minister of Marine, who was most anxious that the Western Sea be discovered. By then it was apparent that Lake Winnipeg was not the salt-water Western Sea.

But there was no advance in force. The reasons for the delay were many; the men still grumbled at the length and hardship of the voyage, which kept them from home over winter. High water interfered with the wild-rice harvest and lessened the food supply in a region where wild rice was a staple and where no Indian corn could be obtained. The fur trade had to be organized and furs collected to pay expenses and satisfy the creditors in Montreal who had financed the venture thus far.

Finally, the perils of Indian diplomacy had to be faced. The Lake of the Woods abutted on Sioux territory, and the Sioux were jealous of their enemies, the Ojibwas, the Monsonis and the Assiniboines, receiving French goods and guns when they themselves were cut off from supply by the second Fox war, not yet ended. La Vérendrye endeavoured to reconcile the two groups, but could not placate the Sioux at the price of offending the forest tribes. In the upshot he had to favour the latter and allowed one of his sons to go on a Cree war party against the Sioux. In 1736 the Sioux struck back, and on Massacre Island of the Lake of the Woods they killed Jean-Baptiste, eldest son of La Vérendrye, the missionary Father Jean Pierre Aulneau, and twenty voyageurs. This heavy loss and the other delays made it impossible for La Vérendrye to advance into the Red River valley until 1738.

The organization of the next advance, including the provision of food, was completed by midsummer, 1738. La Vérendrye himself passed rapidly by the Red and Assiniboine rivers to the south-west, partly to build Fort La Reine at the Prairie Portage by which the Assiniboines passed down to Hudson Bay, and partly to investigate the mysterious and unusual people, the Mandans, from whom the Indians of Red River bought corn. The Mandans had no positive knowledge of the Western Sea, and La Vérendrye and his sons turned to the necessary work of occupying the Winnipeg Basin, as they had occupied the line of the Rainy River and Lake of the Woods. In 1740, Fort Dauphin was built at the outflow of Lake Winnipegosis into Lake Manitoba, and in 1741 Fort Bourbon on Cedar Lake on the White River, the western river now known as the Saskatchewan and which La Vérendrye then learned flowed, not west, as he had led Maurepas to hope, but east. The size of this river must have diminished any expectation of finding a great salt-water inlet within easy reach. And it was clear that whatever the plains to the south-west might lead to, it was in the forests north of the Assiniboine and Saskatchewan rivers that furs would be found.

In 1742 La Vérendrye's sons François and Louis-Joseph (the latter, known as Le Chevalier, a trained geographer) went out on the plains again to investigate the Mandans' tales of bearded white men trading from the south-west. They apparently explored the bad lands of the Dakotas, crossed the Missouri and saw the Black Hills, but they did not find any evidence of the Western Sea. If their journey had any significance, it was to suggest that a land which gave rise to rivers such as the Missouri and its tributaries was large indeed. Certain it is that the Canadians were deciding that the best line of advance for the search, and for the fur trade which financed it, was by the Saskatchewan. After 1742 all their endeavours were directed to that river.

The search for the Western Sea was an obligation La Vérendrye had assumed in order to obtain the monopoly which might enable him to profit by advancing into the Winnipeg Basin. But it was of necessity subordinate to the establishment of the fur trade. Maurepas, however, with the suspicion engendered in the Ministry of Marine by experience of Frontenac and succeeding governors and traders, relentlessly and unreasonably questioned La Vérendrye's interest in the search. Beauharnois patiently and effectively guarded La Vérendrye from the minister until 1744, when Maurepas refused any longer to be put off with explanations of the twelve-year failure to find the sea, or at least to push westward more rapidly. La Vérendrye was deprived of his commission – his licence to trade had already been awarded to others – and recalled to Canada.

He had, however, firmly established the Montreal trade as far westward as the mouth of the Saskatchewan and the great water and land crossroads of The Pas. One by one, with an almost surgical precision, the routes by which the Assiniboines and the Crees went down to York Factory had been severed by the Canadian route which led back to Montreal. The best and lightest furs, the pick of each year's hunt, were now going down to Montreal and not to York Factory. The French could not move in sufficient goods nor maintain supplies regularly enough to divert all the furs from the Hudson's Bay Company to Montreal. But, using their superior skill in river transport and as Indian traders, they won the best furs away from the Company along the line of the Saskatchewan and the Winnipeg. The Montreal trade was invigorated, the trade of New France was increased, and the English competition from the north was reduced. La Vérendrye had found an offset to the sapping of the French trade by New York and Pennsylvania competition. It was an offset which might be developed so as to strengthen France in America.

La Vérendrye's work was, of course, only a beginning. For one thing, the reaction of the Hudson's Bay Company had to be met. The only danger its Governor and General Court had foreseen after 1714 was another series of raids from the sea, led by another Iberville. They proposed to meet this danger by building a fortification to give refuge to the Company's annual ship, the fort to be manned by the ship's crew. In 1731, therefore, they began the construction at the mouth of the Churchill of the great stone fortification called Prince of Wales's Fort. Slowly the heavy work of masonry went forward, part of the time under the supervision of the master mason Joseph Robson, who viewed the unenterprising habits of his employers critically. "They slept," he wrote memorably but inaccurately later, "for eighty years by the frozen sea."

The competition of the French after 1732, if not before, in fact permitted no such "sleep." The Indians would henceforth have to be persuaded, by men sent inland, to live at peace with one another, to shun the Canadian "pedlars" and to come down to the Bay. But the first station inland was Henley House, built on the Albany River in 1740. This was an endeavour to check the old competition from Nipigon. At York Factory and Churchill, there was no penetration of the interior plains to compare with that of La Vérendrye until 1750 and later. Then men would be sent inland, not to trade in competition with the French, for they had no way to bring goods up, but to persuade the Indians to disregard the wiles of the Montreal traders and to come down as before to York. This was the coastal trade still, but plied with the aid of interpreters and *coureurs de bois* – really winterers – of Radisson's and Kelsey's kind.

The Company also had English critics as formidable as its French competition. An energetic Irish gentleman, Arthur Dobbs, devoted to the development of British commerce, turned his attention to the Company and became in effect the first "free trader" in the Company's history and an "interloper" as dangerous as the French in the interior. His studies had convinced Dobbs that the North-West Passage was possible and that the Hudson's Bay Company had failed to press the search for it. His criticism led the Company to undertake more voyages north from Churchill, but these, if not disastrous failures, were no more successful than Knight's unfortunate attempts. Dissatisfied, Dobbs procured the dispatch in 1741 of Captain Christopher Middleton, a navigator in the Company's service, to Churchill to explore to the northward. Middleton proved only that Wager Inlet was not a strait. Dobbs, convinced that Middleton had been influenced by the Company's people and aware of the French advance into the Winnipeg Basin, continued his agitation against the Company's monopoly, and procured the dispatch of a second expedition in 1745. It was singularly unsuccessful in revealing any new possibility of a passage, but its return was followed by an attempt to form a company to prosecute the search and to trade in the lands adjoining the passage. This direct assault on the charter of the Hudson's Bay Company provoked the appointment of a Select Committee of the House of Commons in 1749. The report of the committee affirmed the validity of the charter and vindicated the policy of the Company, but the long-drawn episode revealed how quickly the régime of the fur company would come under attack if the lands it held were ever thought to be valuable to England for other purposes than as a fur preserve.

In the north-west, then, La Vérendrye's work had encroached on, but had by no means seriously injured, the British fur trade. In the great Atlantic fisheries also, the English were on the defensive, but against old France rather than New, and against New England as well as old France. The years after 1714 were marked in the Newfoundland fishery by the decline of the ship fishery and the growth of the boat fishery and of residence. Accompanying these changes was the growing dependence of the Newfoundland fishery and population on New England for provisions and the sale of the catch of the boat fishery.

The decline of the ship fishery from England and the growth of population meant the end of the old policy of the past century, of encouraging the ship fishery and of prohibiting residence. Despite official policy, despite the climate and the scant resources of Newfoundland, despite a drain of men to the New England fishing-ships, despite even attempts to remove the residents to Nova Scotia, population grew in the Island. It even began a natural increase, for women formed part of the fishing-ship's complement, and their presence made the "residence" over winter something more than a bachelors' doss-house. In such a colony crime and disorder were prevalent. Finally, in 1723, merchants at St. John's were driven to form a social contract after the school of John Locke, with little result, and in 1729 the British government appointed a governor for the colony. But the governor was simply the naval officer appointed admiral of the summer fishery, and his jurisdiction over the settlements was exercised only during the summer months.

The French fishery after 1715 developed in the main as a ship or bank fishery carried on from France. Only at points on the "French Shore" of Newfoundland, and around the Gulf of St. Lawrence from the north shore to the Strait of Canso, did the French conduct a shore, or dry, fishery. But in these areas it developed greatly between 1714 and 1763 and was known for the superiority of its product. Even these fisheries gave rise to no more than a small resident population on Isle St. Jean, at Gaspé, and at Canso and Louisbourg. The fishery remained more a French than a Canadian or an Acadian industry. The development of a seal fishery out of Quebec on the north shore of the Gulf was alone a wholly Canadian enterprise.

The Acadian fisheries had been taken over by the New Englanders, to whom the conquest of Nova Scotia meant not only the removal of a nuisance, but also a further step in the domination of the Atlantic fisheries. The Acadians of Nova Scotia, cut off by British rule, gave themselves up to the pastoral life of their farms and sea-meadows. They remained a French element beyond the limits of New France, alienated but recoverable. If they had not migrated to Louisbourg and Isle St. Jean in any considerable number, neither had they given in readily to British authority. They had doggedly evaded taking an unconditional oath of allegiance. Their purpose can only be guessed, but it would seem that these stolid peasants were resolved to remain Catholic, French, and neutral. The British government allowed French priests to minister to them and made no effort, beyond repeated attempts to have them take the oath of allegiance, to end their being French. In 1730, finally, the Acadians had obtained their principal object, an acknowledgement, neither official nor explicit but sufficient, of their neutrality. With this, they again became a people without a history, but their neutrality was a deeply significant thing. In the War of the Austrian Succession, despite great temptation to join the French and Canadian forces, they remained neutral.

KC-E

In so far as Canada had added the best of the fur trade of the Winnipeg Basin to it, as the fishermen of Old and New France were prospering in the Gulf and Newfoundland, as the Acadians were still French and Catholic, though neutral, the French empire in America was in fair trim when the War of the Austrian Succession began in Europe in 1740. But in two areas the equipoise of that empire had been and remained shaken. One was in the Wisconsin country, one in eastern Louisiana. The second defeat of the Foxes in 1733 at Butte des Morts had not ended the fierce resistance of that tribe. Another Canadian expedition in 1734 achieved only partial success, and yet another in 1736 suffered defeat. The command then passed to Paul de la Marque de Marin, who gave up the policy of suppression and extermination as impossible, and attempted instead a policy of conciliation. He won the confidence of the survivors, and, by leaving them as the middlemen to the Sioux, had pacified them by 1738. Thus the second Fox war ended, not without a later flare-up; but the damage it had done to the French cause in America was immeasurable. This small and obstinately independent tribe had made the French recovery much slower and much less than it otherwise would have been. Its resistance had greatly aided the Anglo-Americans, and the Canadian belief that their traders had encouraged the Fox resistance had no doubt some foundation.

There was at least no doubt that in the other troubled area, that of eastern Louisiana, the American traders were at work among the Indians. There the powerful tribes of the Natchez, defeated by the French in 1731, and the Chickasaws, with whom the Natchez took refuge, were angered by the attempt of French traders to by-pass them on the Mississippi. Urged on by the traders of South Carolina, the Chickasaws openly fought the French from 1736 to 1740. So dangerous was their assault that Canadians from the Illinois and from Canada, led by Pierre d'Artaguette of Illinois and the second Baron de Longueuil, marched to the aid of Bienville, the Canadian governor of Louisiana, and fought in the southern campaign. The Chickasaws made peace in 1744, but again an Indian conflict, the third in twenty-eight years, had weakened the French in the interior before the great trial of strength was to come.

What had saved the French empire in the interior so far had been the successful Indian diplomacy of the Canadian governors, not least that of Beauharnois. French policy from Canada to the Illinois was one, and there was no conflict or confusion of purpose with Louisiana. But Anglo-American policy with regard to the Indians had been that of individual colonies. Now a change was beginning. A young Irishman, William Johnson, had settled in New York and was to win for himself a position of singular trust among the Mohawks. His influence was to be confirmed in the coming war, and his career was to be the beginning of a unified Anglo-American Indian policy. Such a policy, added to the slow sapping of the French fur trade of the Lakes by the American traders, would strike heavily at French power in America. For Canada had risen and lived by its fur trade and by its Indian commerce and diplomacy. Defeated in these, it might be defeated utterly.

The fate of Canada was being contested on its far borders. But it would be settled not on the borders but at the heart of the country; and the meaning of the word Canada was changing. It signified no longer merely a region where a mission slowly grew and the fur trade flourished. It signified now a country and a people. The northern route and the northern frontier, with their primitive, far-ranging economy, had none the less distilled on the banks of the St. Lawrence a settled, solid community of European townsmen and peasants. Canada, Laurentian Canada, was a residue of the fur trade, sprung from the fur trade, but no longer resting on it and capable of enduring should the fur trade and its empire collapse. Canadians had, in short, become a people in whom was the germ of nationhood, and they would offer a resistance to attack which could be overcome only by final conquest of the heartland of New France.

Of all the aspects of increasing strength in Canada, the growth of population was most striking. In 1713, 18,119 persons were recorded; in 1730, 33,682; by 1739, there were 42,701. The population of Canada had more than doubled in the course of a quarter of a century, although only some four thousand persons, it is estimated, came to Canada from France between 1700 and 1760. These were in the main disbanded soldiers, *engagés*, and special artisans. About a thousand were convicts transported to the colony for relatively minor crimes. For the most part, then, growth of population was by natural increase, and that despite the hardships of frontier life and the recurrent epidemics.

Because the increase was natural, the Canadians were exhibiting even more strongly the traits of character discernible in the seventeenth century. These were a sense of freedom, a quickness to resist authority, a blithe and cocky head-strongness. Frank, and quick to give his trust, the Canadian could be won to attempt almost anything by those he loved, but could not be compelled to do anything by those he disliked. This independence of spirit was encouraged both by the subsistence economy in which he was cradled – no one need go hungry in the parishes of the St. Lawrence – and by the high wages his labour commanded in industry, trade, or the canoe flotillas. The Canadian was an Americanized Frenchman, and the high worth of his labour had made him, like the New Englander and the Virginian, a man assertively independent and "naturally undocile."

The long peace and the ending of the age of the *coureurs de bois* left large numbers of the young men at home for a generation. The numbers needed as voyageurs for the flotillas for Michilimackinac or the Saskatchewan were small. Thus at last Canada had acquired a generation of native-born settlers, men bred to the land in Canada. As a result, the burnings and the clearings went ahead along the river front; the narrow, golden fields deepened their ranks of stooks between the water and the forest. In 1734, 163,000 *arpents* were in cultivation and yielded a million bushels of cereals. Of these the chief was wheat, which was shortly to become the principal export of Canada itself, not counting fur. The horned cattle were multiplying, as were the sheep and the little French horse peculiar to Canada. Canadian agriculture could now support the people of Canada, and the colony was at last independent of the fur trade for survival, if not for prosperity.

The increase in the acreage of cultivated land meant that the seigniories were being taken up and settled by the growing number of tenants. But the policy followed since the decrees of Marly were issued in 1711, that no new grants of seigniories should be made, had with one exception been continued up to 1727. Then the Court allowed the renewal of grants. One was made to the Ursulines of Trois Rivières and one to Beauharnois himself. Between 1732 and 1739 six new seigniories were established on the Richelieu and ten *fiefs* and seigniories on Lake Champlain. These of course were meant to encourage the settlement of the region and to support Fort St. Frédéric – an endeavour that war was to defeat. Similarly, seven grants were made on the Chaudière River between 1736 and 1738; and some settlement began in the wake of the concessions.

Offsetting these extensions of the seignioral lands were revocations under the decrees of Marly. The decrees were not strictly enforced before 1727, but after that date some four hundred forfeitures of lands by tenants to seigneurs were carried out, and after long delay and many fruitless warnings to delinquent seigneurs, no less than twenty seigniories were escheated in 1741. The total effect was to demonstrate that in Canada the seigniorial system was not one of feudal exploitation, but a means whereby the government placed on private individuals the obligation to settle and bring under cultivation the land of the colony.

In its social character the seigniory became more feudal, if anything, and more aristocratic, as agriculture flourished and landholding became not only honourable but in a measure profitable. The majority of seigneurs were religious corporations, military officers, or civil magistrates. Of their standing in their seigniory there could be no doubt. Between the seigneur and the habitant there was, as a rule, a social barrier of some firmness. When a wealthy merchant or fur trader became a seigneur, then indeed the seigneur's privileges, the front pew in the church, burial in the church, and so on, were not so much marks of rank as privileges bought and paid for. But no habitant acquired a seigniory between 1713 and 1744, and the seigniorial class became a more and more exclusive circle. In many seigniories therefore the importance of the captain of militia and even of the *curé* sank relatively to that of the seigneur.

Canada within the Laurentian parishes was an agricultural colony with a youthful rural society made up of people with a strong sense of rank and dignity, though with few impassable social barriers between classes. But it is to be emphasized that Canada was neither wholly agricultural nor wholly rural. One in four of the population by 1741 lived in Quebec, Montreal, or Trois Rivières. To the end of the French régime the tone and direction of Canadian society was military and commercial, as the fur trade required. The *bourgeoisie* continued to be a numerous class, even if it was still largely made up of French merchants and factors, a *comprador* community rather than a true *bourgeoisie*. It is true, also, that more and more industry was developing to buttress the agricultural economy and to add to the exports of the colony. In 1734, fifty-two sawmills were turning out lumber. The shipyards at Quebec continued to develop and worked steadily at building fishing-vessels, ships for the West Indian trade, and even ships for the royal navy; in 1738 one of five hundred tons' burden was ordered. It was the *Canada*, launched in 1742 and followed by four others, the last a vessel of sixty guns. No more were ordered by the king, but shipbuilding flourished at Quebec thereafter.

With shipbuilding the production of pitch and hemp continued. An endeavour to furnish ships' ironwork and other iron was begun by the development of the iron ores of St. Maurice in 1725. For over fifteen years private individuals tried at great cost to make the forges of St. Maurice profitable, but without success. In 1743 the enterprise, hampered by high wages and lack of managerial skill, was turned over to the Crown. It was a reasonably efficient plant and turned out a good deal of iron, including some cannon, but rarely at costs lower than those of imported iron.

The forges were only one of the industries encouraged and even subsidized by the French government. The manufacture of hats was still strictly pro- hibited, as it had been in 1725. On the other hand, the weaving of cloth and woollens was first tolerated and then encouraged; Montreal in 1714 had no less than twenty-five shops devoted to the production of textiles.

The industrial development of Canada was thus considerable, and rather more than might have been expected in a colony of a mercantilist country. Too much of industry remained in the king's hands, however, or was forbidden, for industrial growth to add decisively to the business community.

A more positive result was that by 1744 the excess of imports over exports was giving way to surpluses. Canada was at last beginning to balance its accounts. This might have enabled it to do away with the card money which had remained in circulation, with many new issues. But the two great wars of the two decades following 1744 made the calling-in of the card counters impossible. The trial of the recovered strength of New France, so long delayed, was to be made at last.

As the trial approached, when the outbreak of war in Europe made it certain France and England would before long be engaged, the governors of New France could at least rejoice that Canadian society was now close-knit and strong- textured. The people were hardy, brave, and at home in their country. The church was now organized, a mission church still, with its special tie with Rome, its *curés* still largely movable by the bishop, but with a parochial organization well established, the churches and the presbyteries built, the *fabriques*, or vestries, stolidly discharging their duties. The government was centralized and absolutist in organization, but paternal and humane in spirit. It had no cause to fear the people, and could count on their freely given support even under great strain. In the governor during these years, Beauharnois, Canada had the good fortune to have a fairly able man, conscientious and honest, who worked patiently to strengthen the country. In 1728 he had had the only upset of his government, a violent quarrel with the vain and pompous intendant, Claude Thomas Dupuy, over the administration of the diocese of Quebec following the death of Bishop Saint-Vallier. The Court supported Beauharnois, and Dupuy was recalled. Thereafter the Governor was ably seconded by Gilles Hocquart, who succeeded Dupuy in 1730, at first only as a subordinate officer but from 1732 as intendant. That office continued to be the main executive office of government in Canada, and the intendant's parish representative, the captain of militia, had become the local agent of the central government in civil as well as military affairs, and as such occasionally more powerful than the seigneur. The growing power of the intendant was accompanied by the decline of the authority of the Superior Council, which had now become a purely judicial body. Fortunately, Beauharnois and Hocquart worked as a loyal team, and the old quarrels of governor and intendant were a thing of the past.

Between church and state in these years also there was peace. The church continued to maintain the Christian life of the family and the individual. The parish, if the boundaries coincided, sometimes developed a certain independence of the seigniory, becoming the focus not only of the spiritual but also the civil life of its people. But this was as yet rare. Bishop Saint-Vallier had lived in accord with governor and intendant after his return in 1714, and so did his successors, Bishops de Mornay and Dosquet. This peace was not without its dangers. The French state was persistently Gallican; the king and his officers managed everything, and the church was always subject to a steady bureaucratic encroachment. The relationship of church and state in New France became outwardly Gallican, but no more than outwardly. The missionary spirit and the direct allegiance to Rome were never wholly forgotten or surrendered.

The domestic peace of Canada was, of course, to be broken by the entry of England into the War of the Austrian Succession in 1744. France at once applied the strategy of Louis XIV, to hold in America while seeking victory in Europe. As a result, New France was not significantly reinforced. And at first there was no need. The Iroquois remained quiet, the New Yorkers did not stir during 1744. Both sides realized that this war should begin where the last left off, in Acadia. Canada had as its object the recovery of Nova Scotia, the New Englanders the capture of Louisbourg, by which they hoped to eliminate French competition from the fishery and to crush the privateers that preyed on their shipping. In 1745 the Canadians seized Canso and, without success, raided Annapolis Royal.

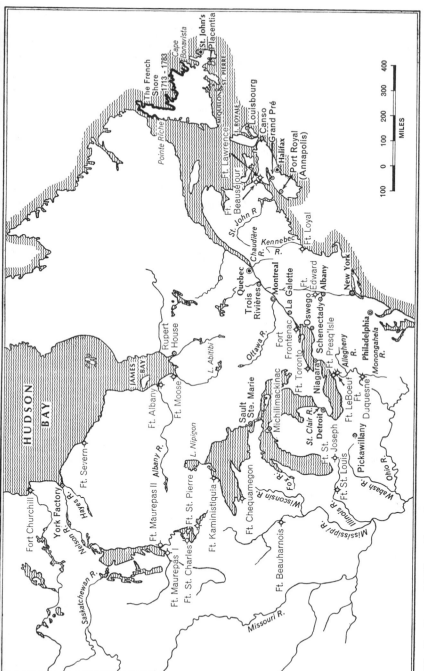

VI *Fur Posts and Military Forts of the French Régime*

It was then the New Englanders' turn, and they directed their attention to Louisbourg.

Louisbourg had been building steadily, if slowly, during the twenties and thirties. When completed, it was a fortification built to European specifications. The only American fortress of comparable strength, though not as elaborate, was Prince of Wales's Fort far up on Hudson Bay. Hence there was talk of Louisbourg being the Dunkirk, or the Gibraltar, of America. Its stone walls and heavy batteries may have seemed to warrant the phrase, but as a fortress it was weak in certain important respects. It was in fact only a fortified harbour. It had no meaning apart from sea power. Its function was to shelter and refresh a battle fleet, but it could perform that function only if the fleet reached it, and meanwhile it was susceptible both to blockade by sea and to attack by land. If an attacking force could put itself ashore and land its siege guns, Louisbourg could be taken, unless relieved by a fleet superior to that which covered the siege.

These weaknesses must have been the study of New England fishermen and governors for years before 1745. When William Shirley, the fiery governor of Massachusetts who had concluded that the French must be driven from America if the Anglo-Americans were to prosper there, decided to act, a force of colonial militia sailed against Louisbourg and took it at small cost and with singular expedition. How well they knew what they were doing is shown by the fact that they took cannon-ball to fit the French guns which they proposed to capture.

This astounding and humiliating defeat at the hands of provincial militia was due, however, not so much to the defects of Louisbourg as to the weakness of the French navy. Commodore Peter Warren of the British navy had covered the New Englander siege operations with no molestation whatever from the French.

The blow to French prestige was severe, and the Court decided to send a naval and military expedition to recover Louisbourg. Though this was a departure from the grand strategy of the war, it was of necessity in the main a naval expedition which would not greatly detract from the war effort of the French armies in the Lowlands and on the Rhine. At the same time the British government encouraged the New Englanders to plan a second campaign, this time against Quebec. The strategy of 1711 was being revived.

Troops were detailed for the British expedition and General James Sinclair was appointed to command it. There was rejoicing in Boston and alarm in Quebec. But the force was not ready in time to sail for Quebec, and the talk of the conquest of Canada in 1746 died down to discussion of an attack on Fort St Frédéric. The French expedition did sail, however, under the Duc d'Anville. It consisted of a powerful fleet and a considerable body of troops. But it was delayed by storms, and when it put into Chebucto (Halifax) harbour in Nova Scotia, typhus broke out among the sea-worn soldiers and sailors. The commander died; the expedition perished. The remnants returned to France, from which d'Anville's second-in-command, Jacques Pierre de Taffanel, Marquis de la Jonquière, sailed as Governor of New France in a second attempt in 1747 to recapture Louisbourg. The English defeated the expedition at sea and captured La Jonquière. Louisbourg was not to be recovered by French arms in America, and as lieutenant for La Jonquière the French court sent out Roland Michel Barrin, Comte de La Galissonnière, soldier, seaman, *savant*, the most brilliant of the rulers of New France. La Galissonnière at once sought to animate the military effort of New France.

The war now shifted to Acadia. Annapolis Royal had been reinforced, and Ramezay had led a force from Canada to Chignecto. Between the English and Canadians in the fall of 1747 lay most of the Acadian settlements. While there was little doubt of their sympathies, the Acadians remained neutral, despite the efforts of the Abbé Le Loutre and others of their priests. When Colonel Arthur Noble, the English commander at Annapolis Royal, advanced to Grand Pré in the winter, Ramezay sent Nicolas Antoine Coulon de Villiers against him. Villiers repulsed Noble, but the Canadians could not hold the settlement and the Acadians did not help them. Neither side was strong enough to win a decision, and the Acadians would not throw their weight to either.

On the New York frontier the war did not begin until 1746. The proposed attack on Canada had led to a muster at Albany for an advance against Montreal, and when the campaign had to be abandoned, Governor Clinton wished at least to attack Fort St. Frédéric. Nothing was done, but the Canadians, seeking to forestall the attack on Canada, struck at Saratoga and destroyed it in November, 1746. Thereafter they kept the frontier aflame, until young William Johnson persuaded the Mohawks to take the war-path once more against the French. They raided as far as the Island of Montreal. In retaliation, Rigaud de Vaudreuil, Canadian son of the former governor, led a war party of five hundred which destroyed the Massachusetts settlement of Northfield. Once more, Canada was using the terror of Indian warfare to fend off the knock-out blow its more numerous opponents would strike, if they could ever collect their strength.

The temper of New York and New England began to burn with a hatred which responded to Shirley's cry of *Delenda est Canada*. To the Americans the peaceful Laurentian colony, with its white churches, the long river fronts of tranquil village after tranquil village, its robed clergy and sisters of charity passing on their errands of mercy and consolation, was coming to seem a nest of bloodstained barbarians, which New England must stamp out if it was to know peace. Such was the character the fur trade and the Indian alliance had given Canada among its enemies. It was in fact a character which sprang from its weakness. The empire of New France was a wilderness empire, maintained by the Indianized war and trade of the wilderness.

Its weakness was not to be proved on this occasion. The war of the Austrian Succession was won in Europe and Asia. The victory of Fontenoy and the

KC-E*

capture of Madras recovered Louisbourg for New France. But in America, the war awaited ever since 1714 had only begun. France, though it had weakened the alliances against it, failed to reap the harvest of its victories in Europe. The Treaty of Aix-la-Chapelle of 1748 only marked the beginning of a truce which was to be filled with preparations for the resumption of hostilities and the final trial of strength in America. Everyone knew this, on the St. Lawrence, on the Hudson, and in Boston. And everyone in command in New France knew that in the final trial of strength the task of New France would be to hold its wilderness empire by means of its Indian allies and the Canadians who could fight alongside them.

ADDITIONAL READING

BREBNER, J. B.   *The Explorers of North America.*
FRÉGAULT, GUY   *La Civilisation de la Nouvelle-France.*
GIPSON, L. H.   *The British Empire before the American Revolution,* Vol. IV.
HARRIS, R. C.   *The Seigneurial System in Early Canada.*
MORTON, A. S.   *A History of the Canadian West to 1870-71.*

CHAPTER 8

The End of French Empire in America
1749-1760

That the Treaty of Aix-la-Chapelle was an inconclusive end to an inconclusive war, every one recognized in both Europe and America. It was a breathing-space, no more. But whereas the cessation of hostilities in Europe led to a great pause while the antagonists re-grouped, in America there was no pause and no re-grouping. The war continued; the only effect of the peace was to silence the guns for a few years. Forces continued to be deployed and strategic points to be seized. Each side conducted itself, wrote the Marquis Duquesne, Governor of New France, in 1754, as though it was "at open war."

The reasons for the continuity of the struggle in America were twofold, stemming both from the grand strategy of France and from the nature of the antagonists and of the conflict in America.

The grand strategy of France in the War of the Austrian Succession, as in that of the Spanish Succession, was to try to win such military preponderance in Europe as to be able to make diplomatic gains in America. Such a policy, however, necessitated the sacrifice of French sea power, and after the battle of La Hogue in 1692 the French navy had steadily declined both in number of ships and in quality of seamen. The French colonies were therefore exposed to capture by English sea power, which might make such gains as to cancel French superiority in Europe. Some at least of the colonies, and of course New France, must therefore be equipped to fight a "holding" action while a decision was reached in Europe.

The nature of the conflict in America was such that no government, not even the centralized government of New France, could fully control or direct the actions of its subjects. New France and the Anglo-American colonies were drifting into collision like two ice-floes moving on converging currents. The competition of the fur trade of New York, Pennsylvania, and South Carolina with that of Canada and Louisiana, the advance of the settlers and land specu-lators of the New England and Virginian frontiers, turned upon the alliances, the shifts and expedients of the Indian tribes of the Acadian rivers and the

Mississippi Valley. New France, New England, New York, Virginia, and South Carolina were drawn so deeply into the tortuosities of Indian diplomacy, their traders and frontiersmen were so far Indianized and barbarized, that the policies and the tactics of Indian policy and Indian warfare were now dominant. Nothing illustrates this more clearly than the enormous increase in the cost of presents to the Indians for both sides from 1744 to 1760.

The strategy of the continuing struggle took shape even before the war ended. The news of the peace negotiations and the consequent cutting down of the supplies for Canada had dismayed La Galissonnière. He protested passionately, early in 1748, "Your letters on the negotiations terrify me. The betrayal with which they threaten a colony at once so useful and so loyal is incredible. I am sure you will not consent to it. These letters bind my arms. . . ." But the approaching end of the war did not change his policy. La Galissonnière was sure that the success of French policy in Europe depended upon the maintenance of a balance of power in America. New France must at least hold while France sought a decision in Europe. If the Anglo-Americans destroyed that balance, England would gain "superiority in Europe." The American balance of power, he saw, was part of the European balance of power; its destruction "would draw after it that superiority that France ought to maintain in Europe." La Galissonnière perceived that supremacy on the Ohio would give supremacy in America, and that supremacy in America would affect, if not determine, the hegemony of Europe. He therefore sought to maintain the American-European balance by urging a revival of French naval power – and in this he had much success after he returned to France – and by strengthening New France where it was chiefly threatened, in Acadia and on the Ohio.

In Acadia he at once and characteristically went on the offensive. There the problem was twofold, to hold the Acadians from eventual adherence to the English and to ensure the provisioning of Louisbourg when restored. To achieve these purposes, pressure must be maintained on the bounds of ceded Acadia, and the lines of communication from the Bay of Fundy to the Strait of Canso across the Isthmus of Chignecto must be kept open. The Governor accordingly not only inspired the Abbé Le Loutre and the other political missionaries to increase their efforts to hold the Acadians loyal to New France and the faith; he also prepared to hold and extend the parts of Acadia not ceded but in dispute. In 1748 Charles Deschamps, Sieur de Boishébert, was sent to occupy the mouth of the St. John River, which he did despite English protests. In 1749, Louis François de La Corne advanced to Chignecto and built Fort Beauséjour to dominate the overland passage to Louisbourg; and the fort had the further purpose of restricting the area controlled by the English to the southern half of peninsular Acadia. For the moment the Anglo-American control of Acadia was reduced to the least degree possible, short of actual expulsion.

Expulsion after 1749, however, would have required more force than New

France alone disposed of. The British conduct of the late war, both diplomatic and military, had been feeble and confused, but it was immediately followed by a determined stroke of imperial policy brilliantly executed. The restoration of Louisbourg to France required that something be done to reassure the New Englanders that they would be protected against a rebuilt Louisbourg. Moreover, in both New and Old England a determination had formed to end the Acadian danger by beginning English settlement in Nova Scotia. Accordingly, the Earl of Halifax, President of the Board of Trade, vigorously advertised for settlers immediately after the peace. In 1749, under Lieutenant-Governor Edward Cornwallis, three thousand British and German settlers were installed at Chebucto, now to be renamed Halifax, and at Lunenburg. Halifax was fortified as a naval base. As a base, it was a counterpoise to Louisbourg; as a fortress, it signified a new imperial policy, really the first true British imperial policy, for it was maintained by British taxes and manned not by colonial militia but by British regulars. The United Kingdom had replied spontaneously and in the same imperial kind to La Galissonnière's forward policy. Cornwallis followed up by building Fort Lawrence in 1750 on the Isthmus of Chignecto to counter Beauséjour. The Acadian frontier was then stabilized.

On the Ohio the Canadians showed the same challenging and offensive spirit as in Acadia. The Ohio Valley had remained a great vacuum in American politics until the 1740's. The Anglo-Americans had not penetrated the barrier of the Alleghenies; the French had followed the Lakes to the Wisconsin and Illinois portages to the Mississippi. Unmolested, the Iroquois had laid claim to all between the Ohio and the Lakes. But by the end of the War of the Austrian Succession, the Iroquois power had dwindled and the vacuum it left was filling. The war diminished the supply of French trade goods and raised the price of what did get through. The western Indians turned to the Iroquois and the English. High fur prices during the war had drawn Pennsylvanian traders through the passes to the headwaters of the Ohio. Two of them at least, George Croghan and Michael Cresap, were able Indian diplomats. Their goods and their promises began to draw the Indians eastward from the Wisconsin and Michilimackinac country, to which they had retreated before the Iroquois in the seventeenth century, and southward from Detroit. New posts, new villages, such as Pickawillany of the Miamis, grew up along the upper Ohio and on its tributaries. Tribal bands, and bands of detribalized Indians and half-breeds, would settle around a trading post. They would negotiate for presents, for the establishment of posts, for the stationing of gunsmiths among them. By 1748 this development had made the Anglo-American fur trade supreme in the Ohio Valley; and after the traders, as Canadians had seen on the rivers of New England, would come the plodding settler and the keen-eyed speculator.

New France, if it was not to expose its vitals to attack, to suffer the loss of the south-west fur trade, and to incur a threat to the lines of communication between

Canada and Louisiana, must advance its effective boundaries to the Ohio, as the second Marquis de Vaudreuil, Governor of Louisiana, had seen as early as 1744. If the Anglo-Americans could be harried off the river, their effective boundaries for some time would be the divide of the Alleghenies, even if the Canadians were as yet in no position to stop the mountain passes themselves. Along the base line of the Ohio, Canada and Louisiana could be pulled more closely together and an area of resistance developed which would maintain the balance of French power in America.

Fortunately for New France, the belief persisted in Canada that La Salle and his Sulpician friends had discovered the Ohio on his first voyage of exploration in 1669. The belief was groundless, but it served the strategy of La Galissonnière. In 1749 he ordered Céloron de Blainville to enter the upper Ohio from Lake Erie, and to lay claim to the valley in the name of Louis XV. Céloron proceeded down the Ohio and took possession of the valley by proclamation and the burying of lead plates at the mouths of the tributaries of the Ohio. But the Indians met the expedition with sullen hostility. A number of times it was in grave danger of attack, and Céloron on his return to Canada reported pessimistically on the ability of New France to expel the Anglo-Americans from the Ohio and break their hold on the Indians. By that time La Galissonnière had returned to France and La Jonquière, freed by the peace, had come to take up his governorship.

La Jonquière, the governor who was to prepare New France for its trial, had neither the genius nor the *élan* of La Galissonnière. He lacked his predecessor's disinterested absorption in the strategy of power. The effect of the change of men, however, was to soften the tone and dampen the temper of Canadian policy rather than to change its direction. For La Jonquière, like so many of his predecessors and his contemporaries, had a sharp eye to the perquisites of office, which in New France meant in the main a share in the profits of the fur trade.

Perhaps this was why it was that in 1750 a more intense exploitation of the western posts on the Assiniboine and the Saskatchewan began. In 1749 La Vérendrye had been restored to favour, granted the Cross of St. Louis in honour of his previous work, and appointed once more the commandant of the western posts. He died in Montreal, however, before he could resume his command. His son Pierre had hastened west, and pushed the French trade up the Saskatchewan. But after 1749, first Jacques Legardeur de Saint-Pierre, then Boucher de Niverville, succeeded La Vérendrye. They too carried on a trade on the Saskatchewan from Fort Paskoyac, founded in 1750, and from posts at or below the junction of the North and South Saskatchewan.

So successful were they in winning the better and lighter furs from the Indians going to York Factory, that they forced the Hudson's Bay Company to send Anthony Henday, Joseph Smith and Joseph Waggoner inland to persuade the

Indians to continue to come down to the Bay. The Hudson's Bay Company was endeavouring to contain the Canadian menace on the Saskatchewan as the Canadians were attempting to deal with the Anglo-American infiltration of the Ohio country. And the Canadian advance to the forks of the Saskatchewan was of course a twin development with the attempted occupation of the upper Ohio. Both were endeavours to hold by extending the fragile empire of the fur trade. The connection was personified in Saint-Pierre, who after his service on the Assiniboine and Saskatchewan from 1750 to 1752, commanded on the Ohio in 1753.

From 1750 to 1752, it is true, the impetus La Galissonnière had given to Canadian policy was allowed to slacken in the Ohio Valley. The Indians were too defiant, the Anglo-Americans too strongly entrenched. La Jonquière hesitated, reluctant to risk war by expelling the traders and forcing the Indians to return to the French connection. As always, any lack of boldness, any want of firmness, was at once perceived and exploited by the Indians. La Demoiselle, a chief of the Miamis, led his people into liaison with the Anglo-American traders at Pickawillany. Despite warnings from La Jonquière and from Céloron at Detroit in 1750, La Demoiselle and the Miamis refused to turn away the Anglo-American traders and withdraw from Pickawillany. Two years passed. Then the French struck. Led by a Wisconsin half-breed, Charles Langlade, a band of Ottawas – still, with all the Ojibwa tribes, the loyal commercial allies of Canada – besieged Pickawillany. They captured and burned it. The traders they sent back to Pennsylvania; La Demoiselle they tortured and ate. Once more the Canadian fur trade had carried commercial competition to the use of force. The Miamis were cowed and the Anglo-American traders were checked.

This brutal blow out of the west actually symbolized a return to the decisive policy of La Galissonnière. La Jonquière, as it happened, died suddenly in 1752. He was succeeded by a nominee of La Galissonnière, the Marquis Duquesne de Menneville. A hard-tempered, incisive soldier, Duquesne was an instrument admirably chosen to resume and carry out his sponsor's policy of making the Ohio an area of strength which would check the Anglo-American expansion. In 1753 he organized, equipped and supplied an expeditionary force of 2,200 men – Troupes de la Marine, militia, and Indians – to cut and fortify a portage from Lake Erie to the upper Ohio and to build a major fortification on that river. Their commander was Marin, the stern warrior who had quieted the Foxes. When Marin died at the outset of the expedition, he was succeeded by Saint-Pierre fresh from the Saskatchewan.

From Presqu'Isle on Lake Erie, the portage was made in the heat and damp of a wet summer to the Rivière aux Boeufs which ran into the Allegheny. The men were haggard with fever and tortured with dysentery. The harassed column advanced down-stream, and built Fort Le Boeuf. When it was well advanced, most of the men were sent back to Montreal, and the remaining three hundred settled down to winter in the new fort, fresh with the fragrance of its green timbers.

They were surprised one day in December when a young man led a party from the forest and approached the fort. It was a Virginian, George Washington, who presented a letter from Governor Robert Dinwiddie of Virginia, by which the Canadians were warned to vacate the lands of King George II on which they were trespassing. Saint-Pierre could only reply that the lands, on the contrary, belonged to Louis XV, and that he was under orders to remain where he had been posted, as he did. In the spring of 1754 the command passed to Claude Pierre Pécaudy de Contrecoeur. He advanced to the forks of the Ohio, where the Monongahela and Allegheny meet. There he found a small American party building a post for the Ohio Company formed in 1749 to obtain a grant of Ohio lands. He forced them to retire, and built between the rivers a fort appropriately named Duquesne.

Washington meantime had retired to Virginia over the mountains, but he returned the following May with a small force for the purpose of driving the Canadians from the forks of the Ohio. When Contrecoeur learned of his approach, he sent out a party under Joseph Coulon de Villiers, Sieur de Jumonville, to check the Virginians' approach. Though under a flag of truce, Jumonville was surprised in camp and shot down by Washington's men. Washington then withdrew to the Great Meadows, where he hastily constructed a fortification he called Fort Necessity. The Canadians, led by Jumonville's brother Louis Coulon de Villiers, and burning to avenge what seemed a treacherous murder, surrounded the force and compelled its surrender. Washington and his men were allowed to return disarmed over the mountains.

Thus Duquesne's campaign had succeeded. The forks of the Ohio had been seized, the build-up of an area of strength had begun, which might stop up the passes of the Alleghenies. But the Anglo-American traders had only been repelled, not finally driven out. The land-seekers, both frontier squatters of Pennsylvania and great planter speculators of Virginia and the Ohio Land Company, were still determined to occupy the rich Ohio lands. Neither were the claims of the British Crown at all diminished. And in Canada the suffering of the men of the great expedition of 1753, and the loss of those who died, coupled with short harvests in 1753 and 1754, weakened and impoverished the colony on the eve of its greatest trial of strength. The occupation of the Ohio had overstrained its resources, which were insufficient for military efforts on a European scale such as the strategy of La Galissonnière had demanded. Its economic strength had been further taxed when in 1749 the laborious and honest Hocquart was succeeded as intendant by François Bigot, a brilliant but corrupt administrator. New France must now fight not only with its sinews strained but with its blood sucked by rapacious officials and unscrupulous contractors.

The death of Jumonville and the capture of Washington were in fact the beginning of the war that was to destroy New France. But as yet it was only a border war, such as had smouldered on the Acadian frontier since 1714. The lines of conflict had yet to be drawn, the character of the struggle and the composition of the opposing forces had yet to be determined both in Europe and in America. The struggle beginning as a frontier war in the forests of the Ohio might be determined in either Europe or America, on the plains of Germany or the banks of the St. Lawrence. What had to be determined in 1754 was, by what combination of powers would the war be fought in Europe, and by what forces, colonial only, or colonial and European, would the fighting be done in America ?

In Europe the traditional combination of England and the House of Austria against France was being weakened by the rise of Prussia. The warfare of France and Austria for the control of the European Lowlands was delivering America to England and Germany to Prussia. This fact had been underlined by France's loss of Acadia in 1713 and Austria's loss of Silesia in 1742. England, for its part, had not only to protect the Lowlands, but also to preserve Hanover. Prussia was a more dangerous menace to Hanover, and therefore more desirable in the role of guardian of it, than Austria could be. France itself was shaken and uncertain. It had failed to gather the fruits of Marshal Saxe's victories in the Lowlands in the War of the Austrian Succession. It had not restored its naval forces, and it therefore could not revert to a maritime and colonial policy, as in the early days of Colbert. Its finances were in disorder; the *parlements* and the people had resisted additional taxes in 1753 and 1754. If France were to fight a great war, then it had better be a coalition war, fought by the great conservative powers of Austria and France to preserve the European balance.

From these considerations came the "reversal of alliances" of 1756. In this changeover, Prussia and England became allies by the Convention of Westminster in January, 1756. In riposte, France and Austria, soon to be joined by Russia, combined to destroy the aggressor in the Silesian War of 1742, and to maintain a continental equilibrium against the equally aggressive colonial power of England.

The policy of the United Kingdom in these years was actually vacillating and confused, but the government was driven by powerful currents of opinion towards the fighting of a war of colonial conquest. The complicating factors were the concern of George II for Hanover, and the timid conservatism of the Whig ministers. The consummate domestic politician, the Duke of Newcastle, was the chief of these adherents of the old Whig system of an alliance with Austria and a continental war. They disliked the reversal of alliances and even more the old Tory policy of a colonial and a maritime war, such as had prevailed in the last years of the War of the Spanish Succession.

Public opinion, however, was growing impatient of these old views. The impatience was partly made up of the desire of the great financial and mercantile interests of London to capture the trade of America and Africa, partly of the old enmity to France, now that it was being inflamed by tales of Canadian and

Indian atrocities on the American frontiers. The people, as distinct from the politicians, called strongly for a war at sea and in America to give England the wealth of Africa and the Indies. In this view, Germany and even the Mediterranean should be treated as secondary areas of conflict. The great area of trial, the points at which absolute victory was to be sought, were not on the Continent, but on the sea approaches to Europe and along the rivers of America. For the English popular temper was at this time profoundly aggressive. The merchants in particular demanded not a war to maintain the equilibrium of the European world but a war which would give the United Kingdom supremacy in trade with the extra-European world. They frankly wished to destroy the balance of the European power in America and to make England supreme there; what the consequences for Europe might be, they did not stop to ask.

This demand for a colonial war and absolute victory in America was to find a voice in William Pitt. Pitt was a superb rhetorician, at times an inspired genius of parliamentary politics, at other times a melancholic madman, but always an embodiment of that drive for commercial empire which had taken his father to win riches in India and which now worked in the counting-houses of London and of Boston and New York. Pitt was a maverick among Whig politicians in that he adhered to Tory diplomacy and strategy, listened to the London merchants more closely than to the territorial magnates, and combined a dislike of Hanover with an unusual and even an exaggerated reverence for the monarchy. From these discordant elements his son was eventually to make a second Tory party. The father in his time could do no such thing; he had to impose a new war policy on George II and on a reluctant Newcastle by his own will and through the growing anger of the country. This was to take time; not until 1757 was Pitt to be in power. But for the moment the important thing was that in Pitt the London magnates and the Anglo-American traders, fishermen, and land speculators found a voice for their aspirations. The British must be supreme in North America. The policy Governor Shirley had urged in 1744 was at last on its way to becoming the policy of Britain: *Delenda est Canada.*

For America, decisions of hardly less moment were taking shape. Washington's defeat was met in 1755 by the dispatch of Major-General Edward Braddock with two battalions of British infantry to Virginia for the capture of Fort Duquesne and the assertion of the British title to the Ohio. Hitherto, except for Hill's expedition in 1711 and the garrisoning of Halifax in 1749, war in the colonies, offensive as well as defensive, had been the business of the colonial militia. Now the United Kingdom was making the matter of the colonial claims one of imperial policy and imperial force.

Precisely the same decision had been made in France, and it was as much the logical outcome of La Galissonnière's strategy as the British reinforcements were a reply to it. The maintenance of the European balance of power in America seemed to call for the use of European troops; so great an issue could not be left to colonial militia, or to the forest tactics of *la petite guerre*. Accordingly, the French court dispatched the Baron Dieskau, a Saxon soldier of fortune, with the regiments of Béarn, Guienne, La Reine, and Languedoc, and reinforcements for the Troupes de la Marine, to the number of some three thousand men in all, for the defence of New France. At long last the Troupes de la Marine and the colonial militia were to have help on a considerable scale in garrisoning the extended fortress system of New France and in fighting the campaign which both sides now took for granted. But, for both, European aid meant European command and European tactics, and in this lay the certainty of friction between European regulars and colonial militia.

In Canada the certainty was, as it happened, made doubly sure by the recall of Duquesne and the appointment in 1755 of Pierre de Rigaud, Marquis de Vaudreuil-Cavagnac. The new governor, fresh from years of office in Louisiana, was an experienced colonial governor. But he was also the son of the former governor, the Marquis de Vaudreuil, and of Canadian birth. Thus he was a colonial and a Canadian, raised in Quebec, trained in the Indian wars in the west, and accustomed to fight *la petite guerre*. As supreme commander, he wished to fight the war in the Canadian manner, by raid, ambush, and dash. But he now had as field commander a European general with European troops, ignorant of Canadian warfare and cocksure as to their superiority over colonials. Here was a source of friction and division, at top and bottom, which boded no good for the defence of Canada.

The British reaction to the dispatch of French reinforcements was to send, while yet at peace with France, a naval force under Admiral Edward Boscawen to capture the transports and the escorting warships. The Newfoundland fogs foiled the British, but two ships with eight companies of soldiers were taken. The ruthless temper of England was thus displayed, and also the government's readiness to treat the war in America as something distinct from the diplomatic manoeuvres then proceeding in Europe. But the attempt also revealed how much New France, committed to holding in America, and needing supplies from France with which to hold, was at the mercy of British sea power.

The operation of sea power is normally slow, however, and for three brilliant years Canada was yet to make war with triumphant success, a success which masked the real weakness of its position. Canadian forces held on the Ohio; they attacked and held on the Ontario and Champlain frontiers; only in Acadia did the defences of Canada give way.

On the Ohio, Contrecoeur spent the spring of 1755 bringing supplies over from Niagara and Detroit, and in sending out patrols along the trails from Virginia and Pennsylvania. By summer the intelligence came in of the advance of the force of British regulars and Virginian militia under Braddock. The British advance was slow and methodical along a road cut and levelled for the passage of wagons and artillery. Clearly the British counted not on surprise but on numbers and fire-power to effect their purpose. Contrecoeur, with his few hundred Troupes de la Marine, militia, and Indians, could neither meet Braddock in open array nor hope to stand a siege in his weak and poorly sited fort. He must use surprise and catch the Anglo-Americans in column in the defiles of the forest.

He sent out a force of less than nine hundred, of whom over six hundred were Indians, under Daniel Hyacinthe-Marie de Beaujeu, an officer of the Troupes de la Marine. The intention may have been to check Braddock's advance at the fording of the Monongahela. As it turned out, Beaujeu, advancing by the forest trail at the head of his motley column, collided with the advance guard of the British. The enemy's reaction was prompt, and Beaujeu and his leading files fell before British musketry and grapeshot. But the untimeliness of this collision was soon redeemed as the Canadian troops and Indians took cover to left and right, enveloping the vivid British column on either flank. Their sniping fire, singling out officers and sergeants, the war-whoops and the incessant and irregular fusillade from concealment, disorganized and demoralized the British regulars. They could neither deploy nor retreat in order. Their platoon fire crashed harmlessly through the brush or murderously into other platoons of their own. Their stout, scarlet-visaged general could neither order nor rally them before he tumbled from his horse with a Canadian bullet in his chest. After three hours the redcoats broke and ran back through the forest in retreat to Virginia. And the Indians and Canadians stepped out among the wounded and the killed to pick up such plunder as they had never known, and to lift for the wigwams of the up country such strings of scalps as Canadian winds had never dried. The Ohio was Canadian, won by Canadian and Indian arms, at least until the Anglo-Americans learned to move and fight in the forest.

The glory of the Canadian victory on the Ohio was to be dimmed by defeat on the Lake Champlain frontier. There New York and New England were marshalling forces under William Johnson for an attack on Fort St. Frédéric, and under Shirley for an advance west to capture Niagara. Johnson had built a fort, afterwards known as Fort Edward, on the Hudson, and had then moved over the height-of-land to Lac St. Sacrement. Here he encamped.

His advance altered the Canadian strategy on the central front. Vaudreuil had planned to use the summer to eradicate that old offence and menace to Canada, Fort Oswego. He had ordered Baron Dieskau with his regulars and a force of militia to capture it. But Vaudreuil had to divert the force up Lake Champlain to prevent Johnson seizing St. Frédéric. Dieskau advanced up Lac St. Sacrement and attacked Johnson's entrenched position. He failed to carry it because he attempted to use his militia and Indians in mass formation as he used his regulars. The Canadians and Indians refused to advance from cover and fought in their accustomed way. Johnson beat off the repeated attacks of the unsupported regulars, and eventually drove them back, capturing the wounded Dieskau. Dieskau had stopped Johnson's advance and saved St. Frédéric, but he left the Canadians convinced that their own methods of warfare were superior to those of European regulars. The rivalry and mutual contempt of the Canadian and European French, already keen, and sharpened during this campaign, weakened the Canadian defence thereafter, as indeed the same jealousy weakened the Anglo-American attack.

No such rivalry could explain or excuse the French failure in Acadia. There Fort Beauséjour, with its growing settlement of Acadians and the fiery political apostolate of the Abbé Le Loutre, had pressed heavily on English Nova Scotia. Yet the post was yielded by its commandant, Louis Dupont Du Chambon de Vergor, to the first pressure of Colonel Charles Lawrence, Governor of Nova Scotia. The French hold on the Isthmus of Chignecto was broken.

Then, at a time when the Anglo-American victory of 1755 and the evident determination of England to destroy French power in America made any such action less urgent, the rulers of Nova Scotia turned to deal firmly with the long evasive, long neutral Acadians. Their numbers, it is true, now made it imperative that their position be clarified; by 1750 the Acadian population was about eleven thousand. Since 1749 Governor Cornwallis and his successors had increased the pressure on these shy but obstinate country folk. The only result seemed to be fresh evasions and an increasing stream of migrants to Le Loutre's fold. Now the war temper was hardening the hearts of the rulers of Nova Scotia. To it was added another factor, the one actually decisive, the land hunger of expanding New England. The Yankee soldiers in their campaigns since 1707, and Yankee fishermen in Fundy, had seen and talked of the fertile acres of the Annapolis Valley and the sea-meadows and broad fields of the Acadians in Minas Basin. Why should these lands be held by potential enemies, by people who only waited for a major French victory to return to their former allegiance?

Lawrence, concerned for the safety of the province, aware that Louisbourg was still French, exasperated by the obstinate belief of the Acadians that they would always be permitted to evade taking the oath of allegiance, now yielded to the steady and subtle pressure of his New England advisers. He organized a mass deportation of the Acadians. It was a thing almost without parallel in its day. It was something not to be justified by any necessity of the time, flagrant as had been Le Loutre's political proselytizing and irritating as had been the sly, peasant obstinacy of the Acadians. In September and October of 1755, British regulars and New England militia assembled the men of the Acadian villages from Annapolis to Grand Pré in their churches and read them the decree of deportation. In the tragic days that followed, the wretched columns of villagers moved down to the waiting transports and sailed for the English colonies below New York. Refugees in the woods, the people of settlements overlooked, made their way to the St. John River, to Isle St. Jean and to Isle Royale and Louisbourg, and even to Canada. Those who found refuge on the St. John or the islands, with the exiles who were to make their way back, would in time reconstitute the Acadian people, but the autumn of 1755 was dark with the tragedy of a folk uprooted and dispossessed.

All the events of 1755 – battles on the Monongahela, on Lac St. Sacrement and at Chignecto, and the exile from Acadia – had taken place while the Crowns of England and France were at peace. But in Europe itself the pretence that peace existed could no longer be maintained, not even by a reluctant and unready France. In 1756 the great powers went to war, seeking such limited gains as the bounds of the European equilibrium permitted. France, its naval power still inadequate for a colonial and maritime war, despite La Galissonnière's victory over Admiral John Byng in 1756, was thus committed to winning such a margin of victory in Europe as would enable it to recoup losses in America. And in America, French strategy was perforce to hold Anglo-American strength – merely to hold, not to divert, as La Galissonnière had planned – and so prevent England destroying absolutely the balance of the colonial empires in America.

This somewhat desperate strategy of France was not one founded on illusion or fancy. For England and its colonies were working their way to a policy which would aim at supremacy in America. After fierce political struggles in 1756 and 1757, effective power passed from the King and the Duke of Newcastle to William Pitt; and this was a victory of the colonial and maritime strategy over the old Whig continental strategy. Pitt did have to make concessions, he did have to undertake to defend Hanover, he did have to say he would win Canada on the plains of Germany. But the European theatre was for England the holding theatre; in America, England would strike with all the force it could command and for absolute victory.

Fortunately for Canada, the force was to be neither overwhelming nor well directed for two more years. The campaign of 1756 opened for Canada with the dispatch of new reinforcements and a commander to replace Dieskau. The reinforcements consisted of the regiments of Berry, La Sarre, and Royal Roussillon; the commander was Louis Joseph, Marquis de Montcalm. The new reinforcements brought up to some six thousand the regular troops sent to the defence of Canada between 1755 and 1759, with four battalions in garrison at Louisbourg. In Montcalm, Canada gained one of France's ablest and most ambitious soldiers. His gallantry, his chivalry and his handsome presence won him devoted admirers then, as they do still.

In the circumstances of New France in 1756, however, Montcalm was no more than an elegant Braddock, who aggravated the clash between the Canadian upholders of *la petite guerre* and the European defenders of the formal tactics of the regulars. Vaudreuil found that the presence of a subordinate field commander in the person of the aristocratic regular soldier, Montcalm, simply served to accentuate the division between Canadians and French in the high command of New France. It meant that the growing national sentiment of the Canadians, which ought to have been directed solely against the Anglo-Americans, was in some measure spent against their allies, the French. It also strengthened that desire for self-government which Canadians shared with Americans, and which had already found expression in their satisfaction at Vaudreuil's appointment as governor.

Vaudreuil was at least able to make his plans prevail for most of 1756. During the winter, war parties raided southwards from Montreal and along the Alleghenies from Fort Duquesne. Then in the summer the deferred attack on Oswego was mounted and carried to completion in August. Montcalm commanded, and claimed the victory, but the strategy was Vaudreuil's. At long last the open wound of Oswego was closed and the Lakes were once more Canadian.

On the Lake Champlain frontier the forces assembled by William Shirley and Johnson were immobile during 1756, and the year passed without any further change. In February of 1757 a Canadian force led by Vaudreuil's brother, François Pierre de Rigaud, Governor of Montreal, attacked the new Fort William Henry on Lac St. Sacrement and captured some prisoners. Then in the summer the new Anglo-American commander, the Earl of Loudoun, drew off the British troops from the New York frontier to attack Louisbourg. The Anglo-Americans were to make Lake Champlain a secondary frontier, and to strike by the sea route on which naval power and sea transport could bring the Anglo-American effort to its maximum. But the slowness of Loudoun's preparations, and a disaster suffered by the British naval squadron supporting him, postponed the siege of Louisbourg until the next year. Vaudreuil and Montcalm took advantage of the thinning forces before them to strike at Fort William Henry. Montcalm captured it in a brilliant victory, marred only by the killing of some fifty prisoners by the excited and uncontrollable Indians. But he was unable to strike across the height-of-land at Fort Edward and carry the war into central New York. Canada's strength was not sufficient to push the attack beyond its own boundaries.

In the next year, 1758, the apex of Canadian fortunes was reached. The strain of three campaigns, however successful, was felt ever more severely. The loss of men, and of manpower from the fields, brought a shortage of food to the colony. Inflation, always severe in New France in war time, was beginning to rage. Its effects and the misery caused by famine were aggravated by administrative corruption. For the intendant, Bigot, not only embezzled from the public funds, but also used his official knowledge and influence to enable a war supply company organized by an associate, Joseph Cadet, to make fantastic profits. Nothing in the history of New France is sadder than this tale of official profligacy, a sure sign that the bonds between France and its colony were ceasing to have any warmth of sentiment or moral validity.

In England, Pitt had at last infused the Anglo-American war effort with vigour, spirit, and comparative honesty. Despite the set-backs suffered by the

Anglo-Americans since 1755, they had steadily built up their resources in men, supplies, and capable leaders. Some twenty battalions of British regulars, or about 20,000 men, served beside ever more efficient American militia. The corps of Robert Rogers' Rangers and the development of rifle companies marked the measure of adaptation the Anglo-Americans were making to the conditions of warfare on the Canadian borders. In 1758 New France would be tried as never before.

The Anglo-American attacks were in the classic pattern, a blow at the Gulf, a blow at the Richelieu. In June the British fleet appeared off Louisbourg; on June 8, Brigadier James Wolfe led his men under heavy fire through a rocky cleft of Gabarus Bay. The walls and harbour defences of the great fortress crumbled under bombardment, and on July 27 Louisbourg surrendered. It was razed, never to be restored or retroceded. But it had held long enough to shield Quebec for one year more. In the west, Brigadier John Forbes doggedly cut a new road over the Alleghenies to Fort Duquesne. Contrecoeur lacked the men and munitions to defend it, and withdrew. Ohio, like Acadia and Isle Royale, had gone; the flanks of New France were driven in.

The centre, however, still held. At Carillon (called by the Americans Ticonderoga) at the entrance to Lake Champlain, Montcalm had placed his 3,500 men in a fieldwork of logs and abattis, distrusting the flimsy stonework of the too small and ill-designed fort. There he had the good fortune to be attacked head-on by General James Abercromby, who employed his magnificent British regulars to try to tear Montcalm's breastwork apart. Time after time like scarlet surf the redcoats and the Highlanders drove into the sharpened branches and criss-crossed trunks, streaming with sweat in the heat and gasping with frustrated fury. They piled up in hundreds before the French and Canadian musketry, until their commander sullenly called the survivors off and retired. Montcalm, despite Vaudreuil's urging, rested on his unexpected laurels and failed to harass an enemy who was still formidable. Proudly Carillon was added to the battle honours of Canada, even if all its fruit was not gathered, and even if it was a last victory in a year of defeat.

How much a year of defeat it was, was shown when the energetic American commander, Colonel John Bradstreet, recaptured Oswego and from there suddenly seized Fort Frontenac. The road to the west and to Louisiana, down which Montcalm had thought a fighting retreat might be conducted, was closed. New France now stood at bay along the St. Lawrence and awaited attack, as in 1690, from Lake Champlain and from the English coming up the St. Lawrence.

So desperate was the situation, so dire the need for aid, that Vaudreuil and Montcalm agreed to send special envoys to France to put the circumstances clearly and firmly before the Court. Michel Jean Hugues de Péan spoke for Vaudreuil, and Louis Antoine de Bougainville for Montcalm. While Bougainville was unfriendly to Vaudreuil, he did make the desperate position of New

France clear at the Court. But he won little succour; little was available, and that would be fortunate to evade the British at sea. Yet, he wrote to Montcalm, "the court wishes you not to capitulate. Keep a foothold in Canada at whatever cost." The strategy was still the same; to hold in America, in the hope of a victory or even a stalemate in Europe. The chief accomplishment of the mission was to discredit Vaudreuil, and to give the supreme command to Montcalm. But Admiral Hawke and the British fleets off the French ports saw to it that little aid passed the Atlantic.

Bougainville, young and gallant, refreshed after a winter in the *salons* of Paris, came back in May, 1759, to a weary and doomed Quebec. The grey town at the foot and on the shoulder of Cape Diamond was not a great fortress; like Louisbourg, it could be taken by a force of sufficient strength to land artillery from the river. Its real defences lay in the rocks, shoals, and treacherous currents of the St. Lawrence, the difficulty of landing near the fortress, and the shortness of the summer. But these, as Phips had shown and as Bougainville had urged, needed reinforcement by batteries and moored ships at the narrow channels. The resources were not to hand. All hopes were therefore pinned on fire-ships which might burn the enemy's ships if he reached Quebec, and on the troops and militia who might deny a landing to him on the north shore. Here was the greatest danger, as Montcalm and Vaudreuil awaited the attack of the new British commander, Major-General James Wolfe of Louisbourg fame, while General François Charles de Bourlamaque faced Amherst on Lake Champlain.

The dangers of the St. Lawrence yielded to the skill of British seamen. On June 26 the British fleet and transports filed slowly out from behind the Isle of Orleans into the great basin below Quebec. A few nights later the attack by the fire-ships was foiled. Wolfe, a fiery, sickly man who was a regimental officer of genius but untried as a general, placed his men in camp on the Isle of Orleans, on the north shore below the falls of Montmorency, some six miles down-river from Quebec, and at Pointe Lévis opposite the city. On the last he placed his batteries, and their fire across the river slowly demolished the Lower and the Upper Town but left the fortifications untouched. The militia of the south shore were beaten off and their villages burned, partly to discourage resistance, more to provoke Montcalm to sally from his lines. When Wolfe attempted a landing on the Beauport flats just above the Montmorency, Montcalm's second-in-command, François Gaston, Chevalier de Lévis, easily beat them off. Everything turned on a landing being made on the north shore before winter drove the fleet back to the sea, and none had been made at the easiest point.

The dispositions of Montcalm and Vaudreuil proved adequate to thwart the ill and anxious Wolfe. Most of their men were entrenched from the Lower Town to the Falls of Montmorency, but strong parties guarded the occasional passages up the cliffs above Quebec as far as the village of Sillery, about three miles upstream. Despite the shortages of food and ammunition, despite the inflation and

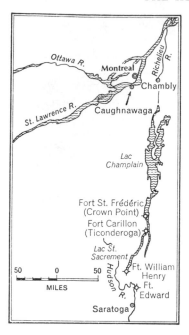

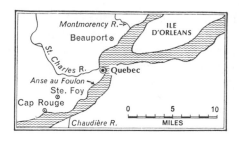

VII *The Hudson-Richelieu Line and the Site of Quebec*

the sight of the burning villages south of the river, Canada's defences held, Quebec was secure, and the approach of winter would drive Wolfe and his fleet down the river. The one disturbing factor was that British warships had passed Quebec and were in the river above the town.

The British commander was indeed desperate. He had failed to see that the vulnerable point of Quebec was its supply line from Montreal, and that the key to victory was to pass a strong landing-force well up the river where the bank was low. Now time was running out; so indeed was his own sickly life. He concentrated his troops on Orleans and at Pointe Lévis. A council of war advised a landing up-stream at Sillery. Wolfe agreed. The troops were moved into place. The ships glided up and down the river like pacing wolves watching for an opening in a herd of musk-oxen. Montcalm, watching them from the Heights of Abraham along the river above Quebec, grew worried. He formed a mobile force under Bougainville to act as a reserve for the posts along the river. As a result the front the French forces had to guard was extended and the centre, the Heights of Abraham, was dependent on the vigilance of the guards and the speed with which Bougainville supported them.

Here Wolfe on his own and secret decision struck in a despairing and headstrong move which had only one thing to commend it, the element of surprise. But surprise was obtained. On the night of September 12, the Anse au Foulon was guarded sluggishly and ineptly by the same Vergor who had surrendered Beauséjour in 1755. Seventy of his hundred men were away on the harvest leave; the rest were insufficiently alert. The British troops landed at the foot of the trail and before the startled Canadians could resist they had cleared the way to the Heights. By sun-up, 4,500 of Wolfe's men were in line and advancing to the plain before Quebec. In shafts of sunlight which pierced the clouds threatening rain, the French scouts could see their scarlet tunics flame, their bayonets flash.

The British were ashore in strength above Quebec. What was best to be done, to try to drive them over the cliffs before they could become stronger, or to bring Bougainville down upon them from up-river, lay artillery fire on their line of communication from the Anse au Foulon, and harass them by musketry from the bush on the edge of the plain? Vaudreuil was for the latter course, and Canadian skirmishers and three field-guns began to fire on the British flank. But Montcalm decided to try to drive the British off the Heights at once, and ordered troops from the Beauport lines below Quebec to concentrate on the plain. When these arrived, Montcalm had a force of some four thousand men, regulars with militiamen incorporated in their ranks. After a brief consultation with his officers, Montcalm ordered his men to attack. They advanced in ragged fashion, firing, their formation being broken by the Canadian militia who, after their style of fighting, threw themselves on the ground to reload. The ragged French charge was shattered by the British volleys crashing out in mechanical unison. French and Canadians alike broke and fled, except for some Canadian militia who held up the British advance by firing from cover on the flanks. Montcalm was mortally wounded and rode bleeding into Quebec. Wolfe had already fallen and was dead on the field. The British had forced a landing, but they had not yet destroyed the army defending Canada, or even taken Quebec.

Vaudreuil now rightly decided that he must save the army and retire to Montreal. All the night of September 13 the troops marched in darkness from the Beauport lines inland and then up the river. No British unit tried to stop them. When Vaudreuil had escaped, Ramezay, commandant of Quebec, decided that resistance in Quebec was impossible and capitulated. The terms that Wolfe's successor, Brigadier Monckton, granted in the Capitulation were generous, for the victors had to get their fleet down-river and their garrison under cover for the winter.

Quebec had fallen before Wolfe's feat of arms, but Canada had not surrendered and the French and Canadian army would fight another year. In the spring Montcalm's successor, Lévis, came down the St. Lawrence to recapture Quebec. General James Murray, who commanded the garrison, chose to meet him at Ste. Foy and there the French and Canadian defenders of Canada, in a bitter, scrambling battle, had their last taste of victory. Murray, defeated, was lucky to escape with his army into Quebec, where Lévis besieged him. When succour came with the first ship up the open river, it was the white ensign of Britain, not the fleur-de-lis of France, that showed on the forepeak above the head of the Isle of Orleans.

Meantime, General Sir Jeffrey Amherst, having failed in 1759 to advance from Fort William Henry in the rear of the withdrawing French and Canadian forces under General Bourlamaque, began to move in the summer of 1760. Johnson had captured Niagara, and Amherst took Fort St. Frédéric but did not push on down Lake Champlain. The Anglo-American forces now marched to converge on Montreal, Brigadier-General William Haviland from Lake Champlain, Murray from Quebec, Amherst from Fort Frontenac. They closed on the city irresistibly. There was no more ordered fighting, but only the last bitter stages of a hopeless resistance. The British fired the homes of the Canadian militia who did not desert, the French of those who did. Canada was beaten to the ground, its armies broken up, its lands, rivers and roads open to the invaders. Finally, the Capitulation of Montreal surrendered all the French empire in America to Anglo-American control. But enough was saved to ensure the survival of what had grown up in that empire, of what had so largely made and defended it, the sixty thousand Canadian people with their faith, their laws and their language. In defeat the empire had collapsed, but, though conquered, the people might still survive as a nation, by natural increase on the narrow farms and by cultural identity preserved in the parishes and towns along the great river, and, no less, by the compact of the capitulations victoriously renewed generation on generation in the resistance to absorption by the victors.

ADDITIONAL READING

FRÉGAULT, GUY   *La Guerre de la conquête.*
GROULX, LIONEL   *Histoire du Canada français,* Vol. II.
STACEY, C. P.   *Quebec, 1759.*
STANLEY, G. F. G.   *Canada's Soldiers* (1605-1960).
~   *New France: The Last Phase.*

THE EMERGENCE OF THE SECOND BRITISH NORTH AMERICA
[1761-1817]

After 1760 France won no advantage in Europe sufficient to recover New France. Only in Newfoundland was France to retain a vestige of its North American empire. Once the British government had decided to keep Canada rather than West Indian sugar islands, the question of the future of the old French possessions was simply how they were to be assimilated to the other English colonies of North America.

The answer attempted was the simple and drastic one of erasing New France from the map and making Canada, renamed Quebec, a colony with the laws and institutions of the other Anglo-American colonies. Assimilation meant uniformity of laws and institutions with those of the older colonies, and eventually even the absorption of the French population by American colonists.

So simple an answer was not to serve. Canada was not to be assimilated to the older colonies, because the causes of the Seven Years' War were still at work; the strategic position of Canada, the competition of the Canadian fur trade, the desire of the western tribes for continued competition, the still watchful imperial interests of France. Canada and its fur trade, and the western Indians, had indeed been incorporated in the new British North America which extended from the Atlantic to the Mississippi, and from Hudson Bay to the Gulf of Mexico. But unless they were reconciled to the new Empire, they might tempt the intervention of a France seeking to reverse the defeat of 1760.

Only a reasonably strong system of imperial defence in British North America could prevent such intervention, but the attempt to provide one provoked resistance in the old Anglo-American colonies. In the circumstances, assimilation failed, and Canada re-emerged as its former self, to survive under the Quebec Act as a fur-trade and military colony. It was designed to hold the western Indians and France in check, but the revolt of the old colonies in 1775 led to a resumption of the old warfare of the Canadian and Indian frontier. When peace returned, Canada survived as a second British North America, a New France which had lost the Ohio but regained Nova Scotia.

The peace of 1783 had in fact begun a new partition of the continent. To the north of the new boundary from the Bay of Fundy to the Lake of the Woods was a British North America still the northern frontier of the fisheries and the fur trade, its population still largely French and Anglo-American. To the latter had been added the United Empire Loyalists, themselves Anglo-Americans but even more hostile than the French to the new United States and its republican institutions. To these elements the British government decided to give British institutions as much like those of the United Kingdom as the circumstances of the colonies would permit. It was hoped that this grant, made to Canada in the Constitutional Act of 1791 in the new spirit in which the other colonies were governed, might effect a constitutional assimilation of both French and Anglo-Americans in one British nationality extending across the Atlantic and secure in North America.

The new experiment in assimilation and the survival of British America itself were at once imperilled by the great wars with revolutionary and Napoleonic France. The dangers were increased by friction with the United States, because of its widespread maritime commerce and its aggressive frontier reaching out to master the continent. But British North America, sustained by British sea power and feeling its way to a separate destiny, emerged unchanged from the years of strain and the War of 1812. That war was the last of the wars for supremacy on the continent, and from its demonstration that British sea power balanced American land power there came, step by step, the peaceful completion of continental partition. British institutions, British military and naval power and an Anglo-American balance of power resulting in the partition of the continent had spun in recurrent interplay the threads of a new Canadian destiny, both French and English, both colonial and national.

CHAPTER 9

The Eclipse and Renewal of Canada
1761-1774

The early winter of 1760 found Canada at peace; after six years the fighting had finally ended. The battles on the Ohio, of lakes Champlain and Ontario, on the St. Lawrence itself were over. War had crossed the threshold; there was no defence any more. As the militia veterans struggled to get the harvest in before the snows fell in the district of Montreal, or to raise shelter for their families in the burnt-out villages up and down the river from Quebec, it was grimly evident that Canada had fought itself out and could fight no more. It was for the conquerors to determine the future.

To the British commanders, the task they had to accomplish on the morrow of the conquest was simple. They had only to keep the Canadians quiet until the war ended and the peace treaty had determined the future of the country. Obviously, the best way to keep the defeated people quiet was to treat them with justice and, if possible, with leniency. The wisdom of doing so was all the more obvious as there was in 1760 little doubt that Canada would be retained at the peace and that the Canadians would become subjects of the British Crown.

Amherst embodied this policy of conciliation in his "Placard," a proclamation posted throughout the districts of Montreal and Trois Rivières. General Thomas Gage was made military governor of Montreal and Brigadier Ralph Burton of Trois Rivières. The inhabitants were to surrender their arms, but might have them returned when it was clear they were to be used for hunting food. The new governors were to appoint to vacancies in the Canadian militia, and the captain of militia in each parish was to settle disputes "with all due justice and equity." The troops were to pay for supplies in money, and trade was to be free. Murray, as governor of the Quebec district, had established a military court of justice in the city, but ordered that all disputes among the people should be settled by the captains of militia, with an appeal to the court at Quebec. Thus, although the office of intendant had ended in Canada, the military régime rested squarely, as the old Canadian government had done, on the broad and familiar shoulders of the captain of militia, the Justice of the Peace of New France.

Similarly, the new régime was conciliatory to the clergy, for no one could be more influential in pacifying or arousing the people. But the relationship was far more delicate than that with the captains of militia. For one thing, Bishop Pontbriand had died before the surrender of Montreal, and could not be replaced, as the British could not tolerate the nomination of a successor by either the Pope or the French king. The grand vicars, Jean Olivier Briand at Quebec and Etienne Montgolfier at Montreal, were treated with respect and responded with a perhaps exaggerated readiness to please. But the Jesuits, Recollects and Sulpicians were watched closely, and the parish clergy were viewed with suspicion. The clergy and their flocks, in short, were allowed the free exercise of their religion, but under surveillance and with a blandness which barely cloaked an abiding distrust. The influence of the clergy on the Acadians could not but be kept in mind.

The Canadians, then, possessed peace and order and the exercise of their religion under the military régime. That régime was justly administered and was made as little oppressive as possible, especially in Quebec, where Murray developed a genuine affection for the Canadian subjects. Himself a Scot with a warm and affectionate interest in his charge, Murray responded readily to the vivacity and charm of the Canadian. As a soldier, he liked that firm mixture of boldness and courtesy which is an especial grace of the Frenchman. And there was much social intercourse between Canadians and British and even some marriages between soldiers and Canadian girls.

These things mitigated but did not alter the impact of the harsh facts of conquest. The Canadians were not free; their future would be determined with no reference to themselves. The future of their laws and their faith was threatened. And Canada had not only been conquered; it had been bankrupted. The currency of card money was worthless, except in so far as the King of France might redeem it, possibly after the loss of the country. Like the South after the Civil War, Canada was reduced to its real assets, its land and its people. The fabric of society had collapsed. The only protection, it seemed, was in the doubtful terms of the capitulations of Quebec and Montreal.

Canadians remembered what had happened five short years before to the Acadians. Those unhappy people were still dispersed in exile, the majority in the English colonies, a large minority in the woods and on the fringes of Acadia. From there they had carried on a guerrilla war with the Abenakis and the Micmacs until 1760. But when Canada fell, they had no choice but to come in and surrender. Some were deported as prisoners of war; some were put to work repairing the sea dikes of Minas, neglected since 1755 and breached by the great storm of 1759, that new-comers might enjoy the lands the Acadians had reclaimed. For in 1758 an Assembly had been summoned in Nova Scotia and the free institutions and good lands advertised in New England. Land-seekers and land speculators had come east out of New England and looked over the diked lands and the uplands. Many were pleased, struck their bargains, and began to move in. By 1763 some five to six thousand New Englanders had joined the English, Swiss, Germans, and Huguenots of Nova Scotia. That was what conquest could mean.

While New Englanders learned how to drain the Minas sea marshes and Canadians waited to hear whether they would be subjects of the King of England or of France, the war drew to its close. In 1761 Spain entered the war against England, but quite failed to check the tide of English victory. In 1762 the Union Jack flew over Havana and Manila. In Europe Russia had withdrawn from the war, and the French and Austrian armies drew back from the decimated but still defiant armies of Frederick, now the Great, of Prussia. British arms had won the greatest and most far-reaching of their triumphs.

In England itself a new king and a new ministry had come to power. George III had succeeded George II in 1760 and in 1761 he and his favourite, the Earl of Bute, had forced from office the inspirer of England's victories, William Pitt. The change was by no means wholly the result of personal intrigue. The new king and Bute had put themselves at the head of a movement of opinion which held that England in defeating France had done enough. For France had begun informal discussions of a peace settlement as early as 1759. To repel these approaches and to go on to humble the House of Bourbon in Spain as well as in France was to invite, declared the peace party, the formation of a European coalition against England. So they insisted on seeking a basis for peace, even if to do so meant a peace settlement less favourable than England might have claimed.

While these political changes were proceeding, and as the war spread to the Spanish empire in the West and East Indies, a debate on the anticipated peace settlement raged in England. To a great degree it focused on the question whether Canada or the great French sugar island of Guadeloupe was to be retained by England. The controversy, in short, was as to whether the old mercantile view, with its emphasis on exotic imports, or the new imperial view of an England entering the industrial revolution, with its emphasis on exports, should determine the character of an expanded empire. It might become more continental and more populous, or more tropical and more commercial. Behind the economic contentions ran one more fundamental. Had the war been fought to increase British commerce, or to win America for the Anglo-American race? If the latter was the aim of British policy, how long could Britain govern colonies which would extend to the Mississippi and be home to turbulent millions?

The preliminaries of peace were negotiated meanwhile and agreed upon late in 1762, the definitive text early the next year. The Treaty of Paris was then quickly ratified. The negotiations went smoothly, except in one contentious field, that of the fisheries. New France was ceded in its entirety, as far west as the Mississippi. The western portion of Louisiana beyond that river was then transferred to Spain. French power was eliminated from the mainland of North America. The Anglo-American aim of 1755 was fully realized, and no check remained, as it seemed, on the sweep of land settlement and speculation between the Alleghenies and the Mississippi.

Only over the fisheries was there trouble. The French court had contested this point strongly during the tentative negotiations of 1761, and Pitt's desire to end French participation in the fisheries and so weaken French sea power was an important element in that intransigence which led to his fall. In 1762, the French raided Newfoundland and captured St. John's and most of the fishing stations. They were expelled before the end of the year, but the attack was an earnest of their interest in the fisheries.

By the treaty, France retained the "French Shore" of Newfoundland and recovered the two islands of St. Pierre and Miquelon in full right on condition that they should not be fortified. These were the sole remnants of French empire in America north of the West Indies, and their retention did help ensure that fishermen were still available to man the Atlantic squadrons of the French navy.

On the delicate question of religion, so important a part of the capitulations of Quebec and Montreal and a matter of great concern to the French negotiators at Paris, the treaty did no more than promise the Canadians "the Liberty of the Catholick religion" and the right "to profess the worship of their religion according to the rites of the Romish church, as far as the laws of Great Britain permit." The laws of Great Britain indeed made it impossible for the British negotiators to allow any more generous phraseology, but what the terms accepted would mean in practice only time and the lawyers would decide.

The great decision, then, had been made, and Canada had been retained. Guadeloupe was restored to France in return for Minorca. England had chosen to acquire territory that would absorb its staple goods, rather than islands that would yield exotics. Finally, the peace had been made, as the war had been fought, for the common benefit of the mother country and the colonies. To put it another way, the war had been a war for the conquest and the destruction of New France, and Canada had been conquered and held for the sake of the American colonies as well as of the mother country. It had been retained to put an end to the French and Indian wars, to the raids, the scalpings, the burnings, and to destroy the slender but ferocious barrier set by Canadian and Indian traders and warriors against the expansion of New England settlement and the commerce of New York and Pennsylvania.

That such a peace would be the result of the cession of Canada was soon to prove a spurious hope. Even while the signatures were being sealed at Paris, even while the debates on ratification were going on, the Indians of the Ohio and the Lakes were rising in protest against the elimination of French power from America. Urging them on were French half-breeds among them, and French traders behind them in the Illinois country, still trading down the Mississipp

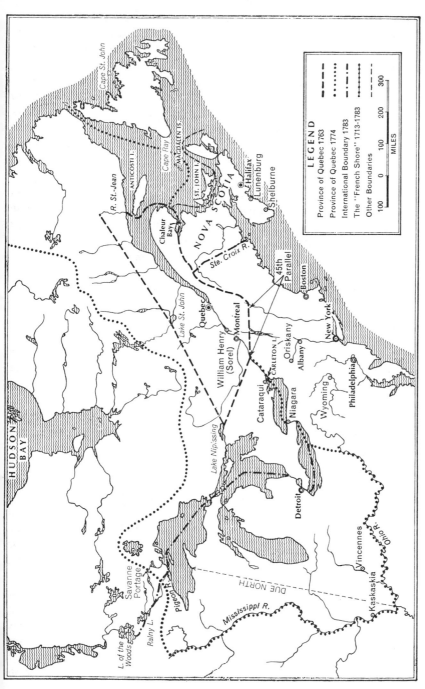

VIII *The Boundaries of Quebec and Nova Scotia, 1763–1783*

to New Orleans. It was almost a revival in the west of the old Canadian coalition of Indian and Frenchman against the Yankee and the Yorker. The Indians regretted the passing of the French, for there was a genuine respect and affection between the two peoples. They resented the ending of the competition for their furs and their favour. They were angered by Amherst's abrupt reduction in the scale of presents. And they sensed that something catastrophic had happened, that in the redcoat soldiers who had come up the Lakes to Detroit and Michilimackinac they had perhaps met their final enemy.

The chiefs therefore hurried to council along the wooded rivers and the forest paths of the upper Ohio and the Lakes. An Ottawa chief, Pontiac, was foremost in urging an attack on the British garrisons. His name was to distinguish the war which broke out in the spring of 1763, the war of ruses and sudden assaults that made the Indians masters of Michilimackinac and smaller posts, and almost of Detroit. The coalition of the tribes extended from the Senecas of New York to the Ottawas and Ojibwas of Sault Ste. Marie, and its intent was to clear the interior of the British. They failed, and Colonel Henry Bouquet's victory at Bushy Run ended the rising. Bushy Run was the last battle of the Seven Years' War, as the Indian rising was the first indication that the cession of Canada had not ensured peace in British North America.

Pontiac's War in fact set off a train of events which ended in the disruption of the new British Empire. It contributed, in the first place, to the scheme of government worked out for the new possessions of the Crown and made official by the Royal Proclamation of October 7, 1763. The proclamation established the boundaries of a new British province of Quebec. The line began at the mouth of the St. Jean River which flows into the Gulf of St. Lawrence just west of the Island of Anticosti, ran up the St. Jean to its head, and then south-west through Lake St. John to the south-east corner of Lake Nipissing. From there it turned back south-eastward to where the 45th parallel of latitude crosses the St. Lawrence above Montreal. Along that parallel it continued east to the "High Lands" dividing the St. Lawrence valley from the Atlantic slope, and then down to Chaleur Bay. Thus all the great west, made an integral part of Canada by Talon, Beauharnois, La Galissonnière and Duquesne, was cut away, and Quebec was practically reduced to the lands of seigniorial settlement, less those of Lake Champlain.

The west was not, however, turned over to the American colonies who had claimed it by charter right. For the time being, the Proclamation decreed, no settlement would be allowed beyond the watershed between the waters flowing directly to the Atlantic and those flowing to the Mississippi and the St. Lawrence. The purpose of this Proclamation Line was partly to gain time to pacify the tribes of the "Indian territory," partly to force south into the Floridas and north into Nova Scotia and Quebec the colonists seeking new lands. But the policy irritated the American traders, land speculators and frontier settlers who wished to cross the Alleghenies; it provided no means of control in the Indian territory, other than military garrisons and Indian diplomacy; and it did not induce New England land-seekers to settle in Quebec. In 1768 the line south of the Iroquois lands was moved westward to the Ohio by the Treaty of Fort Stanwix, but the change gave little satisfaction to the colonists.

Nor were they impressed by the promise of an Assembly and of the enjoyment of the "laws of England," designed, as in Nova Scotia in 1758, to assure the New Englanders that they would find free institutions with the new lands. The reason is not far to seek. In Quebec there had been no expulsion such as that of 1755 from Acadia. There were, on the contrary, over sixty-five thousand Canadians well settled, protected by treaty right, and in fact too numerous to be molested. There could be no hope of "swamping" so large and well-integrated a body of people, unless by the subversion of its laws and institutions.

It did indeed seem that the latter course was intended by the policy of "assimilation" embodied in the Proclamation. The establishment of an Assembly would have meant, without a doubt, the institution of the common law of England with land tenure by free and common socage (in effect, simple ownership), and a set of colonial laws based on those of Massachusetts or New York. The effect on Canadian society would have been destructive in the extreme.

Fortunately for the Canadians and the reputation for humanity of the British statesmen responsible for the government of Quebec, it was not intended that the changes should be abrupt or necessarily sweeping. The instructions prepared for the governor left him discretion as to when he should call an Assembly and, if not too clearly, allowed him to legislate to a limited degree in order to deal with emergencies or to provide necessary regulations. Fortunately also, the new civil governor was James Murray, already familiar with the country and in some ways sympathetic with the Canadians.

It was also fortunate for the Canadians that Murray was antipathetic to the British subjects who had already come into the colony. They were in the main merchants and traders, men who had either come in with the troops as commissaries, or had moved to Canada after the surrender to supply the garrisons and the new market of the Canadian towns and rural districts. Some of them, of course, soon entered the fur trade with the up country, although that had been interrupted by Pontiac's rising. Thus the people whom historians, following Murray's usage, describe as "old subjects" are in some instances to be met under the different and more favourable guise of Montreal fur traders. Some of them were from the British Isles, but many, perhaps most, were Americans. Their commercial habits, their independence and assertiveness, their occasional insolence and rowdiness, grated on the military and gentlemanly sensibilities of Governor Murray and of the officers of the garrison at Quebec and Montreal. The result was a series of incidents – such as George Allsopp's refusal to observe the curfew, and the scandalous affair of Walker's ear – insignificant in themselves but illustrating the clash of officers' mess and counting-room which affected the history of Quebec. For Murray's dislike and distrust of the "old subjects" induced him to defend the "new subjects," even more stoutly than he otherwise might have done, from the grave effects of the policy of the Proclamation.

That policy, as he pointed out to the imperial government, would, if applied to the full, have made the five hundred or so old subjects the masters, in a very real sense, of the lives and property of the defenceless Canadians, through their control of an assembly to which no Roman Catholic could be elected and the possession of offices to which no Roman Catholic could be appointed. The Canadians, for their part, would be excluded from public office, from the administration of the laws, and from all public service. They might be tried in courts in which their language was not allowed, by processes with which they were unfamiliar. In short, laws and government, instead of affording protection, might become a means of exploitation. That the old subjects, even if they were as unscrupulous as Murray thought the merchants of Quebec and Montreal, would have pushed their advantage to the full is most unlikely, but the policy undoubtedly threatened to impose much hardship and more insecurity on the Canadians.

Murray therefore set himself to limit the harm that might be done. After August 10, 1764, when the military régime ended, he issued an ordinance, based on the slender legislative authority of his instructions, by which he established two central courts, with Justices of the Peace as local magistrates. The superior of the two central courts was that of King's Bench for major cases and appeals, but the inferior court, that of Common Pleas, was especially designed to serve the Canadians. All judges and magistrates, of course, had to be Protestant, and the laws to be applied were the laws of England. But both courts were instructed to use French law to settle cases arising before October 1, 1764, and "to determine agreeable to Equity, having Regard nevertheless to the Laws of England, as far as the Circumstances and present Situation of Things will permit, until such time as proper Ordinances for the Information of the people can be established by the Governor and Council, agreeable to the laws of England." Moreover, Roman Catholics were allowed to serve on juries; and, on the ground that no English lawyer in the province understood French, Roman Catholics were allowed to plead cases before the Court of Common Pleas.

Murray went as far as he could to make the new mode of government tolerable to the Canadians. In this he was aided by his council, the nominated members of which he had chosen for their sympathy with the Canadians. Negligence or differences with Murray kept the less sympathetic *ex officio* members from attendance, and as a result Murray's group became the effective council. Moreover, as he steadily refused to summon an Assembly, this council in fact became the legislature, so far as one existed, for Quebec until 1775. As Murray had observed as early as 1762, in his opinion the Canadians were not yet "ripe for such a government as prevails in our other colonies." Thus the plain intent and purpose of the policy of 1763 was defeated, in part by Murray but perhaps more by its sheer inapplicability, in reason and humanity, to the circumstances of Quebec.

This partial reprieve of the Canadians from the operation of the policy of 1763 did not relieve them from the threat to their church. Its position and its future were insecure. Not only were its lay members ineligible for public office and for those careers by which so many of the leading families of Canada had maintained themselves; the want of a bishop, coupled with the withdrawal of some clergy to France, and the decease of others, also threatened to reduce the clergy to ineffectual numbers, or to make it necessary to maintain the church, as had been done in Acadia and in Ireland, by smuggling out youths for ordination and running in priests. The possibility of such an underground existence for the church did not seem fanciful in 1764, when it was plainly the intention of the new government to encourage the establishment of a Protestant clergy.

On this matter of religion, Murray was not as sympathetic as in matters of justice. He plainly viewed the church with suspicion and felt it necessary to keep the *curés* under observation and the higher clergy agreeable to government. For this reason, when the clergy revived in 1764 the practice of electing a candidate for consecration as bishop, in place of royal nomination, and put forward Grand Vicar Montgolfier of Montreal, Murray intervened swiftly and decisively, not to prevent the consecration of a bishop but in favour of Grand Vicar Briand of Quebec. The Governor had found Briand pliable and accommodating since 1759, and he wished to have as head of the church in the province a man who would work easily with the government. When the papacy declined to accept a nomination by election, a new course was adopted. The Governor's candidate, Briand, was in effect nominated and in 1766 unofficially approved by the British government, and went quietly to France for consecration.

If the perpetuation of the Canadian clergy was thus assured, the church was still in a position much inferior to the position it had enjoyed in New France. For one thing, the church in New France had never been merely an association of individuals for public worship and mutual support. It had cared for all that belonged to the spiritual side of man's nature and for about half the business of society. In material terms, it had not only its clergy and churches to maintain; it had also its schools, its hospitals and other works of charity to support. The secular clergy and parish churches were supported by the tithe, and the alms of the faithful were an addition. But the tithe was no longer recognized by law as a charge on the natural produce of the soil. The other works of the church had been carried on by means of the rents of the landed endowments, gifts and bequests, and extensive missionary aid from France. Now the last was cut off and the endowments of some orders were threatened with confiscation such as the Jesuits had suffered. Such losses would injure the whole fabric of the church and a large part of the fabric of Canadian society.

Nevertheless, if Murray's attitude to the church was a cold and politic one, he was still a friend, and the only friend, to whom the Canadians could turn in their uncertainty and distress. When the "old subjects," acting through the Grand Jury of Quebec in October 1764, attacked Murray's measures and tricked seven Canadians into signing the address of the jury with them, the seven, when undeceived, indignantly protested and declared their support for the government. This was followed by an address expressing approval of the new legal situation and of Murray. It was signed, so its endorsement ran, "by the principal Inhabitants of Canada." The old subjects, however, had business connections and political friends in London. Their protests, cleverly brought to the attention of the Board of Trade, which sifted colonial business for the Secretary of State who handled colonial affairs, brought about Murray's recall in 1766.

It was a sad ending of a term of office marked by justice and humanity, if also by much bad temper. But the irascibility of the Governor and the brawling of soldiers and merchants should not obscure the fact that Murray was the victim of an impossible situation. The policy of immigration and assimilation had not been well considered and almost at once proved to be ill-founded. The New England overflow went to Nova Scotia and the middle colonies or was absorbed by the valleys of New Hampshire and Vermont, now free of Canadian war parties. Without immigration and assimilation, the scheme of government sketched in the Proclamation was as impossible as it was unjust. It was unjust because by the law of nations the laws of the conquered continued in force until replaced by the conqueror. In Quebec, until an Assembly was called under the Proclamation, there was no adequate means of replacing the old laws with the new – including the laws of England, whatever that loose phrase might mean – or of levying new taxes. Murray had therefore temporized, partly out of humanity, partly out of uncertainty, partly because he was governor of a newly conquered colony containing almost half the British garrison of North America. That garrison might have to deal at any time with another Indian war or a Canadian revolt or, most likely, with both at once. The circumstances were not altogether those in which a prudent governor would choose to drive some seventy thousand people to revolt by the subversion of their laws and their religion, in a country which was intimately known to their experienced guerrilla fighters and which could not be relieved except in the months from May to October.

The fall of Murray punctuated but did not resolve the tangle into which the policy of 1763 had thrown the legal and political affairs of Quebec. And the social and economic interests of the Canadian people were affected by the cession quite as painfully as law and politics were by the policy of 1763. The destruction of New France and the reduction of Canada to a province of British North America had been accompanied by the supersession of the Canadian official class by a British one, and of the Canadian commercial class by an Anglo-American one. The top of Canadian society had been sheared off as by a glacier, but not with glacial slowness. The elimination of the Canadian bureaucracy and *bourgeoisie* was abrupt and brutal. As it was the principal aspect of the transformation wrought in Canadian society by the conquest, it must be looked at in some detail.

The military capitulation of New France had meant, of course, that the officers and men of the regular troops became prisoners of war and were returned to France. With them went the chief civil officers and their suites of officials. Even the Canadian governor, the Marquis de Vaudreuil, went, for a ceded Canada would afford him no such position as he had held in Louisiana and in his native land.

Such people had to go. In addition, any inhabitant of Canada, French or Canadian, was free to remove himself with family or property until eighteen months after the conclusion of the treaty of peace, which proved to be August 10, 1764. Until that date it would not be fully known how many people would avail themselves of this right. Nor is it easy now to determine how many did in fact go. The best estimates suggest that up to two thousand Canadians – native Canadians – had left by that date.

The composition of this group is also somewhat uncertain. That there was among them a high proportion of officials, soldiers, and men of law and business seems clear, and would of course be natural. The political, legal, and business ties with France ensured that such people would have connections there, and these may well have seemed to promise a better future than Canada would do. What is clear is that many of the *noblesse* who lived by the profession of arms or by holding public office went, and with them much of the breeding and bravery of Canada.

The migration to France, however, was a limited one both in numbers and in quality. It seems not to have been the decisive element in the transformation of Canadian society. The decisive element was the cutting-off of opportunity that the change of régime brought about. The Canadian *noblesse* and the seigneurs could no longer count on serving as government officials, or as officers in the Troupes de la Marine or even the colonial militia. They could not hope to be commandants of western posts. Neither could they hope to provide for their sons by obtaining such positions for them, or for their daughters by marrying them to young men so provided for. And how long could bright young men hope to make a career of the law if the laws were changed and the bench closed to Roman Catholics? Even the old and honoured post of captain of militia had disappeared, the captains being replaced by Protestant justices of the peace.

If prospects of official appointment were slight at best, the same lack of opportunity blocked the path of the Canadian merchant and trader. Not only was he impoverished by the collapse of the card money. His connections and his line of credit with the merchants of La Rochelle and Bordeaux had been severed by the war and then by the British laws of trade and navigation after the peace.

KC-F*

If he sought to replace his creditors and forwarders in France by turning to London business houses, as some Canadian merchants did, he not only found his new Anglo-American competitors established before him; he also found few willing to deal with him, and practically none with the necessary resources. Thus the *bourgeoisie*, never too strong and still largely French at the cession, lost its French members and perhaps some of its Canadian ones, and was so weakened that it failed to restore itself after 1763 and dwindled away.

In Quebec itself, either retailing in the colony or forwarding goods to the up country, the Canadian merchant found busy Anglo-American competitors at work and already in possession of the trade of the west. A Canadian trader could not, after all, be wholly trusted in the west after what the Illinois traders were thought to have done to provoke Pontiac's rising. By the time that suspicion had died down and the fur trade was fully restored, most of the Canadian traders had gone under or had become retailers in the Quebec towns and villages. The great trade of Canada was not for them. The wonder is that a few, like François Baby, actually stayed in business in the fur trade.

The result of this suppression of the Canadian official and merchant class, not so much by British policy as by the brutal logic of the events of 1760–63, was that Canadian society lost many of its natural leaders, while its middle class, so far as it survived, became largely clerical and, after the Quebec Act, also legal. It became, that is, partial and lop-sided. At the same time, Canadian society became what it had never really been before the cession, predominantly agricultural and rural. The habitant survived and multiplied, but the *bourgeois* was henceforth a Scot, or even an Englishman or a "Bastonnais," a Yankee. The voyageur survived, but only as the *engagé*, the hired hand, of the alien *bourgeois*. These changes were the ultimate effects of the cession, except for those which lie too deep for history to plumb.

The new Canadian *bourgeoisie* consisted, of course, of the "old subjects" of Murray's aversion. But, however much their manners and their political views may have offended the irascible governor, their business ability and their sense of what was profitable were keen and alert. They began, as agents of London mercantile houses, to supply not only the local markets and the garrisons of Quebec but also the western fur trade. Like their French predecessors, they supplied traders who ventured up-country with canoes laden with trade goods and manned and guided by the Canadian voyageurs who had served La Vérendrye and Saint-Pierre. On their return with furs these men, the "bourgeois" of fur-trade parlance, paid their debts and took their profits, if any. The Montreal traders then settled with their London houses and the cycle was complete.

The fur trade of Canada was thus being revived, and in more auspicious circumstances than it had known for a century. For Montreal had in fact great natural advantages over Albany and Philadelphia, and the great human resources of Canadian canoe-craft and Indian goodwill. To these were now added the cheaper and superior goods of English manufacture and the long and abundant credit of the London houses. The fur trade of Montreal, alone of Canadian concerns, was an actual beneficiary of the war and the peace.

The trade built up slowly until 1768. The freedom allowed from 1760 to 1763 was checked by Pontiac's rising. Thereafter only licensed canoes were allowed to go west. But in 1768 a new policy left the fur trade to the control of the separate colonies and the old rivalry of New York and Canada revived. The trade was soon in full swing at all the posts of the Lakes and to the south-west on the Ohio, and Montreal traders were even on Red River in the north-west. The old fur-trade pattern was re-emerging under the new political lines of 1763, and the north-west was becoming again a hinterland of Montreal.

As a result, the Hudson's Bay Company maintained its policy, begun with Anthony Henday's great journey of 1754 to the country of the Blackfoot Indians, of sending winterers inland. They anxiously and on the whole successfully at first sought to keep the Indians coming to York Factory and Churchill. These inland expeditions were excelled by Samuel Hearne's great feat of travel to the mouth of the Coppermine River on the Arctic coast between 1769 and 1772. Hearne was investigating the mines, and the result of his journey was to alter the concepts held respecting the width of northern America. But the inland winterers failed to check the "pedlars," as they contemptuously called them after 1770. As a result, by 1774, the Company was forced to send Hearne inland to build Cumberland House on the route between the Saskatchewan and the Churchill to meet the competition of the Montreal Nor'Westers.

If the fur trade was reviving, even though in the hands of English traders, another old Canadian trade, the seal fishery of the north shore of the Gulf, had been cut off by the Proclamation of 1763 as the west had been. The district east of the St. Jean River had been given to Newfoundland by the Proclamation, and the fishery was suppressed for fear that it might become a means of smuggling French goods into Quebec.

In this, as in the cutting-off of the west, Canada had been deliberately sacrificed to interests of older British colonies. The importance of the fisheries question in the debate on the possible terms of peace had made the English look much more closely at the condition of their own fishery in Newfoundland. The prevailing theory was that the fishery was conducted from England by fishermen who returned to England each fall. The fishery was thus "a nursery of seamen" in which men were trained to the sea, and from which they might be pressed in time of war. The actuality was that a "resident" fishery had grown up which was supplied from old England and increasingly after 1713 from New England. Moreover, many of the fishermen who went out each year from England and Ireland either remained in Newfoundland or, probably for the most part, joined New England ships to enjoy the high wages and plentiful food they offered.

The "nursery of seamen" had therefore become a mere slogan the fishing

interests of the English west country used when they wished to obtain legislation or bounties from the government of the United Kingdom. In the general
review of colonial affairs which the Seven Years' War provoked, this situation
was examined and the determination formed to make the "nursery of seamen"
a reality by ensuring that the fishery was once more carried on from England by
fishermen who returned there. Captain Sir Hugh Palliser was appointed in 1764
as governor – that is, as the naval officer superintending the fishery during the
summer months – with instructions to apply the policy. Because of changes of
government, his recommendations were not acted upon until 1775. They were
then embodied in what was known as Palliser's Act, by which bounties were
offered and penalties imposed, all designed to exclude the New Englanders from
the fishery and to ensure the return of fishermen to England. The Act was a twin
of the Quebec Act, in that it withdrew from the American colonists to some extent the opportunity for the unregulated exploitation of the British North
American empire which seemed to be theirs after 1760.

The reservation of the Newfoundland fisheries for English fishermen could
be contemplated because, of course, the New Englanders now had entry to
those of Canso, Cape Breton, and Gaspé, from which French competition was
eliminated. The New England fishing schooners did move in increasing numbers
into the Nova Scotian fisheries, and fishermen began to settle the many harbours
of the Atlantic shore of Nova Scotia.

The chief New England interest in Nova Scotia, however, still continued to
be its lands. By 1775, it is estimated, there were seventeen or eighteen thousand
people in the colony, most of them New England farmers. They were settled in
the Annapolis Valley, about the Minas basin, and at the site of former Fort
Beauséjour. Only a few other colonists, mostly Irish, joined them. The Acadian
problem gradually disappeared as some of these unhappy people, perhaps two
thousand in number, were allowed to settle in the peninsula of Nova Scotia,
on the St. John River, and on the Island of St. John. Even there the Acadians were
to be outnumbered when the Island was made a separate colony in 1769 and
given an assembly in 1773. The predominant New Englanders created an agricultural and New England hinterland to military and British Halifax. They
brought with them the New England township and town meeting, and by so
doing alarmed the Halifax authorities, who accepted with reluctance a modified
township system, combined with counties and under the eye of Justices of the
Peace appointed in Halifax. They used the Virginian model of local government to offset the New England democracy. The new settlers were Congregationalists, while Halifax was in the main Anglican, and religion as well as
political custom widened the gulf between capital and hinterland. Rural Nova
Scotia had ceased to be Acadian and had become American, if already American
with some sense of difference. But in 1775 the Halifax oligarchy still controlled
the dissenting, democratic New England hinterland. Nova Scotia was still at

bottom a garrison and a naval base. Still more important for the future, however, it was becoming a rival of New England in the fisheries and in shipping.

Meantime, the difficulties of the Province of Quebec had brought about a reversal of the policy of 1763. The change began in 1765, even before Murray's recall. In that year the law officers of England gave it as their opinion that the Roman Catholics of Quebec were not subject to the disabilities of those of the United Kingdom. The Board of Trade then began an earnest if desultory discussion – punctuated by the political changes of this period of political instability in England – of the problems and confusion of the laws and institutions of Quebec.

The way out of the difficulties was indicated in 1766 by the newly appointed Attorney General of Quebec, Francis Maseres; namely, that the authority of the imperial parliament would be required to settle the three main matters of religion, laws, and a revenue. Maseres later altered his views, however, and came to approve in a measure the policy of assimilation of 1763. This last, with one fundamental change, was the policy put forward by the Board of Trade in a report completed in July 1769. The Board found that the province was in "the greatest disorder and confusion," and recommended that "a complete Legislature" should be established, by admitting Roman Catholics to the Assembly, and that this legislature should deal with the questions arising from the condition of the courts, laws, and religion. Its recommendations might have made the policy of 1763 workable by substituting the assimilation of institutions for the assimilation of people. But the British government would not act until it had fully considered the opinions and recommendations of Murray's successor.

This was Colonel Guy Carleton, who came out to administer the colony in 1766 on Murray's return to London, and became governor in 1768. A cold, reserved Ulsterman, he was a contrast to the warm and irritable Murray, and at first seemed opposed to the views and policies of his predecessor. But Carleton, like Murray, was a soldier and one of the conquerors of Canada. He was convinced of the likelihood of a French war of *revanche*, and he observed the American resistance to the Townshend duties of 1767, which followed that to the Stamp Act in 1765, with a growing feeling that serious trouble with the colonies would afford France its opportunity. Like Murray, he developed a liking for the courteous and soldierly Canadian *noblesse* and for the habitant's respect for rank. He began to see the Canadians not as potential enemies but as possible allies. Certainly, he declared, the policy of assimilation had failed; "so that," ran his famous phrase, "barring Catastrophe shocking to think of, this country must, to the end of Time, be peopled by the Canadian Race."

Carleton had thus come to share Murray's opinions as well as to hold his office. He shunned the "old subjects" and was sympathetic to the "new." Above all, he studied how the Canadians might be reconciled to British rule so that Quebec might be a bastion of British power in America when the need should come to withstand French attack. He thought Quebec should be given institutions and laws suited to its French inhabitants, both in justice to those inhabitants and in order to ensure their loyalty to British rule.

Carleton concluded it would be possible, by concessions to the Canadians in religion, laws, and government, to make them willing British subjects and so revive the old structure of Canadian society. He saw in the clergy, the *noblesse*, and the seigneurs the natural leaders of the Canadians; and he proposed, by throwing open careers to the *noblesse* and seigneurs and by restoring the legal position of the clergy, to bind the Canadians to the British Crown through their leaders. The policy was intelligible, but Carleton mistook the leaders of the Canadian people and exaggerated the unity of Canadian society. The leaders were the captains of militia rather than the seigneurs, and there were independent minds among the Canadians.

In 1770, worried by the report of the Board of Trade and by Maseres's recommendation that Quebec be given an English code of law, Carleton returned to England, where he was to remain until 1774. A new ministry had just been formed, that of Lord North. It enjoyed the support of both the King and the House of Commons, and could do whatever it was moved to do. It none the less proceeded with exceeding slowness in Canadian affairs, with the result that its legislation for Quebec appeared not as a separate attempt to deal with the affairs of that peculiar colony, but as a measure designed to penalize the old colonies for their resistance to the tea duty of 1773.

There is perhaps no other explanation for this delay than the obvious ones of routine and slowness of communication. Step by step the cumbrous machinery of memorandum and draft, petition and counter-petition, made its way through the three years after Carleton's return. It was decided late in 1770 to do without an assembly and to give the governor and council power to legislate for an indefinite period. Since 1768 the traders and council of Quebec, alarmed by the revival of colonial control of the fur trade, had been seeking a westward extension of the boundaries of Quebec, but the government was doubtful as to what to do in this dangerous matter. What laws Quebec was to have bestowed on it remained in doubt till the end, when events forced a decision, one long foreshadowed, of British criminal and French civil law.

While the British lawyers and administrators groped their way towards a just and liberal mode of dealing with the difficulties of Quebec, another aim, that Quebec should be made a loyal garrison colony, was shaping British policy. The Canadians must be reconciled, to make Canada loyal against French attack. Carleton had not departed from this conviction, formed as early as 1767 and reinforced by subsequent events. While he had no wish to use Quebec to curb the colonies, he did intend that Quebec should not become a base that France might use to aid colonial revolt. He was now supported by William Knox, a British official and pamphleteer, who feared the growing independence of the

American colonies and urged the necessity of checking it. From 1768, as Under-secretary to the new Secretary of State for America, Knox was able to bring his fears and his ideas to bear. He and Carleton saw the problem of British power in America in much the same way, but Knox was the more imaginative of the two. He it was, and not Carleton, who now urged that the way to give the Indian territory reserved by the Proclamation of 1763 the administrative control it lacked was to re-annex it to Quebec. The control of Indian affairs and of the fur trade, thus centred at Montreal, could be put in the hands of the Government of Quebec. Control of the vast interior would then not pass to the ultra-demo-cratic colonial assemblies of the old colonies. And a further check would be given to the western ambitions of the colonies which had been frustrated ever since the Proclamation Line of 1763. The proposal was accepted late in 1773, and became a major part of the new legislation for Quebec.

The terms of the Act provided for the re-drawing of the boundaries to restore the Labrador coast with the seal fishery to Quebec. The western boundary was now extended along Lake Ontario and Lake Erie to the Ohio and the Mississippi and northward from the confluence of those streams. To the north the boundary followed the height-of-land. The boundaries and charter rights of other colonies were "saved," but in effect the French advance to the Ohio in 1749 was for the indefinite future confirmed by act of the British parliament. The Act then went on to assure the free exercise of the Roman Catholic faith; the clergy were to have their accustomed dues (that is, the tithe) from members of the church, and Roman Catholics were freed from the need to subscribe to the Test Act and provided with a special oath of allegiance. Civil law was to be the old Canadian law, which allowed no trial by jury, but criminal law was to be British. The land law remained seigniorial but was modified to provide for grants in free and common socage. Finally, the Act established a council, with the power to legislate but not to tax, except for public buildings and roads. To repair this last de-ficiency, Parliament passed the Quebec Revenue Act, which imposed duties on spirits imported into the colony.

In intent, it is to be observed, the Act was meant to deal finally with some matters, provisionally with others. The religious provisions were permanent. The legal ones were not, nor was the recourse to a legislative council. It was assumed that the laws would be changed, and that the constitution might be revised. Nor were the claims of the old subjects meant to be forgotten, as Carle-ton's new instructions were to show, for example, by ordering the introduction of jury trial in civil cases. But events were to give the Quebec Act a finality which would have surprised its drafters.

The Act, however, did neatly use the parliamentary sword to cut the knots the Proclamation of 1763 had tied in the affairs of the Province of Quebec. It gave a province which had not conformed to the standard pattern, which had failed to become English, Protestant, and devoted to representative government, a special and unique constitution. That constitution was perhaps not ill-devised, but if it was meant to restore the old Canadian form, it was attempting more than its drafters seem to have realized. The great mainspring of the old system was lacking, the office of intendant. His agents, the captains of militia, were forgotten. And that humane and genial paternalism, one expression of the old French genius, was hardly to be captured in an Act of Parliament or by alien administrators.

The restoration of the civil law, on the other hand, was not merely the ending of a tangle, it was simple justice. So also were the religious clauses. In terms of the policy of the Act, however, the important question was whether the grant of simple justice would stir the Canadians to active gratitude. The attitude of their leaders might determine that, and it would be for the governor under the new constitution to deal with them.

The policy of the Act, in the last analysis, lay neither in its recognition of the unique character of Quebec in British America, nor in its measures of justice to the Canadians and their church. It lay in the complete, if not wholly intended, reconstitution of the old Canada of the French régime from the Gulf of St. Lawrence to the Mississippi and from the Ohio to the height-of-land. This tremendous reversal of the policy of 1763 meant that British America was now divided, deliberately and, as it proved, against itself. One part was self-governing and on the verge of revolt. The other, half alien, half Indian, was to be governed as the first model, not only of the British crown colony, but also of the American and Canadian "territory." The two halves of British America looked all too like antagonists in a second struggle for control of the west and supremacy in America. An empire of trade once more faced an empire of settlement. The Quebec of 1775 was the Canada of 1755, but with an even greater gulf between the Canadians and their leaders than existed in the latter year. Whether he could bridge that gulf was the main question which faced Guy Carleton when he returned in 1774 to resume his duties as governor of the colony – a Canadian and Indian colony, a military post and garrison, which was now to be called on to play once more its old role in America.

ADDITIONAL READING

BREBNER, J. B.   *The Neutral Yankees of Nova Scotia.*

BURT, A. L.   *The Old Province of Quebec.*

MACNUTT, W. S.   *The Atlantic Provinces: The Emergence of Colonial Society.*

MARTIN, CHESTER   *Foundations of Canadian Nationhood.*

WADE, MASON   *The French Canadians, 1760-1945.*

CHAPTER 10

The Canadian War of Independence
1775-1791

Canada since 1760 had been embedded in the British Empire in North America. Its limits had been reduced and its outline lost in the imperial organization of 1763. By the Quebec Act of 1774, however, something like its ancient limits reappeared on the map, and something like its former frame of government was restored. Now the shock of the rebellion of the old colonies was to liberate Canada from its bondage to the Anglo-American imperialism of 1763 and restore it, if in altered circumstances, to its old independence in America.

Canada's part in the rebellion of the old colonies was intimate and fundamental. Canada was a cause of that rebellion, both because its conquest had freed the American colonists from their dependence on England for help against Canada, and also because the legislation of 1774, necessary to meet Canadian conditions, was offensive to the sentiments and temper of the colonists. Thus the Quebec Act was grouped by the colonial patriots with the Acts passed to reduce Boston and Massachusetts to order after the Boston Tea Party. And it was at once assumed that the Quebec Act was intended to conciliate the Canadians, not only to ensure that they would not join France in a war against Britain, but also to win them to support of the British in a struggle with the colonies. Canada, in short, had re-emerged in its old colours as the enemy of New England and New York.

Canada had therefore to be conquered once again, but this time by American means and for American ends alone. The means chosen were propaganda and invasion. In September 1774 the Continental Congress, in an open letter, appealed to the Canadians to join the revolting colonies. In the winter of 1774–75 American agents, sure of hospitality among the merchants of Montreal, were in Canada advocating the cause of rebellion and spreading fear and distrust of British intentions in the new Act. Then, in May 1775, Ethan Allen with his "Green Mountain Boys" seized Ticonderoga and Crown Point, and Benedict Arnold of Connecticut seized and briefly held St. Jean on the border. The purpose of these captures was twofold, to obtain cannon for the siege of Boston and to open the route to Canada.

When Guy Carleton, now a major-general, had returned to Canada in September 1774 to resume his governorship and to inaugurate the régime of the Quebec Act, he soon found Canada stirring with unrest and menaced with invasion. The new government was not to begin in favourable circumstances or to have time and peace to take root and adapt itself to Canadian society. It began as a war government and acquired a war temper it was never to lose. When on May 1, 1775, the Quebec Act came into force, Carleton gave it an application and a direction not intended by the imperial government. He did so because the Act had not produced the effect he had hoped for among the Canadians, and because of the impending American invasion.

That invasion, authorized in June 1775, was launched at the end of August. It followed the old pattern of a thrust at Montreal combined with a thrust at Quebec. But whereas the attack on Montreal followed the traditional Champlain-Richelieu route, that on Quebec was a daring march overland by the Kennebec and Chaudière rivers. As the Americans could not go by sea in face of British naval power, Benedict Arnold led them by land in a march of heroic endurance and great wastage of men and material.

Canada was ill-equipped to repel the invaders. Carleton had stripped its garrisons in the fall of 1774, when he still hoped the Quebec Act would enable him to raise a force of Canadians to aid General Thomas Gage, the British commander-in-chief in Boston. Only two battalions remained, and they were below strength. For the rest, Carleton had to rely on the Canadian militia, the Indians, and volunteers. Of these the Indians were the least unreliable. The old subjects, one source of volunteers, were shot through with rebel sympathies. The Canadians were not moved to spring to arms against this renewed attack; in a quarrel of the English and the "Bastonnais," their interest was uncertain. Any merits the Quebec Act might have were not evident to the habitants, nor had there been time to demonstrate them. In any event, the Act did not recapture the old humane and paternal spirit of the *ancien régime*. There was nothing to warm the hearts or excite the courage of the old captains of militia, the natural leaders of the people. The Act was directed to the clergy, the seigneurs and *noblesse*. The seigneurs and *noblesse* had rarely, however, except by personal merit such as the Le Moynes possessed, been the immediate leaders of the habitants; most of them were actively loyal, but the habitants did not respond in numbers to their appeals to defend the country against the invaders, and the loyalist activities of the clergy were often resented. Carleton got few soldiers. The majority of the habitants remained neutral, but not all. Some hundreds of them in fact joined the invaders and were embodied in two small regiments. Revolutionary ideas were by no means alien to Canadian minds, and from this time on there were Canadians who shared the ideals of self-government which fired the "patriots" of the old colonies to the south. So general was the American influence that from the invasion onwards it became the usual practice to elect the officers of the militia. Thereafter Canada was to have a "patriot" and democratic element eager for self-government as a means to preserve French nationality.

On September 4, the invaders under Generals Philip Schuyler and Richard Montgomery reached St. Jean and besieged it. St. Jean was to hold for two months, and the Canadian militia were to rally in some force to defend Montreal. But numbers told, and when news reached Montreal early in November that Arnold was before Quebec, Carleton left Montreal and just managed to avoid capture on his way down the river to Quebec.

There, with about eighteen hundred men, of whom over five hundred were Canadian militia, he faced the combined forces of Arnold and Montgomery. The situation of both sides was hazardous, not to say desperate. The Americans had about as many men as Carleton, but they had no siege guns and were exposed to the rigours of the Canadian winter. Their Canadian followers, not too ardent in their new alliance, soon began to desert. The two generals therefore decided to try to carry Quebec by assault. Their attack, launched in the early morning of December 31, resulted in the death of Montgomery, the wounding of Arnold and the capture of four hundred Americans.

Even this brusque repulse did not break the siege. Arnold held on sternly and reinforcements came up in March. As many again were ordered, for Congress knew that if Quebec was to be taken, it must be before relief reached it by the open river in the spring. But the Americans failed to muster sufficient strength before the soiled snow-drifts had melted and the ice pack had gone grinding down the river. On May 5, 1776, the first British vessels arrived as Carleton's cannon barked in welcome from Cape Diamond.

The besiegers withdrew wearily and at once, but there was no close pursuit. It was impossible, at first. Then, when the way had been prepared by British victories at The Cedars and Trois Rivières to overrun the sick and shattered Americans, Carleton deliberately slowed the pursuit up the Richelieu. Everything pointed to the total defeat of the invaders – disease in their ranks, the now active hostility of the habitants, the crushing superiority of the British regulars. But Carleton was not prepared to strike home, as he hoped that the Americans might yet be conciliated if not driven too hard. He gently herded them up the Richelieu-Hudson line, 150 Canadian *congressistes* going with them into exile. By midsummer Canada was once more clear of enemy forces. As it was to prove, Canada would be free from American invasion for almost forty years.

It might, however, still be a base for operations against the new revolutionary power which had come into being on July 4, 1776. But Carleton did not choose to use Canada as a weapon to destroy the infant United States. To him the mortal enemy was France, and he believed that once the Americans had been shown that they could not defy British authority, they could be won back to loyalty in the Empire. He therefore cleared the Americans from Lake Champlain but turned back from an attack on Crown Point. A thrust from Canada through New York was to be committed to other hands than his.

The expulsion of the Americans from Canada was accompanied by their repulse in Nova Scotia. There an attempt to seize Fort Cumberland, the successor to Beauséjour on the Isthmus of Chignecto, was defeated in November 1776. As Washington pointed out, the Americans could not bring sufficient force against Nova Scotia because of British "strength at sea." It was well that this was so, for the population of Nova Scotia outside Halifax was disposed by its New England origin to sympathize with the New England revolt. This sympathy was, however, to give way to hostility as New England privateers captured Nova Scotian prizes, and as prize-money began to be earned by Nova Scotian privateers sent to sea in reprisal. Caught between British sea power and their natural affection for New England, the majority began to seek, like the Acadians before them, to be "neutral."

If Carleton, back in Canada, had declined to use Canada against the revolted colonies, he had at the same time refrained from initiating the new régime of the Quebec Act. For almost two years Canada was governed by military law and proclamation. Carleton had anticipated the lapse of government after May 1, 1775, by a proclamation of April 26 in which he provided for the administration of the law by six conservators of the peace. In June, military law was proclaimed. The Legislative Council provided for in the Quebec Act, the members of which were named in Carleton's instructions, was not summoned until August. And it passed no laws, because the Canadian members and their English allies refused to have jury trial in civil cases; the old civil law of Canada was not to be modified now that Canadian voices could be raised in its defence.

In midsummer, 1776, the Americans having been expelled, civil government was restored, but not until January 1777 did the Legislative Council meet again. In the interval Carleton had governed by proclamation and with the advice of a "privy council," an inner group of the Legislative Council – Lieutenant-Governor Hector Cramahé, Hugh Finlay, Thomas Dunn, John Collins and Adam Mabane, all confidants of the Governor. But Carleton had feared to call the full council together because death, illness, capture by the Americans and absence in England had left it a body he feared he could not control. In particular, six of the seven original Canadian members were for the above reasons unable to attend.

The summoning of the council could not be delayed indefinitely, however, and Carleton faced the twelve remaining members at Quebec in January 1777. The council then proceeded to establish at last the form of government intended by the framers of the Quebec Act. It enacted a system of law courts and of legal procedure. It instituted the old civil law and English criminal law, but without making the changes ordered by the imperial government in Carleton's instructions as governor under the Act. The criminal law was not made more humane, and the writ of *habeas corpus* was not made a statutory right. In civil law the council again refused to provide for trial by jury and declined to introduce English mercantile law. Thus the new council refused to remedy the old grievances of the merchants of Quebec, and so perpetuated an injustice which had lasted since 1764 and which the framers of the Quebec Act had intended to remove.

The fact was that Carleton had succeeded in continuing under the new régime the old anti-merchant, or French, party of Murray's and his own first governorship. The members of the French party were the English members of the old council, with whom the Canadian councillors now aligned themselves. Its leader was Adam Mabane, a Scots physician of gentle disposition and rigid and reactionary views. This so-called French party was to dominate the government of Canada for the next dozen years. The opposition within the council was at first slight and ineffective.

In extenuation of its dominant role and reactionary policy, the French party could plead that it governed a country at war. For in 1777 the British war plans provided for an expedition from Canada against New York by the Richelieu-Hudson line. The object was to dominate that largely loyalist province and sever New England from the middle and southern colonies. The command was not given to Carleton, who had quarrelled with Lord George Germain, the British Secretary of State, but was committed to Major-General John Burgoyne. A smart soldier, a man of fashion and a popular playwright, "Gentleman Johnny" Burgoyne was to advance by Lake Champlain to Albany, to make contact with British forces operating up the Hudson. An expedition from Oswego to the Mohawk Valley was to create a diversion for him as he attempted to cross the divide from Lake George to Albany.

This diversion, although under the command of Lieutenant-Colonel Barry St. Leger, was to be composed of Indians and "provincials," that is, American loyalists. These Indians and loyalists were from New York itself, in the main from the Mohawk Valley. New York was not only one of the most loyal of the colonies; it was the most like Canada, feudal and aristocratic in bent, and with a considerable commitment to the fur trade and a major Indian element, the confederacy of the Six Nations. It was in the Mohawk Valley that feudalism, the fur trade, and Indian diplomacy were most prominent. The master of all three until his death in 1774 had been Sir William Johnson. Next to him, if at a distance in both fame and wealth, was John Butler. With Johnson's death, his mantle had fallen on his son John and his nephew Guy. Neither possessed the flair or the energy of Sir William, but the leadership of the Mohawk Valley loyalists fell to them, together with John Butler and Joseph Brant, the Mohawk chief who was Sir William Johnson's brother-in-law by his marriage with Molly Brant.

With the outbreak of the revolution the Johnsons failed to dominate the

Mohawk Valley and had to retreat to Canada with Butler at the beginning of 1776. There they organized the King's Royal Regiment of New York and the corps which came to be known as Butler's Rangers. These loyalist forces fought as scouts and light infantry in their own country, often indeed fighting their way to their own homes to remove their families to Canada. With them fought the loyalist Indians of the now divided Six Nations, in particular Brant's Mohawks; of the other tribes, only the Oneidas and Tuscaroras joined the revolutionaries in full force. Burgoyne and St. Leger might hope to be joined by many such loyalists as they advanced.

The campaign of 1777 therefore began with bright hopes as Burgoyne's spruce redcoats and well-drilled Hessians filed in their boat brigades up the broad Richelieu and the long mountain trench of Lake Champlain. But St. Leger, although he defeated the American militia at Oriskany, failed to capture Fort Schuyler (once Stanwix) and had to retreat. He thus failed to make a diversion for Burgoyne, whose thrust lost its vigour as the drag of his supply line grew. Burgoyne received no help from Sir Henry Clinton at New York, and, entangled in the woods and surrounded by the swarming New York and New England militia of Generals Horatio Gates and Benedict Arnold, was forced to capitulate in October.

The surrender at Saratoga was to bring France into alliance with the Americans, for the long-awaited chance to weaken the victor of 1763. This consequence of Saratoga, the only major campaign directed from Canada across the Richelieu-Hudson watershed at New York, made the battle one of the decisive battles of world history. It was quite as decisive in Canadian history. The surrender of Burgoyne's army ensured the independence of Canada in America. Neither France nor the United States could allow the other to possess Canada, and after 1778 Canada was in fact secure from attack, although the Marquis de Lafayette was to propose its conquest in 1779, and Washington was making plans for its capture in the early winter of 1778, and again in 1780 and 1781. But Canada's enemies were each careful to thwart the other's intent, and cancelled one another out.

Canada, if in fact made secure by this paradox, was by no means out of the war, or indifferent to its outcome. By the Quebec Act, and the results of the war down to 1778, Canada had resumed its ancient boundaries and former amplitude. From Quebec to the Illinois, from the St. Lawrence to the Saskatchewan, the old French empire was reconstituted. And once more, as in the days of Frontenac, Canada sought to defend its barbarous empire of the Indian fur trade by the *petite guerre*, the war of raid and burning, of ambush and terror.

Yet, if Canada seemed to fight in the old manner for the old prizes, it was not Canadians who fought. The Canadian militia after 1776 did military corvées when compelled or well paid. Some from Detroit or Michilimackinac, among them that Charles Langlade who had destroyed Pickawillany in 1752, raided on the Ohio or the Mississippi with the British. But the warfare waged from the bases of The Cedars and Carleton Island on the St. Lawrence, and out of Niagara, was fought by American loyalists, the Royal Highland Emigrants, and Brant's Indians. It was a New York civil war, with the weaker side striking from Canadian bases, and the local object was not so much to hold Canada as to win New York. But in the very process of so fighting, the loyalist New Yorkers became Canadian and fought for the independence of the northern economy and its wilderness country.

The fighting of 1778 to 1782 was not as local or as sporadic as it seemed. As under Frontenac, it was concerted warfare with a major strategic object. By raiding into New York and Pennsylvania, Johnson's "Royal Greens" and Butler's Rangers were destroying Washington's sources of supply for his campaigns in New Jersey and Pennsylvania and compelling him to divert forces, as in Sullivan's expedition to western New York in 1779. But it was a fearful kind of war, which combined the horrors both of civil and Indian warfare and left fierce hatreds and bitter tales behind. There was in fact no massacre by the loyalists at Wyoming, or Cherry Valley, or German Flats, but the raids inspired the fear and hatred from which the legends of massacre sprang. The New York frontier was tearing itself in two and the agony was bitter and lasting.

The same kind of warfare ran westward along the Ohio. From Detroit the Indians and the loyalist guerrillas, such as that villain of American folklore, Simon Girty, struck at the American settlers seeping into the Ohio Valley even as the war went on. In 1778 Virginians under George Rogers Clark captured Vincennes in the Illinois country, and Henry Hamilton, Lieutenant-Governor of Detroit, was taken in attempting to recapture it. Clark also took Kakaskia on the Mississippi, but both were retaken by British war parties before the war's end.

After Spain entered the war in 1779, the raiding parties struck at St. Louis itself. And at the end all the south-west to the line of the Ohio and the Mississippi remained firmly and wholly Canadian. Even New York up to the watershed was held, from Carleton Island, Oswego, and Niagara – a possession as it were sealed by the death of the young and gallant Walter Butler, nephew of Colonel Butler and bravest of the Mohawk Valley loyalists, in rearguard action at West Canada Creek in 1782.

While Canada fought to preserve its southern boundaries from American attack, its traders were adding new areas to its domains in the far north-west. Much as the Anglo-American penetration of the country of the Lakes after 1713 had turned French eyes to the north-west and set in train La Vérendrye's endeavour to redress the threatened loss of the south-west by opening the north-west, so now the injury done the trade of the south-west by the war stimulated the penetration of the north-west which had been renewed after 1764.

That penetration had forced the Hudson's Bay Company to come inland and build Cumberland House in 1774. But the Company's occupation of a commanding site on the Saskatchewan and Churchill River systems had not stopped the advance of the Montreal "pedlars" into new beaver country which not even the Canadians had penetrated. In 1775 Alexander Henry, Joseph and Thomas Frobisher and Peter Pond wintered to the north and south of Cumberland House. They had, with the probable exception of Pond, combined their stocks. The pooling of resources was a response to the costs and slow returns imposed by the increasing distance from Montreal. In this need to combine was the origin of the North West Company.

The new method of pooling trade goods was used to penetrate the Mackenzie River basin when in the fall of 1777, as the net was tightening around Burgoyne at Saratoga, the Montreal traders on the Saskatchewan combined their resources to send Peter Pond into the country of the Athabaska River. There Pond discovered the richest beaver country of the trade for the next forty years. There also he first heard of a great river which might flow into the Pacific at Cook's Inlet, as he began to conjecture when he returned to Montreal in 1784 and learned of Captain James Cook's survey of the north-west coast in 1776–78. Such a river would make possible the exploitation of the new beaver country from the Pacific. This idea was to be the inspiration of Alexander Mackenzie's later journeys to the Arctic and the Pacific.

The pooling of interests in the north-west was accompanied by similar combinations at Montreal, and by 1778 men were commonly speaking of "the North West Company." In 1779 a sixteen-share concern was organized, and this was renewed in 1783. In that year the south-west and north-west trades were separated, but the North West Company did not succeed for many years in obtaining what it sought, a monopoly of the Canadian trade with the north-west.

In any event, it had to face the competition of the Hudson's Bay Company, which had seen with dismay its territory of Rupert's Land invaded by the new competitors from Canada and was striving ineffectually to resist. As in the days of the competition from French Canada, the Hudson's Bay Company relied heavily on its ability to tap the Athabaska country from Churchill to maintain dividends. But the Frobishers' advance to Frog Portage on the Churchill River in 1775 and Pond's invasion of the Athabaska itself in 1777 cut into that last preserve. And before counter-measures could be taken, the French, with the revived naval power they possessed in the War of Independence, struck at Prince of Wales's Fort. A squadron commanded by Jean François de Galaup, Comte de La Pérouse, captured and dismantled the fort, and also took York Factory and emptied its warehouses. This stunning blow to the British company of course helped its Canadian rivals at a critical moment in their developing competition. Once more the question was raised of whether the north-west was to remain a maritime hinterland of London or become part of the continental hinterland of Montreal.

Meantime, back at the seat of government in Quebec, the war government continued. Carleton had not yet revealed his instructions for the guidance of the Legislative Council; he continued to govern through his illegal "privy council"; he himself, at outs with the home government and perhaps disillusioned by the failure of the hopes he had placed in the Quebec Act, became increasingly sullen and arbitrary.

How much in the ascendant the Governor and the French party were was shown by the dismissal of Chief Justice Peter Livius in 1778. Sent out to succeed Chief Justice Hey in 1777, Livius had shown himself an able and independent judge, as he had already done in New Hampshire. As such he was increasingly worried by the illiberal and unsatisfactory character of the courts and the laws. When the Legislative Council met in April 1778, Livius moved that the Governor be requested to lay his instructions before it. Carleton took offence at this action of the Chief Justice's, and when Livius found in favour of Richard Dobie, one of the Montreal merchants opposed to Carleton's policies, the Governor dismissed the Chief Justice from the bench. And the scandal did not end with Carleton's arbitrary act. Not only was Livius not reinstated in Quebec; no successor was appointed for eight years. The case of Chief Justice Livius demonstrated that in the system of government which had developed under Carleton there was no place for impartial and independent administration of the laws, as there had been under the French régime, when the intendant might check the governor, or as there was under the British constitution.

Carleton's system, however, did not depend on Carleton. It was entrenched with the French party and sustained by the war. This fact was demonstrated when Carleton was recalled and replaced by Lieutenant-General Frederick Haldimand in June 1778. Haldimand, a Swiss soldier of fortune, was to prove himself a skilful and effective defender of Canada, and a wise and urbane administrator, remembered in Canadian tradition for his kindness to the loyalist refugees from the American war.

But Haldimand's appointment and tenure of office made little difference in the mode or spirit of the government of Canada. The laws were not liberalized and the French party under Mabane continued to dominate the council. Canada was still governed for the Canadians, and the only Canadians were French. The one major change was the result of the dismissal of Chief Justice Livius. The imperial government had learned from that episode of the existence of the "privy council" and Haldimand was ordered to discontinue it. Another was that in the absence of a chief justice, Mabane and other councillors who were not trained in the law acted as justices so far as they could, and the colony was thus deprived of the legal skill and intelligence which might have kept the processes of law more regular, if not more substantially just, than they could be kept by men not trained in the law. The incessant warfare between the governor and the French party on one side and the mercantile minority on the other continued down to Haldimand's retirement in 1784.

By that time peace had been concluded. The negotiations had followed on the surrender of Cornwallis at Yorktown in 1781 and Lord North's resignation in 1782. His successors, the Rockingham ministry, opened informal negotiations at once, and these were continued during the summer and ensuing winter. The British negotiators were in a weak position. Not only had English forces suffered repeated defeats by land and sea; Parliament had by resolution demanded that hostilities with America cease. The British cabinet in consequence had little room to manoeuvre or to break off unsatisfactory negotiations. They therefore sought to divide the Americans from their French and Spanish allies. This division, if accomplished, would not only afford Britain a chance for a more advantageous peace than its military position warranted; it would also give it a better chance to gain the great prize of the peace, the trade of the United States. Finally, the two Secretaries of State, Charles James Fox and the Earl of Shelburne, desired a peace of genuine reconciliation with the Americans, although they differed as to the mode in which it should be made. Thus the negotiations opened with the likelihood that Canadian interests, so stoutly and so fully maintained during the war, would be sacrificed to accomplish Anglo-American reconciliation.

How great a factor this was in the negotiations was revealed by the first informal proposal of Benjamin Franklin, the first and always the principal American representative. In order that the Americans and the British might be perfectly reconciled, Franklin smoothly suggested, Canada in its entirety should be ceded to the United States. King George III's insistence that Franklin must be trifling and the realization by the Cabinet that some British American territory must be held as a refuge for the persecuted loyalists, prevented this proposal receiving serious consideration. None the less, despite the refusal to cede all Canada, the British desire to be conciliatory was so evidently sincere that Franklin and his colleagues, John Jay and John Adams, in effect proceeded to make peace without their allies. The only question thenceforth was how great a sacrifice of British American interests would have to be made to bring the Americans to a separate peace.

As the negotiations went on, however, the British position strengthened, partly because of Admiral George Rodney's naval victory of the Saints in the West Indies in 1782, partly because of the successful defence of Gibraltar, and partly because the Portland ministry, successor to that of Rockingham, fell. The rivalry of Fox and Shelburne, which had weakened both ministries, was ended by the resignation of the former and by the latter's heading a cabinet of his own. Shelburne wanted a peace of reconciliation, but, as a disciple of Adam Smith, he wished to have the settlement include a commercial treaty of reciprocity.

The negotiations therefore resolved themselves into prolonged exchanges on the boundaries, the fisheries, the loyalists, and the pre-revolution debts owing to British merchants. On the question of the boundaries, Franklin and his colleagues had replied to the refusal of the proposal of total cession by suggesting, as their instructions ordered, a boundary from the 45th parallel of latitude to Lake Nipissing and thence westward. Such a line would have cut off the peninsula north of lakes Ontario and Erie and confined Canada pretty much to the Ottawa route to the west and to the Precambrian Shield. Finally, it was decided to begin the boundary at the mouth of the St. Croix, run it to the highlands between the Atlantic and the St. Lawrence, follow the highlands around to the 45th parallel, and then either follow that parallel westward to the Mississippi or take the centre line of the St. Lawrence and the Great Lakes. The former would have cut off the Ontario peninsula, as Franklin's line would have done, but it would have given British America the tip of the Michigan peninsula and upper Wisconsin. The British cabinet chose the line of the Lakes. From Lake Superior the line was to follow the fur traders' route to the north-west angle of the Lake of the Woods, and from there to run due west to the headwaters of the Mississippi, which the negotiators supposed to lie in that direction. In short, Canada between the Lakes and the Ohio, and the Ohio and the Mississippi, together with the lands of the Six Nations, was ceded without a shadow of military necessity, for the goodwill of the United States. The new boundary was one with no historic, political, or geographic meaning and is to be explained in terms of the desire to conciliate the United States and, by means of reciprocal trade, to recapture the trade of the former colonies. British America in British eyes was the fortress of Quebec and the naval base of Halifax, to which were subjoined the fur trade, which would cross any boundary, and enough fertile land to settle the loyalist exiles. No one in London dreamt of founding a second North American nation.

Nor did any one in British America. When the traders of Montreal, where the south-west trade was still much larger than the north-west, heard of the preliminary terms of peace, they were frantic with anger. They foresaw not only the ultimate loss of the region of the Lakes and its trade to a revived New York fur trade. They expected the immediate loss of their goods at the up-country posts in an outburst of Indian warfare touched off by the surrender of the Fort Stanwix boundary of 1768 and of the Indian territory without the tribes' assent. Their representatives in London hurried to press the government to reverse the surrender, but it was already too late. The pressure nevertheless began that policy of postponing the actual transfer of the posts in the ceded territory which became British policy for the next decade. The motives of the merchants themselves were purely commercial.

The fur traders' protest did, however, reveal the character and extent of the blunder which had been made in the drawing of the boundary. The loss of the Ohio Valley certainly freed Canada from an ambition, thrust on it by French imperial policy in 1749 and British in 1774, which was beyond its capacity to realize and inconsistent with the character of the northern economy. Twice a cause of war, it would have led to renewed war. But Great Britain had also ceded what was indubitably and vitally Canadian, the right bank of the St. Lawrence and the country of the Upper Lakes; and by abandoning its Indian a llies a France had done in 1763, but with much less cause, it had risked another Indian war more deadly and prolonged than Pontiac's. The result was actually to be years of friction with the United States.

The commercial convention, which was to complete and indeed to be the chief feature of the peace settlement of Paris, never took shape. An outburst of mercantilist feeling in England helped defeat Shelburne and the project of a reciprocal treaty of commerce. The citizens of the United States were allowed no commercial privilege in the Empire. On the contrary, it was planned that the fish, timber, and flour of British North America should replace those of the old colonies in the West Indian trade, as Colbert had once planned that those of New France should do.

The desire for conciliation also largely explains the extraordinary privileges granted American fishermen in British waters on the coasts of Newfoundland, Nova Scotia, and the Gulf of St. Lawrence. The New Englanders were acknowledged to have the "right" to fish on the Grand Banks and other banks of Newfoundland and even to take fish on the British shore of the island. They were also granted the "liberty" to dry and cure fish on the shores of Nova Scotia, the Magdalen Islands, and Labrador, as long as the shores remained uninhabited.

It may be noted at this point that, in the treaty of peace with France, the French rights and possession of St. Pierre and Miquelon remained unaffected, except that the French Shore was shifted to run from Cape St. John to Cape Ray.

The matter of pre-revolutionary commercial debts is only indirectly of interest to Canadian history, by its connection with the military posts on the western lands yielded to the United States by the treaty. The vexed question of compensation to the loyalists for the confiscation of their estates got no further than an undertaking that Congress would recommend to the several states that such reparation should be considered. Nothing came of this; it is to be presumed that on neither side did the negotiators fully realize that the clause was a mockery. When the Montreal merchants had made evident the danger involved in turning over the western posts, the failure to obtain recourse to the American courts or compensation for loyalist losses was made a pretext for the continued retention of the posts.

The loyalists of the American Revolution were those who had endeavoured to maintain the connection with the Crown of the United Kingdom, or to avoid the violence of the revolutionary party. They were for the most part conservatives; some of them were highly militant conservatives, some pacifist (Quakers and Mennonites). One extreme was High Tory in belief, and proclaimed the illegality and sinfulness of resistance to constituted authority; the other was quite non-political. The great intermediate majority were, however, like the revolutionaries, Whiggish by persuasion. The one thing all loyalists had in common was loyalty to the Crown and a desire by means of that allegiance to preserve the unity of the Empire both across the Atlantic and in America. From this arose their designation of United Empire Loyalists.

In the course of the war since 1776 the loyalists had suffered political persecution, mob violence and confiscation of estates except where the King's troops had defended them. As a result, thousands of loyalist men had enlisted in units such as Johnson's Royal New York Regiment, Butler's Rangers, De Lancey's Volunteers, the New Jersey Volunteers (or "Skinner's Greens"). But the British commanders never used the loyalists extensively, nor did the loyalists until late in the war rally to the King's colours as vigorously as they might have done. They had expected the King to win, whereas their opponents were rebels fighting with halters around their necks. Loyalist complacency was no match for patriot desperation. As a result of this as well as of British defeats and French inter_vention, the loyalists' cause, despite their numerical strength – and even predominance, in colonies such as New York and the Carolinas – became a losing one. To the end, however, the loyalists never quite comprehended why this should have been, or accepted the fact that it was so. To them their enemies were, and remained, a factious minority whose victory was inexplicable and could not, if there were justice in the universe, be expected to endure.

To many loyalists, therefore, the peace of 1783 was only a truce, which enforced another retreat but did not mark the death of their cause or preclude a renewal of the conflict. The great bulk of the loyalists, of course, had perforce to make their peace with the new régime in the United States. They remained to constitute a strong leaven of conservatism and British sentiment in the new republic. Of the estimated fifty to sixty thousand who were forced to leave for the British Isles, the West Indies, or British North America, the majority were mostly concerned with obtaining a place of refuge, or compensation from the United States for confiscated property, or an indemnity from the United Kingdom for the losses suffered in the cause of imperial unity.

Some, however – the political loyalists, they might be termed – had more public hopes and aims. Of these the chief were Jonathan Sewell of Massachusetts, an exile in London, and Chief Justice William Smith of New York. Smith left New York in 1783 with Sir Guy Carleton, who had been sent out as British commander-in-chief with the melancholy task of surrendering the last imperial territory in the United States, the great port of New York once coveted by Talon.

William Smith's ideals were perhaps more representative than Sewell's, and they were definitely more influential, but both men made the same basic analysis of the causes of the revolution and of what was needed to restore British strength and prestige in America. A Whig himself who had joined the loyalist side late in the day, Smith's thinking on the political problems of an America disrupted by the great civil war of independence took its rise from the Albany

Conference of 1754. That assembly, called to deal with the problems of the western frontier and Indian diplomacy, had recommended the adoption of a plan of union of the colonies under a president-general to be charged with Indian affairs and defence. The plan was approved by neither the imperial nor the colonial governments. But it remained in the mind of the New York lawyer as a project which might have prevented the disruption of the Empire. It now seemed to him one which, if applied in what was left of British North America, might preserve that remnant, rally to it the loyalists who had not yet left their homes, and even attract back to the Empire some at least of those colonies which had now embarked on the doubtful experiment of independence. Even if these hopes failed, Canada might yet be strong enough to check American intervention against England in a European war. Such were the ideas of Smith, Sewell, and other political loyalists. These ideas Smith urged on Carleton, and Carleton on the imperial government, and they were to have some influence on the future organization of British North America.

More immediate than plans of imperial reorganization, however, was the need to remove the loyalists to British North America and to establish them there. Those loyalists who sought refuge in the north moved by one of two routes: by sea to Nova Scotia, or by land to Canada. In the spring and fall of 1783 two fleets of the refugees sailed from the assembly point of New York for the St. John River and for Halifax. There they found the loyalists who had already removed to British territory; there they were later joined by stragglers. Some thirty thousand loyalists thus moved into the Atlantic province, more than doubling its population and contributing greatly to that weakening of New England ties and strengthening of British, which the war had begun in Nova Scotia.

The loyalists changed the social character as well as the political views of the province. The simple fisherfolk and farmers of Lunenburg and the Annapolis Valley were now overlaid by the loyalist gentry, office-holders, commissioned officers and formerly well-to-do people who had been driven out of estates and offices by the victors. The great majority came from the colonies south of New England, with the easy good manners and that almost Elizabethan sense of rank and personal esteem which the gentry and upper class of the middle and southern colonies had preserved. These were now imposed on the hard-bitten rural New England stock in the Annapolis Valley and the early colonists of Halifax and Lunenburg. Many members of the loyalist influx were Anglicans. The leaders were almost invariably both upper-class and Anglican, and thus the little Halifax oligarchy of office-holders and merchants was greatly reinforced in its differences with the farmers and "New Light" Congregationalists and Methodists of the outports, the Annapolis Valley and the Fundy shore.

The loyalists were distributed around the coasts of Nova Scotia at the mouth of the St. John River, at Fort Cumberland, Minas Basin, and Annapolis, and from Halifax eastward around to Canso. Some went to Cape Breton and to the

Island of St. John. The largest group, almost ten thousand in number, were encamped at Port Roseway, which was renamed Shelburne in honour of the architect of the peace. In a number of these places the loyalists joined previous settlers, but in many they were the pioneers. Some of the settlements, notably those along the St. John River, were made up of disbanded loyalist regiments, who settled, as it were, in their ranks and formed a military frontier against the United States.

The hardships of the first months and years were to become part of the loyalist tradition, and they were trying and severe. But perhaps more remarkable was the efficiency with which the British army commissariat furnished provisions, tools, and seed, and prevented in the loyalist settlements the losses and disasters of so many colonial enterprises. The fact that the loyalists were, if not frontiersmen, at least Americans familiar with the climate and soil of the eastern coast of the continent and inured, many of them – and those the leaders and the hardier men – to the life of the camp by years of warfare, powerfully contributed to the absence of extreme privation and loss.

Harder to bear, perhaps, was the slowness with which the loyalists' claims for compensation were heard, sifted, and reduced. Yet again the wonder is rather the speed and fairness that were achieved, and the satisfaction with which the ultimate payment was accepted. What might have left a lingering soreness caused by merit slighted or claims repulsed was so handled as to bind the loyalists closer than ever to the Empire for which they had sacrificed so much.

In the administration of the aid and settlement, however, some difficulties were encountered on the north shore of the Bay of Fundy. There, some 12,000 loyalists had swamped the 2,500 old settlers and perhaps 1,500 Acadians. The new settlers of that region early professed to be discontented with government from distant Halifax by the genial and feckless Irishman, Governor John Parr, and wished for a governor of their own, one prompter in response and perhaps more amenable to the wishes of the Winslows, Chipmans and other leading loyalists. Their desire fitted in with advice Carleton had transmitted to London at the urging of Smith. This was to divide Nova Scotia indeed, but to centralize the administration of the provinces by making the governor of Nova Scotia a senior governor with authority over his colleagues of New Brunswick, Cape Breton, and the Island of St. John. The advice was in part accepted and applied. The lands north of Fundy were separated from Nova Scotia in 1784, to become the Province of New Brunswick. It was, despite Smith's plan, given an independent governor in Colonel Thomas Carleton, Carleton's brother. The new governor was instructed to carry on his administration with the aid of a council and an elected assembly. Thus New Brunswick received a constitution on the Nova Scotian or Virginian model, and was made wholly independent of Nova Scotia. But Cape Breton was made a province with a lieutenant-governor subordinate to the governor of Nova Scotia, and the Island of St. John was similarly united with the oldest of the Atlantic provinces. Despite the separation of New Brunswick from Nova Scotia, William Knox's idea that the future security of the Empire required the application of the old maxim "Divide and rule" seems to have had little influence on the reorganization of the remaining British Atlantic colonies.

Newfoundland received few if any loyalists, but it was to feel the stir of administrative reform that the loss of the old colonies provoked. This, with growing lawlessness during the winters when the naval governor was absent, led to the creation in 1791 of a permanent court of justice under Chief Justice John Reeves. Thereafter law and order were represented the year round in St. John's at least; and in effect, though not yet in form, Newfoundland was acknowledged to be a colony.

In Canada, still known as Quebec, the coming of the loyalists produced more drastic changes. By the Quebec Act, Quebec had been acknowledged to be a French province. Those who had governed Quebec since 1775 had insisted that that was the sole intent of the Act, and had striven to keep the colony Canadian. Although the result was continued strife with the English minority of merchants and traders, they had succeeded.

So firmly was this policy established that even the humane and far-seeing Governor Haldimand had at first endeavoured, while providing for the loyalists who came into Canada during the war, to ensure that the post-war influx should be diverted to the Atlantic provinces and to Chaleur Bay and Gaspé. But the New York loyalists could not be sent down the river. They had seen or heard of the good lands above Montreal; they were, almost entirely, frontier farmers who wanted good farmlands, not the fisheries of the Gulf. Some who came by sea shared their wishes. Thus while some five hundred loyalists were settled in Gaspé, another five hundred had to be brought up to William Henry (now Sorel), and the civilian loyalists out of New York, about six thousand in all, were allowed to go direct to lands along the St. Lawrence and Niagara rivers.

The military units in particular were settled along the St. Lawrence, officers and men in formation, unit by unit, from the seigniory of Longueuil to the Thousand Islands, and then again around Cataraqui, soon to be renamed Kingston, as far as the Bay of Quinté on Lake Ontario. Among them were Catholic Highlanders from northern New York and the battalion of the Royal Highland Emigrants, who named their settlement after their old home, Glengarry of the Macdonells. They were to be joined in 1786 by other Glengarry Highlanders, Macdonells direct from Scotland. On the Niagara River, Butler's Rangers formed a similar military crust along the border. The civilian loyalists extended the river- and lake-front settlements, even on Lake Erie and the Detroit River, or in some places took up land in a second range of lots.

The results of this loyalist settlement in western Quebec were twofold. Quebec was no longer a French province with a merely mercantile non-French minority. That minority was now reinforced by people with a special claim on government; and these people were farmers, who would not quit the province as lightly as a merchant might. In the second place, the Canadians who had resisted American pressure for a century were now reinforced by loyalists with vivid memories of civil war. If Canada was henceforth to be Anglo-French, it was also to be doubly anti-American.

Yet the sharpness and immediacy of these effects of the coming of the loyalists can be exaggerated. With the exception of the military units, the loyalists who had come into Canada were not wholly political loyalists. They were frontier farming folk, many of German, many of Highland stock, some of Quaker, some of Mennonite beliefs. They had come because they preferred monarchy to republicanism, or because they sought a refuge from the violence of the late years of war. A clear title to their lands and a quiet life was the main ambition of many; most of them probably would have no interest in the legal difficulties of Quebec and Montreal merchants; some of them would not even be particularly anti-American.

Yet however unpolitical the interests of some loyalists might be, however busy they were with the heavy and urgent work of establishing themselves on their lands, their coming could not but affect the course of politics in Quebec. For one thing, the lands on which they were settled were regarded as seigniorial lands and their tenure as a seigniorial tenure. Accustomed as the loyalists were to English freehold tenure, the new tenure made them uneasy and early led to demands for a change in the land law. Although the Quebec Act allowed lands to be granted in freehold tenure, the demands for freehold tenure implied a desire for a change in the whole civil law. The loyalists were therefore bound to be regarded by the English mercantile party in the province as allies in their demands for *habeas corpus* and trial by jury in civil cases, as well as in the demand for an elected assembly.

The imperial government was thus confronted with a dilemma. If it allowed the Quebec Act and its system of government to continue unmodified, it would please the Canadians but would at the same time increase the already swelling discontent of the English and the merchants. If it replaced the system of government by the normal colonial system of a governor and elected assembly, it would alarm and anger the French party and the great majority of the Canadians. With this dilemma the Secretary of State, Thomas Townshend, Lord Sydney was to struggle languidly for the next four years.

At Quebec itself the French party of Carleton and Haldimand had continued in the ascendant until the end of the war. Then there was an explosion of anger against the unconstitutional control of the government which this party had exercised with the sympathy and support of Haldimand. Though called the French party, its leaders were still English and its chief still the Scot become

KC-G

Canadian, Adam Mabane. The French members were not significant personalities and produced no leader. On the other hand, the English party, when it
petitioned in 1784 and repeatedly thereafter for an elective assembly, had not
wholly lacked support from those Canadians who continued to hold the liberal
democratic and Voltairian ideas they had learned from the American invaders
and from France.

Quebec was thus not without elements which desired a change; and change
was soon to begin. The anger aroused by the French party's rigid resistance to
changes in the law favourable to the English merchants exploded in the case of
Haldimand v. *Cochrane*, in which the Governor sued a financial agent of the
government, John Cochrane. The Governor's cause prevailed in the Executive
Council, presided over by Mabane. The decision naturally angered the English
party deeply, and in the session of the Legislative Council in 1784 they drove
hard for an ordinance introducing *habeas corpus*. To this Haldimand was prepared to yield, but the French party in the main still resisted, determined to maintain the Quebec Act without addition as the constitution of Canada. The ordinance was none the less passed, and its passing marked the beginning of the end
of the régime of reaction.

In the same year Haldimand left for England on leave of absence. The French
party had lost its best champion at a time when its object of keeping Canada
French was most in jeopardy.

In the absence of the Governor, the Lieutenant-Governor administered the
colony. This was that Henry Hamilton who had been captured by George
Rogers Clark in 1779. After being exchanged, he was appointed to succeed
Cramahé in 1782. Hamilton had resigned his commission on becoming
lieutenant-governor of Detroit in 1775, and he thus brought to his office what
it had never had since the cession, a civilian mind. To him it was manifest that
the demands of the merchants for jury trial in civil cases and other amendments
of the civil code should be met. And his own year of office did see jury trial in
civil cases introduced by a narrow vote in a deeply divided council. But Hamilton's sympathy with those who wished to alter the war-time régime, and the
alarm felt by Haldimand in London at an agitation for an Assembly by the
mercantile party, led to Hamilton's recall in 1785.

He was succeeded by Brigadier-General Henry Hope, who promptly restored
the spirit of the old order, although of course the use of *habeas corpus* and jury
trial continued. The imperial government, however, now realized that some
change must be made, and Sydney and Pitt turned to Carleton as the chief
authority on British America, with his faithful adviser, William Smith. In 1786
Carleton was created Baron Dorchester and was sent out as Governor-in-Chief of
British North America, with Smith as Chief Justice of Quebec. If Pitt had refused to establish a British American viceroyalty with Dorchester as first viceroy,
something of Smith's program was realized in the governorship-in-chief of

all British North America, although the lieutenant-governors continued under the direct control of the imperial government. Above all, Dorchester and Smith were to recommend what changes were necessary for the future government of Quebec.

The second governorship of Guy Carleton was to prove a personal and imperial failure. The reason is to be found partly in his own heavy temperament and narrow outlook. It is to be found also in the fact that he had placed himself in the hands of Smith. But Smith and his ideas encountered an impasse in Quebec from which Carleton was to escape only through the intervention of the imperial government. Smith's hope was that the appointment of a British viceroy in America might lead to a remodelling of the Quebec Act by the use of the royal prerogative. By prerogative Smith proposed to create in Canada a form of government modelled on that of the United Kingdom. Such a government, he still hoped, would draw to British territory many loyalists still resident in the United States. Indeed, he hoped that a British America so endowed might draw back part, if not all, of the still fluid and uncemented union of states to the British Crown.

That hope in 1787 was by no means as visionary as the Philadelphia Convention and the new constitution of the United States, begun in that year, were to make it. It was, however, the remainder of Smith's policy that involved Dorchester with him in the contradiction from which they were to prove powerless to escape. Smith believed that a major cause of the American Revolution had been an excess of the democratic element in the constitutions of the colonies. Arguing as an eighteenth-century Whig from the Aristotelian premise that the best constitution was a blend of monarchical, aristocratic, and democratic elements in equal parts, Smith held that in the constitutions of the remaining colonies the monarchical and aristocratic elements should be built up to balance the democratic, which tended to be all too lively and prevalent in American conditions. By every means the royal prerogative in government and the royal supremacy in religion must be maintained. In this, Smith had the full concurrence of the British statesmen concerned with the colonies. Thus he hoped to attract the remaining loyalists and even perhaps reconstitute the Empire in America by offering British representative government, not in its debased colonial form but in its full perfection.

This particular dream, however, was a repudiation of all that the Quebec Act, the French party, and Carleton had stood for from 1774 to 1786. Representative government, British law, the English language, a further influx of loyalists, a reuniting of what the war had separated – what did this mean but the policy of 1763 elaborated and brought nearer to fulfilment? Smith thus became the enemy of the French party; and Dorchester, aging, ill and helpless, could produce no scheme of government to fit the new circumstances. Neither could he solve increasing difficulties in the law, in trade, and in revenue. The last was becoming increasingly inadequate for the needs of government as Canada ceased to be a great military base fed by a flow of British expenditures. The one thing which he could clearly see was necessary, and which he actually recommended, was the introduction of freehold land tenure.

The consequent drift of Dorchester and Smith was not halted until in 1789 the lethargic Sydney was replaced by William Grenville. Grenville, confident and decisive, with the assurance of the aristocrat, took up the tangled problem of the future government of Quebec and in October, 1789, made the first draft of a clear-cut, conclusive policy. His basic idea was one of Smith's, that the institutions of Quebec should be made, as the institutions of the Atlantic provinces had been made, as much like those of Great Britain as possible. But Grenville took a bold step beyond what Smith had urged. British institutions, Grenville was confident, would not only satisfy the old subjects and the loyalists; they would, he claimed, win the allegiance of the Canadians also. In short, he proposed to assimilate the Canadians to British constitutional government, and so in time end the political differences which had troubled the Province of Quebec since 1764.

Grenville naturally thought of the British constitution as Smith did, and proposed to correct the weakness of colonial government, as it was to a degree being corrected in the Atlantic provinces, by strengthening the governor's prerogatives and also by giving the legislative council definition and making it distinct from the executive council. He even proposed to strengthen the aristocratic element by creating a colonial nobility. But above all he insisted that the colony must be given a legislative assembly, the prime factor in British institutions. Nothing could more forcibly illustrate Grenville's assurance that the possession of British institutions would assimilate the Canadians to British ways and British loyalty.

If there was to be representative government, however, there would have to be, it was assumed, two provinces, French civil law prevailing in one and British common law in the other. One legislature could not legislate for two bodies of civil law. Quebec had therefore to be divided.

Allied in purpose and sentiment with the concept of strengthening the aristocratic element, and also of the assimilative effect of British institutions, was the design to provide for a Protestant clergy. Just as democratic excess had led to revolution in the old colonies, so, it was held, had the failure to establish the Anglican episcopate. Already in 1787 the first step to remedy this defect of the old colonial policy had been taken when Rev. Charles Inglis was made first Anglican Bishop of Nova Scotia. Pitt himself was especially concerned with the provision for a Protestant clergy and this part of Grenville's design had his firmest support.

The proposals were sent to Dorchester for his observations and amendments, and he and Smith criticized them with some severity. Dorchester pointed out that a Canadian nobility was certain to provoke ridicule in the primitive and equal conditions of frontier life. Smith, a stout Presbyterian, was opposed to the establishment of the Anglican Church, but was unable to obtain any change in that part of the scheme. The imperial cabinet then accepted Grenville's clear and comprehensive plan for the future government of Canada in 1790, and in 1791 the British parliament passed the Constitutional Act. The Act embodied the whole scheme of government, except that the boundaries of the new provinces could not be given statutory definition because of the uncertainties caused by the retention of the western posts. A clear structure of government, modelled exactly, as its draftsmen believed, on the British constitution in church and state, was provided in governor, executive council, legislative council, and representative assembly to correspond with King, Privy Council, Lords, and Commons. Each part, executive and legislative, was largely independent of the other, but legislation and taxation required their concurrent action. Membership in the legislative council might be made hereditary, if it should seem fitting to create an aristocracy. The Act further ordered the reservation, for the support of "a Protestant clergy," of what was to amount to about one eighth of all Crown lands alienated, and authorized the founding of rectories for the clergy of the Church of England.

Yet perhaps the most noteworthy feature of the Act was that, while it replaced the Quebec Act as the Canadian constitution, it also embodied its provisions with respect to the Roman Catholic Church and persons, the civil law, and the use of the French language in the courts. The French of Canada were neither left the dominant race, as from 1774 to 1791, nor swamped, as the Proclamation of 1763 had intended and as Smith's proposals had implied. They were embodied in a new Canada, in part French Canadian, in part British American, a Canada endowed with "the British Constitution in Church and State." It was also a Canada which had won free from American control, but at the cost of the Ohio country and of a division of its remaining lands into Lower and Upper Canada. Canada once more, as in 1763, was forced back on the St. Lawrence and the Shield. The traders' routes to the south-west and the far north-west, however, were still open, and the maritime approaches of the Gulf were wholly British American. The only portents of danger were the retention of the western posts and the fact that the debates on the Constitutional Act were famous solely for the quarrel of Charles James Fox and Edmund Burke over the significance of the revolution which was overthrowing the ancient institutions of France.

ADDITIONAL READING

BREBNER, J. B. *The Neutral Yankees of Nova Scotia.*

BURT, A. L. *The Old Province of Quebec.*

HARLOW, V. T. "The New Imperial System," *Cambridge History of the British Empire*, Vol. II.

NEATBY, HILDA *Quebec : The Revolutionary Age.*

SWIGGETT, H. *War Out of Niagara.*

CHAPTER 11

The Survival of British North America
1792-1817

The British North American provinces were a remnant of both the French and British empires. In 1783 the colonies had just escaped being engulfed by the United States as, twenty years earlier, they had been submerged in the Anglo-American empire. Their survival, even as a remnant, had in it something of accident and even of the miraculous; it was by no means assured by the Treaty of Paris, the terms of which were disputed for a decade after its ratification. And despite the remarkable recovery of British power which followed that treaty, the wars of the French Revolution and French Empire were to imperil the security of the colonies and raise anew the question of the absorption of the British American remnants into the United States. Once more, external events and the interests of foreign countries were to threaten to engulf the northern colonies and determine their future in terms extraneous to the interests and needs of those weak and dependent communities.

Of these external events the first and chief was the French Revolution. For Canada it had, of course, a special significance. Not only did it convulse Europe with the hope of nations made free and societies made democratic; it held out two prospects to the Canadians. One was a self-governing and free French society on the St. Lawrence. The other was a revival of the glory that was France before the cession, a France that could restore the ties which the cession had ended. The danger feared by Carleton in 1767, and partly realized in 1778 – the power of a France once more militant and restored in North America – returned with the Revolution in a more vivid and dangerous form. It returned as the menace of a living sentiment and also of an idea armed.

The Canadians, stirred as they had been by the ideas and example of the American Revolution, and informed as many were by the ideas of Voltaire and the Encyclopaedists, were now excited by the French Revolution. The clergy, of course, viewed the increasingly secular course of the Revolution with mounting alarm. All their great and pervasive influence was used to dampen and suppress the tremor of national and democratic sentiment which ran through the cities and parishes. The surviving *noblesse* and seigneurs also viewed the fall of their French equivalents with alarm and dismay. They, however, could do nothing to still the revolutionary quiver in Canada. Such influence as they had had since 1775 was rapidly passing from them to a rising class of lawyer-politicians. It was this educated *élite* that was excited by the principles of 1789. There can be little doubt that at any time from 1792 to 1812, French troops with the tricolour or the eagles would have been tumultuously greeted by a not inconsiderable part of the Canadian people.

If British rule in Canada was thus threatened by the French Revolution, the preservation of British North America from absorption into the United States was similarly menaced by the course of the wars to which that revolution gave rise. The peace settlement of 1783 had not been completed by the negotiation of a commercial treaty of reciprocity between the Empire and the United States. On the contrary, a revolt of mercantilist interests in the United Kingdom had led to the enforcement of all the laws of trade and navigation against the United States. In particular, they were shut out of the trade with the British West Indies in order that British North America might supplant the United States as supplier of the plantations with fish, flour and lumber. Year after year, however, Nova Scotia and Canada failed to meet the needs of the islands, and the ports were opened provisionally to American shipping. But the uncertainty of this emergency trade was of course an irritation to the New England fishermen and shippers. The Newfoundland and Nova Scotian fisheries benefited, as did Nova Scotian and New Brunswick shipbuilding and lumbering. The benefits rested, however, on imperial policies which might be modified by American pressure, not on natural advantages or competitive ability.

The same fragile and provisional character was apparent in British-American relations on the new frontier with the United States west of Montreal. The blunder of the treaty line and the betrayal of the Indians had been cloaked by the retention of the western posts from Oswegatchie on the St. Lawrence to Michili-mackinac. The retention had as its purpose the readjustment of the Canadian fur trade to the new political situation and the persuading of the Indians to make terms with the United States. Using the pretext of the unsatisfied loyalist claims to compensation, the British government had held the posts and had half convinced the western tribes that they had not been abandoned.

The Indians for their part had responded by organizing a confederacy to resist an American invasion of the Ohio. Their principal leader was Joseph Brant, who had visited England in 1785–86 and had satisfied himself that the British would not fight again to defend the Indians' lands on the Ohio. From then until 1791 the Indians raided the American settlements south of the Ohio and endeavoured to hold their lands north of that river. In 1791 they heavily defeated an American force under General Arthur St. Clair which had advanced north from the Ohio. So triumphant were the victors that they began to hope to hold the line of the Ohio, and their British friends dreamed for a while of an Indian neutral territory which would be a barrier between American settlement and Canada. Meanwhile the Montreal traders were free to cross the boundary under the treaty, and the retention of the posts meant that they continued to enjoy all the support which the posts gave the fur trade. Moreover, there were as yet no American traders who could match those of Montreal in skill, capital, or organization.

More noteworthy than the continuation of the south-west trade was the development of that of the north-west. There the pursuit of the ever-retreating beaver frontier, and the pressure of growing overhead costs as trade routes and the trade cycle lengthened, drove the Montreal traders to explore ever new territories. Peter Pond's idea of an outlet to the Pacific had been taken up by a young Scot, Alexander Mackenzie, who had wintered with Pond on Lake Athabaska in 1787. In 1789 Mackenzie had descended the river thenceforth named after him. His hope was to emerge on the Pacific. Disappointed, he returned to his base. Not until 1793 was he free to ascend the Peace River, cross the Rockies and descend the upper Fraser. Stopped on that stream by hostile Indians, he struck westward over the mountains and reached the Pacific "by land." He had again failed to find a river that would link the interior with the Pacific. And not for another fifteen years was the Fraser to be followed to the sea.

It was the Fraser's great sister, the Columbia, that was to be the outlet for the furs of the western interior. The American captain, Robert Gray, had entered the narrow mouth of the Columbia in 1792. British explorers and traders had failed to detect it, although their work was to be the basis of the British claim to the north-west coast. Neither the British nor the Americans who sailed the coast to chart it or to trade for sea otters attempted to penetrate inland by the Fraser or the Columbia. Not even Captain George Vancouver, who from 1792 to 1794 charted the coast northward from the Strait of Juan de Fuca, contributed anything to the linking of the interior with tidewater. It was left to the American expedition of Lewis and Clark to explore the lower Columbia from overland in 1805, revealing part at least of the route between the inland and the sea and thus strengthening the American claim to the coast.

Alexander Mackenzie had made his voyages in the service of the North West Company. That concern had not yet achieved a monopoly of the north-west trade, as Mackenzie was soon to demonstrate by founding his own firm. The competition among the Montreal traders was keen and often violent, and led to the passing of the Judicature Act of 1803 by which the imperial parliament gave the courts of Canada jurisdiction over "the Indian territory." The rivalry between the Nor'Westers and the Hudson's Bay Company was less strenuous, if only because the English company was more peaceful in disposition and more stable in organization. But it was plodding tortoise-like after the North West hare, and in 1793 its traders came in by the Albany and Winnipeg rivers to the

KC-G*

Assiniboine, to make contact on that river, as they had already done on the Saskatchewan, with the buffalo plains and the supply of pemmican which nourished the canoe brigades of the Montreal traders.

The same year, 1793, saw the great war between England and revolutionary France begin. The war at once created two issues between Great Britain and the United States which were to last throughout the course of the struggle. The issues were the rights of neutral traders and the rights claimed by the United Kingdom to search neutral ships for deserters from the Royal Navy. The United States, despite the treaty of 1778 with France, at once adopted a policy of neutrality. Its merchant ships traded with both belligerents, but the British government, seeking to weaken France by naval blockade, steadily tightened the blockade by restricting the rights of neutrals. Normally, American shippers suffered no loss, for the British paid for condemned cargoes, but the British blockade increasingly infringed upon the rights of neutrals. Thus no one suffered, except American seamen wrongly seized as deserters from the Royal Navy; the dispute remained one between governments and did not become a matter of great popular feeling, especially as the dominant American party, the Federalist, was strongly anti-French and pro-British.

With all this, British North America had little to do except in so far as Nova Scotian shippers shared the prosperity of the American, and Nova Scotian privateers captured French prizes. No French attack was attempted until 1797, when a French squadron appeared off the coasts of Newfoundland and Nova Scotia, without, however, doing any damage. The effects of the war, oddly enough, were first felt on the Canadian boundary.

War in Europe meant that Britain could not lightly risk serious conflict with the United States. The hope of any rectification of the frontier and the continued retention of the western posts had therefore to be given up. When John Jay was sent by the American government late in 1793 to negotiate a settlement of the outstanding difficulties between the two countries over commerce, boundaries, and neutral rights, he found the British Foreign Secretary, William Grenville, with an open mind and eager to reach a settlement. The result was the treaty of 1794, commonly called Jay's Treaty. By it Britain undertook to give up the western posts unconditionally. The surrender was carried out in June 1796; the Union Jack came down and the redcoats marched out from the last posts on the territory ceded to the United States in 1783. Much the same pressure from Europe which had forced the surrender of 1783 now completed the work.

The other provisions of the treaty were of comparatively minor importance. It was agreed to appoint an international joint commission to determine the whereabouts of the north-eastern frontier, which had been in dispute since 1783. The Americans were given limited access to the British West Indies, but as the Senate rejected this section of the treaty, no change was effected. The significance of the treaty was that it helped settle the question of the Canadian border and the Indian frontier, and that it ensured, despite its failure to deal with neutral rights or the impressment of American seamen, that peace continued between Great Britain and the United States.

The settlement of the Indian frontier was carried one stage further by the victory of an American expedition under General Anthony Wayne over the western tribes at Fallen Timbers in 1794. The battle was fought within earshot of British-held Fort Miami on the Maumee River. But a clash between the British and American forces was avoided, and in 1795 the Indians yielded by the Treaty of Greenville the lands north of the Ohio from which in 1803 the State of Ohio was to be formed. The tribes, like Canada, had had to withdraw before the weight of the American frontier, swarming, restless, and ruthless.

It was in such circumstances that the Canadian provinces of British North America embarked on their separate courses under their new constitutions. In this their fortune differed from that of the less exposed Atlantic provinces; Nova Scotia, New Brunswick, and the Island of St. John continued under their old colonial constitutions, with the authority of governor and council strengthened beyond what their counterparts in the old colonies had been. From 1792 to 1808 Nova Scotia was governed by John (later Sir John) Wentworth, a New Hampshire loyalist who brought to his office rigid Tory principles and with his wife made the governor's mansion a heady court, excited by the presence of the royal princes, Edward, Duke of Kent, and William, Duke of Clarence, an ever-changing flow of military and naval visitors, and a steady stream of local people who were doing well out of the war. It was the golden age of the Haligonian oligarchy. In these years the gulf between the merchants and lawyers of the capital and the sober farmer folk of the inland counties widened in sporadic struggles over the apportionment of the revenue between expenditures in Halifax and those on roads and bridges in the outlying counties. Except for such friction, and a continued official suspicion of American democratic influence, there was little agitation in the province and no constitutional issue arose, although between 1797 and 1807 Cottnam Tonge, a naval official in the province, did challenge Wentworth and the oligarchy and stir the elements of a popular party until the Governor refused to accept him as Speaker in 1807 and procured his dismissal from the post of Naval Officer.

On the St. John, the loyalist settlements drowsed under the rule of Thomas Carleton and the loyalist cabal which had procured the separate government and made Carleton its puppet. Only the sharp-tongued critic, James Glenie, as a member of the Assembly from 1789 until his departure from the province in 1805, revealed how completely the oligarchy had gathered the power and influence of government into its own hands and used it to endow its members with Crown lands. His supporters seem to have been to a large degree the pre-loyalist settlers who naturally wished to have government function in New Brunswick as it had done in their New England homes. Glenie's career, like that of Tonge, served to reveal the need for, and the elements of, a reform movement to correct the complacent abuses which accompanied permanent tenure of public office.

The Island of St. John (which became Prince Edward Island in 1799) and Cape Breton were quietly adding to their farming population, under minute colonial administrations little developed politically. With Nova Scotia and New Brunswick, the islands experienced the beginning of Scots and Irish immigration. The growth of sheep-farming in the Highlands of Scotland and the pressure of the Catholic peasant population on the land in Ireland was driving Highlanders and Irish across the seas. Poor, accustomed only to the life of the clan or family, usually Roman Catholic by faith, and often, as in Cape Breton, Gaelic or even Erse in speech, these new-comers confined themselves to building their new homes and took no part in politics.

No major political changes occurred in the Atlantic colonies during the years of war, nor in Newfoundland, not yet accounted a colony. But in Upper and Lower Canada the form of government was new in 1792; in the latter province, indeed, much was experimental.

What Pitt and Grenville had done was to grant to the Canadians government on the British colonial model with, as they thought, significant improvements. The result, because of the fact that there were 145,000 French in Lower Canada in 1792 and only 10,000 English, was that Canadians elected a majority of the Legislative Assembly. There were thirty-four Canadians to sixteen English. Had a majority of Canadians been appointed to the legislative and executive councils, the government of the province would have been fully in their hands, subject only to the veto of the governor or of the imperial government. Lower Canada would have possessed, subject to the supremacy of the Parliament of the United Kingdom, a wide measure of legislative independence under the Crown.

That it would have been wise to appoint a majority of Canadians seems apparent now. To grant self-government is to make a gesture of trust. Trust wholly given begets trust; half given, it engenders suspicion. Such magnanimity was not possible in 1791. A slight majority of the legislative and executive councillors (nine out of sixteen and five out of nine respectively) were English, a proportion generous in the circumstances. As the English majority of one consisted of Adam Mabane of the old "French party," the intention was to have a balance of French and English. But the results of not having a French majority – for Mabane died before the councils met – were to be regrettable. A chill fell steadily through the years on the warm generosity of 1791, and the hearty din of cheers and toasts with which it was welcomed by Canadians and English alike died away.

Nothing could have been more unfortunate, for Canadian society was rapidly fitting itself for self-government. In spite of forms of paternalism, it had, through the captains of militia, largely governed itself before the cession. Since the cession it had been increasingly supplying its own *élite* in the priesthood and in the professions of law, medicine, and surveying. The *avocat* especially had risen beside the *curé*; soon the journalist was to join him. And beside them all the local leaders continued to represent the sentiment of their parishes, either as Justices of the Peace or as militia officers, no longer, it is true, as representatives of the all-supervising intendant, but still as local leaders commissioned from Quebec. In these men was material for members of parliament and even ministers of the Crown.

An intellectual preparation for self-government had been at work since 1775. The democratic ideas then absorbed had been cultivated by the educated since. Canadians were not only ready to accept and work self-government; a considerable number were all but ready to demand it. This readiness was now increased by the Constitutional Act and inflamed by the French Revolution with a gust of racial pride. The French, ardent Canadians hoped, might yet give the English some lessons in political liberty

When therefore the first Assembly of Lower Canada was summoned by Lieutenant-Governor Sir Alured Clarke in Dorchester's absence, not only did the voters elect a majority of Canadian members; the representatives showed their temper by electing a Canadian, Jean Antoine Panet, as Speaker, by making French as well as English a language of debate and record, and, more significantly, by caucusing together outside the chamber.

This dispatch in assuming legislative power is perhaps open to misinterpretation. It signified no more than that the Canadians proposed to be masters in their own house; the French majority of 1792 was not anti-English or anti-British, despite the fact that the new councils contained English majorities.

An anti-English and anti-British sentiment was present in the province, however, from 1792 on. The ground had been prepared for it by news of the Revolution, with its promise of a renewal of French strength and glory. Then in 1793 and 1794 French emissaries from the United States began to work on opinion in the province. They were powerfully aided by a pamphlet written by the Canadian Henri Mezière, who went to the United States with a view to reaching France to serve the cause of revolution. Mezière was at once employed by Citoyen Genêt, the envoy of revolutionary France to the United States. In his pamphlet *Les Français libres à leurs frères les Canadiens*, Mezière assured his countrymen that the French, having freed themselves, would free Canada also.

A wave of excitement ran through the parishes. The bishop and clergy, already estranged from the Revolution by the Civil Constitution of the Clergy, used all their authority to damp it down. The government redoubled its war-time alertness. When riots broke out in 1794 against the new militia act passed by the Assembly, an Alien and Sedition Act was passed and arrests were made. When in 1796 there were riots against an act imposing a corvée, some of the agents sent into Quebec by Genêt were arrested and tried. One, David McLane, was condemned as a traitor and hanged, drawn, and quartered at Quebec. The excitement was stilled, but thrilled again through the province when in 1797 the French squadron was on the Atlantic coast. Thereafter the response to French agitation died away. The Canadians were all French in sentiment; a considerable number were revolutionary in sympathy; as a group, but with varying degrees of intensity, they wanted Canada to be free of alien rule. The circulars of Bishop Jean François Hubert, firmly urging loyalty to the British Crown, could cloak but not extinguish this fact of Canadian nationalism which had so far found a vent only in the revolutionary contagion from France.

The unrest excited by the Revolution and the outbursts of 1794 and 1796 instilled a distrust of Canadians in the British officials in Lower Canada. That the agitation and plots after 1796 were often the work of American land speculators with their eye on Canadian land was not realized then, as it has been little recognized since. The local authorities, the governor and his officials, military and civil, were much more suspicious than were the imperial authorities. As a result, instead of Canadians and English in Lower Canada drawing together in self-government, they began to draw apart. In the second Assembly, elected in 1797, the French majority was increased and was even more self-consciously French. The English merchants and the seigneurs elected in 1792 were for the most part not re-elected. General Robert Prescott, who had succeeded Dorchester as governor-in-chief in 1796, warned the Colonial Office that because the Assembly was dominated by the Canadians it was necessary to maintain an English majority in the councils. That majority began to entrench itself in the councils and became the "Château clique" of notoriety.

Especially did they use their position in the Executive Council to make large grants of the unalienated Crown lands of the province to themselves and their friends. These were certain lands, outside the seigniorial limits, that were surveyed about 1791; they lay east of Montreal and the Richelieu, and were for that reason called the Eastern Townships. Some loyalists had settled in them after 1783. After 1791, New Englanders and New Yorkers began to squat on them. But none of the Townships was granted to, or reserved for, Canadians. The lands were deliberately used to enrich the English official and commercial minority and to build up the English population against the Canadian. The English abandoned any trust they may have had in Grenville's hope of "assimilation" by the grant of British institutions. Assimilation they desired more than ever, but they hoped for the personal and cultural assimilation that formal education might produce.

An attempt at such assimilation was made in 1801. In 1793 an Anglican bishopric of Quebec had been created, and the first Lord Bishop, Most Rev. Jacob Mountain, was keenly interested in the provision of education for the young. Then in 1800 the last member of the Society of Jesus in Canada died and the great estates of the order were available for the support of schools. In 1801, with the full support of Lieutenant-Governor Robert Shore Milnes and Bishop Mountain, the Royal Institute for the Advancement of Learning was created. Nominally an attempt to aid education with the resources of the Jesuit estates, it was actually a full-blown scheme of Anglicization, which, however, remained a dead letter in the face of steadfast French opposition.

The English official class had thus revealed the depth of their distrust of French culture and of the Roman Catholic Church. But they did no more for the time being. The other face of the Revolution, its terror, its intolerance, its proscription of the church, had already made itself felt in Quebec. Forty-five *emigré* priests who came to Lower Canada strengthened the church's resistance to Canadian sympathy with revolutionary France and increased its appreciation of British opposition to the Revolution. And, fortunately for the relations of Canadians and English in Lower Canada, the Treaty of Amiens in 1801 allowed the tension of the war years to relax briefly.

Very different had been the history of the sister province of Upper Canada. Upper Canada was a British, not a French, province. It was preoccupied with the Indian and American frontier, not with the Revolution. Whereas the great problem in Lower Canada was to give the Canadians self-government without independence, in Upper Canada it was to found the institutions of government and to create the physical apparatus of civilized society. Lower Canada had been established for well over a century; Upper Canada was in the earliest stages of settlement.

More than that, Upper Canada was a colony in many ways unique. It was the first inland British colony. And its farthest settlements were hundreds of miles from Quebec, the deepest point inland within the grasp of British sea power. The colony thrust like a sword deep into the centre of the continent. Like a sword, it barred the advance of the American frontier, forcing it down on the Ohio lands of the Shawnees and the Miamis, tribes yet unconquered in 1792. Settlement consisted of a line of loyalist regiments and refugees on the St. Lawrence and the Niagara, and the French villages at the old fur posts. It was not even part of the American frontier, the outer edge of occupied territory. It was a typically Canadian settlement, strung out far into the wilderness along the rivers which were the trade routes and war-paths of the fur trade. And its value in 1792 was still that the Canadian peninsula between the Lakes was a piece of fertile ground on which to raise corn and pork for the fur trade.

Had Dorchester had his way and Sir John Johnson been appointed as Upper Canada's first lieutenant-governor, Sir John, raised in the fur trade and Indian diplomacy, would have seen Upper Canada in those terms. But Grenville chose to appoint Colonel John Graves Simcoe, a retired British officer who had commanded the loyalist regiment known as the Queen's Rangers in the Revolutionary War. Simcoe was an energetic man, full of bounce and enthusiasm. But he had a limited sense of reality, and one marvels that the colony came to so little harm at his hands. What he did possess was an extraordinary faith in the virtue of British institutions and more than his share of William Smith's vision of a British North America drawing loyalists out of the United States by the attractive power of those institutions. His task, as he saw it, was to create a British province in the heart of America which would manifest the superiority of British law, British justice, and British government and become a rallying-ground for those on the other side of the border who were still loyal to the Crown.

Behind this grandiose enthusiasm was much practical experience and considerable shrewdness. Simcoe saw clearly enough that both the development and the defence of Upper Canada turned upon communications. On the Lakes this was furnished by the ships of the Provincial Marine of the old province of Quebec. These were lake schooners which freighted private goods. But the Lakes might be dominated by American warships, and roads were therefore necessary. To cut them, Simcoe proposed the formation of a military pioneer corps which could work on roads and public improvements in peace time and defend the province in war. Such a body was organized and given the name of the Queen's Rangers, after Simcoe's old unit. The Rangers began the road system Simcoe planned: the portage road, or Dundas Street, from Burlington at the head of Lake Ontario to the head of navigation on the Thames; Yonge Street from Toronto to Lake Simcoe, also a portage road; and then Dundas Street prolonged from Burlington to Toronto, and the Danforth Road to Kingston. This was perhaps Simcoe's master idea. It exhibited, on the map at least, a Roman simplicity and grandeur, and the roads in fact gave Upper Canada a coherence it had not possessed before.

Yet it is for the ideals he expressed to the first legislature that Simcoe is best remembered. When that body met in 1792 at Newark near the mouth of the Niagara, as the most accessible central point for the scattered settlements of the province, Simcoe emphasized the opportunity the veteran loyalists and hard-bitten pioneers had to make their new institutions, as he put it in dismissing them at the close of the session, "the very image and transcript of the British constitution." It was an ideal which for a generation was to struggle with another and not consciously antagonistic tradition, that of the old American colonial governments. For the legislators Simcoe faced were, whether loyalist or not, Americans. And when they established the common law and freehold tenure, and provided for the eventual extinction of slavery in Upper Canada, they acted in ways not to be distinguished as British or as American. They were Americans living and acting under British institutions not yet fully differentiated from American except in the central fact of allegiance to the Crown.

Another part of Simcoe's dream was his hope that the Church of England might be established in Upper Canada. A petition of 1787 had indeed asked that the Church of England and the Church of Scotland should be established, but the facts were overwhelmingly against an establishment, particularly a merely

Anglican establishment. The great majority of the people were Presbyterian, Methodist, Baptist, Quaker, or Mennonite. The prevailing ideal was that of the voluntary church in a democratic society. But Simcoe's hope was to linger. In 1799 a Presbyterian schoolmaster, John Strachan, came to Canada and, after taking Anglican orders in 1803, began to teach many of the boys who, as it proved, were to govern Upper Canada in later years and to sympathize, some of them, with Strachan's ideal of an establishment even in a society with many voluntary churches.

How ardent was the Governor's dream of a new Britain in the heart of America was revealed by his plans for the capital of the colony. The river La Tranche he renamed the Thames and planned a new London on its mid course, surrounded by settlements and counties named after the suburbs and home counties of London. In the same spirit he changed the name of Toronto to York, that it might be the second city of the province. But York was made the temporary capital in 1794, and the choice proved permanent. A change had come over the Governor's dream; it had altered, as reflections waver on moving water, in the swiftly-running stream of history. Not London by the Thames leading to the old south-west, but Toronto, with its portage road to Huron and the far north-west, was on the main route to the future of British America.

Much indeed had changed when Simcoe retired in 1796. His eager hopes of rallying loyalists from the United States had borne fruit; thousands had come in response to his advertisements in the States. They proclaimed themselves loyalists and took the oath of allegiance. But it was cheap, good land they sought, rather than British institutions, and the result of the influx of late loyalists was to make Upper Canada an American community, not only American as the loyalists were, but also in the sense of being indifferent to the British allegiance, or even of being republican in sympathy. And the Indians, despite Simcoe's strong but ill-judged support, had fallen back before the Americans, and Jay's Treaty had led to the surrender of the posts. The boundary of 1783 was at last drawn along the Lakes, and Upper Canada was merely a British wedge deep in American territory, and no longer a magnet to draw back to the Crown the loose sections of a disrupted republic.

With Simcoe's retirement, the administration of the province was entrusted to Hon. Peter Russell as president and administrator, until General Peter Hunter became lieutenant-governor in 1799. At the same time Upper Canada, like Lower Canada with the Château clique and Nova Scotia with the Halifax ring, came under the control of an official group and its connections. This group continued the favour shown to the loyalists, and the loyalists gave it the sanction of their support. But, as in Lower Canada, the real cement was the influence the group possessed upon the granting of public lands. Leading loyalists, office-holders, members of the governor's official family, all became possessed of tracts of wild lands more or less large and so developed the interests and attitudes of speculators. Thus was formed that group of well-established people, some holders of public office, some the leading business or professional men of their communities, who governed Upper Canada with a jealous eye to their own position and who were finally to be named the Family Compact.

In becoming land speculators, of course, they took a hand in the greatest game then proceeding in the Canadian provinces, the first appropriation of the lands which lay open to settlement because the Indian tribes of what had become Upper Canada had been driven out by the Iroquois in the great wars of the seventeenth century and only a few Ojibwas, known as Missisaugas, had replaced them. In taking up these lands the actual settler played a secondary role. It was the first appropriator who was the active man in discerning the course of settlement, obtaining title, and holding the land until his price was reached. There was as little system in Upper Canada as in the Eastern Townships of the lower province. Both British officials and American land speculators in the last years of one century and the early years of the next were actively at work possessing themselves of as much as possible of the best tracts; on the American side of the line, speculators were even plotting the conquest of Canada to forward their designs. The migration of the late loyalists was of course part of this great speculation, to which Simcoe in his innocence and Russell and Hunter in their greater experience lent their countenance. In this strong American interest in the fertile land of western Upper Canada lay a growing threat to the British possession of the inland colony.

In 1803 that threat was made more dangerous by the renewal of the war in Europe. Britain, which had sought to confine the energies of revolutionary France, now sought to block the imperial ambitions of Napoleon. The first repercussion in America of the new struggle was Napoleon's abrupt and sweeping sale of Louisiana to the United States. The results for British North America were to quicken the westward movement of the American frontier which was seeping through Upper Canada, and to make necessary a re-drawing of the frontier of 1783 west of the Lake of the Woods. A broader effect was to free the United States from the European balance of power, and to leave British North America exposed to the pressure of a United States unchecked except by British sea power.

At that time, however, British sea power seemed the most likely cause of war between Great Britain and the United States, and so of an American attack on Canada, because of the renewal of the searching of American ships by British warships and the removal of alleged deserters by the boarding parties. The shippers and merchants could endure this violation of American rights; the government of the United States could not, bound as it was to defend its citizens. The British continued the practice, despite American protests, until the appalling and indefensible attack in 1807 by H.M.S. *Leopard* on U.S.S. *Chesapeake* off the Virginia capes. War seemed the only possible outcome, but an instant

British admission of wrongdoing and the pacific character of President Thomas Jefferson's administration averted a conflict. An irritation similar to that caused by the right of search was that which arose from the blockade and counter-blockade of the belligerents, the Berlin and Milan decrees of Napoleon in 1806 and 1807, and the answering Orders in Council of Great Britain.

In all this, British North America had little direct concern. British sea power was supreme after Trafalgar and there was no more talk of French descents on the Atlantic coast. Nova Scotian privateers were cruising once more in the West Indies and snapping up prizes. Halifax was alive with shipping and seamen, and Halifax society was once more in the feverish whirl of a war-time garrison and naval town. Canadian wheat in years of surplus flowed out to the West Indies and even to the British Isles.

The war, however, had had some unsettling effects in Lower Canada, where the renewed evidence of French vigour and glory once more touched the national pride of the Canadians. Resentful of the distrust of the English official group and merchants and of the threat of Anglicization in the founding of the Royal Institution, the Canadians could not but feel pride in the new French empire in Europe and struggled vigorously to assert French interests in Lower Canada. Even the Roman Catholic Church, always on the side of the British allegiance but always careful not to acknowledge the royal supremacy in religion, was involved in the racial friction, for in 1805 Bishop Mountain formally questioned the apparent position of the Roman Catholic Church as the established church of the province. A prolonged controversy followed, which died away without resolution, as the imperial government declined to commit itself on this vexed question.

The Canadian politicians, as well as the Canadian church, had a battle to fight. This was a secular conflict fought out in the Assembly over taxation. Funds were needed for gaols, court-houses and other public necessities. The Canadians wished to raise them by customs duties, the English merchants by land taxes. It was the usual struggle of interests, but unfortunately, as a result of the elimination of a Canadian commercial class by the cession, the lines of interest followed national lines.

The controversy became open and bitter when two English papers, the Quebec *Mercury* and the Montreal *Gazette*, attacked the French party for its stand on taxation. As a result, three Canadian lawyers, Pierre Bédard, Jean Thomas Taschereau and Joseph Louis Borgia, founded the French newspaper, *Le Canadien*. It was to be an organ of constitutional discussion and of national and democratic sentiment. It took its stand on British constitutional principles and pressed its attack from that irreproachable if irritating ground. It was this group which first introduced into Canadian political discussion in 1808 the principle that the advisers of the governor might be held responsible by the Assembly for the acts they advised. The object of the attack was the entrenched

English oligarchy, with its official favouritism and its land grants, with its fears of French Jacobinism and its desire to Anglicize the Canadians. The group behind *Le Canadien* was nationalist and democratic in sentiment. But it was most careful to be constitutional in doctrine and pro-British in tone. It perhaps did not represent the great body of the Canadians in any direct way. Neither, however, did the Canadian anti-democrats or High Tories who survived among the seigneurs and *noblesse*.

The English party in 1807 found an active champion in the new governor, Sir James Craig, a kindly man but a military disciplinarian of crisp temper and decisive action. He quickly became alarmed by the spirit shown by the Assembly, which he thought revealed seditious and Jacobinical tendencies. The majority may have been moved by religious prejudice when they challenged the Jewish merchant, Ezekiel Hart, member for Trois Rivières, on the ground that he could not genuinely take the oath, but they were within the law as it then stood. And when they challenged the right of judges to sit in the Assembly on the principle that for them to do so was to imperil the dignity and impartiality of the Bench, they were once more on a sound constitutional footing. The English oligarchy, however, saw the attack on Hart and on Judge P. A. de Bonne as an attempt to undermine their class and their position as a governing *élite*. The election of 1808 was fought violently on the issue, and Craig intervened by cancelling the militia commissions of the proprietors of *Le Canadien*. When the new Assembly none the less proceeded to expel Hart and Judge Bonne, Craig prorogued it in 1809, and when it persisted in the expulsion in 1810, he abruptly dissolved the Assembly. He followed this up by seizing the press of *Le Canadien*, gaoling its printer, putting military patrols in Quebec, and suspending the mails. He arrested Bédard, Taschereau and François-Xavier Blanchet and imprisoned them without trial.

When in the elections of 1810 the electors returned much the same representation, including Bédard and Blanchet, Craig concluded that representative government, at least as granted by the Constitutional Act, could not be allowed to continue in Lower Canada, or that the provinces must be reunited. With the support of the English oligarchy he sent his secretary, H. W. Ryland, to England to urge that the Constitutional Act be revoked. The imperial government with great common sense declined to do so, as it declined to place the Roman Catholic Bishop of Quebec below the Anglican. Instead, it recalled Craig in 1811 and replaced him by Sir George Prevost, a conciliatory French Swiss who might be expected to soothe Canadian feelings – a matter of first importance as relations with the United States grew tense once more. Prevost changed the membership of the Executive Council, appointed Canadians to the Bench, notably Pierre Bédard, and for the time being stilled the strife in Lower Canadian politics. His success proved that the Canadians were neither intractable nor disloyal, but strongly resentful at being excluded from the government of their own country under a colonial version of the British constitution.

This change in political feeling was, as it happened, accompanied by a considerable economic change in Lower Canada between 1807 and 1812. The old economy of course continued. The wheatfields of the seigniorial lands widened. In the Eastern Townships the Yankee farmers from New Hampshire and Vermont continued to settle on freehold lands. From the Townships came first potash, the product of the burning of the forest, and then wheat.

At the same time the Montreal fur trade, booming from 1796 to 1808 as it never had since the days of Frontenac, was going on from strength to strength, not only against the Hudson's Bay Company in the north-west, but also against the American traders who had entered the south-west since the surrender of the posts in 1796. Not even the formation of John Jacob Astor's American Fur Company in 1808 had checked the success of the Montreal traders. From the north-west itself the flow of furs continued undiminished. The Nor'Westers held the Athabaska country, from which they drove the first Hudson's Bay Company men who attempted entry in 1804. From 1805 they were seeking an outlet to the Pacific. In 1808, Simon Fraser descended the river to which his name was given, only to prove that its canyon made it useless as a canoe route. In the same year David Thompson, the great geographer-trader, began to feel his way through the passes of the Rockies north of the headwaters of the North Saskatchewan. Fear of inter-tribal war held him back until 1811, and when at last he made his way to the mouth of the Columbia he found that Astor's American Fur Company had anticipated him by sea.

To these flourishing older trades there was now added the timber trade. After the closing of the Baltic in 1807, the forests of Canada as well as of the Atlantic provinces were called on to meet the urgent demand of the British shipyards and timber merchants. As a result the timber trade of the ports of Quebec and St. John began. The pines of the St. Lawrence and the Ottawa were cut in winter, prepared as masts and spars or squared with the broadaxe, bound in rafts, and floated down to the ports. There the great timbers were loaded on the "timber ships," old ships at the end of their days, and freighted to the British Isles. English capital joined with Canadian skill to create this new great staple trade. British North America had found a staple which for half a century would not lead it, as the fur trade had done, away from the St. Lawrence into the up country and the north-west.

The new timber trade affected Upper Canada directly in that it began the occupation of the Ottawa Valley and gave a new staple, with potash and wheat, to the settlers on the St. Lawrence and Lake Ontario. Otherwise, the province continued after 1803 to pursue the course set for it in the 1790's. It continued to drowse under the British institutions the Constitutional Act and Simcoe had given it. The colonial bureaucracy of Simcoe and Hunter became more firmly rooted under Lieutenant-Governor Francis Gore. The colonial democracy gave them little trouble even if from time to time "American" ideas and sentiments were voiced in the Assembly. Some sharp criticism there was of the officials and their ways, but it came mostly from immigrant Irishmen – William Weekes, William Willcocks, Joseph Willcocks, Robert Thorpe. Usually the stimulus of these critics seemed to be grievance that their own merits were not adequately realized. They were new-comers trying to enter the citadel of privilege, or to rise within it, rather than democrats trying to take it by storm. Only Joseph Willcocks gave promise of becoming a useful and responsible politician in opposition to the bureaucracy. But this group, with another Irish immigrant, W. W. Baldwin, and an Englishman, John Mills Jackson, may have begun the transfer to Canada of the idea of responsible government, the idea that the advisers of the governor should answer to the people of the colony for the conduct of local affairs.

All the time, Upper Canada continued to attract ever more immigrants from the United States. The process of land settlement, especially from the Niagara River westward, was making the loyalist province steadily more American. At Quebec, where the responsibility for defence lay, and at York, the seat of government, anxiety steadily increased as to whether the province could be held when the overwhelming majority of its people were Americans fresh from the United States. And it seemed that little could be done to check or offset the American immigration. The American frontier was the only source of people with pioneer skills. If the lands of Upper Canada were to develop quickly, then Americans were the people, and practically the only people, to do it. The British government had full use, in the titanic struggle with the Napoleonic empire, for all the labour it could muster, as the new factories throve and field was added to field in the drive to grow enough food to replace supplies from the Continent. A Scottish nobleman, Lord Selkirk, was indeed moved by the distress of the displaced and remote Highland crofters and the Ulster sub-tenants to seek relief for them in emigration to British North America. In 1803 he had moved a colony of Highlanders to his lands in Prince Edward Island, and in 1804 began a colony at Baldoon near Lake St. Clair in the Upper Canadian peninsula. But Baldoon was unfavourably located and drew few British immigrants. The other great colonizer of the peninsula, Colonel Thomas Talbot, did try to encourage British immigration, but with limited success before 1812.

The truth was that the peninsula was being absorbed into the American frontier as the Eastern Townships were, and if the slowly soaking tide was to be held back, it must be by war. Once more, as in the days of the French fur trade, war was to be the deliverer of Canada from penetration from the south. But could Canada be defended when so many of the potential enemy were already within the gates?

The prospects, it is true, were not as gloomy as they appeared. The American immigrants seem to have been largely non-political. They were not in the main convinced republicans, although accustomed to self-government. They might be won by British institutions, as Simcoe had hoped. They might remain neutral in a war with the United States. A considerable number of them, being Quakers and Mennonites, were pacifists, and had been granted exemption from military service by provincial law. This neutrality would mean in practice that the bulk of the new settlers would accept the verdict of battle.

Moreover, Upper Canada was still within the Indian frontier of North America. Not only did the Canadian traders still largely control the country of the Upper Lakes; the Canadian government still continued to make annual gifts to the tribes, most of whom lived on American land. Thus the Indians continued to regard the British as tacit allies and supporters. Even more important was the beginning in 1805 of a new Indian confederacy by the Shawnee chief, Tecumseh, and his brother the Prophet. Tecumseh sought to organize the tribes from Canada to the mouth of the Mississippi in a barrier against the American frontier. His brother preached a new religion by which the Indian convert renounced the white man's ways and goods. Tecumseh's success alarmed the American government, and in 1811 General William Henry Harrison marched through the Indian territory to the Shawnee village of Tippecanoe. There he fought a drawn battle and burned the village. In so doing the Americans drove the Indians back upon the support, tacit but real, of the Canadian fur trade and the British territory which at need could be their shelter.

The Indian wars in the west, both Tecumseh's on the Miami and the Red Sticks war in the south-west of the United States, were to blend in 1812 into the war with Great Britain on the maritime issues which had vexed the relations of the two countries since 1793 and particularly since 1807. Those issues were of first importance, but they were the concern of the government more than of the people of the United States. No government could, while retaining its self-respect, fail to protest with the utmost vigour against the infringements of American rights under international law practised by the two belligerents and especially by Great Britain. But the issues were neither popular with the American public nor possible of resolution by any pressure the government of the United States could exert. American traders and shippers were thriving, despite the Orders in Council and right of search. The western "war hawks" of the Congress elected in 1810 attempted to tie the maritime issues to the alleged British support of the western Indians, but there was no great body of opinion behind a war to be fought over the maritime issues.

It is apparent, indeed, from an examination of American voting in 1810, that support for war varied inversely with the sectional interest in maritime matters. Thus the west and south, which had no shipping and were not likely to be engaged in the war, supported the idea of war, while New England and New York, the great commercial and shipping sections, were solidly opposed. The result was that when President Madison declared war in June 1812, it was promptly dubbed "Mr. Madison's War," and the north-eastern states in effect became and remained obstinately neutral, despite the commitment of the nation to uphold their maritime interests by war.

While the United States, with its population of more than seven million in 1810, was a considerable land power, it was not a sea power at all. Its four heavy frigates, greatly as they were to distinguish themselves in single-ship actions, could not hope to weaken British naval strength. If Great Britain was to be fought, it must be by an attack on British North America. But all British North America from Nova Scotia to Lake Champlain was buffered by New England's dogged neutrality. Accordingly, only Canada could be attacked, and the war declared on maritime issues became, as it were by default, a western war fought for the conquest of Upper Canada. The American war leaders had first to "popularize" the war in an indifferent and divided country by winning easy western victories. That of the estimated 75,000 people of Upper Canada possibly over two-thirds were comparatively recent American immigrants was a political fact on which they hoped to base military success. At the same time, and inevitably, since Canada and the Indian tribes were allied by their common commitment to the fur trade, it was also a western war fought to complete the breaking of the power of the western Indians begun at Fallen Timbers and Tippecanoe.

To Americans at large, then, the War of 1812 was an unpopular war which deeply divided the nation, and was in fact to be fought only by American regulars and the sometimes reluctant militia of New York, Ohio, and Kentucky. To the soldiers and rulers of the Canadas it was a very different matter. It was a war which had long been anticipated and so far as possible prepared for. If well fought, it might be used to undo the blunder of 1783, correct the boundary, and protect the Indians. The Montreal supply houses and the up-country fur traders saw an opportunity to gain political security for the south-west trade by bringing the Michigan and Wisconsin country back under British sovereignty. To the loyalists, it was a war to be fought against old enemies now attacking the homes they had made in the Canadian wilderness. These elements, the oligarchs and the military, the fur traders and the loyalists, would fight daringly and even desperately to repel American aggression. To them American talk of "liberation" was a brazen affront.

The American presentation of the war as one to liberate Canadians groaning under the British yoke was not, however, mere persistence in declaring the messianic character of American republicanism. It was propaganda that was no ineffectual. What its effect in Lower Canada might have been, had the words been followed by battalions, can only be conjectured. But it would have won some recruits. In Upper Canada the American propaganda was of course directed to the thousands of American settlers. There it was to be successful in a measure,

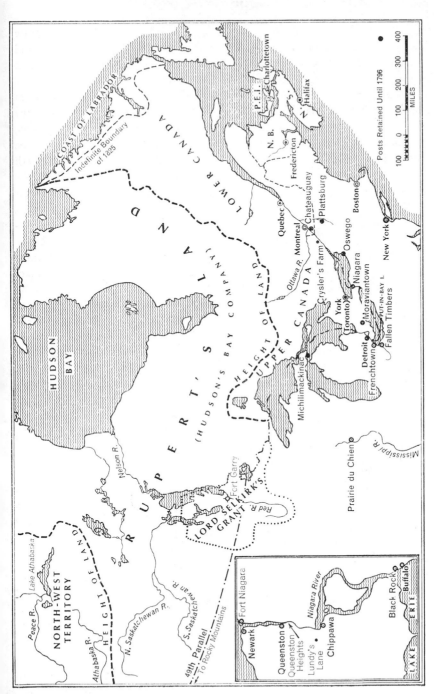

IX *British North America after 1783*

Posts Retained Until 1796

MILES
100 0 100 200 300 400

HUDSON BAY

RUPERT'S LAND
(HUDSON'S BAY COMPANY)

NORTH-WEST TERRITORY

LOWER CANADA

UPPER CANADA

COAST OF LABRADOR

Indefinite Boundary of 1825

HEIGHT OF LAND

Peace R.
Lake Athabaska
Athabaska R.
HEIGHT OF LAND
N. Saskatchewan R.
S. Saskatchewan R.
49th Parallel
To Rocky Mountains
Nelson R.
Red R.
Fort Garry
LORD SELKIRK'S GRANT
Prairie du Chien
Mississippi R.

Michilimackinac
Detroit
Frenchtown
Fallen Timbers
Moraviantown
York (Toronto)
Niagara
PUT-IN-BAY I.
Oswego
Crysler's Farm
Ottawa R.
Montreal
Chateauguay
Plattsburg
Quebec
Boston
New York

N. B.
Fredericton
P.E.I.
Charlottetown
N. S.
Halifax

Fort Niagara
Newark
Queenston
Queenston Heights
Lundy's Lane
Chippawa
Niagara River
Black Rock
Buffalo
LAKE ERIE
MILES

partly by inducing most of the population to be neutral, partly by winning considerable numbers to join the American forces. It was not ludicrous at all for the Americans to profess that they came, not to conquer, but to liberate, as General William Hull did in a famous proclamation made at Detroit.

In these circumstances, Canada could be held only by a judicious mixture of discipline and dash, discipline to out-fight the American militia and dash to win the Indians by early and showy victories. Once more, as in the days of Frontenac and Vaudreuil, Canada had to fight as a light-weight in training against a heavyweight not yet hardened. The six British battalions in the country would supply the discipline. To these were added the Canadian regulars, of whom the Glengarry Light Infantry, a militia battalion of veteran Highlanders, and the Voltigeurs of Lower Canada under a Canadian officer of the British, Army, Colonel Charles de Salaberry, were the chief in 1812.

The indispensable initial dash was to be given by Major-General Isaac Brock who had been in Canada since 1802, had acted as commander-in-chief during the crisis of 1807, and knew the country. An energetic and able officer, of great professional keenness and a singularly candid and attractive personality, Brock gave life to the dreary task of defending Canada, as he was to inspirit the regulars and the militia in the field. In 1811 he became administrator of Upper Canada and commander of the forces in that province. It was Brock who made it possible to use the militia to aid the regulars. He had had no illusions as to what use could be made of the sedentary militia of Lower Canada. In general, they could not be trusted to fight, or even not to join the enemy. How then to separate the loyal elements from the indifferent majority and the disloyal minority? Brock did what Canadian governments have done ever since. He did not use the general levy the militia laws permitted, but called for volunteers. In Lower Canada he suggested, and Craig applied, the principle of "embodying" volunteers from the militia. In this way it was possible in 1812 to raise two thousand militia in the Lower Province. In Upper Canada the volunteers were embodied, under an Act procured by Brock in 1811, as the famous "flank companies" which fought in line with the British regulars and from which the battalion of Incorporated Militia was drawn. Thus the loyal were prepared for the defence of Canada and the great body of the indifferent were left at home.

The war itself followed a clear-cut and simple course. At sea the Americans won some brilliant single-ship actions, but they neither broke the British convoy system nor prevented a British blockade of the coast. The seaboard was slowly closed, except in so far as the British deliberately made exceptions in favour of New England shipping. There was no immediate threat to Lower Canada. In Upper Canada, Brock, faced with great odds, redeemed the situation by great daring. Michilimackinac was captured in mid July by a sudden blow delivered by a few regulars and some five hundred Canadians and Indians. As a result the western tribes were won to the British cause. Then Brock struck at Detroit in early August and the American commander, Hull, fearful of the Indians on his line of communication, surrendered the fort and the Michigan country.

These dazzling strokes regained the south-west and laid the ground for redrawing the frontier; by 1814 all the Wisconsin country as far as Prairie du Chien on the Mississippi was held by British forces, and the boundary of 1783 corrected. In 1812, however, the Niagara border was under pressure and Brock hurried back to hold the river against the New York militia. His death in action at Queenston Heights took the bloom off that victory. But he had saved Upper Canada and was remembered by his men as an English officer who fought in what English as well as French Canadians were coming to regard as the Canadian tradition of surprise and the deft blow, which had saved Canada before.

Thereafter, numbers told. The American command feared to fight the war in the obvious way, by a main stroke at Montreal which would force a withdrawal from Upper Canada, because they still had not sufficient troops for an advance against the strong British force, or enough public support for a major campaign. What was apparent was that victory depended upon naval control of lakes Erie and Ontario, and both sides began to build ships with furious haste. Thus 1813 was marked by an American naval descent on York, where the public buildings were burned, and an invasion of the Niagara peninsula, which forced General John Vincent to fall back to Burlington, the key to the western peninsula and central Upper Canada. Next came Commodore Oliver Perry's naval victory over Captain Robert Barclay at Put-in Bay, which gave the Americans control of Lake Erie and forced Colonel Henry Procter, despite his victory at Frenchtown, to abandon Detroit and fall back up the Thames with Tecumseh. They stood at Moraviantown, but General William Henry Harrison's Kentucky cavalry swept away Procter's weary regulars and Tecumseh died fighting at the head of his Indians. The western front was torn open and the Americans had regained Michigan and held the Canadian peninsula to trade for Wisconsin.

But the Americans failed to capture Burlington by an advance from Niagara after the capture and burning of Newark and the raiding and burning of York. Harrison withdrew to Detroit, and Colonel John Harvey's victory at Stoney Creek drove back the Niagara army. By the end of the year the Niagara frontier was cleared and the American side of the river swept clean of American forces, with Black Rock and Buffalo burned in retaliation for the American destruction of Newark. The war was becoming a war of border vendettas and the burning of "Tory villages" by Americans inflamed by old memories of the War of Independence. For the next year American bushwhackers, such as Andrew Westbrook, raided loyalists' homes in the western peninsula. A war to incorporate Upper Canada or at least the western peninsula into the United States had become a civil war, with the bitterness such a conflict engenders. In a raid on Chatham, Upper Canadian militia early in 1814 captured a number of settlers serving with the American forces; nineteen of these were tried for treason at the

Ancaster assizes, and eight were executed. The issues were becoming more stern than whether Upper Canadian or New York land speculators would dispose of the lands of Upper Canada. The treason of Joseph Willcocks, "Colonel" of a "Canadian" battalion in the 1813 campaign, and late a member of the Assembly of Upper Canada and a critic of the government, indicates the changing nature of the war.

During the war years the Upper Canadian assembly met annually, but the legislators were concerned mainly with the war. In Lower Canada, politics continued as usual. While Prevost had stilled the conflict between Governor and Assembly and refrained from dissolving to challenge the popular party at the polls, the struggle between the Assembly and the oligarchy continued. The executive councillors continued to encourage English settlement in the Eastern Townships; the Assembly continued its opposition to separate representation for the Townships. Finally in 1814, the Assembly, led by James Stuart, who had been dismissed from the attorney-generalship in 1809, impeached Chief Justice Jonathan Sewell – who, like his predecessor William Smith, hoped for the reunion of the Anglo-American people – for, among other things, plotting in 1809 to unite Lower Canada and New England. The accusation was not wholly extravagant, and was of course supported by the Canadian members, who saw this as yet another attempt of the English oligarchy to overwhelm them with Yankee settlers. And in 1814 New England was talking secession. New England provisions fed the British troops and Upper Canadian civilians threatened by famine because of the disruption of agriculture.

On balance, the war was not going badly for Canada east of York. The loss of the western peninsula was offset not only by the holding of the Niagara line, but also by the maintenance of a naval stalemate on Lake Ontario and by the ease with which de Salaberry on the Chateauguay and Colonel J. W. Morrison at Crysler's Farm defeated the attempted invasion of Lower Canada. When Napoleon's defeat early in 1814 released British troops and ships for the war in America, a stalemate had already been reached. The Americans had failed to cut the St. Lawrence route at Montreal. They had failed to master Lake Ontario and were not to do so in 1814.

Yet when the British went on the offensive to recapture territory lost in 1783, they too were unable to command success. They failed to recapture control of Lake Erie, or to retake Detroit. The hard fighting at Chippawa and Lundy's Lane, besides showing that the Americans had acquired a discipline to match that of the British regulars, revealed that stalemate had been reached on the Niagara frontier. Prevost's failure at Plattsburg on Lake Champlain, the first major British offensive, confirmed the stalemate. The one big change effected was the British occupation of Maine early in 1814.

The peace negotiations were already in train at Ghent. The course of the negotiations was relatively simple. Neutral rights and impressment were the major issues, but these were soon dropped from discussion and were not dealt with in the treaty. They were war-time issues which could be forgotten in peace. The British negotiators strove hard, however, to undo the blunder of 1783, and in particular not to abandon the Indians lest they should prolong the war. To these ends they first proposed that the boundary be re-drawn on the basis of what each side held, with an Indian buffer state to be created and guaranteed by both powers. The Americans refused to give up their sovereignty over the territory, and in the end the treaty merely guaranteed the Indians their previous "possessions, rights and privileges." The principle of *uti possidetis* had to be abandoned also, because the American negotiators refused to surrender the country of the Upper Lakes for a mere part of the western peninsula of Upper Canada, or to give up Maine. Neither would they yield to a British demand for naval disarmament on the lakes. Other matters, such as the American privileges in the fisheries, abrogated by the war, and the north-eastern and north-western boundaries, were referred to commissions for settlement.

The Americans had won none of the objects for which they went to war, but they did win the peace negotiations in that they gave up little and regained both Maine and the country of the Upper Lakes. Those interests of British North America were once more sacrificed on the altar of Anglo-American understanding and the boundary of 1783 stood unamended. The Indians were in fact once more and finally abandoned to their fate. The country of the Lakes was lost conclusively and for ever. Canada had been driven back upon the Shield, the fur trade, and its primitive northern economy. Its trade with the old south-west, three times claimed and lost, must henceforth be carried on across an international border finally drawn and firmly fixed.

As though to underline this fact, the peace of 1814 was followed by an outbreak of violence in the north-west. There, on the Red River, Lord Selkirk had planted a colony of Highland and Irish settlers. He did so on the grant of land made him by the Hudson's Bay Company and named Assiniboia. The colony had built up painfully, but peacefully, from 1812 to 1814. Then a quarrel broke out with the Nor'Westers over the export of pemmican, needed by the canoe brigades, from the territory of Assiniboia. The Nor'Westers decided that the colony menaced their trade, aroused the métis against it, persuaded some colonists to move to Upper Canada and drove the rest from Red River. The colony was restored in 1815 but was broken up again after bloodshed in the encounter of the colonial governor, Robert Semple, with the Nor'West leader, Cuthbert Grant, and his métis at Seven Oaks in 1816. Lord Selkirk then set out for the north-west with a force of disbanded soldiers, seized Fort William on the way, and in Red River restored his colony. But the violence had led the British government to appoint a commission of inquiry in 1817 under Colonel W. B. Coltman. The strife was then transferred to the courts of Canada. It had arisen, however, not only from Selkirk's premature scheme of colonization but also from the determination of the Montreal traders to hold the north-west, the more so as they had finally lost the south-west. The result was to bring the deadly struggle of the fur companies to a climax in their union, and to separate the north-west from Canada for half a century. Canada had thus survived the upheavals of the revolutionary and Napoleonic era, but had lost its old connections with the west, and became, or seemed to become, only a settlement on the banks of the St. Lawrence.

ADDITIONAL READING

BREBNER, J. B. *North Atlantic Triangle.*
BURT, A. L. *The United States, Great Britain and British North America*
CLARK, S. D. *Movements of Political Protest in Canada, 1640-1840.*
SMITH, LAWRENCE A. "Le Canadien and the British Constitution," *Canadian Historical Review*, June, 1957.
STANLEY, G. F. G. *Canada's Soldiers* (1605-1960).
WADE, MASON *The French Canadians, 1760-1945.*

THE WINNING OF
COLONIAL SELF-GOVERNMENT
[1818-1846]

After 1815 the British North American colonies, freed from the menace of the great wars, turned to their own concerns. Their social and economic character began to change rapidly as they grew in population, trade, and industry. In particular, the Canadian fur trade withdrew to the far north-west, and lumbering and farming began to produce the principal staples of the northern economy in the St. Lawrence Valley.

With social and economic growth and the British immigration which began after 1815 came a strengthening of the demand for constitutional reform. The colonial governments, partly because they were of the old model, modified but not substantially changed after 1783, and partly because of the reaction caused by the years of war and revolution, had become oligarchies entrenched around the governor of the day. Made up of officials and local magnates, these governing classes, or colonial ascendancies, held office by permanent tenure independent of public opinion, and could when necessary administer the government of their colonies without regard to popular wishes. During the war years few had objected, but after 1818 more and more voices were raised demanding that government be made responsive to public opinion.

These demands were not without effect. In 1828 a Select Committee of the House of Commons agreed that specific reforms were needed. After 1830 the Whig government set itself to put these administrative reforms into effect in the hope of making the colonial governments function in a more popular manner.

The Whig program of piecemeal reform, however, seemed inadequate to the more decided Reformers. These demanded "elective institutions" and "responsible government." Both were meant to make the colonial governments more responsive to public opinion, and they were not mutually exclusive. But elective institutions pointed to the American system of congressional government, while responsible government meant the introduction of British parliamentary procedure and of the cabinet system of administration by political heads of departments responsible to Parliament.

In 1837 the more extreme Reformers, exasperated by the Whig refusal to adopt basic constitutional reforms, such as making the appointed Legislative Councils elective, rose in rebellion but were quickly suppressed. Their failure ruled out the possibility of a constitution with elective institutions and popular sovereignty on the American model. When Lord Durham recommended the introduction of cabinet government as a remedy for the ills which had produced the rebellions, it seemed that colonial reform was to follow along the path of parliamentary government.

The imperial government, however, still believed that responsible government would mean the dissolution of the imperial connection. It therefore simply continued its policy of administrative reforms and coupled them with an attempt to make colonial government popular by means of political management of the legislature by the governors.

This work was brilliantly begun in Canada and Nova Scotia by Charles Poulett Thomson, Lord Sydenham. He and his successors made up their executive councils of heads of departments drawn from the legislatures. They refused, however, to allow any party to compose the full membership of the council. This they did on the instructions of the imperial government, which feared that a party council might either weaken the imperial connection or form a permanent party ascendancy in place of that of the oligarchs. Imperial loyalty without imperial control, and party government without a party ascendancy, were, it was feared, impossibilities in the colonies.

In 1846, none the less, the abolition of the Corn Laws and the old Mercantile System, by ending the economic basis of imperial control, made these fears of party ascendancy, colonial democracy and imperial dissolution suddenly irrelevant, and opened the way to colonial cabinet and parliamentary government under the Crown.

CHAPTER 12

The Last Years of the Oligarchic Ascendancy

1818-1828

There was a note of finality about the close of the War of 1812. It was one of the decisive wars of history. In the first place, it revealed that while the Americans could, once they organized themselves, conquer Canada, the British navy could at any time blockade the coasts of the United States. It was on this balance of power that the security of British North America was to rest for the remainder of the century. In the second place, the United States and Canada were both freed from the European balance of power by the war. The United States went on to practise isolation and to realize its manifest destiny to dominate the Americas. British North America, for its part, ceased to be, as it had been since 1744, a pawn in the great game of European-American power politics. Made dependent by its primitive staple economy and scant population, it remained tied to Europe, but as long as British sea power was supreme, it was isolated from the European system of power and protected against the American.

It was the simple, structural finality of the new circumstances, and the clarity with which they were appreciated by the extraordinarily able Americans and Englishmen who dealt with them, that explained the ease and speed with which the conventions of 1817 and 1818 were concluded. These were the genuine peace settlement. By the Rush-Bagot Agreement of 1817 the Great Lakes were disarmed, except for police vessels and until notice of change was given. In 1818 the fishing privileges of 1783 were revised, with the Americans excluded from territorial waters except for certain privileges along stretches of the shores of Newfoundland and Labrador, and the right to obtain wood and water. The "liberty" of 1783 was thus partly lost. Another convention of the same year accepted the 49th parallel of latitude as the boundary from the Lake of the Woods to the Rockies; the British gave up the line to the Mississippi, as the Americans had given up the latitude of the north-west corner of the Lake of the Woods. The same convention provided for the joint occupation, for a ten-year period, of the Oregon country of the Pacific slope between the Spanish and the Russian territory.

KC-H

By 1818, except for the north-eastern frontier, which it proved to be impossible to determine at that time, all Anglo-American difficulties had been settled or at least dealt with provisionally. The long peace had begun along a border which, though not unfortified, was not again to be crossed by invading armies. The limits of British and American power in North America had been defined for the time being, and the boundary across the continent recorded the result. But what was delimited by the boundary? On the one side, clearly, a proud and vigorous nation, devoted to republican principles and resolved to dominate the Americas. On the other, apparently, only a half dozen weak and separate colonies ranged along the northern boundary of the Republic. What kept them in being except the imperial power of England? Little indeed as yet, but that little was capable of growth. In Nova Scotia and New Brunswick there was a strong British patriotism, born of a sense of having shared the trials and triumphs of the great wars. In Lower Canada the sense of Canadian nationality battered ever harder at the shell of English commercial and political control, proving itself in politics, journalism, and literature. And in Upper Canada the sword had stopped the process of Americanization. There "the war," as it was to be remembered for three generations, had made Canadians of the loyalist Americans and the mere settler Americans; the American aggression had kindled the spark of nationalism, and beside the French Canadianism of the lower province an English Canadianism was beginning to glow and flame in the province of the Lakes.

In their economy as well as in sentiment the British North American colonies had emerged transformed from the epoch of the great European wars. The timber trade and privateering, the demand for fish and wheat, the garrisons and the fleets, had poured money into the colonial economy. With trade and money had come an increase of population. The population of all the colonies in 1792 was about 230,000; in 1818 about 796,000. The War of 1812, moreover, had settled finally the division of English-speaking America and the boundary line of demarcation. There was to be no more thought of a south-west or a Maine recovered, of an Indian buffer against the United States, or of access to the Mississippi. The old imperial Canada of the fur trade had finally ended, and the fur trade itself was rapidly withdrawing to the far north-west.

There was in the British territories in North America, of course, ample room both for a remote and far-extended fur trade and for colonies of settlement and commerce. Those territories were as imposing in extent as they were limited in population and wealth. From the Atlantic colonies and the valley of the St. Lawrence they stretched north-west over thousands of miles of wilderness, rock and forest, river and lake, ancient and lonely as a planet uninhabited, to Mackenzie's river and that Arctic coast and archipelago which Captain John Franklin began to explore from inland in 1819. No one outside the Hudson's Bay Company considered that hinterland as of more than passing commercial

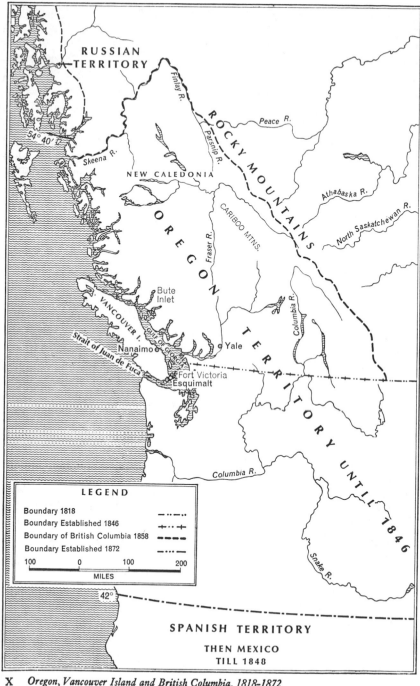

RUSSIAN TERRITORY

54° 40'

Finlay R.

ROCKY MOUNTAINS

Peace R.

Parsnip R.

Skeena R.

NEW CALEDONIA

Athabaska R.

CARIBOO MTNS.

North Saskatchewan R.

O R E G O N

Fraser R.

Columbia R.

Bute Inlet

VANCOUVER I.

GULF OF GEORGIA

Strait of Juan de Fuca

Nanaimo

Yale

T E R R I T O R Y   U N T I L   1 8 4 6

Fort Victoria
Esquimalt

Columbia R.

LEGEND

Boundary 1818	— ·· — ··
Boundary Established 1846	— + ·· + —
Boundary of British Columbia 1858	— — —
Boundary Established 1872	— ·· — ··

100   0   100   200
MILES

Snake R.

42°

SPANISH TERRITORY

THEN MEXICO

TILL 1848

X   *Oregon, Vancouver Island and British Columbia, 1818–1872* or scientific interest. No one at all considered it, after Selkirk died in 1820, as territory which might be occupied by civilized communities. The settled British North American colonies were to have no western and no northern destiny, and for their part now lost their interest in the old up-country. They had for the next half century to work out their future in terms of their local resources and internal growth, and of their need to draw the trade of the American midwest, now rapidly filling up, through Montreal and the St. Lawrence.

The resources of the colonies were nevertheless great, as was their extent between the Atlantic coast of Newfoundland and the Detroit River at the tip of the Upper Canadian peninsula. But between 1791 and 1815 there had been little political change in the colonies. The imperial connection and the political structure of each colony was what it had been in 1792. Not only had the wars allowed no time for the devising of change; the long resistance to revolutionary France had created a reactionary temper in the United Kingdom which viewed any change as but the first tremor of a revolutionary avalanche. A similar temper, fortified by the long possession of office and of property, prevailed in the entrenched oligarchies of the colonies, at St. John's, Halifax, Fredericton, Quebec, and York. The authority, patronage and prestige of government were the unchanging possession of a small official, legal, and commercial group in each colony. These men had come to regard their permanent retention of office as part of the legitimate order of things. Often able, always loyal, remarkably honest and devoted to duty in the circumstances, the colonial office-holders and political leaders were sternly pro-British and anti-American, monarchist and anti-republican, authoritarian and anti-democratic. But the British North American colonies were well into the nineteenth century, and their own colonial democracy, inspired by British, French, and American democratic ideas, would soon seek to challenge the oligarchs' perpetual possession of office. Like the British Tories and the American Federalists, the colonial bureaucrats were legitimists, but, unlike those politicians, they had never to seek re-election. They were kept in office by the laws, instructions, and authority of the imperial government. To challenge them would seem a challenge to the Empire itself.

In 1815 there were few signs anywhere that the long rule of the office-holders was likely to be questioned. The oldest and least settled of the colonies, Newfoundland, was still, officially, not a colony but a fishery. British policy still assumed that the fishery was carried on from England, and the Acts which had required that it should be so carried on were left on the statute books until 1824. But the resident population had steadily grown and in 1816 had increased to over fifty thousand. Such a community could no longer be left without permanent government, and in 1817 the governor was made resident. The custom of appointing a naval officer as governor continued for some time yet.

The island still remained dependent on the fishery for the support of its population. In the fishing economy the merchants of St. John's were now dominant, troubled not at all by English rivals and relatively little by New England competitors. They outfitted the fishermen of St. John's and the outports on credit, and the fishermen were constantly in debt to them. The same dominance was to be carried into politics when at last Newfoundland became a colony. Such politics as the island had immediately after 1815 consisted of stirrings of discontent against the St. John's merchants and factors.

The economic structure of Nova Scotia was at bottom somewhat like that of Newfoundland, though much more diversified, but it possessed a political life Newfoundland was not to begin for almost twenty years. The merchants of Halifax dominated the commerce of the province, and Halifax was not merely the political capital but the seat and place of business of the governing class. Many members of the Assembly were Halifax men elected for the outports or the farming counties; nearly all members of the Councils were Halifax residents. But Nova Scotia was an older political community and a much wealthier society than Newfoundland. Its population in 1817 was estimated to be over eighty thousand people. To fishing it added farming, lumbering, shipbuilding and shipping. Halifax was a garrison and naval base, enriched by soldiers' spending and naval prize-money. And the New England and loyalist background gave rise to an easy political assurance, a spirit of casual independence, and a deliberate cultivation of the manners and mode of the gentleman, which were far from the radical outbursts and strident complaints of St. John's. The merchants of Halifax were men of the world; they mingled with officers and gentlemen, with lawyers and doctors. They were not, as their counterparts in St. John's often were, traders isolated in a raw community of masters and servants, or mere factors sent to wring everything possible from capital invested.

By 1815 Nova Scotia had enjoyed representative government for almost sixty years. The system of government which had developed was odd, but workable. The governor was the usual colonial official, but his position had been made remarkably independent of popular pressure by his possession of the control of a large Crown revenue, territorial and fiscal in the main. His council, formed under his instructions, was at once executive, legislative, and judicial in function, like the councils of the old colonies. Its members were appointed during pleasure and in fact for life. They thus enjoyed longer terms of office than the governors, whom they tended to make their agents, and than the Assemblies, which they tended to dominate. By a curious reversal, the council in its legislative capacity actually held the power of the purse. It controlled the permanent revenue, the Assembly only what revenue it cared to vote taxes for, always in these years much less in sum than the permanent revenue. Thus the council, by refusing to pass a money bill, could deny the expenditure of that excess of the permanent revenue over the amount needed to pay official salaries, and thus cut off the greater part of the public expenditure for the year. This was made up of the grants for roads and bridges which the Assembly men from the outports and the outlying counties had been sent to Halifax to obtain. The Assembly, moreover, tended to be dominated by its Speakers, who could look to become officials or councillors in due course and therefore tended to act as the agents of the governor and council in the Assembly – in short, as government leaders. Thus the constitution of Nova Scotia was one suited to its own circumstances, resembling only in fundamentals either its British parent or its American cousins. It admirably served the purposes of an able governing class of entrenched officials and councillors, a bland oligarchy which was accepted at this period by the fishermen and farmers without much question and with no organized opposition. The path of the Nova Scotian democracy was not so much blocked by an entrenched oligarchy or a dominant merchant class, as it was thronged by a suave Whig gentry which avoided offence and kept its ranks open to able new-comers.

In New Brunswick much the same genial political temper prevailed. In a province where the loyalist migration was still dominant, it was natural that politics should take its tone from the colonial Whiggism the loyalists had brought from New England and the middle colonies. But there were two differences between New Brunswick and Nova Scotia. New Brunswick had its commercial capital in Saint John and its political capital in Fredericton, not both combined as in Halifax. And in New Brunswick the timber trade created a dominant industry which threw up masterful capitalists and gave to the economy of the colony something of the harshness of that of Newfoundland.

The constitution of New Brunswick had developed much like that of Nova Scotia, with a small official oligarchy dominating a council possessing executive, legislative, and judicial powers, the members holding office for life. In a population estimated at 74,000 in 1824, the non-loyalist elements, Acadian, Irish, and Scottish, were yet so little incorporated into the political community that the loyalist society continued to accept the rule of the timber and shipping capitalists of Saint John. There was little evidence that the dominant oligarchy was greatly resented and there had been little political friction in New Brunswick since the return of James Glenie to England in 1805. A quiet provincial society lived a life of unresentful poverty or carefully preserved gentility, and made no great expenditure of energy except when the timber drives came hurtling down the St. John out of the winter woods.

Across Northumberland Strait the population of Prince Edward Island exceeded twenty-two thousand in 1822. Settlers had continued to come to the fertile lands of the Island, despite the quitrents demanded by the absentee landlords. The small colony was developing in the main as a farming community, but with considerable lumbering and fishing to vary its economy.

The land issue ensured the existence of a "democratic" party in the Assembly, but both governor and councils were dominated by a Charlottetown oligarchy. The subordination to the governor of Nova Scotia had ended when the Island was placed under Dorchester in 1786. As Dorchester and his successors exercised no authority, the effect was to restore the Island's separate status which was unchallenged by 1815. Under its governors the executive and legislative councils were a minute, undifferentiated body.

The Assembly now possessed some organization and tradition; it was working out relations with the councils and was winning independence of the governor. This last was accomplished in a prolonged quarrel in the session of 1818, which ended in the recall of the governor. The organization in 1811 by J. B. Palmer of a "Club of Loyal Electors" to oppose the proprietors and control the Assembly had led to fears of "Jacobinism" and to Governor C. D. Smith's abstention from convoking the Assembly from 1814 to 1817. When it met in 1818, the Club challenged the right of the Governor to veto an appropriation for road-building.

Cape Breton was still governed by governor and council only. No assembly had ever been summoned, as the population of Acadians and Gaelic-speaking Highlanders was thought to be too scanty for representative government. In 1820 the colony was judged too small to be viable and was reunited with Nova Scotia, the only measure ever to modify the partition of 1784.

The Atlantic provinces, in their populations, their political institutions and the tone and modes of their societies, belonged to the British American world of the Atlantic seaboard. Wholly British by allegiance and partly British, partly American, by descent, they possessed in speech and manner much of the gentleness of old English and New England life. They were not to know the rigour and stridency of the economic pressures, race friction, and political strife of the Canadas until later in the century when the Scots and Irish new-comers entered politics with Celtic fervour and with new and difficult issues. In moving from the Maritimes to the Canadas in 1818, the traveller entered a new political climate.

In the Atlantic provinces the rise of democracy, when it came, was to be a matter of fishermen of the outports and farmers of outlying counties rising against the local oligarchies. Up to 1815 the voters were, however, either too little organized to challenge the oligarchies or not enough moved by any difference of interest between themselves and those who controlled the political life of the colonies. In Lower Canada, the circumstances were altogether different. Lower Canada was an older and a comparatively sophisticated political community, with a growing political class versed in political controversy since 1774. It was larger; in 1822, its population was 427,465, larger than that of the rest of British North America put together, Finally, its population was divided into a French majority and an English minority, the former subordinate, the latter dominant in both commerce and government. As a result, the political structure of Lower Canada tended to follow the contours of race, and the division between oligarchy and democracy, which existed only potentially in the Atlantic provinces, was active and intense on the lower St. Lawrence. The Lower Canadian oligarchy, made up of English officials, speculators in the lands of the Eastern Townships, and merchants, with a minority of Canadian seigneurs and *noblesse*, had distorted the constitution to make it, not the instrument of self-government it was meant by Pitt and Grenville to be, but an instrument of minority rule and majority subordination.

As a result, the democracy of Lower Canada, that of the Canadian habitants of the seigniories and the *bourgeoisie* of the cities, was not only fired by the ideas of the American and French revolutions. It was also the burning democracy of a repressed nationality; and in Lower Canada, as in Ireland, democracy and nationality went hand in hand, except for a small number of English members who allied themselves with the Canadians. Nor did the democracy go leaderless. The oligarchy was English and not a kindred and familiar one. It thus never succeeded in absorbing the able and the eloquent who rose from the ranks of the democracy. A long succession of governors, Sir George Prevost excepted, failed to win the confidence of the Canadians and refused to bestow office upon them. As a result, the *collèges classiques* of Lower Canada were turning out lawyers, journalists, and doctors in numbers that commerce and the professions could not employ and for whom the public service offered no place. Thus the able or the troublesome men, who in Halifax were quietly absorbed into the ample bosom of the oligarchy, in Quebec continued to storm the palisades of power and incite the democracy to discontent.

The whole situation was to be summed up in the career of Louis Joseph Papineau. Clever, handsome, educated, well-to-do, Papineau was equipped in all respects to be a successful political leader. But the only office that was open to him was the speakership of the Assembly. To this he was elected in 1815 and he held it almost continuously until 1837. But as Speaker he was not the friend of the administration in the Assembly: he was the leader of the opposition, with the power to stop all legislation and without the least hope of ever attaining ministerial office. For Papineau and the Canadian democracy the constitution was frustration systematized, alienating the majority from power and therefore from responsibility. These men, however, were by no means social radicals, or reformers. They were a new *élite* seeking power to rule the Quebec of the *habitant*, the parish, and the seigneury as it had always been and as they wished it to continue to be.

In Upper Canada the social and political structure was much more like that of Nova Scotia or New Brunswick. The racial difference of the lower province was absent, as was the revolutionary tradition. But the tone and temper of politics was to become more and more like that of Lower Canada and less and less like that of the Atlantic provinces. For one thing, Upper Canada was territorially large, and its population was growing rapidly. In 1814 there were 95,000 people; in 1824, 150,000. For another, its oligarchy possessed, as exhibited by the Governor's dismissal of Willcocks and Thorpe from office, a harsh temper which perhaps derived from the mobbings of revolutionary New York and the border warfare. The same temper flared up anew in 1818 when Robert Gourlay, a new-comer and an excitable and voluble Scots busy-body, circulated a set of questions and organized a convention which seemed to reflect on the progress of the colony under the ruling oligarchy. Gourlay was harried, imprisoned, and deported; the critic of the oligarchs was an exile until 1836. Much of this fierce intolerance un-doubtedly derived from the fact that the governing group of Upper Canada had since the days of Simcoe endowed themselves and their connections with thous-ands of acres of public land. They were land speculators on a greater scale than that of the Château clique in Lower Canada. Their lands, perhaps not ill-gotten under the conditions of that day, they held in the face of a rising population of settlers urgently interested in obtaining cheap and accessible land quickly and with certainty. To question progress, as Gourlay did, was to turn away the settlers whose coming raised land values. To question government was to threaten to deliver Upper Canada to an agrarian democracy which might attack, by squatting or by enactment in the Assembly, the great potential wealth of the speculators' lands.

This was the lion in the way of the democracy of Upper Canada, and this was the chief of the elements which made the oligarchy relatively unpopular in Upper Canada. Because of the loyalist element and its reinforcement by middle-class British immigrants, as well as their own considerable ability and public spirit, the bureaucrats and land speculators of York and the small lake-front towns were normally able to keep a majority in the Assembly. But they failed on the whole to recruit the ablest of their critics to their own ranks; they seemed some-times to prefer to repress them. The Upper Canadian oligarchy failed to make itself coincident with the propertied and professional classes of the colony. More than elsewhere, therefore, the way was open for the rise of a democratic political party and the beginning of public controversy on matters of principle.

If the political life of the British American colonies was still comparatively peaceful, and its institutions little developed and differentiated in the years after 1815, in the remainder of the British possessions political institutions were so elementary as scarcely to deserve the name. Selkirk's colony had survived the fur-trade war and in 1818 was struggling to exist in a country which seemed persistently hostile. The Highland, Irish, Swiss, and Polish settlers were governed by a Governor of Assiniboia, who in 1818 was Alexander Macdonell. The governor was aided by a small council appointed by the proprietor. This was the form of government until 1834, when Assiniboia was restored to the Hudson's Bay Company and much the same form of government continued.

The vast remainder of the British American empire consisted of Rupert's Land, extending north of the northern watershed which was the boundary of the Canadas from Labrador to Lake Superior, and thence along the American boundary to the Rockies. Beyond Rupert's Land was the area later called the North-Western Territory. Both were governed after 1821 by the Hudson's Bay

KC-H*

Company's Governors and Councils of the Northern and Southern Departments, the former meeting annually at York Factory or Norway House, the latter at Moose Factory or Fort William.

Beyond the Rockies in the jointly occupied Oregon country there was no organized society. The Hudson's Bay Company posts existed among the native tribes in virtue of their utility to the Indians. The posts themselves were directed by the Council of the Northern Department, but in these territories, as in the Athabaska and Mackenzie River country, there was neither law nor government, only the jurisdiction of the courts of Canada under the Judicature Act of 1803. Rupert's Land and the far north-west had no other political connection with the Canadas and had ceased to be part of the economic structure of British America.

That structure was powerfully influenced after 1815 by the imperial system of which it was a segment, the old mercantile system as revised under the stress of the American Revolution and the Revolutionary and Napoleonic Wars. Its main features were the granting of a preferred position to colonial timber in the British market and the endeavour, continued down to 1830, to preserve against American competition at least part of the British West Indian market for the shipping and produce of the North American colonies. The colonies, that is, were still encouraged to be suppliers of materials needed by the metropolis and the tropical colonies. Their manufactured imports were supplied by British industries, although the former prohibitions on colonial manufacture were not kept up. They were in fact unnecessary, as British production was so much cheaper. The general effect was to keep the colonial economy a simple one, devoted to the production of staple goods.

The years after 1815 were to see the old system considerably modified. The changes which affected British North America were the Free Port Act of 1818 and its amendments, which helped to preserve the position of Nova Scotian and New Brunswick shipping in the West Indies down to the treaty of 1830 with the United States. By the "reciprocity treaty" of that date, American shipping was allowed to trade with the British West Indies, but British colonial shipping was admitted to American ports. Despite the competition, Nova Scotian and New Brunswick shipping throve. For the rest, the general change in the old colonial system was to transform a protective system into a preferential one. In the 1820's, however, the timber of British North America enjoyed such a margin of preference as to be in fact protected, and Canadian wheat enjoyed varying degrees of protection under the successive Corn Laws passed from 1815 to 1842. The colonies remained well sheltered under the revised system and the development of the staple trades in timber and wheat was fostered as part of an imperial economy. There can be no doubt that the colonies benefited greatly from imperial protection during these years, and that without it their development would have been much slower. Two other major consequences were that the imperial preferential system was also a powerful commercial and political prop of the oligarchies and that the Canadas were encouraged to develop the St. Lawrence as a route for British commerce with the American midwest.

Internally, the economic changes were in the main those of growth along established lines. In Nova Scotia perhaps the chief development was in the art and business of shipbuilding. Not only did its builders perfect the Nova Scotian schooner both for fishing on the banks and for coastal trade; they also played a part in the development of the clipper ship, and Donald McKay, greatest of the clipper builders in America, was a Nova Scotian trained in New York.

In New Brunswick the St. John and Miramichi River trade gave rise to the logging industry as it was to be in the northern pine zone from Fundy to the Mississippi. Here developed the river drive of the squared timber and the masts down the river, the lumber camp, the lumberjack, the peavey, the term "Main John" for the woods boss. Here began that seasonal change from farming to lumbering which was to hold back New Brunswick farming so long, and which, in its alternation of barracks life in the woods and family life on the farm, was to give the British North American male his curious combination of roughness and domestic puritanism. The cutting of the pine woods of the St. John and the rivers of the North Shore on the Gulf of St. Lawrence dominated New Brunswick for a generation, created the dynamic of its political life, and furnished the one great staple of its economy.

The Canadian timber trade out of Quebec was somewhat different, although it, too, took the young men, as the fur trade had done, into the woods for the winter. At first small groups of men brought out the timber for sale to British buyers at Quebec. Only later did big timbermen like those of New Brunswick appear in the Canadas. Lumbering went hand in hand with farming, especially in the Ottawa Valley, but only along the forest fronts did farming become tied to the timber trade. The Canadian farm economy was as a whole independent, and like that of Prince Edward Island it soon produced a surplus. By 1815 Lower Canada was exporting flour and wheat in quantity, and soon after, Upper Canadian flour was being carried down the St. Lawrence in freight boats and on the great timber rafts. The appearance of steamships on the St. Lawrence and the Lower Lakes furnished tows for the timber rafts and transport for flour and wheat.

The development of Upper Canadian lumbering and farming, however depended upon the improvement of the navigation of the St. Lawrence. Canal construction began in 1819 when a company was formed to dig the Lachine Canal, first attempted in 1690. The Rideau Canal, supplemented with canals on the Ottawa River, was begun in 1826 and completed in 1834, to furnish an alternative military route to the St. Lawrence. It proved to have little commercial utility. The canals on the St. Lawrence between Lachine and Kingston were improved in 1817 from the work of the Royal Engineers during the War of Independence, but only slightly. Work on them awaited the reunion of the

Canadas. Between 1824 and 1829, after many difficulties, the first Welland Canal was dug, to attempt to hold for Canada the trade the Erie Canal of New York was drawing across the boundary.

The growth of colonial democracy was aided by this economic development and also, after 1815, by an increase in migration. The American influx into the Canadas ceased with the War of 1812 and the subsequent opening of the Indian territory west of Ohio, but as a result of unemployment combined with over-population in Ireland, the Highlands, and parts of the English countryside after Waterloo there began a great movement of British migration which was to continue for thirty years. Some small part of this migration was aided by government, as in the Rideau River settlements of British veterans made with imperial assistance after 1815. Much the greater part, however, was voluntary and individual. The result was that the Americanization of British North America, which, in a sense, had begun with the loyalists, was ended. This in itself was a blow to the oligarchic system, which at bottom was that of the old colonies. Now British North America was to become more British in sentiment and tone. The former tenants, the unemployed workers, the independent yeomen, were all eager for political freedom in the New World. Many were political radicals; all believed in free institutions. And their coming prepared the way not only for a revolt against the colonial office-holders but for the choice of British constitutional expression for the new Canadian democracy.

Into all the colonies, but especially Newfoundland, New Brunswick, Upper Canada, and the cities of Quebec and Montreal, the great migration brought a large infusion of Irish, both Protestant and Roman Catholic. The Highland Scots continued to flow into Cape Breton and eastern Nova Scotia, making a New Scotland indeed. In Lower Canada the Canadians, still the great majority, had new grounds to fear that they might become a minority in the land of their ancestors. Resentment of this danger added to the growing bitterness of the political conflict in that province. Correspondingly, of course, as the British minority in Lower Canada began to increase, the oligarchy thought even less in terms of accommodation with the French. The old mirage of racial assimilation began to dance once more on the political horizon of the Lower Canadian compact, with all its invitation to disaster. If the post-war migration prepared the way for a rising against the office-holders, it also threatened the peace of Canada by seeming to menace the nationality and autonomy of the French.

Still another and even more potent force making for the rise of colonial democracy was the development of the free Protestant churches in the Atlantic provinces and the Canadas. The result was a great, often muffled, often bitterly articulate struggle between the principle of a semi-established church, with toleration for other churches, and the principle of free, voluntary and legally equal churches in a neutral state. The ecclesiastical result was a victory for the latter principle; the political result was to be, it is scarcely too much to say, the creation of the Canadian democracy and the overthrow of the political establishments from St. John's to Toronto.

The creation of the Anglican diocese of Nova Scotia was the first attempt after the American Revolution to found and provide for an established church, and it had been defeated by two facts: that the Anglicans were a minority, and that an establishment was unpopular. Contributing to this defeat were the too domineering efforts of the second Bishop Inglis to have the position of his church recognized, and the opposition of Anglican laymen who realized that an establishment could not but harm their church, a minority among the Baptists, Presbyterians and Roman Catholics of the colony. Similarly in the diocese of Quebec, Bishop Mountain's strenuous efforts to have the Church of England recognized as the established church had been thwarted by the imperial government's unwillingness to offend the Roman Catholic bishop and clergy, and by the claim of the clergy of the Church of Scotland to belong to the "Protestant clergy" for whom the clergy reserves of the Constitutional Act had been provided.

Mountain's successor, Bishop Charles James Stewart, ceased to push the claims of the Church of England in Lower Canada, and that church in fact became a voluntary church, only nominally connected with the state. But the idea of establishment and the Christian state was upheld with zeal by Rev. John Strachan, now of York, Upper Canada. Strachan's efforts to maintain the primacy and state connection of his church in Upper Canada led, of course, to much hostility towards the Anglican Church among the other churches, and to its identification with the oligarchy and the propertied class.

The Church of Rome, despite the fact that in Lower Canada it too was semi-established, with its right to tithe its own members, and its bishop a member of the Executive Council and in receipt of a salary as councillor, did not incur any such odium. It was not identified, for all the care the imperial government took to maintain its goodwill, with the oligarchs and the possessing classes. In Lower Canada it was, on the contrary, identified with the Canadians who were in opposition to the political establishment; and the church was, in a broader, subtler, and more comprehensive way than the national democratic movement, the vehicle of French nationalism.

In other provinces the Roman Catholic Church had its beginning as the church of the immigrant from lands where it had been the church of the oppressed. In the Atlantic provinces (as in Montreal) it tended to continue its role of defender and leader of its flock in secular as in spiritual affairs. In Upper Canada the bold and vigorous leadership of Bishop Alexander Macdonell, coupled with the military loyalty of the Glengarry Scots, had won a special respect for the Roman Catholic Church which was to aid the growth of religious toleration in Canada. And increasingly in the 1820's the British American provinces, especially Nova Scotia, led the English-speaking world in the admission of Roman Catholics to political life and office. The Catholic voter, as the limitations and prejudices which stood in the way of his entering public life were removed, steadily became more active in public affairs and won eminence in politics and the law. There was long a tendency to preserve the group loyalty which had enabled Catholics to survive in their Scots and Irish homelands. But the British provinces won from their Catholic citizens a loyalty which neither American democracy nor Irish sympathies would weaken in the future.

It was far different with the Protestant free churches. They in all their variety were religious democracies themselves, with every man his own priest, and with authority coming from the congregations of the faithful. Their religious beliefs and practices led directly to social and political equality; to the equality both of churches and of men. The Methodists and the Baptists were the largest of the Protestant sects. The Baptists took over the New Light Congregationalist churches in Nova Scotia, and largely held them even against the devoted ministry of such Methodists as Rev. William Black. In the Eastern Townships the Congregationalist churches had begun to lose members to the Church of England, or to the Wesleyan Methodists. In Upper Canada the Methodist churches tended to absorb quickly all rural Protestants and many Anglicans as well. The Methodist "class" supplied the frontier pioneer with the religious discipline he needed, the "circuit" system provided the loneliest settlement with the aid and exhortation of men of natural eloquence and fervent feeling, whose quickness and strategy the parochial churches usually failed to match.

The one great handicap of the free churches was that their ministers either came from the United States or were educated in American seminaries. The colonies were included down to the War of 1812 in American Methodist "conferences." These American affiliations were sometimes used by their critics and rivals against the Methodists, other than the British Wesleyan, and indeed against other sects with similar ties. The aspersion on the loyalty of the sectarians was unfounded, but their American connections tended to confirm their democratic leanings and assist the leaven of reform. It was this of course that was feared.

The concept of an established church carried with it, despite the principle of toleration, two corollaries that were objectionable to the free churches. One was that only the clergy of the established church might perform the rites of marriage and burial. The other was that education should be under the control of the established church, in contrast to the public school of the American states, which, with its absence of religious discrimination, appealed to most of the free denominations. The Roman Catholic Church, on the other hand, believed that education as well as spiritual ministration must be in the hands of the clergy, and of course insisted on having its own schools. At the same time few congregations of any church could afford to support their own denominational school. The first schools, then, were for the most part "parish" schools, usually but not necessarily under Roman Catholic or Anglican influence, and almost always supported by grants of public funds. To these, in the English colonies, grammar schools and colleges were slowly added; in Lower Canada, the *collèges classiques*.

In all the colonies but Lower Canada, therefore, a struggle began to create non-denominational schools supported out of public funds. The Anglican Church sought to maintain control of higher education by founding King's College in Nova Scotia in 1789-1802 and King's College in New Brunswick in 1824, and by obtaining in 1827, under John Strachan's leadership, a grant of Crown lands to support a King's College in Upper Canada. The Roman Catholic Church struggled to support parish schools, and to win some public funds for them, with a measure of success which was to lead to the "separate school" in all the colonies. In Lower Canada it had an early and decided success, the Assembly gladly voting money for denominational schools. As a result, the failure of the Royal Institute in general education was assured. Thus the Catholic Church was slowly and painfully working its way to an accommodation with the state in all the colonies. The ministers of the Protestant churches, however, were deprived by law of two major functions of their ministry, the marriage and burial of members of their churches. At the same time, members of those churches faced the prospect of having to have their children seek higher education in Anglican institutions with state support, or of having to provide their own academies and colleges. It was a situation incompatible with the principles of the Protestant churches and the social order of the colonies.

Such was the background of the struggle that was beginning for constitutional reform and a liberal democratic society in British North America. It began at different dates in different colonies, in Lower Canada in 1815 – the preliminaries date from 1806 – in Upper Canada in 1820, in Nova Scotia in 1830, the other colonies following at irregular and scarcely to be dated intervals. In New Brunswick a struggle of another character began in 1824 when Thomas Baillie became Commissioner of Crown Lands and attempted to end the free cutting of timber. In the Canadas and Nova Scotia, however, the struggle was essentially one to dislodge the oligarchy and to make the colonial administration responsive to public opinion and popular will. The result of success would be the undoing of the work of the post-Revolution administration of the Empire, which had been the strengthening of the governor's position as against the Assembly, the creation of a revenue independent of vote by the popular branch of the legislature, the buttressing of the executive government by the establishment of legislative councils as second chambers, and the semi-establishment of a state and official church. The result would also be to put control of local affairs and the disposition of local patronage in local hands.

In Lower Canada from 1806 to 1818 the political conflicts had not been wanting in constitutional principle. The position of judges in the councils and Assembly

, was clearly a violation of the doctrine of the separation of powers. The impeachment of Chief Justices Sewell and Monk in 1814 was also of great constitutional interest as it further illustrated the division between the Assembly and the other branches of government. That of Justice L. C. Foucher, although never completed, did in fact win for the Assembly the right to impeach, never before conceded. But none of the conflicts had revolved around an issue which touched the fundamentals of power. In 1818 such a struggle opened. Up to that date the permanent revenue of the Crown, the casual and territorial revenues, and the returns from the duties imposed by the Quebec Revenue Act of 1774 had nearly sufficed to meet the ordinary expenditure of government. When they did not, advances were made from the imperial funds of the Military Chest. The Canadian governor had at his disposal revenues not annually voted by the legislature. The moneys for other expenditures were raised by taxation voted in the Assembly and Legislative Council. In 1810 the Assembly offered to vote all expenses, but the offer was not accepted, because to do so would have been to give the Assembly control of supply. In 1818, however, the governor, Sir John Sherbrooke, had insufficient funds from the permanent revenue to meet the costs of government. He asked the Assembly to vote the difference, which, not realizing its opportunity, it did.

In the next year the Assembly declined to vote the amount needed to supplement the permanent revenue until it had examined all the proposed expenditures and voted them item by item, from both the permanent and supplementary revenues. What an opportunity was here to bring the members of the Château clique – its lordly bishop, its long-secure bureaucrats, the heads of the English party – to account, to criticize their discharge of their duties, to lower their remuneration, and to make the will of the Assembly, which voiced the will of the people, prevail in the government of Lower Canada! The Duke of Richmond, who had succeeded Sherbrooke in 1819, at once saw the danger, that the Assembly was grasping at the control of government through the control of expenditure which the old colonial assemblies had exercised, and refused to allow the Assembly to assume control of the permanent revenue. He and his successor, Lord Dalhousie, were firm in maintaining that the executive government of the colony was, under the theory of imperial rule developed after 1783, to be independent of popular control. The English party was of one mind with the Governor, so much did its own mercantile and real-estate interests accord with the policy, and used its control of the Legislative Council to vote down the Assembly's supply bills then and thereafter. But the Assembly persisted year after year, especially when in 1823, a year of depression, the Receiver General, John Caldwell, was found to be almost £100,000 in arrears of public moneys in his charge. The Canadian popular party then had manifest proof that the bureaucracy was corrupt as well as irremovable.

The strife thus begun in 1819 was annually renewed throughout the next decade. In place of the fleeting skirmishes of former years there came the recurrent yearly shock of the irresistible Assembly colliding with the immovable legislative and executive councils, and this mutual frustration inevitably built up over the years into mutual exasperation.

The tension in Lower Canadian politics was suddenly increased in 1822 by a secret and unexpected attempt to reunite the Canadas. The division of the old province of Quebec in 1791 had never been accepted by the English minority of Lower Canada, and particularly not by the merchants of Montreal. To them, it had destroyed the unity of the St. Lawrence commercial system, and now that funds were needed for canals it weakened the credit of the Canadas. It had also denied them the political aid of the English of Upper Canada. In addition, there was to be a vexatious practical problem of the allocation of the proceeds of the Quebec Revenue Act between the two provinces. And allocation there had to be, as the duties were levied on goods consumed in Upper as well as in Lower Canada; but how to make it had never been decided to the satisfaction of both provinces.

The reunion of the Canadas would solve this problem, as it would restore the unity of the St. Lawrence and strengthen the credit of the Canadas. The English party therefore went to work quietly in London to use the problem of the division of customs duties to bring about a union of the provinces. Lord Bathurst, the Colonial Secretary, was agreeable, and the project had reached the stage of a parliamentary bill when the protests of the startled French and critical comments from Upper Canada stayed its course. It was not proceeded with thereafter, and a Canada Trade Act was passed in 1823 to provide for a division of the duties. But for the French Canadians the Union Bill raised once more the spectre of 1763, the threat of enforced assimilation, and brought the sudden realization that the English party in Lower Canada felt no compunction about changing the rules of the game in order to have its way. The trust without which free government is impossible, and which the imperial government had never extended to the Canadians by giving them majorities at all levels of government, the Canadians could not give to the English of Lower Canada who had attempted the manoeuvre of the Union Bill of 1822. The episode added to the build-up of bitterness.

The Colonial Office under Lord Bathurst made little further effort to resolve the conflict and kept the able but unpopular Dalhousie firmly to his task of repelling the democratic forces. In 1827 Dalhousie, following a general election into which the Governor threw the full patronage and influence of the government in the hope of winning enough seats to vote a civil list, vetoed the election of Papineau as Speaker on the ground that his utterances against the government had exceeded permissible limits. At the same time, with the death of the Prime Minister, Lord Liverpool, the long Tory resistance to reform began to weaken. With the advent of George Canning as Prime Minister, the liberal Tories began to influence government. Spring was in the air, and the waters of reform began to trickle down the frosty front of the inveterate Toryism of post-Waterloo government.

In Upper Canada, the course of politics had been less troubled. In the opinion of the greatest of Upper Canadian Reformers, Robert Baldwin, the reform movement began there in the Assembly in 1820. That is to say, critics of government appeared who proposed specific reforms. There was as yet no opposition party, and no drive for power such as characterized the Lower Canadian Assembly. But a series of questions began the process of dividing opinion in the country and in the Assembly, and the rudiments of political principle and party formation began to appear. The Alien question was one such, from 1820 to 1824. It concerned the national status of Americans who had been British subjects before 1783 but had come to Canada as American citizens. Were they to be regarded as British or American? Could they be naturalized? The major issue was that, if aliens, they could not hold land, and the majority of land titles in the province were affected. The government used the doubt to disqualify Barnabas Bidwell from sitting in the Assembly and to attack his son, Marshall Spring Bidwell, one of the earliest and ablest of the Upper Canadian Reformers. The attack on the Bidwells aroused such opposition that critics of the oligarchy had a majority in the Assembly elected in 1824. In 1828 the Assembly of Upper Canada passed an act naturalizing all people resident in Upper Canada for seven years prior to March 1, 1828, and set the vexed question at rest.

A second and even more important question was that of the Clergy Reserves. The great areas of these, their frequently favourable location, the fact that none had yet been sold, made them a practical matter of land settlement. The prospective distribution of the returns also made them a denominational question. The Church of England clergy were determined, especially Strachan, to claim them all for the clergy of that church. In 1819, however, the Church of Scotland as an established and Protestant church was declared by the law officers of the Crown to be entitled to a share proportionate to its numbers in the Canadas. Little was realized from the Reserves, either Clergy or Crown, until in 1824 the Canada Company was formed to invest in the public lands of Upper Canada, including the Reserves, and to place settlers on the land of the Huron Tract. With this beginning, the Clergy Reserves ceased to be merely a grievance in principle and became a grievance in fact as well.

The prospect of the two churches being endowed with public lands, and the Church of England possessing a monopoly of higher education with the grant of the charter of King's College, invited challenge by the other churches. They found an outstanding champion in Egerton Ryerson, a Methodist minister and editor of the church paper, the *Christian Guardian*. A bold, eloquent, but essentially moderate man, a loyalist and one-time Anglican, Ryerson successfully challenged the Ecclesiastical Chart which Strachan prepared for the Colonial

Secretary on the respective numbers of clergy and adherents possessed by the various churches of Upper Canada. In this Chart the number of Anglicans was much exaggerated and that of the Methodist ministers stated in highly inaccurate and prejudiced terms. As a result of the controversy, Ryerson brought the great weight of his church to the side of the reformers, who consequently won control of the Assembly for the second time in 1828. Neither Ryerson nor the Methodists were to be always on the side of reform, but they did on this occasion decisively help to precipitate the formation of the reform movement.

Loyalists like Ryerson, indeed, and the Methodist Church generally, which separated in 1828 from the American conference, could not fully support the growing radical element in the reform movement. This new element, sprung from British radicalism and inspired by the Jacksonian democracy which was triumphant south of the border, was personified in William Lyon Mackenzie. A shrill-toned, bristling terrier of a man, Mackenzie was the strident champion of a host of causes. He was also a critic of righteous and irritating pertinacity. Neither his personality nor his behaviour made him an admirable character, but he was a journalistic gadfly driven to sting the complacency of the colonial bureaucracy. An outburst of scurrility in his *Colonial Advocate* in 1826 had fired a mob of young members of the ruling set to break his press and scatter his type. The provocation had been great, but the attack was shameful. The courts, however, did their duty, and Mackenzie was awarded generous damages. His election for York in 1828 and 1830 and his repeated rejection by a Tory-controlled assembly after 1830 for libel of the Assembly made him a popular hero, the Wilkes of Upper Canada. With Mackenzie, Upper Canadian political life assumed the vigour and the bitterness of that of Lower Canada. The colonial torpor, the bland loyalist complacency, were ended.

The political controversies in the Canadas were but faintly echoed in the Atlantic provinces. The struggle for representative government in Newfoundland was much more elementary than the party warfare that was developing in the Canadas. Popular agitation had won reform of the courts and municipal government for St. John's in 1824, and in 1832 a mixed Assembly, partly appointed, partly elected, was established to make Newfoundland at last a colony governed as other colonies were. In New Brunswick a recurrent struggle to contest the appropriation of the revenues had gone on, with the Assembly usually prevailing. After 1824 it merged with another issue, the disposal of the timber lands of the province. Hitherto the timber had been cut freely, without fee or licence. The new Commissioner of Crown Lands, Thomas Baillie, sought to introduce a system of lease and sale, for the profit of the Crown and himself. The attempt was bitterly resisted by the "merchant democrats," as a historian of New Brunswick ironically calls them. As Baillie married the daughter of William Odell, a member of the oligarchy, this struggle became one within the governing group, but it had little constitutional significance except to reveal that access to the timber stands was the one great issue of New Brunswick politics.

The course of politics in Prince Edward Island was little more significant, except that the Assembly did establish the right to criticize the administration and procured the recall of the absurd Governor C. D. Smith in 1825. But only in Nova Scotia did conflicts begin from which parties were to take their rise and create an active political life. There the attempt of the second Bishop Inglis after 1825 to maintain an Anglican monopoly of higher education by preventing public funds being voted for the support of Pictou Academy, a Presbyterian institution, provoked denominational controversy which, like that over the Clergy Reserves in Canada, began a cleavage of political opinion. The attack was led by the Anglican Tory, T. C. Haliburton, later famous as the creator of Sam Slick, the hero of *The Yankee Clockmaker*. Then in 1830 a conflict between the Assembly and the Executive over a failure to collect the duty on brandy broke at last the spell which the Halifax oligarchy had maintained over the rural electorate. In this debate began the rise of Joseph Howe, the flamboyant editor of the *Nova Scotian*, who was to give the province a cause and a leader to evoke the latent democracy of the outports, the Fundy counties, and the Baptist chapels.

The discontents in the Atlantic provinces were not yet serious, but those in the Canadas – over the control of expenditure in Lower Canada, the rejection of Papineau as Speaker, the want of separate representation and courts in the Eastern Townships, the recurrent friction between governor and assembly in Upper Canada, the dismissal of Judge John Walpole Willis, and above all the vexed questions of the Clergy Reserves and King's College – came to a head in 1828. The Colonial Secretary, William Huskisson, received petitions with thousands of signatures from the popular party in Lower Canada, the inhabitants of the Eastern Townships, and the Reformers of Upper Canada. The first group protested against Dalhousie's treatment of Papineau and demanded control of supply by the Assembly and a change in the Legislative Council; the Townships sought separate representation, courts capable of dealing with freehold land tenure, and a union of the Canadas; the Reform party criticized the principle of church establishment as embodied in the Clergy Reserves and the charter of King's College. Among these grievances of principle were more specific matters – the division of the revenue from customs between the provinces, the question of mortgages on land in Lower Canada, the still unsettled defalcation of the Receiver General, Caldwell, in Lower Canada, the disposition of the Jesuit Estates, the independence of the judges.

In England the resignation of Lord Liverpool in 1827 had marked the beginning of the end of the long period of Tory reaction which had begun with the French Revolution. The liberal current was beginning to run strongly in British politics; the repeal of the Test and Corporation Acts in 1828 and Catholic Emancipation in 1829 revealed its force and direction. As a result, the liberal members of the House of Commons, of whom Sir James Mackintosh was Agent for Lower Canada, were able to obtain the appointment of a Select Committee to inquire into the grievances complained of in the petitions. The report of the Committee was an all but complete acceptance of the complaints and contained a series of proposals designed, with one exception, to remedy them.

The exception was the request of the Eastern Townships for the union of the provinces. The Committee did not think that the circumstances and situation of the Canadas required a change so drastic. It did, however, recommend that the Townships be granted separate courts and their own judicial districts, that the law be simplified respecting the sale and registration of freehold land and clarified respecting mortgages, and that the change from seigniorial to freehold tenure be made without the Crown demanding the share in the commutation. In the matter of supply it recommended that the Assembly be given full control except for a "civil list" to cover the salaries of the governor, the executive councillors and the judges, the amount to be voted for the life of the king and not annually. It urged that provision be made for the proper audit of all public accounts. The Jesuit Estates it thought should be used for purposes of education. The legislative councils, it strongly recommended, should be given a more independent character by having a membership distinct from that of the executive councils. The Committee agreed that the judges should not be members of either council.

While prepared to say that the Jesuit Estates should be used for purposes of education, the Committee found itself at a loss with respect to the Clergy Reserves. Although it obviously disliked the discrimination the Reserves made between the churches of England and Scotland on the one hand and the free churches on the other, it could not see how the proceeds might be divided, nor did it recommend that the Reserves be used for some secular purpose, such as education. It was, however, definitely of the opinion that the Charter of King's College should be altered so as to eliminate any religious test for faculty or students.

The Committee concluded its report with a censure of Dalhousie for his treatment of Papineau and by urging the necessity for "an impartial, conciliatory and constitutional system of government" in the Canadas. The report of the Committee and the implementation by Governor Sir James Kempt, on instructions from the Colonial Office, of its recommendations with respect to the voting of the expenditures of the province and the introduction of French and pro-French members in the councils, brought an immediate relaxation of tension in Lower Canada. And it was a clear signal that the practices and politics of the years of the oligarchic ascendancy were not in keeping with the changes proceeding in the political life of the United Kingdom.

ADDITIONAL READING

CLARK, S. D. *Movements of Political Protest in Canada, 1640-1840.*
CREIGHTON, D. G. *The Empire of the St. Lawrence.*
KILBOURN, W. *The Firebrand.*
LOWER, A. R. M. *Canadians in the Making.*
MARTIN, CHESTER *Empire and Commonwealth.*
OUELLET, F. *Histoire économique et sociale du Québec, 1760-1850.*
WADE, MASON *The French Canadians, 1760-1945.*
WALSH, H. H. *The Christian Church in Canada.*

CHAPTER 13

The Reform of the Colonial Constitutions

1829-1838

As the decade of the 1820's approached its end, it was as apparent in the Canadas as in the United Kingdom that constitutional reform in church and state was imminent. The course of politics, in Lower Canada especially, had clearly revealed the fundamental defects of the constitution of 1791. Simply as a constitution it was defective; but as a constitution for a British American society, whether French or English, it was in large part irrelevant. Moreover, in a society by a majority French and a minority English, it had functioned so as to bring out and acerbate national rivalries.

The constitution of 1791 suffered from two defects, both of which sprang from the fact that it was an attempt to reproduce in Lower Canada, so far as was compatible with colonial dependence, the British constitution in all its elements. One was that the constitution of independent branches did not work in Lower Canada as it did in the United Kingdom. Two of the theoretically independent branches, the governor and the legislative council dominated by the English party, had united in opposition to the third, the assembly, dominated by the French majority. The intended checks and balances of a constitution became in practice the recurrent collisions of two racial factions, and politics, quite unnecessarily and quite misleadingly in terms of the real issues of the province, thus became racial.

That result, however, was only an exaggeration of a second and basic defect in the constitution of 1791. The fact that there were French and English in Lower Canada only helped to bring it to view. The constitution of the United Kingdom had developed in an aristocratic society, and in its eighteenth-century phase was a profoundly aristocratic constitution, a true reflection of the hierarchical structure of English society. It functioned not as a system of checks and balances, an academic concept of the previous century early discarded, nor by the convention of cabinet government, not yet defined. It functioned by means of royal patronage and influence, used by the king and his advisers to procure a majority in the House of Commons. Before the development of organized democratic parties, this was the only way a majority could be formed to support a ministry. Moreover, the advisers of the king sat as members of either the Lords or the Commons.

An even more striking case of parliamentary government by patronage and influence had been in evidence in Ireland before the Union of 1801. Corrupt as were British politics, Irish politics were infinitely more so because patronage and influence were used among the small numbers of the leaders of the Protestant ascendancy in Ireland to support the government of the English Lord-Lieutenant, an extra-Irish, if not an alien, executive. Among the thousands of Irish immigrants to British America must have been many who remembered and understood the nature of this external and irresponsible government which ruled by patronage and influence.

In the British North American colonies, however, and in Lower Canada in particular, the governor, though invariably from the United Kingdom and responsible to the Colonial Secretary, had very little patronage and might have very little influence. Colonial government had few offices, and these were held by life tenures as a form of property. It had no titles to give and no honours to bestow, for no hereditary aristocracy had been created under the Constitutional Act and no colonial was judged worthy of an imperial honour or title. Any influence a governor might possess depended upon his personality, his ability to step outside the jealous circle of his little court and council, and on the tone of the society of the colony. Where the loyalists predominated, as in Fredericton or York, where there were garrisons, as in Halifax or Quebec, a governor might exercise much social and even political influence, and in Nova Scotia and Upper Canada this influence might extend throughout the province and affect elections. Finally, in none of the colonies was it customary for members of the executive council to sit in the assembly; on the contrary, a largely concurrent membership in the legislative council in the Canadas practically prohibited them from doing so. Thus the governor was also precluded from having a direct influence on the assembly, while he controlled the legislative council.

Nowhere, then, was there any patronage and influence comparable with that of Great Britain. For British American society in all provinces consisted simply of a population of farmers, fishermen and workers, with a small *bourgeoisie* of merchants, doctors and lawyers in the few small towns. It was a society at once poor, simple, and with few class distinctions. In such a society a constitution which relied on an aristocratic element for its functioning was in fact irrelevant. As Papineau protested, the United Kingdom had applied "the aristocratic principle in full force and vigour in the Canadas, the social structure of which was essentially democratic, when everyone without exception lives and dies a democrat; because every one owns property; because no one is more than a small property-owner." Alexis de Tocqueville could not have been more perceptive, and the statement is the stronger from the fact that Papineau was himself a seigneur.

The social and economic equality of colonial society was reflected in the colonial electorate. In all the colonies the property qualification for the franchise was low; it had to be, or there would have been few voters. There was no property qualification for members of the assembly. Thus the number of voters was large, too large to be affected by such influence or patronage as a colonial governor possessed. It was only by a wide diffusion of petty patronage, such as expenditures on roads and bridges, that the electorate could be reached, and these the assemblies – except in Lower Canada where such expenditures were few and their use as patronage was rendered unnecessary by the national cohesion of the French – jealously and pertinaciously kept within their own control, to the bafflement and frustration of the governors and the oligarchies.

The actual functioning of the constitution in Lower Canada, then, had been reduced to a deadlock because the assembly could not affect the administration of government and the governor could influence neither the assembly nor the electorate – unless, like Prevost, he was prepared to speak French and admit Canadians to office; and those gestures were only palliative, with no lasting effect. The popular party of Lower Canada, with an exception to be noted later, had accepted the constitution as it stood, and insisted on the assembly's independence of the governor. They had repelled Dalhousie's advances, refused to allow him to exercise influence, and reproached the few Canadians who were offered and accepted office. To be of "*les gens en place*" had come to be regarded not as a coveted honour but as a betrayal of a cause. This intransigence of the Canadians was of course a response to the intransigence of the English in the councils, but both served to exaggerate the institutional gulf between the council and the assembly and to bring out the inherent defects and social irrelevance of the constitution.

In Upper Canada, although the constitution was identical with that of Lower Canada, and the social order much the same, the governor and councils were able to keep the oligarchic ascendancy on a more popular basis. The British American composition of the population and the province's history accounted for this. The ease with which charges of disloyalty, sedition, or being alien, could be used, enabled the governor and oligarchy to employ the influence and authority of government to suppress criticism and even to expel critics.

It was not therefore altogether the defects of the constitution or its failure to correspond with the social facts of the colony that made for disharmony between the executive government and the popular assembly in Upper Canada. The same issues there, such as control of supply, did not lead to the exasperation and deadlock that they caused in Lower Canada, and it might well have proved possible, as the Select Committee of 1828 hoped, to make the constitution of the province reasonably responsive to popular opinion for some time, once certain adjustments had been made and civil governors of some parliamentary experience and tact had replaced the post-Waterloo soldier governors.

It was not so much the constitution of the state as the principle of church establishment that provoked a general and sustained opposition to the "constitution in church and state" in Upper Canada. Even a limited establishment, with freedom of conscience and worship, was contrary to the religious principles and the social ideals of the great majority of the population, including some members of the churches of England and Scotland. The Reformation ideal of the Christian state had given way to the principle of the complete separation of church and state. An establishment was regarded as religious discrimination and social pretension; nor did toleration help, for in such a society as had come into being in Upper Canada, mere toleration would not be tolerated. All churches, like all men, were to be free and equal.

Some fundamental changes, then, were necessary in the constitution of 1791 in the Canadas. Although the issues were not so starkly drawn in the Atlantic colonies, they existed there also, in Nova Scotia and Prince Edward Island. In New Brunswick the conflict of governor and assembly, by contrast, was lacking. Except for the internal struggle with Thomas Baillie, the structure of the constitution coincided well with the social and economic order of that province, dominated as it was by the timber trade and with its proletariat leaderless and politically indifferent. In all three provinces, however, any constitutional adjustments would have to be preceded by the separation, in personnel and function, of the executive and legislative councils. Until that was done, none of the colonies would be abreast of the constitutional development of the Canadas or possess a constitution the same in outline as that of the United Kingdom. In Newfoundland the development of a fully elective assembly, as well as of separate councils, had yet to take place.

By the opening of the decade of the 1830's, however, there could be no doubt that the government of all the colonies would have to become more popular and that the changes necessary to this development would have to take place. The flame of colonial democracy, beginning to burn in Nova Scotia and Upper Canada and already blazing in Lower Canada by 1828, was thereafter, despite the relaxation brought about by the recommendations of the Select Committee, to be fanned by the July Revolution of 1830 in France and the struggle over the Reform Bill in England in 1831 and 1832. The post-Waterloo period had ended and the age of reform had begun. The ideas of nationalism and democracy in Europe, suppressed in 1815 and 1820, were traversing the continent again. As the excitement spread to the Netherlands and Poland, it spread to British North America also. In the United Kingdom the Whigs and liberal Tories came to power under Earl Grey and great expectation sprang up of liberal reform in colonial as well as domestic government.

The Whig government did indeed try to meet these expectations, but with the same reservations and lack of imagination as were to characterize their decade of domestic reform. The rapid succession of Colonial Secretaries up to 1835 did nothing to improve their grasp of colonial matters, although this disadvantage was greatly offset by the ability and clarity of purpose of the permanent official, James Stephen. The true colonial reformers were the Radicals, who gave the government intermittent support but none of whom was in the Cabinet. These Radicals ranged all the way from men such as Joseph Hume, Sir William Molesworth, and Arthur Roebuck who, as followers of the utilitarian philosopher Jeremy Bentham, advocated the emancipation of the colonies, to those who believed that the colonies might be given a large measure of self-government within a liberal Empire. Of the latter, the young and brilliant Charles Buller was to be the chief, and his ideas were shared by Lord Durham, a member of the Cabinet but wholly concerned with the Reform Bill, and Lord Howick, the son of Earl Grey, not yet a member of the Cabinet. Thus the colonial democrats had allies in Parliament but no effective spokesman in the government during the period of Whig reform.

The result of this situation was that although the Whigs wished to improve the working of the colonial constitutions they had no new idea with which to approach their task. Their remedies were those of the Select Committee of 1828 as sharpened and defined by James Stephen: the surrendering of control of Crown revenues to the assemblies in return for a civil list; the separation of the councils in the Atlantic provinces; the appointment of civilian and conciliatory governors; and a sustained attempt to establish harmony between the executive and the assembly. Without any change in the constitutions the last could only mean, of course, a deliberate use of the influence and patronage of government to win elections and control the assemblies. In short, the Whig purpose was not to change the colonial constitutions but to make them work by a liberal spirit favourable to the popular parties in the colonies. The Whigs were disposed to look sympathetically at the constitutional difficulties of the British American colonies and to see, with the eyes of practical parliamentarians, in what respects the operation of the colonial constitutions differed from that of the imperial parliament. From there it was but a step to the carrying out of a series of reforms which would bring the functioning of the colonial governments to correspond more closely with that of the United Kingdom. The effect of these piecemeal adjustments of the colonial constitutions would be to convert them from the old colonial model as modified after 1783 to something resembling the British parliamentary system before 1830.

The first and chief of such adjustments was that concerning the control of Crown revenues, which by an Act passed in 1831 was given to the assemblies on condition that a civil list be voted to pay official salaries without further vote during the lifetime of the king. An additional proposal was that money should be voted by the assemblies only on the recommendation of the governor and never on the motion of a member of the assembly. This would have made possible the introduction of the British system of an annual budget for the expenses of

238 THE KINGDOM OF CANADA

the public services. Another and quite different measure was the proposal to separate the executive and legislative councils in the Atlantic provinces, and to separate their membership in the Canadas, with the exclusion of the judges from both. In two of these measures the Whigs had some success: Upper Canada in 1831 and New Brunswick in 1837 voted a permanent civil list, and three Atlantic provinces at last saw their councils separated – New Brunswick in 1832, Nova Scotia in 1837, and Prince Edward Island in 1839 – while the separation of the personnel began in the Canadas. Newfoundland had not yet reached the stage of constitutional development in which these refinements were necessary.

That, however, was the extent of Whig success. In Lower Canada matters quickly returned to the old lack of harmony after the initial success of Sir James Kempt's conciliatory policy. Papineau, embittered by Dalhousie's treatment of him – despite Dalhousie's recall – and disillusioned by the Select Committee's insistence on a permanent civil list, began to abandon his admiration for British institutions and to take American radical democracy as his ideal. The Whig proposal of a surrender of Crown and statutory revenues in return for a permanent civil list completed his disillusionment, for this was the new government urging the old policy. The killing of Canadians by the troops in an election riot in 1832 caused further bitterness and led to the refusal of the Lower Canadian Assembly in 1833 to vote supplies at all. As it persisted in this refusal in the next three years, the deadlock was renewed and intensified.

Thus the effect of the measures proposed by the Whigs was only to increase, especially in Lower Canada, that division between the assembly and the executive which was the fundamental characteristic of colonial government in British America. The colonial constitutions were based on the divided powers of independent elements: the assembly, the legislative council, and the governor and executive council. In the old colonies the assemblies had dominated the weak councils and the harassed governors who were largely dependent on the assemblies for supply. In the United Kingdom the development of the cabinet system had of course ensured that the Crown and Parliament would work in harmony. But in the post-revolutionary colonies all elements were actually independent to a great degree. The result could be, and in Lower Canada after 1833 it was, a partial or complete deadlock in the making of laws and the voting of supply. To strengthen the assemblies by giving them the power of appropriation, while making the legislative council independent of the governor and giving the governor, the judges, and the civil servants security of tenure by means of a civil list, was only to intensify the deadlock in provinces such as the Canadas and Nova Scotia, where the division between the assembly and the executive coincided with class or national or denominational divisions. Only where the dominant economic interest in the colony dominated the assembly also, as in New Brunswick, were the Whig proposals to prove effective.

In consequence, the democratic movements of the Canadas went ahead to formulate their own proposals of constitutional reform. In Lower Canada, Papineau's party, then at the summit of its power with nearly all the Canadian middle class and habitants, the Catholic Irish with their rapidly growing numbers, and radical democrats from the Eastern Townships in its ranks, embodied their grievances and their proposals for reform in the Ninety-two Resolutions which were approved by the Assembly in 1834. The Resolutions were a prolonged and verbose complaint against the imposition of an oligarchical constitution on a democratic society, an English oligarchy on a French democracy. But the only constitutional change it urged was that the legislative council should be made elective.

The democratic surge of Lower Canada was matched in Upper Canada. In 1834 Mackenzie, backed by the Reform majority elected in that year, presented a Seventh Report on Grievances. Like the Ninety-two Resolutions, the Seventh Report was an extensive criticism of the prevailing system of government. It provoked Joseph Hume to write that the colonies should be freed from the "baneful domination of the Mother country," but like the Resolutions it proposed one central constitutional remedy, that the legislative council be made elective, although it urged also that the executive council be made "responsible."

This seeming lack of fertility in the Canadian democrats is at first sight surprising. Men so prolific in grievances might have been expected to be more productive of remedies. The fact is, however, that the elective Legislative Council, in itself a considerable reform, was only the fraction of the iceberg that showed above the surface. The democrats had a full political program in mind. It was the application of the elective principle to all offices, including that of governor; it was the "elective system" of Papineau. They were, in tendency at least, republican democrats who might aspire not only to establish democratic government in the Canadas but also to win independence. But they did not present their whole program at once because they would have been content with less for the time being, because they had not yet despaired of aid from a liberal Imperial Government, and because they were not sure that independence was possible without annexation to the United States, or, in Lower Canada, that annexation in any case was desirable. In this uncertainty they asked for no more than was possible within the existing colonial constitution, the election of the members of the second chamber of the legislature.

That this was the radical democratic position is revealed by Mackenzie's curt dismissal of another proposal in 1834, that of "responsible government." He understood it clearly and fully; he thought it essentially aristocratic and conservative, and judged it to be quite inadequate to the needs of the Canadas. Only an elective, congressional system would satisfy the demands of popular sovereignty, and allow the people to drive the oligarchs from their places of power and profit and institute an economical and democratic system of government in which the interests of the habitant, the small farmer and the working man would be considered as well as those of the merchants, lawyers and bankers.

For the Reformers were attacking an economic and social system as well as a constitution. Papineau and his radicals were striking at the English bureaucrats, land speculators, seigneurs, mortgage-holders and bankers in their assault on the legislative council. Mackenzie and the more radical reformers of Upper Canada had a social and economic program which would have eliminated the land speculator, reduced the power of banks and the Canada Company, and made the agrarian democracy supreme over the local compacts – the outposts of the "Family Compact" of Toronto, as Mackenzie termed it in a too well-remembered epithet. In Canada, as in the United Kingdom and the United States, the democratic program aimed at the creation of a new social order of free and equal men, not merely at a new constitution.

It must be recognized that the British North American colonies did have three clear choices of constitutional development in 1834. One, that of the Family Compact, was to maintain the existing constitution with its checks and balances and permanent councils. A second, that of the more radical Reformers, was to remodel the colonial constitutions on the pattern of the new state constitutions over the border. (There was not necessarily in this view any desire for annexation to the United States.) The third was to make the existing constitution work on British parliamentary lines.

The second was that most actively canvassed. To have made the Legislative Council elective would practically have made the constitution like that of an American state, even without an elective governor. Moreover, it would have been a relatively slight change, since the Canadian legislatures in many important respects functioned as the old colonial assemblies had, or as the American state legislatures did. The assemblies practically possessed the financial initiative, for example, and any member could propose a money bill; there was thus no government control of expenditure through a budget. The assemblies worked extensively through committees upon which they bestowed executive powers such as supervision of road-building and the disbursement of public funds, including the reimbursement of their own members for the services rendered. They had thus assumed major executive functions and distributed their own patronage to a degree which made their attacks on the oligarchies not so much crusades of the poor and righteous as aggressions of equals and rivals. The Speaker of such an assembly was not a mere chairman, but a House leader, almost a tribune of the people, opposed to the senators and the consul of the colonial republic. In a constitution so organized, the radical democrat was inevitably disposed simply to complete the work of constitutional organization by perfecting the separation of powers and by providing for a second chamber responsive like the first to public opinion, even if through a differently constituted electorate. Such changes constituted a simple, obvious, and entirely democratic program.

The real objections to the program were not so much constitutional – all the proposals might have been combined with responsible government – as they were traditional and national. The radical changes were more in the American congressional than in the British parliamentary tradition. And every one who critically contemplated the program concluded that it implied independence and assumed, no doubt correctly, that independence would mean annexation. (The free soil of Canada might by 1845 have nicely balanced the slave soil of Texas.)

The radical democratic program therefore opposed to the constitution of the colonial oligarchy a program of reform which seemed to bend the development of the colonial constitution towards republicanism and annexation. But such a course was unwelcome to those of loyalist stock, to the majority of the new British immigrants, and to the clergy and the political conservatives and moderates of French Canada. After 1834, Papineau's hold on the representatives of the Quebec district of Lower Canada weakened and slipped; he was left with the radicals of the Montreal district and the Richelieu Valley. And in Nova Scotia and Upper Canada the great majority of the people supported neither the oligarchs nor the democrats. Reforms many of them desired, often democratic reforms, but they wished to achieve them by British methods and within the British connection. The development of what it had become customary by 1834 to call "responsible government" is not properly to be grasped unless it is first understood that it was a proposal essentially traditional and progressive which could be supported by moderate men whether of liberal or conservative persuasion.

The idea of responsible government was widely known, if not clearly understood, among politicians in British North America by 1834. Yet it was first clearly enunciated in its final form of colonial cabinet government as late as 1828 by Dr W. W. Baldwin, father of Robert Baldwin. In that year the elder Baldwin wrote the Duke of Wellington as Prime Minister, urging adoption of the principle of "the presence of a Provincial Ministry, if I may be allowed to use the term, responsible to the Provincial Parliament, and removable from office by His Majesty's representative at his pleasure and especially when they lose the confidence of the people as expressed by the voice of their representatives in the Assembly; and that all acts of the King's representative should have the character of local responsibility, by the signature of some member of this Ministry."

This, perhaps the most pregnant sentence in Canadian political history, was written by a moderate Reformer. So also was a similar but more extended plan of "responsible government," which it was claimed was written about 1811, perhaps by a member of the Baldwin circle, and which was published anonymously in the *Upper Canadian Herald* in 1829. In 1829 John Neilson, of Lower Canada, an advanced Reformer, called for the "accountability" of ministers. And in 1830 Ogle R. Gowan, a Tory and an Orangeman, seems to have published a pamphlet calling for "responsible government" as necessary to make the Constitutional

Act of 1791 work as the British constitution did. Thus even before the functioning of cabinet government had been openly and formally recognized in the United Kingdom, both Reformer and Tory writers, of whom two were Anglo-Irish and all were opponents of the narrow and nativist Family Compact, had clearly defined it in Upper Canada, and one, Baldwin, had suggested how it might be used in a colony.

Responsible government had, of course, origins much more remote. It originated as the constitutional principle that some one of his ministers should be responsible for every public act of the king. The process for enforcement of responsibility was impeachment. This was all that was meant by Grattan and other Irish statesmen who talked of the "responsibility" or "accountability" of Irish ministers to the Irish parliament after it had achieved legislative independence in 1782, and by the Earl of Mornington, writing on Irish affairs in 1793. Another Irish statesman, Lord Castlereagh, had even advanced the final principle of the joint responsibility of ministers in debate in the House of Commons in 1806, a debate that almost certainly was noted in Canada. It was this kind of responsibility that the Assembly of Lower Canada had debated in 1808 and to which a writer in *Le Canadien* had referred in 1809. So it may be that Ireland gave to Upper Canada the idea which those Anglo-Irish Canadians the Baldwins, father and son, were to inject into the constitutional development of British North America; but Lower Canadians also, following their own political genius, had advanced from the position of 1809 to Etienne Parent's statement of 1833, in which he spoke with simple lucidity of "the formation of a provincial ministry, on the model of the Imperial ministry, which might give unity, coherence, consistency and finish to our legislation."

In itself, the idea of Baldwin and Parent had all the simplicity of genius. It would bring the discordant executives and assemblies into harmony by an established and constitutional process. But there were many obstacles in the way of realization. Like elective institutions, responsible government seemed to point to colonial independence, and although Baldwin had proposed the answer to that objection – that responsible government should operate only in local affairs – the instant reaction of British statesmen was that cabinet government was incompatible with colonial dependence. If granted, it would, in their view, make a colony wholly self-governing, since responsibility could not be divided. Moreover, no cabinet, or ministry, existed in the colonies. The executive councils were composed partly of non-political officials, partly of political advisers. None of these needed to be a member of the assembly or the legislative council, and the assumption on all sides was that none could be a member of the assembly or, after the separation of the councils, of the legislative council. Until the political advisers were made political heads of departments also, and the non-political officials civil servants, and the convention adopted that all ministers must be members of the legislature, responsible government as cabinet government could not be applied in British North America. This state of affairs was a genuine impediment it took many years to clear away completely. Before there could be a colonial cabinet government there had to be colonial departments of government under political ministers.

These two proposals for reform, an elective Legislative Council, or a responsible cabinet, dominated the years 1834 to 1837. But it was the pressure exerted by the stoppage of supplies in Lower Canada that prompted the Whig secretary of the colonies, Lord Glenelg, to replace the unpopular governor, Lord Aylmer, for whose impeachment the Ninety-two Resolutions had called, with Lord Gosford, and to make Gosford head of a royal commission to inquire into the difficulties of government in Lower Canada. Gosford was a typical colonial appointee, well-intentioned and incapable, of the weak and troubled Melbourne ministry. At the same time an eccentric adventurer, Sir Francis Bond Head, who had fortuitously acquired a somewhat spurious reputation as a reformer, was sent to replace Sir John Colborne in Upper Canada. Both governors were instructed to attempt to obtain harmony between the legislature and the executive. The intention was to free the governor from the control of his councils and to strengthen his authority by enabling him to win popular support in the assembly. Gosford, however, did not publish this part of his instructions, while Head published his in full. The result was to create distrust of Gosford's intentions among the now excitable Patriotes, as the followers of Papineau were beginning to be called. As they became aware of the increasing disapproval of the Catholic hierarchy and the subtle withdrawal of support by the moderates of the Quebec region, Papineau's followers, while decreasing in numbers, became more extreme.

The work of the Gosford Commission was thus prejudiced from the first. Nor did it find a solution for the problems vexing the province. The Commissioners were bound by their instructions not to recommend either an elective Legislative Council or the responsible government the Assembly now demanded as well. Papineau and his followers were actively boycotting the buying of British goods and becoming more outspokenly republican. The English elements began to draw together in defence. Supply remained unvoted and the government was carried on by officials paid out of army funds. Gosford failed to break what had become a constitutional deadlock in Lower Canada.

In Upper Canada events pursued a very different course. Head was determined to obey his instructions and to live up to his reputation as a reformer. He therefore invited two known Reformers, the sober and cautious Robert Baldwin and Dr John Rolph, to enter the Executive Council. Baldwin received the invitation with misgivings, as he had stated his desire to see responsible government introduced and was aware that Head did not mean to grant it. But Baldwin entered the council on the understanding that he was free to urge his views on his colleagues. He did so effectively. When a dispute arose between the

KC-I

impetuous governor and his council over the extent to which he was obliged to seek their advice in matters of patronage, all six members, including four reckoned as Tories, resigned on the ground that they could not be responsible for acts on which they were not consulted. This was responsible government in an older and more elementary meaning than Baldwin had in mind. It was none the less responsible, if not cabinet, government, and was significant of the fact that all shades of opinion, Tory as well as Reformer, except the Compact bureaucrats and the radical democrats, had accepted in some measure the idea that the government of the colony must be accountable to the legislature of the colony, always saving the British connection. For by now Baldwin could submit to the Colonial Secretary, Lord Glenelg, a memorandum in which his concept of responsible government was put with perfect clarity: it was "having the provincial Government, as far as regards the internal affairs of the Province, conducted by the Lieutenant-Governor (as representative of the Paramount Authority of the Mother country) with the advice and assistance of the Executive Council acting as a Provincial Cabinet, and composed of men possessed of the public confidence, whose opinions and policy would be in harmony with the opinions and policy of the Representatives of the People."

Head himself subscribed to the general doctrine of responsibility in his own eccentric way. He was, he said, responsible to the Colonial Office. And this stand, he predicted, the electors of Upper Canada would support. He proved his point by dissolving the Assembly, by using his patronage and the fear of American republicanism and annexation ruthlessly, and by fighting the ensuing election in person. Ryerson, alarmed by the radical and republican tone of the extreme Reformers, threw the powerful support of the *Christian Guardian* to the Governor. The old loyalist elements and the new British immigrants, the members of the Catholic Church and the Loyal Orange Order voted for the Governor. It was a mortifying defeat for the Reformers, yet Head's precipitate recourse to Tory democracy conceded to a degree the Reformers' claim, as Baldwin noted. But the defeat threw the leadership of the reform movement into the hands of the extremists – Mackenzie and the agrarian radicals – who opposed the real-estate speculators, the banks and merchants, the economic compacts of Toronto and the lake-front towns. The same deadlock seemed to have been reached in Upper Canada as in Lower Canada. The radicals in both provinces were soon discussing together plans for a rebellion in 1837. Constitutional agitation seemed to them to have failed.

While the politics of the Canadas moved towards deadlock, exasperation, and violence, Nova Scotia was entering on a contentious but dignified constitutional debate. Joseph Howe stood out as an eloquent leader in the nascent democracy of the colony. Of loyalist stock, a man self-educated but with a native genius for the compelling word and vivid gesture, Howe was a passionate Nova Scotian and a fervid Briton. In his hands, the colonial democracy could never incur a charge of disloyalty, of republicanism, or of doctrinaire impracticability. In 1837 he persuaded the Assembly to pass a resolution calling for an elective Legislative Council "or such other reconstruction of the local government as will ensure responsibility to the Commons." The cause of reform in the senior Atlantic province now had a champion and a goal. The other provinces were stirred by the issue, even the new assembly of Newfoundland requesting a responsible system in 1838; but none had developed or adopted the clear-cut Baldwinian formula.

In New Brunswick, indeed, responsible government was to win its only influential advocate in the young Lemuel Allan Wilmot; to other politicians of the St. John valley and the North Shore it seemed only to threaten the Assembly's control of provincial and local affairs without ensuring them control of the one thing of major interest, the timber lands of the Crown. When in 1837 they succeeded in procuring Baillie's dismissal and in exchanging a civil list for control of Crown lands, they had achieved their goal and thereafter regarded responsible government with suspicion and even hostility.

Early in the same year, the imperial government took the Canadian question out of the hands of Gosford. It proposed to deal with the situation by appointing the legislative council from all interests in the province and the executive council from both the assembly and the legislative council. This, with a distribution of provincial patronage among all elements, would, it was hoped, restore harmony to the working of the provincial constitution. These proposals were embodied by Lord John Russell in his Ten Resolutions, laid before the House of Commons in March 1837. In the Resolutions, however, the authority of the imperial parliament was also invoked to break the financial impasse, and the colonial executive was empowered to override the assembly and to make provision for the supply denied since 1833. Thus the local democracy was, on this issue, to be overridden by the imperial parliament; and it would have been, had Russell not altered the offending Resolution.

The threat, however, was sufficient to provoke an outbreak, and the political crisis came quickly to a head. It was intensified by the severe commercial crisis of 1837, and by the total failure of wheat farming in the overpopulated Montreal and Richelieu Valley districts. Now, though French settlement in unoccupied parts of the Townships had begun, a heavy price was to be paid for the policy of exclusion attempted by the Château clique, for it was this policy that led to the rebellious outburst of the swarming seigniorial lands and the beginning, after the Rebellion, of French emigration to New England. The English merchants were in distress, the Canadian farmers were in despair. The press of both languages began to use a tone of increasing menace, and Lower Canada began to break up into its discordant parts. The French divided into the more conservative parishes of the Quebec region and the lower river, and the more excitable parishes – more so because more economically distressed, and more irritated by contact with the English – of the Richelieu and Montreal regions. The English of the Townships tended to draw back into their hills as the politics of the lowlands moved towards violence. The English of Montreal, both the supporters of the English party and the moderates, organized against the Patriotes, and became more and more conscious of their position as a minority ascendancy in the midst of an angry and mutinous majority. The Catholic Irish kept to themselves. Throughout the summer of 1837 the situation became steadily more revolutionary.

The idea of revolution had been implanted in Papineau's following as early as the July Revolution of 1830 in France. The revolutionary temper had grown markedly after 1834 and swiftly since 1836. Since the former date a Permanent Central Committee had guided the radical wing of the democratic party. It had started and extended non-importation, non-consumption agreements directed against British goods. Following faithfully the American antecedents, it had organized committees of correspondence to direct the movement and take over the government. A society called Les Fils de la Liberté completed the reproduction of the American model in August 1837. Papineau had continued to lead the Patriotes while still preserving his hold on thousands of professional people, rural merchants, and Canadian farmers who were essentially moderate. He was not as radical a democrat as the English Wolfred Nelson or T. S. Brown, or the Canadian André Ouimet, or Dr. Cyrille Côté. He was more a nationalist than a republican democrat and sought rather the emancipation of the Canadians than the creation of a republic. Papineau nevertheless struggled to hold the leadership and maintain the unity of the party he had led so long, but more extreme men were taking it further and faster than he wished. Thus he presided at the meeting at St. Charles in October at which revolutionary resolutions were adopted by the representatives of six counties which in effect made them a republic. The Patriotes were withdrawing the government of the province from the authorities, and Papineau had to go along with them or lose his position as leader.

As the crisis developed, the Roman Catholic hierarchy's growing distrust of the democratic and revolutionary tendencies of the Patriotes became open and outspoken opposition. The bishops of Quebec, Montreal and Trois Rivières urged their people to remember their duty to obey the constituted authorities. Their exhortations had widespread effect, and they marked the first definite breach between the church and the democratic nationalism of the Patriotes. The Patriotes of course were angered at what they considered this clerical interference in politics, and not all the clergy agreed with, or even obeyed, the bishops. For the next half-century clericalism and anti-clericalism were to disturb the politics of Lower Canada.

Gosford, advised by the veteran soldier, Sir John Colborne, concentrated at Montreal all the troops in Canada except the Quebec garrison and waited for an overt move by the Patriotes. The English of the bureaucratic party were not so restrained. They had organized a Constitutional Society and the more violent were enthusiastic members of the Doric Club whose members clashed in the streets of Montreal with the Fils de la Liberté. Montreal, a turbulent and riotous city always, half Paris, half Belfast, was in one of the most violent periods of its history. And the English extremists were daily inflamed by the anti-French philippics of Adam Thom, a Scots lawyer, who urged the need to keep Canada English even at the cost of its ceasing to be British. The government would have no part in such extremes, but insisted on giving no provocation and on allowing the rebels to reveal the extent and measure of their designs. The Constitutional Society was suppressed. Then, when fighting between the Doric Club and the Fils de la Liberté began, the government decided to arrest the leaders of the Fils. Papineau fled from Montreal on November 13, and the first ill-prepared risings followed.

The authorities were ready. The regular troops moved out into the areas of revolt. The volatile, mutinous French section of Montreal was held quiet. The English militia aided the regulars and gave a fiercer temper to the work of repression. The expeditions sent out to break up the assemblies on the Richelieu met some resistance at St. Denis and St. Charles, but quickly broke it. In the Deux Montagnes country north of Montreal, there was a savage slaughter of rebels at St. Eustache. The risings were not organized or co-ordinated. There was no effective military command. Most of the political leaders, including Papineau, had fled over the border in the first days of the fighting and left their followers to fly or surrender. The soldiers under Sir John Colborne had crushed a desperate rising which had failed to organize-the genuinely revolutionary situation in the Montreal and Richelieu parishes.

In Upper Canada the discontent was sporadic and individual. The freedom-loving blacksmiths who hammered out pikeheads were few and pathetic. Angered as the Reformers had been by Head's electoral victory, and distressed as business men and farmers were by the economic crisis of 1837, only Mackenzie was active in organizing revolt. In view of the thoroughness of the Reformers' political organization before 1837, this was both surprising and revealing. Only some rural townships seemed disposed to combine for revolutionary action; the great body of Reformers and all the leaders remained quiet. There were some meetings and musterings "beyond the ridges" north of Toronto, but no systematic political or military arrangements had been made when it was learned that the revolt had broken out in Lower Canada. Yet the situation in Upper Canada was tempting. Toronto seemed to be an easy prey for a resolute rebel band to seize. Head had insisted on sending all the regular troops to Montreal, confident, and rightly as it proved, that the militia would deal with any rising. The rebels accordingly rose, as they had agreed with their Lower Canadian fellows to do.

On December 7, Mackenzie led an ill-organized but daring attempt to capture the exposed capital and its arsenal. He was defeated at Montgomery's Tavern on Yonge Street by an equally ill-organized militia and fled for the American border. There was no rising anywhere else in the province, despite the economic distress and political discontent. The government and the loyal militia dominated the situation easily and at once.

Such were the rebellions of 1837. Their repercussions did not end with that year, for their effect was far beyond the force the rebels had commanded. Fumbling, feeble and foredoomed as the rebellions were, they had demonstrated that the colonial constitutions of the old colonial model were no longer workable. Canadian democracy and French nationalism had broken the mould of the oligarchic ascendancy.

In Lower Canada the constitution had in fact collapsed and was soon to be suspended by the imperial parliament. In Upper Canada, it is true, the constitution had been triumphantly sustained. But to the imperial government French Canada was Canada, and the collapse of the system of 1791 in Lower Canada meant that a revision of that system had to be considered for both the Canadas and indeed for all the British North American colonies.

If the rebellions destroyed the old oligarchic ascendancy, they of course did nothing to indicate what might take its place. The outcome of the conflicts was at first a purely negative suppression. In Lower Canada the gaols were filled with Patriotes under arrest; scores had fled across the border; other scores hid out in the sugaring huts and loggers' shanties in the bush. In Upper Canada, Mackenzie escaped across the Niagara River and formed a centre of resistance on the Canadian soil of Navy Island. There he defied the militia under Lieutenant-Colonel Allan MacNab of Hamilton, while supplies reached him from the American shore in the S.S. *Caroline*. But the dashing MacNab, and the no less daring Head, were not men to suffer a defiance of this kind. A party under Commodore Andrew Drew cut out the *Caroline* and towed her away in flames to sink in the Niagara.

The aftermath of the rebellions thus had an international as well as a domestic aspect. While the courts of Upper Canada tried two of Mackenzie's lieutenants, Peter Matthews and Samuel Lount, for high treason; while these two honest and misguided men swung for treason in the spring of 1838; while something like a Tory terror spread around Toronto and in the London district, where a rising had just failed to break out; and while Reformers and plain democrats began to plan to move to the United States, the refugees were being acclaimed as heroes in Buffalo and Detroit, and aid was being organized by the democrats, the Irish, and the lawless. Soon the Hunters' Lodges were formed to liberate Canada from British tyranny, and the slack laws and not too friendly governments of the United States at first did little to stop these threats to the peace of Canada. The Canadian militia had therefore to remain on the alert during the summer of 1838. As the British of Lower Canada exulted at having beaten the

French into submission, the Tory temper of Upper Canada rode triumphant over republican treason unmasked and American aggression repelled. It was a stern, an ugly and a sterile temper in both provinces.

Fortunately, a better tone prevailed in the imperial government. Melbourne and Glenelg realized that they must insist on reform in Canada and might use the rebellions to hasten its coming. Gosford was recalled, and Head's resignation accepted, to make room for the appointment of a politician of the first rank with full powers to govern, to report, and to recommend a new form of government for the Canadas.

The man nominated, John George Lambton, Earl of Durham, was not altogether happily chosen, nor was he selected solely in the hope that he might find an answer to "the Canadian question." Proud, quick-tempered, difficult, and the hope of the British Radicals as a future prime minister, Durham was chosen by his distrustful colleagues not only because he might end the Canadian troubles but also because, if he failed, the Canadian question which had broken so many governors might damage Durham's career also.

This vain, sulky and egocentric man, bearing the fate of the Melbourne government on his shoulders, was sent out with unprecedented powers as High Commissioner and Governor-in-Chief of British North America. He reached Quebec at the end of May, 1838. At once he struck a new note in the conduct of public affairs in Canada. His bearing was regal, his retinue lordly, and he held court in a fashion never seen in Quebec before, not even in the days of Frontenac. Durham put government in Canada on a new footing. It was to be neither military routine nor civilian humdrum as in the past; he made it stately, stirring and dynamic, and the impulse was never quite to fade during the remainder of the century.

Nor did his new approach end there. He also did what no Canadian governor had done since the days of the first Vaudreuil: he opened direct communications with the great power to the south, not with the government directly, but through the British minister at Washington. For Durham saw not only that rebellion in Canada invited American intervention, but that to avert that intervention it must be made clear to the government and people of the United States that the imperial government meant to deal with rebellion and its consequences and would emphatically repel invasion and repress border incidents. He also saw that a discontented and backward British America could not long be kept from seeking union with a progressive and prosperous neighbour. Firmness, friendliness, and the intent to reform Canadian institutions must therefore be shown to Canadians and Americans alike. In that spirit, while on tour in Upper Canada later in the summer, he crossed the Niagara River into Lewiston and with Lady Durham moved freely through a curious and friendly crowd. He was certain, and in this he was to be backed by the imperial Foreign Secretaries of the next decade, Palmerston and Aberdeen, that good relations with the United States were necessary if the Canadian question was to be resolved.

At his seat of government in Quebec, Durham faced two tasks. One was to govern Lower Canada. The other was to organize the inquiry he had been commissioned to make into the government of the Canadas and other North American colonies. As it turned out, he had only five months in which to attempt both these major tasks; his term was cut short because of the circumstances of his mission and his handling of the government of Lower Canada. Not only had Durham left a critical Prime Minister and Cabinet behind him; the Tories were prepared to use his mission as an occasion to bring the tottering government down, and his old colleague, the eccentric and egotistical Lord Brougham, was watching for an opportunity to discredit him. Durham with his usual arrogant carelessness had given the Tories grounds for criticism in choosing as members of his personal staff two men with unusual abilities but dubious pasts, Thomas Turton and Edward Gibbon Wakefield. The latter was a gifted writer on colonial subjects and had elaborated a theory of colonial land settlement. Both proved useful but Durham might have found equally able men with records less open to carping, as he did in another member of his staff, the brilliant Charles Buller. The result was that Melbourne, harassed by Tory criticism of Durham's retinue, had made ready to sacrifice Durham if need be, rather than suffer defeat.

In the government of Quebec, Durham began well by honourably dismissing the council which had governed the colony under Sir John Colborne since the suspension of the constitution of 1791 by the imperial parliament. He then appointed five members of his own staff to his council and so avoided making commitments to either the English or the French.

But his first major problem was to dispose of the political prisoners held since December. It was impossible to try them, for no French jury would convict. Durham dealt with the matter by obtaining confessions of guilt from nine of the chief prisoners. These he then banished to Bermuda, over which he had no authority, and granted an amnesty to all the rest. This measure was well accepted by both sides in Canada. He followed it up by proclaiming, though he had not the power to do so, that Papineau and the other chiefs of the rebellion were to be permanent exiles, forbidden to return to Canada on pain of death.

This disposition of the punishment of the rebels was dramatic, dictatorial, and effective; the French-Canadian public was pleased and relieved that there was to be no extended proscription. But it was not in accord with British law or the terms of his commission and instructions. In the Lords the savage Brougham pounced, and the Tories took up the cry. The Whig cabinet under the attack declined either to repair the defect in the ordinance of banishment or to approve the proclamation. Durham felt his position had become impossible, and resigned. He reached England in December 1838.

While Durham was on the sea, a second rising, planned in the United States and aimed at the "liberation of Canada," flared along the border. The invaders proclaimed a Canadian republic in Lower Canada, but few joined them and they were quickly driven over the border. In Upper Canada a party under Nils Von Schoultz, a Polish exile, was captured at Prescott on the St. Lawrence. From Detroit another band crossed into Canada, only to be scattered by the militia and to have four of their number shot out of hand on the orders of Colonel John Prince. Durham's resignation had seemed to indicate that the imperial government was after all paltering with the Canadian question and that an attempt to liberate the Canadas might succeed. But the ready and successful defence meant that there was to be no republic of Canada on the St. Lawrence. There was, on the contrary, to be a fundamental reform of the colonial constitution, for Durham was to accomplish in his Report what he had failed to do in his government of British North America.

ADDITIONAL READING

CLARK, S. D. *Movements of Political Protest in Canada, 1640-1840.*
CREIGHTON, D. G. *The Empire of the St. Lawrence.*
KILBOURN, W. *The Firebrand.*
LOWER, A. R. M. *Canadians in the Making.*
MARTIN, CHESTER *Empire and Commonwealth.*
NEW, C. W. *Lord Durham.*
WADE, MASON *The French Canadians, 1760-1945.*
WILSON, G. E. *The Life of Robert Baldwin.*

CHAPTER 14

The Definition of Responsible Government

1839-1846

While the Lower Canadian militia and the hard-drilled regulars still tramped the snowy roads of the border counties in December of 1838, Durham was closeted in London with his advisers. Together they were completing the report that was to crown his brief and stormy mission and, they hoped, retrieve his reputation from the effects of Brougham's invective and Melbourne's cold-hearted sacrifice. The result of their labours was the famous Durham's Report which has always been considered the principal outcome of the rebellions and the beginning of a new era in the history of Canada and the Empire.

That a report of such significance should have been produced in five months is to be explained by several factors. One was the ability and originality of Durham's staff. Another was the nature of the views with which Durham came to Canada. But it was due above all to the fact that he found in Canada two men each of whom held a clear and trenchant idea about colonial government. On these two ideas Durham seized with a magnificent quickness of apprehension, developed them, and adapted them to the purposes of his mission. One of the men was Robert Baldwin. Durham met Baldwin briefly on his tour of Upper Canada, and Baldwin sent him the letter he had written to Glenelg in 1836, with its all but complete definition of colonial government. The other was Adam Thom, the Scots-Canadian lawyer till lately editor of the Montreal *Herald*, who in his *Anti-Gallic Letters* had made himself the voice of the English party in Quebec. Thom was articulate, dogmatic and domineering, a British immigrant who had no feeling for the peculiar texture of Canadian life and no intention of accepting the French as equal fellow-subjects. Durham appointed Thom to his staff, and he was a member of the committee which prepared the material on municipal government for Durham's Report. That Durham should have employed such a man was an indication of the attitude he was to adopt towards the French as a group, and exposed him even in his official family to the influence, powerfully evident from outside also, of the English party and the Montreal merchants who saw in the rising of 1837 not an outbreak of desperate peasants, precipitated by reckless demagogues, but a final and open manifestation of the disloyalty of all French Canada. Lower Canada should therefore be kept British by union with Upper Canada.

Durham had come to Canada with two leading ideas in mind. One was that a federation of British North America should be attempted. The other was that the government of the colonies should somehow be given the popular impulse and administrative efficiency the government of the United Kingdom was acquiring under the influence of administrative reformers inspired, like Robert Peel, by the example of the younger Pitt, or, like Durham himself, by the utilitarian ideas of Jeremy Bentham.

In Canada, however, Durham learned that the Atlantic provinces, even though the idea of an intercolonial railway from Halifax to Quebec was already under discussion, were by no means ready to think of political union with the Canadas. They were immersed in their own political problems and in the development of their provincial economies. Moreover, federation implied some kind of provincial self-government within the federation, and it was increasingly borne in upon Durham that neither his own government, nor the government of Upper Canada, nor, still more emphatically, the English party of Lower Canada, would accept any restoration of self-government which would allow the French to dominate the Assembly of Lower Canada again. The English party were determined to maintain the ascendancy the rebellion had allowed them to establish. To thwart them in this would drive them into the arms of the United States.

Federation was therefore impossible at that time. In place of it, Durham had to bring forward the old idea of restoring the pre-1791 unity of Canada. To do so, of course, offered great financial and material advantages through the development of the traffic of the St. Lawrence. But it would also have the effect of confronting the French majority in Lower Canada, said to number about 450,000, with a British majority in a united Canada – 150,000 in Lower Canada with 400,000 in Upper, rapidly increasing through immigration. In short, to propose a union of the Canadas was to revert to the policy of the Proclamation of 1763; the purpose would be to swamp the French.

That Durham should have assumed so illiberal an attitude, and expressed it in the brilliant rhetoric of the Report, is not easily explained. His liberal sentiment took account both of individuals and nations; his protest to the Czar of Russia on behalf of rebel Poland had been more than formal. But he had no such feeling towards the nationality of French Canada. For French Canadians as individuals he had every generous concern. For their nationality he had only a forthright disdain. He thought it a pitiful provincialism, from which wisdom counselled it was right and necessary to rescue the French Canadian by the example and the vigour of British institutions. It can only be said that his complacency was the complacency of Macaulay, his zeal the zeal of Governor-General William Bentinck abolishing suttee in India, his outlook that of Adam Thom.

If, however, Durham was prepared to stifle French-Canadian nationalism, he did not mean to deny Canadians, whether French or British, the benefits of self-government. That the colonies should have self-government was his second conviction. He did not even mean to deny them the blessings, as the nineteenth century saw it, of nationality; he repeated his sense of the need of creating "a national feeling" in the Canadas if they were to remain in the Empire and independent of the United States. For Durham saw the answer to the Canadian question in a free and generous grant of self-government by means of responsible government as Robert Baldwin had defined it.

Such a grant he urged in the first great recommendation of his report. As one experienced in cabinet government, he saw that the old executive councils must go and be replaced by cabinets made up of responsible heads of departments who were members of the legislature. He saw that money votes must originate with the Crown. He saw that the assemblies would have to surrender their control of local works and local patronage to municipal authorities. He saw also that Baldwin's definition was incomplete, in that it did not state what matters should be reserved for imperial control. Durham named them: "The constitution of the form of government – the regulation of foreign relations, and of trade with the mother country, the other British colonies, and foreign nations – and the disposal of the public lands." With those recommendations and that added definition, Durham urged the grant of responsible government as it was used in the United Kingdom. But the grant of self-government was to be to a Canada in which, by his second major recommendation, the provinces were to be united and the French would be outnumbered by the British. It was impossible for the French to see then, as it is easy to forget now, that without the Union and the "swamping" of the French, Durham could not have recommended the grant of responsible government.

The Report did much to vindicate Durham's Canadian policy in London and it was to affect greatly the development of British colonial policy. In British North America its immediate reception was more mixed. In French Canada it was received with natural and bitter resentment. Durham had accepted and exaggerated the imputations of their English-Canadian enemies, that all French were rebels at heart and that their national sentiment was the fruit of a backward and provincial society. The English of Lower Canada rejoiced at the prospect of outnumbering the French in the proposed union, but even so they had little interest in responsible government or the other recommendations of the Report.

In Upper Canada the Assembly, dominated by the conservative majority elected in 1836, angrily exposed the numerous and serious inaccuracies of the Report. The Legislative Council even more strongly opposed both the union and responsible government. The former would simply saddle Upper Canada with the troubles of Lower Canada; and responsible government, they saw and said clearly, would destroy the old colonial constitution of 1791 with its separation of independent powers by making the executive subordinate to the legislature. But the Upper Canadian Reformers, near despair, were rallied once more by Durham's endorsement of responsible government. Even more important was the seldom noted fact that many moderate Tories, independent of the small Compact group, decided that responsible government as defined by Durham was something they could accept, always provided the independence of the governor and the permanence of the British connection were safeguarded. It was, in short, a system of government, not a party, that had been condemned by the events of 1837 and Durham's Report.

The impact was equally decisive, the reception equally enthusiastic, among the Reformers in Nova Scotia. There Joseph Howe was struggling to formulate his desire to make the provincial government responsive to the popular will rather than merely expressive of the interested benevolence of the Halifax gentry. He was suddenly struck by the clarity of the Report in revealing the great and effective differences between the institutions of the colonies and those of the mother country. But why should there be such differences, when colonists as well as Englishmen, or Scots, or Irish, were loyal British subjects? Howe put the question elaborately in his *Four Letters to Lord John Russell*, when Russell, speaking on Durham's recommendations, reaffirmed his belief that responsible government was inadmissible in a colony. The *Letters* are one of the classics of Canadian political literature and an argument as eloquent as Durham's for colonial self-government.

The other Atlantic provinces were not as much aroused as Nova Scotia. New Brunswick was not merely indifferent but actually hostile to responsible government. Nor did it seem to offer much of substance to Prince Edward Island or Newfoundland. But it was plain that whatever the imperial government might do with the recommendations of the Report, the development of colonial self-government had entered a new phase. It was no longer the demand of colonial rebels and provincial politicians; it was the recommendation of an imperial state paper, and was to become in time even more a goal of imperial policy than the prize of colonial reformers.

The Melbourne government, however, on the advice of Russell, who had become Colonial Secretary in succession to Glenelg and Normanby, decided to unite the Canadas but not to grant responsible government. A bill to unite the colonies was introduced in 1839 but was withdrawn to await the winning of the consent of the Canadian governments by the new Governor-in-Chief. This was Charles Poulett Thomson, President of the Board of Trade since 1834, who had declined the Chancellorship of the Exchequer to take the hazardous Canadian post. Thomson was a member of an old commercial family and had specialized in finance and commerce since his entry to the House of Commons. Influenced like Durham by Benthamite radicalism, he was essentially an administrator in the Pittite tradition, brisk, efficient, and incredibly industrious. He had accepted

the view that responsible government as Durham had defined it was impracticable in a colony. Yet, like his friend and chief, Lord John Russell, he was
aware and freely admitted that the government of the colonies, since it could not
be carried on in defiance of public opinion, must somehow be carried on in accord
with it. Like Durham he saw that the colonies suffered from obsolete and inefficient institutions, and like Durham he resolved to replace them with the best
reformed British models. Thomson was superbly confident that hard work,
efficient administration, and "House of Commons management" would produce
government that would be popular without being "responsible" in British North
America. He came, in short, to fulfil the old pre-Durham policy of the Whigs
and to be, as a friendly critic was to write, "the Castlereagh of the Canadian
Union."

Nothing in his brief Canadian career was to destroy Thomson's confidence
that he could do all by management. And Russell gave him a free hand and firm
support; in a famous circular dispatch of October 16, 1839, he implemented a
principal item of Colonial Office policy and freed colonial governors from dependence on executive councillors appointed during pleasure, and in effect for
life, by the instruction that they might remove councillors when the public
service seemed to require it. Thomson thus became master of his council as his
predecessors had never been. (At the same time, though not intentionally, a
long step had been taken towards creating one of the prior conditions of responsible government.)

Thus empowered, the new governor set briskly to work. Thomson had no
difficulty in winning the consent of the Special Council of Lower Canada to the
union and a civil list, or in setting in train the work of administrative reform there.
The antiquated, costly and inefficient machinery of the old colonial régime was
ruthlessly reconstructed by one of the ablest administrators of his generation.
In Upper Canada he had to deal with a suspicious and defensive Assembly and
Legislative Council. But by holding out hopes of "responsible government"
through the assurance that government would be carried out "in accord with the
well understood wishes of the people," by the bait of a settlement of the Clergy
Reserves, the most vexed issue in Upper Canada, and by personal influence on
members, Thomson carried approval of the union. He also won acceptance of a
civil list and of an Act to divide the proceeds of the Clergy Reserves propor-
tionately among the Protestant denominations for purposes of education.

Thomson had thus laid the ground for the imperial Act of Union, which was
passed in the spring of 1840. But before he turned to the task of instituting the
union of the Canadas, the Governor went to Nova Scotia to deal with a conflict
which had arisen between the Reformers in the Assembly, led by Joseph Howe
and Herbert Huntington, and the Lieutenant-Governor, Sir Colin Campbell.
The Reformers had interpreted Russell's October dispatch as opening the way
to responsible government. Campbell, quite correctly, denied the validity of

this inference. Thomson intervened tactfully and persuaded Campbell to take some Reformers into the executive council. At the same time he induced Howe and two others, for Huntington refused, to enter a council still largely made up of the old permanent members. This in fact was what Russell and Thomson meant by talking of governing in accord with popular wishes; the governor would govern with the aid of a council of which the membership would be varied from time to time to accord with changes in the legislature and in public opinion. But the council would be a council and not a cabinet, still less a cabinet made up of members of one political party.

The Governor's intervention in Nova Scotian politics was an indication that he had more than merely Canadian tasks to discharge. Relations with the United States continued to be strained. Not only did the Hunters' Lodges continue their threat to the frontier. An indiscreet Scots Canadian named Alexander McLeod, who was well known in New York as one who had helped cut out the *Caroline*, had been arrested as an accessory to the death of an American killed in the affair. The possibility of his being condemned by a New York jury put Anglo-American relations in jeopardy. And the still unsettled north-eastern frontier now threatened to make serious trouble. Its settlement could no longer be delayed, because discussion of a railway between the Atlantic provinces and Canada pointed to the need of ensuring a route through New Brunswick, and the lumbermen of that province were disputing timber tracts with the loggers of Maine. In 1839 this flamed up as the "Aroostook war," with the rival lumbermen supported by the police and militia of the province and the state respectively. An outbreak of violence might have occurred at any time. Thomson's fear was that the Americans would so infiltrate the districts in dispute that British rights would be forfeited before they could be established by treaty. The imperial government agreed with his desire that a firm line should be taken, and in the course of the next year Foreign Secretary Palmerston was to create the conditions for the settlement of the north-eastern boundary, which was accomplished in the Webster-Ashburton Treaty of 1842. Meantime, the Foreign Secretary's firmness scored a success in the acquittal of McLeod and the ending of that incident.

Important as were Anglo-American relations in 1840, the passage of the Act of Union was perhaps more important. The Act was followed by Thomson's being made Baron Sydenham of Sydenham and Toronto. Rewarded thus for his work in bringing about the Union, Sydenham had now to put it in force in Canada. The Act was a comparatively simple one, and not nearly as detailed as had at first been intended. The provision of municipal institutions, for example, was left for Canadian action. Union, moreover, was not complete; the model was rather that of Scotland with England in 1707 than that of Ireland with England in 1801. There was to be, it is true, only one legislature and one administration. But two bodies of law continued to exist. Neither the civil law of Lower Canada nor seigniorial tenure was affected by the Act. Nor were the special rights of the Roman Catholic Church in Lower Canada touched. Thus a duality continued which was reflected in the appointment of two sets of law officers, Attorney-General East and Attorney-General West, for example, and in the growth of two school systems. On the other hand, French was not to be a language of record or debate.

In the Union there was also to be equal representation of the two sections which were the old Upper and Lower Canada, now Canada West and Canada East. Each section was to have forty-two members in the Legislative Assembly; the number of representatives might be altered by a two-thirds majority of the Assembly, but the principle of equality of representation must be retained. The result was a major injustice to the French Canadians, the number of whose representatives was much smaller than the French population warranted. The union, in short, was a gigantic gerrymander. A high property qualification of £500 of real property was set for members. The members of the second chamber, the Legislative Council, were appointed by the Governor General in Council for life. The membership was to be not less than twenty. No provision was made for its equal distribution between the two sections.

One other outstanding feature of the Act was its incorporation of Durham's recommendation that money bills should be introduced only by a member of the government. Few measures did more to make over Canadian government on the modern British pattern. At a stroke this section of the Act of Union ended the proposal of expenditures by private members, the "log-rolling" to distribute expenditures among constituencies, the waste and inefficiency of uncontrolled spending by members of the Assembly, which had characterized the old colonial assemblies. By the same provision, the introduction of British budgeting, with government control of expenditure, became possible.

The Act of Union was followed by an Act to deal with the Clergy Reserves. The Upper Canadian Act obtained by Sydenham having been ruled inadmissible by the law officers in the United Kingdom, an imperial Act was passed which took account of the legal objections and provided for a division of the Reserves among the denominations for religious purposes. Thus the principle of state provision for religion was preserved, while that of an exclusive establishment was abandoned. But this "plural establishment" was to prove little more acceptable than the old dual one. The "voluntary principle" of some denominations and many individuals was to keep alive the demand that the Reserves be secularized. For the moment, however, the Reserves ceased to be a matter of political contention.

Sydenham was pleased with the two measures but concerned at the need to legislate for municipal institutions in Canada. He feared that no Canadian assembly would give up the "jobbing" and patronage involved in voting money and private bills for local works. To strengthen his hand, he therefore put through the Special Council of Lower Canada a municipal ordinance which would serve as a model for Upper Canada. The latter province had had counties since Simcoe's day, governed by lord-lieutenants and Justices of the Peace on the English model, with local taxes assessed at need by the grand juries. Lower Canada had nothing of the kind; indeed, the elementary form of local government provided by Justices of the Peace and captains of militia had crumbled away as the militia system was allowed to disintegrate in the 1820's and 1830's. The last vestiges of the old French system had disappeared and left nothing to take its place. The only kind of local government left was the ecclesiastical *fabrique*, the parish vestry charged with the upkeep of the church edifice. The Justices could not function as local government officers without the framework of the county and the stimulus of assize justices and the grand juries. But neither of these belonged to the traditions of the seigniories or of the townships. Thus Sydenham was creating a system of local government in Lower Canada; in Upper Canada the need was to infuse a measure of popular control into a system hitherto jealously controlled by the provincial government.

Sydenham approached the organization of the new central government of the Union with the same determination to create modern, efficient British institutions in place of the archaic colonial ones. But to attempt this, he found he had to begin by doing most of the work himself. No colonial politician, not even Robert Baldwin, knew just what had to be done to make the machinery of government efficient, not to say responsible. Before local cabinet government could be attempted, the conditions and practices of British parliamentary and local government had to replace those of the old colonial constitutions of 1791.

But Sydenham found not only no politician he did not have to train; he also found no political parties. The Family Compact and the Château clique had never been more than small groups of officials and lawyers, together with a few business men. The ultra-Reformers scarcely numbered more. The great body of moderate opinion, whether liberal or conservative, was not organized. Many people, and particularly the Methodists whom Egerton Ryerson swayed, were quite independent of party. Parties had yet to be made and the techniques of party government learned before Canadian politicians could take over and develop the machinery Sydenham was creating.

In these circumstances Sydenham had to "manage" the new administration and the new legislature as he had managed those of Upper Canada in 1839. And he began by rigging and influencing the election. Not only did he draw the electoral boundaries of Quebec and Montreal so as to deny the French four seats; he also toured Upper Canada in 1840 and conducted a subtle campaign "to break up the exclusive power of the Compact on the one hand, and repress the violent radicals on the other," in order to ensure the return of moderate men, whether Reformer or Tory, who would support his administration. He did not stump the province like Head, but he campaigned no less effectively.

Sydenham was to preserve to the end the combination of a legislative program designed to give Canada efficient British institutions and the personal management of an adept and experienced politician. But he had no intention of admitting that government "according to the well understood wishes of the people" should mean government by a party cabinet. He would choose able men of political influence as heads of new departments and members of his new executive council. They would make up something far more like a British cabinet than anything the colonies had hitherto seen. But it would be a coalition of individuals, and Sydenham would be its directing head. It was very like the mode of government practised by George III from 1770 to 1782, the "departmental system" in which ministers were held individually responsible to the king, except that some of Sydenham's advisers were old permanent officials carried over into the new régime.

It was in this system that Robert Baldwin, appreciative as he was of Sydenham's administrative capacity, found it impossible to serve. Made Solicitor-General in February 1840, he was invited to become a member of the executive council of the Union and did so in February 1841 without, as he thought, compromising his principles and his concept of responsible government. He explicitly warned Sydenham he had no political confidence in the three Tory members of the council.

The election of the first legislature of the Union seemed to make it necessary for Baldwin to act, for it had undoubtedly resulted in the return of a majority of Reformers. In Canada West only six or seven Compact Tories were returned, and the same number of extreme Reformers. The remaining thirty were moderate Reformers or Conservatives, all of whom accepted responsible government to some degree and nearly all of whom were elected to support Sydenham. In Canada East, it is true, only about twenty French Reformers had been elected, partly because of Sydenham's gerrymandering and partly because of the violence of the English party at the polls. Among the defeated was Louis Hippolyte Lafontaine. This able, earnest and sober man had succeeded Papineau as chief of the French Reformers, and the difference in their characters demonstrated the change in the party. Where Papineau was effervescent, Lafontaine was restraint itself. When Papineau had become embroiled with rebellion, Lafontaine had taken no part. Steady, reserved, and determined, he was the pivot of Canadian politics for the next decade.

The leaders of the English Reformers recognized his quality. Baldwin and Francis Hincks, a clever, dynamic Irish immigrant who had espoused the cause of reform in 1836, had both been in touch with him before the election. They had seen that the coalescence of the Reformers of the two sections would both prevent the political suppression of the French and ensure the triumph of responsible government. Lafontaine had seen this too, despite his resentment at the Union, and he responded to their approaches.

The seal was now put on the union of the parties by having Lafontaine returned for North York, one of the two seats Baldwin had won. (It was a not unusual practice of that day for prominent politicians to contest more than one seat.) The spectacle of a French Canadian sitting as member for one of the York constituencies outside Toronto was a vivid illustration of how political principle had been put before racial sentiment. French and British Reformers were to unite to bring about responsible government. Moreover, Lafontaine's decision was one of the most crucial in Canadian history. He might have led the French members in a boycott of the Union; he might have led them in a permanent opposition bloc in the House. His decision to work with the English Reformers saved Canada from the fate of Grattan's Ireland and Gandhi's India, and made a plural and a liberal society possible in British North America.

Baldwin accordingly held a caucus of the Upper Canadian Reformers at Kingston, which Sydenham had chosen as the capital of the Union, to concert upon whom they would put forward for election as Speaker and to learn if they would act as a united party. They had agreed to support a French Reformer as Speaker, in order to test the support the government would have, but many of them felt too much obligation to support Sydenham to be ready to oppose his administration. (The fact is, many were still thinking in terms of the old system; this was indicated by their desire to elect Baldwin as Speaker in the old style, as leader of the popular branch of the legislature.) Baldwin was, however, supported in his determination to request Sydenham to remodel the council by replacing the three Tory members with Reformers or moderate Conservatives. When Sydenham curtly refused to consider this, Baldwin resigned.

Baldwin had asserted his principles, but popular opinion supported Sydenham, as it did when he cleverly accepted the Reformers' candidate for the Speakership. And the Governor then triumphantly drove through his program, which was topped by a proposed imperial guarantee of a loan of £1,500,000 for debt conversion and public works. Ably aided by the adroit "Sweet William" Draper and the loyal and steady S. B. Harrison, Sydenham performed a tour de force as governor, prime minister, and parliamentary manager.

He completed his reorganization of the departments of government by the establishment of the Board of Works, forerunner of Public Works. He put through municipal legislation for Canada West similar to that already in force for Canada East, despite Reformer opposition to the wardens and treasurers of the counties being appointive and not elective officers. He had a school act passed providing for a system of public elementary education. A host of minor measures followed. On only one major bill, for the setting up of a bank of issue, was he forced to delay.

Few could resist the magic of a politician so adroit, few oppose a program so sound, well organized, and necessary. The truth was that Sydenham had promised and performed so much that only a few extremists had consistently resisted. Even Francis Hincks, the most vocal of Reformers in 1839 and 1840, was so captivated by the administrative efficiency and financial skill of Sydenham that he began to support the administration and ceased to follow Baldwin.

Sydenham had in fact, in his two brief years and one legislative session, established the system of British parliamentary administration in Canada in place of the old colonial system of divided powers and archaic routine. He, with Durham and Russell, had done in this respect what Pitt and Grenville had failed to do, and he had approached even to the crowning development of parliamentary government, despite his flat opposition to responsible government in what he called "its inadmissible sense" of cabinet and party government. For when, late in the session, Baldwin challenged the administration on the point of principle by moving a set of resolutions declaring responsible government an indispensable mode of conducting the government of Canada, Sydenham's riposte was to have Harrison substitute substantially the same resolutions, except for a phraseology which lent less support to an interpretation of responsible government as cabinet government. But the end of the session, and the ending of Sydenham's life by a riding accident at the same time, left one urgent question hanging over Canadian politics. Could even Sydenham have got through another session without admitting more pronounced Reformers, and the French Reformers, to seats in the council? It is generally agreed that he could not have done so. The magic was becoming familiar, the great patronage of the new government had been committed, there was no second £1,500,000.

The money that Sydenham had made available for public works was spent chiefly on canals on the St. Lawrence between Lake Ontario and Montreal. Throughout the decade, the work of blasting, digging and lock-building went forward, and by 1848 a waterway for vessels of nine-foot draught ran from Kingston to Lachine. Thousands of penniless immigrants, mostly Irish seeking the cash needed to settle on the land, toiled at the wheelbarrows and the hoists.

The great program heaved Upper Canada out of the depression of the late 1830's. The expenditure of the loan not only gave work to the immigrant, it also spread money through the river- and lake-front towns and started it trickling among the new farms on the back concessions. There each annual wave of immigrants from the British Isles quickly learned, or quickly failed at, the frontier skills of "chopping," "burning" and "breaking," and with axe and flame edged back a township range or two the scarcely penetrable ranks of the hardwood forest of the St. Lawrence lowlands. There also they learned the frontier practices of mutual help, the "bees" to "burn" a neighbour's chopping or to "raise" the frame of his new barn. The old American stock and the earlier British settlers in "the bush" had created a rural economy and society of farm and market town into which the new-comers were soon incorporated and became, with the sons of pioneers, fresh assault troops in carrying the frontier of blazed forest trail and squared field on squared field back towards the granite shoulders of the Shield and westward across the Ontario peninsula towards the waters of Huron, Champlain's Freshwater Sea. Upper Canada in the 1840's entered on a surge of growth which made it by 1850 a wealthy, a populous and a British province.

In Lower Canada that tale of prosperity was not repeated, except in the Eastern Townships into which the British immigrants also flowed. On the seigniorial lands the native population mounted, while the habitant was slow to recover from the failure of his one-crop agriculture and found it ever more difficult to plant his sons out on the land of his native province. The welling increase pushed back the ranges of settlement into the rear lands of the seigniories, towards the Notre Dame mountains to the south-east and the slopes of the Laurentides of the north-west. But the land could no longer absorb the increase. French-Canadian youngsters in small parties, and soon by hundreds, began to go over the border, first to work for spells in the manufacturing towns of New England and take their wages home, and then to settle and remain. The Québecois, like the Acadians and the English, became a people of a dual allegiance. But French Canada was not prospering in the 1840's; it was suffering the first of the great population haemorrhages of Canadian history – a poignant background of Lower Canadian politics, during these years when Canadian institutions and the Canadian temper were formed.

The contrast with Upper Canada was painful; that with the Atlantic provinces was scarcely less so. There also, natural increase and the mounting British immigration, together with a prosperity marked by the growth of the Bank of Nova Scotia, founded in 1832, and of the Cunard Steamship Line, begun in 1840, caused the population of the provinces to mount at a rate never again to be attained. The Scots in eastern Nova Scotia, the Irish on the North Shore of New Brunswick, a mixture of both in Prince Edward Island, increased the numbers and altered the composition of the population of the seaward provinces. The range of the composition was marked at one extreme by the Gaelic-speaking Highlanders of Cape Breton and on the other by the mounting numbers of the Acadians on the Upper St John. In these provinces, as in the Canadas, the strengthening of the British element quickened the transformation of British American politics from the old colonial model of the late eighteenth century towards contemporary British practice. This transformation Sydenham had begun in administration, and the advocates of responsible government wished to carry it into parliamentary politics under his successors.

Sydenham's successor was Sir Charles Bagot. Bagot had been appointed by Sir Robert Peel, who had become prime minister in 1841, with Lord Stanley as colonial secretary. Bagot had to face the task of either maintaining Sydenham's system or replacing it by one in accord with the facts of colonial life. The facts were that Sydenham's system, based on the exclusion of the French from office, could not be maintained on practical any more than on moral grounds. An amiable but able diplomat, Sir Charles had a diplomat's sense of the disposition of power in a situation, and was soon aware of the fact that his ministry could not face a second session with any confidence. In the spring of 1842 he succeeded in winning Francis Hincks to enter the council as Inspector General of Public Accounts, the office which later became that of Minister of Finance. But much more was necessary. Draper and Harrison advised the Governor that this was the case, and both also advised him to seek to bring some French members into the council on what Harrison termed "the principle of extension." This was to add French members to the existing council in an official coalition, but not to reconstruct the council around the French. When Lafontaine was approached, he made it clear that no French Reformer would join the council without Baldwin. And Baldwin would not agree that pensions should be given to two retiring members who were not political ministers but permanent officials from the old régime. Not even that cheap price would the political purist pay for the liquidation of the old order. The principle of extension collapsed, Bagot was forced to give way, and Baldwin, with Lafontaine and two other French Reformers, entered the council.

The result was not a new council; neither was it a reconstituted one. It is true that it was and is called the first "Baldwin-Lafontaine ministry," and that Baldwin and Lafontaine were the men of greatest weight in it. But the old ministry did not resign as a body; the only members to leave the council were two pronounced Conservatives, William Draper and Henry Sherwood, and the two permanent officials who had been made political officers by Sydenham. It is indeed difficult to understand the stir that the new appointments made until it is remembered that the change did mark the collapse of Sydenham's personal system, that Baldwin and Lafontaine came in as avowed upholders of responsible government in Sydenham's "inadmissible sense," and, above all, that the French had been admitted to the council. The full import of the last, as was realized by everyone, was that it marked the collapse of Durham's attempt to denationalize the French Canadians. The new ministers certainly had more freedom and authority than their predecessors and indeed thought, themselves, that they had achieved responsible government. But it was the admission of the French that made the change outstanding, for they were still regarded as "rebels" by many Canadian Conservatives and were still distrusted by the Colonial Office as unfriendly to the British connection. Small wonder that Bagot was worried over the reaction at home to his daring.

He did not live to face the consequences. His delicate constitution began to give way in the fall of of 1842, and he submitted his resignation. By spring he was dead, and Canada had claimed the life of another governor.

To succeed Bagot, Stanley chose Sir Charles Metcalfe, a distinguished official in India for many years and a successful governor of Jamaica at a time when the island was torn by the aftermath of the abolition of slavery. Metcalfe was a stiff administrator but a man of liberal mind and kindly human sympathies. There was little in his character to provoke the trouble that marked his term of office. But he was undoubtedly given a special and private mission by Stanley, who had accepted Bagot's inclusion of the French and Baldwin in the council but was undoubtedly perturbed by consideration of its possible consequences.

That mission was to see that responsible government as party government should not result from Bagot's act. Government in Canada was not to be allowed to become wholly like the cabinet government of the United Kingdom. It was not to become, that is, government in which a party with a majority in the assembly should form a cabinet of party members only, on the principle of ministerial solidarity, and use the patronage of government to maintain its majority and to influence the next election. In a colony, and particularly in Canada, Stanley was sure the result would be to entrench the popular party in power by a tenure as enduring and exclusive as the former oligarchies had possessed. An oligarchic ascendancy would be replaced by a popular and a French one. It would also reduce the governor to a position of no influence in local affairs. This would weaken the imperial connection, which Stanley saw as depending on the retention of authority and patronage by the governor as well as on the loyalty of a free people.

It must be admitted that it was easy to see the Reformers entrenching themselves in power. The colonies had no experience of alternating governments, and all parties seek to maintain themselves in office indefinitely. It was easy, if mistaken, to see the Reformers, still thought in England to be under the influence of American ideas and institutions, using a position of permanent power to weaken the tie with the metropolis. Thus it was understandable that the Colonial Secretary should tell the Governor it was really the Tories and Conservatives who were to be looked to as the last resort if the imperial connection were threatened. In consequence, Metcalfe was to abstain from giving his ministers his full and exclusive confidence. He was even to maintain relations with the Opposition and to see that some patronage went to them.

The result was that shortly after Metcalfe took up his duties early in 1843 a coolness developed between him and his ministers. They soon felt they had reason to believe they did not possess the Governor's undivided confidence. Metcalfe was undoubtedly greatly influenced by a talk his private secretary, Captain J. M. Higginson, had had with Lafontaine. In that discussion Lafontaine made it clear that he believed the ministers ought to be consulted on all matters, including patronage. Higginson, who must be presumed to have expressed no view that Metcalfe would not have approved of, demurred, and argued that the governor must possess a measure of independence, especially in matters of patronage.

Such a discussion could have no formal outcome, of course, but Higginson's report of it helped convince Metcalfe that his ministers meant to insist on enforcing their own policy in local matters and in using the patronage to maintain their position. This, he reported to Stanley, he would never agree to, as if he did the prerogative power would be abandoned, the governor would become a figurehead, and the imperial connection would in effect be dissolved. Metcalfe proceeded to keep in touch with the Opposition, to appoint some of them to office on his own initiative without consulting his ministers, and to grow further and further away from Lafontaine and Baldwin.

Matters thus drifted on through the session of 1843. The main items of business were bills to deal with the Orange Lodges and the university question in Upper Canada. Irishmen had been pouring into British America in hundreds of thousands since the first potato famines of the 1820's. They brought their political and religious rivalries with them, and their habits of conspiracy and violence. The violence of Canadian elections was undoubtedly increased by the importation of Irish electoral practices, still rife with eighteenth-century corruption and dominated by the shillelagh. The Protestant Irish brought with them the Loyal Orange Order, which became an ally of the Tories and Conservatives and an offence to the Reformers. When Baldwin sought to curb the Order by his Secret Societies Bill, Metcalfe said nothing, but when it passed he reserved it for the approval of the imperial government. The ministers felt that he should have advised them of his objections before the bill was introduced. The University Bill was an attempt to secularize Bishop Strachan's King's College, but with provision for the affiliation of denominational colleges to the new university. This measure ran into so many cross-currents of opposition that its passage was doubtful and the ministers were embarrassed by their own legislative offspring.

This was the moment they chose to challenge Metcalfe on his practice of bestowing patronage on their political opponents. The Governor refused to agree with their demand that they be consulted in all appointments to public office, and all the ministers, including those who were ministers when Bagot reconstructed the administration, resigned. The sole exception was Dominick Daly, an old permanent official whom Sydenham had induced to enter public life but who now declined to behave like a politician.

The issue of patronage was a real one and, in this phase of the development of responsible government, the central one. But there is no doubt that the ministers had wished to escape their embrassassment in the matter of the university bill by raising another issue and hoped, by resigning, either to make Metcalfe submit or to provide themselves with a good election cry. In this they miscalculated, and their miscalculation illustrates how their concept of politics had outrun the two elements they had to work with, the Colonial Office and its governor, and Canadian public opinion. Metcalfe held on stubbornly with only Daly to aid him, and then prorogued. He found his first political minister in Draper, his first French minister in D. B. Viger. Slowly he built his council up to six with Draper's help and the adherence of D. B. Papineau, brother of the rebel. The delay of course arose from the necessity both of having some French members and of keeping the council non-partisan. A Tory council might have been formed at any time, but to have done so would have been to concede the principle on which Baldwin and Lafontaine had stood.

In the course of these attempts at reconstruction, Draper revealed the same kind of liberal-conservative statesmanship as had induced him to resign to make way for Lafontaine in 1842. The situation was basically the same. The ministry could not be sure of a majority without the support of the French. The French must therefore be brought into the government. Metcalfe agreed; he had no intention of reversing what Sydenham had accepted in the Baldwin-Harrison resolutions, or of proscribing the French from office. When he had a working council, Metcalfe dissolved the first legislature of the Union in September, 1844.

The ensuing election was the most violent in Canadian history. Neither side spared any effort at corruption or intimidation. The Irish navvies working on the new canals marched into constituencies to hold the polls for the party that paid them. But Metcalfe and Draper had gauged the sentiment of Upper Canada aright. While the French increased their number of representatives in Lower Canada, in Upper Canada an appeal to loyalty, powerfully backed by Egerton Ryerson, carried the great body of moderate opinion. Many felt, as did Ryerson, that Baldwin and Lafontaine had tried to make the governor a cipher and had imperilled the British connection. They had no thought of opposing or repudiating responsible government, but the responsible government they were prepared to accept left a central position and a definite independence to the governor.

As a result, the ministry had a small majority in the second parliament and was able to carry on, with considerable reconstruction from time to time, until 1847. It was, however, difficult to maintain a majority from divided English Canada when French Canada was still united by fear and resentment of the Union. Approaches made to Lafontaine in the summer of 1845 through R. E. Caron, Speaker of the Legislative Council, found Lafontaine implacable. He would come in only on his own terms and he could not forget the election of 1844 and the charges of disloyalty. It was this failure to win French support that made Draper's ministry so weak, rather than Metcalfe's opposition to responsible government as Baldwin had defined it. This feeble ministry carried on for the remainder of the Governor's term of office. Metcalfe, stoically enduring the ravages of cancer, finally capitulated; he resigned and retired to England, to die in 1846. As it happened, the old colonial régime died with its heroic defender, but this was because of events in England and Ireland, not because of any sudden triumph of responsible government as understood by Baldwin or by Draper.

How tentative the idea of responsible government was, meanwhile, even in Lafontaine's mind, is shown by the emergence of a new idea in the French press. It was that of the "double majority," the concept that legislation for either section of the province should be carried only by a majority of the representatives from that section. The survival of French law under the Union invited the development of such a conception. But it meant a dual administration, with the two halves possibly of opposite political complexion, and it was therefore incompatible with the development of cabinet solidarity on which responsible government depended.

Draper's ministry, then, was a responsible but non-party one with a majority in Parliament, and responsible government as Baldwin defined it had suffered a defeat which might have been of considerable duration, had it not been for major changes outside British America which made possible the recovery and then the triumph of the Reformers. These changes were the settlement of the Oregon dispute with the United States and the abolition of the Corn Laws in the United Kingdom, both in 1846.

The Webster-Ashburton Treaty had settled the north-eastern frontier, but it had not really restored harmony in Anglo-American relations, disturbed since 1837. Now the strained relations with England were made part of the election strategy of the Democratic party, which had been defeated in the election of 1840. The dominant southern wing wished to annex the republic of Texas and perhaps acquire other territory from Mexico, for the expansion of the slave economy. But to carry the northern wing for such a project, some northern expansion was necessary. The Oregon territory, jointly occupied since 1818, furnished the pretext. The Hudson's Bay Company had successfully eliminated American traders, but it was helpless to oppose American missionaries and settlers. From 1838 to 1843 these were moving into the lower Columbia valley in increasing numbers. An attempt to offset them in 1841 with immigrants from Red River failed. In 1843 the American squatters formed a provisional government and demanded union with the United States.

The Democrats took up the issue and launched the famous slogans of "The annexation of Texas and the re-annexation of Oregon" and "Fifty-four forty, or fight," the latter a demand for the whole of Oregon up to Russian Alaska. This belligerence was dealt with quietly and firmly by the British Foreign Secretary, Lord Aberdeen, after the Democrats had won the election of 1844. When Metcalfe was relieved in 1845, his successor was Earl Cathcart, commander of the forces in America. The defences of British America were readied. A military survey of the far western territories was made. In 1846 a detachment of troops was sent to Red River. But Aberdeen of course wished to negotiate a settlement, and it soon became apparent that President Polk intended a war with Mexico, not with Britain. A compromise was reached by which the territory was divided at the 49th parallel to the Gulf of Georgia and thence along the Strait of Juan de Fuca. This sensible settlement of an intricate dispute, and the involvement of the United States in increased sectional tension after the Mexican War, removed from British America the pressure the United States had exerted since 1837, and so diminished the fear that the British connection was in danger from Canadian radicalism.

Important as the relaxation of tension between the United States and the United Kingdom was, it was much less important in its consequences than the abolition of the Corn Laws. Since 1839 the Anti-Corn-Law League of England had conducted an ever more effective agitation against the protection of British agriculture. The League demanded the free importation of grain. The formation of a Conservative ministry, which drew much of its support from the agricultural interest, seemed a set-back for the League. But Prime Minister Peel was convinced that the United Kingdom, with its booming industries and its swelling population, must move towards freer trade. Budget by budget, measure by measure, he led his party towards that unannounced goal. The Canada Trade Act of 1843, which admitted Canadian wheat and flour – even if ground from American wheat – was in fact a means of admitting American wheat under the colonial preferential rates of the Corn Laws. It delighted the Montreal business men and led to increased investment in flour mills.

Peel undoubtedly meant to reach his goal by measured steps and with compensation for agriculture. But in 1846 his hand was forced by the great Irish famine. The potato crop had failed in 1845. Most of Ireland's eight million people depended on the potato as the staple of their diet. Famine raged all that terrible winter, and thousands began the bitter and despairing migration to the ports of British America. The Corn Laws were suspended early in 1846 – in effect, repealed – to let in supplies of grain, and such was public opinion in England that an emergency relief measure became, as every one knew it must, a national policy of free trade, and of free trade not only in food, but in all goods.

Peel had resigned rather than suspend the Corn Law. But Lord John Russell, now Whig leader, failed to form a ministry, and Peel came back to carry the repeal with Whig support and then resign early in June 1846. Russell then formed a government, with Lord Grey, Durham's colleague and brother-in-law and a believer in colonial self-government, as Colonial Secretary. After the years of political inertia before 1837, and the years of friction since, constitutional change in British North America was to set in at a revolutionary pace following the commercial and imperial revolution begun by the coming of free trade.

ADDITIONAL READING

COUPLAND, R. *Durham's Report.*
CRAIG, G. M. (ed.) *Lord Durham's Report.*
DUHAMEL, GEORGES *Le Rapport du Lord Durham.*
HODGETTS, J. E. *Pioneer Public Service, 1841-67.*
KNAPLUND, P. (ed.) *Letters from Lord Sydenham to Lord John Russell.*
LUCAS, SIR CHARLES (ed.) *Lord Durham's Report.* 3 vols.
MARTIN, CHESTER *Empire and Commonwealth.*
TUCKER, G. N. *The Canadian Commercial Revolution, 1845-51.*

THE NATIONAL
PERIOD

THE FOUNDING OF
NATIONAL INSTITUTIONS
[1847-1873]

When the Commercial Revolution of 1846 made colonial democracy possible, it opened the way to colonial nationality. British Americans proceeded after 1846 to use the new powers of self-government to remake the institutions under which they lived. In doing so, they created the patterns of national life embodied in the union of British North America in 1867.

The democratization of municipal government, the separation of church and state in Upper Canada, the incorporation of religious societies in Lower Canada, the evolution of the separate school in all the provinces, the abolition of the law of primogeniture in the Common Law provinces and of seigniorial tenure in Lower Canada, the drafting of the code civil *in the latter – all these and a host of similar reforms were the work of the colonial democracy which was given its head in 1847. The powers of self-government were used in the British provinces to create a liberal democratic society and in Lower Canada a French and clerical society resting on a civil democracy.*

The Commercial Revolution of course had economic as well as political consequences. Cast out from the Eden of the protected British market into the depression of 1847, the colonies groped their way past the lures of annexation to a pattern of colonial protection, railway construction, and reciprocal trade with the United States. As the imperial ties slackened the continental ones tightened. The full pattern appeared in the Grand Trunk Railway, begun in 1853, and the Reciprocity Treaty of 1854. By that time British America was prosperous as never before and British Americans had learned that railway construction to develop the export trades was the key to prosperity.

Self-government and the reform of local institutions did not, however, provide a stable basis for parliamentary government in Canada. The Act of Union, in conferring equal representation on Lower and Upper Canada, made it possible for laws affecting Lower Canada to be passed by an Upper Canadian majority, or vice versa. With the national and religious differences which existed, the result was growing resentment, the attempt to meet the difficulty by the convention of the double majority, and the Upper Canadian demand for representation by population. The trouble was that the Canadian democracy was not a simple and uniform one ; it was French and English, it was Roman Catholic and Protestant. And the same colonial democracy, by ensuring the survival of the French-Canadian nationality, made it necessary to create the institutions of a plural, or bi-national, society.

This necessity was reinforced after 1857 by the need to form some pattern of economic expansion more profitable than that of the Grand Trunk Railway and the Reciprocity Treaty had proved to be. The new formula was an Intercolonial and a Pacific railway, and the development of British American trade in the northern half of the continent from the Atlantic to the Pacific.

Even more urgent after 1861 was the need to unite against possible pressure from a North defeated or a United States reunited in the Civil War. To none was the danger more apparent than to the British government, which by 1864 saw the union of the colonies as an imperative necessity.

Out of this coincidence of imperatives came the project of British North American union in 1864. In three swift years that project was carried to completion in a bi-national union under a parliamentary monarchy in which minority rights were safeguarded. When the North-West was annexed, the Red River resistance and the Manitoba Act made it clear that neither French nor English, but both conjointly, were to determine the future of the union. By 1873 it remained only to build the railways east and west and to bring in the island colony of Newfoundland. Out of the colonial democracy of 1847 had come the native institutions, the bi-cultural society and the national union of the colonies under the name of Canada.

CHAPTER 15

The Formation of Canadian Institutions
1847-1856

The break-up of the old colonial system was a shock as violent and a change as revolutionary for English Canada as the conquest and cession of 1759–63 had been for French Canada. It meant the end of a system of European connection which had sustained and nourished the British North American colonies even while they chafed at certain of its restraints. Its permanence the colonists had taken for granted; demands that it should be ended they had treated as treasonable; to maintain it they had expended their treasure and shed their blood. Now at a stroke the imperial government had swept the whole system of commercial protection away, without hesitation or regret, and the stroke threatened to carry with it the old concomitants of military defence and mutual trust.

The results of the revolution were twofold. On one hand, the psychological effects were sharp and deep. The British North American patriot, especially the loyalist Tory, felt that his loyalty had been betrayed. And loyalty wounded leads quickly to a passionate rejection of the object of loyalty. Moreover, the British loyalist of the Canadas had bitter memories of what seemed a recurrent British tendency to forgo Canadian interests, as in the boundary treaties from 1783 to 1846. On the other hand, the weakening – the destruction, as many felt it to be – of the ties of the British connection released British America to the full gravitational pull of the United States, its markets and its institutions, and that in a year when "Manifest Destiny" was at high tide and great new areas of the continent were being drawn by conquest and occupation into the American union. It might well be, the bitter reflection ran, that British America also would find a better and more secure future in continental union.

These effects of the ending of the old colonial system meant that British America, particularly Canada, faced a crisis after 1846 in which it seemed that the separate existence of the colonies might well be ended. All those things that had kept them separate for three centuries – the northern economy, the consequent dependence on Europe, the monarchical loyalty of a dependent people – all, it seemed, might be terminated unless the colonies should achieve, as Durham

KC-K

had prescribed, "some nationality of their own." Certain it was that the next few years would hear much talk of ending the imperial connection and of annexation, and see much groping for new departures and new directions in British North American life.

There were, of course, other consequences more immediate and concrete, some economic, some political. For a time there was a continuation and even an increase of the prosperity that British North America had known since 1841. It was caused by the shortage of foodstuffs in the British Isles, a continuation of the shortage that had begun in 1845 and had precipitated the abolition of the Corn Laws. The flow of grain and flour from the St. Lawrence kept up until the fall of 1847. Then the flood of grain from the Baltic and the Black Sea into the free English ports, and the diversion of American grain to American ports now that the colonial preference was gone, caused the Canadian grain market to collapse. From that time on, Canadian wheat would have to be sold in a competitive market, pitted against the grain of the prairies of Illinois and of the steppes of the Ukraine. In late 1847 the great British railway boom also broke sharply and ruinously, bringing restricted credit and depressed prices in all lines of business.

By the end of 1847 the magnitude of the blow the Laurentian trading system had received was apparent. Since 1821 the Montreal business men, supported by their outliers in Kingston, Toronto, and Hamilton, had developed the commercial system based on the navigation of the St. Lawrence. They had created a banking system which fed out through its branch banks the credit to take off the harvests and bring down the timber drives. From the development of the trade of the Canadas they had gone on to aspire to draw the trade of the American middle west down the St. Lawrence. The Union itself, the canal construction inspired by Sydenham, and the Canada Trade Act of 1843 had finally crowned their ambition and much money had gone into shipping, grain warehouses and flour mills between 1841 and 1846. But it was a precarious system they had fabricated. It was first threatened in 1845 by the American Drawback Act, which allowed a refund of the duties on Canadian produce shipped through the United States. Then came the abolition of colonial preference on colonial wheat and on flour ground from American wheat, along with the repeal of the Corn Laws. The trading organization of the St. Lawrence was reduced to its Canadian limits; indeed, it was further diminished as the produce of western Upper Canada was drawn down the Erie Canal. Yet it was denied the use of its natural advantages, for the Navigation Laws still closed Montreal to the foreign and American shipping, the competition of which might have continued to draw American grain to Montreal. Not until 1849 was this handicap to be removed. Meantime many firms went bankrupt; all faced an uncertain and, as it seemed, a restricted future.

The gloom and apprehension of the Montrealers were natural, but exaggerated.

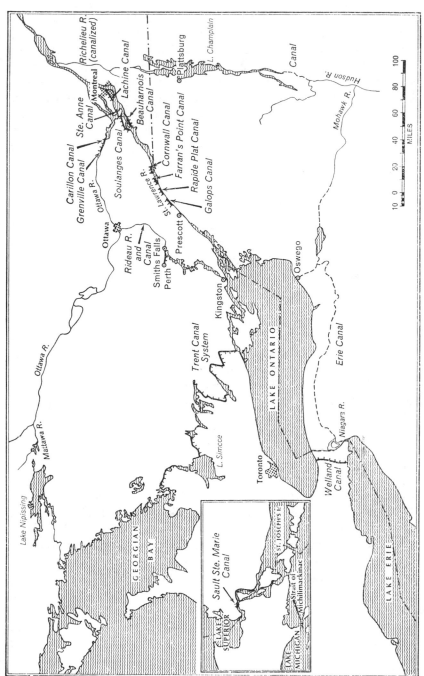

Ottawa R.

Mattawa R.

Lake Nipissing

GEORGIAN BAY

L. Simcoe

Toronto

Kingston

Oswego

LAKE ONTARIO

Erie Canal

Niagara R.

Welland Canal

LAKE ERIE

Trent Canal System

Ottawa

Rideau R. and Canal

Smiths Falls

Perth

Prescott

St. Lawrence R.

Galops Canal

Rapide Plat Canal

Farran's Point Canal

Cornwall Canal

Beauharnois Canal

Soulanges Canal

Ottawa R.

Grenville Canal

Carillon Canal

Ste. Anne Canal

Lachine Canal

Montreal

Richelieu R. (canalized)

Plattsburg

L. Champlain

Canal

Hudson R.

Mohawk R.

MILES

10   0   20   40   60   80   100

LAKE SUPERIOR

Sault Ste. Marie Canal

ST. JOSEPH'S I.

Strait of Michilimackinac

LAKE MICHIGAN

XI   *The Canals of Canada*

Elsewhere in British North America the shock of the commercial revolution was not nearly so great. The Atlantic colonies were not as hard hit by the ending of the old protective system, although they did suffer and there were riots of unemployed in Saint John. The timber duties were retained, though much reduced, until 1851 when the other colonial preferences went; and much of the fish of the colonies had always been sold in competitive markets. After the repeal of the Navigation Laws in 1849, the shipbuilding and the shipping of the Atlantic provinces had indeed to operate under fully competitive conditions. But the cheapness of their timber and the skill of their builders and seamen kept the ships of Nova Scotia and New Brunswick on the seven seas for another generation. The fifties were to see the rise to ocean supremacy of the clipper ships. Nova Scotia and New Brunswick designers never sought to turn out the speediest ships, but built for cargo space and sea endurance as well as speed. Their ships were famous for all three qualities and found a ready market until the last decade of the century. It was the slow replacement of the wooden sailing-ship by the iron steamship that caused the shipping of the Atlantic provinces to decline.

The comparative buoyancy of the economy of the Atlantic colonies suggests that the gravity of the Canadian depression was exaggerated because all factors in the depression were concentrated in the Canadian metropolis of Montreal. The rest of Canada did not suffer as severely as did the grain-exporting city. Canadian timber still enjoyed the colonial preference, and the Canadian economy could be diversified. The depression, moreover, was not merely the result of the abolition of imperial protection; it was in great part the periodic down-turn of the business cycle. And almost at once a remedy for British free trade and American tariffs was proposed. It was a treaty of commercial reciprocity with the United States, by which, in natural products at least, the Canadian share in the export trade of the American west might be retained and Canadian grain sold on equal terms with that of the northern states. But to negotiate such a treaty would take time. Surrounded as they were by commercial failures, falling prices, and collapsing real-estate values, the Montreal business men were developing the moody desperation from which rash action springs.

Nor was commercial depression all. There was additional cause for gloom along the St. Lawrence. The year 1847 saw the onset of the sick and desperate hordes of destitute people who had escaped from famine-stricken Ireland. By the thousands they were pouring into every North American port from Baltimore to Quebec. The great seepage of emigrants out of Ireland which had grown for many years now became a torrent of refugees. The poorest and most destitute came on the old, poorly-found ships of the Canadian timber trade. Many perished at sea of disease and hunger; many landed fever-stricken at the quarantine station of Grosse Ile only to die in its crowded halls. The survivors moved up the river, bringing their misery, their diseases and their helplessness to Montreal and the towns and settlements of Upper Canada. In Saint John and the ports on the North Shore of New Brunswick the fugitives were fewer but the sickness and misery no less. Private charity both French and English, as well as government aid, strove to deal with this avalanche of human misery, and much was done to alleviate the distress and to aid the passage of the immigrants. But much resentment, both French and English, was kindled against the British government which had allowed the Irish poor to sink into such misery and become charges on a distant people, burdened with their own difficulties and not responsible for the condition of Ireland. And to the population of British America, notably in New Brunswick, Montreal, and Upper Canada, were added hundreds of thousands of people who had no love for England, "repealers" who wanted Ireland restored to its old self-government and who thrilled to the news in 1848 that "Young Ireland" had rebelled. The poverty and anger of the Irish added one more tension to the strain on the public temper of the Canadas in these critical years.

The economic and social results of the commercial revolution of 1846, when aggravated by the slump of 1847, were thus of the first order of gravity, and even menacing. The political consequences were quite as drastic, but these at least pointed to a new order in which British America might develop along fresh lines. The Colonial Secretary, Lord Grey, was a doctrinaire believer in colonial self-government. His appointment meant that the Prime Minister, Lord John Russell, despite his stand of 1837 on the limits of colonial self-government (maintained right down to his approval of Metcalfe's policy as governor) was now prepared to accept the political consequences of free trade. The commercial reason for retaining the colonies had gone; there remained only considerations of prestige and affection. Prestige neither Russell nor Grey placed very high; the affection they valued greatly. But a union of sentiment and ideals did not require the central direction and imperial control that the old Empire had required. The authority of the governor no longer had to be so decisively paramount as in the past. Colonial self-government, responsible government "in its inadmissible sense" and as defined by Baldwin, was now actually desirable from the imperial point of view. Moreover, it would now be possible, Grey and Russell hoped, to realize the old Whig and Radical desire to reduce the cost of the colonial governments to the British taxpayer. Colonial self-government was to mean colonial self-support.

Grey at once set himself to deal with the inflamed political situation in Nova Scotia and Canada. The attempt to govern on the Sydenham-Metcalfe plan of a responsible but coalition ministry had resulted, in both provinces, in the refusal of the Reformers after 1843 to enter a coalition. Only Tories or bureaucrats would, but it was impossible to fill the councils with them, as that would have made the council a party ministry of the kind the Reformers were demanding. Neither Falkland in Nova Scotia nor Metcalfe in Canada had succeeded in bringing a single Reformer in, and both accordingly governed with what Howe dubbed "fragmentary councils." In Canada, quiet prevailed under the soldier governor, Lord Cathcart, who succeeded Metcalfe for the duration of the Oregon crisis; but in Nova Scotia, Lord Falkland was seriously at odds with his council.

New Brunswick, by contrast, had shown not the slightest interest in responsible government since its Assembly obtained control of the casual and territorial revenues in return for a civil list in 1837. There Sir John Harvey, the hero of Stoney Creek and a conciliatory administrator, was working amiably with a mixed ministry. Grey now turned to Harvey to replace Falkland, and in a dispatch of November 3, 1846, instructed him to act, and to let it be known he would act, as a constitutional head of government, above party, with no predilections and prepared to work impartially and cordially with either party. In short, Harvey might agree to a party ministry. In his new government he first attempted to repeat his New Brunswick success with a "mixed" council. The attempt failed, and led late in 1847 to a general election in which the Reformers won a sweeping victory. Harvey then cordially accepted a Reform ministry led by J. B. Uniacke on January 28, 1848. Responsible government in its full, unqualified sense was an established convention in Nova Scotia from that date.

Canada followed close behind Nova Scotia. Grey had accompanied the transfer of Harvey to Nova Scotia by the appointment of James Bruce, eighth Earl of Elgin and Kincardine, as Governor-in-Chief of British North America to succeed Cathcart. Elgin, like Metcalfe before him, had just completed a successful term as governor of distraught Jamaica. The younger son of a Scottish peer, and a brilliant scholar, he began a promising political career with his election to the Commons in 1841, but at once lost his seat and his prospects of a parliamentary career by the deaths of his father and elder brother. Failing election to sit as a Scottish peer, he never became in fact what he was by ambition and temperament, a Peelite Liberal-Conservative parliamentarian. The appointment to Jamaica saved him for public life, however, and in that province he first revealed those qualities of insight, detachment and moral integrity which enabled him to govern men by influence, and in Canada to preside with something close to genius over the transition from the governor who was an active executive officer to a governor who was a constitutional monarch. For if there was to be responsible party government in the colonies, the governor would by the same token have to become a constitutional monarch of the type that had been in evolution since the attempt of George III to govern through Lord North had failed and royal influence had broken down with defeat in the American war. This Elgin perceived with the clarity of a first-rate mind; this he realized in the strong crosscurrents of Canadian politics with the tact and insight of a master politician.

The fact that Elgin was a Conservative was no bar to his appointment by a Whig government. Not only had he not been active in politics; in November 1846 he had married as his second wife a daughter of Lord Durham, and he shared with Grey, who was Durham's brother-in-law, the determination to vindicate Durham's impetuous insight in recommending for Canada responsible government as practised in the United Kingdom.

When Elgin arrived in Montreal, early in 1847, he found the Draper ministry still in office and still incomplete. Draper was deeply worried by his failure to win further support from French Canada. Not even the restoration of the use of French as an official language of debate and record in 1846 had diminished the French distrust of the English Tories. Draper had been able to strengthen his ministry by bringing in John Hillyard Cameron, a young and brilliant High Tory from Toronto, who replaced Henry Sherwood when the latter resigned. But when D. B. Viger also resigned, Draper was unable to find a replacement from French Canada.

In the spring of 1847, however, Draper did make a notable addition to the Upper Canadian members of the council. This was John A. Macdonald, a genial and somewhat jaunty young Conservative with a liberal cast of mind, who had been elected for Kingston in 1844. His gifts of good-fellowship, his unusual knack in debate, his deft efficiency as a committee-man, had already distinguished him among the rather heavy, wordy, and pushing politicians of the Assembly. Draper had noted Macdonald's promise, and in appointing him to the council on the eve of his own resignation he was designating his heir as leader of the liberal, or moderate, Conservatives.

On Draper's retirement the ministry was reorganized by Henry Sherwood, who returned to the council as Attorney-General West. The Sherwood-Daly ministry, as it was called, for the irremovable Dominick Daly still continued in office, contained only D. B. Papineau from French Canada and was in fact an attempt at a party ministry without French support. It met the Assembly with a frankly Conservative program of legislation, including an attempt to settle the university question by using the King's College endowment for all the denominational colleges. This was Macdonald's proposal. It was conservative in that it preserved the principle of endowment, and liberal in that it proposed to endow all denominations. But the bill was defeated, and the defeat illustrated the general weakness of the government. It was all too evident that the tide of opinion in the province was running in favour of the Reformers. Finally in December, having brought in two French members from the Legislative Council, the ministers advised Elgin to dissolve the Assembly and went to the country to fight the election as a party government.

It was a hopeless contest. The Reformer memories of 1844, the ineffectual performance of the administration since, a growing division between the old High Tories of Compact days – led by MacNab, Sherwood, and Cameron – and the moderates, of whom Macdonald was chief, were probably sufficient to defeat the administration. But the commercial and agricultural depression of late 1847 was itself enough to bring down any government. The Reform party won a sweeping majority; in Lower Canada few Tories were returned, and scarcely any from Toronto westward.

The defeated ministers, as was not unusual in those days when many new members of the Assembly were not committed to any party, decided to meet the House in late February and test the strength of their support. They were at once defeated heavily on the election of the Speaker, and resigned. Elgin then called on Lafontaine to form a ministry, which he did in early March. It was a straight party administration, for even Dominick Daly had been forced to resign, and responsible government in its fullest sense was as clearly and decisively established in Canada as in Nova Scotia.

The way to responsible government had been prepared by the reorganization of colonial government since 1839, the experience of working Sydenham's responsible government through "mixed councils," and the growth of something like party solidarity in the Reform parties of Nova Scotia and Canada since 1842. But its establishment was assured when the commercial revolution of 1846 removed the need for the colonial governor to function as the agent of a connection founded on the imperial regulation of commerce. That connection must now rest on the very different ground of common ideals and common institutions. Before this basic fact could become clear, the debris of the old colonial order had to be burned away and the compatibility of the exercise of full responsible government and the maintenance of the imperial connection demonstrated. This was to be done in the turbulent and revolutionary years of 1848 and 1849.

When the post-Waterloo system created at Vienna finally collapsed in 1848, liberal and national revolutions erupted across central Europe. Liberal ideas were to be speedily thwarted but the idea of nationality under conservative guidance was in the next twenty years to re-draw the boundaries of Europe between the Rhine and the Carpathians, as it was in the same period to remake the map of British North America.

British America in 1848 was by no means immune to the revolutionary contagion, or to the influence of the revolutionary ideas. The most direct impact on Canadian sentiment came from the February Revolution in France, the Young Ireland rising in Dublin, and the great Chartist demonstration in London. Young French nationalists in Montreal listened ardently to Papineau, back after his years of exile in France, unchanged, unrepentant, and full of the radical ideology which created the Second Republic. Soon "*les rouges*" were to have their own set of ideas – radical, republican, anti-clerical – and their own journal, *L'Avenir*. So also the still swarming, still afflicted Irish welcomed the news that Young Ireland had struck. And in the Upper Canadian peninsula, the country of the Reformers, American-settled and American-influenced, Chartism gave a British complexion to the radical-democratic ideas held by both Chartists and Jacksonian Democrats. The establishment of responsible government, that moderate, traditional and British achievement, had occurred just as Canada was beginning to ferment with political ideas little short of explosive.

How various and widespread were the effects of the commercial revolution of 1846 and the political revolutions of 1848 was illustrated by the unrest and political agitation even in isolated and primitive Red River. There a quarrel between private traders and some officers of the Hudson's Bay Company had blown up into an agitation by the half-caste people of Red River – the French métis and the English half-breeds – against the monopoly and the government of the Company. Petitions asking for free trade and self-government were sent to Washington and London in 1846. The arrival of troops, sent nominally because of the Oregon dispute, quieted the agitation, but it flared up again in 1849 at the trial of Guillaume Sayer for trading furs contrary to the monopoly rights of the Company. The armed métis gathered to intimidate the court; and when Sayer was found guilty, with a recommendation for mercy, they interpreted the verdict as an acquittal and proclaimed that trade was free. Thereafter, it was. And Louis Riel, a métis educated in Lower Canada, headed a committee which demanded that representatives of the métis be appointed to the Council of Assiniboia; that Adam Thom, once an aide of Durham's, and Recorder of Rupert's Land since 1839, be dismissed; and that French be used as well as English in the courts of the settlement. This was the voice of the "new nation" of the métis making itself heard on Red River just after the year of revolutions. Only on the Pacific coast did peace prevail. There in 1849 the Hudson's Bay Company, under imperial direction, founded the colony of Vancouver Island to preserve the British share of the Oregon territory from American occupation.

The tumult on the banks of the Red amid the buffalo-hunters of the plains attracted little notice. More startling, as well as more serious, was the violent riot by a Tory mob in Montreal. The outburst was the result of Tory opposition to a Rebellion Losses Bill and to the establishment of a party government of Reformers on the institution of responsible government by the Whig government of the United Kingdom. There was in fact ground for criticism and opposition in the way the Rebellion Losses Bill, intended to compensate those who had suffered losses in the troubles of 1837–38, was presented to the Assembly. The truth was that the French ministers were resolved to carry the bill, cost what it might, and their English colleagues were embarrassed but forced to remain silent. It was thus a first test of cabinet solidarity under responsible government. But the intent and substance of the bill were unexceptionable, being no more than an act of justice to the French sufferers in the rebellion, and an act intolerably de-layed. In Upper Canada, compensation had been paid before the Union to those who had established claims for damages suffered as a result of the rebellion. Similar compensation to those who had claims in Lower Canada had been delayed by the political struggles of the Union, until the Draper ministry appointed a commission to consider claims in 1846, and in 1847 learned that perhaps a vote of £100,000 would meet all legitimate demands. There the matter stood, however, and no further action was taken.

It was this incomplete Conservative measure that Lafontaine took up in 1849; his bill called for the provision of £100,000 for the satisfaction of claims. Its terms failed to define what grounds of claim were legitimate, however, and Lafontaine failed to state the government's position on how claims were to be decided. Many who were actually in rebellion in 1837 had not been convicted in court. But some of them had suffered damage from the operations of the troops putting down the rebellion. Were such unconvicted rebels to receive compensation for damages resulting from measures necessary to the defeat of the rebellion? On the face of the bill it seemed they would, and the government did not attempt to offer a formula which would discriminate between the legitimate claimant and the former rebel.

Thus the Tory opposition felt they had grounds for objecting to the measure and they bitterly, if unavailingly, opposed it in the Assembly. This was of course their right and duty. But when the bill also passed the Legislative Council and was ready for Elgin's assent, the Tory leaders turned to questionab le measure to induce the Governor General to reserve the bill. To petition him to do so, as they did, was proper; to demonstrate against his signing it, as they did, was allowable. But to incite the Protestant Tory mob of that turbulent city – in which Orange and Green, French and Irish, confronted one another like Kilkenny cats – to demonstrate against the royal assent was to resort to intimidation by violence, and the attempt ended in arson and manslaughter.

Elgin, for his part, had disliked the bill but thought it a local measure and therefore one on which he must accept the advice of his ministers. He accordingly drove down from his residence at Monklands on the mountainside through the swarming narrow streets, where the mob shouted threats and the Montrea militia cavalry were plainly fraternizing with the roughs and the gentlemen who made up the mob. But when he emerged after assenting to the bill, the demonstration burst its intended limits and became a prolonged and disastrous riot. Elgin was pelted with stones and eggs; his carriage barely made its w ay out of th crowd, thanks to efforts of the Toronto cavalry, who, much as they sympathized with the mob, did their duty. But the Montreal cavalry, sons of the business gentry and the old oligarchy, "sat laughing in their saddles" as the Queen's representative fled before the rioters.

The mob then turned to the burning of the Parliament Buildings and the sacking of Lafontaine's house. The city, unpoliced and full of unemployed, did not quiet down for some days. The Government and Parliament of Canada were all but forced to cease functioning by the violence of some elements of the political party whose watchword was loyalty and whose first concern was law and order.

The encouragement of rioting, outrageous and disgraceful in any citizen, was peculiarly so in conservative and respectable persons. But leaders of extreme,

Compact Toryism, like MacNab, had not learned to respect the conventions of parliamentary government. Accustomed to think of himself as a member of a loyalist garrison in a continent given over to democracy and in a province threatened, as he saw it, by a French ascendancy, the Canadian High Tory had developed the ascendancy mentality of a Protestant and British garrison. When he found himself excluded from power, as all representatives of his party were for the first time in 1848, he was gravely angered and alarmed. He did not think the opposition loyal; he did not expect the alternation of party governments, the easy ins and outs of the parliamentary game. He assumed that his own ascendancy, modified though it had been since 1841, had been replaced by a rival ascendancy, French and crypto-republican, which would be as exclusive and perhaps as enduring as his own had been in Compact days. That was why MacNab said in his rough and reckless way at the height of the Rebellion Losses agitation, "If we don't make a disturbance about this, we shall never get in." The Reformers had been caught voting public money to pay rebels; what better chance would there be to expose them for what they were, and discredit them forever!

Such was the temper which had played with riot, and led to the burning of more than the Parliament Buildings. In those flames the good name of the old Compact Toryism was consumed. With it went the hope of Montreal to be the political capital of Canada. As Elgin wrote from the security of Monklands to explain to Grey why he felt obliged to assent to a measure the policy of which he questioned; as the troops still patrolled the streets, and as Parliament took up in its temporary quarters in the Bonsecours Market the great and laborious program of the Reform ministry, Montreal returned to an uneasy peace, aware that an epoch was ending.

But the death throes of the old Toryism did not end with the Montreal riots of the spring of 1849. There was little revival of trade that year, little indication of a change for the better. The repeal of the Navigation Acts did not come into effect until January 1850, and did not affect the shipping rates of 1849. What seemed certain was that imperial protection was gone beyond recovery; what was most uncertain was the future of Canadian trade and of the traffic of the St. Lawrence.

Increasingly men were coming to the conclusion that the commercial revolution had left the imperial connection void of either economic or political meaning. And those who came to that conclusion also assumed, and rightly in the circumstance of the day, that British America could not be independent. They therefore saw annexation to the United States as the inevitable destiny of Canada, and since inevitable, as something to be hastened.

It was chiefly the Tory business men of Montreal who thought the imperial connection had become economically meaningless; and now that the Rebellion Losses Bill had passed, they found it equally devoid of political significance. Some Tories elsewhere in Canada, and some in New Brunswick, had come to the same conclusion. The British American *bourgeoisie* had always sat light to patriotic sentiment and political ties. Resident rather than domesticated, it had lived in a world of commerce rather than one of political nationality.

Some Reformers also interpreted the commercial revolution and the grant of full responsible government as foreshadowing the virtual end of the imperial connection. Radical reformers saw responsible government as a compromise which fell far short of popular sovereignty, elective institutions, and the cheap and honest government which the radical principles of Mackenzie had promised. Peter Perry, the old Reformer, had become an annexationist and won a by-election without repudiating his views. Other Reformers, such as Caleb Hopkins, who held similar opinions were sufficient in number to embarrass Baldwin. And in Lower Canada, Papineau and the Rouges were talking freely of the need for republican institutions and annexation to the continental republic.

It was, however, the exasperated and desperate Montreal Tories who made an open and spectacular avowal of their annexationist aims in a manifesto issued in October 1849. Since imperial protection was ended, they declared, Canada must assure its commercial future in union with the United States. The signatures on the manifesto were those of leaders of Montreal business, the bearers of names long honoured in Canada. The old imperial patriotism, the vaunted loyalty of the Tory, had been publicly disowned by a large number of the prominent men of the party. That some Reformers should be annexationists surprised no one; in the Tory it was a denial of everything in his tradition since 1776. But in the Tory, support for annexation sprang from frustration caused by a loyalty spurned and a world turned upside down. In the radical it rested on a long-nurtured preference for reason over tradition, and the republic as against the monarchy.

There can be little doubt that, as a consequence of the uncertainty which followed in the wake of the commercial revolution, the annexation rot had sunk deep in certain areas and classes. As colonial dependence ended, few Canadians of the extremes of politics, the High Tories and the democratic radicals, were prepared to think in terms of an independent Canadian nationality.

Fortunately, the men in charge of events, Lafontaine, Baldwin, Hincks, Elgin and Grey, believed both that the imperial connection still possessed meaning and validity and that a self-governing colonial nationality was the immediate goal of Canada. The government, therefore, firmly and implacably dismissed from office every Justice of the Peace, colonel of militia, or other holder of a royal commission or honour who had signed the manifesto. The action made it clear that annexation talk verged on treason and would be punished. This firm stand stopped the rot completely in the Tory party and drove it underground among the radicals, where it was to smoulder until the end of the century.

The chief results, then, of the flaring passions of 1849 were that the old High Toryism and the old democratic radicalism had reached their historic terms in

Canada. The old Toryism had burned itself out in the Montreal riots and the fury of the Annexation Manifesto. The oligarchic arrogance, the ascendancy mentality, the constitution of checks and balances, the independent and permanent executive, the hierarchic concept of a society of gentlemen obliged to serve the public and of ordinary people who did the work of the world, these had become ineffectual anachronisms. And the old radicalism, rational, international, abstract, found itself outmoded in the new age. In a year or two Papineau was to retire permanently to his beautiful Montebello and a long Indian summer of gentlemanly leisure. Mackenzie, glad to be back in homely, oddly tolerant Canada from the bosom, strangely chill when tested, of the republic whose glories he had sought to establish there, remained a lonely figure, cantankerous and pathetic, the financial gadfly of successive legislatures.

The end of the old Toryism and the old radicalism was beneficial to Canadian politics and to the Tory and the Reform parties. Extremes that had dealt in violence and annexation were removed. Henceforth all parties were to play the political game according to the parliamentary rules; and in parliamentary government the centre governs, the moderate men rule. The Tory party could now adapt itself to responsible government under a saner, more flexible, more liberal kind of Toryism, the conservatism of Macdonald. And the Reform party had in its new radicals, the Clear Grits, and in the Rouges, a left wing which was for a generation nationalist in its leadership. Indeed, in the Clear Grit headquarters there was talk of "Young Canada"; and the literary voice of the Grits, William McDougall, was to be one of the inspirers of the later movement, "Canada First."

All this was far from being apparent in 1849, however, and Tories and radicals alike floundered about in confusion, seeking new directions. In the suddenly organized and most incoherent British American League – annexationist, imperialist, nationalist, all at once – they sought the new orientations together. At a conference held in Kingston in December 1849, and watched with keen attention by the Canadian public, they even stumbled on the old idea of William Smith and of Durham, the federal union of British America. This was the key to the future and the vehicle for the Canadian nationality which was to give life and purpose to the floundering colonies of British North America. But no one recognized it as such at the time, although the idea was to lodge in the mind of John A. Macdonald.

If the events of 1849 were turbulent and the minds of men confused, there was order and discipline in the government of Lafontaine and Baldwin. With responsible government achieved, they could undertake, after the brief and comparatively barren session of 1848 and the disturbance of the Riots, that program of reform legislation to which responsible government was but the prelude and means.

The program was noteworthy first for the volume of legislation it produced.

No less than two hundred bills were passed, a clear indication that with responsible government Canada had adopted the practice of continuous and specific legislation which distinguishes modern democracies.

Even more striking, however, was the diverse use the two sections of the Union made of the new powers of self-government. The legislation for Lower Canada was conservative and designed to strengthen and perpetuate a conservative and clerical society. The school system, denominational before 1841, continued to be so, and its Roman Catholic section came increasingly under the care and management of the religious teaching orders. The incorporation of ecclesiastical and religious orders made up a large part of the Lower Canadian legislation between 1841 and 1853, when a general act of incorporation was passed. Of reform in the sense of remodelling institutions there was little. None was desired by Lafontaine and his followers; they were defenders of French nationality, not radical critics of the social order. The one great measure that was in agitation and would produce a change in the basis of French-Canadian society, the abolition of seigniorial tenure, had been the subject of a royal commission appointed in 1844. But action was held up by Lafontaine's insistence that the rights of the seigneurs should be adequately protected. It was apparent that the French Reformers were conservative nationalists, and that they would use responsible government more as a means to defend the privileges of French Canada than to change its institutions. This conservative character in Lafontaine's following explains in part the rise of the Rouges.

Upper Canadian legislation was in the main very different. The vague socia and political ideal held by Grenville, Simcoe, and the conservative loyalists, of a social order governed by a recognized gentry, with the character of a Christian state preserved by an endowed church, was now to be finally discarded. In its place was brought forward the ideal of the democratic and rational, if also Christian, society, already so fully realized in the United States. The change, though neither simple nor complete, was to be a drastic and decisive one.

Its principal architect was Robert Baldwin, that devout low-church Anglican who, though a pupil of John Strachan, had defied the Compact and undone much of the work of his former tutor and present father in God, the Bishop of Toronto. Baldwin thought that Strachan had placed the Anglican Church in an invidious and impossible position by his attempts to maintain the whole apparatus of an establishment. The Anglican Church in Canada, he held, simply did not possess the historical position which made the establishment defensible in England.

This aspect of Baldwin's thought determined the character of his university bill by which the University of Toronto was established as a secular corporation supported by the land endowment given to Strachan's King's College. Baldwin's Act by no means settled the university question in Ontario – denominational universities and colleges were to survive under a new Act in 1853 and some were to federate with the University of Toronto later in the century – but it did indicate the trend of moderate opinion in Upper Canada to the view, already expressed in the system of common schools, that the state had a prime obligation to support learning and could do so, in a society of many churches, only on the neutral ground of secular knowledge.

Like Lower Canada, Upper Canada had had a public schools system since 1841, but had developed it as a non-denominational system. The first Act was faulty and Baldwin accepted the ideas of the Superintendent, the Reverend Egerton Ryerson, in rejecting an uncompromisingly secular bill prepared by Malcolm Cameron in 1849 and moving the adoption of the one prepared by Ryerson in 1850. The new Act continued the non-denominational public system, but it did allow a measure of relief to individual Roman Catholics who wished to have separate public schools for their children. This willingness to yield to the conscientious scruples of the French, Irish, and Scots Roman Catholics, in Canada as in the Atlantic provinces, was beginning to give British American public education one of its main characteristics, the separate school. Further concessions were made in 1853. But Canada West resolutely refused to accept the denominational system of Canada East, whatever smaller concessions it might have to make to a majority drawn from Canada East.

The next great measure was the Municipal Act, a large and cumbersome measure which replaced Sydenham's District Councils Act of 1841. Its chief feature was that it made the wardens and treasurers of counties elective instead of appointive. Thus local government in Upper Canada became fully democratic; in Lower Canada the Ordinance of 1840 had remained in force until 1845, when it was abolished and elective parish and township councils established. In 1855, after a trial of county municipalities, the basic institutions of parish township, town, and village were finally established, each with its elective council. No comparable development of incorporated and elective municipal institutions was to take place in the Atlantic provinces until the 1870's and 1880's.

Two other chief measures, one of 1849 and one of 1850, completed the Baldwinian reforms in Upper Canada. The Act of 1849 reformed the Court of Chancery. It was a long step in the direction of a simpler legal system and that merging of equity with common law which legal reformers had long urged in the interests of cheap and speedy justice. To Baldwin his Act was a final step and his most cherished achievement, but it proved to be only the penultimate step before the abolition of Chancery. The Act of 1850 was also a legal reform, the abolition of the rule of primogeniture in the inheritance of real estate. Henceforth all children, male and female, were to have equal right of inheritance, subject only to the right of bequest. The old feudal principle of inheritance by the eldest male, a cornerstone of hierarchic society, gave way to the principle of equal rights in a society of equals, a theory compatible with the general tenor of a democratic society of civil equals, in which the rights of women were beginning to approximate to those of men. The measure was to be one of the fundamental premises of Canadian society. Nothing could have more clearly signalled the end of the Tory social ideal of perpetuated property and social hierarchy; nothing more clearly indicated the advent of democratic and social equality. This was the work done by the free-thinking and rationalist Jefferson in Virginia seventy-four years before. In Canada, most typically, it was the achievement of a devoted churchman who had none of the Virginian's facile optimism, nor his faith in the goodness or indeed the equality of men, but carried the measure because he thought it was required by the social conscience of his day.

None the less, despite his action in the university question, Baldwin was reluctant to act on one other great measure which had already agitated Upper Canadian society and which came to the fore again in 1850, that of the Clergy Reserves. Lafontaine also was reluctant. The former as an Anglican, the latter as a Roman Catholic, could not easily give up the principle of the state endowment of religion as a manifestation that the state itself was Christian. But the principle of the separation of church and state, and the more radical "voluntary" principle, that there should be no state support of religion, were held by too many Upper Canadians for the settlement of 1841 to be left unchanged.

This was indeed true of other issues. Lafontaine's stand on the abolition of seigniorial tenure, Baldwin's on the Court of Chancery, their attitude towards the abolition of the Clergy Reserves, all indicated that they had carried reform as far as they were prepared to go. The great centre coalition led by Lafontaine and Baldwin was breaking up, partly through internal weakness, partly from external pressure. Its main purpose had been achieved in the establishment of responsible government and the great reforms of 1849–50. Its leaders and its core were becoming conservative and their feeling was expressed in Baldwin's words, "Il faut jeter l'ancre de la constitution." But large elements of the public were not prepared to leave the issues of the Reserves, seigniorial tenure, and the Court of Chancery where they stood in 1850. The reform of institutions was not yet finished in Canada.

The institution of responsible government and its use to carry out the laws and reforms the two Canadian peoples wanted was accompanied by a devolution on the colonies of those services still administered by the imperial government. In 1851, for example, the Post Office became a provincial service; in 1854, Indian affairs were transferred. But the attempt of Lord Grey to have the colonies assume the charge of the most fundamental of services, that of defence, was unsuccessful. Self-government did not yet mean self-defence. At the request of the colonial governments, the imperial garrisons remained in Canada and New Brunswick; at the naval base of Halifax there was no question of withdrawal.

Not all the legislation of 1849 and 1850 touched on fundamentals, and there were political leaders, notably Francis Hincks, who thought, as Sydenham once had done, that it would be well for Canada if fundamentals were left at rest and more attention given to the practical business of economic development. Certainly there was call for the latter. Canada was faced with a major commercial depression and with the sudden supersession of its magnificent canals, completed in 1848 at great cost, by the advent of the long-distance railway. In Lower Canada, the emigration of French Canadians from the rural districts to the New England factory towns continued. To the competition of the Erie Canal with the St. Lawrence was now added the competition of the New York railways. All these things urgently required strong and decisive action by government, if only because they underlay the political discontent and annexation sentiment of the day.

That which lent itself to the readiest and most effective action was the development of railways. In 1850 Canada had only sixty-six miles of railway in operation – the line from Laprairie opposite Montreal to the Richelieu River, which had been in use since 1836. Since that date there had been repeated talk of a line to the Atlantic provinces, to unite British America and give Canada a winter port, but nothing had been done until 1848 when a line had been surveyed by Major William Robinson, R.E., for the War Office. A strictly commercial proposal to build a line to Portland, Maine, had resulted in 1845 in the organization of the St. Lawrence and Atlantic, the purpose of which was to connect Montreal with Portland by a line through the Eastern Townships and Maine. The company had accomplished little, however, as it had encountered the collapse of the British railway boom. Other lines were also being organized, the Great Western to carry American traffic from Niagara to Windsor, lines running north from the St. Lawrence and Lake Ontario to haul farm produce and lumber to the waterfront, and a line from Halifax to Windsor in Nova Scotia.

Canada clearly had to add railways to its canals, if it was to continue to compete for the carrying trade of the American west. And the cities, towns and farms of both sections of the province suddenly realized, as all America had, that the railway was a matter of commercial life or death. The problem was how to raise the needed capital; and therefore government, which in British America had from the first provided or helped to provide canals and locks, for commercial as well as military reasons, must assist also in the construction of railways. It was now the supple and clever Hincks who originated the legislation which made the state the underwriter of private railway development in Canada. His Guarantee Act of 1849 gave a government guarantee to the bonds of railways up to five per cent interest when the railway had completed half the construction proposed. The same act empowered the municipalities to use their financial resources to assist railway construction.

The Act was extensively used and helped stimulate the railway boom of the mid fifties. But even without it there would have been an outburst of railway development in British America. Both British contractors and British financiers were anxious to begin investment and construction in the Empire, as the main work of building the railway network of the United Kingdom was already done.

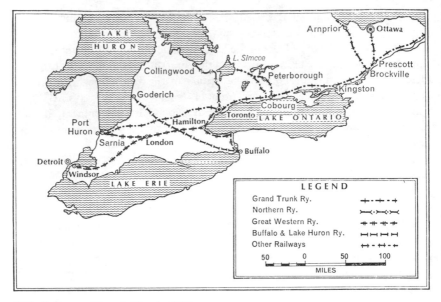

XII *Railways of Canada West by 1860*

And for a time it even seemed that the great enterprise of the Intercolonial might go ahead. Joseph Howe was pushing it vigorously from Halifax and Lord Grey was interested in the building of a military line by immigrants who would settle the country through which the line passed. The government and people of New Brunswick wanted a line to run westward into New England, but Howe was persuaded to favour a line to Canada by the St. John valley, which would aid the New Brunswick westward line, and was convinced that the imperial government guarantee promised for the military line along the North Shore of New Brunswick might be used for the St. John valley line. The imperial government declined to agree, however, and the Intercolonial project suddenly collapsed in the spring of 1852.

Hincks, who represented the Canadian government in the negotiations, promptly turned to the English capitalists who were interested in building railways in Canada, and worked out with them the scheme which became the Grand Trunk Railway Company. The new company was to build, with the backing of the Guarantee Act, a line from Montreal to a junction with the Great Western Railway. An amalgamation with the St. Lawrence and Atlantic was worked out, but none, as it proved, with the Great Western. The object was to build a high-standard through line, as expressed by its name of Grand Trunk, to draw traffic from the Middle West. By the new means of the railway, Canada still pursued the quest of a trade carried by the St. Lawrence route and drawn in large part from the United States.

Meanwhile another line of development, of more significance to the future, had begun. That was a movement along the edge of the Precambrian Shield in search of new land, new timber berths and, above all, minerals. Since the organization of the Geological Survey of Canada in 1842, its director, William Logan, was beginning to reveal the vast Precambrian background of the Laurentian valley. Prospecting increased in the 1840's and Canadian mining companies began to press along the north shores of Huron and Superior. In 1842 the town of Bruce Mines had been founded, and in the early 1850's the Montreal Company opened the Wellington copper mine there. This westward movement along the Upper Lakes was the groundwork for a new Canadian penetration of the northwest.

The main interest of Canadians, however, was still the trade of the American west. The amount of traffic would obviously be conditioned by American commercial policy. While the comparative costs and services of Canadian railways and canals would be the decisive factors in determining the movement of American goods by the St. Lawrence route, such a movement would be part of general commercial relations and would tend to increase if the total volume of transborder trade increased. Hence arose the feeling of many that annexation was a solution to this problem as to others. It was to deal with the feeling and satisfy it by other means that Hincks in 1851 made the first of those approaches to the government of the United States which after many delays were to produce a treaty providing for reciprocity of trade in natural products.

In commercial relations with the United States, the colonies themselves could now do much, for the Russell government in 1846 had granted them the power to make local tariffs. In 1847 to 1849 Canada and the Atlantic provinces for the first time made provision for their own customs service and imposed their own tariffs. The Canadian tariff included duties on American agricultural products competing with Canadian products in the home market. Such duties were imposed in response to the demands of the farmers, but they might be used to create pressure in the United States for reciprocity, just as a stricter enforcement of the terms of the Fisheries Convention of 1818 might soften New England's opposition to a treaty admitting British American fish. In 1852, in which year a treaty still seemed remote, the Atlantic squadron of the British navy was ordered to enforce the convention more strictly than in the past.

By that year the political scene in Canada had altered considerably. The growing conservatism of Lafontaine and Baldwin had stimulated the rise of the Rouges in Canada East and of the Clear Grits in Canada West. In turn, the presence and the pressure of the Rouges caused Lafontaine and the great body of the French members to become still more conservative. This division of the French bloc which had been formed to resist the union, and had won the grant of responsible government and the restoration of the French language to official use, in fact forced the French majority to think and act politically, and in the process to realize that they were conservative. But their increased conservatism did not weaken them. The party of Lafontaine, the Bleus, continued to hold the majority of the members from Lower Canada and remained the cornerstone on which a parliamentary combination in the Canadian Assembly had to be built.

The effect of the rise of the Clear Grits was different. They did not remain a somewhat isolated minority, as did the Rouges in Lower Canada; they threatened to become the Upper Canadian majority. They were strong in the populous counties in the western peninsula, the old home of radicalism. They had in the Clergy Reserves an issue which embarrassed the conservative Reformers and brought them more support than their radical democratic platform by itself would ever have done. Their first impact on the political structure was somewhat accidental when in 1851 they supported a motion of William Lyon Mackenzie's to abolish the Court of Chancery. The motion won a majority of the Upper Canadian members, and Baldwin, cut to the quick, insisted on resigning. Lafontaine, weary of political life, followed him. Elgin asked Hincks to form a ministry, which he did with the aid of A. N. Morin, Lafontaine's successor. Hincks included two representatives of the Grits in the Upper Canadian section of the ministry, and thus was able to continue in substance the Lafontaine-Baldwin coalition known as the Reform party.

The Grits were not happy in the association, however, and the new combination also failed to contain that new force in Canadian politics, the journalist George Brown. For in 1842 Brown, a Scot, had come to Toronto with his father from New York, where they had found American democracy uncongenial. They began a paper addressed to the Scottish community and upholding the religious principles on which the Free Church of Scotland was based. In 1843 the Browns began a second paper to support the Free Church, just formed as a result of the disruption of the Scottish Kirk. The next year, George Brown launched the *Globe* and made it an organ of Reform opinion. A bitter opponent of Metcalfe, Brown soon made himself a leading man in the Upper Canadian Reform party, taking an active part in its affairs and in the election campaign of 1847 and subsequent by-elections. A strong believer in the British connection and British institutions, he earnestly and effectively fought the annexation sentiment of the old radicals. He also found the hard, bright radicalism of the young Clear Grits little to his taste. But his own profound belief in the voluntary principle, animated as it was by the "Papal Aggression" controversy in England in 1850, led to Brown's breaking openly with the Lafontaine-Baldwin Reformers for their lukewarmness in the matter of the Clergy Reserves.

To Brown thereafter, the separation of church and state became the central issue of Canadian politics. In the general election of 1851 Brown entered the Assembly and at once established himself as one of the foremost men in the House. Able, forceful, self-assured, he was in public a man of dogmatic and uncompromising temper. He disliked and distrusted the clever and flexible

Hincks. He feared and denounced the ecclesiastical legislation of Lower Canada and the power of the French vote. He sought to break up the coalition on which the Hincks-Morin ministry rested. Brown wanted true political parties, resting on some body of principle, not expedient groupings sharing the spoils of office and dispensing the sudden and abundant largesse of the railway era. A man who seemed to see only two colours, black and white, he sought to create a clear-cut Liberal party which would separate church and state, and govern democratically by majority rule based upon representation of the people according to population. In 1851-52 the first census of the Province of Canada, by revealing that the population of Upper Canada had come to exceed that of Lower Canada, gave a local application to the principle of representation by population. By the provision of the Act of Union which gave equal representation to the two sections of the Union, Upper Canada was to be under-represented after 1851. This to Brown meant that the Canadian Union was seriously imperfect; he therefore moved a resolution in 1853 for representation by population "without regard to a separating line." In the end, Brown's aspirations would break up the Union. In the immediate future they were to break up the Hincks-Morin ministry and drive the conservatives of Upper and Lower Canada together in a body of political strength which in the main would govern Canada for the next forty years.

The Hincks-Morin ministry served to mask and confuse the new alignment which seemed in fact necessary in Canadian politics, the formation of a parliamentary Conservative party purged of the ascendancy temper, and a Liberal party freed of the drag of the clerical nationalism of French Canada. These ssues were submerged by the lush prosperity of the great railway boom in which Tories like Sir Allan MacNab combined with Reformers like William Hamilton Merritt, the inspirer of the first Welland Canal, under the slogan attributed to Sir Allan: "Railways are my politics." Ministers of the Crown sat on the Board of Directors of the Grand Trunk, and it took even the Clear Grits and the Rouges a little while to realize that such a practice jeopardized the public interest.

Not even an unexampled and ever-growing prosperity could drown two older issues, however, or do more than delay the break-up of the Reform coalition. One issue was the Clergy Reserves; the other, seigniorial tenure.

When it had become apparent in 1850 that a majority of the public of English Canada was deeply dissatisfied with the settlement of the Reserves by the imperial Act of 1841, Baldwin and Lafontaine had subordinated their own views and decided that the imperial government must be asked to repeal the Act. Hincks and Morin agreed in their turn, although they refused to introduce, as the Grits urged, a Canadian bill to indicate to the imperial government what action they would take when permitted. The Russell government had agreed to a repeal but did not bring the matter forward for fear of failure in the session of 1850, and in that of 1851 they gave way to the first Derby ministry, a minority Conservative government. The new Colonial Secretary, the Tory Sir John Pakington, simply refused to seek repeal of the imperial Act. The Clear Grits and George Brown, already distrustful of what they suspected was procrastination by the Canadian ministry under French influence, then claimed that Pakington's refusal was a denial of responsible government. In 1853, however, the Aberdeen government agreed to repeal the Act, which was done early in 1854.

At the same time that Hincks was under merciless attack by Brown, with his cry of French domination and his demand for representation by population, Morin was under steady pressure from the Rouges to abolish seigniorial tenure. The tenure was no longer a protection to the French who in growing numbers since 1837 had been overflowing from the seigniories into the Eastern Townships and New England. Indeed, as many seigneurs were business-like Anglo-Scots, the tenure had become a mere set of commercial relations such as it had not been in the French régime. The difficulty, however, was still the issue of compensation to the seigneurs, with all its implications for the rights of property. But clearly, as Morin saw, it would be better for conservatives to carry such a reform, if it was inevitable, than to have the Rouges do it, tinged as they were with "socialism."

It is probable that the Hincks-Morin ministry would have carried the secularization of the Reserves and the abolition of the tenure with compensation, had it survived the session of 1854. But Hincks had been involved in two scandals, one involving the purchase of railway stock, one the purchase of land at Pointe Lévis for sale to the Grand Trunk. His political reputation was gravely injured by this participation in the corruption of the day. Early in 1854 he was also absent in England and in the United States with Elgin for the final negotiation of the Reciprocity Treaty. That long-sought agreement came too late to restore prosperity, for a great boom was well under way by 1852 and was driven even higher by the wheat prices of the Crimean War. It was also much too late to restore the fortunes of Francis Hincks. He therefore took refuge in a declaration that, since the representation of each section was to be increased to sixty-five, matters so serious as the Clergy Reserves and seigniorial tenure should be submitted to a new and enlarged assembly. The old assembly was dissolved; and after the general election, the ministry failed to command a majority in the House and Hincks resigned.

Hincks was defeated by the Clear Grits voting with the Conservative opposition. The defeat redounded to the advantage of the Conservatives, however, not to that of the Grits. At last the opportunity had come to bring about what Elgin had foreseen in 1847, and what Draper and Macdonald had been preparing the Tory party to accept, the union of the French conservatives with the English. On Hincks's advice, Elgin sent for MacNab, and MacNab succeeded readily in forming the MacNab-Morin ministry, on the basis of the coalition of the French Reformers and the English Conservatives. This coalition was to become a party, the Liberal-Conservative party, the main vehicle of Canadian national purpose for the next generation. Once more, as under Sydenham in 1841 and under Lafontaine and Baldwin in 1848, the moderate but progressive centre dominated Canadian politics and ensured the continuance of the monarchical and parliamentary tradition and the establishment of Canadian independence.

The new ministry at once carried the secularization of the Clergy Reserves and the abolition of seigniorial tenure, with compensation; the last vestiges of the work of Pitt, almost the last vestiges of the work of Talon and the French intendants, were obliterated. In English and Protestant Canada the principles of the separation of church and state and of voluntary support of religious institutions had won a large if not a complete victory (the rise of the separate school constituting a victory for the opposing principle). The Church of England began to develop modes of self-government and, step by step, moved from its ties with the Crown to a position of full autonomy. Thus the Protestant churches, now private associations, faced the Church of Rome, semi-established in Lower Canada and united by allegiance to Rome and a growing hierarchy – a situation that was one of the origins of later church union. In Lower Canada, land was at last to be treated as a commodity charged with no special obligations and committed to the support of no particular way of life. The great basic reforms of the century were all but completed. Well might Elgin, his work done, retire, to be succeeded by his former Oxford examiner and like-minded friend, Sir Edmund Walker Head, late lieutenant-governor of New Brunswick.

In the other colonies of British North America the shock of the commercia revolution and the coming of responsible government brought no such stresses as affected Canada and posed no problem requiring such a resolution as that of 1854 in Canada. The Tories of New Brunswick and Nova Scotia were not as high-tempered as those of Canada, and were not at all addicted to the use of violence and riot. The evolution towards the common pattern of the new colonial constitution was advanced when responsible government began, to some degree at least, in New Brunswick in 1848, in Prince Edward Island in 1851, and in Newfoundland after the separation of the Executive from the Legislative Council in 1855. But in all these colonies, less politically advanced than the Canadas and Nova Scotia, the prevalence of faction and the undifferentiated character of the constitutions delayed the full institution of responsible government for years after these traditional dates. The relations of church and state, and of denomination with denomination before the law and in the public school system, had to be worked out in the Atlantic provinces also. This was done, there also, step by step, and left the churches voluntary societies in a state attached to none of them but with varying measures of public support for denominational schools, ranging from the state separate schools of New Brunswick to the church-controlled ones of Newfoundland. Thus the Atlantic colonies acquired much the same basic institutions as Canada.

In Canada, political life was comparatively placid from 1854 to 1856. The boom now reached its peak; the rapid building of the Grand Trunk, the Great Western and the Northern railways, with many smaller ones, war prices for wheat, and the sale of natural products under reciprocity in the American market, gave Canada the most prosperous years of the century. The reform of institutions continued, but only two significant changes remained to be attempted; the rest was done by way of amendment of existing legislation. One of the major reforms was the Act of 1856 which made the appointive Legislative Council elective. Both Grits and Tories had demanded this since 1849, the Grits to make the council democratic, the Tories to make it an effective second chamber by means of the property qualification required for election. The other significant reform was the establishment of a commission in 1857 to codify the civil law of Canada East. The project was initiated and eagerly watched by George Etienne Cartier, a blunt, pugnacious railway lawyer, who had been a proscribed rebel in 1837 and who by 1856 had succeeded to the leadership of the Bleus. The work was completed in 1866 and the French civil law, so antique, so confused, the object of so much dispute, was at last systematized and simplified. At the same time the modernization of the judicial system of Lower Canada, long needed but not attempted by Lafontaine, was carried out. These measures signified that, twenty years after 1837, one half of United Canada was French in law and in the administration of the law, and that French was one of its official languages, a language taught in Roman Catholic schools supported by public funds.

Such a development found many opponents in Upper Canada, and their leader was George Brown. In the *Globe* and in Parliament, Brown had continued his strident crusade to diminish "French influence" and Roman Catholic encroachment, as he saw them, by creating a liberal, anti-clerical party of Clear Grits and Rouges. By 1856 he was succeeding in both Lower and Upper Canada. His cause throve, particularly after the government forced through, with Lower Canadian votes, in the last days of the session of 1855 when many Upper Canadian members had gone home, another amendment to the School Act which strengthened separate schools. But the more Brown succeeded, the more he cemented the Bleus to the Upper Canadian Conservatives. The coalition of 1854 was beginning to fuse as a party.

One obstacle to the fusion, however, was the continued leadership of the genial, bluff and incompetent old High Tory, Sir Allan MacNab. Finally in 1856, the English Conservatives felt that enough had been done for the "gallant knight," and MacNab was forced to give way to Macdonald. Morin had retired early in 1855 and had been succeeded by Etienne Pascal Taché, who continued as leader of the new ministry. One notable feature of the Taché-Macdonald ministry was the inclusion of George Etienne Cartier, who became Macdonald's lieutenant and chief by turns but was his loyal colleague and faithful friend without a rift until Confederation. The bond between the two men was a rare example of political friendship, excelling in its quality of real affection the partnership of Lafontaine and Baldwin. That such a friendship was possible revealed how far Canada had travelled from the politics of ascendancy towards the concept of a dual culture in one political nationality.

To continue to develop such a society in one nationality had become the peculiar destiny of Canada, and such was the character of Canadian freedom under its monarchical and parliamentary institutions, that the process was to be one not of denying differences and stressing uniformities, but of admitting differences while seeking union. As yet it was an instinctive process, a trend still only half realized, but the man who stood, by the intuition of genius, at the point of realization was John A. Macdonald.

To realize the half-apprehended goal, Macdonald had, against the clear-headed, narrow-edged, dogmatic battering of George Brown and the Clear Grits, to maintain the Union at all costs, whatever its defects and whatever the racial and religious friction of its working. He had to preserve the credit of the government for the great works to be undertaken by a small population. He had to bridge sectional cleavage and chill sectarian fervour, however much they might be stimulated by the religious animosities of the Gavazzi riots of 1853 in Quebec and Montreal, or the failure of a Catholic jury to convict a Catholic accused of the murder of the Protestant Corrigan in 1856. To do all this, Macdonald had to maintain a majority if possible, a respectable number at least, of Upper Canadian Conservatives to prevent Brown pointing a triumphant finger at a parliamentary majority based on the steady French bloc of the Bleus.

It was to prove an ever more impossible task for Macdonald, or any other. Once the policy of assimilation had failed, as it did almost at once, the Union became an attempt to govern a dual society – plural, it might almost be said, with the arrival of the southern Irish – by a unitary government. As this was a parliamentary government responsive to a free and vigorous democracy, the result was the recurrent clash of two groups of opposed interest, the French conservatives and the English radicals. Only so long as some intermediate body of opinion such as the Upper Canadian conservatives could be found to act as a buffer could the Union endure. Only so long as the sectional interests would coalesce could something like parliamentary party government be carried on. Without these shock-absorbers, one side or the other would find its most intimate concerns being regulated by the votes of its political opponents and sectarian antagonists. The unitary drive of the majority vote was racking the structure of the Union, and its frame was being steadily loosened and warped by the strain. Equality of sectional representation could not be tolerated indefinitely; the double majority was not a workable convention; representation by population the French could not really be expected to accept. In the circumstances, it was not surprising that in 1856 A. A. Dorion, the able intellect of the Rouges, should have suggested a federal union of the Canadas. Only in federation could Canadians have both self-government and union, but it was to take a decade of trial and a wider range of union to bring this about.

ADDITIONAL READING

CARELESS, J. M. S.   *Brown of the Globe.*
CREIGHTON, D. G.   *John A. Macdonald: The Young Politician.*
HODGETTS, J. E.   *Pioneer Public Service.*
MOIR, J. S.   *Church and State in Canada West.*
WALSH, H. H.   *The Christian Church in Canada.*

CHAPTER 16

The Creation of Political Union
1857-1867

The year 1856, then, saw not only the last of the great constructive measures of reform set in train; it saw also the emergence of new issues and the first formidable challenge to the Union itself. From 1856 the trend of events in Canada was in new directions and perhaps towards new goals. And events outside Canada were to reinforce that trend and compel Canadian statesmen to turn, however reluctantly, from their absorption in domestic politics to study horizons long clear and suddenly clouded, to examine new landmarks which had risen to view and to scrutinize the old afresh.

Relations with the United States had been good for a decade after the Oregon treaty. Then British recruiting of soldiers for the Crimean War, especially by an over-patriotic and indiscreet Joseph Howe, led to a fierce outburst of American resentment in 1856. So serious was the situation that the British forces in America had to be heavily increased and the special training of volunteers from the Canadian militia begun. Canadians were reminded how precarious Canadian peace and independence would be if they depended on Canadian resources alone, a contingency which often seemed not unlikely with the growth of indifference in mid-Victorian England to the fate of the British American colonies.

It was not only by invasion across the New Brunswick or Canadian borders that the United States threatened the security of British America. Peaceful penetration by American settlers, as Texas and Oregon testified, was always a more serious menace than the movement of American troops. And now there were new developments which might result in additional loss of British territory to the Republic and the closing of the north-west, the region of destiny, to Canada. These developments were in the Red River and the Fraser River valleys.

Since the wresting of a free trade in furs from the Hudson's Bay Company in 1849 by the embattled métis, the trade had steadily grown. It was carried on by Red River cart brigades with St. Paul in what had become the Territory of Minnesota in the same year as the Sayer trial. A firm economic tie was knit between the Red and the upper Mississippi, and a few American traders even moved into the Red River Settlement. Others might follow; and even if the Hudson's Bay Company by skill of experience and weight of resources were able to render these intruders comparatively harmless, it could not deal so easily with traders south of the border, who could act in concert with the petty traders of Red River without being amenable to the laws of Assiniboia or the control of the Company.

For this reason, when Sir George Simpson in the summer of 1856 received news of the appearance of an American cavalry detachment near the border south of the Red River Settlement, he had applied at once for the dispatch of a contingent of British troops to Red River. This was granted without delay, and in 1857 a considerable force of the Royal Canadian Rifles, a British unit recruited and stationed in Canada, was sent to Red River, where it was to remain for four years.

The presence of this force assured the Company that Americans at the border would not be able to foment trouble in the Settlement. But the quiet ensured by the Rifles did not prevent Red River and the whole north-west coming prominently to the fore in 1857. Prospectors had discovered gold in the bars of the Fraser late in 1856, and a great rush from the United States began into the vast and empty Pacific slope, unoccupied save for a few Hudson's Bay Company posts. The prompt extension by James Douglas, without authorization, of his jurisdiction as governor of Vancouver Island over the mainland prevented any questioning of British sovereignty. And the British government, uncertain of the future of the enormous and vaguely known territories, was wondering if the fact that the Hudson's Bay Company's licence to trade, renewed in 1838, was to expire in 1859 might lead to Canada's assuming responsibility for the north-west. Indeed, in 1856 Robert Lowe, a Little Englander member of Palmerston's government, had visited Sir Edmund Head and made it apparent that he and those who thought like him wished Canada to take over the British inheritance in North America. As a result of such thinking, Henry Labouchere, the Colonial Secretary, decided late in 1856 to have a committee set up to examine the question of the future of the Hudson's Bay Company. He invited Canada to be represented at the hearings.

Thus at a time when the oft-repeated attempt to capture the trade of the American west was again encountering difficulty in the mounting embarrassments of the Grand Trunk Railway, the region which had strengthened Canada in the days of La Vérendrye and of the North West Company was once more looming from its remote distance as a possible source of strength, as a market, and as a place of settlement. And the British desire to be rid of the north-west was matched by the eagerness of some Canadians to claim the region for Canada. For years a small number of Upper Canadians with experience of the north-west and centred on the family of Miles and Alexander Macdonell, Selkirk's lieutenants, had dreamed of renewing the ties between Canada and the north-west. They

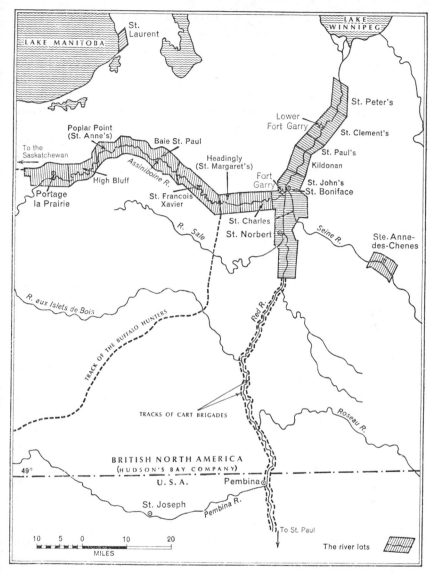

XIII   *The River Lots and Parishes of Red River*

were strong opponents of the Hudson's Bay Company and one of their number John McLean, had published in 1849 his *Notes of a Twenty-five Years' Service in the Hudson's Bay Territory*, a bitter attack on the Company's conduct of its trade. Now the railway boom suggested the means to accomplish their object.

They found support in Toronto, where the idea of western expansion caught the imagination of George Brown and William McDougall, now an editorial writer on the *Globe*, and of a group of business men in that city. The *Globe* began an agitation for the acquisition of the north-west and a revival of the old French claim against the Hudson's Bay Company to all the land as far as the Rocky Mountains. The idea of acquiring the Red River country for Canada appealed to the Clear Grit Reformers of western Upper Canada; they were concerned to find new land for settlement by themselves or their sons, as the good lands of Canada had all been taken up, to the shores of Huron and the rocks of the Shield.

As a result of the *Globe's* campaign and Brown's interest, a committee of the Assembly was appointed early in 1857 to go into Canada's claims. The committee of the House of Commons was appointed at the same time in England to consider the Hudson's Bay Company's licence and the future government of the north-west and the Pacific slope; and the Canadian cabinet, although cautious with good reason about incurring the costs and hazards the acquisition of the north-west would bring, dispatched Chief Justice William Draper to represent Canada's interests before it.

The appointment of the Canadian committee was followed by the dispatch of an exploring expedition in the summer of 1857 under the direction of George Gladman, an old Hudson's Bay Company man, soon to be replaced by Professor Henry Youle Hind of the University of Toronto. The expedition was to examine the route to Red River and the resources and climate of the Red and Assiniboine. At the suggestion of the Royal Geographical Society, the imperial government also dispatched an expedition under Captain John Palliser to examine the possibility of railway construction from Lake Superior to Red River and across the Rockies, and to report on the agricultural possibilities of the southern districts of Rupert's Land. The British committee, after extensive hearings, recommended the organization of a government over the gold-rush country and the piecemeal transfer to Canada for settlement and organization, if Canada were willing, of the fertile southern districts of Rupert's Land in the Red and Saskatchewan valleys.

The sudden British concern with the north-west and the Pacific coast contrasted oddly with the lack of interest which had led to Alaska being neutralized during the Crimean War at a time when a few warships might have added it to the British possessions. The new alertness signified a drastic change in the development and destiny of Canada. From 1857 on, Canadian statesmen and business men had to think in continental terms once more, as in the days of Frontenac and of William McGillivray. The Laurentian provincialism, the preoccupation with the American middle west which had set in after 1821, was ending. United Canada was threatened with disintegration and restless with a need to expand. If there was to be an attempt to end the racial friction in

Parliament, to replace the Union by a federation, it would in all likelihood be a federation to unite the whole of British North America.

It was certain by 1857 that the Canadian Union could not much longer contain its two sections on the terms of 1840, and it was soon to be evident that as a union Canada could not expand. Since the general election of 1854, George Brown and the Clear Grits had hammered hard at the implications of the census of 1851 and the principle of equal representation in the Union. It meant, as they saw it, the government of one section, Canada West, and that steadily the more populous one, by representatives from the other. It therefore meant also the government of a community in the majority Protestant by a community in the majority Roman Catholic. To the radical democrats, to British immigrants like Brown, unreconciled to the large, loose tolerance of Canadian life, to earnest Protestants reared in fear of popery, this was an intolerable situation, and they set themselves to end it, without thought of the consequences to Canada at large. What was at work was a clash of the radical democracy of the Clear Grits, with its belief in popular rule exercised by the majority vote of individuals, and the conservatism of Catholic and Orange Canada. This latter strange pair were united by their common belief in the corporate personality of church and nation, and in the development of society not so much by the rational decisions of legislation and administration as by the organic growth of tradition and custom.

Representation by population was of course an outstanding example of the radical belief in the importance of numbers. The conservative defence of the Union, which had become by a twist of events not an instrument to destroy the corporate nationality of the French but a barrier to defend it, was an example of how the conservative may come to defend almost any power that is. As a practical issue, representation by population was admirably designed to attract votes in Upper Canada, with its radicals ready to put all to the test of the majority, and its British Protestants sensitive to the cry of "French domination" and Catholic encroachment. At the same time, however, it operated to injure the Rouges of Lower Canada and to strengthen the Bleus, because to vote for the Rouges seemed to invite the imposition of a hostile Protestant domination over Lower Canada.

The anxiety of Brown and his Protestant followers was, it must be said, not mere bigotry, but concern aroused by one of the great trends of the century, the victory of ultramontane over liberal Catholicism. In Canada it revealed itself by the increasing pressure for separate schools for Roman Catholic children, and in Quebec by a strengthening of the ties with the Catholics of France. The contemporary anti-Catholic feeling in the United Kingdom and the United States, where Catholics were minorities, of course, stimulated the fears of Protestants in British America where the members of the two groups were in balance. But what was chiefly feared was the direct challenge the ultramontane Catholicism of

Pope Pius IX presented to liberal and democratic principles. This raised questions, not of religious toleration but of the sovereign power in society. Which was to govern, church or state, was the question raised by the ultramontane rejection of the doctrine of popular sovereignty. To the will of the people expressed in the nation state, the ultramontane opposed the moral authority of the church, the objective nature of law, and the weight of custom.

In practice these profoundly conservative views led to clerical intervention in politics, and in Europe even to the creation of political parties. No direct conflict occurred, however, between the apprehensive Protestants of Brown's following and ultramontane Catholics in Upper Canada. That contest was to be waged in Canada East between the ultramontanes and the Rouges. The Rouges were anti-clerical democrats, and some were free-thinkers. To pursue their own studies they formed the Institut Canadien, a reading and debating society in which works of free-thought and prohibited books were available. In 1858 the Institut was attacked by Bishop Ignace Bourget of Montreal, an ardently ultramontane prelate, and the first shots were exchanged in a conflict which was to last for a quarter of a century.

The political struggle of these years was conducted and understood in the above terms by the participants. But it is also to be seen as the organization by Brown and the Grits of the developing metropolitan interests of Toronto and the sectional interests of the then Canadian West against the economic domination of Montreal and the Laurentian trading system. The position of Montreal was upheld by the Conservatives and the Bleus. But they were on the defensive. To the Grand Trunk and the trade of the American west, Brown opposed the Northern Railway from Toronto to Lake Huron, and beyond it a Pacific railway; to the trade of Montreal by the St. Lawrence, the trade of Toronto on the upper lakes; to the habitants bound to the banks of the St. Lawrence and the Ottawa, the restless farmers of Bruce and Huron counties ready to move on to the prairies of Minnesota or Red River. The sectional rivalry within the Union touched every aspect of life; and the most heated, the religious, was practically the least significant.

As a result of this sectional rivalry, the general election of 1857 gave the Reformers a majority in Upper Canada and the Bleus a sweeping victory in Lower Canada. The two sections of the Union were once more in opposition, as after the election of 1844, and the tacit acceptance and normal use since 1848 of government on the double-majority principle, by a coalition of a majority from each section, was no longer possible. It was true that no responsible statesman since Lafontaine, except John Sandfield Macdonald, a Liberal and individualistic Catholic Scot from Glengarry, had adhered to the double majority as a principle. There nevertheless remained the fact, as Baldwin had felt in 1851, that it was embarrassing for a political leader not to be supported by a majority from his own section, and Macdonald now felt the same embarrassment.

The Macdonald-Cartier administration carried on, but Macdonald's position was weakened. And the administration faced the need finally to settle one of the most contentious sectional issues of the Union, that of the seat of government. Fixed in Kingston by Sydenham, it had been removed to Montreal in 1843 on the insistence of the French members of the first Lafontaine-Baldwin ministry. Montreal had forfeited its claim by the riots of 1849, and thereafter the capital had moved every four years, at great expense to the taxpayers and to the serious impairment of the public service, between Toronto and Quebec. The legislature could deal with the location of the capital only by a straight sectional vote, which might decide the question but certainly would not settle it. Macdonald, urged by Head, adopted the solution of referring the matter to the Queen, who in 1857 announced that her choice had fallen on what most Canadians still called Bytown. This small lumber town, recently renamed Ottawa after the river on which it stood, had been recommended by Head to the Queen as being a compromise between the sectional claims of Quebec and Toronto and also, unlike Kingston, a place at some distance from the frontier. This royal award the legislature would be asked to ratify in the session of 1858.

The critical year of 1857 had been made more critical by the onset of one of the most severe of the cyclical depressions of the century. The railway and war boom of the mid fifties collapsed that year, and in Canada the weight of the depression was aggravated by the increasing difficulties of the Grand Trunk Railway. An enormous undertaking, with the added cost of the Victoria Bridge at Montreal, it was built lavishly to European standards and with a broad-gauge track. By 1855 the government, committed by the Guarantee Act as well as the intimacy of political ties between the railway and members of the Cabinet, had had to make an advance to keep construction going. The advance had to be repeated in larger amounts in 1856 and 1857. The depression now greatly increased the burden of the railway on the government, the more so since, as a trunk line built to carry through traffic, it had to be completed to Sarnia before it could operate as it was designed to do. When completed, its broad gauge was to prove an obstacle to the movement of American freight from American railways. It was a heavy part of the embarrassing burden of difficulties the weakened government carried as it faced Brown and his triumphant Grits in the session of 1858.

The depression was no less burdensome in the Atlantic provinces. In Nova Scotia it was aggravated, as in Canada, by railway construction, the extension of the government's line of railway from Halifax to Truro. In none of the provinces did it produce a political change, but it did start the provincial governors, if not the governments, thinking of economies to be achieved by the union – the reunion, actually – of the two mainland provinces and Prince Edward Island. Beyond this, however, there was little disposition to think the situation required a new approach or a larger setting to remedy the evils of the depression. The Atlantic provinces were still reasonably content as self-governing colonies of the Empire and with the export and maritime economy based on timber, shipping, and fish, especially as long as the Reciprocity Treaty continued to give them entry to the markets of New England.

In Nova Scotia a proud provincialism had flowered not only in the achievement of responsible government and in the foundation of economic institutions such as the Cunard Steamship Company and the Bank of Nova Scotia, but also in the creation of a local literature of respectable quality and a racy character. And in New Brunswick the genteel society of Fredericton, nourished amidst the roughness of the timber trade of the St. John and the corruption of New Brunswick politics, was preparing the ground for the talent of Charles G. D. Roberts and Bliss Carman.

In Canada it was different. Society in Canada was also provincial in the sense that its tastes and values were imported, from the United Kingdom in the main but also from Boston and New York. In Canada, however, an authentic national note was being sounded, only here and there but unmistakably; and this was in fact only the anticipatory expression of a steady movement towards national expansion and national union in British America.

The accents of nationality were uttered of course in two idioms, French and British Canadian. Each was almost wholly peculiar to itself; the significant thing is that they had something in common. The French, like the English, had used self-government to shape their institutions to their liking. Much more than the English, they had begun the creation of a literature; François-Xavier Garneau's *Histoire du Canada* – the retort to Durham's charge that French Canada had no history – and Octave Crémazie's verse meant that the French Canadian, like the Nova Scotian, could see his native scenes described in a native idiom and his present made intelligible by the interpretation of his past. His literature, like his politics, was defensive still; his art – the wood-carving and the metal work, for example – was like his mind, still cradled and conditioned by the church. But in Joseph Edouard Cauchon and Joseph Charles Taché, French Canada in these years produced vigorous nationalists and expansionists who saw, the former in his *L'Union des provinces de l'Amérique Britannique du Nord* (1865) and the latter in his *Des provinces de l'Amérique du Nord et d'une union fédérale* (1858), a wider union as a necessity and the north-west as the key to a common destiny of the two Canadian stocks.

French nationality was ethnic and cultural; it was also American, made so by two centuries of life by the St. Lawrence. Even the resumption of ties with France in the visit of *La Capricieuse* in 1855 and the appointment of a French consul to Quebec in 1858, made possible by the clerical element in the Second Empire, did not lead to any deep renewal of sentiment. But in British Canada the old American element of the loyalist and post-loyalist settlers had to a great extent been overlaid by the scores of thousands of English, Scottish and Irish immigrants since 1815. By 1858 the leaders of British Canadian society were almost wholly British born. The old native element was not eclipsed, but it was heavily outnumbered. As a result, the English-Canadian sense of nationality was as powerful as the French, yet it was basically a British nationality, a transplanting to Canada of a sentiment which was largely of British nurture. But because it was British and not American, it had the same effect as a native Canadian nationalism and was, with French Canada, the explanation of the continued independence of Canada in the mid century. Because it was British, it blended easily with the loyalist tradition, itself made nationalist by the War of 1812. Once more, as in 1776 and 1812, Canada was saved from absorption into American continentalism by the extra-continental connections which its economy demanded and which its history had nourished.

British-Canadian society, then, was provincial but not backward, and certainly not unenlightened. It was indeed an extremely vigorous and aggressive society. Its prevailing political tone might be moderate and its literary and artistic achievement slight, but it was a clear-thinking, outspoken society, in which individuals cherished strong convictions and deep feelings and acted on both. As one studies this society, the impression takes shape that already a Canadian sense of achievement had formed and that a Canadian conceit, brave, firm, and rather attractive, was definitely in the air. What else could have led young George Denison of Toronto to enter the Czar of Russia's competition for the best treatise on the training and handling of cavalry and win it against the soldierly pens of Europe? And if there were few writers and artists to which Canadians might point, the truth was that British Canadians as yet had felt little need for native interpretation of the local scene – it was to come soon – or a Canadian version of the great themes of art. The painter Cornelius Krieghoff was patronized in Lower Canada, as was Paul Kane in Toronto after he had gone west to paint Indians, but no one yet took pride in them as Canadian artists. Canadians were sturdy provincials, content to import their cultural needs.

Again, however, as in French Canada, there were men who did not hesitate to strike a national chord in politics. One of these was Alexander Morris, son of that William Morris who had helped to build up McGill University and to found Queen's. A Canadian intellectual of his generation, Morris delivered in 1858 the lecture published under the title *Our Hudson's Bay and Pacific Territories*, in which he spoke with assurance of "a northern nationality." Like Cauchon and Taché, Morris was well in the van of Canadian nationalists, but already the passionate oratory of the new Canadian, Thomas D'Arcy McGee, late Irish rebel and Irish-American journalist, was preparing the ground for the Canada First young men who set out to possess the north-west.

If, then, 1857 was the turning-point in events between 1841 and 1867, it was not a turning towards defeat or even towards frustration. There were in British America, and especially in Canada, forces at work and men of the genius to bring the colonies, the slow product of a northern economy, into line with the great movement of the century, unification by commerce, railways, and the spirit of nationality. That Canada was feeling the impulse of the movement was indicated when A. T. Galt, president of the British American Land Company of the Eastern Townships and the Grand Trunk Railway, a forceful, able, and imaginative business man, moved a set of resolutions in the Assembly calling for a federation of all British North America.

Any attempt at a larger union, however, would spring from the working of the existing one. The Union of 1840 was in fact one of the first of the attempts to create a political framework for a society of two communities. It had become, through the strength of French nationality and the grant of responsible government, an attempt to create a free government for a plural society. The Union did not, however, allow either the French or the English that independence in local and domestic matters which is a prime condition of success in the government of plural societies. Upper Canada was becoming more and more resentful of its legislative subordination to a majority drawn largely from the French of Lower Canada.

The result of the Grit gains in the election of 1857 was an immediate trial of strength when the new legislature met in 1858 on the most tender sectional issue, and the one on which the government would suffer a defection of its French supporters, the seat-of-government question. A vote went against the Macdonald-Cartier government on a resolution opposing the Queen's choice of Ottawa. While the ministry was sustained on the subsequent motion to adjourn the debate, Macdonald and Cartier decided to resign in order to try the Grit leader, Brown, with the temptation and the compromises of office. They precipitated by doing so one of the most agitated week-ends of Canadian political history. It was on a Friday that Brown all too readily accepted the invitation of Governor Head to form a ministry, undeterred by Head's warning in writing that he did not feel bound to grant a dissolution in the event of the failure of the new ministry to win a majority in the House. With the leader of the Rouges, A. A. Dorion, as Lower Canadian colleague, Brown succeeded in forming a ministry over the week-end. The two men based it on the acceptance of representation by population coupled with constitutional checks to safeguard the French minority; it was the essential agreement on which the later Confederation was to rest. But Brown and all his colleagues, under the law as it then was, had to resign their seats on accepting office. The new ministers could not enter the Assembly and the personnel of the new administration was therefore announced on the Monday by a private member without any statement of policy. Straightway a motion of want of confidence was moved by the Conservatives and carried. This, though technically permissible and within the rules, was ungenerous and wholly contrary to the best traditions of parliamentary usage. The Assembly ought to have adjourned until the ministers had been returned and could attempt to win a majority in the House. Head then refused Brown's request for a dissolution and the ministry had perforce to resign.

The anger caused among the Liberals by this humiliating upset of Brown, who had entered office with men whose views and policies he and his supporters had publicly denounced, even if he had privately reached agreement with them on principle, was promptly increased manifold by the events of the next few days. Head first asked A. T. Galt, a former Lower Canadian Rouge turning Conservative, to form a ministry. Galt tried and failed. Head then turned to Cartier, who succeeded, and who brought Galt in as Minister of Finance on Galt's condition that the government put forward a plan, such as he had already proposed, for the federation of all British North America. Macdonald was Attorney General for Canada West, but second to Cartier because of the new disposition of strength in the party since the general election.

The new ministers at once faced the necessity of resignation which had so harmed the late administration. They evaded it, however, by a legalistic expedient which infuriated Brown and the Grits and which remains notorious as the "double shuffle." A recent Act had provided, in order to reduce the number of ministerial by-elections required when a member of the legislature became a minister of the Crown, that a minister in changing from one portfolio to another within a month of acceptance of the first, need not seek re-election. The former ministers now took a sharp advantage of this section of the Act by assuming new portfolios when first sworn in and then within a bare two days reverting to those they had held in the Macdonald-Cartier government. In three cases at law, the legality of their action was upheld by the courts, but the sharpness of the expedient was as evident then as it is now.

Moreover, the harm done was serious and might have been deeply injurious to the development of Canadian nationhood. Brown had of course been precipitate; he had to learn that a statesman could not use the unmeasured language of Victorian journalism and not be called to account for it. It is most doubtful if by the usage of the day he had any claim to a dissolution. None the less, Brown had been, as he was to be again, the great moderating and patriotic force in the Liberal factions. He was not a radical, and he was warmly devoted to British institutions and the British connection. But after the trickery and humiliation of 1858, Brown and the *Globe* for several sombre and dangerous months denounced responsible government and advocated a new constitution on the American model in an Upper Canada freed from the Union. This was the road to annexation. In the end Brown returned to his original convictions, but he had been sorely tried.

That men of the stature of Macdonald and Cartier had resorted to such shifts was a reflection on their political sensibility. It was also a further major symptom of the rapidly developing organic disease of the Union that sectional antipathies were destroying the incipient party system without which the responsible government of the Union was impossible. Galt's insistence on an attempt at federal union, even if inspired by other considerations, was therefore timely and auspicious.

Cartier probably had doubts about committing the fate of French Canada to the experiment of a federal union, and Macdonald probably felt that the time was scarcely ripe. Galt's proposal was nevertheless proceeded with at once in September 1858, particularly because of the warm encouragement it received from Head. It was necessary, of course, to invite the Atlantic provinces to consider the plan and to inform the imperial government. But only one of the provinces replied before hearing from the Colonial Office. That one was the key province of New Brunswick, and its reply was to the effect that it was interested in a legislative union of the Atlantic provinces as well as a general federation. The desirability of a Maritime union was the strongly held view of the province's influential governor, J. H. T. Manners Sutton. In London the Canadian proposal, which had not been preceded by any explanation from Head, startled and angered the new Colonial Secretary, Sir Edward Bulwer Lytton. His staff had not informed him that his predecessor, Labouchere, had encouraged Head to proceed with a scheme of British American union. As a result, the response from the Colonial Office was discouraging. Nova Scotia then replied in a decidedly negative manner, and New Brunswick accepted Manners Sutton's preference for Maritime union. Only the two island colonies rather surprisingly showed some disposition to consider the proposal. Finally, the Colonial Office made it clear that any future proposal must be made only on its authorization, and must come from all the provinces concerned.

Meanwhile a Canadian delegation of Cartier, Galt, and John Ross, a politician and railway man, had gone to London to seek imperial help to finance the province's commitments for the building of canals and railways and the construction of the Intercolonial Railway, and to discuss the proposal for a British American federation. It is not surprising, in view of the reaction of the Colonial Office, that the delegation should have been put off politely in the matter of federation and have quite failed to move the imperial government to take up the lead given by Canada. Bulwer Lytton was indeed fired by the Fraser gold rush, the creation of British Columbia, and the expiration of the Hudson's Bay Company's licence, to contemplate a chain of colonies from the Pacific and the north-west joined with the eastern and central provinces by the imperial connection and perhaps a railway. The Canadian proposal of 1858, however, he thought nothing but a political manoeuvre, as in a measure it was, and firmly refused to encourage the Canadian initiative.

As a result, British American federation dropped out of view, while Maritime union continued to be discussed sporadically in the Atlantic provinces. On the Pacific coast Lytton had acted decisively, although it meant more colonial disunity, in bringing about the creation of the colony of British

Columbia in 1858. Fortunately Douglas continued to govern both island and mainland for a time, but again a situation had been created which would call for another "Maritime union." In Rupert's Land and the north-west nothing was done. The licence was allowed to expire without renewal in May 1859. But the question of the validity of the Hudson's Bay Company's charter, raised by Canada, impeded with its legal thickets Canada's path to the north-west, and Lytton failed in an attempt to have Canada bring the charter before the Judicial Committee of the Privy Council.

The exploring expeditions finished their work and completed their reports. Hind was enthusiastic about the possibilities of settlement in the Red and Assiniboine valleys. Palliser, however, was discouraging with respect to railway construction between Lake Superior and the Red, and distinctly discouraging as to the prospects of settlement on the plains to the south of the Saskatchewan valley and west of those of the Red and Assiniboine, the area thereafter known as "Palliser's triangle." Both made it evident that agriculture was possible in the Red and Saskatchewan valleys. The Toronto Canadians interested in the north-west had meanwhile formed the North West Transportation, Navigation, and Railway Company. They had even engaged the support of Sir Allan MacNab and Viscount Bury, the superintendent of Indian affairs from 1854 to 1856, and obtained a contract to deliver mail from Lake Superior to Red River by a British route. An eager offshoot of the *Globe*, the *Nor'Wester*, founded in Red River in 1859, publicized the prospects of the north-west for agricultural settlement and urged the annexation of the territory to Canada. But all these bright hopes faded as quickly as they had kindled. The decisive turn of events in 1857 seemed only to have led to failure and frustration by the end of 1859.

There was, nevertheless, a basic strength and purpose which meant that the impetus of 1857 would be resumed. For one thing, George Brown had returned to his original course. He and the *Globe* ceased to urge the dissolution of the Union and the substitution of a written for a parliamentary constitution. And in the Reformer Convention of 1859, Brown and McDougall held the Reformers to the plank of a federal union of the Canadas and to that of the annexation of the north-west. The main goals of Canadian destiny were thus kept in view.

Among the difficulties which had to be dealt with at once was the plight of the Grand Trunk Railway. It had nearly pulled down the leading Upper Canadian bank, the Bank of Commerce; it had nearly pulled down the Macdonald-Cartier government; and it had set the Cartier-Macdonald ministry looking for fresh credit in Britain and new revenue in Canada. The latter quest had produced the Cayley tariff of 1858 and the Galt tariff of 1859. For the first time, duties in Canada were raised not only to increase revenue but to give "incidental protection" to the new industries which had sprung up in the 1850's with prosperity and the coming of the age of iron and steam with the railway. Galt's tariff was so protective that it brought a protest from British manufacturers and the Colonial

Office, to which Galt responded with a carefully reasoned defence of Canada's right under responsible government to make its own fiscal decisions. But the Grand Trunk, though furnished with a third rail for cars of standard gauge and though now seeking local as well as through freight, was still not paying, or promising to pay. Canada had failed to capture any considerable share of the traffic of the American west.

To study this situation and to recommend a remedy, the directors of the Grand Trunk sent a representative to Canada in 1861. This was Edward Watkin, a brisk, clear-headed and dogmatically confident man. Watkin came, saw, and recommended that the basic policy of the Grand Trunk be continued, but that the quest for through freight be diverted from the American middle west to the British north-west and the Pacific. This grandiose idea, as it was in 1861, of extending the Grand Trunk to the Pacific of course raised again the question of the future of the Hudson's Bay Company territory, now practically lying derelict with the government of the Company increasingly ineffectual as respect for its authority drained away. From Watkin's recommendation was to come, in 1863, the purchase of the Hudson's Bay Company by the International Financial Society, made up of members and associates of the Grand Trunk, with a view to building a telegraph line and ultimately a railway to the Pacific. Among these men was Sir Edmund Head, who had completed his term of seven years as Governor General in 1861. In the United Kingdom he kept up his interest in British America and the north-west and was elected Governor of the new Hudson's Bay Company in 1864.

Long before that date, however, Canada had welcomed Head's successor, Lord Monck, an able and placid Irish peer, and had lost much of its active interest in the north-west because of the outbreak of the Civil War in the United States. The war abruptly raised the matter of Canadian defence, interest in which had declined since the awakening of 1856. At first, sentiment towards the American war in British America was pro-Northern because it was anti-slavery. But when the war began to be seen as a war not for ending slavery but for preserving the union of the states, opinion altered, and much sympathy for the South developed, especially in conservative circles. This change of sentiment, with Secretary of State W. H. Seward's anti-British attitude, prepared the temper of British America for the "Trent Affair." The American warship *San Jacinto* had stopped the British mail-ship *Trent* and removed two commissioners of the Confederate States. The breach of neutral rights almost led to war, because of the long-simmering rivalry of the two countries and because of the relief a foreign war would have given to the tension that was destroying the Union. So serious was the threat that heavy reinforcements, including two battalions of the Guards, were rushed to Halifax in the late fall and moved overland by sleigh to Canada. Fortunately the new president, Abraham Lincoln, refused to be swept into a war with England, and the emergency passed.

It had revealed, however, the seriousness of the situation of the colonies, and particularly that of Canada, as neutral neighbours of the war-divided republic. Canada was no longer as defensible as in 1812, when the forest still allowed only three or four narrow entries into the country. Now the whole frontier from the Richelieu to Sault Ste. Marie was faced by a populous countryside and open to approach by a network of railways and canals. The truth was that, in a war, Upper Canada and perhaps all Lower Canada down to Quebec would have to be given up. To gain British help to hold even Quebec, however, Canada had to demonstrate that it was prepared to tax itself and fight in its own defence. To do this meant to put the militia on a respectable footing and above all to increase the numbers and improve the training of the force of volunteers begun in 1856.

This the government set out to do. A commission of inquiry into Canadian defence was appointed. The Department of Militia was created and the office was assumed by John A. Macdonald. In the session of 1862 Macdonald introduced a Militia Bill which provided, as recommended by the commission, for an active force of 50,000 men. It was to be raised by volunteering or, if necessary, by ballot from the militia, at a cost of about $480,000 during the first year for the training and equipping of 30,000 men. The Cartier-Macdonald government was old, corrupt, and incapable of restoring itself to health and vigour. It took a bold line on defence because it was ready to court defeat. The legislature and public opinion, particularly the French members and French Canada, were in fact not prepared for a measure so forceful and so costly. The bill was defeated, the government resigned, and the defeat did much more harm to the reputation of Canada in the United Kingdom than it did, as it happened, to the defence of Canada in America.

The result was a serious and prolonged debate between the Canadian and the imperial government over the responsibility for the defence of British America. The imperial view was that the United Kingdom should aid the colonies if they made substantial provision for their own defence. If they would not, then the United Kingdom would be relieved of the obligation to help the colonies and freed from the fear of war with the United States over Canada when engaged in war in Europe. The colonists, and particularly the Canadians, argued that any war in British America would be caused not by the colonies but by rivalry between the Empire and the Republic. The colonies themselves were not likely to be attacked on their own account, and the militia was enough to ensure against such danger as there was.

The immediate dangers of the Civil War to Canada proved to be the dangers not of military attack but of neutrality on the outskirts of a war which was, like all the wars of democracy, a war of principle and opinion. Such wars admit of no real neutrality, and Canadian opinion and sentiment were involved from the first. That Canadian opinion was opposed to slavery goes without saying; the Canadian provinces had been among the first American communities to abolish the institution. But Canadians had mixed feelings; if they approved the anti-slavery cause, they also instinctively felt, as people repeatedly threatened with American attack, that the South, whether within the Union or without, was a makeweight against the expansive energy of the North which British America had so much cause to fear. A resultant danger was that the South, seeking to divert the forces of the Union, would use a sympathetic Canada as a refuge for escaped prisoners and as a base for plots and even raids against the North. This danger did materialize, in the last years of the war, and some pro-Southern Canadians perhaps eased the way of Confederate agents. (The attitude of the colonial governments was of course circumspectly correct, and their performance fairly efficient, with two exceptions late in the war.) The militia system was also improved and the training of volunteers put on a better footing by the new ministry. While never adequate for the defence of the frontier, the volunteers at least gave Canada a military force such as it had not possessed since 1814.

John Sandfield Macdonald had succeeded Cartier in 1862. With L. V. Sicotte, a Bleu who had parted from Cartier and John A. Macdonald on the seat-of-government question, he formed a ministry which, while Liberal, was not Clear Grit. The fluidity of Canadian politics was still such that a permanent division into two parties of firm Conservatives and doctrinaire Grits was impossible. Too many members were independents – "loose fish," in the language of the party caucus – too many voters were new-comers to Canadian politics, for stability of party organization to prevail. For over a year Canada was to be governed, weakly and incoherently, by this mildly left-of-centre coalition.

The Macdonald-Sicotte ministry is best remembered by its professed adherence to the doctrine of the "double majority," significant at this juncture as an implied alternative to representation by population, and not less by its prompt but silent shelving of that doctrine when it was put to a serious test. That was in the Separate School legislation of 1863. The Roman Catholics of Upper Canada had not been content with the concessions of 1853 and a further set in 1855. The Macdonald-Sicotte government was sympathetic, and in 1862 R. W. Scott of Ottawa was allowed, as a private member, to bring in a bill to improve the position of the separate schools. The bill was withdrawn and much revised, and in 1863 the ministers felt obliged to support it individually. It passed by a general majority, but against a majority vote of the Upper Canadian representatives. Although the ministry continued in office, the vote was the end of the "double majority" principle and of much of the reputation of the administration.

It had already done badly, indeed behaved badly, in renewed negotiations over the Intercolonial Railway in 1862. The emergency of 1861 had again made evident the desirability of the railway for defence and had reawakened the interest of Nova Scotia and New Brunswick in a project that would aid their own incomplete and moribund railways. The British government offered to guarantee the necessary loan, the three colonies had agreed on the costs, when the whole scheme was brought to nothing by the refusal of the Canadian representatives to accept the requirement of the imperial government that a sinking-fund should be provided. In extenuation, it must be noted that much had been made by the ministers, when in opposition, of the extravagance of the late Conservative government; the administration was economizing, as it was when it also declined to subsidize without imperial aid a telegraph line to the Pacific coast. The Macdonald-Sicotte cabinet consisted of provincial politicians who had failed to sense the new currents which had begun to flow in Canadian politics in 1857.

The troubles of the makeshift ministry increased after the passage of the Separate Schools Act in the spring of 1863. In the summer Macdonald asked for a dissolution and was granted it. He then reorganized his ministry, substituting A. A. Dorion of the Rouges for Sicotte, and gaining the support of George Brown by making electoral reform an open question. The government had moved left and in the election it made major gains in Upper Canada, offset in part by losses in Lower Canada. The Canadian parties could not escape from the old pattern of opposing majorities in the two sections.

Talk of union, federal or legislative, general or local, continued in desultory fashion in Canada and the Atlantic provinces, but no action was attempted. The Civil War ground on; in September, the battle of Gettysburg underscored the inevitability of the Confederacy's defeat. But British America continued to drowse through the oft-repeated manoeuvres of provincial politics, regardless of the day when the North would be triumphant in a reunited republic and unchecked beside a British North America divided and unorganized, most of its vast spaces having not so much as a flag, much less the uniforms of soldiers or police, to exhibit sovereignty. Canadians, lulled by the prosperity the war had brought, bemused by the labyrinthine politics of the Union, drifted spellbound, incapable of moving to put British America in a posture to face the perils the end of the war would bring.

The political trance, however, could not last. In March 1864 the Macdonald-Dorion government, conscious of loss of support in the Assembly and the country, suddenly tendered its resignation. Sir Etienne Pascal Taché then contrived to form a Conservative ministry, of which two former Liberals, Michael Foley and Thomas D'Arcy McGee, were members. The new government survived until mid June. Then it too was defeated. With its defeat the fabric of Canadian politics crumbled. What party, what political combination, could possibly take the place of the late ministry and replace its torpor by activity, its weakness by vigour, its drift by purpose?

At first men anticipated another shuffle of the worn and greasy political cards. Monck turned first to Fergusson Blair, then to Alexander Campbell, both independents, but neither could find the material with which to build a ministry. Then the unexpected, the almost incredible, happened, though it was actually the consequence of many changes of thought and many imperceptible preliminary moves. The crisis turned on three men, John A. Macdonald, George Brown and George Etienne Cartier. Macdonald had never lost his sense of the ripening destiny of British America, or his feeling that at the point of ripeness the idea of a general federation might give a decisive and forward turn to Canadian politics. From time to time since 1861 he had made cautious and most tentative approaches to Brown with a view to joint action to resolve the growing paralysis of Canadian politics. Brown had not responded, but his own thought had moved steadily from representation by population through a local federation to the contemplation of broader schemes and the sinking of personal and party considerations in order to end the clash of Upper and Lower Canadian opinion. Brown was ceasing to be an impatient journalist editorializing on the floor of the House, and was maturing to statesmanship. And Cartier, staunch champion as he was of the rights of his people under the Act of Union, had come to see that some new framework must be found if the rights of French Canada were to be preserved. To stand on the Act of Union indefinitely would imperil, not safeguard, those rights.

When therefore the intermission without a government had lasted some days, Brown let it be known through Alexander Morris that he was prepared to enter a coalition to attempt a federation. An informal exchange of views with Macdonald on the floor of the House confirmed his readiness. At once a coalition, consisting of the Bleus of Lower Canada, the Conservatives of Upper Canada, and the Brownite Liberals of Upper Canada, was formed under the titular headship of Taché. Four Liberals entered the ministry, of whom one, on Macdonald's insistence, was Brown. The purpose of the coalition was to attempt, not a local federation of the Canadas, as Brown had intended, but, as Macdonald urged, a general federation of British North America.

When the ministry had been formed and the session wound up, an approach was at once made to the Atlantic provinces to win their assent, as required by the Colonial Office, to proposing to the imperial government the union of British America. In the Atlantic provinces the project of a legislative union of those provinces had been revived in the fall of 1863 in Nova Scotia and also by Lieutenant-Governor A. H. Gordon of New Brunswick. The two governments, with that of Prince Edward Island, had agreed to send delegations to meet at Charlottetown in September 1864. Now came the Canadian proposal for a general federation, followed by a request to be allowed to send a delegation to Charlottetown to discuss it there with the representatives of the three Atlantic provinces.

The Atlantic governments agreed, partly because some of their influential men, such as Dr. Charles Tupper – the most powerful Conservative in Nova Scotia, just become premier – favoured a general federation, partly because all the talk since 1858 of union, legislative or federal, general or local, had not crystallized opinion in the Atlantic provinces, and the governments were prepared to hear yet another proposal. Moreover, when the conference met on September 1, the Canadian delegation persuaded the Atlantic delegates to agree to meet in Quebec in October, with representatives of Newfoundland invited, to discuss a general union. The issue of Maritime union was therefore postponed. The Canadian delegates went to Halifax and Fredericton to enjoy Maritime hospitality and to speak at large and excited meetings of the promise and prospects of the proposed union of all British America.

So sudden and dramatic a setting-out on an adventure so hazardous and so great is to be explained by the long years of germination of the idea of British American union. Since the days of the Albany Congress the idea had been kept alive in one form or another; since the dark days of annexation talk in 1849 it had recurred steadily and rhythmically as the means to strength and independence. And now it had finally recurred in its fullest form, a federation of all British America, simply because no smaller union was possible. Atlantic union was not really practicable without means of communication at all seasons, ˜nd there was none in the Gulf of St. Lawrence in winter. Nor was it feasible, without a system of local government – and there was practically none in the Atlantic provinces at that date – for one government to function over so large a territory. A local federation of the Canadas was not enough, for Upper Canada wanted not only freedom from the French majority in domestic matters; it also wanted, and the Brownite Liberals especially, to annex the north-west and build a Pacific railway. But Lower Canada could scarcely agree to the annexation of the northwest unless this were offset by guarantees of its historic rights in the new union, and by the adherence of the Atlantic provinces to the union to balance the indefinitely growing population of Upper Canada. Neither would Lower Canada and the Atlantic provinces assent to the cost of building a Pacific railway unless that were matched by the building of the Intercolonial. Only a general union, balanced with all the care and precision of a cantilever, was practical in 1864.

Moreover, Canadians and Maritimers alike were aware that after the Civil War a restored American Union might well use its vast military strength to remould the continent to its heart's desire. Public sentiment in the colonies had become more anti-Northern as the fortunes of the South declined, and after the Battle of Gettysburg it was edged with a certain hostility. This was resented in the northern states, and Canadians and Maritimers were increasingly blamed for the activities of Southern agents in Canada and the Atlantic provinces. These activities led in 1863 to the attempt to free Confederate prisoners on Johnson Island in Lake Erie and to the capture of the American vessel S.S. *Chesapeake* off Saint John. Despite the persistent correctness of the colonial governments in maintaining neutrality, despite the presence of some thousands of British American soldiers in the Northern armies, despite steady support given by the *Globe* to the cause of the Union, relations were strained when, even as the Quebec Conference sat, a band of Southerners raided St. Albans, Vermont, from Canada, robbed the banks, and killed three citizens. The preliminary trial of the raiders proceeded slowly, and Judge C. J. Coursol, eventually deciding that he had no jurisdiction, released them. The anger of the North, inflamed by the raid itself flared anew, and it seemed in December of 1864 that by spring the colonies might be drawn into the ferocious struggle south of the border.

This danger underlined – it did no more – the need to bring about Confederation. That need had already been fully accepted by the Colonial Office. The proposal of British American federation now produced in London none of the asperity and opposition it had in 1858. On the contrary, Colonial Secretary Edward Cardwell was firmly and even emphatically a supporter of the federation of all British North America. In this he represented the view of the imperial government that the union of the colonies would diminish the likelihood of American attack and so reduce the possibility of England's being weakened in Europe by war in America.

Such were the unstated premises on which the conference that opened at Quebec on October 10, 1864, was to proceed, and such were the circumstances in which it acted. The conference was made up of delegations of the governments of Canada, New Brunswick, Prince Edward Island, Nova Scotia and Newfoundland. It was a conference, that is, of governments responsible to their provincial legislatures. It was not a convention of delegates popularly elected. And this meant that the constitution of the new union, when ratified, would rest, not on sovereignty of the people, a principle not recognized in British constitutional theory, but first on the authority of the provincial legislatures and finally on the sovereignty of the imperial parliament. As British Americans rarely tired of insisting, their governments were not democracies, but parliamentary sub-monarchies under the Crown of the United Kingdom.

The conference met privately and acted with dispatch. There were few hitches and no crises. The Prince Edward Island delegation early displayed and steadily developed a dislike for the terms of union accepted by Canada, New Brunswick, and Nova Scotia. The Newfoundland delegation, on the other hand, was in general agreement, despite the fact that the terms elaborated really did not meet the peculiar circumstances of either island colony.

The main points of agreement, however, were quickly reached and were of a massive simplicity. The union was to be a general union, legislative as far as possible but with federal features; by implication the legislative union of the Atlantic provinces soon came to be dropped from consideration, and by general consent the wholly legislative union of British America that Macdonald desired was put aside as impracticable for the time being. The form of government was to be British, responsible, parliamentary, and monarchical. The legislature was to be bicameral, a parliament to consist of a Legislative Council and a House of Commons. Members of the Upper House were to be appointed for life from regions rather than provinces, twenty-four from each of the two Canadas, which with federation were to become separate provinces, and twenty-four from the three Atlantic provinces, with four more from Newfoundland. Each region, then, was to have twenty-four members, and Newfoundland four. The representation in the Lower House was to be based on provincial population; the number of representatives for Lower Canada was fixed at the sixty-five it had under the Union, and that for the other provinces was to be calculated by dividing one sixty-fifth of the population of Lower Canada into the population, by the latest census, of each other province.

In the matter of the allocation of powers there was agreement, in the light of the break-down of the American Union and because of experience of British imperial institutions, that the general government should be given supreme powers and the provincial governments allowed exclusive ones sufficient for merely local purposes. It was, in short, to be a legislative union modified by the federal element of the allocation of powers, but with an overriding power in the general government. It was thus to be a unique structure of government which resembled no other so much as it did that of the British Empire since the introduction of responsible government. Under this allocation, the central government was given a general power to legislate for "the peace, welfare and good government" of the union, and twenty-nine subjects of legislation were assigned – by way of instance, but not restrictively – to it, and sixteen exclusively to the provincial assemblies. The financial terms were equally unique: the general taxing powers were unlimited; the provinces could levy direct taxes only, but the general government was to pay subsidies calculated at eighty cents a head of population, make grants for public buildings, assume all provincial debts, and pay those provinces whose debts *per capita* were less than that of Canada five-per-cent interest on the difference, or as it was termed, a debt allowance.

Safeguards for the rights of French Canada, and of religious minorities in education, were among the main features of the scheme of government elaborated at Quebec. French was to be an official language in Lower Canada and in the general government and courts. French civil law was protected by making property and civil rights a provincial subject. The right of Roman Catholic and Protestant minorities to separate schools was especially safeguarded, and education was made a provincial subject. The fruits of the experience of the Canadian Union and the Atlantic provinces in these matters were preserved and generalized. And to the French representatives at Quebec these aspects of the scheme of union were fundamental and decisive. Scrutinized as they were by their compatriots, the French members of the conference could accept no plan of union which did not improve as well as maintain the position French nationality had won for itself in the Union. To them, as to their successors, the new union would be in effect and in law a pact between the two peoples and two cultures. They accepted it, they defended it, in terms of the "co-ordinate sovereignty of the two Canadian peoples," thus emphasizing the essential federal element in the proposed scheme of government.

Such was the general structure and character of the union proposed by the Quebec Conference. It was a strictly practical and wholly conservative document in both content and spirit. It neither professed to enshrine an ideal nor claimed to advance a principle. It added not one voter to the electorate, and secured no right, old or new, to the subject. The reasons for this austere practicality are plain. The union of British America was proposed, not to achieve sought-after privileges and liberties but to preserve an inheritance of freedom long enjoyed and a tradition of life valued beyond any promise of prophet or of demagogue. Confederation was to preserve by union the constitutional heritage of Canadians from the Magna Carta of the barons to the responsible government of Baldwin and Lafontaine, and, no less, the French and Catholic culture of St. Louis and Laval.

The results of the conference were embodied in sixty-nine resolutions, to which three were later added at Montreal to make the seventy-two resolutions of the Confederation scheme. These now had to go to the provincial legislatures for ratification.

The delegates had agreed that the Resolutions should be submitted only to the legislatures for ratification, not to the people in plebiscites or to the electorates in general elections. Ratification by the legislatures was constitutional; it was also expedient, as it was most doubtful whether a popular vote would ratify the Resolutions. Indeed, without much more information than they had, it was certain that the voters in New Brunswick and Nova Scotia at least would repudiate the plan their governments had accepted.

The plan for legislative ratification was quickly shattered. In New Brunswick the legislature was within a few months of expiring. So unfavourable was the first reaction of the public to the reports of the Quebec Conference that Premier S. L. Tilley, the suave Saint John business man and Reformer who had been in office since 1857, was forced to promise, in an endeavour to stop the growing opposition, that he would not act until a new legislature had been elected. He might still have put the scheme before the old legislature, formally and with full and official explanations, but he was hurried into a dissolution by Lieutenant-Governor A. H. Gordon, who was strangely confident that the supporters of Confederation would be returned.

The news that New Brunswick was to have an election strengthened the rapidly gathering opposition to Confederation in Nova Scotia. There Joseph Howe, driven by poverty and ambition, had accepted in 1862 an imperial appointment as Fisheries Commissioner under the Reciprocity Treaty and so had missed the movement for that union he himself had sometimes eloquently advocated. He might, in view of his earlier advocacy, have been expected to support the concrete proposals of the Quebec Conference. But his real desire was for an imperial rather than a Canadian federation, and moved perhaps in part by rivalry with the young and hard-driving Tupper, certainly by sympathy with the injured provincial pride of his fellow Nova Scotians, he came forward in loud and determined opposition to Confederation. So rapidly and fiercely did the storm build up that Tupper did not venture to put the Quebec Resolutions before the Assembly. Taking a lead from a renewed proposal for Maritime union, he carried a resolution in favour of that cause, thus at least averting until times might change for the better the actual defeat of the Confederation scheme.

During the same months of late 1864 and early 1865, Prince Edward Island's legislature had decided it wanted neither Confederation nor Maritime union. The Newfoundland government took no action on the Resolutions in the face of growing suspicion and hostility to the idea of union with the mainland.

Thus when the Resolutions were laid before the Canadian Assembly in February, the prospects for the adoption of Confederation, which had seemed so promising in October, were rapidly dimming. Its proponents, Macdonald, Brown, Cartier, McGee, spoke strongly and ably in its support. They had, they declared, prepared the creation of a new nationality. They had provided for the perpetuation of monarchical institutions in America. They had drawn up a scheme of government strong enough to avoid the evils which had befallen the United States and to discharge all the great tasks laid upon it. This scheme, said Macdonald, had "all the great powers of government." But within it, Brown echoed the assurances of Cartier, the rights of the French and of minorities were amply and securely safeguarded.

The criticism of the Opposition, led by A. A. Dorion and Christopher Dunkin of Lower Canada, pointed to the perhaps excessive interest of the Grand Trunk Railway in the scheme, and to the fact that the new government would be as much or more affected by race and section, even in the Cabinet, as ever the government of the Union had been. The criticism was a criticism of details, however; the basic principles of the scheme were not actually attacked. Only in the Atlantic provinces and at a later date in central Canada was the question of the rights of the provinces in Confederation to be raised.

The debate was, in sustained thought and parliamentary eloquence, the greatest of Canadian parliamentary history, as indeed the occasion demanded. Ratification was assured by the majority the coalition possessed. The government feared, however, some attempt at amendment by the Rouges which might draw away the votes of their French supporters. They therefore insisted that the scheme was in the nature of a treaty or compact among the provinces, which might indeed be rejected but which could not be altered. By doing so they succeeded in obtaining ratification of the Resolutions as submitted, and at the same time they confirmed the French members in their insistence that Confederation was a pact unalterable in its fundamental principles except by the consent of all parties to it. On this understanding, unmistakable though by no means explicit, the Resolutions were approved.

Before the vote, however, the Opposition was cheered by the news that the anti-Confederationists had scored a sweeping victory in New Brunswick, the indispensable province. It was all very well to put the victory down to American railway money, to which indeed it was in part attributable. The north-eastern American railways were backing "westward extension," the building of a line from Saint John into Maine, and wished to stop the building of the Intercolonial. But New Brunswickers had taken the American money because they disliked Canada and Canadians, because some feared the economic effects of Confederation, because the Roman Catholics were apprehensive of how it might affect their church, and because their provincial politicians had bridled at the charge that their province was being "sold to Canada for 80 cents a head."

For the moment, then, the cause of Confederation was checked; and for all any one could tell, indefinitely. Within the year, however, it was to be revived and on its way to completion. Three things led to the revival: the American abrogation of the Reciprocity Treaty, the Fenian raids, and the determination of the imperial government to lessen its own responsibilities in North America by setting up the confederation. American anger at the St. Albans raid had assured the termination of the treaty, already threatened and only renewed for one additional year in 1865 by the extraordinary impression Joseph Howe had made at the Detroit Convention of the American Chambers of Commerce. But it would now expire in March, 1866. In addition, because of alarm and irritation at the growing Confederate activity in British America and the anti-Northern tone of most of the press, the United States early in 1865 took steps to end the Rush-Bagot convention of 1817 by which the Great Lakes had been disarmed. It also threatened to review the trading privileges by which Canadian imports and exports moved in bond across American territory. These were drastic measures, which would injure all British America. No part would suffer more from the ending of Reciprocity than New Brunswick, and when the new anti-Confederation leader, A. J. Smith, returned from Washington early in 1866 convinced that there would be no speedy renewal of the Reciprocity Treaty, his cause and that of "westward extension" had suffered a mortal blow. Any economic benefits Confederation might bring would have to be considered again.

To these economic considerations, the need for defence against Fenian filibustering was added in 1866. The armies of the Republic marched no farther after Lee's surrender at Appomattox, either across the Rio Grande or the St. Lawrence. But many of the Irish veterans were re-enlisted in the service of the conspiratorial Fenian Brotherhood, founded to free Ireland by acts of terror in Ireland and the United Kingdom. Some of its leaders now believed that an attack on British North America would assist the cause of Irish freedom by embroiling the United Kingdom with the United States. Macdonald had organized an intelligence service in 1864 under Gilbert McMicken, stipendiary magistrate of Windsor, to watch Confederate agents. He had begun to disband it at the war's end, but now he built it up again to deal with the Fenians. It soon had its agents planted in the very councils of the Brotherhood, and the Canadian and New Brunswick governments never lacked speedy and accurate information of Fenian plans and movements.

They suffered, however, the cost and effort of manning the long frontiers with militia against the raids which, however ineptly planned and organized, spelled loss and death to the homes and villages of Canada and New Brunswick. The effect was to strengthen the Confederation cause in New Brunswick, because the Fenian raids put in an adverse light the Americans who seemed to tolerate these criminal plots against a friendly neighbour, and commended a scheme which would strengthen British America against such lawless attacks.

In these circumstances, the anti-Confederation government grew steadily weaker. Finally Lieutenant-Governor Gordon, acting on explicit instructions that the imperial government wished Confederation carried, dismissed the Smith ministry. His doing so gave the anti-Confederationists the cry of responsible government in danger, but Tilley, again in office and taking no chances, for with Macdonald's help he had raised a campaign fund in Canada, carried the province for Confederation in May, 1866. Tupper for his part was able to get a general resolution through the Nova Scotia Assembly in favour of continued negotiation for a union of British North America, but without reference to the Quebec Resolutions.

The two provinces then sent delegations to London to assist the Colonial Office in the drafting of a bill based on the Quebec Resolutions, with such amendments as might be agreed on. The Canadian delegates were held up by political obstacles. Brown, convinced that Reciprocity might have been saved, had resigned from the coalition. Taché had died and been succeeded by Narcisse Belleau. And in early June the Fenians made a raid across the Niagara River. It was the most serious of the raids, and ten Canadian militiamen were killed and thirty wounded in a sadly bungled engagement at Ridgeway. But nothing could have given more impetus to Confederation than this bloodshed on Canadian soil by raiders out of the United States. If British North America was not to be treated as a pawn in Irish politics and Anglo-American relations, the colonies had to develop the strength to win respect at Washington and along the border.

In November the delegates all met in the Westminster Palace Hotel and began the delicate task of revising the Quebec Resolutions under Macdonald's chairmanship. No great changes were made. The financial terms were made more generous, but not sufficiently, as events were to prove. The protection given the Protestant minority of Quebec in educational matters was made general. The building of the Intercolonial was made a binding undertaking of the union. The most vexatious question was the composition of the upper chamber: how to preserve sectional equality while providing for the future admission of Prince Edward Island, and for possible deadlock. The Island was to have four of the Atlantic provinces' twenty-four seats, it was decided; and three Senators, or six, might be appointed in the event of deadlock, in equal numbers from the three sections.

Most significant, perhaps, was the decision as to the name and style of the new Confederation. A Maritime delegate had proposed, and all agreed, that it should be called Canada. But Canadians and Maritimers alike wished and expected it would be called the "Kingdom of Canada." That designation signified at once the creation of a new nationality and the continued link with the Crown of the United Kingdom. But wind of this proposal had reached the United States, where anti-monarchical sentiment was deep and also politically profitable. The Legislature of Maine passed a resolution expressing its opposition and the matter was also raised in Congress. No formal objection was made to the government of the United Kingdom. But what was done was enough to alarm the Colonial Office, worried by the serious state of Anglo-American relations, and the Canadians were asked to find a designation less offensive to American susceptibilities. Once more Canadian sentiment and interest were sacrificed to Anglo-American considerations. The new union was accordingly termed the "Dominion of Canada" by the Queen at the request of the delegates – a historic term, but one of little meaning in English and of even less when translated into French as "la Puissance." This failure to define accurately and with due solemnity what was in process, the establishment of a new nation under the British Crown, was to cost Canada much confusion of thought in the next two generations.

The immediate issue, however, was to have the completed bill ratified. The British political situation was extremely brittle in early 1867, with the Conservatives in office as a minority government for the third time since 1852. Also, Howe was hard at work in London at the head of an anti-Confederation delegation, seeking to stir the Radicals and Little Englanders to oppose the bill. But nothing came of either danger, and the British North America Act was passed with general support, to come into force on proclamation by the Queen. Only Lord Carnarvon, Cardwell's successor as Colonial Secretary, succeeded in touching on what the occasion meant for Canada and for the United Kingdom: "We are laying the foundations of a great state," he said, "perhaps one which at a future day may even overshadow this country. But, come what may, we shall rejoice that we have shown neither indifference to their wishes nor jealousy of their aspirations, but that we honestly and sincerely, to the utmost of our power and knowledge, fostered their growth, recognizing in it the condition of our own greatness."

It was decided that the date of proclamation should be July 1. Lord Monck had already decided that there was only one man to fill the office of Prime Minister, John A. Macdonald, now to become Sir John. Macdonald accepted the task of forming the first ministry. Little more could be done until the first Dominion election constituted the first House of Commons of the new Dominion parliament. Then the new government would have to set itself to the great mandatory tasks of Confederation: the building of the Intercolonial, the acquisition of the north-west, the bringing of Newfoundland, Prince Edward Island, and British Columbia into the union. Thus the first Dominion Day, celebrated with church services, parades, band music, picnics and fireworks from Halifax to Sarnia, was a day rather of beginning than of ending; of endeavours planned, rather than achievements reviewed. Much as had been done already, it was only that an undertaking greater still might be attempted.

ADDITIONAL READING

CARELESS, J. M. S. *Brown of the Globe.*

CREIGHTON, D. G. *John A. Macdonald: The Young Politician.*

GROULX, LIONEL *Histoire du Canada français*, Vol. IV.

KERR, D. G. G. *Sir Edmund Head: A Scholarly Governor.*

MARTIN, CHESTER *Foundations of Canadian Nationhood.*

SKELTON, O. D. *The Life and Times of A. T. Galt.*

TROTTER, R. G. *Canadian Federation.*

WAITE, P. B. (ed.) *The Confederation Debates in the Province of Canada, 1865.*

WHITELAW, W. M. *The Maritimes and Canada before Confederation.*

WINKS, R. W. *Canada and the United States: The Civil War Years.*

CHAPTER 17

The Establishment of Independence
in America
1868-1873

The federation of the Canadas, Nova Scotia, and New Brunswick on July 1, 1867, realized the schemes of unification from that of William Smith to that of Alexander Galt, and also the aim of the three years of intense political endeavour from 1864 to 1867. The new union, however, had yet to "stiffen in the mould," as Macdonald put it; and there was the rest of British North America to be brought in, from Newfoundland to British Columbia, and from the forty-ninth parallel to the northern tip of the northernmost arctic island. The Dominion had not only to acquire those vast territories; it had to demonstrate that it could organize, govern, and hold them. Canada had to brave the possible intervention of the United States as it rounded out its territories and strove to develop the national spirit that would give unity to the transcontinental political structure. And to achieve a transcontinental union as the basis for independence in America, the new national government had first to organize itself, assist in the organization of the provinces, and placate the open and angry resistance of Nova Scotia to Confederation.

The first ministry of the Dominion had been planned before July 1 and was simply installed on that day. Lord Monck now became Governor General of the new Dominion. In inviting Macdonald to assume the office of Prime Minister Monck had told him that in the new circumstances the old dual French and English first ministry of United Canada would be discontinued, and that the office of Prime Minister should be single and pre-eminent. This change in the character of the office of first minister was to prove one of the most outstanding produced by Confederation. Macdonald had already chosen his cabinet. It was simply the Canadian coalition of 1864, less George Brown, continued with both Liberals and Conservatives added from the Atlantic provinces. The continuance of the Liberal-Conservative coalition which had brought about the union was not as remarkable as the careful choice of cabinet members to ensure sectional and communal representation within the cabinet. So important was this principle that Thomas D'Arcy McGee, despite his great service to the cause of Confederation, had to stand aside in favour of a man of little eminence, an Irish Catholic from Nova Scotia. Thus the principle that the cabinet itself should be representative, which had governed the composition of cabinets before Confederation, continued to do so in the Dominion, as Christopher Dunkin had predicted in the Confederation debates.

Otherwise, the new government at Ottawa was the old government of Canada enlarged to give representation to the politicians and the interests of the Atlantic provinces of the union. The departments of government were the former Canadian ones, to which a Department of Marine and Fisheries was added in 1868. The offices occupied were in new buildings – striking examples of the architecture of the Gothic Revival – lately completed on Parliament Hill for the use of the government of the now vanished Union of the Canadas. While it was inevitable that Ottawa should be the capital, the circumstances had the effect of making the new government seem very much a "Canadian" affair.

The constitution of the Parliament of Canada proceeded more slowly. The process of deciding which of the Legislative Councillors of the provinces should be appointed to the new Senate went forward with much deliberation and privacy as the politicians weighed the services and merits of the numerous aspirants, until the writs could go out to summon the representatives of the great geographical sections of the union to the Red Chamber of their retired and somewhat perfunctory debates. Their co-equal power with that of the House of Commons was from the first regarded as a latent power, latent but necessary to the stability of the union.

The writs for the House of Commons called for return in August, and that month saw the first national election of Canadian history. The government was victorious by a large majority, but the opposition Liberals gained seriously over the coalition in Ontario, and in Nova Scotia only two supporters of Confederation were returned to Parliament. This lack of support in Nova Scotia was a matter of concern and embarrassment to the new government, and the early success of the opposition in Ontario and Nova Scotia was the ground for that continued opposition to a strong general power which was to emerge as the doctrine of "provincial rights" after 1880. None the less, November 1867 saw the first parliament of the Dominion of Canada assembled in Ottawa.

The formation of the Dominion government was accompanied by the setting up of two new provincial governments, those of Quebec and Ontario, the old Lower and Upper Canada reconstituted but with fewer powers than they had possessed before 1840. Their constitutions were actually parts of the British North America Act itself and were alike, except that Quebec preferred a bicameral legislature while more radical and frugal Ontario insisted on a unicameral one. The new governments were not at once wholly separated from that of the Dominion. The law allowed members of Parliament to be members of the provincial legislatures. Macdonald used this fact to try to keep a hand on affairs in Quebec and Toronto. In Ontario he also helped set up a coalition government under John Sandfield Macdonald, which he hoped might assist him to maintain his strength in that province. In 1872, however, Ontario was to be captured by the Liberals, who at once ended "dual representation"; and the prohibition soon became general.

If the installation of provincial governments, with the lieutenant-governors, ministries and departments of government and legislature, and the status of provincial capital for Quebec and Toronto, were something of a restoration in Quebec and Ontario, in Fredericton and Halifax the chief effect of Confederation was a considerable diminution of power and prestige. The governments of Nova Scotia and New Brunswick no longer maintained and called out their provincial militias; these were incorporated into the militia of Canada. Their postal systems became parts of the Dominion system. Their legislatures no longer levied customs duties, their politicians no longer recommended tide-waiters for appointment. The customs revenue drained off to Ottawa, and Ottawa appointed – with local advice, it was true – the customs officers as well as the militia officers. The continuity of the institutions of each province was unbroken; no new provincial constitution was necessary; but the proud legislature of Nova Scotia was reduced in its power, the shrewd politicians of New Brunswick were left with only the shreds and husks of patronage.

It was little wonder, then, that after 1867 there remained much opposition to the union. British North America was, after all, a set of dispersed, highly parochial communities which had little intercommunication even in the summer season. The communities were made up of singularly self-sufficient and hard-headed people who kept to hard facts and sure returns. Confederation had been an amazing tour de force carried by a political élite who with imperial support had overcome the provincialism of the continental colonies, if not of the islands.

In the continental provinces of Ontario, Quebec, and New Brunswick, the provincialism of British America had been overcome largely by the magic of the new means of transport, the railway, which meant so much to the mainlanders. Even there, objection, not so much to union as to the kind of union carried in 1867, still lingered to nourish the Liberal opposition and ultimately to produce the "provincial rights" tradition of Canadian politics. But it was in peninsular Nova Scotia, where there was no railway magic at work, that opposition to Confederation was open, organized, and in control of the province. There every member of the Conservative party had been swept out of the provincial legislature by the "repealers."

The union was, then, still incomplete and faced with opposition on its Atlantic front. In the north-west the prospects were equally doubtful. In 1865 the government of United Canada, at the insistence of Brown, who had entered the coalition of 1864 partly to ensure the acquisition of Rupert's Land and the North-Western Territory, had taken up with the Colonial Office the question of acquiring those territories. But it had proved no more possible to reach an agreement with the new Hudson's Bay Company than with the old. The two extremes still held; Canada denied the validity of the Company's charter, and the Company was endeavouring to obtain a price for its rights to the territory and government of Rupert's Land.

Meantime, the authority and influence of the Company as the government of Rupert's Land was rapidly decaying. Free traders multiplied, checked only by the competitive power of the Company, while the Canadian party – the Canadians and their sympathizers left after the agitation of 1857 in Red River – and their organ, the *Nor'Wester*, undermined the Company by ceaseless attack. Ordinary men increasingly ignored the authority of the Council and Courts of Assiniboia. There were repeated gaol-breakings in Red River between 1860 and 1870. The Sioux war in Minnesota in 1862 threatened to bring American troops over the border in pursuit of the refugee bands. The wintering partners of the Company were suspicious that their interests had been overlooked in the sale of 1863, and they only half-heartedly maintained the hitherto unflinching front of authority which had kept Indians and free traders respectful. And the Indians and métis grew restless, as the buffalo retreated westward and the Sioux refugees from the Minnesota massacre roamed their lands, and as "the Canadas" talked ever more freely of taking over the territory.

Beyond the mountains, in British Columbia and Vancouver Island, there was also talk of impending change. The gold-diggers of the Fraser had pushed up the tributaries of that stream into the Cariboo country where the gold was traced in the beds of ancient creeks long buried beneath the mountain terraces. But the richest diggings of the Cariboo were soon exhausted and by the mid sixties the gold rush was over. The miners drained away, business fell off, the government revenues dwindled. After the boom, contraction was necessary; private business economized, and the two governments sought to reduce their expenditures. One way of reducing the costs of government was to unite the two colonies. This the imperial government did in 1866, when Vancouver Island and British Columbia became the colony of British Columbia with its capital at Victoria.

More than economy was needed, however, to end the depression, and ambitious men looked to political union and a transcontinental railway to set a new boom going. The union might be with the United States, with which communications were so easy, or with Canada, remote as it was. For there were Canadians and a "Canadian party" in the Pacific colony, particularly in the Cariboo diggings, where the Canadian Dr. R. W. W. Carrall was a correspondent of Sir John Macdonald. But the parties of union were opposed by a colonial party, or compact, led by Governor Frederick Seymour and made up of the old Hudson's Bay Company families and the British officials who feared the loss of their offices and their pensions. This local oligarchy was to resist the talk of union successfully for two years more.

They could do so the more effectively in that they could point to the vast distance between Canada and British Columbia. It was known of course that Canada proposed to build a Pacific railway, but it had first to acquire Rupert's Land, and was bound by the Act of Confederation to build the Intercolonial Railway. Both would prove heavy undertakings; the Pacific railway was one of yet unexampled magnitude, and it was thus easy to argue that it was beyond the resources of Canada.

These tasks of consolidation and expansion in the Confederation and the remainder of British North America had, moreover, to be carried out along the northern border of an irritated and rapacious republic whose citizens time after time had poured into the territory of neighbouring countries and then clamoured for their annexation to the United States. The public of the United States was angered, and with ample cause, by the losses inflicted on American merchant shipping by the Confederate raiders, *Alabama* and *Shenandoah*, built in British ports and armed by British firms. The "*Alabama* claims" for damages, however, as stated by American politicians and the American press – the total cost of the Civil War; the cession of British America – passed all reason, and not unnaturally suggested a disposition on the part of the United States to exaggerate a legitimate grievance for aggressive purposes.

Coupled with this menace were the difficulties arising from the ending of the Reciprocity Treaty in 1866, especially the refusal of American fishermen to forgo the rights they had enjoyed under that treaty in Canadian territorial waters. This disposition to override the rights of the weaker neighbour was also revealed in the careless tolerance shown by American authorities towards the Fenians, still plotting raids on Canadian soil after the repulse of 1866.

That a good many Americans thought that the great convulsion of the Civil War, with its destruction of the internal balance of power in the Republic, might well work itself out in the absorption of British America into the United States was apparent in the American press. The editors of the northern city journals were well aware that the English Liberal party, and the Little Englanders of whatever party, viewed with a growing indifference the continuance of the tie between the United Kingdom and Canada. They knew that English politicians like John Bright thought Confederation the occasion for ending the connection amicably but definitely. The powerful chairman of the Senate Foreign Relations Committee, Charles Sumner, a fanatic supporter of the *Alabama* claims and an outspoken advocate of annexation, was a correspondent of Bright's and knew the drift of Little England sentiment. At the same time, so fierce was anti-British sentiment that Anglo-American relations were perhaps in their most intractable condition since 1776. Probably, however, most of the furore consisted of the historic Anglophobia inflamed by British and Canadian sympathy with the political cause of the South during the Civil War. The only considerable bodies of sentiment for annexation, coupled with some determination to realize it, had their centres in certain railway interests in New England and in St. Paul, Minnesota, where hopes had developed that all the Red River and Saskatchewan country might be drawn by trade and railway construction into the Republic.

It was against this background of American irritation and hostility that the work of Confederation was to be completed. And even within the Dominion there was still open or covert opposition. To the desire for repeal, some Nova Scotians added the hope of annexation to the United States. A group of Montreal business men were similarly infected. Then there were the Americans and American sympathizers in Red River and British Columbia. All these were disposed to thwart, though not necessarily committed to thwarting, the continuance or the completion of Confederation.

There were two elements in the Nova Scotian resistance to British American union. The first was the proud provincial patriotism of the chief of the Atlantic provinces. Nova Scotia was a British colony and an Atlantic community. In a way it was almost a nation, with its own literature and traditions. It lived by the sea, looked to the sea, and was distrustful of the pull and weight of the continent. It was this spirit, fiercely stubborn, that Howe had aroused in opposition to Confederation. The second element was commercial. The end of Reciprocity was to Nova Scotia in 1866, particularly to the fishermen and the coal-miners who had sold their fish and coal in New England, what the ending of the old Commercial Empire had been to the Montreal merchants in 1849. As in that crisis, the effects were greatly intensified by a severe economic depression. And just as the passage of the Rebellion Losses Bill had seemed the political completion of a commercial catastrophe, so in Nova Scotia the passage of the British North America Act seemed the last straw of the economic depression. The imposition of the Canadian tariff, lowered though it had been to effect Confederation, seemed certain to complete the commercial ruin of the fisheries, mines, and shipping of Nova Scotia, dependent as these were on the export trade to the United States.

As a result, the fierce agitation for the repeal of the union was underlain by a growing sentiment for secession and annexation to the United States. Many Nova Scotians felt that the province could not stand alone and if freed from Confederation might have to seek entry to the Republic. These beliefs were freely and widely expressed in the press and from the platform after July 1867. They were probably even more widely held in private. Those who voiced them included people of prestige and authority; among them were the Premier, William Annand, and the Attorney General, Martin Wilkins.

But the provincial patriotism of Howe, to which he had appealed in his compatriots, would never turn to annexation; it was a British as well as a provincial patriotism. In Howe's hands resistance to the union would never become a tool to effect annexation. Howe was therefore the key to the appeasement of the movement for repeal. The Nova Scotian members under his leadership did not boycott the House of Commons, but used their seats there to make a strong but constitutional protest against the union. And when Howe led a delegation to London in the spring of 1868 to seek repeal, it was not too difficult for Monck and Tupper to counter the efforts of the delegation. The Colonial Secretary, the Duke of Buckingham and Chandos, returned a courteous but firm rejection to the petition of the Nova Scotians. Howe, now assured that the United Kingdom would not undo the Act of Confederation, listened to Tupper's urging that he turn his influence and talents to persuading his fellow Nova Scotians to accept the inevitable, in return for a revision of the financial terms of union. Later in the year Macdonald, Cartier, and John Sandfield Macdonald, who was a personal friend of Howe's, visited Halifax while a repeal convention was in session and were influential in persuading Howe and his supporters to refrain from extreme pronouncements.

From then on the anti-Confederation forces were divided. Howe agreed to accept a seat in Macdonald's cabinet and to campaign for re-election as a supporter of Confederation on a platform of "better terms." These were financial terms only; no legal or constitutional element of the British North America Act was to be altered. The terms were worked out early in 1869, and in effect simply repaired a real injustice by extending to Nova Scotia revised financial terms similar to those granted to New Brunswick in 1866. Howe carried the county of Hants in a bitter contest, aided by supporters of Confederation such as Adams G. Archibald. But two other by-elections were lost to repealers. The movement against Confederation continued; in June, 1869, the Anti-Confederation League was actually renamed the Annexation League. Thereafter Howe's example, and returning prosperity, caused repeal and annexation sentiment to decline. But a lingering resentment against Confederation remained in the ancient province and was to reappear in times of stress for many years. The Nova Scotia resistance was the first demonstration that a provincial agitation could force a change of policy in Ottawa; and, as it happened, it was to be followed by the resistance of the métis in Red River.

Before that storm broke in the north-west, however, calm seemed to spread over the Atlantic region. The conciliation of Nova Scotia was accompanied by reports that the government of Newfoundland, after years of indifference, was beginning to consider joining Confederation. The reports were undoubtedly tinged by the optimism of the Lieutenant-Governor, Anthony Musgrave, but they were encouraging. Negotiations for union were cautiously opened with Prince Edward Island and a generous offer was made to buy out the remaining landlords and compensate the Island for its lack of public lands. The Intercolonial, after serious contention in the federal cabinet, was going forward. It was laid down along the North Shore of New Brunswick, not by the St. John valley, and it was a public work, built and operated by government. The eastern wing of the Dominion then seemed to be in a fair way to completion. It remained to balance it by beginning the construction of the western wing in Rupert's Land.

The work was in fact well in hand. Early in 1868 William McDougall, one-time Clear Grit and Young Canada writer, now a unionist Liberal minister from Ontario, had moved resolutions in Parliament requesting the imperial government to grant Rupert's Land and the North-Western Territory to the Dominion. After an interval, the Duke of Buckingham cabled that a delegation would be welcome, and in haste McDougall and Cartier were dispatched to London to negotiate for the transfer of the north-west to Canada.

One intended member of the party was left behind in the hurry. He was Charles Mair, a student of Queen's University who had just published one of the first volumes of Canadian verse and had assisted McDougall in collecting material on the north-west. In his leisure hours Mair had found companionship with other young intellectuals in the raw new capital, especially Henry J. Morgan and R. G. Haliburton. Their talk was of literature and the greater destiny of Canada. McDougall was something of a mentor to them, and his Young Canada was soon to be outshone by their Canada First. For in these young men the spirit of Confederation found a dwelling and an utterance. Hitherto it had found adequate expression only through one voice, which in fact inspired Canada First. That was the voice of D'Arcy McGee, stilled when in February, 1868, McGee was shot down for his Canadian patriotism by a Fenian skulker in Ottawa. Mair and his friends as yet spoke only among themselves, but their accents were the accents of Canada's manifest destiny to occupy and settle the north-west, explored and occupied for over a century by Canadian traders, French and English. The only pity was that among them was no Joseph Cauchon, no Pamphile Lemay, no Louis Riel.

Mair was compensated for not going to London by being dispatched to Red River. In that distant settlement the crops, the buffalo hunt, and the fisheries had all failed, and famine threatened the poor and the improvident. Relief funds were raised in St. Paul and in Canadian cities, and a relief grant was voted by the Ontario legislature. The funds were used to buy flour and seed wheat in Minnesota, which were carted to Fort Garry and distributed. But the Dominion government chose to aid the distress in Red River by beginning the cutting of the roads on the land and water route between Fort William and Fort Garry which had been recommended by the Canadian engineer, Simon J. Dawson, of the exploring expedition of 1857-59. A party with Mair as paymaster was sent west in late September, 1868, to buy provisions and to begin the hiring of Red River labour to cut a road from Ste. Anne des Chênes to the north-west angle of the Lake of the Woods. Naturally but unfortunately, these Canadians entered into friendly relations with the leader of the "Canadian party" in Red River, Dr. John Christian Schultz.

Schultz, a bold and able man, was determined to open the north-west to

Canadian settlement. In his urging of union with Canada, he had offended the local Hudson's Bay Company officers and had somehow aroused the distrust of the Roman Catholic missionaries at St. Boniface. The attitude of both the Hudson's Bay people and the missionaries spread to the French element in Red River, the French-Canadian traders and the métis buffalo-hunters and freighters. The distrust was extended to the Canadian road party and the motives of the Canadian government. No one in Red River had yet realized, no one had been at pains to explain, that the acquisition of the north-west by the Dominion would be the joint achievement of French and English, Catholic and Protestant Canada. The French at Red River feared that it would be what had seemed to threaten in 1857-59, a union with predominantly Protestant and English Ontario. And Schultz and Mair, and the little coterie of Canada First men in Ottawa and Toronto who now welcomed Schultz to their midst, did represent a Canadian "manifest destiny" that was purely British and Protestant.

As if to underline the point, Louis Riel, son of the man who had led the métis in 1849, came back to Red River in July 1868 from Montreal and St. Paul where he had been a student, and an observer of Canadian and American politics. Politically, he had been raised in the school of Papineau, but his education was clerical. His role, consciously inherited from his father, was to be the champion of the French element in the north-west. The possibility was thus rapidly developing at the end of 1868 that the acquisition of the north-west, unless handled with considerable tact in Red River, might divide French and English in Canada and impair the co-operation which had made Confederation possible.

Meanwhile, in London, Cartier and McDougall had spent the winter of 1868-69 in negotiation. They insisted that the British government, possessing the sovereignty of Rupert's Land, must deal with the Hudson's Bay Company. They refused to commit Canada to buying out the Company. They stood fast on these points while the Duke of Buckingham gave way to Lord Granville, Colonial Secretary in the new Liberal government of Prime Minister Gladstone. Finally Granville decided the Company must be compelled to settle, and practically forced them to accept the Canadians' reluctant agreement to have Canada pay £300,000 and grant some thousands of acres of land around the Company's posts, together with one twentieth of the "fertile belt" of the north-west, in order to extinguish the rights of the Hudson's Bay Company in Rupert's Land. The Company was to surrender the territory to the imperial government on receipt of the money from Canada, and the imperial government was to transfer the territory to Canada, at a date to be agreed upon later.

No one, however, neither the Hudson's Bay Company, nor the imperial nor the Canadian government, officially informed the Hudson's Bay officers in Rupert's Land, or the people of Rupert's Land, of the terms or date of the transfer, or of what their condition was to be after the transfer. In the absence of official information, rumour bred prolifically, and the conviction grew among the

French that "the Canadas" meant to take over the country and dispossess them. Under Riel, they determined in the fall of 1869 to resist the unconditional transfer of the north-west to Canada. Bishop A. A. Taché, on his way to the Oecumenical Council at Rome, warned Cartier of the impending trouble, but the minister paid no more attention than to order the dispatch of some army rifles to Fort Garry.

The suspicions of the métis had been fed by the arrival in August of a Canadian survey party, sent out to make surveys before the rush of settlement expected in 1870. The head of the party, Lieutenant-Colonel J. S. Dennis, obtained permission from Governor William Mactavish to proceed with the surveys, and exerted himself to avoid offending local feelings. No private property was surveyed. None the less, on October 11, Louis Riel and a party of métis stopped the survey of a base line from the Principal Meridian to Ste. Anne des Chênes in order to challenge the right of Canada to make any survey in Rupert's Land.

The métis then organized as they did on the annual buffalo hunts and elected a council with a president and secretary. The president was a nonentity; the secretary was Riel. They barricaded the public highway along the Red River at St. Norbert south of Fort Garry to search travellers and carts for dispatches and the government rifles. On October 31 they turned back at Pembina, on the border, the governor-designate of Rupert's Land, William McDougall, who had been sent out to assume the government with the aid of a provisional council on the date of the transfer, for which December 1 was finally chosen. On November 2, the métis seized and garrisoned Fort Garry. Riel then attempted to unite the settlement behind him under a provisional government which would negotiate terms of union with Canada.

In his resistance to the transfer Riel set aside the constituted government of the Hudson's Bay Company, on the plea that it was decrepit, and neither the council of the métis proclaimed on December 8 nor the provisional government finally set up in February had any validity in British law. But his military position, impregnable while winter lasted, and the fear of American intervention, forced the Canadian government to negotiate. The negotiations were begun by the agents it sent to Red River, of whom Donald A. Smith of the Hudson's Bay Company was chief, and delegates sent by the provisional government with a Bill of Rights agreed to in a convention of the people, but seriously modified by Riel and his associates. The Canadian government called Bishop Taché back from Rome, and in his hands the terms agreed upon were given their final form. But the Canadian ministers refused to grant an amnesty for the acts of the resistance, particularly after it was learned that on March 4 an Ontario man named Thomas Scott had been shot for being insubordinate as a prisoner and striking his guards. From this act, and from the refusal to grant an amnesty, much trouble was to come. But in May, 1870, the terms of the transfer were embodied in the Manitoba Act, which created a province of that name in the Red River valley.

Riel thus won the self-government he thought necessary to protect his people, and the French language and denominational schools were established by law in the new and tiny province on Red River. The public lands, however, remained under Dominion control and the North-West Territory under a colonial régime directed from Ottawa. And policy, pushed on by British and Protestant sentiment outraged by the execution of Thomas Scott, called for the dispatch of a military expedition. A force, part British regulars, part Canadian militia, was sent out under Lieutenant-Colonel Garnet Wolseley, to warn the United States that the United Kingdom supported the union of the north-west with Canada and also to discourage an attack by the plains Indians on Red River. The Wolseley expedition reached Red River on August 23, and Riel, who had waited anxiously for an amnesty, realized at the last moment that none was to come and fled into exile. A new lieutenant-governor, Adams G. Archibald of Nova Scotia, appointed as an alternative to one from either Ontario or Quebec, followed Wolseley, and civil government under Canadian sovereignty was instituted in Manitoba and the North-West Territory on September 5. The Dominion then extended to the Rocky Mountains and the Arctic Ocean.

With the annexation of the north-west, the way was open to union with British Columbia beyond the Rockies. In that colony the cause of union had become even more insistent since 1866. The North Pacific had ceased to be the backwater it had been shown to be in the Crimean War. Russia had since seized the Amur valley and advanced to warm water on the Pacific; in 1867 the United States had purchased Alaska, though with mingled misgiving and indifference. In the colony, the economy was still depressed and the government nearly bankrupt. Increasingly, however, the question of union became not whether union was to be with the United States or with Canada, but whether there could be union with Canada. The American annexationists were few and dwindling, and their significance came increasingly to lie in the use the Canadian or the colonial party might make of them to help its own cause.

The debate between the two major parties ran high. It was inflamed both by feeling between the island and the mainland and by that between British and Canadians. As in Red River, the Canadians had made themselves disliked by their drive and pertinacity, and earned the designation of "oatmeal Chinamen" from the easy-going colonists because of their readiness to work hard for the going wage. The two antagonisms, of island for mainland and of colonists for Canadians, combined because the island was the centre of British officialdom and settlement, while the Canadians led opinion on the mainland. An exception was the flamboyant and erratic Amor de Cosmos, originally a Nova Scotian named William Alexander Smith, whose *Daily Colonist* of Victoria was an early and ardent advocate of union with Canada.

The colonial party of British officials and their supporters was firmly in control of the Legislative Council, the majority of whose members were appointed by the Colonial Office. This fact gave the Canadian party fresh fuel for their agitation. They demanded popular control of the council and, as they assumed that union with Canada would bring with it provincial status and responsible government, the demand for union thus became a democratic as well as a Canadian cause. In British Columbia as in Red River, Confederation would mean popular government and the end of a colonial régime. The old Canadian contest of the 1830's was being fought out anew on the Pacific slope.

Little impression was made by the Canadian agitation on the entrenched British officials, supported as they were by Governor Frederick Seymour, or on the old British and Hudson's Bay element, personified by the popular Dr. J. S. Helmcken. Indeed, when in September, 1868, de Cosmos organized a convention at Yale which called for immediate union with Canada, the introduction of responsible government, and the reduction of official salaries, it was commonly spoken of by members of the colonial party as the "Yale Conspiracy," with mutterings of "treachery" and "disloyalty."

In all this there was nothing the Canadian government could do directly. But the Prime Minister did keep up his correspondence with moderate Canadian partisans, such as Dr. Carrall and Dr. R. W. Powell. Macdonald also continued to keep before the Colonial Office the project of complete British American union. The desirability of maintaining a footing on the North Pacific and of devolving North American responsibilities on Canada induced the imperial government to come to Canada's aid. In 1869 Governor Seymour died and was replaced by Anthony Musgrave, who had tried actively, though unsuccessfully, to carry Newfoundland into Confederation.

Musgrave, fortunately, soon made himself popular with the colonial party and used his popularity to diminish the prejudices and fears with which they had viewed union with Canada. In October 1869 he published a dispatch from Granville which announced that the imperial government had decided that union with Canada would afford British Columbia its best future prospects. A petition for annexation to the United States, bearing forty-three signatures, to which sixty-one were later added, only had the effect of arousing public opinion in favour of union with Canada. Then, when the acquisition of Rupert's Land and the North-West Territory was about to remove a last remaining obstacle to union, Musgrave was able to have a resolution in favour of union moved by members of the Executive Council who had hitherto been at best lukewarm towards Confederation.

The terms sought were assumption of the colony's debt, responsible government when the local administration was ready, a railway to the east, and a public works program. After some confused debate caused by the reversal of the officials' stand, the resolution passed, and Musgrave appointed a delegation of three, Dr. Carrall, Joseph Trutch, and Dr. Helmcken, representative of the three main elements in the colony, to go to Ottawa to discuss terms of union with the Canadian government. They arrived at the end of May, shortly after the Manitoba

KC-M

Act had been passed, and as the Wolseley expedition was being launched. Canadian expansion, checked by the Red River resistance, was now driving ahead once more, and the Canadian government was determined that there should be no repetition of the Red River errors and no second check. The British Columbia delegates were warmly welcomed by the impetuous Cartier, for Macdonald had collapsed during the passage of the Manitoba Act, and the negotiations went forward with a swing.

The delegates received better terms than they had dared ask for and went home dazed by Canadian generosity. The province was to institute responsible government when its own government saw fit. The colonial debt would be assumed by the Dominion and the standard provincial subsidies would be paid on a liberal over-estimate of the population. The national government would endeavour to have the naval station maintained at Esquimalt and would guarantee a loan to build a dry-dock in that port. The province would control its public lands except for a strip along the line of the proposed railway. And with respect to the railway Cartier simply overrode the modest requests of the delegates. He committed the Dominion to begin the railway within two years and to complete it within ten of the date of union. He had to overcome resistance in his own party by obtaining assurance from Trutch that the terms need not be interpreted literally; he met opposition from the Liberals by declaring that the terms would bring no increase in taxation. A tithe of such liberality would have kept peace in Red River; the British Columbians were awed into grateful acquiescence.

As a result, opposition to union died away. The colony moved serenely towards responsible government and union through the remainder of 1870. The proportion of elected members in the Legislative Council was increased, and every constituency elected a supporter of Confederation. In January the terms of union were accepted unanimously and the Legislative Council drew up a provincial constitution modelled on that of Ontario. Canada had penetrated to the Pacific indeed. The remaining preliminaries went through without a hitch and on July 20, 1871, one year to the day after Manitoba, British Columbia became a province of Canada. Bound to the St. Lawrence since 1821, Canada had garnered at last its full heritage of the rivers explored by French and British from the St. John to the Fraser and the Mackenzie, and stood on the Pacific and the Arctic, one united British America, a transcontinental empire under a constitutional monarchy and a parliamentary democracy.

That such had been the outcome, in the face of American pressure and growing British indifference, was something of a miracle, the result of repeated demonstrations that Canada, its people as well as its governments, had deliberately chosen to remain British and not to become American. That this choice was in effect a choice of national independence was not yet clear.

Two events of 1868 had seemed to point to stronger American pressure on Canada and a weakening British resistance to such pressure. One was the election to the United States Presidency of General U. S. Grant as the candidate of the Radical Republicans, among whom were Charles Sumner of Massachusetts and Zachariah Chandler of Michigan, the leading American expansionists. The other was the formation of Gladstone's Liberal ministry, with powerful Little Englanders like John Bright and Robert Lowe at its board. And the high point of the campaign to browbeat the imperial government into ceding Canada in settlement of the *Alabama* claims had been reached when in April 1869, under the bitter leadership of Sumner, the Senate Foreign Relations Committee had rejected a draft treaty, known as the Clarendon-Johnson treaty, as a wholly inadequate settlement of American claims. Had the Grant administration elected to follow the lead given by Sumner, the threat to Canada might have become serious indeed.

The new Gladstone ministry also seemed to be about to behave as anticipated when in place of Monck, the grave, persistent architect of Confederation, they appointed a "mere Bart.," Sir John Young, as Governor General. It is true no man of higher rank and reputation could be found, as the Canadian parliament had reduced the salary of the office. But Young had not the character or the strong imperial sense of either his predecessor or his successor, and he may have had some notion, as a speech in Halifax in 1870 was to suggest, that he had been sent to preside over the last days of the British connection in Canada. The idea was definitely abroad that Confederation was the prelude to separation. And American opinion was sure that separation would mean the end of Confederation.

Fortunately for Canada there was, except in Minnesota, no real drive towards expansion in the United States. The victorious North was war-weary; its armies had been disbanded or were busy occupying the prostrate South. The war debt was heavy. The American people were absorbed in the expansion of industry, the reconstruction of the South, the occupation of the trans-Mississippi and Pacific west. The United States had become a united nation and was becoming an industrialized society; the expansive democracy and land-grabbing imperialism of the Democratic era were diminishing forces. In consequence, the demand for the cession of Canada had become largely a matter of congressional oratory and diplomatic pressure. There were real hopes and real desires for the acquisition of Canada, but no American money was to be spent and no American blood was to be shed for it. Many Americans were sure that Confederation would fail and annexation follow, but few were moved to hasten the inevitable. As a result American policy was diffuse and vague. The one really serious issue was that of the *Alabama* claims. President Grant himself was wrapped up in the Cuban rebellion and a personal scheme to annex Santo Domingo. The policy of his Secretary of State, Hamilton Fish, towards Canada was that of waiting for the ripe fruit to fall, but of not making any great effort to shake the tree.

This attitude was founded on the belief that the great mass of Canadians wished to become American and were only deterred by the influence and authority of the upper circles in business, politics, and society. Once these were undermined, as seemed likely under a Liberal government in England, by the withdrawal of imperial sanction and support, the unreal structure of Canadian Confederation would, it was held, collapse, and Canadians would gratefully seek their true home in annexation to the United States. American public opinion was utterly blind to the birth of Canadian nationality, probably because its own historic experience led it to believe that nationality could spring only from revolution.

None the less, shallow as the American desire for annexation was, mistaken as the American reading of Canadian sentiment might be before 1870, any one of a number of issues between April 1869 and June 1870 might have led to a crisis. The first of these and the most insistent was that of the fisheries. When the Reciprocity Treaty ended in 1866, the British American fisheries once more came under the Convention of 1818, by which American fishermen had no right to fish within the three-mile limit along the British shores, except in Newfoundland, and none to enter British American ports except to obtain wood, water, or provisions. That is, they could neither buy bait nor sell fish. In dispute was their alleged right under the Convention to fish in bays less than six miles wide at the mouth. But under the Reciprocity Treaty they had been able to fish in all the British American waters and to trade in British American ports. These rights they were reluctant to give up, partly because the New England fishermen had always believed that they had an inherent right to fish without restriction in the north-eastern fisheries. Partly also in the sly hope that they would wear down British resistance, the Yankee skippers persisted in fishing within the three-mile limit and trading in the British American ports.

This situation was one of the problems faced by the new Canadian government and its Department of Marine and Fisheries headed by Peter Mitchell, its Minister from New Brunswick. Mitchell continued the policy of Nova Scotia and New Brunswick before 1867, that of tolerating the New England boats within territorial waters but of charging a licence fee of fifty cents a ton, with a view to squeezing the New Englanders out by increasing the fee, or, preferably, inducing the American government to renew the Reciprocity Treaty.

Though legally justifiable, this policy was dangerous. It assumed a power to enforce licensing if the New Englanders evaded the Canadian patrol boats, as they did when the fee was raised by stages to two dollars a ton in 1869. It also assumed that the imperial government would then enforce the Canadian regulations by means of the Atlantic Squadron of the Royal Navy, and that the United States might think the fisheries of sufficient importance to renew the Reciprocity Treaty in order to obtain free entry to them. None of these assumptions was valid. As a result, the imperial government became increasingly worried by Mitchell's strong line and the danger of an incident in the fisheries.

In 1870 it declined to enforce the licences with the vigour which alone would have ensured that the majority of the American vessels were licensed, and induced the Canadian government to suspend a prohibition of American fishing vessels trading and trans-shipping fish in Canadian ports. The American government, knowing that sentiment among the public against the renewal of reciprocity was overwhelming, simply formed the impression that the Canadians were hot-headed and irresponsible. Thus the fisheries issue was inflaming Canadian-American relations and embarrassing the United Kingdom at a time when Canada most needed England's support, and when that support was becoming most doubtful.

If the Canadian attitude in this matter irritated the American government, the revival of Fenian activity in 1869, on top of the American refusal to consider Canadian claims for the expense and damage suffered in the raid of 1866, equally irritated Canadian opinion. Late in 1869 the Fenian leader, John O'Neill, began to plan another attack on Canada. The Canadian militia was kept alert. The Canadian Irish were loyal. As before, Macdonald had kept his police vigilant. Known now as Dominion police, they were still directed by Gilbert McMicken. McMicken promptly sent Macdonald news of the Fenian intentions and this was relayed by him to Sir Edward Thornton, the British minister at Washington, for transmission to the Government of the United States. Nothing was done. Americans were inclined to think that the Canadians exaggerated the danger, and no northern politician wished to offend the Irish vote. O'Neill was allowed to organize two attacks on Quebec from Vermont in May, 1870. Both invasions were turned back by the Canadian militia after an exchange of rifle fire and O'Neill was arrested and gaoled in the United States. The hopes of deluded Irish patriots, the savings of Irish chambermaids, were thus futilely squandered, the Fenians became even more ridiculous without ceasing to be a murderous menace, and Canadian sentiment hardened still further against the United States.

When therefore Wolseley's arrival at Fort Garry had clinched the annexation of the north-west, and the terms of union with British Columbia were ratified, Canadians not only felt that a new continental and national destiny was assured them. They were also quite sure they had no desire to become citizens of the American republic. The work of the Viking seafarers and the Bristol and Norman fishermen, of the missionary and fur-trade explorers, had been re-enacted and confirmed in new political terms and for new economic purposes. The northern economy had given rise to a northern nation. The northern way was now to be laid in iron to the Pacific. But any turning aside, any faltering from the path, had been ruled out by the harsh language of the American press and the crude pressure of the American annexationist politicians. Canadians could and would walk their own way in North America.

The many factors at play in 1870, the Red River resistance, the Fenian stir-rings, the ever-troublesome fisheries, had fallen towards that conclusion by mid 1870. But Canadian-American and Anglo-American issues still had to be settled diplomatically. The outbreak of the Franco-Prussian war in July confronted the United Kingdom with dangers in Europe that made it desirable, as in 1794, to settle without delay the disputes with the United States. And the already ex-pressed determination to withdraw all British troops from Canada, including Quebec but excepting the naval base of Halifax, meant that British backing for Canada in negotiations with the United States would be diplomatic backing at most.

Hamilton Fish, the American Secretary of State, had suggested privately the setting up of an international joint commission to seek a settlement of the fisheries dispute. Lord Granville, Foreign Secretary of the United Kingdom, employed John Rose, formerly a Canadian politician and now an Anglo-American banker, to sound Fish on the conduct of such a commission and the prospects of widening its scope. Late in 1870 it was agreed that both governments might commit themselves to the proposal of a commission to settle all outstanding issues. Then the Gladstone government made a new departure. It appointed Sir John Macdonald a member of the commission.

The appointment was significant because by it the British government recog-nized Canada's status as an emergent nation and gave something of a reply courteous to President Grant's less than neighbourly reference, in a message to Congress, to the way "this semi-independent but irresponsible agent" had exer-cised the power "delegated" to it by the United Kingdom in policing the inshore fisheries. It was embarrassing for the Canadian Prime Minister, however, be-cause Macdonald was at once a national leader and an imperial delegate, and would be held responsible by the Canadian electorate for any sacrifice of Canadian interests for the sake of Anglo-American harmony. Canadians were convinced by warrant of long experience, as they thought, that when the United Kingdom and the United States agreed, it was at the expense of Canada. The danger of the appointment was clearly seen by Macdonald and his colleagues, but it was im-possible to decline. They had to seek a favourable settlement with the United States and must try to retain British support in reaching one.

The negotiations soon found the British and American commissioners moving rapidly towards substantial agreement. Fish had prepared the ground well and the British were determined to settle. But Macdonald was bound to try to trade the fisheries for a reciprocity treaty and to obtain compensation for the Fenian raids. The latter the Americans abruptly and firmly refused to consider, on the ground that it was not on the agenda. On the former, they made two offers, the more generous of which was the free entry of fish, coal, salt, and firewood in exchange for the freedom of the inshore fisheries. Macdonald could not accept such terms and face the Maritime electorate, as he must do in the coming year.

Something like deadlock occurred as the dogged and isolated Canadian held out against the American refusal to see the Canadian position and the unconcealed impatience of his British colleagues. Finally, the imperial government undertook to compensate Canada for the Fenian raids. Canadian fish was given entry into the American market in return for the freedom of American fishermen to fish in Canadian waters. The exchange was admitted to be unequal, and Canada was to be awarded monetary compensation, the amount to be determined by a commission. The freedom of navigation of the St. Lawrence – though not of its canals – was exchanged for the same privilege on the Yukon, Porcupine, and Stikine rivers in the far north-west in perpetuity, and on Lake Michigan for ten years, to be renewable thereafter until denounced. A decision on the boundary between American and Canadian islands in the Straits of Juan de Fuca, referred to the new German emperor for arbitration, upheld the American claim and gave control of the Haro channel to the United States. But, above all, the *Alabama* claims were to be settled by the same process of international arbitration.

Such were the main terms of the Treaty of Washington. They ended the aggravated friction between the United States and the United Kingdom which the Civil War had caused, mostly by reducing the *Alabama* claims to dimensions acceptable to British pride and to common sense. The treaty dealt with certain specific and important issues between Canada and the United States, and although it permanently settled none of them it did register, indirectly, grudgingly and ungraciously, American acceptance of the fact that the Republic was faced from sea to sea by an independent American nation, as free, as well-organized and as stable as itself, but founded on an explicit and final rejection of American institutions and of American manifest destiny. A superficial victory for Grant and Fish, the Treaty of Washington was in fact the greatest diplomatic check the United States had accepted since its foundation. It had agreed to share the continent with a self-governing Canada; the continental imperialism of the pas was ended with the ending of British imperial power in America.

For Macdonald and his colleagues in the Cabinet there was no such clarity of outcome, and no such certainty for the future. The United States still seemed a formidable menace to the infant Dominion. The British connection, the indispensable alliance upon which the survival of Canadian independence turned, was weakening, perhaps ending. John Rose, Canadian Minister of Finance at Confederation, had since 1869 been the specially accredited agent of the Canadian government to that of the United Kingdom, to ensure that the interests of Canada were kept before the imperial government and the tie maintained in its true character of an alliance of governments. There was still imperative need to prevent the Little Englanders having their way and persuading the Gladstone cabinet to abandon Canada. The new transcontinental union, as Macdonald said, was still in "the gristle," not yet "hardened to bone." In the second half of 1871 all yet remained to be organized and consolidated, and the life of the first parliament of Canada was to expire in 1872.

If the government coalition, now really the Conservative party once more, was to continue and complete the work of nation-building begun in 1864, it would have to win the election of 1872. To do that it would have to overcome the liabilities of its record, the still-simmering discontent in Nova Scotia, the amnesty question in Manitoba, renewed by an abortive Fenian raid in 1871 in which Archibald had accepted support from Riel, the over-generous terms of union granted British Columbia, the failure to get reciprocity in the Treaty of Washington.

There were offsets, of course. The disappointments of the Treaty of Washington could be eased by the British compensation for the Fenian raids in the form requested, an imperial guarantee of a loan of £2,500,000 to build the Pacific railway. The railway itself, as a national undertaking and an economic enterprise, would win the government powerful moral and material support. Moreover, the failure to obtain reciprocity and the consequent growth of national sentiment brought support to the growing demand of Canadian manufacturers for protection. Macdonald dealt with the demand in his usual perceptive fashion when he seized on a phrase increasingly in vogue, the phrase "National Policy." He used it to give particular interests a national setting and to lead selfish ambitions to transcend themselves by serving a larger purpose. A promise of industrial protection pointed to the need to strengthen and round out the economy of the old Canada if it was to bear the burden of developing the new. At the same time Macdonald won votes in the new industrial towns of Ontario and laid the foundations for a Tory democracy by his Trade Unions Act of 1872 which freed trade unions from the operation of the Common Law doctrine of conspiracy. That the occasion for this was a strike by the printers of the *Globe*, hotly resisted by George Brown, only underlined the difference in the political philosophies of the two giants of Confederation.

The phrase "a national policy" seemed likely at that time to take on a force and currency which in fact it did not do till later. In Ontario there was a conscious, public effort to arouse a national spirit. The men of Canada First, spurred by their experience in the acquisition of the north-west, now began a campaign to arouse the Canadian public to a sense of the magnitude of what was going forward in the Dominion. They had acquired a new leader in the brilliant young W. A. Foster, whose lecture on "Canada First – a New Nationality" sounded the keynote of their campaign. Supporting no party, indeed deliberately non-partisan, Canada First was preparing the bullets some politician might fire.

These preparations for the election were subordinate, however, to the main task of building a Pacific railway to bind the north-west and British Columbia into the union. The Cabinet had already decided that, unlike the Intercolonial, the Pacific railway would be built by a private company. The construction of the line, however, would be subsidized by money grants and land grants from the fertile belt of the prairies. The problem was to find the capitalists willing to undertake the gigantic enterprise, the greatest yet planned in railway construction. By mid 1871 one group had come forward; the bulk of their backing was American, something to give the government pause, as an American-built railway might be left to rust lest it compete with the rival American line, the Northern Pacific. Then Sir Hugh Allan, the steamship magnate of Montreal, came forward, but with the same American backing. Also, it was imperative that the company have support from Toronto as well as Montreal, lest the former rivalry of the two cities for the trade of the north-west, shown in the excitement of 1857-59, be revived. A separate company was organized by Sir David Macpherson in Toronto, and the problem then was how to exclude the Americans and combine the two companies. The government undertook the task, but negotiations dragged out over the question of whether Allan or a Toronto man was to be president.

Unable because of this dispute to get the decks cleared for action, the government went into the election with the organization of the Pacific railway incomplete. They were faced by formidable opposition. In Ontario, John Sandfield Macdonald's provincial coalition had gone down in 1871 before the Liberals led by Edward Blake, a brilliant scion of the Baldwin-Sullivan clan. In Quebec, Cartier was in difficulties, stemming partly from his role in the Red River troubles, partly from the enmity of Sir Hugh Allan in railway politics. And in the Maritimes, anti-union sentiment and disappointment at not obtaining reciprocity would seriously affect the government's chances. The result was a confused and bitter election, in which promises were recklessly showered on the electorate and campaign money was freely asked and freely spent. Much of it was money furnished by Allan to Macdonald.

The government carried the election and the Canadian Pacific Railway Company was then organized under Allan as president and with the Americans excluded. But the Americans were annoyed at the exclusion and saw to it that the Opposition obtained copies of their correspondence with Allan and of the ministers' demands on Allan for campaign funds. The result was a demand in the session of 1873 for a parliamentary select committee to inquire into the circumstances surrounding the granting of the charter to Allan's company. After some political manoeuvring, and some uncertainty as to the power of Parliament to authorize a committee to take evidence on oath, the facts of American influence and of campaign contributions emerged in all their nakedness. While it was not established that the charter was given to Allan for improper reasons, the "Scandal" was too notorious for the government to continue in office. Macdonald placed his resignation in the hands of the new Governor General, Lord Dufferin. The leader of the Liberal party, Alexander Mackenzie, a dour and righteous Scot, quick and confident in debate and of an angular honesty, formed the first Liberal administration in Dominion history.

The Conservative government had fallen with its work of national organization incomplete. Much had been done, indeed a titanic achievement stood to its credit. Even amid the confusion of 1873 one more stone had been added to the building when Prince Edward Island joined Confederation on liberal terms. And the Department of the Interior had been set up to administer the North-West Territory and the Dominion lands, and the North-West Mounted Police created to keep the peace on the western plains. But Newfoundland was still outside the union; the Intercolonial was incomplete; the Pacific railway project had collapsed in ruins; and in 1873 a black depression swept over the country. All that had been done might be jeopardized by what the Conservatives had failed to do, to strengthen the national economy with a national policy and to bind the transcontinental union with a transcontinental railway.

Yet it was by no means an ill thing that the great task of nation-building should be placed in the hands of the Liberals. As the Opposition they had been the critics of Confederation. They were not yet a national party, but rather the representatives of provincial political parties. It would be well to have them carry national responsibilities and face national issues. Confederation was too great an undertaking to be left to one party, or to rest on the support of one set of partisans. The Liberals trying where the Conservatives had failed, whatever their success or failure, would knit Canada more firmly as a nation.

ADDITIONAL READING

CREIGHTON, D. G. *John A. Macdonald : The Old Chieftain.*
MORTON, A. S. *A History of the Canadian West to 1870-71.*
MORTON, W. L. *Manitoba : A History.*
ORMSBY, MARGARET *British Columbia : The History of a Province.*
SMITH, GOLDWIN *Canada and the Treaty of Washington, 1871.*
STACEY, C. P. *Canada and the British Army, 1846-1871.*
STANLEY, G. F. G. *The Birth of Western Canada.*
THOMSON, D. C. *Alexander Mackenzie : Clear Grit.*

THE DEVELOPMENT OF
NATIONAL POLICY
[1874-1921]

The process of uniting British North America was checked by the Pacific Railway Scandal, the fall of Macdonald's government, and the great depression of 1873. To continue the work of creating a nation on the northern half of the continent, it was first necessary to devise an economic policy which would attract people and capital to the country and especially to the empty north-west. It was not less necessary to kindle a national spirit and convert the colonial self-government of 1847 into a national autonomy within the Empire which would reconcile national purpose with imperial association, and the two nationalities of Canada in one nationhood. The Canada First movement in Ontario and the parti national *in Quebec were the growing-points of the urge towards a national autonomy leading to independence. Tasks so great required a corresponding strength of purpose, and the chief significance of the change of government in 1873 was that it led to no change of goal; national development, national autonomy, national unity, were still the aim of policy.*

The change of government did lead to a change of pace, however, and the Liberal government of Alexander Mackenzie, harassed all its days by the severe depression and falling revenues, failed to give the country the leadership it required. The Conservatives were able in consequence to return to power with a "National Policy" of economic development which added tariff protection of manufacturing to railway construction and the export of staples. Aided by the return of prosperity, they were able to complete the Pacific railway in 1885, and round off the work of Confederation begun twenty-one years before.

What was completed had then to be defended. In the national elections of 1887 and 1891 the Liberal party sought to replace the National Policy by Commercial Union, or Unrestricted Reciprocity, with the United States. The Conservative victories in those two elections were among the decisive events in Canadian history. For such victories to be lasting, however, more than a national policy of material development was required. The old provincial loyalties continued strong and new ones developed with the new provinces. The judicial interpretation of the British North America Act step by step gave those loyalties legal sanction and a political authority never intended in 1867. The Saskatchewan Rebellion and the execution of Louis Riel revived the ultramontane nationalisme *which had first flared up after the Red River troubles. A cultural conflict began, which raged around the schools of Manitoba and drew fresh strength from the Boer War and the question of imperial defence. Canadian nationality threatened to divide into two channels, the French* nationalisme intégral *of the Quebec extremists, and the British nationalism of the imperialist extremists of English Canada.*

Neither Macdonald nor Laurier, in their turn, gave any countenance to either extreme, and moderate opinion in Canada supported them. The adoption of the National Policy by the Liberals after 1896, and the prosperity of the great boom which followed, rendered the tensions of the cultural conflict less dangerous and allowed the development of a sentiment of nationhood sufficient to defeat both extremes.

That sentiment was terribly tried by the War of 1914–18, and Canada emerged from it at once crowned with national autonomy and divided by racial and social conflict. The conscription election of 1917 had alienated Quebec from the rest of Canada, and the Winnipeg Strike and the farmers' entry into politics had revealed the powerful class antagonisms of Canadian society. These lesions would have to heal if Canada was to develop its unique nationhood and play some part as a nation among nations. And Canadian statecraft would have to produce a more complex national policy than that of 1878.

The Struggle to Hold the North-West
1874-1885

The Conservatives had gone out and the Liberals had come in at the beginning of one of the greatest of the century's depressions, that which began in the fall of 1873. Thus the new Prime Minister, Alexander Mackenzie, had not only to take up the unfinished work of his predecessor; he had also to attempt to carry out the work of nation-building with severely straitened means. The want of revenue and the depression of trade and industry circumscribed the Liberal adminis-tration for the five years it was in power.

If economic conditions were bad, however, the political circumstances were singularly favourable. The Conservative party was discredited and shattered by the revelations of 1873. Its two chief leaders, Sir John Macdonald and Sir George Cartier, were particularly and directly implicated. Macdonald's genius, tarnished as it was, was still at the service of the party, which would not hear of his resigning, but Cartier had died in May 1873. He left a void which his heir in Quebec, Hector Langevin, an able and attractive man but one afflicted with an opaque personality, was never to fill. The party as a whole was shaken and disheartened. The triumphant Liberals had only to ride down the scattered ranks of their opponents.

As Prime Minister, Mackenzie succeeded in forming an administration starred with two exceptional names and possessed of a high average of ability. One name was that of A. A. Dorion, the Rouge leader from Quebec. The other was that of Edward Blake, a brilliant lawyer of wilful and eccentric genius, perhaps the most intellectual and least effective of Canadian statesmen. The erratic quality of Blake was wholly peculiar to himself, yet it somehow exemplified the uncertain character of this Liberal ministry. The Liberals and especially the Rouges had been the opponents and critics of Confederation from the beginning. Their strength was in the provinces, particularly Ontario; they had not yet really fused into a federal party. And in their leader they possessed a man of industry, courage, and flawless integrity, but not a man capable of weld-ing the elements of his following into a party conscious of a national character and of a role in the national life. This Blake had the capacity to do, but Blake neither consistently supported his chief nor frankly challenged his leadership. The party and the government in consequence remained less than the sum of their members and were weakened, not strengthened, by the possession of power.

Nevertheless, when Mackenzie obtained a dissolution in order to have a parliament free of the corruption of Sir Hugh Allan's money, the Liberals triumphed across the country and gained a comfortable majority in the House of Commons.

In the election, however, Louis Riel had been returned for Provencher in Manitoba, and actually took the oath and signed the roll as a member of the House before he was recognized. The new parliament and government then found themselves challenged to deal with the amnesty question which had been kept in the background since 1870. Even if Riel had not dared Parliament to accept or reject him, the arrest and trial of his lieutenant, Ambroise Lépine, in Manitoba would have forced the issue. Lépine was convicted by a mixed French and English jury of the murder of Thomas Scott. Public sentiment in Quebec strongly adhered to the belief that the resistance of the métis in 1869 had been warranted and that its leaders should be treated with clemency. But Orange sentiment in Ontario was resolute in demanding the punishment of the slayers of Scott, and the general public shared the belief that his execution was a crime which called for the conviction and punishment of those responsible.

The Commons appointed a Select Committee to inquire into the circumstances of the Red River resistance and the nature of the terms agreed on with the delegates of the provisional government. The inquiry revealed that the ever sanguine Cartier had gambled on the imperial government's granting a general amnesty and had in consequence misled Father Ritchot, the only delegate concerned with the amnesty, and also Bishop Taché. Clearly, the expectation that an amnesty would be granted had been created, and it would only be politic to meet that expectation. But to do so would anger Ontario, from which the Liberals drew most of their strength, without doing them much good in Quebec, where they were weak. From this dilemma the government was rescued by Lord Dufferin. Dufferin was the first of the governors-general who made the ceremonial duties of the office more important than the administrative. But he was also one of the last of the active governors-general, and was always ready, if not too ready, to assume a personal responsibility. He now took it upon himself to recommend to the imperial government that Lépine's sentence be commuted to a term of imprisonment and the permanent forfeiture of political rights. The Canadian cabinet was then able to have Parliament grant a general amnesty, which included Riel and Lépine, but on condition of five years' banishment. Riel withdrew to the United States, and the unhappy after-effects of the Red River troubles seemed to have been ended.

In Manitoba itself a weak provincial administration dominated by Lieutenant-

Governor Alexander Morris was slowly organizing the civil government on the lines of that of Ontario and on the basis of the common law. Ontario, not Quebec, was to give its laws and institutions to Manitoba, except in education. Population was coming in, slowly but in numbers sufficient to swamp the old Red River stock. It was almost wholly British or Canadian in origin, except for some hundreds of Icelanders and of German Mennonites from Russia.

Beyond the boundaries of Manitoba lay the North-West Territory, governed by the Lieutenant-Governor of Manitoba with the aid of a territorial council, and from 1873 under the new Department of the Interior. The first great task was to make some provision for the administration of the law. Justices of the Peace had been appointed and the trade in spirits had been prohibited. In the early summer of 1874 the North-West Mounted Police, assembled and trained in Winnipeg and Lower Fort Garry in the fall and winter of 1873, were ready to begin the policing of the plains. The force set out in a great march along the international boundary, first to warn off American whiskey-traders and to clear them out of Fort Whoop-up in the Blackfoot country, and then to post themselves where they could watch the Indians and the frontier. By fall this task had been carried out and the detachments were in their posts throughout the Territory. Morris could then get on with the prolonged diplomacy involved in making treaties with the Indians from the Lake of the Woods to the Rockies. Archibald had begun it with Treaty Number 1 in 1871, and all the tribes of the plains, including the great Blackfoot confederacy, were in treaty and moving on to their reserves by 1879.

To pacify and police the plains was one task, and one brilliantly performed. To build the Pacific railway across the plains and meet the terms of union with British Columbia was another, and it was not to be performed as undertaken, nor, in any of its aspects except the tremendous surveys of the Shield and the Rockies, was it to be managed with more than bare competence. The Liberals had in fact opposed the terms as extravagant and beyond the capacity of the country to fulfil. They were right, and Parliament had supported them in adding to acceptance of the terms the proviso that they were to be fulfilled only if this did not lead to an increase in taxation. The fall of the Macdonald government, and the failure to complete the surveys sufficiently to choose the route through the mountains to the coast, resulted in failure to fulfil the first condition of union with British Columbia, that the railway be begun within two years. British Columbia protested. When the embarrassed Mackenzie finally got round to dealing with the protest, it was only to begin to seek a modification of the terms.

The Liberal administration was in the unhappy position of having to honour a commitment the terms of which it thought unreasonable and indefensible. It was, moreover, impracticable to carry out the terms in a time of commercial depression and shrinking governmental revenues. Early in 1874 Mackenzie therefore sent James D. Edgar to Victoria as agent of the national government.

He was to report on public feeling in British Columbia and try the temper of the provincial government by suggesting certain modifications of the terms of union respecting the construction of the railway. These were postponement of construction until the surveys were completed, and the construction of a wagon road and telegraph line along the route of the railway. When the surveys were completed, the sum of $1,500,000 was to be spent annually on construction. To these terms, the immediate construction of a railway from Esquimalt to Nanaimo might be added.

There was much to be defended in the suggestions, as the resources of the national government were limited and the task of making the surveys through the practically unexplored ranges of the Rockies was an enormous one which could only be carried out slowly. But British Columbian feeling was impatient and exacting, and all the doubts about union with Canada revived and were inflamed. Premier G. A. Walkem suddenly questioned Edgar's credentials, and Edgar withdrew his proposals. The legislature had already passed a resolution that no change of the terms of union could be accepted unless submitted to the people for approval. And now Walkem sought authorization to go to London to protest against any change in the terms of union.

Before Walkem set out, the Colonial Secretary in the newly installed Conservative government, Lord Carnarvon, offered to arbitrate the differences, provided his decision were accepted as final. The Canadian government at first refused to entertain the offer, as did that of British Columbia. But on consideration, the latter in August and the former a few weeks later agreed to accept Carnarvon's terms as a basis of settlement. Carnarvon's terms were the completion of the Esquimalt to Nanaimo railway as soon as possible (a necessary sop to Vancouver Island), the pushing of the mainland surveys with vigour, the immediate construction of a wagon road and telegraph line from the east, a minimum annual expenditure of $2,000,000, and the completion of the railway from the Pacific to the head of Lake Superior by the end of 1890. These terms were accepted by the Mackenzie government and approved by Parliament in March, 1875, except for the rejection of the Esquimalt and Nanaimo railway by the Senate.

They were also fiercely criticized by Edward Blake, who had resigned from the government mainly because of the sending of Edgar to British Columbia. And many other Liberals felt that Canada was being made the victim of the exigent demands and the mainland-and-island rivalry of British Columbia. The result of Blake's criticism was to revive the old condition that the railway should not cause an increase in taxation. Nor was opinion in British Columbia content, particularly in view of the continued Liberal evasion of the terms of union. Mackenzie was frankly warned that British Columbia might seek to secede.

Thus beset, Mackenzie sought to restore unity to his party and to hold British Columbia by bringing Blake back into the Cabinet, this time as Minister of

Justice, on new terms for the building of the railway. There was to be no further appeal to the Colonial Secretary. Blake, strong in the Canadian nationalism he had taken over from his interest in the Canada First movement, insisted on that. The Island railway was not to be built by the national government. In compensation for delay in building the main railway, the province was to be paid the sum of $750,000, and $250,000 for the Esquimalt dock. The effort failed, however. The Legislature of British Columbia rejected the new terms in January 1876, appealed to the Queen, and threatened secession from the Dominion.

When the relations between Canada and its Pacific province had come to such a pass, Lord Dufferin, still the active viceroy, felt he might intervene. He visited British Columbia in the late summer of 1876. There he used his great personal charm and romantic Irish vocabulary to soothe excited feelings and to create assurance in the good faith and honesty of purpose of the Canadian government. In this he did a considerable service. But when he sought on his return to persuade Mackenzie to agree to a conference on more favourable terms with representatives of British Columbia, he precipitated a serious controversy over his right to press advice upon his ministers, and was forced to withdraw from the position of mediator he had assumed. As a result, nothing further was done to modify the last terms proposed by the Mackenzie government, and British Columbia, continued to seethe with discontent and to threaten secession through 1877 and 1878.

While relations with British Columbia developed in this unhappy fashion Mackenzie had been endeavouring to press on with the piecemeal construction of the railway to the Pacific. He had sought to get construction of the railway started in 1874 by a private company. In the depression none came forward. He then abandoned the Conservative plan of having one company build the whole line with the aid of grants of land and money. Instead he proposed to call for tenders from contractors for four different sections of the line, and to aid construction by a land grant of 20,000 acres a mile and a subsidy of $10,000 a mile. The government might take over all or any of these sections on payment of the cost, less the land grants and plus ten per cent of the remainder. No time was fixed for the completion of the road, but a line to the border in Manitoba, to join the St. Paul, Minneapolis and Manitoba Railway, was to be pushed in order to make a connection with the American railway system. On this basis the Mackenzie program went forward. The Pembina line to the border was opened late in 1878, and considerable sections of the line from Fort William to Winnipeg were building by that date. But relatively little progress had been made in linking British Columbia with the rest of Canada, and it was this delay that caused the discontent in the Pacific province.

In the east the construction of the Intercolonial had gone steadily forward and was completed in 1876. This line was never to earn a profit; its cost explains much of the difficulty in honouring the terms of union with British Columbia, and its much-disputed North Shore route remained a standing grievance in the rest of New Brunswick. Its completion, however, fulfilled a political necessity. The work of adding railway communication to political union thus proceeded, but without the bright speed and imaginative daring of Macdonald's day. For the time being, the *élan* had gone out of Canadian nation-building.

The major reason for this was of course the depression. But some part of the responsibility for the loss of impetus must be ascribed to the Liberal party and the Mackenzie administration. The party, not yet a national party in organization or spirit, was partly provincial in character and, despite the strongly imperial and nationalist sentiment of Mackenzie himself, partly continentalist in outlook. It was also dominated by the numbers and strength of its Ontario contingent. There was no Maritimer to match Tupper or Tilley, no Quebecker, when Dorion retired to the Bench in 1876, to equal Cartier or even Langevin in Canadian outlook and national purpose, not even when Wilfrid Laurier entered the Cabinet as the most promising of the younger Rouges. And the temper of Ontario was fiercely provincialist, seeking not so much to weld diverse sections into national unity as to impose the institutions and outlook of Ontario on the rest of the country. The old ascendancy temper, drawn from Ulster and kept alive by conflict with Quebec and the pressure of the United States, still affected the public mind of Ontario, whether Liberal or Conservative.

Nor was the task of national leadership lightened by the curious relations between Mackenzie and Blake. The upright and narrow Mackenzie was always overshadowed by the giant intellect of his lieutenant. And Mackenzie's steadiness as a leader was recurrently shaken by the vagaries of Blake – his resignation, his public utterances, such as the outburst at Aurora in 1874 which was inspired by the Canada First group and darkly hinted at a score of things, including independence – and by his conduct as a colleague in the government. The public could not but wonder who was prime minister and what the course of national policy was.

Yet if it lacked a strong national purpose and inner harmony, the administration had many accomplishments to outbalance its few specific failures. In 1874 it had responded swiftly to an opportunity to discuss reciprocity with the United States. George Brown, now a Senator, was sent as a special envoy to Washington and with the British minister there negotiated a most favourable treaty with the Secretary of State, Hamilton Fish. It was a brilliant piece of diplomacy, even if it was rejected by the American Senate and the still growing protectionist spirit of the United States. Similarly, the administration might claim some credit for the successful outcome of the fisheries award in 1875 under the Treaty of Washington. Canada received $5,500,000 in compensation for the admission of American fishermen to its inshore waters. It is true that the administration found no answer to the dumping of American goods in Canada. After raising the tariff in 1875 to an average level of 17½ per cent, the Mackenzie government decided not to increase it further, as to do so would make the rates protective. Here the free-trade principles of the Minister of Finance, Richard Cartwright, a former Tory but an economic liberal, gave Liberal policy a rigidity from which the party fortunes were to suffer.

In political reform the government was more fortunate. The Elections Act of 1874 brought in vote by ballot, a further step in making political democracy individualistic, and provided that all voting should be done on a single day across the country. Blake also had the satisfaction of carrying the measure Macdonald had set his heart on, the establishment of a Supreme Court. It was a court of appeal from the Canadian courts, but appeals might be made from it under the royal prerogative to the Judicial Committee of the imperial Privy Council. Not until 1888 was the right to appeal stopped, and then only in criminal cases. Nevertheless, the establishment of the Supreme Court in 1876 was an important step in completing the work of Confederation.

To these measures must be added the establishment of the Royal Military College at Kingston in 1874, with the purpose of furnishing the militia with a core of professional officers. The withdrawal of the British regulars in 1871 made it necessary for Canada to begin to supply its own standards of military competence. In the different and even more unfamiliar field of social legislation, Parliament passed the Prohibition Act of 1878, the first national venture in the regulation of the sale and consumption of spirits. It was a venture that was to have many consequences in both social polity and constitutional law.

In these varied accomplishments the government was responding to public pressures and applying party principles rather than implementing a national policy such as the unfinished state of the Dominion demanded. But in one area Mackenzie and Blake did have a national policy and did advance Canada towards national stature. That area was the constitutional position of the Governor General. Dufferin's dashing discharge of his viceregal role and his intervention in matters of policy had led to his being forced to submit to his ministers on the matter of the terms of union with British Columbia. Mackenzie stated the position of his government firmly:

I embraced the opportunity to tell [him] that Lord Carnarvon and he must remember that Canada was not a Crown Colony (or a Colony at all in the ordinary acceptation of the term), that 4,000,000 of people with a government responsible to the people only could not and would not be dealt with as small communities had been sometimes dealt with; that we were capable of managing our own affairs, and the country would insist on doing it, and that no government could survive who would attempt, even at the insistence of a Colonial Secretary, to trifle with Parliamentary decisions.

Blake followed up by insisting that the instructions issued to the Governor General be altered to ensure that Dufferin's successor did not conceive his functions in as ample terms as Dufferin had done. The alterations prohibited the use of the pardoning power except on ministerial advice, a somewhat curious consequence of Dufferin's assistance to the Mackenzie government in the Lépine case. As a result of the changes the conversion of the Governor General into a constitutional monarch, begun by Elgin, was completed when the Marquis of Lorne succeeded Dufferin in 1878.

The divisions, the achievements, and the growing embarrassment of the Mackenzie government were accompanied by the recovery, at first gradual and hesitant, then swift and confident, of the Opposition. The Conservative party of Macdonald had fallen because the fast pace of its empire-building and the handicaps imposed by Macdonald's responsibility for the Treaty of Washington swept it into a mood of reckless desperation of which the outcome had been frantic dependence on "another ten thousand" from Sir Hugh Allan and the humiliation of the Pacific Scandal. For that fall the only remedy was time. The public would not forget, but in time it would cease to be shocked. In time the sins of the Conservatives would be lost to sight before the inevitable shortcomings of the Liberal government. The Opposition was therefore subdued and discreet during the sessions of 1874 and 1875. Macdonald indeed contrived to play with his usual distinction the new role of the reserved, but helpful, elder statesman.

Then in 1876 the rejection of the reciprocity treaty, the continued depression, the outcry in British Columbia, the gathering anger of industrialists at American dumping, the government's failure to lead, gave the Conservatives their opportunity. In the session of 1876, Macdonald saw that the issue shaping up was that of the tariff. And Cartwright's doctrinaire adherence to the principles of free trade placed the ball at his feet. He did not come out for protection; to do so might have alienated the bulk of the voters. He came out for "reciprocity of trade, or reciprocity of tariffs." He hinted at protection of some kind for everyone, for farmer as well as manufacturer. He talked of a "national policy" deliberately and repeatedly, and made the transient phrase of 1872 a political slogan for 1878. And then, the session over, Macdonald began to attend a succession of political picnics throughout Ontario in the summer of 1876 which assured him that the Scandal was behind him and the country ready to support a broad-based National Policy of tariff protection and railway construction. The same desire for tariff protection was present in Quebec as a strong element in the *nationaliste* movement there.

The recovery of the Opposition and Macdonald's seizure of the political initiative was not countered by the Liberal government. It plodded stolidly on with piecemeal measures and the piecemeal construction of the Pacific railway. It had failed to transcend its internal divisions and its provincial outlook. And the contrast with the reinvigorated and confident Conservatives was vivid as the general election drew near.

The Conservatives were also helped by a resounding controversy which broke out in the Province of Quebec. That province had resumed in 1867 the thread of its own provincial life, broken by the suspension of the constitution in 1838. In the provincial as in the national field, the Bleus, the party of political moderation and of gallicanism, remained in the ascendant and formed the first ministry, that of P. J. O. Chauveau. Chauveau was the lieutenant of Cartier in Quebec as J. S. Macdonald was Sir John Macdonald's in Ontario. The Rouges were in opposition and no stronger provincially than they were nationally. But Quebec politics at once began to reveal their own distinctive character. The ultramontanes were moving towards the formation of a Catholic political party, and "l'affaire Guibord" was to rock the province in the middle seventies. For, since Bishop Bourget's attack on the Institut Canadien in 1858 and 1859, the ultramontanes had been stirred and strengthened by events in Europe. The unification of Italy in 1860, the support given the papacy by France and inspired by ultramontane influences behind the Empress Eugénie, the defeat of Garibaldi's threat to Rome after 1866, all served to arouse the Catholic sentiment of Quebec. This found expression in the sending of a contingent of French Canadians as Papal Zouaves to Rome in 1868. The growth of ultramontane influence showed in the increasing strength of the Jesuits in the dioceses of Montreal and Trois Rivières, the latter the seat of Bishop Laflèche, as ardent an ultramontane as Bourget of Montreal. All these things had made the two bishops and their political followers more urgent and more aggressive. Beneath their gathering zeal lay a determination to challenge the pretensions of the lay state. And in the ultramontane *Programme* of 1871 they began to attack the gallicanism of the Bleus.

In the new ultramontane creed in Quebec, Catholicism helped the growth of *nationalisme*, that is, nationalism as an emotional and practical union of race, language, family and faith. The old fact that the church had been the main vehicle of French culture and sentiment might now appear in a new dress, the dress of a Catholic political party. It was this fusion of religion and race that made the ultramontanes in 1870 the champions of the Catholic missionaries of Red River and Riel in their resistance to the taking over of the north-west by Protestant Ontario.

It also helped to bring into being the first *parti national*, the French equivalent of the English "Canada First," and like it in part a reaction to the implications of events in the north-west in 1869–70. Young Rouges, breaking away from the Institut Canadien, weary of the failure of their party to end Cartier's control of the province and his steady subordination of French-Canadian claims to national ends, formed the Parti National to bring honesty, clarity, and purpose into provincial politics. In 1872, L. A. Jetté as their candidate defeated Cartier n the federal election. Little else came of this first *nationaliste* group; but its nationalism might fuse with that of the ultramontanes to produce a Catholic and clerical party, and this was already apparent by 1872.

What the ultramontane temper could be was revealed in the Guibord affair. In 1869 Joseph Guibord, an undistinguished but resolute member of the Institut Canadien, died excommunicate in Montreal, and his widow and friends sought to have him buried in a Roman Catholic cemetery. The ultramontane *curé* refused to bury in consecrated ground one who had been excommunicated, and the mob of the ultramontane city rioted when burial was attempted. Guibord's body was interred in a Protestant cemetery while a civil action was begun against the *curé*. The case finally reached the Judicial Committee, which found in 1874 that burial in a Christian cemetery was a civil right and could not be denied on ground of death while excommunicate. In the test of strength between church and state, the state, secular and neutral, had prevailed, and the body of Guibord, guarded by more than twelve hundred soldiers, was buried in concrete and scrap-iron in the Catholic cemetery. Bishop Bourget promptly declared the burial plot no longer consecrated, and the issue, so fiercely fought, was left in suspense.

The rise of *nationalisme* and ultramontanism produced no immediate change in the parties or government of Quebec. The Bleus were returned under Chauveau in 1871. On his retirement in 1873, he was succeeded by Gédéon Ouimet. Ouimet's government fell as a result of scandal in 1874, but the Bleus continued in power under Charles Boucher de Boucherville, a descendant of the Pierre Boucher who had helped save New France in 1661.

The pressure of the ultramontane clergy on the Rouges, none the less, became disturbing as the ultramontanes insisted that the *Programme* be adopted, that the clergy should have immunity from the law as a separate order, that the same clergy had a duty to intervene in politics, and that it was sinful for a Catholic to be a Liberal. The attack on secular politics extended even to Laval University at Quebec, where the faculty was too liberal in temper for the zeal of ultramontane and jealous Montreal. In reply to the ultramontanes, the young Wilfrid Laurier, himself a moderate Rouge, argued in a speech of singular discernment and eloquence before the Rouges of Quebec in 1877 that British Liberalism was not anti-religious. He declared that French-Canadian liberalism was not the anti-Catholic and anti-clerical liberalism of Europe, but the tolerant variety of Great Britain. The speech made Laurier a national figure. It opened the way for the survival of the Liberal party in Quebec, and for a discreet intervention by Rome to moderate the temper of the ultramontanes.

The Liberals, however, national as well as provincial, now became involved in a bitter quarrel, provincial in origin and wholly French in character but with serious consequences for the national party. Mackenzie had appointed as Lieutenant-Governor in 1877 Luc Letellier de Saint-Just, a stiff and uncompromising anti-clerical Rouge. Alone and unprompted, but worried by the course of the administration's legislation, Letellier came to the conclusion in

1878 that de Boucherville had not accorded him consideration befitting the dignity and responsibilities of his office. After a strained exchange of correspondence, he dismissed his premier. There were few precedents for such an act in constitutional usage, but in fact the quarrel in its beginning and its course was a Gallic one fought out solely in terms of Quebec politics and personalities. Letellier actually found a new premier in Henri Joly de Lotbinière, a Swiss Protestant, who fought a general election in March 1878 and won for the Rouges a majority of one in the legislature. Joly held on until October 1879. But Letellier's high prerogative action did nothing to help the national Liberals in the general election of September 1878. In Quebec as elsewhere they went down before the irresistible Conservatives returning to the power they had forfeited in 1873. And the victors had to concede their incensed Quebec followers the vengeance they demanded, and dismiss Letellier, a *coup* for a *coup*.

The Conservative victory was conclusive and comprehensive. In every province but New Brunswick they won a majority, and in Parliament they had a decisive majority of seventy. They had been brought back to office by a ground swell of discontent with the Liberal failure to protect national industries and carry forward the national purpose of consolidating the transcontinental Dominion of 1871. It was because the Conservatives spoke like men who intended to carry out that purpose that they were elected.

The objects of the party were simple and clear. The national economy must be strengthened. The diplomatic and financial support of the United Kingdom must be secured. The Pacific railway must be hastened to completion. Finally the north-west must be organized and welded into the national framework. That the north-west was the main object of concern, the area of strategic interest, Macdonald made clear by himself taking the portfolio of the Department of the Interior.

The national economy was to be strengthened by the national policy of protection. Neither then nor later was Macdonald or his party opposed to reciprocity. They were merely sure that it would not be obtained by allowing the dumped goods of American factories to smother the development of Canadian industry. It was plain that in the modern world the development of industry was the way to national power. Canada should no more allow the United States to block its industrialization than the United States had allowed Great Britain to check the rise of the industries of New England and Pennsylvania. Finance Minister Tilley therefore called in the manufacturers, learned their needs, and in the budget of 1879 raised the tariff rates to protective levels on a wide variety of goods. The textile mills of Sherbrooke, the iron furnaces of Hamilton, the farm-implement plants of Brantford and Waterloo, would now be secure from the price-breaking incursions of American goods. On most items, of course, the rates had to stand at revenue levels, for the customs yielded the greater part of Canadian revenue. But the Conservatives had fulfilled their pledge "to make the tall chimneys smoke" and had given the economy of central Canada the strength to bear the cost of building the Pacific railway and of holding the west.

Macdonald himself had gone to England to seek imperial support for his resumed program of nation-building. He wanted an imperial guarantee for a loan for railway construction, and imperial help in turning immigrants to the north-west the railway was to open. The somewhat touchy nationalism of Mackenzie and Blake had chilled a reviving British interest in the colonies. Macdonald was as good a nationalist as Blake, but he knew that British support was still necessary for Canadian independence and would be so for years to come. Yet he wanted British support – the British alliance, as he thought of it – on Canadian as well as British terms. The care of Canadian interests must be in Canadian hands. He had therefore to ask the appointment of, in effect, a Canadian diplomatic officer in London – a "resident minister," as he suggested; the High Commissioner, as the officer was finally called. A. T. Galt was appointed at once and began the vital work of encouraging immigration to Canada and of seeking new commercial openings for Canadian goods.

Macdonald had obtained his guarantee and revived the British alliance. Canada was accepted finally as the trustee of British interests and honour in North America, a trust symbolized by the transfer to the Dominion in 1880 of the vast and vacant Arctic Archipelago, of which so much had been revealed by British navigators from Baffin to Franklin.

The arctic islands extended Canadian territories far towards the Pole and gave the country a depth to match its breadth. A thousand miles south of them, the empty north-west of the Indian and the métis was at last beginning to yield to the farmer and the market town. After a decade of trial, Manitoba was at last being settled by a rush of farmers from Ontario. In the rural districts of the old province, smitten by the wheat midge, the "Manitoba fever" was burning and settlement "parties" were being organized to possess the land where the plough ran free of stone or stump. British farmers who had been suffering from the competition of prairie-grown wheat were beginning to come to Manitoba just as the Mennonites and Icelanders ceased. And Bishop Taché was eagerly reclaiming from Massachusetts French Canadians who came to found new French villages by the Red and along the upper Pembina.

Out in the North-West Territory the old way of life was ending also. The great buffalo herds were shredding away; the last bands were being shot down by wandering métis. These inveterate nomads for the most part could not bring themselves to settle. They were reluctant to bind themselves either to the lands granted them in Manitoba or to the river fronts they held on the Saskatchewan. Neither did the Indians, Blackfoot or Cree, find it in them to sit on their reserves like women after the years of freedom on the plains. Like a night wind on the prairie, a great uneasiness, vaguely menacing, was stirring and breathing across the rolling grasslands and empty skylines of the North-West Territory. And the scarlet-coated police, feeling their own Indians growing restless, had had to watch with steady vigilance Sitting Bull's sullen Sioux, refugees from the victory over Custer on the Little Bighorn, and barred by American cavalry until 1879 from return to their own hunting grounds. As the Sioux had tried to do, the old inhabitants of the Canadian plains might yet sweep the new away, unless the railway were built to bring in more new-comers and, if need be, troops.

The Pembina line at least was at work, and west of Fort William the construction crews were driving the grades through the rock and muskeg – a novel and costly barrier to the road-builder. The surveyors were still at work from the Ottawa to the Pacific, running the surveys of the great northern route Sandford Fleming had laid down on the map, north through the muskeg and jack pine of the divide between the Lakes and Hudson Bay, across the Red at Selkirk, between the Manitoba lakes to the Saskatchewan, by the Yellowhead Pass to Bute Inlet, and across to Vancouver Island. The telegraph line had followed this northern route from Winnipeg to the Saskatchewan; and British Columbia was still hoping for the Bute Inlet route, the crossing to the Island, and the railway from Nanaimo to Esquimalt.

The new Minister of Railways, the hard-driving and ever confident Charles Tupper, first proceeded to revise Fleming's concept drastically, then to discard both it and the great engineer himself. His northern route was to await another builder, while the Pacific railway took a more southerly line. The first decision, announced in 1879, was to follow the Fraser valley to a mainland terminus. The government would not undertake to build the Esquimalt to Nanaimo railway (thus inheriting Mackenzie's quarrel with British Columbia), but it did begin at once to push construction eastwards up the Fraser. At the same time the work between Fort William and Winnipeg was quickened. With these preliminaries and Macdonald's British guarantee, the way was open at the end of 1879 to entrust the building of the railway to a new company and complete the revision of the route.

It was now possible to find such a company. The Conservatives had not only been victorious in 1878; they had also been lucky. They had returned to office on the rise of a wave of prosperity, a short sharp boom which crested in 1881 and broke in 1882. But its impetus and duration were enough to carry the Pacific railway well on its course to completion. And in Manitoba the boom completed the work of the Manitoba fever by drawing thousands of immigrants to the prairies; in 1881 Manitoba's boundaries were widened and its southern park belt quickly overrun and settled.

The men who were to take up the government's offer of aid to a private company had already acted together and established a reputation as successful railway builders and financiers. The crash of 1873 had bankrupted the St. Paul and Pacific railway which was building from the Mississippi to the Canadian border. In 1876, two former Canadians living in St. Paul, J. J. Hill and N. W.

Kittson, combined with Donald A. Smith of the Hudson's Bay Company and George Stephen of the Bank of Montreal to buy the line cheaply. In 1877 and 1878 they built the reorganized railway, the St. Paul, Minneapolis and Manitoba, to the border where it joined the government line to St. Boniface. Thus all goods for construction of the prairie section would pass over their line.

They now formed the core of the syndicate with which Macdonald negotiated. The government had offered $25,000,000 and 25,000,000 acres of land to the company which undertook to complete the line, together with the portions of the line already built. These were valued at $31,000,000 and the lands at $38,000,000. To these terms were added exemption from customs duties of capital imports for construction, exemption from local taxation in the north-west forever, and the prohibition for twenty years of the construction of any line of railway running to the border.

For these very large concessions the company, the Canadian Pacific Railway Company, was to build the line and operate it in perpetuity. The charter did empower the Governor General in Council to limit net earnings to ten per cent on capital, but it made no other provision to protect the public interest. The magnitude of the task and the imperious need of completing it are written across the face of the charter.

The new company brought with it a new policy. It first completed the scrapping of Fleming's northern route in all sections. From the Ottawa to Fort William, in order to use cheap water transport of construction material, it decided to keep as close as possible to the Lakes. In the prairie section the line was diverted from Selkirk to Winnipeg, the Assiniboine, and thence across the short-grass plains of Palliser's Triangle to the valley of the Bow. It was thought safe to make this great change on the advice of the botanist, John Macoun – in fact an enthusiast misled by the wet years of the late seventies – but it was done to close out the rival Northern Pacific and perhaps also to avoid the cost of pre-empted townsites on the northern route. The change involved the abandonment of the easy grades of the Yellowhead Pass for the steep lift of the Kicking Horse and the unknown obstacles of the Selkirk and Golden ranges.

The construction of the line, however, had been entrusted to a man who brooked no obstacle, William Van Horne, a dynamic and forceful American, a tireless and slogging driver with a gift for the commanding phrase and the decisive gesture. A master of American methods of railway construction and an organizer of genius, he gave to his daunting task a flawless loyalty and an irresistible *élan*. How completely Van Horne made the railway his own project is shown by his insistence that the line could be built along the north shore of Superior, as the government for political and military reasons required that it should be, while the former Canadian, J. J. Hill, withdrew from the company rather than be party to such economic folly.

Under Van Horne the pace of construction quickened and worked up to record achievements. By 1882 the line from Fort William to Winnipeg was completed; by 1883 the rails had reached the Elbow of the South Saskatchewan and the grade the valley of the Bow, and the surveyors were deep in the forests of the Selkirks and the Golden range, while the blasting reverberated from the sections building along the cliffs of Superior's northern shore. Van Horne was racing against the Northern Pacific, building to the south across Dakota and Montana; against the overhead of constructed and unused track; against the chill of the next down-turn of the business cycle.

The rapid building of the railway did not end the trouble with British Columbia. The mainland was pleased with the Fraser route and the terminus at New Westminster, as was first planned. But the Island was not, and Macdonald and Tupper declined to carry out the Carnarvon terms respecting the Esquimalt and Nanaimo railway, or to pay the compensation the Liberals had proposed. The Governor General, the Marquis of Lorne, tried to soothe Island feeling during his visit in 1882 and even to persuade his ministers to make some concession. But nothing was to be done until 1884 when they agreed to give $150,000 towards the building of the Island railway and to take over the Esquimalt graving-dock with a payment of $250,000 and assumption of its cost to date, in return for a block of land in the Peace River to compensate for alienated or rocky land in the "railway belt" granted by the original terms of union. In this manner the terms were finally fulfilled as the Pacific railway neared completion.

The Canadian Pacific was only well launched towards its goal when the government had to turn to other preoccupations. Macdonald was preparing for the next election by carrying out the redistribution of seats required by the British North America Act after the decennial census.of 1881. The redistribution was frankly designed to improve Conservative chances in Ontario by putting together counties and townships in which Liberal votes predominated. This "hiving of the Grits" was done in the spirit of the age in which political advantages were as frankly taken as they were hotly resented. And the gerrymander of 1882 rewarded its contrivers, for in the general election that year the Conservatives increased their following in Ontario and enlarged their majority in the country.

The same year saw another triumph for Macdonald. As the chief designer and director of a strongly centralized federation, he had watched with his usual keen but detached interest to see whether the courts would uphold his concept of the constitution. In the case of *Russell* v. *the Queen*, decided by the Judicial Committee of the Privy Council, his highest hopes were realized. The Committee held that the regulation of the trade in spirituous liquors was a subject of national jurisdiction under the "peace, order and good government" clause of Section 91 of the British North America Act. It was not a matter of provincial jurisdiction under the property and civil rights subsection of Section 92.

The decision in *Russell* v. *the Queen*, however, was perhaps the summit of

Macdonald's achievement as the great centralizer of the constitution. (In 1885 he was to carry his long-planned Dominion Franchise Act, which created a uniform property franchise for national elections, but this the Liberals rejected after 1896 in favour of the manhood suffrage of most of the provinces.) From then on he had to face and fight incessantly two distinct but related things, the growing political movement for provincial rights, and a series of judicial decisions which weakened the national and strengthened the provincial governments. The doctrine of provincial rights had been latent in the Rouge and Clear Grit criticism of Confederation. As the party most in opposition since 1867, they naturally tended to support the provinces in any differences with Ottawa. And they had in fact been much more successful in provincial than in national politics. This was especially true in Ontario, which Blake and Oliver Mowat had captured for the Liberal Party in 1871 to begin a period of party dominance that endured for over a generation. Mowat, once Macdonald's law partner, was an assured and aggressive individual, an able lawyer and a shrewd politician, who gave his province able and honest government and his political opponents no quarter. And he embodied perfectly the attitude of his wealthy and powerful province to Confederation. It had one third of the total population, and one third of the representation in the Commons. More important, it furnished the major part of the will, intellect, and public spirit which enabled the great loose-jointed continental state to function. All these things Ontario and Mowat both knew and said. But if Confederation was built around Ontario, Ontario was not to be imposed upon by the corrupt French and the greedy Maritimers. It was the special office of the Premier of Ontario to see that his province was not made subservient to adventurers at Ottawa, men drawn from every part of the Dominion, and ready, all of them, to try to seize upon the hard-won wealth of the "banner province." In short, the spirit of nationalism Macdonald strove to create was even in the foremost province of Canada likely to be smothered by a quick and hostile provincialism.

In Nova Scotia the provincial Liberal party was equally parochial, but where the Ontario Liberal was inclined to see Confederation as a convenient form for the expansion of the power and influence of Ontario in Canada, Nova Scotia Liberalism was still coloured by the dour anti-Confederation spirit of the "better terms" struggle. Many Nova Scotians had as yet given no inner assent to the union with Canada, and the Liberal party expressed their sullen resentment. That resentment welled up again in the depression of the mid eighties and returned the Liberals to power in 1884, the beginning of a tenure of power even longer than that of the Liberals in Ontario. The party's temper was shown by the passage of a resolution calling for secession from Canada. The new premier, W. S. Fielding, a bland and courtly man of the old Nova Scotian moderation, let the hot fit pass, but he was as determined as Mowat to maintain provincial rights, if not as pertinacious in asserting them.

Mowat in 1884 was just about to win two signal victories for the rights of his province. The ground for them had been laid by a decision of the Judicial Committee in 1883 in the case of *Hodge* v. *the Queen*. In this case the court held that the provincial legislatures were sovereign, not subordinate, within the limits of their powers under Section 92. The governing concept of 1864, that the general legislature was supreme and the local ones subordinate was blown away by this cold draft of legal logic. In its place the federal principle of co-ordinate and separate sovereignties was established. A body in which the representative of the Crown joined with the representatives of the Commons was a parliament, by whatever name called and with powers however limited. The finding suited to perfection the Ontario pride which insisted that the legislature meeting in Toronto was a provincial parliament, not a legislative assembly.

Now the Judicial Committee, which saw Macdonald's constitution not as the centralized empire he had intended, but as a clear-cut federal system, settled two issues long and bitterly contested between the Ontario and the federal government. One was the Rivers and Streams controversy, the other the Manitoba-Ontario boundary case. Both were struggles, essentially political and over rival lumber interests, between the Dominion and Ontario, Macdonald and Mowat. Neither in itself raised any constitutional issue. Both were decided in favour of the Ontario contention, and the result was to strengthen the cause of provincial rights. The union of 1867 was beginning to alter its character; the great concentration of power which had produced Confederation was dissolving.

The dissolution of national powers, serious as it was for the long run, was soon forgotten in the wave of revolt which swept over the north-west in 1884. There the land boom had collapsed in 1883. The wheat crop of that year was seriously injured by frost, and the summer of 1884 was dry. Prices fell, the freight rates of the new railway seemed high, the service was erratic. The barely settled farmers were badly worried; the deflated land-speculators were desperate.

Nor were they alone. The Canadian Pacific itself, now sprawling in hundreds of miles of raw grade and fresh-cut ties across the plains, was running into financial difficulties. The cash subsidy was consumed; the sale of bonds was sagging as the stock-market dropped, and the sale of lands as immigration slackened. The Grand Trunk, still committed to the trade of the American midwest, was hostile, and its opposition began to tell on the London market as its directors strove to deny their rival the money it needed to keep the track thrusting forward. In 1883, George Stephen had to come to the government for aid. A loan was made. It was the story of the Grand Trunk in 1856 over again, as Macdonald must have remembered while he watched Tupper move a resolution in the session of 1884 to give the Canadian Pacific a further loan of $6,000,000. Next year the story was repeated, the aid this time being a loan against the lands of the railway. The depression was threatening to make the railway, major national effort that it was, drag down the credit of the country to ruinous levels.

Keeping the Canadian Pacific building, however, did nothing to allay discontent on the prairies. There the railway was built and was itself a grievance. The settlers' discontent found utterance in two protests, one in Manitoba and another on the Saskatchewan. The farmers of western Manitoba organized a Farmers' Union in the fall of 1883. If they had a model, it was presumably that of the Farmers' Alliance in the states to the south. The only farmers' organization in Manitoba before had been the Grange, and it barely existed there, although strongly established in Ontario. The Union held a convention in Brandon at which, in imitation of Riel's provisional government, a "bill of rights" was drawn up asking for lower freight rates and lower tariffs. Land speculators and Opposition politicians flocked to the support of the Union. In 1884 a second convention was held in Winnipeg at which the hotheads got control. A resolution declaring that immigrants should keep away until conditions improved angered the business community and a motion calling for secession alienated many farmers. The Union rapidly broke up thereafter, but in it the western farmers had made their first organized protest against railway rates and the national tariff.

The discontent of the farmers in Manitoba was matched by discontent on the Saskatchewan. There the white settlers who had sought the banks of the Saskatchewan in anticipation of the coming of the Pacific railway were angry at the choice of the southern route, and they were even more afflicted by frost and by low prices than were the Manitoba farmers. But behind them was a discontent more vague and more formidable, the discontent of those who belonged to he old, doomed, vanishing life of the plains, the métis and the Indians.

The resistance of the Red River métis had not saved them from what they feared, the ending of their way of life. It had saved French culture in the west and the character of Canada as a plural society. But it had not preserved the buffalo hunt, the cart brigade, the semi-nomadic way of life based on winters spent on the river fronts and summers spent on the plains. In the majority therefore the Red River métis had sold their river lots and the scrip to their land grants and joined their brothers on the Saskatchewan where the old life might last a little longer. There they had increased the river-front settlements at Batoche and along other stretches of the Saskatchewan. There they went out to run the straggling remnants of the buffalo herds. But they sensed that their trek had not saved them from the ever-accelerating onset of the railway and of settlement.

The plains Crees along the Saskatchewan were even more disturbed than their kindred, the métis. The passing of the buffalo not only cut off the principal source of their food, raiment, and shelter; it was so catastrophic as to seem to their earnest primitive minds a divine condemnation of the Indian way of life. The régime of the reserves offered no compensation; it was irksome, confining, and degrading. The agriculture it offered was women's work; the rations and

CHAPTER EIGHTEEN, 1874-1885

blankets it afforded were given coldly. For the first time in Canadian history, Canadians of European descent faced the prospect of an Indian rising of the American kind, a desperate resistance to settlement. In the fur trade the whites and the Indians had been partners and allies. Quarrels there had been, some savage, as when the Indians, maddened by smallpox, had turned on the Montreal traders on the Saskatchewan in 1781. But there had been no wars, and in Canada a live Indian was a good Indian. In 1884 this long partnership was on the verge of ending.

The danger was serious; serious enough to move Charles Mair, a resident at Prince Albert since his return to the north-west, to go east to warn the government. The government – that is to say, Macdonald as Minister of the Interior – had already been warned and was alert. The requests of the métis for a river-front survey had been met. Their demands for a new land-grant had not, simply because the experience with the 1870 grant had revealed that this was no way to help the métis. How to aid them was a puzzle not solved then or since. Nor was a better way conceived for assisting the Indian than the treaty régime, as none has been yet. Macdonald hoped the discontent would be checked by the passing of the first shock of the depression and by the example of moderate men.

There is no reason to doubt that it might have been, had men not turned, on the Saskatchewan as in Manitoba, to the precedents of 1869. The Manitoba farmer had drawn up a "bill of rights"; on the Saskatchewan they sent for Riel.

Riel, since he had escaped arrest in Ottawa as Member of Parliament for Provencher in 1874, had spent some time in a Quebec asylum and some time in Vermont. In 1879 he had returned to the west and settled with a colony of métis in Montana. There he became an American citizen and taught school. But he never forgot the part he had played in Manitoba's founding, the unhappy lot of his people, and the personal wrongs which he believed himself to have suffered. The mental tension which had always marked him, and which had led to his confinement in the Beauport asylum, now revealed itself in his melancholy broodings over the past. When therefore the emissaries of the Saskatchewan métis reached him in the late summer of 1884, he answered their call and returned with them to Batoche, the principal métis settlement.

Once more the council of the métis decided on resistance in order to win terms from Canada. Once more a provisional government was proclaimed, with Riel as its president. But there the parallel ended. This time there could be no semblance of legality as excuse for a provisional government. To take up arms now would be rebellion against a legally constituted and actually functioning government. The Queen's writ ran on the Saskatchewan and this time there was to be no show of unity, genuine or enforced, between whites and métis. The few whites who had encouraged the métis, either out of sympathy or to provoke a war that would revive business, soon fell away. And the sympathy of the Roman Catholic missionaries, so apparent on the Red in 1869, turned to full opposition on the

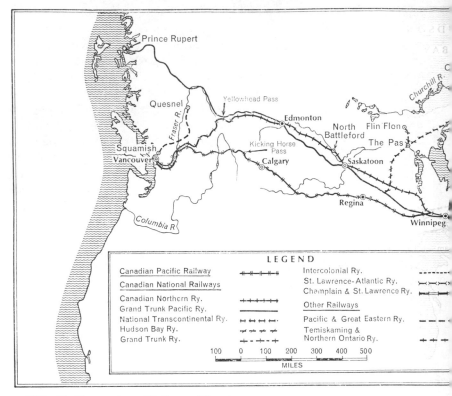

XIV   *The Transcontinental Railways of Canada*

Saskatchewan as Riel attempted to usurp the place of the church by assuming the role of prophet.

There were also two major factors not present in 1869. One, always awesomely in the background in Red River, was the active alliance of some Indian bands with the métis and the possibility of all the plains tribes, including the great Blackfoot confederacy, rising to sweep the whites from the west. The other was the fact that the Canadian Pacific was sufficiently near completion to enable troops to be moved from central Canada in fewer weeks than it had taken months to do so in 1870. That, coupled with the fact that Riel did not come out in open rebellion until March of 1885, when his men defeated a force of police and volunteers at Duck Lake, thus forfeiting the winter's six months of protection, made the effective power of Canada much greater than it had been in 1870. There were also the Mounted Police and behind them the Canadian militia, already stiffened by the elements of the Permanent Force created in 1883.

Riel's demands for his people, embodied in yet another bill of rights, did

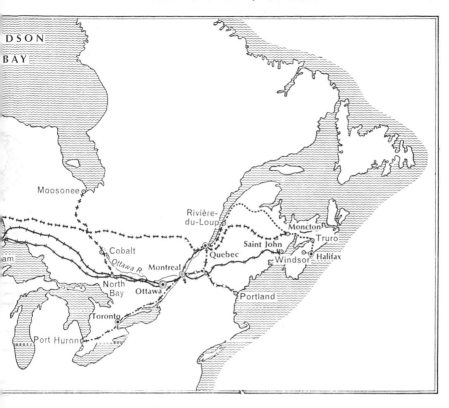

touch on some real grievances, such as the need for increased representation of
he people in the Council of the Territories, but they did not present a program
of practical substance which the government might have granted without be-
rayal of its responsibilities. And Riel harmed his cause by his grasping personal
demands and his erratic visions of the north-west made a home for the oppressed
nations of the Catholic faith. However laudable this purpose, the Canadian
government can hardly be blamed for refusing to continue its private negotiations
with him, or for sending in the troops to suppress the rebellion.

The first in the field were the Manitoba militia. But Van Horne drove his
construction crews to carry the eastern militia across the gaps in the line of the
Canadian Pacific. The result was that by May three columns were advancing
north from the line of the Canadian Pacific to Batoche, to Battleford and Edmonton. Had Riel allowed his able lieutenant, Gabriel Dumont, buffalo-hunter
and plains guide, to harass the main column advancing on Batoche as it crossed
the plains, the fighting might have been grimmer. But Riel refused, and at

KC-N

Batoche the impatient Canadian infantry swept over the rifle pits and broke their brave opponents on the back reaches of their river lots. In the flight Dumont escaped, but Riel was captured. The other columns were less swiftly and spectacularly successful, but the Cree chiefs, Poundmaker and Big Bear, were forced to surrender, and the Blackfoot tribes did not rise. By August the north-west was pacified, and Canada had demonstrated that what it had taken it could hold.

The Saskatchewan Rebellion was a sad affair, and it was to have even sadder consequences; consequences which began to work out their evil course when on November 16, after all appeals had failed, Riel was hanged at Regina. But the rebellion did help the Canadian Pacific Railway by demonstrating, with war's vivid drama, how essential the railway was to the nation's existence. It was now possible to have Parliament pass the final loans which brought the east and west lines together high in the Golden range at Craigellachie. There on November 7, 1885, a little group of directors and managers, of whom Donald Smith and Van Horne were chief, met with the bearded construction crews to drive the last spike. There were no journalists, no distinguished visitors, no golden spike, such as had marked the completion of the rival Northern Pacific, and its concurrent bankruptcy. The Canadian line, in dour Canadian fashion, would not so tempt the gods. Smith stepped forward and solemnly pounded the iron spike down, and the clang of the hammer rang dully along the mountain slopes until the cheers broke forth as the last blow thudded home.

But however the grim Canadian spirit might belittle the feat, the world's longest line had been completed; it had been built without financial failure, as it was to be operated without bankruptcy. British and French capital, American engineering and managerial skill, had contributed to this. But the essential factor, the loyal partnership of private enterprise and government aid, had been Canadian, as the inspiring vision, far-ranging yet harshly practical, had been Canadian also. The scant five million people of 1881, with few resources and great daring, had made good their claim to half a continent, had held the north-west, had shown that what they held they could develop.

ADDITIONAL READING

CREIGHTON, D. G.   *John A. Macdonald: The Old Chieftain.*
DE KIEWIET, C. W.   *The Dufferin-Carnarvon Correspondence, 1874-1878.*
and UNDERHILL, F. H.
MACNUTT, W. S.   *Days of Lorne.*
ORMSBY, MARGARET   *British Columbia: The History of a Province.*
RUSSELL, PETER H.   *Leading Constitutional Decisions.*
SHARP, P. F.   *Whoop-Up Country: The Canadian-American West, 1865-1885.*
SKELTON, O. D.   *The Life and Letters of Sir Wilfrid Laurier,* Vol. I.
STANLEY, G. F. G.   *The Birth of Western Canada.*
THOMSON, D. C.   *Alexander Mackenzie: Clear Grit.*

CHAPTER 19

The Struggle to Maintain the Nation
1886-1897

The execution of Riel gave rise to a bitter and prolonged reaction which convulsed the course of national politics for the next decade. In Ontario it had been demanded and applauded by the Orange element as the punishment of treason and a vindication of loyalty. In Quebec, Riel was defended, despite his apostasy and megalomania, as the symbol, indeed as a hero, of his race. The suppression of the rebellion and the execution of Riel were interpreted as the deliberate refusal of English Canada to admit the French to full partnership in the northwest. Macdonald had remained unmoved, refusing to grant reprieve or commutation. The outburst in Quebec he believed to be a "fire of straw"; his cabinet and party, he was confident, would hold together. In the latter connection he was correct, but in the former gravely mistaken. Riel's death made Quebec *nationalisme* a political force.

In Montreal the execution had been followed by a mass meeting of people of all shades of opinion on Sunday, November 22, 1885. On the Champs de Mars that day the oratory was torrential. Even the temperate Laurier declared that he himself would have shouldered a musket with the métis on the Saskatchewan. But the orator of the occasion was Honoré Mercier. A one-time Bleu, then a member of the Parti National in 1871, Mercier had become a Liberal politician. Now he saw a chance to snatch Quebec from the Conservatives by reviving the concept of a *nationaliste* party based on language, faith, and race. Since 1882 the Parti Bleu had in fact been divided between its old-guard Gallicans and the ultramontanes, or *les castors*, as they were nicknamed. The time was now ripe to exploit the division, widened by the Riel agitation. The extremes of Ultramontane and Rouge would unite to crush the Gallican Bleus. But Mercier, quick as he was to see this prospect, was not just a calculating politician; peasant born, he felt the emotion that he aroused, the vehement pride in being French and Catholic which was the French response to the execution of Riel.

The Ontario reaction was similarly passionate. The frustration expressed in that province, however, sprang not from the events of 1885 but from those of

1870. Riel had been condemned to death for treason, but the demand in Ontario for the carrying out of the sentence was inspired by the desire to avenge the death of Scott. And behind this primitive clamour of the Orangemen was a wider, stronger, more dangerous sentiment, the conviction of English Ontario that Canada was a British country in which the English language and laws and institutions must prevail. Quebec was a regrettable exception and must be kept within the bounds established at Confederation.

Both views, the French nationalism of Quebec and the British nationalism of Ontario, were so inimical to the Canadian concept of a political nationality with cultural plurality that the very foundations of Confederation were shaken by the dispute. Fortunately, Macdonald's cabinet held firm. The Quebec ministers, although they strove fiercely for commutation of Riel's sentence, stood fast despite the thunder of the *nationaliste* agitation. Even the demagogic Adolphe Chapleau, the one man who might have snatched the leadership of a maddened province from Mercier, put his duty to the nation before the call of his race. Their courage was to be justified, for when the events of the rebellion and its suppression were debated in the session of 1886, the issues divided the Liberals even more than they did the Conservatives. Only some seventeen Conservative French members voted against the government, and they quickly returned to the party fold.

The government was therefore able to weather perhaps the most savage political outbreak in Canadian history, and to carry out reforms in the administration of the North-West Territories. These now consisted of three, Assiniboia, Saskatchewan, and Alberta, organized in 1882, as well as the unorganized territory which was to become the districts of Athabaska, Franklin, Mackenzie, Ungava, and Yukon in 1895, Keewatin remaining under the Lieutenant-Governor of Manitoba until 1912. The Territorial Council was enlarged, its powers were increased, and the Territories were given the right to elect four members to the House of Commons for Assiniboia, Saskatchewan, and Alberta. Two senators also were to be appointed. Once again Riel had quickened the pace of political development in the west, some small return to be set against the terrible hazards of his method.

Political reforms in the North-West Territories did nothing to check the agitation in Quebec. There Mercier continued his vehement campaign for a *nationaliste* government, and in an October election his candidates won a majority of the provincial seats. After some delay, Mercier formed a cabinet in January 1887. Provincially Quebec, for the first time since Confederation, was governed by a ministry which was based, not on political principle, but on language, race, and faith. Laurier, it is true, had withdrawn from the position he had taken on the Champs de Mars and henceforth steadily refused to accept race as a basis of political union. By so doing, he showed his quality, for that refusal might well have cost him his position as leader of the national Liberals from Quebec.

Any paltering by Laurier with provincialism, whether the fiery racial provincialism of old Quebec or the brash sectionalism of new Manitoba, would have greatly strengthened the forces which were now racking the Dominion. The depression which had begun in 1883 had deepened. It had been aggravated by short crops and the tightness of money caused by adherence to the gold standard at a time when the flow of new gold into the market was insufficient for the needs of industry and agriculture. As a result, economic distress welled up in political discontent. In Nova Scotia, for example, the depression was intensified by the completion of the long decline of the wooden ship. Both shipbuilding and shipping suffered. The ills that afflicted Nova Scotians were, however, blamed on Confederation rather than on economic causes. In 1886, Fielding once more brought in resolutions calling for the province to secede in order to join a maritime union or to become a simple colony again. In Manitoba the farmers were still clamorous against the freight rates charged by the Canadian Pacific Railway and its alleged failure to build branch lines. Under their pressure, the provincial legislature chartered railway lines to join up with American railways, only to have them disallowed by the Ottawa government in order to protect Section 12, the "monopoly clause" of the railway's charter.

In all the provinces economic distress and political discontent were at work, inflaming tempers and eroding the national morale which Confederation and the building of the Canadian Pacific had created. In Quebec and Ontario the new industries had given rise to the phenomenon, first experienced in the Quebec dock-workers' riots of 1877, of mass industrial unemployment. And this failure of the National Policy, as the Liberal opposition described it, was underlined by the increased flow of emigration to the United States. Many immigrants had always moved through Canada and the Maritimes to the United States. Now, however, it was the high proportion of native-born Canadians, as well as the increase in numbers of emigrants, that caused the concern at the "exodus." Between 1871 and 1880, 383,269 Canadians, both French and English, had entered the United States; in the years between 1881 and 1885 alone, the number entering was 392,802. Many of these were native Canadians – French going to the textile towns of New England, or English to the cities and farms of the midwest and north-west.

The loss of population, the continuance of the depression, the aftermath of the Riel agitation, these were not encouraging portents for the general election that could no longer be postponed. The inevitable was faced in February 1887, in a campaign which was comparatively quiet and which resulted in a comfortable Conservative victory. The Macdonald magic, the new men in the government – John S. Thompson of Nova Scotia and George Eulas Foster of New Brunswick, to name only two – with Chapleau in Quebec and Macdonald himself in Ontario, gave heart to the party and, with the support of the Canadian Pacific Railway and the industries growing under the National Policy, ensured the Conservative victory in an election in which for the moment no great issue stirred the electorate. Macdonald had neatly caught a lull between the Riel agitation and the next great issue, that of commercial union with the United States.

Before Macdonald faced that issue, he had to take the measure of a new leader of the Opposition. Edward Blake had twice led the Liberals to defeat, in 1882 and now in 1887. Aloof, sensitive, driven by a powerful, abstract intelligence which could remember neither name nor face of a party colleague, Blake could not bear the frustration of the repeated defeat. He insisted on resigning. He insisted also that Wilfrid Laurier succeed him. The party, with some slight hesitation, agreed; Laurier, with distinct reservations, accepted after a time. This was Blake's greatest service both to his party and to Canada. For he gave his party in Laurier a man who would win a majority in Quebec to add to the usual Liberal majority in Ontario. And he gave Canada a French politician who would meet and defeat the *nationaliste* politics of Mercier. For the courtly scholar and graceful orator, the man who preached in Quebec that British Liberalism was neither anti-clerical nor free-thinking, was, though proudly French, a Canadian who claimed all Canada for his country. Laurier matched Macdonald in the deep humanity from which alone could spring the sympathy and tolerance to lead a political nation with a plural culture through the clash of section, race, and creed. His election as Liberal leader was the assurance that Canada would surmount the cleavages opened by the depression and the passions aroused by the execution of Riel.

The lull which saw the Conservatives returned to office soon gave way to new troubles. One was that the fiery Mercier gave the discontent of the provinces a lead and a focus by calling together at Quebec a conference of provincial premiers. Four of the other six responded, only those of Prince Edward Island and British Columbia abstaining. The five premiers – three Liberals, with the *nationaliste* Mercier and the discontented Conservative Norquay of Manitoba – met at Quebec in October 1887, in evident parody of the conference of 1864, and there proceeded to discuss the fundamentals of Confederation. Their meeting and their public statements made it evident that in their eyes Confederation was a compact of the provinces which the provinces might modify or rescind. So much had the concept of Canadian nationhood, as held by the political leaders of five provinces including Quebec and Ontario, altered from the centralization of the legislative union envisioned at the first Quebec conference.

On this demonstration of provincial discontent and partisan calculation Prime Minister Macdonald turned a deliberate and expressionless back. He would not be a party to a gathering which had no place in constitutional usage and which was held with so little regard to the national interest. But the meeting was to be in some sense parent of the Dominion-Provincial conferences of a later date.

Another trouble of the vexed year 1887 was the renewal of the ancient irritation of the Atlantic fisheries. Since the termination of the fisheries clauses of the Treaty of Washington, in 1885, the Convention of 1818 had governed the relations of American and Canadian fishermen in the Canadian waters left open to the former by that convention. But the development of shipment of fish by rail and of refrigeration made it more desirable than formerly for American fishermen to use Canadian inshore fisheries and the facilities of Canadian ports. Canadian fishermen, facing the American tariff on their catch, naturally became impatient with this competition. The government responded by beginning to enforce the letter of the Convention, particularly with respect to the interpretation of the word "bay" and to the purposes for which American fishing vessels might resort to Canadian ports. In midsummer of 1887 an American vessel was seized and a clear indication given that Canadian rights, as interpreted by Canadians, would be upheld.

The American reaction was the usual one of annoyance that Canadians should attempt to use their position in the fisheries, as was supposed, to force the negotiation of a commercial agreement. This feeling could easily be fanned into a strong anti-British outburst by an appeal to the anti-British sentiment of the Irish. But the cabinet of President Grover Cleveland, though sensitive, as a Democratic administration, to the Irish vote, was a capable government of moderate temper. The Secretary of State, Thomas F. Bayard, readily accepted the proposal of a Joint Commission to attempt to settle the difficulties, either by a renewed commercial treaty or by an agreed definition of the disputed terms of the Convention. The British delegates were Sir Charles Tupper, Sir Lionel Sackville-West, British minister to Washington, and Rt. Hon. Joseph Chamberlain. Any hope of a commercial treaty was quickly ruled out, but a satisfactory treaty of definition was drafted. Early in 1888, however, it was defeated by a Republican majority in the Senate. There followed an Act authorizing retaliation by the stopping of bonding privileges if Canada should persist in enforcing its interpretation of the Convention. In the upshot, the matter was settled by administrative agreement, by which American vessels paid a licence fee and the Canadian government allowed them to ship fish and buy ice from Canadian ports.

The failure of the Fisheries Treaty of 1887 by no means ended the interest aroused in American-Canadian commercial relations that year. The railway, the telegraph, and the rise of the industrial economy had bound Canada and the United States in an ever more close-knit web of daily commercial transactions. Men and money were drawn both ways across the border, and the new connections naturally gave rise, especially in time of business depression, to the idea that the commercial relations between the two countries should not be hampered by tariffs or other fiscal restrictions. Two business men were moved to action by these considerations; one was an American, Samuel J. Ritchie, who had invested in the complex ore-body discovered at Sudbury, Ontario, in 1886, and one an expatriate Canadian, Erastus Wiman, who had prospered in New York and owned telegraph lines in Canada. Acting together through the Canadian Club of New York, they proposed the commercial union of the two countries.

Though probably unaware of it, they were the business heirs of Thomas Dongan and Sir William Johnson, reaching out from New York for the wealth of the north-west. And American politicians, quickly taking up the idea in regions where it was favoured, introduced resolutions in Congress for commercial union with Canada.

The idea was also taken up at once by Edward Farrer, the susceptible and volatile editor of the *Globe* of Toronto. Under him the *Mail*, a Conservative organ, had reacted so violently to the Riel agitation in Quebec that it had declared it would rather Confederation should break up than Ottawa submit to the pressure brought to bear to commute Riel's sentence. Now the *Globe* hurtled off under Farrer's erratic guidance into the advocacy of commercial union, which at that time might well have meant an end to the National Policy and the work of building a nation in the northern half of the continent. This aberration was only another manifestation of the chaotic state of conviction and sentiment in Canada in the late eighties. For commercial union, on analysis, clearly meant the adoption of the old American belief that the North American continent was destined to be united under republican government. Political union would not of logical necessity follow commercial union, but the latter would destroy the industrial development without which Canada could not hope to become a modern nation with North American standards of efficiency and power. A Canada so weakened would certainly become politically subordinate to the United States.

The advocacy of commercial union quickly produced a reaction. Ever since Confederation a growing number of people in the United Kingdom, some of them colonials, others with experience of the colonies, had been opposing with increasing activity and success the anti-colonial spirit of economic liberalism. In 1884 they organized the Imperial Federation League, not so much in the hope that the Empire might be federated in any formal way as in order to keep the idea of empire before the British public and to promote co-operation between the United Kingdom and the colonies. A branch of the League was formed in Halifax in 1884 and another in Montreal in 1885. But no great activity followed until in 1887 a branch was organized in Toronto expressly to combat commercial union. Thus British imperialism confronted American continentalism, extreme against extreme. Neither party accepted the idea of a Canadian nation politically independent and economically self-sustaining, not subordinate to the United Kingdom and not destined for absorption into the United States. The temper of both was extravagant. How far Farrer was prepared to go was to be revealed in 1891. How far the leader of the Toronto Federationists would go was stated quite bluntly by its leader, George Denison, author of *Modern Cavalry*, member of Canada First, police magistrate; when he had exhausted all constitutional means of protest, and he obviously expected to exhaust them quickly, he would, he declared, lead a riot. In Denison spoke the old loyalist temper of Upper Canada, crossed with that of the Irish ascendancy, fearless, outspoken, and utterly ruthless.

Denison found his chief opponent not in Edward Farrer or in Erastus Wiman, but in Goldwin Smith. Smith was an Oxford radical, a one-time Regius Professor of History, who had later taught at Cornell University in New York State. In 1871 he had joined relatives in Toronto, where he married a lady of wealth and family, the widow of W. H. Boulton, and settled comfortably in the Boulton home, the Grange. Smith was a clear-cut example of the economic liberal of the nineteenth century, hyper-rational, void of sentiment, and insensitive. With these qualities he combined great clarity of thought and diction, a nervous prose style and a life-long habit of public discussion. He had been the friend of the Canada First young men and alert to the first stirrings of national sentiment in Canadian letters in the 1870's. But the National Policy and the Canadian Pacific Railway, the great attempts to realize economically and politically the geographic and natural unity of Canada, seemed to him to fly in the face both of reason and of nature. The great depression of the second half of the 1880's seemed to him to confirm his opposition to Canadian nation-building. He became the advocate of commercial union and the prophet of continentalism. "The continent," he wrote, "is an economic whole."

Smith was a lone wolf, politically as intellectually. But he said with his unrivalled sharpness what a good many Canadians were thinking. The Clear Grit radicalism of the 1850's, with its annexationist sympathies, had never died out of Canadian Liberalism. It was stirring again. Farmers harassed by debt and the lowest prices of the century, business men not assisted by the National Policy, all who traded across the border, the transient and rootless journalists, all these listened to the lure of commercial union. And in the Liberal party itself there were outspoken advocates. Of these Richard Cartwright, who had been Mackenzie's Minister of Finance, was the chief. An economic liberal with a decisive mind and an edged tongue, Cartwright saw in the loss of population and the depression of trade the result not of the business cycle and a faulty monetary mechanism but of the protective tariff and Conservative extravagance. He found a remedy in commercial union and the reversal of the National Policy. In March of 1888 Cartwright and his supporters persuaded the Liberal caucus to approve a resolution for debate in Parliament which called for complete reciprocity of trade in natural products and manufactured goods between Canada and the United States. The debate went on for three weeks in the Commons, and was then voted down by the Government majority. But the Liberal party had adopted the policy of economic continentalism.

This momentous issue, one of the most fundamental that could be posed in Canadian politics, was not at once debated as it should have been. A new storm of political passion was blowing up; or rather, the storm of the Riel agitation was returning in the form of a cultural conflict which involved the existence of Canada as a plural society. It was a conflict partly western and sectional, partly central Canadian and cultural, but with the two strands crossing and flashing on contact like live wires swinging in a storm.

The western strand began in Manitoba. There the provincial administration of Premier John Norquay, a native of Red River, had become a Conservative and party administration as a Liberal opposition developed in the legislature under the leadership of Thomas Greenway, a former supporter of Alexander Mackenzie at Ottawa. Norquay had won better financial terms for his straitened province in 1886, but his position steadily weakened as Macdonald's government disallowed the railway charters which the legislature passed to satisfy the demand that there should be competition with the Canadian Pacific Railway. Finally in 1887 the desperate Norquay defied Ottawa and attempted to build a railway to the border, only to fail to raise the money needed. He fell from power when his Provincial Treasurer was proved to have advanced money illegally to another provincial railway. His Conservative successor gave way to Thomas Greenway early in 1888.

Greenway, like all Manitoban political leaders before him, came into power with the support of the French element in the province. But a redistribution of seats and a sweeping electoral victory freed him from any further need for French support. After pressure on Ottawa, he had also won the prize denied to the long-suffering Norquay, the ending of the disallowance of railway charters. The federal government professed to believe that the bumper crop of 1887 proved the necessity for further lines, and persuaded the Canadian Pacific, in return for a loan, to give up the "monopoly clause." Greenway now built the Red River Valley Railway to the border, but the too lenient terms of his lease of it to the Northern Pacific in 1889 cost him powerful Liberal support. He and his Attorney General, Joseph Martin, were thus in some need of a new political issue to give a new direction to Manitoban politics when in 1889 the cultural conflict in central Canada entered Manitoba.

The eastern strand, in this new phase of the political storm, began in Quebec when Mercier dealt with an old question, the Jesuit Estates. The great land-holdings of the Society of Jesus, the fruit of their great missionary endeavour of the seventeenth century, had passed to the British Crown after the cession. At the death of the last surviving member of the order in Canada in 1800, the income was made available for educational purposes. It continued to be so used after Confederation. But the Society, which returned to Canada in 1842 and was incorporated by Mercier in 1887, pressed intermittently for the restoration of the Estates. The restoration was of course part of the ultramontane program, and Mercier had to respond to the pressure. In 1888 he passed an act by which the Jesuits accepted a payment of $400,000 – the Estates may have been worth five times as much – with $60,000 given to the Protestant schools, for a full and final settlement. Any dispute concerning the settlement or the distribution of the money was to be referred to the papacy for final adjudication. In French and Catholic terms, the settlement could scarcely have been more moderate, fairer, or more conclusive.

It seemed quite other to British and Protestant eyes. The *nationaliste* movement, with its shrill emphasis on race, language, and creed, had stirred a strong reaction in English Canada. The ascendancy temper of Protestant Ontario was never stronger, or more inflamed. To the recurrent Protestant resentment of a militant and advancing Catholicism since the Ecclesiastical Titles controversy of 1851 had been added the bitter rivalry of Catholic and Protestant Irish since the famine years when their strife was transported to Canada and the United States. And in the 1880's the Irish abscess, the morbid result of English mis-government and Irish muddle, had burst in agrarian outrage and the Home Rule agitation, and its poison was flooding along the veins of British politics, Anglo-American relations, and the delicate tissue, the barely knit fibres, of the plural Canadian community. The Irish, Catholic and Protestant, were the largest English-speaking group in Canada in the census of 1881. The explosive quality of Canadian politics, the lack of good humour and easy common sense in public life at this time, was the result not only of French vehemence but also of Irish pugnacity, which counted no cost and overlooked no point of dispute. How intimate the Irish connection with Canada might be was shown by the fact that Thomas Scott, shot in Red River, came from the Irish estates of Lord Dufferin; and that Lord Lansdowne, Governor General from 1883 to 1888, was an Irish landlord threatened with Fenian assassination.

It was a man of this background who now chose to make the Jesuits' Estates Act the object of attack. Dalton McCarthy, Irish born and Canadian educated, a large, handsome, bold-mannered man, was a leader among the younger Conservatives and might, had he added a shade of discretion to his natural qualities, have aspired to succeed Macdonald. But he chose rather to give his fiery nature free rein than earn a reputation for that reserve and detachment which marks the Canadian statesman, subject always to demands from con-flicting interests. The Jesuits' Estates Act was a fence at which McCarthy rode with all the fury of his kind. He sought to serve no personal or political end. He simply meant to strike a blow at the intervention, as he saw it, of the papacy in Canadian affairs and at the *nationaliste* thesis that the French were a permanent and an equal element in Canada. In McCarthy the ascendancy temper, which would brook no admission of equality with a group held to be subordinate, was personified and aroused. In the session of 1889, Colonel W. E. O'Brien and McCarthy moved a resolution in the Commons, calling on the government to disallow the Act. The debate was loud and furious, as Orange and ultramontane battled in open argument on the floor of the House. But the parties, under the cool direction of Macdonald and Laurier, abstained from commitment to a cause so hopeless – the Act being undoubtedly within the powers of the pro-vince – and from engaging in a contest of bigotry with bigotry. Only thirteen members, "the noble thirteen" of Protestant Ontario, voted for the O'Brien resolution.

Defeated in the Commons, McCarthy turned to the country. In the summer of 1889 the Equal Rights Association was organized to protect the rights of Protestants against the alleged encroachments of the Roman Catholic Church. That summer McCarthy spoke up and down Ontario, preaching the danger of French aggression and Catholic domination, and in the fall he journeyed west to Manitoba. In that province and the Territories he found the French language an official language in governments, courts, and schools, and the schools the separate schools of Quebec. In a fiery speech at Portage la Prairie he so kindled his Orange audience that Hon. Joseph Martin, member for Portage and Attorney General, rose on the platform and declared that the provincial government would abolish the denominational school system in Manitoba and replace it by a secular one. The leaders of the Liberal party agreed to do this because of the feeling McCarthy had aroused against the separate schools system and because of their own need to distract attention from the bargain with the Northern Pacific Railway. Thus the sectional discontents of Manitoba fused with the cultural conflict McCarthy was agitating, and the two flamed through another six years of national controversy.

Back in Ottawa, McCarthy carried on his campaign by moving for the abolition of the official use of French in the North-West Territories. This, with the action of the Manitoba legislature, would undo the work of Riel and Taché and the terms on which the north-west had consented to union with Canada in 1870. The equality of the French in the north-west, and by implication in Confederation, which Riel had asserted and which the Parliament of Canada had accepted, was being deliberately attacked and piece by piece destroyed. The wheel of misunderstanding and violence was coming full circle: Scott had opposed Riel; Riel had shot Scott; Riel had been hanged; his death had set Quebec aflame; Ontario had flared up in angry response. Now the doctrine of a British ascendancy was being written into the constitutional law of Manitoba and the Territories. English Canada was replying to French nationalism with a British nationalism; and each was claiming that its nationalism was the only Canadian nationalism.

It was of course inevitable that such a struggle should focus in the schools. In the central provinces the public schools issue had been settled before Confederation and carefully safeguarded for both provinces by the rigid clauses of Section 93 of the British North America Act. In the Maritimes denominational schools had always been accepted, if only on a practical basis and not without serious controversy. In 1871 New Brunswick had terminated public support for denominational schools; it was alone in doing so. A prolonged controversy had followed, but the right of the province to make such a change under Section 92 was not successfully challenged in the courts, and Macdonald had refused to disallow it. Even there, a gentleman's agreement eased the position of the Catholics. A request for denominational schools had been a most important part, undoubtedly proposed by Bishop Taché, of the terms of the Manitoba Act. In Section 22 of the latter, the safeguards of Section 93 of the B.N.A. Act, confirming the possession of denominational rights held by law or practice at the time of union, were re-enacted. As a result, Manitoba had a dual system of public schools, Roman Catholic and Protestant, from 1871. After some opposition and modification in the mid seventies, the system continued without public dissent until 1890. Then at a blow it was swept away and replaced by a uniform system which, if not wholly secular, was definitely neutral and allowed no religious instruction or any but the most formal religious exercises. The legal ground for this action was the contention that the church schools in Red River before the union had received no support from public taxation.

The abolition of a system seemingly guaranteed by the British North America and Manitoba Acts and enjoyed for twenty years seemed to the Roman Catholics of Manitoba a manifest injustice. Three possible remedies were available: disallowance, a decision in the courts that the Act was *ultra vires* of the province, or remedial legislation by Parliament under Section 93. With an election coming on in the midst of the cultural conflict, disallowance would have been most embarrassing for the federal government, and the Manitoba Catholics were persuaded to seek redress in the courts. Not for three years was the final verdict on appeal to be given.

The strife of race and culture which was involved in the Manitoba Schools Question was the most strident of political issues, excepting only that of commercial union. And, like commercial union, it tended to distract attention from changes and events at least as important for the future of Canadian society. The racial and religious controversies came out of the past, were a conflict of extremists only, and were inflamed by memories of historic wrongs – the tragedy of the conquest, the oppression of Ireland. But changes were taking place in the structure of the Canadian economy and Canadian society which would give rise to new conflicts and new relationships not less vital than those of race or church. These were the development of the industrial economy, the organization of labour, and the rise of the farmers' organizations.

The industrialization of Canada had been proceeding quickly since 1850. Sawmills, shipbuilding, flour-milling, meat-packing, cheese-making, were the chief secondary industries. Other industries were a degree more remote from primary production; the manufacture of agricultural machinery by blacksmith-inventors like Daniel and Hart Almerrin Massey and J. F. Frost, and iron casting and working in strategic centres such as Hamilton. The great staple trades in raw or semi-finished goods – timber, sawn lumber, wheat, fish, gypsum – still dominated and imposed their pattern on the Canadian economy. But along the St. Lawrence and the Lakes, at the mouth of the St. John, and around the coal of Cape Breton and eastern Nova Scotia, industries were multiplying in number and growing in size.

After the adoption of a protective tariff in 1879, the rate of this growth and multiplication increased. And the prospect of a wider market in the west, even though its realization was delayed, led to an increase in scale. New industries sprang up, such as cotton textiles; old ones, such as woollens and furniture-making, were stimulated. Wood-pulp mills and hydro-electric power plants appeared, foreshadowing the great electrical plants of the next century.

This increase in scale was followed in the second half of the eighties by the beginning of industrial combination. The depression, American example, and the profits to be made by eliminating or diminishing competition, were conducive to combination in a number of industries such as the milling of oatmeal, sugar-refining, and cotton manufacture. Canada was thus passing swiftly to the stage of high industrial capitalism with its drives towards monopoly. The contrast was striking between the Senate Committee of 1887 on the Food Resources of the North-West and the Commons Select Committee on Combinations in 1888. One discussed the extinction of the prairie buffalo, the other the rise of the industrial tycoon. Nothing could be done for the buffalo; and an Act passed in 1889 forbidding combinations in restraint of trade was no more successful in checking the multiplication of mergers.

The degree to which the Canadian parliament was involved in the problems of the new industrial order, even while McCarthy was beating the Protestant drum and Mercier bringing the odour of incense into Quebec politics, is shown not only by the Select Committee on Combinations but also by the Report of the Royal Commission on the Relations of Labour and Capital in 1889. The day of the parliamentary blue-book had dawned in Canada. The report revealed, of course, that with industry had come industrial labour, and with labour, organization for mutual help and collective bargaining.

The history of organized labour in Canada dates back at least as far as 1827, in which year there is note of a society of Quebec printers. But the various unions of which there is record were local, scattered, and impermanent down to the 1840's. The way was led by the typographers' unions. The Typographical Society dates from 1844 and a struggle with Peter Brown, father of the editor of the *Globe*. The English Society of Amalgamated Engineers came in with the Grand Trunk Railway, as did that of the Carpenters and Joiners. American unions appeared later in the fifties, either by forming branches in Canada or by entering into affiliation with Canadian unions. The Iron Molders Union was such a one. Canadian unions early became international.

These first unions were mutual benefit societies rather than collective bargaining agents. The strength of the unions was too slight, public opinion too adverse, and their status in law too precarious, for much to be attempted. The first great victory was won by the Toronto Typographical Society in 1872 when it struck for the nine-hour day, against the vehement opposition of George Brown, whose liberal philosophy held no place for collective bargaining. Macdonald scored heavily off his old opponent by enacting in Canada the substance of Gladstone's Trade Unions Act of 1871. The Act freed unions from the operation of the common-law doctrine of conspiracy in restraint of trade. Henceforth unions might organize and act without fear of prosecution as illegal associations.

The rapid development of Canadian industry in the next decade was accompanied by a parallel development of labour organization. The craft unions tended to combine in local trades and labour councils. The industrial unionism of the Knights of Labour in the United States entered Canada and flourished in the 1880's even in Quebec, after initial difficulties over the secret oath of membership. In 1886 the Trades and Labour Congress of Canada was organized, an attempt, largely successful in central Canada, to bring into one general organization both the craft unions and the industrial unions of the Knights of Labour. Ambitious as it was, the Congress was only a beginning, but its existence was clear evidence that Canadian society was entering a new stage of development as far removed from pioneer agriculture and lumbering as that stage was from the way of life of the prairie métis, just destroyed by the Canadian militia on the banks of the Saskatchewan.

The organization of labour was accompanied by the rise of the farmers' organizations. The early agricultural societies had been formed to improve the practices of agriculture rather than to improve directly the status or the income of the farmer. In the early 1870's a new kind of organization came in from the United States. This was the fraternal organization known as the Grange. Its original purpose, which was always retained, was to make the farmer a more articulate and familiar member of a literate and scientific society. But the local Granges almost at once began to use their influence as organizations to press government for remedial action on such matters as railway rates, elevator storage charges, and other matters affecting the storage and transport of farm produce. In certain American states the Grangers even went into politics.

The Grangers did not do so in Canada, but in the next decade they were succeeded, though not displaced, by a more militant farmers' organization, also of American origin, known as the Patrons of Industry. The Patrons did everything the Grangers did, but they added a special emphasis on co-operation. They indeed implanted the idea of co-operation, both for buyers and producers, among Canadian farmers, and they made a number of attempts, most of which were early failures, at co-operative enterprises such as manufacturing binder twine. But the Canadian Patrons, unlike the Grangers, did favour the idea of the farmers entering politics to achieve their aim of a better relative position in the new industrial economy. Some Patron candidates were elected to the Ontario legislature in 1894 but their fate there was succinctly described by Goldwin Smith as that of "a flock of sheep between two packs of wolves" – meaning the old parties. None the less, the simple symmetry of the two-party system in Canada was to be distorted more than once again by an agrarian third party, and this emergence of economic issues meant that the politics of race and bigotry was to retire to the background in the 1890's.

Literature and science perhaps also suggested that the future would belong to forces other than those of racial and religious difference. The Royal Society of Canada, founded on the initiative of the Marquis of Lorne in 1882, was now making progress in its task of stimulating French and English savants, in both the humanities and the sciences, by bringing them together in joint endeavour and mutual emulation. A group of English poets had responded to the national spirit of Canada First, and reflected its ardour in some, though not the most characteristic, of their verse, notably that of Charles G. D. Roberts of New Brunswick. More characteristic was the response of others to the general questions of the day, William Wilfred Campbell's to the problems arising from the theory of evolution, and Archibald Lampman's to the social questions of the time. Most significant of all was Lampman's quiet conclusion that in art there was "only one standard for all the world." In this there was no place for parochial bigotry or provincial prejudice. The poets at least were thinking of a Canadian life free of the passions that racked it.

That it might be so was Macdonald's plea in the Commons debate in February, 1890, on McCarthy's bill to end the official use of French in the North-West Territories. "Let us forget this cry," he pleaded, "and we shall have our reward in seeing this unfortunate fire, which has been kindled from so small a spark, extinguished forever, and we shall go on, as we have been going on since 1867, as one people, with one object, looking to one future, and expecting to lay the foundations of one great country." But the fire was not to be dampened down in his lifetime, and when it was, it was to be by Laurier, not yet in 1890 quite ready to succeed Macdonald as a national statesman.

Nor was there to be peace on the other front on which the Canadian nation was under attack, that of continentalism. The Republican administration of President Benjamin Harrison, its foreign policy inspired by Secretary of State James G. Blaine, an anti-British politician from Maine and a persistent wooer of the Irish vote, was definitely cool towards Canada. The fisheries dispute had faded into the background, but the dispute over fur-sealing in the Pacific was steadily growing more dangerous. There the American government was attempting to carry out a legitimate policy by illegitimate means. The fur seals, recklessly hunted at sea, were threatened with extermination. To preserve them, the American government began to capture Canadian sealing vessels at sea and to force them to desist from taking seals. It was necessary to regulate the pelagic sealing, but the American action was counter to international law, unless the Bering Sea were to be treated as a closed sea – in itself a claim counter to international law and practice.

Any attempt to negotiate a settlement of this issue, or a new fisheries agreement, would raise the question of a new commercial agreement. Late in 1889 the fur-sealing issue led to proposals that it be negotiated and, after opposition from Blaine to the appointment of a Canadian, Charles Hibbert Tupper, son of Sir Charles, was sent to Washington in February 1890. The Americans proposed a close season in pelagic sealing, to be imposed at once, while a mixed commission studied the habits of the seals. The Canadian government demurred, as a close season at sea without one on the islands would simply deliver the whole annual catch to the Americans. The negotiations stalled on the Canadian objections and the Americans resumed their seizures of Canadian vessels. The dispute was then referred to arbitration, which went against the American claims, and a convention in 1894 put into force for four years the regulations recommended by the arbiters. Meantime, the McKinley tariff, a high protective tariff, came into effect with serious damage to the sale of Canadian products to the United States.

Newfoundland, from its self-governing isolation, now entered the scene and proceeded to negotiate a fisheries and commercial treaty of its own, the Bond-Blaine Convention, and the Colonial Office suggested that Blaine might be ready to discuss such a treaty with Canada. Macdonald suspected that Blaine's real purpose was to force Great Britain out of America by dealing with British America piecemeal, but by December he had no choice but to agree to the opening of informal talks. Then Blaine, annoyed at a Canadian disclosure that there were to be talks, discussed trade relations openly with Edward Farrer of the *Globe*. This was a studied insult to the official Canadian representation and in effect repudiated any intention of receiving a Canadian delegation. The whole proceeding seemed a deliberate attempt to expose Canada's commercial weakness, and it had to be defied by the Macdonald government. The result was the calling of the general election of March 1891, to be fought on the issue of commercial union, or, as the Liberals now proposed to call it, unrestricted reciprocity. Shaken by the defeat of 1887, the leading Liberals had not only thought it necessary to replace Blake with Laurier; they also believed the party needed a new and definite policy. Cartwright persuaded Laurier that commercial union, modified to unrestricted reciprocity, was such a policy; and the Liberals seemed to have provided themselves with a popular cry.

The Conservative party was not in good shape to fight an election. Its chief was old; Macdonald reached his seventy-sixth year in 1890. Still active, still capable of great effort, he none the less could scarcely bear the strain and shock of Canadian politics much longer. All his old colleagues, except Hector Langevin in Ottawa and Tupper in London, were gone, to provincial politics, to retirement, or to the grave. There were able men among the young, but only Sir John Thompson showed the force and authority of a statesman. And Tupper was too distant to help, and Langevin was passing under a cloud of disgrace. Minister of Public Works for many years, and administering that lucrative department with a freedom that the times and the political *mores* of his province allowed, Langevin had become the victim of those whose corruption he had tolerated. Israël Tarte, a Quebec Bleu, had begun the exposure of a trail of political corruption which led from Mercier's Quebec to Langevin's Ottawa. In Ottawa his charges centred on the misappropriation of public funds, and on political payments made by Thomas McGreevy, a contractor. As yet, only the charges were public; nothing had been proved. But Langevin was, practically speaking, out of action unless his name was cleared.

In addition, the government faced the long record of depression and hard times since the completion of its last great work, the Canadian Pacific Railway. It had little to put forward to offset the disillusionment of Canadians with the

fruits of the National Policy. And it had to meet and turn back the vigorous
Liberal campaign for unrestricted reciprocity, with its promise of free trade in
all commodities with the United States. It had, in short, to persuade the Canadian
electorate that the policy of nation-building was still to prevail; that the continental inclinations of the Liberals in fact endangered the prospects of Canadian
nationhood in the British Empire. Macdonald himself saw the issue in these
terms and his election manifesto contained the famous words: "As for me, my
course is clear. A British subject I was born, a British subject I will die. With my
utmost effort, with my latest breath, will I oppose the 'veiled treason' which
attempts with sordid means and mercenary proffers to lure our people from their
allegiance."

It might have been difficult to draw the issue in those terms, because the word
reciprocity was a magical one to the Canadian electors; it spelled a return of the
good times of the 1850's and 1860's. But fortunately for the Conservative cause
the highly questionable activities of Edward Farrer of the *Globe* were revealed
to the Conservative leader. Farrer had written a pamphlet the purpose of which
is uncertain but which presumably was an argument for unrestricted reciprocity,
and in this he outlined the measures by which the United States government
might force Canada into commercial union; the ending of bonding privileges,
for example, or the raising of duties on certain imports. Galley proofs of part
of the text were conveyed to Macdonald. He read from them with dramatic
effect at his meeting, accused the author of collaborating with Blaine and other
anti-Canadian elements in the United States which were endeavouring to break
Canada economically, and delivered his ringing manifesto. From then on, the
Liberals were on the defence against the implication, if not the charge, of disloyalty. The drive was taken out of their campaign, and the victory which might
well have been theirs was denied them. Continentalism was defeated, and defeated
not only in the country but in the Liberal party. That is to say, it was finally
defeated; and the narrow electoral victory of the National Policy in 1891, won
by means often dubious, was perhaps the most decisive in Canadian history.

The narrowness of the margin was shown by the fact that Quebec and Ontario
split evenly. The heartland of Canada was half continentalist; only the outlying
provinces voted national in the majority, and they under more than usual pressure
of party patronage and the influence of the Canadian Pacific Railway, which stood
to lose most by any slackening of the east-west flow of traffic. And the victory
was bought at the price of Macdonald's death in June, 1891. He never recovered
from the strain of the campaign and he died without knowing how final was the
last of all his victories.

It is easy, and it has been customary, to over-stress the difficulties of the
Conservative party after the election of 1891. Recent study has shown that the
National Policy softened the rigours of the depression, and that Canada in
some ways was better off than the United States. Nor did the party suffer for
lack of electoral support; it in fact carried nearly all the by-elections from 1892

to 1896. The ill effects of Chapleau's withdrawal were much less than thought. What was lacking was the firm ascendancy and prevailing leadership of the old chieftain.

There was no heir apparent to Macdonald. Dalton McCarthy had forfeited his once brilliant prospects. The McGreevy scandal had overwhelmed Langevin, as the related corruption had driven Mercier from office in Quebec. The ablest member of the Cabinet, Thompson, was not only a Roman Catholic; he was a convert to Roman Catholicism. The party feared the Orangemen might not accept his leadership. After much uncertainty in the party, the Governor General, Lord Stanley, called Senator J. J. Abbott, a one-time signer of the Annexation Manifesto and a life-long Tory, to be Prime Minister. Abbott failed, however, to recognize the ablest of the Quebec Bleus, Chapleau, as Langevin's successor as party leader from Quebec. Chapleau consequently retired to the office of Lieutenant-Governor of Quebec. His going meant that the Bleus were slackening in their loyalty to the Conservative party, which now relied, more and more, on Castor support from Quebec. In 1892 Abbott retired, and was succeeded by Thompson without a murmur from the Orange Lodges. The legal brilliance, political courage, and transparent honesty of this least known of the greater prime ministers of Canada had made nonsense of the petty calculations of prejudice and bigotry.

It was Thompson, then, who had to face the re-emergence of the Manitoba Schools Question. After passage through the Manitoba courts and the Supreme Court of Canada, the former declaring the Act *intra vires*, the latter *ultra vires*, of the province, the Judicial Committee of the Privy Council held in 1892 that it was within the powers of the province. The Roman Catholics of Manitoba then applied to the Governor General in Council for remedial legislation under Section 93 of the British North America Act. But it was no simple matter to grant the petition. There was a legal doubt as to whether Section 93 applied to Manitoba. And behind the Schools Question lurked the greater question of provincial rights. Remedial legislation meant the supersession of provincial by national legislation. The party which passed such legislation could be sure that such an "invasion" of provincial rights would be used to its detriment in every province of Canada. The Cabinet therefore referred the question of jurisdiction to the Supreme Court.

If the Conservatives hesitated to embark on coercion, the Liberals had to be equally cautious. For Laurier to have flatly defended the right of Manitoba to legislate as it had done would have been to suffer attack in Quebec, where the hierarchy was strongly championing the Catholic minority of Manitoba. He therefore took refuge in the fable of the wind and the sun, extolled the virtues of "sunny ways," and refused to commit himself to a specific line of policy, urging the superiority of conciliation over coercion in terms of polished generality.

Thompson might perhaps have dealt with so deft an opponent, but in 1894 he died suddenly while in the United Kingdom and a guest of the Queen at

Windsor Castle. His death was a tragic loss to Canada and a disaster for the Conservative party. He was their last man of national stature. The leadership passed to Sir Mackenzie Bowell, a Senator and a past Grand Master of the Orange Lodges. Bowell was a dry, rigid man of slight ability, quite deficient in all the major qualities of political leadership. His choice as leader was an acknowledgement of the power in the party of the Orange element of Ontario and the West. It had been the extremists of this element who had led the attack on the Manitoba Schools system, and on the official use of French outside Quebec. They were themselves resisting Mowat's cultivation of the Catholic vote in Ontario, and defending their own concept of Canadian nationalism. But in doing so they slowly convinced the French voters of Quebec that they could not rely on the Conservatives to uphold the rights of French Canadians outside Quebec. Under Bowell, therefore, the Conservative government waited paralysed for some delivery from the dilemma of remedial legislation. If no remedy was attempted, Quebec was lost; if any, Ontario.

With the Schools Question still in suspense in 1894, two new questions had arisen. One was the extension of Confederation by the admission of Newfoundland. The possibility that the island would reconsider the decision of 1869 was the outcome of Canadian concern for the need to present a common front to the United States in negotiations that became necessary after the fishery clauses of the Treaty of Washington ended in 1885. Moved by this concern, Macdonald had made informal approaches to some Newfoundland politicians in 1888. Nothing came of these. In 1891, however, the Newfoundland government, weighed down by debt incurred largely in building a railway across the island and angered by the Canadian resistance, exerted through the Colonial Office, to ratification of the Bond-Blaine convention, did none the less consent to listen to unofficial proposals of union from the Canadian government. These led to an unsuccessful preliminary conference at Halifax and, after renewed preparations, to a full-scale conference at Ottawa in 1895. It, too, failed. The hard-pressed Canadian government was unable, because of fear that the provinces would demand an increase in their grants, to offer financial terms acceptable to the Newfoundland government. Nor was the British government ready to assist either by guarantees or pressure as it had done in 1866. Thus Newfoundland continued to be the strategic and diplomatic anomaly it had been since 1867.

The other question was the future of Canadian fiscal policy, left open despite the electoral result of 1891, and still agitated by the Imperial Federation League. The League was now disintegrating but it left two legacies, one to Canada, one to the United Kingdom. The latter was the idea of colonial participation in imperial defence, the former the idea of imperial preference. The Conservative party in Canada had already shown some inclination to take up the question of imperial preference in order to bring about the restoration of the system ended in 1846–49, but any such suggestion ran into the as yet unbreached wall of British adherence to free trade. In consequence, imperial preference remained in the background for the time being. In the same way, imperial defence, first raised at the Colonial Conference held at Queen Victoria's Golden Jubilee in 1887, was to break on the rocks of colonial nationalism. Thus the Colonial Conference held in Ottawa in 1894 dealt with neither imperial preference nor defence. It considered only the lesser if still important matters of imperial communications. Conservative fiscal policy remained unchanged in substance, although certain tariff rates, notably those on agricultural machinery, had been lowered in G. E. Foster's budgets of 1893 and 1894.

The fiscal views of the Liberal party, on the other hand, were changing rapidly and extensively. The defeat of 1891 had been intensified when Edward Blake published the letter in which he resigned his seat in West Durham and in effect supported the Conservative charge that unrestricted reciprocity was the first step to political union with the United States. Liberals like Laurier and Mowat were hurt and angered by the allegation. But it had point. There were Liberals, and not insignificant ones, who meant that commercial union should lead to political union. Their views might be defended on the grounds that the reunion of the English-speaking peoples was a greater object than the building of a Canadian nation. But it was none the less a repudiation of that nation and of all its past, and the fact of Canadian political leaders discussing annexation with the editor of the New York *Sun* was not one that could be defended by loyal citizens. Laurier in the national party and Mowat in Ontario let it be known they would have nothing to do with this higher internationalism of Goldwin Smith and Richard Cartwright, and their influence prevailed. After 1891 the Liberal party rapidly became a national party which might be entrusted with national policy and the national destiny. The Liberal Convention of 1894 confirmed this return to the Liberalism of Brown, Mackenzie, and Blake, in particular by substituting a low-tariff policy for the unrestricted reciprocity of 1891.

As the Liberal party threw off the infection of continentalism and began to knit together as a national party in spirit as well as in organization, the leadership of the Conservative party was disintegrating still more in face of the question of remedial legislation in Manitoba. The question of jurisdiction had gone to the Supreme Court, which held that the national government need not take remedial action, and to the Judicial Committee, which held that such action was necessary. The issue of the Manitoba Schools Question was squarely before the Bowell administration early in 1895, and the dilemma it faced was now inescapable. At first Bowell tried to avoid the horns of the dilemma by private negotiations with the Manitoba government in order to arrive at an agreed basis for the remedial legislation. None was found; the political prospects of intransigence were perhaps too tempting for it to be possible for Greenway and his Attorney General, the incisive and hard-driving Clifford Sifton, to agree to any terms. Bowell also failed to strengthen the Bleu wing of the Quebec party when Chapleau refused to return to Ottawa at his request.

The double failure caused a crisis of confidence in the Cabinet. In the atmosphere of a "national emergency" declared as a result of the Venezuelan crisis which seemed likely to lead to war between Great Britain and the United States, and in a state of internal dissension caused by personal animosities as well as political tension, the stronger leaders of the party took a desperate step. Seven members of the Cabinet made up their minds that Bowell could not lead the government through the difficulties of the Schools Question. In January 1896 they presented their resignations direct to the Governor General, Lord Aberdeen, without submitting them to the Prime Minister. This demonstration of disorder and division greatly weakened the administration before the public. So serious was the situation that Aberdeen, perhaps influenced by the ardent Liberalism of the exuberant Lady Aberdeen, even considered calling on Laurier to form a government. At the last minute the breach was closed, and Sir Charles Tupper returned from his office of High Commissioner in London to enter the Cabinet and lead the party in the Commons. All the ministers who had resigned were reinstated except Charles Hibbert Tupper, who remained out lest the presence of both himself and his father in the Cabinet should provoke criticism.

Sir Charles took over with his usual bluff courage, but the damage had been done. The Bleus were alienated in Quebec and were following Tarte to the support of Laurier; the silent Chapleau said nothing to stop them. And in Ontario the Orangemen were shaken from their customary allegiance to the Conservative party. The classic dilemma of Canadian politics, that to win Quebec was to lose Ontario, held the government to a choice of evils; evasion was no longer possible. A Remedial Bill was drafted, and Tupper undertook to drive it through the House. But the life of that parliament was approaching its end. The uncommitted and confident Liberals, sure in the knowledge that Ontario could be won and that the Bleus of Quebec, shepherded by Israël Tarte, were ready to come over, had only to talk the measure out until Parliament expired "by the efflux of time." This they undertook, aided by Orange Conservatives, and the government was forced to go to the country on the Schools Question, without time to raise or define any other issue. Tupper replaced Bowell as Prime Minister at the end of the session, but he failed to persuade Chapleau to join his administration. As a result, all his French colleagues were ultramontanes.

The Manitoba Schools Question was the central issue of the election of 1896, but it was by no means the only one. In Manitoba, where the Greenway government had twice been returned to office since 1890, the issue was regarded as closed. Manitoba without any sense of paradox returned six Conservatives to two Liberals in the election, so little did it believe in the possibility of coercion. In the Atlantic provinces the tariff issue, Liberal low tariff *versus* Conservative protection, was infinitely more important. And in Quebec, tariff policy, and in Ontario the prohibition of the sale of spirituous liquors, were major issues. But in popular opinion and in historical memory it was the Schools Question that was central; it epitomized the last phase of the cultural conflict, and was the issue in spite of which a French Canadian was elevated to the prime-minister-ship of Canada. For it was plainly evident that the voters of Quebec voted for Laurier despite public injunctions of the hierarchy to support the Bleus. They also expressed their conviction that Orange influence would make any remedial action by the Conservative government minimal if not ineffectual. Thus they made the Conservative party what they feared it had become, the English and Protestant party of Canada. How decisive their act was is shown by the fact that the Conservatives carried 72 seats against 79 Liberal in the rest of the country. The Liberals won 49 seats against 16 Conservative in Quebec, which gave them a majority of 33 in the House (with 4 McCarthyites and 3 Patrons).

Coercion had failed; conciliation had won. Compromise was the order of the day, and Laurier and Greenway arrived at a compromise on the school question which allowed bilingual teaching, in French or another language with English, instruction by a teacher of the same religion as that of the pupils, and religious instruction under prescribed and limited circumstances. The Orangemen of Ontario and Manitoba fumed; the Roman Catholic hierarchy of Quebec and Manitoba remained hostile until at Laurier's request the papacy quietly inter-vened. But the issue was out of politics and for all practical purposes it was at an end. For the time being, and in its ultramontane and educational form, the cultural conflict died away.

It died away in the dawn of a new prosperity. Low prices, low freight-rates, and South African gold had laid the foundations of a new boom. In the aureate decade that followed 1897, men turned away from prejudice and bigotry, and often from principle, in order to prosper. In the new prosperity the Liberals could take over the National Policy which at long last began to yield returns. The first Fielding tariff of 1897 was distinguished by two things, the moderation of its reductions and its grant of British preferential rates without demanding a British preference in return. The Liberal victory had not meant the end of the National Policy; it was to mean, in fact, its further elaboration to meet the needs of an expanding and diversifying national economy. The development of Canadian nationhood was to continue, with a Liberal emphasis but without a repudiation of Conservative purpose.

ADDITIONAL READING

CREIGHTON, D. G. *John A. Macdonald: The Old Chieftain.*

SAYWELL, J. T. *The Journal of Lady Aberdeen.*

SIEGFRIED, ANDRÉ *The Race Question in Canada.*

SKELTON, O. D. *The Life and Letters of Sir Wilfrid Laurier,* Vol. I.

THOMAS, L. H. *The Struggle for Responsible Government in the North-West Territories.*

WARNER, DONALD F. *The Idea of Continental Union.*

CHAPTER 20

The Opening of the Northern Frontier
1898-1911

By 1897 the prolonged depression which had lasted with only one minor boom since 1873 was ending in every walk of life, and in spirit as well as in fact, for confidence returned with prosperity. The basic conditions of economic recovery had been taking shape for some time. Since the late eighties the discovery of gold in South Africa had been slowly bolstering the monetary base of the gold-standard countries. Both prices and wages had fallen during the long depression, and now revived. Ocean freight-rates, of particular significance to Canada, had declined, creating a stimulus to the export of grain. Once effective demand for wheat, lumber, wood pulp and minerals strengthened, Canada would experience a boom.

In fact, the conditions necessary for the realization of the National Policy of industrialization, east-west railway traffic, and western settlement had at long last come into being. In fields where Macdonald and the Conservatives had sown, Laurier and the Liberals were to enter and reap. This good fortune of course carried to completion the transformation of the Liberal party into a party committed to support and develop the National Policy.

Still another factor contributed to the conditions favourable to the realization of the National Policy. The frontier of free homestead land was closing in the United States. American farmers who for generations had provided for their sons by placing them on new land had now to turn to the plains north of the 49th parallel. European immigrants who for a generation had favoured the institutions and lands of the United States over those of its neighbour had now to turn to Canada. British immigrants, of whom a vast majority in the past had gone to the Republic, now began to consider favourably the prospects of settlement in the Canadian west. The result was to be the last great land rush of North American history and the settlement of the Canadian prairies from the border to the northern forest belt and the prairies of the Peace River district.

The quickening pace of prairie settlement meant that wheat now succeeded timber, as timber had succeeded fur, as the leading export staple of the Canadian economy. It was the export of hard spring wheat, used to strengthen the flour of soft winter wheat, that furnished freight to the railways and canals, profits to the millers and grain merchants, and a stimulus to British lending for Canadian development. At the same time the flow of wheat eastward set up a counter-flow of capital, goods and men westward, and Canadian manufacturing boomed with the "wheat boom" of the first decade of the new century.

The realization of the National Policy by the settlement of the prairies and the wheat boom was accompanied by the extension of wheat-growing north-ward. The experiments of the Dominion Experimental Farms since the 1880's had introduced some earlier-maturing varieties of wheat and were soon to lead to the breeding by Charles Edward Saunders of the great spring strain named Marquis. As a result, Canadian settlement in the north-west was to spread to a distance north of the border attained nowhere else in Canada. The development of the north-west, then, was a phase of a new orientation in Canadian growth, an orientation to the Precambrian Shield and the Mackenzie and Yukon valleys. After the completion of the east-west transcontinental axis of the National Policy, Canada was turning, as the nineteenth gave way to the twentieth century, to the development of its own distinctively northern economy.

The economy of the Canadian northland had continued since 1870 to be the old economy of the fur trade. No one, other than the fur traders or the scientists of the Geological Survey of Canada, had penetrated the rocky southern rim of the Shield or the northern forest, muskegs, and arctic prairies beyond. The lumbermen, it is true, had cut off the pine of the southern valleys and sand ridges in central Canada, and were now beginning to cut into the spruce of the Shield itself for wood pulp. But it was the prospector and the miner who were to create the new Canadian northern frontier of the twentieth century.

They first did so on the Klondike, a tributary of the Yukon River, in 1896. The Klondike strike was a placer gold strike, and the rush that followed in 1897 and 1898 was the last of the great gold-rushes on the Pacific slope which had begun with the California rush in 1849. Its first prospectors were the survivors of those who had combed the valleys and creek-beds of the Rockies from Cali-fornia to the Arctic Circle. The Yukon goldfield, then, gave rise to the last example of an old type of mining, not the first of a new kind which Canada was soon to know along the edge of the Precambrian Shield.

If the last, however, the Yukon rush was perhaps the most far-reaching in its effects. It swept away the lingering remnants of the long depression in Canada and released a great outburst of energy which made itself felt through the world economy. It drew into the Yukon, British Columbia, and the prairies many people who never saw the gold, and much capital that was merely attracted to the magnetic neighbourhood. The effect of prairie settlement in stimulating the "Laurier boom" was no greater than, was perhaps secondary to, that of the gold rush. The drama, the suffering of the Trail of '98, the sudden riches and the garish high life of the last of the great mining camps, were an advertisement the railways and the real-estate promoters of the prairies could not rival in their utmost extravagance.

It was not lost upon public opinion or the Government of Canada that this galvanic stimulus of an economy so long inert had come from the farthest north-west. The National Policy of industrial protection and railway construction was as a result to enter a new phase in which it would become a policy of aiding the development of natural resources, and henceforth there was to be a new emphasis on the importance of developing the north.

But it was not only northwards that the Canadian economy was broadening its range. In the 1890's the mineral deposits of southern British Columbia had been discovered. For a few years, ores from the mines at Rossland and in the Slocan district were transported to American smelters by pack-horse and river-boat, and the Great Northern Railway of J. J. Hill. This mineral wealth was one of the offsets to the prevailing depression of the early nineties and one factor in the recovery experienced in the last years of the decade. In 1897 the Canadian Pacific Railway, anxious to deny this territory to its new rival, the Great Northern, sought aid from the federal government to build through the Crowsnest Pass near the border to the mines. Parliament voted a land grant and a subsidy to the railway in return for reductions in freight rates on grain and flour moving east and on designated farm supplies moving west. In this agreement the development of Canadian resources was tied to the encouragement of the east-west flow of trade.

The beginning of the exploitation of the minerals of the Shield also helped to broaden the base of the economy, though its chief importance was that it brought about the new northward orientation. In 1883 the construction of the Canadian Pacific had led to the discovery of the mineral complex at Sudbury, and the beginning of the mining of its nickel ores. But no further discoveries occurred until in 1903 the construction of the Temiskaming and Northern Ontario Railway led to the uncovering of the silver and other deposits at Cobalt. From this discovery was to come the opening of the mining districts of the southern Shield from the Porcupine in Ontario to Flin Flon on the Manitoba-Saskatchewan border.

In central Canada, in consequence, as well as in the north-west, the economy was being broadened as the northern frontier of the fur trade was transformed into a mining frontier, rich in the precious and base metals needed to finance and feed the industrialization of Canada and the established industries of the United States and Europe.

The development of the northern economy was at first accompanied by the decline of continentalism. The significance of the preference granted on British goods by the Liberal budget of 1897 was that it tended to increase the east-west flow of trade in Canada and through Canadian ports. When difficulties created by the most-favoured-nation clause in British treaties with Germany and Belgium had been removed by the termination of those treaties in 1898, the unconditional British preference became a permanent part of Liberal tariff policy. It was a low-tariff measure which harmonized with the National Policy.

That the preference was unconditional was one of the main points Laurier made in his various addresses when in 1897 he represented Canada at the celebration of the Diamond Jubilee of Queen Victoria. In all the emotion and tumult of the imperial pageantry the courtly Canadian prime minister, bearing his new designation of Sir Wilfrid somewhat uncomfortably, as a one-time Rouge, quietly emphasized that what Canada had offered it had offered without condition or commitment. In the same spirit he firmly and decisively resisted pressure from the dynamic Colonial Secretary, Joseph Chamberlain, to consider an imperial customs union. Canada would retain control of its own tariff, whether the suggestion of surrender came from London or from Washington.

That is not to imply that Canada had not much to do with Washington in these years. It is true that the emphasis on trade with Britain, coupled with the surging vigour of the wheat economy, bound Canada to trade overseas rather than over the border and reduced the pull of the continental market to its lowest intensity since 1846. The Canadian desire for reciprocity had never been wholly quiescent since 1866 and was never abandoned even in the flood-tide of the National Policy. It was now more subdued than ever before, partly because of the quickening pace of restored prosperity, partly because the McKinley tariff of 1891 had been succeeded by the even higher Dingley tariff of 1897. But the desire for a reciprocal trade continued, particularly in the Atlantic provinces and in border communities, and there remained also the recurrent or unresolved issues of American-Canadian relations.

One of these was the Bering Sea Convention, the term of which was to expire in 1898, with all the dangers of reviving the friction over pelagic sealing. To avoid this and deal with other matters, such as that of the boundary of the Alaska panhandle, now made urgent by the Yukon gold rush, it was agreed to refer these and other outstanding issues to a Joint High Commission for settlement. The Commission, the British half of which consisted of Laurier and one other Canadian minister with the British ambassador, met in 1898. The Commission dealt amiably and successfully with all matters but two. One was reciprocity; it was soon apparent that nothing was possible because of the American commitment to a protective tariff. The second was the disputed boundary of the Alaska panhandle. On this no progress could be made and in 1899 the Commission reported that it was unable to reach a settlement. An attempt to reach a political settlement by obtaining an American concession in Alaska in return for the surrender of British treaty rights (under the Clayton-Bulwer Treaty of 1850) in a Central American canal failed because of the British need of American friendship during the Boer War. The Americans saw no reason to forgo the title implied by seventy years of undisputed possession by the Russians and themselves. That was plain. What Canadians failed to realize was that since the Venezuelan crisis of 1895–96, Great Britain was finally and fully withdrawing from the Americas and leaving them, with Canada, to an unconditional American hegemony. The crass imperialism of the Republican party at the end of the century was partly the cause, partly the result of this withdrawal.

After that loss of British bargaining-power, not only was there possibility of trouble in the disputed area when President Theodore Roosevelt sent troops to uphold the American claims, but a steady hardening of the American attitude over the next four years. Thus the prospects of a friendly accommodation, never good, became steadily worse. They were never good because the Canadian and imperial governments, faced with the terms of the Anglo-Russian Treaty of 1825, which were vague and bore little relation to the terrain to which they were to apply, had done practically nothing between 1870 and 1896 to prepare a case and prevent claims from being solidified by a quarter of a century of tacit acquiescence by Canada. The practical dispute since 1897 was whether the boundary was such as to leave the head of one or more inlets in Canadian territory and so to allow Canadians access by sea to the Yukon. Moreover, the belief that all the territory in dispute was gold-bearing sharpened the need for settlement. The difficulties of interpretation were whether the terms called for an unbroken band of territory around the heads of the inlets and whether the Portland Canal at the southern end of the panhandle ran north or south of the islands in Dixon Inlet. In the way of the Canadian claim stood not only twenty-five years of negligence – the legal strength of the American position – but also the determination of Seattle and Tacoma to hold the Yukon trade, the belief that the land in dispute was rich in gold, and the headstrong imperialism of Theodore Roosevelt. The Canadian government had then attempted to reach a diplomatic settlement by bargaining; it found however that, because of British withdrawal and United States intransigence, it had made claims so extensive that it had overreached itself in terms of a settlement by arbitration or by judicial process. The British government, for its part, was anxious to persuade the Americans to let the "bumptious provincials," as Henry Cabot Lodge called the Canadians, down as easily as possible. It finally persuaded the reluctant Americans to accept a judicial settlement.

The two governments, it was agreed, would submit the dispute to settlement by a tribunal of six "impartial jurists of repute." Whether any national, of whatever repute as a jurist, could really be impartial in a matter of so much controversy was a doubtful question. It was made irrelevant by Roosevelt's appointment of three American representatives all of whom were publicly and previously committed to upholding the American view that the treaty called for an unbroken band of territory around the heads of the inlets. They were in fact approved by the Senate only because they were so committed.

The two Canadian members of the British half of the tribunal shared the anger of the Canadian public at Roosevelt's seeming bad faith and cool disregard of the letter and the spirit of the agreement. Thus the British member, Lord Chief Justice Alverstone, was put in a very delicate position. When on the matter of the unbroken band of territory he found with the Americans against the Canadians, he did no more than he was bound to do. But when he supported a division of the islands in Dixon Inlet in what was a political rather than a judicial decision, and one actually suggested by himself, he brought down on himself and the United Kingdom the wrath of an embittered Canadian public. Humiliated by the Americans and, as it seemed, betrayed by the British, Canadians in an outburst of anger decided that in the future they must handle their own business with the United States in their own way. It was an unreasonable reaction, largely directed against the United Kingdom, but it fed the growing nationalist spirit which sought freedom at once from British imperialism and American continentalism. Nothing did more to sharpen the Canadian sense of nationality than the Alaska boundary dispute and its settlement.

The way had been prepared, however, by the Boer War of 1899–1902. That war was the outcome of the impact of industrial society, represented by the mining community of Johannesburg, on the pastoral community of the Boer republics. Boer society was undergoing the shock of industrialization at a time when Canadian society, both French and English, was being transformed by the same pressure. The Boer War would have affected Canada no more than had the native wars of South Africa, if the rise of the industrial and military power of Germany and the United States – not to mention that of the old rivals, France and Russia – had not made the United Kingdom look to its military and naval resources. One result was an attempt by the imperial government to persuade the self-governing Dominions both to put their own defences in order and to undertake some contribution towards imperial defence. This had hitherto been a responsibility carried by the Royal Navy, the British Army, and the taxpayers of the United Kingdom, with little help from the colonies. The new Governor General, the Earl of Minto, and the new officer commanding the militia, Major-General Hutton, had endeavoured both to improve the efficiency of the Canadian militia and to interest the Laurier government in imperial defence. They found the Minister of Militia, Frederick Borden, a convivial Nova Scotian dispenser of patronage, a surprisingly ready and able reformer of an obsolete and inefficient militia. But Borden's reforms, approved by his colleagues, aimed to create a Canadian militia, uncommitted to use in imperial defence.

No British American colony before 1867, nor Canada since, had ever officially taken part in a British war outside North America. Canadians had served individually in the imperial services, or in imperial units raised in Canada, such as the 100th Regiment, or the Sudan expeditionary force. But because of the pressure exerted by the Colonial Secretary, Joseph Chamberlain, and the

British racial sentiment built up by the Imperial Federation League, the outbreak of the Boer War led to a demand that a Canadian contingent be dispatched to South Africa. The government was caught unawares by the strength of the pressure, and promptly divided. Laurier himself was disposed to think that President Paul Kruger had been unjust in denying the franchise to the immigrants in the Transvaal, but he had no intention of surrendering control of Canadian policy to Chamberlain, or of having his party split in Parliament by yielding to imperialist sentiment. For it was soon apparent that such sentiment was not general in the country, even outside French Canada. The old Canadian belief that Canada's only military obligation to Britain was to defend itself against attack by the United States was still widespread. The Venezuelan crisis of 1895 had renewed it. The result of division in the Cabinet and the country now was that the government authorized the raising and equipping of a contingent not to exceed one thousand men and to be commanded and paid by the British Army. A second contingent followed on the same terms, and some auxiliary forces were also sent, together with Lord Strathcona's Horse, raised by the former Donald A. Smith. In addition, Canadian troops relieved the British garrison of Halifax. In all, over eight thousand Canadians served in one way or another the cause of Empire in the Boer War.

The practical compromise of volunteers serving under British command and on British pay did not entirely preserve party or national unity. Henri Bourassa, a young Liberal follower of Laurier, a grandson of Papineau and the son of an artist, cultured, capable, reflective, perhaps the best Canadian mind in the public life of his generation, spoke out in opposition, and he alone spoke for French Canada more authentically than did Laurier burdened with his national responsibilities. At this point the rift opened which in the end was to break Laurier's power. For Bourassa, speaking as a patriot and a citizen of all Canada, declared that Canada as a nation had no interest and should take no part in the imperial wars of Britain. He won the heart of Quebec by so speaking, and he was heard beyond Quebec. The rift, however, would widen because behind the nationalism of Bourassa, still Canadian, still more than French-Canadian, the narrower *nationalisme* of Mercier had found a fresh voice. That voice was Jules Paul Tardivel, ultramontane and fervently *nationaliste*.

Nor did the cause of imperial defence benefit by the war. General Hutton, eager to promote the cause he believed he had been appointed to advance, was dismissed for trying to force the hand of the Cabinet. The matter became a private constitutional issue when Minto, convinced Hutton was being made to suffer unjustly, insisted on protesting to the Colonial Secretary against the dismissal. (When Hutton's successor, Dundonald, in 1904 publicly criticized the Minister of Militia for political interference in militia promotions, Minto, believing him to be constitutionally in the wrong, said not a word for him.) Canadian forces would be controlled and disposed of by the Canadian government alone. In 1904 the Militia Act was amended to make it clear that the armed forces of Canada could be used only for "the defence of Canada" whether on Canadian territory or elsewhere.

The Boer War thus brought Canadian national sentiment to the point of deciding whether it was British or exclusively Canadian. It also brought the advocates of imperial defence squarely up against the fact that the cabinets of the self-governing Dominions were responsible exclusively to their parliaments for the commitment of men and money to war, and could not take direction or respond to pressure which was not in harmony with a united public opinion in the Dominion. This hard fact of the autonomous nationality which had grown out of Durham's formula for colonial self-government determined Laurier's stand at the Colonial Conference of 1902. There Chamberlain pressed hard for colonial commitments to aid the military and naval defence of the Empire. Laurier evaded any such commitment for Canada; he made it clear that Canada had its own preoccupations and that any military or naval undertakings of the Canadian government would be made in the immediate interests of Canada by the Canadian government alone. In short, Canada might be expected to go to war when the power of the United Kingdom was threatened, for that involved the security of Canada. But Canadian forces would not be committed to colonial wars which did not affect the position of the United Kingdom as a great power. The British alliance, so necessary to Canadian independence, was continued, but the terms of the alliance remained unwritten and the Imperial Defence authorities had to plan without knowing what aid Canada might contribute in a major war. Most Canadians, including the Cabinet, were too isolated in fact and mood from the tensions of Europe and the preoccupations of world power, too absorbed in cultural defence or economic development, to realize how in fact, while aspiring to independence, they remained dependent on Britain in the most vital matters of national security.

The Boer War also combined with the Alaska boundary dispute to drive Canadian national sentiment into a new channel. Fear of American continentalism à la Roosevelt combined with fear of British imperialism à la Chamberlain to make thoughtful Canadians, such as Bourassa in Quebec and the distinguished Manitoba lawyer, J. S. Ewart, believe that Canada must assume full control of all aspects of its affairs and achieve, under the Crown, complete independence. Under the title of the *Independence Papers*, one of which was entitled "The Kingdom of Canada," Ewart began to press the idea of full and formal independence. His thought and Bourassa's flowed together in instant harmony; the sentiment which informed their ideas found a popular expression in the rapid spread of the Canadian Clubs and the beginning of the use of "O Canada" as a national anthem in English Canada. Here was the beginning of a national sentiment, not exclusively French or exclusively British, but indigenous to the land and history of Canada.

If the external irritations of the Alaska boundary and the Boer War produced so strong a sharpening of Canadian national feeling, they by no means set the tone of the early years of the Laurier régime. That tone had in fact been set by Laurier's easy rhetoric proclaiming that the twentieth century would be Canada's century as the nineteenth had been that of the United States. The tone was one of hazy, golden optimism and plunging, materialistic opportunism, as Canadians began at last to draw the dividends of the National Policy and exploit the resources of the north. After so many years of austerity, wealth at last came to the government and business men of Canada and both struck out in reckless development and careless expenditure, confident that the growth of the country would buoy up any undertaking.

In nothing was this more evident than in the railway policy of the Liberal government. It had begun cautiously enough. The Conservative administration had made no land grants after 1890, and the Liberals now adopted the policy of making none. They did, however, continue to aid construction by money subsidies and guarantees of bonds, and as they had taken over the National Policy of tariff protection, so also they assumed the related policy of aiding railway construction which would increase the east-west flow of traffic.

But only the Canadian Pacific Railway joined central Canada to the north-west. The branch lines of the Canadian Pacific and independent lines funnelled the rapidly growing wheat crops of the prairies down to Winnipeg and the single line to Fort William. Thus there was a possibility of the funnel choking up, and other Canadian railways saw the Canadian Pacific enjoying the quickly mounting profits of long-haul freight returns from wheat moving to Fort William and goods going out to the rapidly spreading settlements of the north-west. Both Canadian and American railways bestirred themselves to win a share of the profits, the former by building north of Lake Superior, the latter by building from Duluth across the border.

The first rival of the Canadian Pacific in the north-west was a new and upstart line, the Canadian Northern. In 1896 two Canadian railway contractors, William Mackenzie and Donald Mann, purchased the charter of a Manitoba railway which was to run from Gladstone, on the Manitoba and North Western, to Dauphin. Having also obtained a provincial subsidy of $6,000 a mile, they built the line. They then began to extend north and west to follow the Saskatchewan Valley line that Sanford Fleming had planned for the original Canadian Pacific. They thus resumed, as the name they chose for their line indicated, the northern theme Canadian railway builders had dropped when Van Horne pulled the Canadian Pacific south to keep out the Northern Pacific. Mackenzie and Mann next sought to find an outlet east by Winnipeg to the Lakes. In 1901 an agreement with the Manitoba government gave them the necessary assistance in return for a reduction of freight rates, and in 1902 the Canadian Northern reached Port Arthur on Lake Superior. By 1905 it had reached Edmonton in the north-west. Haphazardly financed, cheaply built and cheaply operated, the most Canadian of Canadian railways, the Canadian Northern was a second major railway which had opened the northern prairies to settlement and laid a second line to the Lakehead.

It was inevitable, once at the Lakehead, that the Canadian Northern should wish to enter central Canada with its rich, year-round traffic. Mackenzie and Mann began to buy small lines there at once. Another possibility existed, however, and one which at first glance was both simple and in the interest of the railways and the country. The Grand Trunk Railway had fallen into the background of national development since the acquisition of the north-west, built as it was to the old concept of capturing the trade of the American midwest. While it had ceased to be the concern it was in the 1860's, it had never recovered from the initial extravagance of its construction or the faulty judgement that traffic could be pulled from the midwest past New York to New England ports. Nor had it greatly extended its system. In 1888 it had entered Chicago, but there its development ended. Its debts remained mountainous, its dividends nil.

Now, however, it saw its supplanter in government favour, the Canadian Pacific, begin to thrive on the traffic of the Canadian north-west. Here might be an opportunity to earn dividends at last. Charles M. Hays, an able American, was made general manager and the Grand Trunk set itself to obtain a Canadian connection with the north-west. The sensible and obvious thing was for the Grand Trunk to combine its eastern lines with those of the new Canadian Northern, and for the united company to build the connecting link through the wild country north of the Lakes. Canada would thus have acquired one more transcontinental system – sufficient, surely, to handle even the traffic of Canada's century.

The formulation of a national railway policy was in fact neither simple nor obvious. Railways were still politics. The Canadian Pacific was traditionally a Conservative line which had served the party well in past elections. The Liberals too wanted a railway attached to the fortunes of their party, and friendly financial interests in Montreal and Toronto were eager for the profits of construction backed by public credit. The union of established lines would not achieve these ends. Neither would it meet the many regional demands for new construction, especially in central New Brunswick and in the Quebec City region struggling to overcome the loss of traffic up the deepened river to Montreal. The Grand Trunk with its American connections and American outlets was suspect as an agent of national policy. Mackenzie and Mann were suspect for other reasons, not least a conspiracy of Hugh Graham of the Montreal *Star* with Andrew Blair, Minister of Railways, to force the Cabinet to support their plans. Laurier refused to be intimidated and the result was the resignation of Blair from the Cabinet. But clearly the time had come for government action. There seemed no end to the demand for railways, particularly for railways to develop the north and "deepen

KC-O

the country." The cumulative effects of the Klondike rush, the work of the Geological Survey, the reports of the "clay belt" farming country south of James Bay, built up a conclusive appeal which made it possible to satisfy all the hungers and ambitions involved – construction in the Maritimes, traffic to Canadian winter ports, the Quebec bridge over the St. Lawrence, another line to move prairie wheat to seaboard, the opening of northern British Columbia.

The result was the Liberal railway policy outlined by Laurier in 1903. From Moncton, by Quebec and the northern clay belt to Winnipeg, the government would build a National Transcontinental line. It was an undertaking of appalling magnitude, involving as it did the bridging of the St. Lawrence and thousands of miles of construction through the rock and muskeg of the Shield. Its scale is indicated by one of the arguments made in favour of its northern route, that the diminishing curvature of the earth would shorten the line. When completed, this line would be leased for ninety-nine years at three per cent of construction cost to a subsidiary of the Grand Trunk Railway, the Grand Trunk Pacific. This company, for its part, would build from Winnipeg to Prince Rupert on the Skeena River, by the Yellowhead Pass.

The Canadian Northern was left free to enter central Canada and to build a third transcontinental line to the Pacific at Vancouver with the help of provincial and even federal guarantees. Thus Canada might have not two but three major railways, and few thought them too many. The grandiose undertaking of a national northern line leading to Canadian ports on Atlantic and Pacific expressed the buoyant, nationalist spirit of the day at the same time that it fed a thousand personal and regional ambitions and created a Liberal political following which extended across scores of parliamentary constituencies. The railway policy of the Laurier régime was the supreme expression of Canadian national purpose in the decade, as it was the apogee of the North American blending of politics and railway-building. There had never been anything like it before, not even the building of the Union Pacific, as there was never to be anything like it again. In this at least, Canada had bettered its American instructors.

The tremendous expansion of the Canadian railway system had in the first instance been inspired by the rapid growth of agricultural settlement in the north-west. Since becoming Minister of the Interior in 1896, Clifford Sifton had whipped the immigration officers and the Canadian Pacific into a search for immigrants in the United States, the British Isles, and central Europe. The northward movement of American farmers was augmented; out of the industrial cities of Great Britain a massive movement began; and a third major element was added to the population of the country by European immigrants of whom the Ukrainians of Austria-Hungary and Russia were to be the largest group. The north-west, heretofore predominantly French and British Canadian, now became a polyglot area in which the Canadian experiment of combining political nationality with duality of culture was extended to include a plurality of cultures.

In 1901 there were 419,512 people in Manitoba and the three prairie Territories; by 1911 there were to be 1,322,709 in the prairie provinces.

Rapid settlement fed the movement for self-government. Assiniboia, Saskatchewan and Alberta, the three prairie Territories, were in fact colonies of the Dominion. Since 1888 when the elected members came to number twenty-two of the twenty-five members of what was from that date the Legislative Assembly of the Territories, a struggle for responsible government had gone on, repeating within Canada the old struggle within the Empire before 1848. By 1901 Ottawa had step by step yielded to its Territories what London had once granted British North America.

By that date, however, the agitation was for full provincial status. The population of the Territories made the possession of provincial powers and revenues a matter of some urgency. When and how provincehood was to be granted was a matter of practical decision, for the Dominion had established no statistical or other test of the time when a territory might become a province. The public opinion of the Territories was strongly opposed to the addition of any part of the Territories to Manitoba. It was divided as to whether the Territories should be one province, or more. But there was practical unanimity in demanding a speedy grant of provincial status.

When both federal parties promised to grant provincial autonomy in the federal election of 1904, the principle was settled, though not the time or the terms. The Laurier government, returned with a majority increased over that of 1900, at once proceeded in the session of 1905 to implement its promise. It decided on two provinces running from the international boundary to the 60th parallel of latitude, one to be named Saskatchewan, one Alberta. These were to have constitutions like that of Ontario in every respect but one. As in Manitoba, the federal government would retain possession of the natural resources. Generous financial terms were provided, which met one of the chief expectations of provincehood.

The transfer of jurisdiction to the new provinces, however, aroused one grave controversy and awakened echoes of the cultural conflict of the preceding decade. The Territories had had separate schools since 1875. At first these resembled the separate schools of Quebec; by 1901 they were more like those of Ontario. The French and Catholic minority might, that is, have separate schools in defined circumstances, but the school system was no longer dual and denominational. When the Autonomy Bills were introduced it was found that they made provision for the kind of school system the Territories originally had. Laurier, under pressure from the Catholic hierarchy, had thought it proper to attempt to restore the educational rights the minority had been granted by the national government. But the clauses provoked a fierce outcry, and Clifford Sifton, under criticism for his administration of the Yukon and the north-west, chose to resign from the Cabinet on the issue. So heavy was the pressure exerted on the

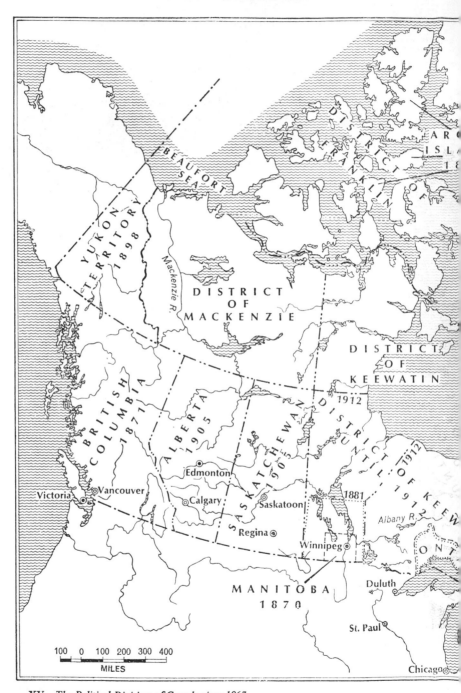

XV   *The Political Divisions of Canada since 1867*

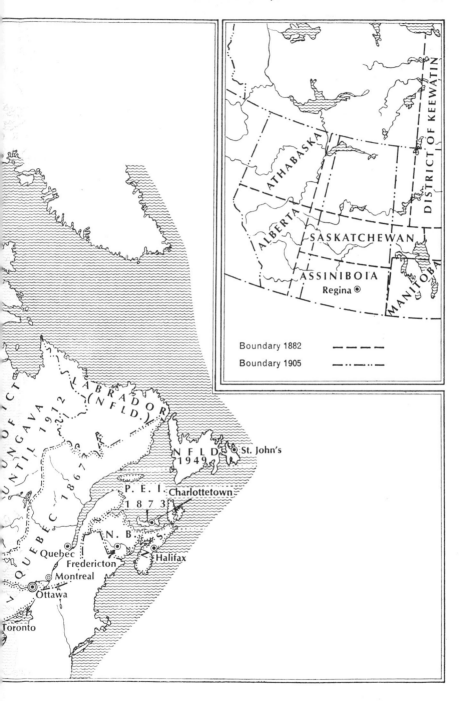

Boundary 1882 ------
Boundary 1905 --·--·--

government that Laurier was forced to amend the clauses so as to establish in the new provinces the school system the Territories had had since 1901. In the outcome, he had irritated Protestant Canada, lost an able if much criticized minister, and further strengthened Bourassa in Quebec. And Bourassa's nationalism, hitherto pan-Canadian, now began to approach the narrower, clerical *nationalisme* of Tardivel and the ultramontanes. Once more the development of the north-west had powerfully and dangerously reacted, as in 1870, on the growth of Canadian nationality.

The creation of the eighth and ninth provinces of Confederation had other repercussions. Manitoba was left a comparatively small province within its boundaries of 1881–84, "cabined, cribbed, confined," as Premier R. P. Roblin complained. And its financial grants from the Dominion government were not as generous as those given to the new provinces. Accordingly, Roblin's Conservative government began a sustained campaign for extension of the boundaries of Manitoba to the north and for an increase of the grants from the federal government.

As the Atlantic provinces and British Columbia also felt that the grants they received were no longer adequate or just, the Laurier administration attempted in 1906 to make the various financial settlements, undertaken in the original British North America Act and as the later provinces entered, at once uniform and final. The attempt was not wholly successful, as British Columbia at once appealed to London against the settlement. The Colonial Office refused to intervene, but did remove the words "final and unalterable" from the enabling Act. Thus the recalcitrance of the Pacific province dashed the slender hopes of uniformity and finality. And the three prairie provinces had a continuing grievance in the national control of their natural resources. The question of the financial relations of the Dominion and the provinces was certain to come up again.

Except for Manitoba, Conservative since 1899, and British Columbia, still not divided on party lines so much as by regional rivalries, the Laurier government as a rule enjoyed good relations with the provinces. All the provinces, with the exception of these two and Ontario, which turned out Mowat's party in 1905, continued to have Liberal administrations. Quebec was already far advanced in the Liberal régime which began in 1897, when the Conservative successors of Mercier lost power, and which was to last a long generation into the future. The federal Opposition, led since Tupper's retirement in 1900 by Robert Laird Borden, an earnest, gentlemanly, and able Nova Scotian, had therefore begun to talk the language of provincial rights, but so far to little effect.

Relations with the provinces, however, and especially those between the Prime Minister and the Province of Quebec, were to be greatly affected by relations with the Empire. The question of imperial defence grew graver year by year as Europe divided into two alliances of the great powers and as the German navy built in ever more challenging rivalry with the Royal Navy. At the Colonial

Conference of 1902 and again in that of 1907 the Dominions were asked to consider the formation of an Imperial Council and to contribute ships to the Royal Navy. At neither conference would the Canadian delegation have anything to do with the proposed council. Laurier also declined to commit Canada to the contribution of ships or money to the United Kingdom, but said Canada was contemplating the establishment of its own navy. The intensification of the naval race that year aroused imperialist opinion in Canada and forced the government to embark on the formation of a naval force in 1910.

The decision and the delay in implementing it were caused both by counter-pressure of imperialist and *nationaliste* on the government, and by Laurier's knowledge that he could lose Ontario quickly to the imperialists as he might lose Quebec slowly to Bourassa. The election of 1908, which was hard-won by a government obviously growing old and seriously discredited by lethargy and corruption, led to some loss of support to imperialist sentiment in Ontario. In 1909 the rate of German building provoked a crisis in British naval policy. In the upshot the government introduced a Naval Service Bill in the session of 1910. It provided for the building of five cruisers and six destroyers, and the formation of a naval force and naval college. All were to be under Canadian control, except that in emergency the government might place Canadian naval forces under the command of the British Admiralty. Mild compromise as it was, the bill was fiercely criticized by the Conservatives as trifling in the face of the German menace, and by the Bourassa *nationalistes* as delivering Canada to British imperialism.

Bourassa now began to despair of the wider Canadian nationalism of his earlier career. He helped Olivar Asselin and Armand Lavergne with the founding of *Le Devoir* in reaction to the Naval Bill, as a paper to express the views of the *nationalistes*. He associated himself with Asselin, the leader of the movement, and in so doing he joined forces with clerical *nationalisme*, the integral French nationalism of Quebec. In 1908 Laurier had carried Quebec by appealing to the young men to follow "the white plume" of his silver hair. After the Naval Bill, the young men went over to Bourassa, as was shown with startling force later in 1910 when the by-election in Drummond-Arthabaska, fought on the naval issue, was lost by a Laurier Liberal to a *nationaliste* candidate.

The *nationaliste* movement was obviously a reaction to the pressure on Canada generated by the tension among the great powers in Europe. But more profoundly it was a reaction of rural Quebec and its clerical leaders to the impact of industry on Canadian society. This was perhaps at its maximum in Quebec, where the early textile industry and the later hydro-electric and wood-pulp industries were at least as quickly and extensively developed as in Ontario. In Quebec the upset of rural by industrial society was aggravated by the fact that capital and the managers of industry were almost always English Canadian, when not American. To the prospect of being conscripted to fight the wars of imperialism was added the much more immediate likelihood of becoming the wage slave of an English industrialist. The personal fortunes of French Canadians, then, were threatened, and also the culture of French Canada, by the harsh impersonal forces of an urban and industrial revolution under English direction. The intensity of *nationaliste* feeling sprang as much from fear of the effect of industrialization as from hatred of British imperialism.

It was not only Quebec which was being upset by the growth of industry. Since a hydro-electric plant had been built at Niagara Falls in 1895, power plants had been spreading rapidly along the edge of the Shield in Quebec and Ontario, and on the Winnipeg River in Manitoba. Canadian engineers quickly solved the various problems arising from the use of ice-bound rivers. Not only the pulp and paper industry but a host of light industries sprang up to exploit the availability of cheap electric power. The old and new industries pulled labour from the farms into the spreading towns, adding to the industrial production of the country and to a growing resentment in the rural districts. Between 1901 and 1911 the rural population of Canada increased by 17.16 per cent, the urban by 62.25 per cent. In 1900 the value of all agricultural production in Canada was $364,437,305; in 1910, $760,316,804. In the same years the value of manufactured goods produced was $481,053,375 and $1,165,975,639. Even as the north-west realized the hopes of 1870 and became one of the great agricultural regions of the world, Canada was rapidly becoming an industrial society.

The growth of industry was accompanied by the growth of organized labour. Since 1886 the older craft unions had continued with the Knights of Labour in the Canadian Trades and Labour Congress, many of the craft unions of which were affiliated with the American Federation of Labour. In 1903 the Knights and their sympathizers were expelled and the larger craft unions reorganized the Trades and Labour Congress. Those expelled formed the Canadian Federation of Labour, first known as the National Trades and Labour Congress. It was an exclusively Canadian association, which barred international unions from membership but was open to either craft or industrial unions. It was to have a severe struggle to maintain itself against all the factors which made alliance with the American unions desirable.

These were organizations in central Canada. Labour in the prairie provinces did not join the eastern federations, partly because of distance, the influence of immigrants, and the desire for more radical policies. In British Columbia the radical union, the Industrial Workers of the World, was strong among the lumber workers. Thus organized workers were not only a minority of the labour force. They were also divided among rival organizations, and while the growth of organized labour was impressive, labour had yet to win an influential place in the economy and was far from doing so in politics.

The divisions of labour were increased by the situation in Quebec. Not only did the language and the rural background of Quebec labour stand in the way of unionization. The Roman Catholic Church and the *nationalistes* actively opposed the formation of unions by the Federation of Labour, or the Labour Congress. They assisted instead in the formation of Catholic unions which might indeed bargain with the employer, but which left the workers under the eye and influence of their *curés* rather than under the hand of an English Canadian or an American union organizer. These unions were devised, that is, as buffers against the impact of industrialization, in the hope that they might prevent the disintegration of the parish and the family by urban and industrial life.

Under the surface of so much that was familiar, the railway-building and western settlement, the mining frontier, and the differences with the imperial government, a new and strange society was growing up in Canada. Not all Canadians were unaware of it, or noting its presence were surprised by it. Two young men, for example, William Lyon Mackenzie King – a grandson of the rebel leader of 1837 – and O. D. Skelton, were studying sociology and economics at Chicago and Harvard. Both in due course were to enter the public service of Canada. Earnest, insinuating, persistent, King did so early in 1900 under the eye of William Mulock, Postmaster General, who wished King to reorganize the Bureau of Labour as a Department. He was impressed by King's ideas and thought he should be given a chance to apply them. King believed that the division of society between employers and labour should be modified by providing means for conciliation and for the pressure of public opinion to induce a settlement. He rose rapidly as deputy minister of the Department of Labour, and with Mulock's encouragement entered Parliament in the election of 1908 and became Minister of Labour in 1910. His ideas were not popular with labour, which interpreted attempts at conciliation as favouring the employer. King's settlement of the prolonged strike on the Grand Trunk Pacific in 1910 was so interpreted. None the less, King was a portent of the new industrial society which was coming into being on the southern fringe of a country still mostly northern wilderness and raw agricultural frontier, as yet dominated by the ideals of hard-working, independent folk who knew little of cities but their names and nothing of industry but its products.

When the material growth caused by the new industry was so marked, it was natural to ask whether there had been a corresponding growth of mind and spirit. Contemporaries were reasonably sure there had not been. Rupert Brooke's experience was pointed, but typical. When his New England friends learned that he was going to Canada, they were horrified at the journey to "the country without a soul," and pressed books upon him for his spiritual sustenance. And what Brooke enjoyed in Canada in 1912 was the natural beauty of the Winnipeg River. There he was the guest of "Ralph Connor," pen name of Charles Gordon, the clergyman novelist who had made a fortune by his novels of manly violence in which a masculine virtue always triumphed. Even in conservative writers like Sir Gilbert Parker, an admiration of physical violence combined with moral restraint was manifest and fundamental. This proneness to violence and ardour for righteousness characterized the popular Canadian literature of the day, and undoubtedly expressed the naive Canadian puritanism sprung from the pioneer experience, in which usually a little more effort, stoutly applied, had put things right. It was the same spirit which was turning many men's minds from the older theology to the new "social gospel," which was driving the Prohibition cause towards victory, and which in the Progressive movement a decade later would carry a non-political element into politics. Canadians were becoming an educated but not a sophisticated people.

An educated people they were becoming increasingly as secondary-school systems were completed, and as universities grew and multiplied. The secondary schools were still grammar schools, systematically provided but continuing to serve only a select minority of pupils proceeding from the primary grades. The universities and colleges were slowly emerging from their denominational status west of Quebec, and even in the Atlantic provinces and Quebec a widening interest in secular and scientific knowledge was beginning to effect a change in curriculum. In Ontario and westward the same interest was producing a revolution. The provision of instruction and means of research in science required more support from government and led to more government control through boards of governors in part at least appointed by government. In Ontario and Manitoba the federation of denominational colleges with the state university begun in Ontario in 1886, survived the rise of the science departments. But in the three western provinces the new universities were wholly secular institutions with a strong emphasis on applied science. With this development, and the continued growth of the Royal Society of Canada, the humanities and sciences in Canada had an organization and a backing they had never possessed before. The foundations were laid for continuing such work in science as Ernest Rutherford had initiated at McGill and such scholarship in the humanities as John Watson had established at Queen's. From the universities were to come the trained minds which might solve the problems of a complex polity and plan the adjustments of a society turning to industry and becoming less dependent on the great occupations of the past, forestry and agriculture.

Even the character of agriculture, however, was changing. For half a century farm machinery had been reducing the manual labour in farming and increasing the capital overhead. The farmer sold more and more on the competitive world market opened to him by the railway, while buying more and more from protected industries, among which was the one that produced farm machinery. To this situation he had responded by organizing, by turning to co-operative buying, and occasionally by political action. In Ontario the Grange still functioned. In 1902 it was joined by the Farmers' Association, and the two united in 1907. In the north-west the Patrons of Industry had disappeared, but in 1901 the farmers of Assiniboia organized the Territorial Grain Growers' Association to force the

Canadian Pacific Railway to allow farmers to load grain cars without having to sell through an elevator. The organization spread to Manitoba and grew in Saskatchewan. In Alberta it was matched by the organization of the United Farmers of Alberta. From the associations sprang the United Grain Growers' Grain Company in Manitoba and Alberta and the Saskatchewan Co-operative Elevators in that province, both attempts to free the farmer from dependence on the Winnipeg Grain Exchange for the sale of their grain.

While these organizations remained strictly non-political, they of course exerted great pressure on the provincial governments and obtained much legislation helpful to agriculture. To bring the same pressure to bear on the national government, the prairie and Ontario organizations formed in 1909 the Canadian Council of Agriculture, which would press for the regulation of terminal elevators and a lowering of the tariff on farm machinery and agricultural necessities in order to cut down the costs of production on the farm. Here was an incipient challenge to the National Policy of protection and the east-west flow of trade. It increased when the farmer felt the rising costs of production as shipping rates and the prices of manufactured goods rose in the last stages of the boom, which had been renewed after a sharp but short set-back in 1907. The Council arranged a march on Ottawa of about a thousand farmers from the north-west and Ontario late in 1910. Their leaders met with the Cabinet, and made known the wish of organized agriculture that the balance between agriculture and industry be adjusted by lowering the tariff. The Cabinet made no promise, but it was impressed by the size and the seriousness of the delegation.

This demonstration by the organized farmers against the cost, to them, of the National Policy – they took little account of any benefit – closely coincided with a change in attitude towards trade with Canada in the United States.

General relations with the United States had been quiet since the furore of the Alaska boundary award. From that blow to Canadian *amour-propre* had come the determination of the Canadian government to handle Canadian affairs. In 1909 the Department of External Affairs was established, on a modest basis and really as a branch of the Prime Minister's office. No separate minister was to be appointed for many years. At the same time, growing difficulties over the use for power or irrigation of the water of streams flowing across the international boundary led to the setting up of a Permanent Joint Commission to settle such disputes by judicial process. The Commission itself, in the long and honourable tradition of the joint commission going back to that set up under Jay's Treaty, soon had a number of practical successes to its credit. It became yet another of those institutions and conventions by which the long, articulated frontier was administered, and which had proved to be necessities on a boundary which united rather than divided.

As well as these two developments, one an indirect outcome, one a direct, of

American-Canadian relations, the years between 1903 and 1911 saw some ancient irritations brought to an end. The Anglo-French colonial settlement of 1904 ended the régime of the "French Shore" in Newfoundland. In 1909 the Hague Tribunal finally settled, largely in Canada's favour, the recurrent fisheries disputes arising out of the Convention of 1818. These two settlements removed the last of those international servitudes which British America had inherited from its colonial past. Finally, the Canadian view of the controversy over pelagic sealing in the Bering Sea was also upheld, and in 1911 Canada ratified a Convention to protect the seals. Three long-standing causes of friction thus passed from the headlines into the textbooks.

Nowhere was this relaxation and ending of friction more apparent than in commercial matters. The American tariff had remained high since 1897. In 1909, following the Republican victory of 1908, it was raised even higher in the Payne-Aldrich Act. A reaction followed in the United States, as the increased tariff was blamed for a rising cost of living. The great newspapers, hurt by higher duties on Canadian newsprint, joined the outcry against the tariff and began to advocate reciprocity with Canada as a means of alleviating the cost of living. The result was an approach by the administration of President William H. Taft to the Laurier government with a proposal that an agreement for reciprocal trade be discussed. The surprised Canadian cabinet saw in this not only the possibility of getting what had been desired since 1866 and given up as hopeless in 1898, but also an immediate answer to the demands of the organized farmers. They responded favourably and an agreement for reciprocal trade in natural goods and some manufactured ones was quickly reached.

The agreement was not a treaty, which the American Senate might have rejected, but was a reciprocal undertaking to be ratified by concurrent legislation. When it was first introduced into the House of Commons, the government was complacent and the Conservative opposition daunted. Then criticism began to erupt across the country. All those interested in the east-west flow of trade – the railways, the railway towns, the manufacturers, all those fearful of American continentalism – began to denounce the agreement as a surrender of the Canadian birthright to the United States. Even Clifford Sifton led eighteen dissident Liberals of Toronto in publishing a manifesto against the agreement. When the Opposition took up the cry the issue of the next election was drawn, and the Laurier government went to the country.

In Ontario and the north-west, reciprocity was the issue. As the campaign developed, all the latent Canadian fear and dislike of the United States as a nation foamed to the surface. The bitter memory of the Alaska boundary award, the ancestral memories of "the war" (of 1812), fed a current of sentiment into the interested desire to protect the national economy against continental inroads. American politicians and even the courtly President himself made statements which said or implied that the eventual destiny of Canada was absorption into the American union. Every such statement played into the hands of the Canadian Conservatives as proof that the dangers of reciprocity were real. In the Atlantic provinces there was less emotion and a clearer view of the material advantages of the agreement.

In Quebec, however, reciprocity, while important, was subordinate to the still seething issue of the Naval Service Act. The Conservatives left the campaign there to Bourassa and his *nationalistes*; indeed, they had little choice, for a Conservative could hardly get a hearing. The result was unfortunate, for the *nationalistes* had no more affinity to the Conservatives than to the Liberals. The Liberal hold on Quebec, unshaken since 1896, was now loosened, not by the national Conservative party, but by a provincial movement with no federal responsibilities whatever.

The great Liberal defeat, however, was in Ontario and Manitoba; the Conservatives won seventy-two out of eighty-six seats in the former, and in the latter eight out of ten. The Liberals carried only Alberta and Saskatchewan; the maritime provinces of east and west were divided. Borden had a majority of Conservatives and *nationalistes* combined in the new House of Commons.

So ended the Laurier régime, shattered by a too easy return to the continentalism the Liberals had shed in the 1890's, and by one extreme of the Canadian nationalism they would have been well advised to defend against the American approach. Between 1891 and 1911 Canada had made it clear repeatedly that it was jealous of subordination to either British imperialism or American continentalism. With both it must have dealings, since both served either interest or sentiment in some parts of the country, and since one was necessary to offset the other. But the one note sounded throughout the campaign of 1911 by both the defenders and the opponents of reciprocity was the note of determination to maintain Canadian nationality. The great unresolved difference was the split over naval defence, as here there was, it seemed, a deep cleavage over what constituted the defence of Canada.

For the moment that problem faded into the background. As the new government of Prime Minister Borden took over, the boom ran on; there was war in the Balkans but it seemed unlikely to spread. The new government took up the work of its predecessor, especially in pushing the frontier north. The Hudson Bay Railway in Manitoba was pushed vigorously by the national government, as was the Temiskaming and Northern Ontario Railway by the government of Ontario. In Alberta, the Alberta and Great Waterways Railway and the Peace River Railway were pushing into the northern half of that province. All Canada, still booming, vibrant with national confidence, was pushing northward, finding unity in the north and realizing that northern destiny which had always claimed it and which now seemed to promise so much wealth and power.

One thing was not then as clear as it was to become later. The products of the northern frontier, unlike those of the southern prairies, went largely to the

United States, so that the new northern frontier was reviving the continental ties of the mid-nineteenth century, whereas the northern economy in the past had on balance operated to preserve a tie with Europe. The old economy had helped maintain the British connection, that alliance which, while it had so often sacrificed peripheral Canadian interests, had kept Canada free. But these changes and incipient contradictions were made unimportant by the outbreak of the Great War in Europe. The British connection suddenly and imperatively demanded that the weight of Canada be put into the balance in Europe, as the weight of Britain had so often been put into the balance in America.

ADDITIONAL READING

BORDEN, ROBERT LAIRD *Memoirs*, Vol. I.
DAWSON, R. MAC GREGOR *William Lyon Mackenzie King.*
DONNELLY, M. S. (ed.) *Laurier: A Study in Canadian Politics* by J. W. Dafoe.
EASTERBROOK, W. T. *Canadian Economic History.*
and AITKEN, H. G. J.
SHARP, P. F. *The Agrarian Revolt in Western Canada.*
SKELTON, O. D. *The Life and Letters of Sir Wilfrid Laurier*, Vol. II.

The Rise of the Industrial State

1912-1921

The outcome of the election of 1911 had been not so much a Conservative victory or a Liberal defeat as a reaffirmation of national purpose. Canadians were determined, and paradoxically this was true whichever way they voted, not to be subordinate to American economic requirements or to British imperial policy. English Canada had stressed the one, French Canada the other, but the two cultural groups were not as far apart as they seemed. And all Canadians were united in the resolve to continue to develop the economy, to add industry to agriculture and lumbering, and to bring the north into the main life of the nation.

They wished to go on as they had for the past decade. Canada had indeed advanced materially. The census of 1911 revealed that the population had grown from 5,371,315 in 1901 to 7,206,642 in 1911. Wheat production had risen from 55,572,368 bushels to 132,077,547 bushels for the same years; fish, from an annual value of $25,737,154 to $34,668,000; minerals, from $65,797,911 to $103,220,994; export of forest products, from $33,099,915 to $56,334,695; manufactured goods, from $481,053,375 to $1,165,975,639. The old Canada of the primary staples was greater and more productive than ever, but a new Canada, urban and industrial, was growing up under the cover of the old staple economy. The population of Montreal had grown from 254,278 in 1901 to 490,504 in 1911; Toronto, from 218,504 to 381,833; Winnipeg, from 42,340 to 136,035; and Vancouver, from 27,010 to 100,401. The number of industrial workers in trade unions had risen to 160,120 by 1912 in 1,883 locals. Impressive as the figures of industrial and urban growth were, the Canadian economy still derived its strength from the great staples which yielded its exports and attracted the capital for growth. Both exports and capital were now obtained also from the development of the northern frontier, which fed minerals to Canadian and American smelters.

The unchecked impetus of the boom kept alive the interest in northern development, and one of the first things the administration of Prime Minister Borden had to do was to deal with the northern extension of the boundaries of Manitoba.

That province had been firmly Conservative since 1899, and its government had aided materially in the victory of 1911. Borden had promised the boundary extension, the denial of which had been a grievance since the creation of Saskatchewan and Alberta in 1905. The claims of Saskatchewan to part of the territory between Manitoba and the 60th parallel, and the opposition of the Roman Catholic missionaries at The Pas to being brought under Manitoba's School Act, were now removed, but the national government encountered opposition from Ontario. That province asked that its north-western boundary be extended west from the Albany River to a line drawn due north from the point where its western boundary reached the Winnipeg River. The line passed west of the western shore of Hudson Bay and would have cut Manitoba off from tidewater. The claims of the two provinces, twice at odds over expansion, were reconciled when the boundary of Manitoba was run north from its north-eastern corner to Island Lake and thence north-eastward to a point due north of the junction of the Ohio and the Mississippi, a last echo of the boundaries of the Quebec Act. Ontario was given a corridor five miles wide across Manitoba territory to Nelson or Churchill, whichever should be made a port. The north-western extension of Ontario was balanced by the cession to Quebec of the former Hudson's Bay territory from the height-of-land to Hudson Strait. The route and terminus of the Hudson Bay railway were thus to be in Manitoba, and Ontario and Quebec fell heir to enormous portions of former federal territories, vast, unexplored, unknown, but desired for the dim promise the north held out.

The national government was divesting itself of great territories and considerable responsibility for policing and surveying, but there was still an enormous domain to be administered. The Yukon had remained a Territory, with its council and with a representative in Parliament, but placer mining had given way to dredging of the gravels, and population had fallen greatly. The Mackenzie valley, the central arctic prairies and Keewatin stretched from the Porcupine Mountains to Hudson Bay. The first explorers since Hearne, Thomas, Simpson, Franklin, and Richardson had been going in to the territory between the Mackenzie and the Bay – J. B. and J. W. Tyrrell, Ernest Seton-Thompson, and Agnes Deans Cameron – and writing of its caribou and musk-ox, and its swift summer rivers and ice-cold lakes. Greatest of all was Vilhjalmur Stefansson, who carried on anthropological studies in the Mackenzie delta in 1906-7 and on Coronation Gulf in 1908-12. He succeeded in interesting the Canadian government, for the first time since 1880, in the vast and little-known archipelago of the High Arctic. He was dispatched on an expedition in the *Karluk* in 1913 to explore the western islands and to inform the government of what it laid claim to in the ultimate north. When the *Karluk* was lost, Stefansson none the less drove on with a few companions, living off the country, to traverse the ice-fields of the Beaufort Sea and to demonstrate that a new attitude and new methods were needed in arctic exploration and development.

While Stefansson made his way to the outermost reaches of the arctic archipelago, the great boom which had partly inspired and partly been generated by Canada's turning north at the century's opening had faltered and ended. For some years the conjuncture of favourable factors which had made possible the settlement of the north-west – high wheat prices, low freight and ocean rates, cheap land values, and a massive inflow of capital – had been altering to its disadvantage. Wheat prices fell off somewhat, freight rates rose decidedly, land values soared, and in 1912 loans to the Balkan countries at war diverted British and European capital from Canadian homesteading and railway-building to the purchase of munitions and the payment of conscripts. In 1912 the rate of development in Canada fell off sharply and in 1913 unemployment was increasing, investment limited, and business slow. So it remained in 1914. Perhaps the interests hardest hit in the country were the Grand Trunk Pacific and the Canadian Northern railways. The former was building along the Skeena to the new port of Prince Rupert, the latter down the Fraser to Vancouver. They found it more and more difficult to raise capital to meet the costs of mountain construction. The wheat crop of the prairies, enormously as it had grown, from 23,456,859 bushels in 1900 to 194,083,000 in 1911, did not give enough revenue to meet the costs of boom-time construction and of the profitless miles of mountain and Precambrian line. And only the national government could have met the cost of the corrupt profusion which characterized the construction of the National Transcontinental from Quebec to Winnipeg, again through hundreds of miles of wilderness yielding no traffic.

Men had seen the sharper recession of 1907, however, and they hoped that 1912 would prove no worse an experience. The new government seemed to have little need to worry about the economic future. Its problems were political. There was first that of the Quebec *nationalistes*. As there were twenty-seven members of the Commons from Quebec who were not Liberals, and who ranged all the way from *nationalistes* who had been Liberals, through Conservatives who were *nationalistes* only for convenience, to plain Conservatives, it was from their numbers that Borden found the representatives of Quebec in his cabinet. Just as Laurier in 1896 had had to bring a former Bleu like Israël Tarte into the cabinet, so Borden now had to accept an out-and-out *nationaliste*, if former Conservative, in F. D. Monk. The other Quebec members, W. B. Nantel, L. P. Pelletier and C. J. Doherty, were straight Conservatives. It could not be claimed that it was a harmonious cabinet; the gap between the opponents of the Naval Bill and the advocates of full aid to the United Kingdom was too great, and Monk was to resign on the issue in 1912. But it was a representative and a national cabinet.

The Conservatives faced another issue which might have become one of some magnitude. Like the Liberals in 1897, they faced a Senate dominated by the appointees of the long years of their opponents' rule. As the Liberals were persuaded that the Conservative victory in 1911 was a chance one, not reflecting the real mind of the country, they soon began to use their majority in the Senate to defeat government measures in the hope of forcing a dissolution and a fresh appeal to the voters. In particular, the Senate voted down the government's bill to aid the construction of highways in 1912 and 1913. In the latter year its bill, a money bill to provide an emergency contribution to imperial defence, passed the House only after the introduction and application of closure to end Liberal obstruction. Then in the Senate, when an attempt at compromise failed, the Liberal majority deliberately voted the bill down. The government, with three years of Parliament yet to run, chose to ignore the challenge contained in this, the most extraordinary use by the Canadian Senate of its co-ordinate power of legislation with the Commons.

The issue, of course, was only secondarily a constitutional one. Primarily it was the old issue of what practical relations there were to be between an autonomous Canada and the empire of which it was a member. Borden had refrained from being explicit on this point in his election manifesto in 1911. Too many of his followers from English Canada thought it imperative, however, in the interests at once of Canada and of the Empire, to aid Great Britain in the naval race with Germany, for the government not to act now that the Conservative party was in power. Accordingly Borden went to London in the summer of 1912 with Pelletier and Doherty to discuss with the imperial government what aid was needed. Borden urged his own strong conviction that if Canada gave aid, it must, in return for that aid, be given admission to the secrets of policy and a voice in shaping policy. In this way he was trying to bridge the gap between the need to sustain Canada's oldest and only ally and the need to conciliate the strong *nationaliste* sentiment of Quebec.

He did in fact obtain assurances satisfactory to him from the government of Prime Minister Asquith, and returned to Canada to prepare a bill to make a money contribution towards the building of ships for the Royal Navy. It was then that Monk resigned. *Nationaliste* sentiment was also inflamed by the promulgation in 1913 of Regulation 17 by the Ontario Department of Education. The Regulation forebade primary instruction in French in the French-settled school districts of eastern Ontario, as well as in other French communities throughout the province. *Nationalisme* was moving now towards a resumption of the cultural conflict of the late eighties, and it was provoked by the same spirit of resistance to French claims as McCarthy had aroused in English Canada in 1889. In such circumstances Monk could not remain in the national cabinet. Borden replaced him by Louis Coderre and drove ahead with his bill, only to see it defeated in the Senate. Here the matter stayed while Borden waited for a change in the Senate and attempted to initiate shipbuilding in Canada. Meanwhile, the Canadian Navy, consisting only of two old cruisers purchased as training-ships, languished, and the Royal Navy received no battleships.

Fortunately for Canada, the issues which blocked the development of naval policy did not interfere so drastically with the reorganization of the militia. Canada, apart from the Atlantic provinces and British Columbia, had little naval tradition; it had everywhere a military one which might have been nourished into a considerable national asset. The tradition was that the military strength of the country rested in the militia, and the military virtues of the citizen soldier were initiative and dash. After 1904, however, the development of Canadian military policy was not in the Canadian tradition. The Militia Council set up in 1904, besides ensuring civilian control of the army, did do something to improve the training and equipment of the militia, but the acceptance in 1909 by the Imperial Defence Conference of central supervision by the newly organized Imperial General Staff resulted in the standardization of training, equipment and doctrine throughout the Empire. The centralization of imperial defence, so stoutly resisted in naval matters where it might well have been accepted, was unintentionally allowed in army matters, where it was objectionable on important grounds of national sentiment and military spirit. The result was that much of what might have been distinctive and useful in the Canadian militia was eliminated, not least its ability to appeal to the martial tradition and national pride of French Canada.

The truth was that Canada was being drawn by events and by its own history towards the battlefields of Europe where the issues would be contested by mass and conscript armies. Such a type of warfare was beyond Canadian means and repugnant to the Canadian genius. If Canadians were to fight such a war, it had no doubt to be as an adjunct to some greater power, and in a spirit not Canadian. But in a war in which a *corps d'élite*, heavily armed and unconventional, might have proved useful, the Canadian forces were in fact to be trained in the conventional drill and tactics of the British Army, and equipped with the same weapons.

No one saw at the time that the Canadian military tradition was being set aside. The real task seemed to be to bring the Canadian militia, now less riddled with politics than in 1904 and working much more steadily at its duties, to the level of the British Territorial Army. At this, little progress had been made before 1910. Then serious improvements began. In 1911, before the change of government, the planning of an overseas expeditionary force was started, but in extraordinary secrecy, lest it be the object of political attack in Parliament or the press. The planning for the expeditionary force continued down to 1914, as a strictly professional task carried out in the national interest. The staunch imperialist who was Minister of Militia in the Conservative government, Sir Sam Hughes, did not materially add to the improvement of the militia, or to the strength of the commitment implied in the planning of an expeditionary force.

The fact was that in a war in which the power of the United Kingdom was seriously threatened, Canada in its own national interest had little choice but to give what support it could. The United Kingdom was the sole external connection Canada had to place in the balance, moral if no longer military, against the United States. In law, moreover, Canada could not be neutral and was therefore liable to attack, if in relatively little danger that any attack would be made on its territory. As Laurier had frankly said to Dundonald in 1902, the Monroe Doctrine protected Canada from aggression. It was true on the other hand that only the Parliament of Canada could decide the time, the character, and the weight of the Canadian war effort. But when the United Kingdom declared war on Germany on August 4, 1914, it did so for all the King's Dominions, and Canada was at war with Germany.

War had long been anticipated, yet it took everyone by surprise. Everyone sensed that the coming war of the great powers would turn the course of civilization, yet few, bred as men were in the habits of peace and the doctrine of progress, could convince themselves that such a war could happen. The members of the Canadian government were in much the same position as the public. What they had expected had happened, yet they were not really ready for it. How should they proceed? The Cabinet looked at, and brushed aside, a suggestion that they should ask for a dissolution and a mandate for the war effort. There was no need for such a manoeuvre. The German invasion of Belgium united a Canada which might have been divided. Laurier declared that Canada had but one voice and one mind. There can be no doubt that he spoke for French Canada and his party, and for the whole nation, at that time. Yet it must be recognized that the German invasion of Belgium, though it silenced, did not eradicate the *nationalisme* of Quebec and the deep-rooted isolationism of old-stock Canadians, whatever their origins. After the first shock, universal belief that the war would soon be over masked the doubts many Canadians felt, and would openly express before many months, about unlimited commitment to the great European trial of strength.

The declaration of war was followed immediately by the scrapping of the mobilization plan elaborated since 1910 and the substitution of a new scheme which involved the organization of numbered battalions in place of the traditional militia units. This personal act of the Minister of Militia, well-intentioned, but against tradition and national pride, illustrates how far the subordination of the Canadian military doctrine to that of European soldiers had gone. The Military Districts were called on to fill quotas by voluntary enlistment, and to move the recruits to a new camp constructed during August at Valcartier in Quebec. In October, 33,000 men of the Canadian Expeditionary Force sailed for England, where they were trained as the 1st Canadian Infantry Division, complete with supporting arms. The eager men prepared for battle and its testing of their quality and Canadian hardihood with the "rigid humility" Rudyard Kipling noted in them on parade. In January, the first unit, Princess Patricia's Canadian

Light Infantry, went into the trenches in which the war was being conducted, against all the doctrine of the staff colleges, at the imperious teaching of the machine-guns.

The relation of the Canadian force to the British Army was uncertain and delicate. In the past, all Canadian units serving abroad had been integrated into the British Army. The same procedure might have been followed in 1914 and in a measure it would have contributed to the military efficiency of the imperial forces to have done so. But the Canadian Expeditionary Force was the outcome of national decision and national will. The government and the force itself were determined that it should remain a national formation, under national command so far as possible. The status of the serving soldiers was defined by the Canadian government as that of active militia serving abroad in the defence of Canada, and the Canadian militia unquestionably came under Canadian command. From this decision had followed the organization of the Expeditionary Force as the 1st Division, which the War Office of the United Kingdom was not allowed to break up for use as reinforcements. The first commander of the division was an English officer, but he was succeeded by a Canadian and as new divisions were formed Canadians were appointed to command them.

The Canadian force grew and developed its own command in action. The first engagement of the 1st Division was the fierce defensive action of the Second Battle of Ypres in the spring of 1915, when the Canadians stood fast on the edge of the first gas attack of the war and held the German advance. But it was in the prolonged and savage fighting on the Somme in the summer of 1916 that the Canadians showed their national quality. In these grim actions they showed all the dash and fighting fury of the old days but coupled with it a command and sense of *matériel* that was North American. The work of the Canadian artillery became outstanding. This new quality sprang from the skill and outlook of the engineers and workers who had traversed the muskegs of the Shield and penetrated the gorges of the Rockies. Much of the success of the Canadians as attack troops derived from their insistence on an abundance of equipment and munitions and their ruthless use of metal to spare the expenditure of men.

The flaming national spirit of the first contingent waxed stronger as the military reputation of the Canadian forces grew. The units became the expression of the sense of nationhood which had been growing so strongly since 1812, and which had found little expression in art or literature, though much in the political creation that was Canada. The result of this national spirit, which broke the bonds of its British training and showed itself in the mixture of self-reliance and self-discipline that marked the Canadian, was that the first two Canadian divisions were formed into the Canadian Corps in 1915 and placed under a Canadian commander, Lieutenant-General Sir Arthur Currie, in 1917. Currie was a teacher and real estate man, and a militiaman in the artillery who had emerged as one of the successful soldiers of a war in which few reputations were made and many lost. A hard, plain man, with the gift not only to command but also to win respect, Currie was not a brilliant general. Yet if he is to be rated second to the Australian Monash among the senior British commanders, it is doubtful that he was second to any other, even Haig. A sound administrator as well as a captain of rare tactical insight, what he attempted he accomplished, and what he ordered his troops to take they took. The first action of the full Canadian Corps, not yet under Currie's command, was the storming of Vimy Ridge on Easter Day, 1917, a landmark in the course of Canadian history because it was the first major victory of the war won by Canadian arms alone. And in the fall of that bitter year the Canadians took Passchendaele, the last blow of the desperate campaign in which the British armies sought to engage the military force of Germany, freed from the Russian front, until the French recovered and the Americans came in force.

The year 1917, however, was the great year of crisis in the war, as it was perhaps for the twentieth century, and the heavy losses of the Canadian Corps in the savage fighting of the summer reflected the shattering events of that year of crisis in Europe as surely as they precipitated a crisis in Canada itself. In Canada, voluntary recruitment was coming to an end. The drain on the manpower of a nation of eight million people, the growing demands of industry, the continuing demands of agriculture and forestry, all contributed to reduce recruiting to figures insufficient to maintain the Canadian divisions at strength. And the Canadian divisions, unlike those of other armies, were kept up to strength. But beyond 1917 lay, it was thought, at least two more years of war, until the new ally, the United States, could bring its enormous manpower and undrained resources to bear. Only conscription, the soldiers claimed, could keep the Canadian Corps intact.

This demand for conscription arose in a political situation in which national unity was seriously deteriorating. The *nationalistes* of Quebec and the farmers of the north-west were both engaged in agitation which could become dangerous to national unity. Since 1913 Bourassa, Asselin, and Lavergne had ceaselessly denounced the proscription of French as a language of instruction in the schools of Ontario. They saw this as a denial of the full equality of the French and their language throughout the whole of Canada. As a result, Bourassa's nationalism became ever more a defensive, Quebec *nationalisme*, resembling that of the Castors which preceded it and that of the Abbé Lionel Groulx, which followed. Fresh cause for agitation was given the Quebec *nationalistes* when the Legislature of Manitoba in 1916 abolished the use of French and all languages other than English as languages of instruction in Manitoba schools, and passed a Compulsory Attendance act.

The same year saw the Canadian Council of Agriculture, in anticipation of the general election which the law required, issue a statement of the organized farmers' political demands under the title of "The Farmers' Platform." It was a demand for a lower tariff, public ownership of railways and certain other public services, and a graduated income-tax. Nominally a non-partisan document, it was in fact a low-tariff manifesto which if carried out would have brought about a serious modification of the protective tariff and the National Policy. The organized farmers had not ceased to regard the defeat of the reciprocity agreement of 1911 as a national disaster.

The intention of the Council was that the Platform might be taken up by one of the major parties, or by individual candidates. It was not yet thought of by many as a possible rallying point for a new party. None the less, there had been a steady growth of disillusion with the old parties and an increasing demand for a new approach to politics, particularly in the prairie provinces but also in Ontario. The Liberal government elected in Manitoba in 1915 had been elected by a non-partisan vote. The recurrent scandals in provincial and municipal government had sickened people, and the corruption was blamed on party politics rather than on the great boom and the easy moral standards of Canadian public life. The sentiment was strengthened by the influence of the Progressive movement in the United States, itself a response to similar evils. And in North Dakota a Non-Partisan League was formed in 1917 which was to spread quickly into Saskatchewan and Alberta, carrying with it not only a repudiation of party politics but also a strong spirit of isolationism.

In addition to the political weaknesses developing in the nation, there were economic stresses of great force and complex impact. The national economy was left to function without government control until 1917. The only economic measure adopted by the government had been to take the Canadian dollar off the gold standard in 1914. Lack of control, coupled with war-time demand, led first to recovery from the depression of 1912 and then to a steady rise of prices. One result was the progressive weakening of the new railway companies; in 1916 the Smith-Drayton-Acworth Royal Commission was appointed to study the plight of the two embarrassed railways, and in 1917, partly on its recommendation, the Canadian Northern was taken over by the government. Another was a rise in the price of wheat, so great as to affect the United Kingdom's ability to pay for it. A Wheat Board was therefore set up in 1917 to buy the annual crop at a fixed price. Until 1917 the general price rise was not too serious in its effects; then it became inflationary and a cause of public unrest. At the same time many individuals and firms made great profits from the war. This "profiteering" – often, as it seemed, rewarded with knighthood – was bitterly denounced and led to the growing demand for the imposition of an income and corporation tax. War-time demand also quickened the industrial growth of Canada, not only in established industries, such as textiles and steel-making, but in new industries such as the production of cellulose and chemicals and the manufacture of aircraft. The foundation of the National Research Council of Canada in 1916-17 to aid industry by research was an illustration of the rapidity of the growth of new industrial needs. With the growth of industry, the labour force and labour unions grew also, especially the radical industrial unions of the Pacific coast and the prairie provinces. The war was making Canada an industrial state, with the strength and the stresses of an industrial state.

Such was the Canada that Prime Minister Borden left in the spring of 1917 to visit England and assess the position of the allied powers. In the war, changes far more drastic than those shaping up in Canada were on the verge of happening. The Europe of the nineteenth century was about to collapse; the revolutionary and totalitarian twentieth century was about to emerge. The French offensive in Champagne was to drive the over-tried French infantry to mutiny; Russia was drifting out of the war and into revolution; Italy was exposed by its bitterly won and exhausting advance in the Isonzo to the flank attack and disaster of Caporetto. The United States, in not the least revolutionary event of the year, would commit itself to intervene in Europe; but until its weight told, the forces of the British Empire must sustain the cause of the Allies.

In these circumstances the military effort of the Dominions, now nearing its maximum, became of major significance. The time was therefore ripe for an attempt to define the working relations of the governments of the Empire, or the Commonwealth, as some were already beginning to call it after Lord Rosebery's use of the term in 1894. Hitherto, despite the assurances given Borden in 1912, the government of the United Kingdom had in fact decided policy in all matters of war and diplomacy. But the establishment of a separate and distinct Canadian military command, aided by the appointment of a Canadian cabinet minister resident in the United Kingdom, necessarily led to some modifications. It meant, by an inescapable logic developed from the same premises of parliamentary control of the nation's resources and parliamentary ratification of its policies, that a separate and distinct Canadian foreign policy would emerge. How were the facts of national war efforts and national foreign policies to be reconciled with the association of the autonomous Dominions in the Commonwealth? How were the Dominions in fact to be given "an adequate voice" in making policy?

The coalition government of Prime Minister Lloyd George was seized of the issue, and prepared to be flexible in considering and adopting means to meet the situation. The means employed was the creation of an Imperial War Cabinet which was given control of policy-making and to which representatives of the Dominions and India were appointed. Thus Borden sat as the representative of Canada in a "cabinet of governments" in which the major policies of the Empire in continuing the war and preparing for the peace were decided. The War Cabinet seemed to be an expedient which reconciled the nationhood of the Dominion with association in the Empire by setting up a body responsible to all the parliaments of the Empire for the making of common policy. There were even hopes that this war-time expedient might become a permanent institution to give direction to imperial policy at all times.

With this hope in mind, it was possible for the Imperial War Conference which met in April, 1917, to begin a redefinition of the imperial relationship. In its Resolution IX it called for a "readjustment of the constitutional relations of the component parts of the Empire" in a post-war conference; and it affirmed its belief in the need for a full recognition of the Dominions as "autonomous nations" and of "the right of the Dominions and India to an adequate voice in foreign policy and foreign relations," with provision for consultation. The Conference thus pointed the way to a new concept and working relationship in the imperial association, but assumed that it would be a relationship realized in common policy, not in the separate and distinct national policies of the United Kingdom and the Dominions.

More urgent than the intricacies of imperial relations was the pressure for reinforcements to replace the casualties of the Somme and to enable the British forces to bear the weight of the German troops released from the eastern front by the disintegration of the Russian armies. Borden came home convinced that Canadian reinforcements must be found and that they could be found only by the introduction of compulsory military service. Returns at the recruitment centres had fallen off, as the demands of agriculture and industry grew, from 30,000 a month to a mere 6,000. The returns from Quebec had been particularly disappointing. French Canadians did not feel the pull of British sentiment which drew many English Canadians to the colours, and they felt no comparable sentiment for France. Many were frankly isolationist and questioned Canada's interest in the war. Recruiting in the province had been badly mismanaged. Attempts were made, but without success, to raise French units with French officers on the model of the famous 22nd Regiment. Recruiting was not vigorously organized under French direction, and no intelligent effort was made to enlist the willing help of leading French public men. The weakness of the French section of the Cabinet contributed to this bungling. And the failure to appeal to French pride and sentiment played into the hands of the *nationalistes*, who became increasingly critical of Canadian participation as their anger grew against Regulation 17 in Ontario and the Manitoba School Acts of 1916.

As Quebec had yielded, by April 1917, only a little over half of an estimated fifteen thousand French recruits to the Canadian forces in France, it had quite failed to keep pace with the rest of the country, including the French population outside Quebec; and English Canada grew resentful of the fact, which it tended to view as the result of a lack of national patriotism in French Canada. One result of this situation was that conscription would amount to the coercion of Quebec by an English majority. It would also mean, in fact, compulsory service in that province alone, since the rest of the country could yield relatively few more recruits. None the less, a registration of manpower had already been set in train, in order that the government might know what men were available. Now that Borden knew how compelling the need for manpower was, the means necessary to obtain Canadian reinforcements could be adopted, if the political situation allowed.

Before the conscription crisis of 1917 is considered, it is necessary to note certain circumstances in which it was undertaken. Although the Canadian government and people had so far adhered to the idea that a volunteer army was superior to a conscript one, as Australia was to do throughout the war, the United Kingdom had adopted conscription in 1916 (except in Ireland) and the United States had done so on entering the war in April 1917. The effect of these powerful examples was reinforced by public demands similar in kind to the demand for conscription in that they aimed at achieving "equality of sacrifice" by a graduated income-tax and by the curbing of inflation. Both measures were as revolutionary as the introduction of conscription, and both were introduced in 1917. And the actual bankruptcy of the Canadian Northern Railway and the threatened collapse of the Grand Trunk, which imperilled the national credit, helped create in government and Parliament a drastic and critical temper which made it seem imperative that conscription, among other things, should be carried at whatever cost to national unity.

The question of conscription was indeed fundamentally a question of national unity, and Borden approached it in national terms. He sought to deal with it by a union of the two national parties in order to prolong the life of Parliament, as had been done in 1916, and carry a Military Service Bill through a united House. Thus the conscription question became a question of "union" or coalition government in the first instance, and of the need for appeal to the people in the second. The decision at this point came to rest on Laurier. When Borden first asked him in May to join a union government under another prime minister than Borden himself, Laurier faced a decision of cruel import. If he joined a union government, he would lose most, if not all, of Quebec to Bourassa and the *nationalistes*. If he did not, he must lose much of the English following of the Liberal party, particularly in the north-west, where conscription was strongly demanded. In short, whatever he did, he could not contribute to national unity. He therefore stood on two clear principles. He refused to enter a coalition. He affirmed his personal conviction that the principle of voluntary military service was best, and would in fact yield more recruits than compulsion. The practical question then became, could Laurier hold his English Canadian following?

The first effect of his decision was to ensure that there would be a general election. The life of Parliament could not be prolonged now that agreement was lacking. The second effect was, as the government had to proceed with the Military Service Bill at once, that the measure split the Liberal party. The strain of the war effort, the growth of non-partisan sentiment, the example of the United Kingdom, had already started a sentiment in favour of union government among many Liberals in 1916. Now union government was demanded particularly in Ontario and Manitoba, where the powerful *Manitoba Free Press* and its editor, J. W. Dafoe, made it a special cause, as a means of carrying conscription. The split in the Liberal party was made public both by the vote on the Military Service Bill in July and at a conference of western Liberals in Winnipeg in August. The Laurier supporters did indeed succeed in carrying the conference, but the western "Unionist" Liberals then broke away.

Borden was now free to negotiate with the leaders of the Unionist Liberals. There was much reluctance among the Liberals at first to accept Borden as prime minister; the stature he had achieved as a national leader was not yet appreciated. When this difficulty was overcome, the formation of the cabinet of the Union Government went forward quickly. A special feature of it was the introduction of T. A. Crerar, a Liberal but also president of the United Grain Growers' Grain Company and a representative of agriculture. That this was his intended character was revealed by the fact that Henry Wise Wood, president of the United Farmers of Alberta and a non-partisan, was also invited, but declined.

The new cabinet when formed in October consisted half of Conservatives, half of Unionist Liberals, under Borden as Prime Minister. It was designed by its creators – Borden, Sir Clifford Sifton, J. W. Dafoe, N. W. Rowell – to be a new government; a government of national concentration with a special commission to fight the war, to deal with the reorganization of the railways of the country, and to limit political patronage and carry the Civil Service reform on which Borden himself had set his heart in 1912. It was, in short, conceived as a government of national purpose set up to deal with a national crisis and to realize, after the prevailing and corrupt partisanship of the past, the ideal of honest government through a capable and disinterested Civil Service.

The new government, however, faced a general election in a nation already deeply divided and strained by three years of war and a mounting inflation. It might well face defeat in the election called for early December. Certain it was that the election would be bitterly contested, for many Liberals had taken fierce exception to two measures passed in August and September which they alleged were designed to tilt the electoral balance in favour of the government. These were the Military Voters Act, which provided for taking the vote of the armed forces overseas, and the Wartime Elections Act. The latter enfranchised women who had relatives serving in the forces and disfranchised persons of German speech, those of enemy alien birth naturalized since 1902, and conscientious objectors. It was alleged that the enfranchisement of women next-of-kin was meant to load the vote for the government which had carried conscription, and that the disfranchisement was a blow aimed at the Liberal party in the prairie provinces, where the immigrants had tended to give their vote to the party in power at the time of their settlement. These Acts of course continued in effect under the Union Government, which proceeded to add to their undoubted bias against the Opposition by granting exemption from military service to farmers' sons and to agricultural workers when it became apparent that opposition to conscription was such, even outside Quebec, as to imperil the future of the government.

The campaign, though bitter, was waged with some restraint, for the cleavage was not fundamental. The question was not whether the war should be fought, but only how it should be fought. The government was returned but the Liberal party polled a large part of the popular vote and elected eighty-nine members. Sixty-two of these, it was true, were from Quebec, as sixty-two of the government's hundred and forty-eight were from Ontario. The government's majorities, however, were narrow in many seats outside Quebec, and in some the decision was made only by the overseas soldiers' votes. Quebec seemed far more isolated than it actually was; the shock to national unity was less damaging than it might have been.

It was tragic that there should have been a shock at all. However high-minded the architects of Union Government, and no men in Canadian history had been more so, the temper they displayed and the policy they enforced in carrying out conscription were gravely mistaken. In the government of a federal and a bi-cultural state a majority on fundamental issues of policy is not enough. At bottom, Canada must be governed by concurrent majorities of French and English. The conscription issue of 1917 was not in itself fundamental, but it was made a trial of wills between French and English Canada by the upsurge of the old Anglo-Canadian ascendancy temper under the strain of war. The result was a set-back to national unity it was to take a generation to make good.

In French Canada, the greatest potential source of recruits, only about fifteen thousand were obtained by conscription. Not only did the custom of early marriage win legitimate exemption for many. The whole French population tacitly conspired to defeat the obnoxious law, and in Quebec City the attempt to enforce it resulted in fierce rioting in the spring of 1918. The rest of the country yielded a total of sixty-eight thousand; less than in three months' voluntary recruiting in 1915. In Canada, the election revealed, there were limits on the power of government. A law not founded on local assent could not be enforced in any part of the country by any method that public opinion in the rest of the country would support. Quebec in its heart knew this, and a motion for secession in the legislature found little support there and scant echo from the public.

On the other hand, the conscripts made up the main body of the reinforcements for the Canadian Corps in 1918, some forty-eight thousand. The remainder had to be found by using the men of the planned 5th Division as replacements. The formations of the Corps were thus kept up to full strength when Allied and enemy formations were depleted. It was this fact, together with their discipline and spirit, that made the Canadians the formidable shock-troops they had become. After the great German offensive of the spring of 1918 had been held, and the Allies passed to the offensive, it was the Canadians who with the Australians started the roll-back of the Germans on August 8 from their deepest penetration at Amiens. Their part here and in the breaching of the Hindenburg defence line added to the weight the Canadian Army had given to Canadian statesmen at Westminster and in the planning of the peace.

This was of the utmost importance to Canada, because the definition of Canada's position in the Empire and the world was involved inextricably with the making of the peace settlement. If the Dominions took no distinct part in making the peace, if the United Kingdom acted publicly for an undifferentiated Empire, the definition of imperial relations at a future Imperial Conference would be of little significance.

Borden, with the support of General J. C. Smuts, Prime Minister of the Union of South Africa, and W. M. Hughes, Prime Minister of Australia, insisted in the Imperial War Cabinet during its sessions in 1918 that the Dominions should be represented at the Peace Conference by their own national delegations.There was resistance, as the Foreign Office felt that such representation would end, as it was to do, the diplomatic unity of the Empire. The Dominions prime ministers had their way, however, Borden insisting that the Canadian expenditure of blood and treasure entitled it to a place like that of Belgium, or any independent small power. As a result, a Canadian delegation, headed by Borden himself, sat in the Peace Conference and assisted in the deliberations of the General Conference and its committees. Borden was even given the serious responsibility of meeting delegations of the contending governments of Russia on the Isle of Prinkipo in the Sea of Marmara, but the conference did not take place. If it had, Canada might have found its representative acting in a mediating role between the Bolshevists and the victor powers, as the Canadian government was in fact doing between the United States and the United Kingdom during the intervention by American, English, Japanese, and Canadian forces in Siberia.

Similarly, Canada won with the other Dominions distinct and individual membership in the League of Nations, which the Conference created in the hope that the League might revise as well as maintain the peace settlement. Thus Canada first emerged in its own right as a nation in the community of nations. But its representatives at Paris, and the supporters of the government in the House of Commons, paid more attention to the new status so fully recognized than to the new duties perhaps too lightly assumed. Only the Liberal opposition voiced some of that North American isolationist opinion which was to defeat ratification of the League in the Senate of the United States.

The entry of Canada into the League did not in fact indicate that the interests of the government or public of Canada had greatly widened. The dispatch of the expeditionary force to Siberia had been done under British pressure. When the troops were recalled, the episode was closed and forgotten. The orientation of

Canada continued to be towards Europe; to the Pacific and Asia, Canada remained comparatively indifferent. Indeed, Canada had wearied of external adventure and precipitate growth in national stature, as was revealed by the widespread Canadian opposition to the appointment of a Canadian minister to Washington, even after the United States had agreed in 1920 to receive one.

Thus Canada's emergence as a member of the League of Nations was not at first accompanied by a development of the staff and apparatus of diplomacy, or the evolution of a Canadian foreign policy. Borden was made a member of the British delegation to the Washington Conference on Naval Disarmament in 1921–22; but this was only an attempt by the government of the United Kingdom to apply Borden's own "adequate voice" theory. In practice it was no advance on Macdonald's status in the negotiation of the Treaty of Washington fifty years earlier.

The development of a distinct Canadian diplomacy had to wait on that redefinition of imperial relations for which the Imperial War Conference had asked in 1917. Such a redefinition was not attempted in the Imperial Conference called in 1921 to prepare for the Washington Conference. There, however, Borden's principle of the adequate voice was given a brilliant demonstration, somewhat to the dismay of the United Kingdom. A major issue of policy was whether the United Kingdom should renew the Anglo-Japanese Treaty of 1902, which was about to end the second decade of its existence. The government of the United Kingdom was disposed to renew. But the renewal was vehemently and successfully opposed by the new Prime Minister of Canada, Arthur Meighen, a brilliant lawyer and fiery debater who had succeeded Borden in 1920. Meighen insisted that the treaty, although it specifically exempted the United States from its operation, was strongly disliked in that country. The goodwill of the United States, he insisted, was of far more value to the countries of the Empire than the Japanese alliance. Certainly it was to Canada, which would have been invaded in any war between the United States and the alliance. He persuaded the Conference; and despite Australian objection, Canada, speaking through Meighen, ensured that there should not be even the appearance of balancing power against the United States.

While Canada was thus becoming an international power of some influence, the government and public at home were struggling with the aftermath of the war. The inflation which had begun in 1917 had rapidly increased in the next three years. Wages had not kept pace with the increase in the cost of living, and the families of industrial and other wage-earners began to suffer. The unrest in the larger cities was evident. The rapid demobilization of the troops in 1919 brought thousands of men back to a labour market which was becoming competitive as war production ceased. The organization of unions went ahead rapidly, as men turned to unionization as a means of keeping up with the mounting cost of living. In the western provinces a radical industrial union took shape, the Canadian One Big Union, or O.B.U.

The O.B.U. sought to establish by strike action the right to collective bargaining, a legal right but one not yet recognized in practice by many Canadian employers. Some O.B.U. leaders were Clydeside radicals; some were affected by the ideas of the Social Democrats who had come with the great migration of the first decade of the century from Germany and Russia. In particular, the leaders of the O.B.U. were attracted to the doctrine of the general strike, which was thought of as a means to rapid establishment of the right to collective bargaining. At a convention in Calgary in 1918 at which the O.B.U. was organized, these and other views, some quite revolutionary, were uttered freely. They were reported to the government by its agents. The Russian Revolution had made all democratic governments sensitive to any indication of socialist subversion. As a result, the Royal North-West Mounted Police suddenly found themselves with the new duty of internal security on their hands, a national duty which was largely to replace the old territorial task of policing the plains of the northwest. The reports of the undercover men put the national government on the alert for any indication of revolutionary intent.

Meantime, strikes began to multiply across the country. In 1918 a strike in the building trade in Winnipeg reached major proportions. The next year, following much wild and some revolutionary talk, two great strikes took place in Vancouver and Winnipeg. That in Vancouver was prolonged and fierce. But the Winnipeg strike was a carefully organized sympathetic strike, and to it the attention of the country was directed for six weeks during May and June. The strike became a trial of strength between the strikers and public authority. Unfortunately for them, the strikers lost the sympathy of the general public almost at once. When at length the strike ended, the original striking unions won the right to bargain collectively. But the national government arrested ten of the leaders of the sympathetic strike. They were tried on charges of sedition and seven were convicted and sentenced to terms of imprisonment. The strike also led to the introduction of Section 98 into the Criminal Code of Canada; by this the government was empowered to proceed against "unlawful associations" without the usual restraints imposed by Canadian law. Thus the Winnipeg strike advanced the cause of collective bargaining and at the same time, owing to reaction against the imprisonment of the strike leaders, which aroused much popular sympathy, and against Section 98, it hastened the coming of political action by Labour. But it also helped condemn the use of the sympathetic strike and placed radical movements in Canada under police surveillance and the threat of legal prosecution.

Both the advances made and the set-backs suffered indicated the drastic temper of the times. In agriculture also, explosive pressures were building up. The war had brought high prices for farm produce, but high costs also, and a mounting indebtedness incurred at high interest rates. The condition was aggravated by the increasing use of machinery. Only continued high prices could keep the industry solvent. By the end of the war the pressures were already severe, and the leaders of organized agriculture were convinced that aid could best be given to the farmer by relieving him of the costs which the national policies of industrial protection and subsidization placed upon agriculture.

Their views were proclaimed in a revised version of the Farmers' Platform of 1916, issued in 1919 under the challenging heading of "The New National Policy." The program of the Canadian Council of Agriculture was, even more than in 1916, a low-tariff one, coupled with reciprocity with the United States, free trade with the United Kingdom, and a large measure of public ownership of utilities, including the railways. The intent of the Council was to furnish ideas to the political parties, with the hope that one or other of them might adopt a large part of the program.

The strategy of the Canadian Council of Agriculture, however, was that of a vanished age. During the eight years since 1911 the farmers' organizations had grown in number, with one in every province, and each organization had grown in membership and in wealth. The United Farmers of Alberta, the Grain Growers' Association of Saskatchewan and the United Farmers of Ontario fully represented agriculture in their provinces and their annual conventions spoke almost without contradiction for the farmers of those provinces. And it was in these provinces that Canadian farmers, feeling that their organizations had done all they could do and that it was not enough to meet the needs of agriculture, determined to enter politics. By political action they would seek to change the conditions under which the farmer worked, with his labour lost to the cities and the new industries, his costs rising, his outlay of cash steadily increasing, with agricultural debt mounting although the individual farmer's credit was often scant and dear. The decision was often to go into politics as "farmers'" candidates, particularly in Ontario and Alberta. The movement began when a farmer candidate won a provincial by-election in the riding of Manitoulin, Ontario, in 1918. The next year saw a farmer win a by-election in Alberta and another the federal seat of Assiniboia. Clearly a new wind was stirring on the prairies and in Ontario.

The national and provincial governments were actively aware of the demanding mood of the voters. The political parties set themselves to appeal to the labour vote and the farm vote. The Liberal party had particular occasion to prepare a new program to lay before the electorate. Early in 1919 Sir Wilfrid Laurier died, troubled in his heart by a party divided and a Quebec alienated. But his death gave his party the opportunity to elect a young leader for the new age and to draft a platform that might attempt to suggest remedies for the current evils. It was an occasion also for an attempt to reunite the party and win back those voters who had supported the Union Government in 1917. The convention held at Ottawa in August, 1919, was a great political achievement. The party was reunited; a platform was adopted, so forward-looking in its proposals that some were not to be implemented for twenty-five years; a leader was chosen, not the veteran Fielding of Nova Scotia, nor the young William Martin of Saskatchewan, but William Lyon Mackenzie King of Ontario. As grandson of the rebel he stirred Grit hearts; as the favourite of Laurier he was acceptable to Quebec. Because he was learned and progressive in outlook he might appeal to the restless farmers, and since he was well known as a labour conciliator, he might appeal to labour without repelling the middle class. Rarely had a candidate been more "available"; never in British history had a choice of leader prepared a party for more years of power. The Liberal party had reason to be pleased with the work of the convention.

The Union Government meanwhile was facing the issues of the day in terms of the responsibilities of office. It had established Canada as an autonomous nation in the Commonwealth and the world. It had also to deal with domestic issues. Of these the chief was the future of the second of the two bankrupt railways, the Grand Trunk and Grand Trunk Pacific. In 1917 the majority, or Drayton-Acworth, report of the royal commission on the railways had recommended that the two systems, the Grand Trunk and the Canadian Northern, be united and operated by an independent commission. The government, having assumed the direction of the Canadian Northern in 1917, brought it together with the government-owned lines in 1918 as the Canadian National Railway. In 1919 the Grand Trunk had to be taken over and a beginning made at creating a system from the hodge-podge of lines to which the government had fallen an embarrassed and reluctant heir.

The great issue was not so much the national ownership of railways as the preservation of the national credit. At the same time it was imperative to be just both to the shareholders who might lose their investments (to the injury of future borrowings, including those for the management of the war debt) and to the taxpayers who were having to assume liability for bonds which were heavily depreciated, when not worthless. It was not an easy task to accomplish under the critical scrutiny of organized farmers and labour in a world in which Socialist parties were taking over government after government and while the business community pressed its own interests privately. The government defended the public interest with success, but the political result was that as conscription had estranged Quebec, so the nationalization of the railways alienated the Canadian Pacific Railway and the financial interests of Montreal from the Union Government and the Conservative party.

In addition to laying the foundation of the future Canadian National Railways, the Union Government carried two other measures of permanent significance. One was the amendment of the Civil Service Act, by which the Civil Service Commission was set up and competitive examinations established as the principal

KC-P

means of recruitment – the foundation of the capable and disinterested national service of the subsequent generation. The other was the Dominion Franchise Act, which created the uniform national franchise carried by Macdonald in 1885 and repealed by the Liberals in 1897. By this act the franchise was also extended to women, as it already had been in a number of provinces. The uniform franchise now belonged to all adults not civilly incapacitated, and Canada had nearly completed the slow and unruffled evolution of its democracy.

These measures carried, and the tasks of the Union Government discharged, Prime Minister Borden felt free to retire, after an achievement comparable with Macdonald's. The parliamentary caucus elected Arthur Meighen to succeed him. Ontario-bred, Meighen had practised law in Portage la Prairie, Manitoba, and entered Parliament in 1908. He soon made a parliamentary reputation as a brilliant and ruthless debater. During the war that reputation grew. An incisive mind and a cold courage made Meighen the man to take those bold risks the cautious and the mediocre shrink from. He had introduced the Military Service Act, and Quebec remembered it against him all his public career. He had carried the Wartime Elections Act and was remembered for it by the voters he had disfranchised. But the proud imperiousness which made him contemptuous of risk made him also a devotee of the well-turned phrase and the apt word, a lover of literature and a connoisseur of style. Too intellectual to be wholly at ease with Canadian politicians, too tense to be gentle with the slow-witted and woolly-minded, he might have fared more pleasantly at Westminster than he did at Ottawa. But in 1920 he rose to the eminence of first place, an eminence that was to prove at once precarious and brief.

The scene the new Prime Minister saw before him was still troubled and unlike that surveyed by either of his predecessors since 1896. A third party was emerging in national politics. In the winter of 1919–20 certain western members began to sit apart and to call themselves "Progressives." They grouped themselves around T. A. Crerar, who had resigned from the Union Government in 1919 because he could not support the government's budget. This, with the growth of political action by the farmers in the provinces, meant that the two old parties would face a three-cornered contest in many a rural riding. There could be no thought of continuing the Union Government after the Liberal convention of 1919. In 1920 the government proclaimed itself a party administration supported by the National Liberal-Conservative party – the Conservative party with the parliamentary Liberal Unionists. When to go to the country would depend on the turn of events.

The course of events proved to be steadily more unfavourable to the government. The United Farmers became a large and separate group in the Manitoba legislature in 1920. The United Farmers of Alberta swept that province in 1921. A similar movement in Saskatchewan was only headed off by a quick dissolution by Premier William Martin, also in 1921. The same year saw farmers emerge as the largest group in the Ontario legislature. This irruption of the farmers into politics was the result of the collapse of agriculture prices in 1920-21. The main cause of this collapse was the abolition of the Wheat Board in 1920. Finally the defeat of a well-known supporter of the Conservative party by a farmer candidate in a national by-election in Medicine Hat in September, 1921, decided the issue. The farmers were in revolt against the old political parties and the old National Policy; they wanted a new national policy to ensure the old significance of agriculture in Canada. Meighen sought a dissolution and went to the country in December.

He went as the defender of the National Policy against the attack of the farmers, not only of the north-west but of Ontario. It was a major attack, for the Progressives hoped to carry seventy-five seats in the prairies and Ontario – seventy-five out of two hundred and thirty-five. It was an attack made in the old language of low tariffs and low railway rates. But it was really a new attack, made by the old agricultural interest on the new industrial order which the National Policy had called into being and the war had inflated. For the agricultural interest was not only in difficult economic circumstances; it was losing its long supremacy. Canada was ceasing to be a nation of farmers and lumberjacks represented in Parliament by lawyers. In the census of 1921 the rural population was 4,436,041, the urban 4,352,442; agricultural production $1,403,686,000, industrial $2,747,926,675. Meighen, then, though he appealed to the memory and inheritance of Macdonald, was speaking for the present and the future. He appealed in crisp, clear-cut terms for the development of a national economy in which industry and agriculture might support one another, in which the Canadian dependence on exports might be lessened and the economic strength of the country consolidated.

The Liberal party under King took no such high or clear-cut line. It campaigned on regional issues; it assailed the government's use of Orders in Council as an arbitrary war-time habit needlessly kept up in peace; it outmanoeuvred the farmers' candidates in Ontario; it won the election. The Progressives took sixty-five seats, not seventy-five – a sectional triumph short of a national victory. The Liberals had a hundred and seventeen members, sixty-five from Quebec; the Conservatives were reduced to a mere fifty, largely from Ontario; there were three independents. Meighen's trenchancy, the farmers' heavy-handed grappling with fundamentals, had not prevailed against the resentment of Quebec, the skill of the Liberal organization, and the obscure star of William Lyon Mackenzie King.

ADDITIONAL READING

ARMSTRONG, E. H. *The Crisis of Quebec.*
BORDEN, ROBERT LAIRD *Memoirs,* Vol. II.
EASTERBROOK, W. T. *Canadian Economic History.*
and AITKEN, H. G. J.
GRAHAM, ROGER *Arthur Meighen: The Door of Opportunity.*
LOGAN, H. A. *The History of Trade-Union Organization in Canada.*
MCNAUGHT, K. W. *A Prophet in Politics.*
MORTON, W. L. *The Progressive Party in Canada.*
STANLEY, G. F. G. *Canada's Soldiers* (1605-1960).

THE REALIZATION OF
THE KINGDOM OF CANADA
[1922-1968]

The rifts in national unity brought into Parliament by the election of 1921 made it clear that the task of national statesmanship was to restore the unity of purpose from which Confederation had sprung. That unity of purpose had to be expressed in new terms and pursued in the light of new social concepts and new forms of external association. In simple terms, the national government had to recover an authority to match the fact of national independence, and exercise that authority to realize social justice and maintain independence in association with the Commonwealth.

It was not an easy task. The work of nation-building for which the national authority had been made so strong was in fact completed. There was no such land rush to supervise and no such need for railways as the pre-war years had seen. The development of the northern frontier was a task for the provinces. The new urban and industrial society, the new motor traffic with all its demands, strengthened provincial rather than national powers and revenues.

Only in the field of imperial and external relations did national development continue towards legislative independence, a process completed by the Statute of Westminster in 1931. By that time the evolution of national autonomy had practically reached its end, but the restoration of national unity at the same date was at best superficial.

It was on a national structure so weakened that the great depression of the 1930's fell. The provinces soon proved financially incapable of meeting the costs of relief which were their constitutional obligation. The national government had to help them all, out of its unlimited power to tax, and had in effect to take over the weaker ones, almost as the United Kingdom had to suspend responsible government in Newfoundland.

Out of these trials, however, came a new sense of national purpose and a new sense of the obligations of the social order. Clearly the powers of the national government must be sufficient and must be used to sustain the national fabric; clearly the nature of modern economic society was such that collective action through the state was needed to ensure the welfare of the individual and the family.

The War of 1939–45 further strengthened the renewed sense of national purpose. Every effort was made to avert a re-enactment of the national division of 1917. Every national party agreed that the powers of the national government should be used to avoid a return, after the war, to the poverty and depression of the thirties. Only from Quebec was there dissent, and in Quebec the provincial government sought the same goals by provincial action. After 1945, therefore, Canada went forward under a greatly strengthened national government. An event symbolic of the new sense of national purpose was the completion of Confederation by the entry of the ancient province of Newfoundland in 1949.

The achievement of full national stature, delayed still for the want of agreement on how to amend the national-provincial section of the British North America Act by Canadian process, nevertheless reached its climax in the proclamation of Queen Elizabeth as Queen of Canada. Canadian nationhood had reached its full historic evolution in the Kingdom of Canada.

In history, however, there is neither pause nor ending. Canada had achieved its national destiny thus far in a world of novel and terrible dangers, not to be met by national strength alone. To meet them Canada had become in 1940, with the setting up of the Permanent Joint Defence Board, the ally of the United States for the defence of America, and in 1949 a member of the North Atlantic Treaty Organization for the defence of that western Europe from which Canada had sprung. The Canadian nation, committed in its origins to association with the French and British empires, was now committed in its national power and monarchical independence to association with its American and Atlantic neighbours for the defence of common values transcending the bounds of nationality.

That such was the destiny of Canada was accepted by the world, and by most of its own citizens. But the road of destiny proved both rough and crooked during the eight years that began in 1960. The causes of this frustration were three, and all were internal to Canada. The first was that the provinces found by experience that they could not accept undiminished the federal power built up by war and post-war prosperity. To fulfil their responsibilities they needed more revenue, perhaps more power. The second was that an important minority of French Canadians had not accepted the concept of Canadian nationality current from 1918 to 1960. To preserve the French language and culture, they asserted, Quebec needed more powers, perhaps even independence. The third was the disarray of the two major parties caused, apparently, by the career of John Diefenbaker, actually by the changing nature of politics in an age of mass democracy, preponderantly urban, and the coming of instant communication by television. Until the political changes were stabilized, there could be no solution of the problems of a federal state, a bilingual country and a constitutional set-up traditional in form but under dynamic pressures. The question in 1968 was, therefore, had such a stabilization begun with the election of a new-style politician, Pierre Elliott Trudeau, as Prime Minister?

CHAPTER 22

The Decline of the National Government
1922-1935

The results of the election of 1921 reproduced in Parliament the racial and sectional cleavages intensified by the war and its aftermath. Those results spelled out in parliamentary terms what the press and politics had made clear since 1919, that the main task of the national government would be the restoration of national unity. The composition of the new House made it equally clear how difficult that task would be. Canada was divided into its component elements. Even the largest of the parliamentary groups, the Liberal party, drew more than half its strength from Quebec and much of the remainder from the Atlantic provinces. There was no national party in Canada, and no group with an effective parliamentary majority.

There was, however, one obvious way of creating a majority and forming an administration with support from all sections. That was to negotiate an alliance of the Progressives with the Liberals. Prime Minister King had addressed himself at once to this undertaking and had initiated talks with T. A. Crerar and with E. C. Drury of Ontario. Both men were willing to enter a ministry with the Liberals, but their followers refused. By no means all the Progressives, and certainly not all of those who had elected them, were agrarian Liberals in revolt against the tariff and the old party system. Some were former Conservatives, and even more were resolute agrarians who had broken finally with the concept of party government to turn to the new idea of government by economic groups. Their desire was to act as the delegates of their constituents and to remain an independent group in Parliament, committed neither to support nor to oppose the administration. Such a position was scarcely in the parliamentary tradition, but it faithfully respected the sentiment of their constituents. Both Crerar and Drury failed to win the Progressive members-elect to adopt any other position. As a result they had to decline to enter the new administration.

Prime Minister King had then no choice but to form a wholly Liberal cabinet. The outcome of the Progressive refusal was unfortunate. Not only was the new government less national than it might have been with Progressive support and

Progressive members, even though a minister was found for every province; it was also less liberal, for while the alleged conservatism of certain of its members, such as Sir Lomer Gouin, was much exaggerated, nearly all the Cabinet, with the exception of the Prime Minister, were men of a more conservative cast of opinion than were the leading Progressives. The Progressives, moreover, having refused to commit themselves to the support of the Cabinet, also declined the responsibilities of official opposition. They would only undertake to vote for "good" legislation, and to oppose "bad." In consequence, the Conservatives under Arthur Meighen became the Opposition. Yet the Cabinet, commanding only half the House, was in fact dependent on Progressive support, and thus some communication had to be kept up with the leaders of the group. The result on the one hand was growing suspicion between the more extreme Progressives and their leader, T. A. Crerar, and on the other, weak and irresolute government. The preservation of the life of the administration and the restoration of national unity necessarily took precedence over the claims of reform legislation and of a vigorous national policy.

Not the least serious manifestation of the state of national unity in Canada after 1921 was the new temper of the *nationaliste* movement in Quebec. The leadership of Bourassa, however fiery, had never challenged that Anglo-French compact which was the foundation of Canada. But Bourassa was now withdrawing from the leadership of the nationalists, and it was passing into the hands of intellectuals prepared to push nationalist principles to the limit. The Reverend Lionel Groulx had, like Garneau, turned to history to find the origins and the justification of nationalism. His dignified but unyielding statement of the historical case for French national existence in Canada was turned by some of his youthful disciples into advocacy of a Laurentian republic, French, clerical, and independent. But the main endeavour of the later nationalists was to assert French equality in law and language throughout Canada, by the co-equal use of French on stamps and banknotes, for example, with the goal of a Canada completely bilingual. Once more the cultural conflict flared, with the vital difference that in 1921 there was no countering English clamour. The rapid development of Canadian nationhood in the new concept of Commonwealth prevented that calamity. And if Laurier had gone, his sense of Canadian destiny and his political courage had been transmitted to Quebec's new Liberal leader, the gigantic and cheerily indomitable Ernest Lapointe, the ally and counsellor of Mackenzie King for the next quarter-century.

Not unnaturally in such circumstances, the new administration achieved most, and won most distinction, in external affairs. The French-Canadian Liberals and the Progressives could be united by a policy of nationalist independence and practical isolation in Commonwealth and external affairs. The King government was given an opportunity to make an isolationist and nationalist stand in its first year of office. The new Turkey of Mustapha Kemal had defied the Treaty of Sèvres, by which Greece was to receive the Ionian coast, and by which an international régime was to control the Straits. The Greeks were driven from Asia; and at Chanak, Turkish troops confronted the British forces which were occupying a zone south of the Dardanelles. War between the United Kingdom and Turkey seemed imminent, and the Colonial Secretary, Winston Churchill, warned Turkey publicly, without having consulted the Commonwealth governments, that it would be war with all the Commonwealth nations. This seeming attempt to commit Canada to war without the agreement of its government aroused much resentment in Canada. It thus enabled King to score a resounding success by a flat and public refusal to be committed to any measure of Commonwealth co-operation except after consultation and by decision of the Canadian government or Parliament.

This negative and isolationist attitude was popular throughout the remainder of the life of the government. In the Imperial Conference of 1923, King stuck resolutely to the same position, powerfully reinforced by the presence of the great Liberal editor, J. W. Dafoe, and by the special adviser to the Canadian delegation and later Deputy Minister of Exernal Affairs, O. D. Skelton. The idea of "an adequate voice" and consultation for co-operation was in effect killed in this important conference. Canada thus paved the way for the more extreme nationalism of the Union of South Africa and the new Irish Free State, which could only lead to the complete dissolution of the legislative supremacy of the imperial parliament and with it the diplomatic unity of the Empire. In the latter connection, the negotiating and signing of the Halibut Fisheries Treaty with the United States in 1923 without any representative of the United Kingdom taking part at any stage was a clear assertion of the diplomatic autonomy of Canada.

The same spirit of isolation governed Canada's participation in the work of the League of Nations. Not only did Canada oppose plans for strengthening the means of collective security, such as the Draft Treaty of Mutual Assistance and the Geneva Protocol in 1923 and 1924, and serve notice it would not be a party to the guarantees of the Locarno Pact in 1925; it also attempted by resolution in the League assembly to make the obligation under Article X of the Covenant, that of aiding a member of the League when attacked, dependent on geographical neighbourhood. The resolution – "the Canadian resolution" – never passed the Assembly, but it became operative in spirit after 1924 and governed the interpretation of the Article. Canada thus withdrew into North American isolation almost as effectively as the United States; and in consequence of these withdrawals the League, which had been intended as the means of revising an imperfect peace settlement, became instead the instrument by which the imperfections were maintained.

Canada in fact, during these years, was trying to go back to the world before 1914. The government had returned the army to its pre-war standing and had only just maintained the navy and the infant air force. The country was pre-occupied with its domestic divisions and with endeavours to resume the great material development it had known in the first decade of the century. National politics continued to revolve around the ancient issues of tariff and railway policy, even while signs were multiplying that new issues were rising to dominance. The exhaustion and shock left by the war were nowhere more evident than in the sterility and anachronistic quality of the national politics of the decade. An age had collapsed in 1917, but men still lived amidst its ruins, and their first effort was to rebuild an edifice the very bricks of which dissolved in their fumbling hands. The new industrial age had brought with it a new collectivism, neither that which the Liberal had feared nor that which the Socialist had advocated, and the principles of the old individualistic society of private enterprise and free trade no longer made full contact with social and economic reality. But few in Canada, and no politician, unless the Prime Minister himself, saw that this was so.

National politics were therefore almost wholly concerned with issues that were pre-1914 in origin or in spirit. One of these was the tariff. Nominally the low-tariff party, the Liberals might have been expected to respond to the Progressive pressure for a considerable reduction in the budget of 1922. But the Minister of Finance was that W. S. Fielding who had continued and developed the National Policy after 1897, and the existing tariff was largely the work of his hands. Moreover, the heavy burden of the war debt meant that few reductions could be contemplated as yet in the revenue items of the tariff. The Progressives now faced the fact that if they voted with the Conservatives to defeat the government on the tariff, the result would be to make Meighen, the avowed protectionist, Prime Minister, and bring on another election. That prospect they could not face, and thus the Progressives largely failed in their most important aim, although considerable reductions were made in 1924 and 1925 when Fielding had retired and government revenues had risen with renewed prosperity. The tariff remained substantially unchanged, despite the revolt of the farmers against it.

Only a national movement, it was evident, could have altered the tariff. The Progressives had more success in matters of railway policy, because in the regulation of the railways they found more support from other sections of the country than they did in tariff matters. The new Canadian National Railways was still critically viewed by financial and business interests, both as an experiment in public ownership and as a charge, in its annual deficits, on the national revenues. To have it fail, and allow its component lines to be sold, seemed to many both sound business and good national policy. The Progressives, however, were devoted to the principle of public ownership and saw the maintenance of the Canadian National Railways as a means of rate regulation. In this they had much support from those with vested interests, such as railway workers, in the many constituencies in which the national lines operated. The Canadian National was therefore maintained and its organization was entrusted to Sir Henry Thornton, an able American railway man, who set out to give the Canadian National the efficiency of a privately operated system, and who had it earning surpluses in the prosperous years of the late twenties.

On the inflamed issue of the restoration of Crowsnest Pass rates, the Progressives had much more trouble and much less success. The rates had been suspended by Order in Council in 1918 to meet the war-time inflation, and the suspension continued until 1922. Then the suspension was renewed until 1924, except that the Progressives and western Liberals won the restoration of the rates on grain and flour moving east. The railways then sought the renewed suspension of all the rates, and again, after a bitter struggle, Parliament by statute in 1925 applied the rates to grain and flour moving east, and in 1926 to the same commodities moving west to the Pacific ports. Railway regulation, like the tariff, was thus maintained by sectional political pressures as a complex of sectional compromises. But in neither tariffs nor railway regulation had any new national policy been introduced; only the basic old one had been maintained.

Among the more advanced Progressives, however, new ideas were emerging. Two members of the "Ginger Group," as it was dubbed, were labour politicians returned to Parliament as a result of the Winnipeg strike and the general industrial unrest of the post-war years. Chief of these was J. S. Woodsworth, a former Methodist minister, who had joined the labour movement in Vancouver and Winnipeg. A fervent idealist in the old Methodist tradition, a social reformer of a prophetic more than a political bent, Woodsworth entered politics in a heroic endeavour to make society more humane. His immediate and special causes were the repeal of the discriminatory Section 98, introduced into the Criminal Code at the time of the Winnipeg strike as a weapon of intimidation against labour organization, and the provision of old-age pensions. But his principal work was a work of the spirit. More than any other Canadian public man, he helped transform Canadian politics from the politics of special and sectional interests to the politics of collective concern for the welfare of the individual in a society collectively organized.

The agrarian members of the Ginger Group, mostly from Alberta, shared his spirit, but some of them, and the Calgary Progressive, William Irvine, were also influenced by monetary theories brought by Populist Americans into Alberta, and were attracted by the new doctrine of Social Credit advocated by a British engineer, Major C. H. Douglas. Here they were groping for a new concept, that of the control of monetary policy, not by the allegedly automatic working of the gold standard and orthodox banking practice, but by national institutions and national policy. Their heterodox and pre-Keynesian ideas were spread on the public records in hearings before the Standing Committee on Banking in 1923, and were portents, little appreciated at the time, of a major change in monetary policy in the future.

Another change that received little notice at the time was the steady growth in the power and prestige of the provincial governments. This came in part from the fact that the new mining economy and, to a degree, the new manufacturing industries were based on the development of provincial resources with provincial encouragement. Hydro-electric energy, the wood-pulp and paper industry, the precious and base metal mines, were all provincial concerns. In addition, the multiplying use of the automobile, with the accompanying demand for improved roads and the new sources of revenue in licences and gasoline taxes, came under provincial jurisdiction and required provincial action. But the most important factor was the transfer of power from the national government to the provincial governments by a long series of decisions of the Judicial Committee of the Privy Council. This had begun with *Hodge* v. *the Queen* in 1883 and culminated in *Toronto Electric Commissioners* v. *Snider* in 1925. The general effect of the decisions was to place upon the provinces responsibility for the enactment and administration of a great new corpus of law, comprising labour, welfare, and social security legislation, which was coming into being in response to the needs of the industrialized economy and of an urbanized society. The old individualistic social order of nineteenth-century agriculture and of the early industrial revolution, with its principles of individual responsibility and governmental laissez-faire, which still seemed to be the inspiration of political action at Ottawa, was rapidly giving way in the provinces to an increasing measure of governmental intervention in economic and personal life and a rapidly growing acceptance of the ideal of a basic social welfare achieved by collective action.

The one thing the Judicial Committee failed to do in its fundamental remaking of the Canadian constitution was to confer on the provinces financial powers commensurate with their legislative responsibilities. The taxing power of the national government remained unlimited, that of the provinces confined to direct taxation. This situation was relieved only by the use of income, succession, and corporate taxation, itself a major element of the new order, and by the taxation of motor vehicles and motor fuel. But the time might well come when the financial resources of the provinces would be inadequate for the discharge of their ever-increasing responsibilities.

It was, however, in Ontario, Quebec, and British Columbia that these developments were most evident. The Atlantic and prairie provinces were moving slowly into the new order, but on the whole the former were still living in the post-Confederation depression and the latter in the "boom" mentality of settlement. The more the central provinces and British Columbia went ahead, the greater became the sectional differences between them and the Atlantic and prairie provinces. Because the prairie provinces had benefited by the vigorous national policies of the Laurier régime, it was to the national government that they turned for aid. Neither they nor the Atlantic provinces were inclined to look to the development of local resources by local means for the growth of prosperity. Neither realized that the national government, for the time being at least, was powerless to initiate again such policies as had accompanied the great development of the first decade of the century. Still less did either realize that the external conditions which had favoured those policies were passing away.

The Progressive revolt was of course the major effort of the agrarian west to achieve national policies which would aid the western grain-grower. But the prairie provinces also sought to encourage a resumption of the immigration and land settlement which had accompanied the prosperity of the past. In the middle and late twenties both were resumed in volume reminiscent of that before 1912; the remaining lands of the prairies were taken up, and the frontier pushed farther northward than before. But the limits of land settlement and agricultural development, as then practised, had almost been reached, although only a bold man would have dared to say so, and no one would have believed him in a society still devoted to the mystique of the boom.

The three prairie provinces were in fact at these very times striving to bring two chief elements of the old colonial and settlement régime to an end. All three steadily pressed Ottawa to surrender the "natural resources," that is, the remaining Crown lands of the provinces, with compensation for the alienation of those granted by the national government. Such a surrender would mean that the purposes of the Dominion had been fulfilled and that the homestead era of land settlement had ended. After various delays, a royal commission was appointed to assess the compensation due, and in 1930 the Crown lands were transferred to the prairie provinces. The transfer marked the end of the constitutional inferiority of the provinces created from the national territory. It marked also the ending, as it happened, of the period of western expansion and settlemen which had begun in 1870. It did little, however, to prepare the provinces to adjust their agrarian economies to the changed conditions of the world of 1930.

In the Atlantic provinces the same basic conditions of a hinterland area adversely affected by the national tariff policy and lack of capital for the development of local resources were coupled with the absence of northern frontiers for provincial development. Moreover, emigration rather than immigration had for two generations been the rule, and this loss of population both reflected and augmented the depression of the region. The Progressive movement had penetrated to the farmers of the Maritimes and laid the foundation of some radical discontent, but the Maritimers refrained from protest or talk of secession as in the past. They generally put their faith in the Liberal party at this period and followed the veteran Fielding and the young J. L. Ralston in seeking relief by pressure on that party. In 1926 they were rewarded by the appointment of a royal commission on Maritime claims, which recommended and obtained a reduction of twenty per cent in freight rates in the region. Its other recommendations for the encouragement of industrial growth in the Atlantic provinces were less easy to apply and did not lend themselves to national legislation.

The depressed condition of the Atlantic provinces contrasted with a general economic recovery in the rest of the country, even in the prairie provinces. Much of the recovery consisted of a partial restoration of the old wheat economy which had underlain the Laurier boom. By 1923 wheat prices were recovering on the free market and the western farmers began to reduce their indebtedness and to deal with the problems of plant rust, the concentration on wheat farming, and the rising overhead costs of an ever more mechanized industry. But their experience with the stable prices attributed to the Wheat Board had implanted an abiding distrust of the free market. When the farmers' organizations failed in their attempts to have the Board continued, agrarian leaders, other than those of the United Grain Growers' Grain Company and the Saskatchewan Co-operative Elevators, turned to the idea of pooling, or co-operatively selling, the wheat crop as a means of levelling the seasonal fluctuations of wheat prices. In 1923 and 1924 an agitation for the formation of pools swept the prairies, and by 1926 pools were established in all three provinces with a Central Selling Agency handling the great bulk of the western wheat crop. The movement was sustained during the first years of organization, not only by the enthusiasm which had gone into the election of Progressive candidates in 1921 but also by improved prices and yields. It seemed that the wheat economy had "come back" organized co-operatively. More important, perhaps, was the fact that a majority of western farmers had broken with the principles of economic liberalism and had devoted themselves to the principles of co-operative marketing, to be aided, if necessary, by state intervention in the marketing process.

The recovery of the wheat economy was accompanied by a revival of immigration. British and European immigrants once more passed in annual crowds through the immigration halls of Winnipeg and spread out over the wheatlands. The British were often aided by the Empire Settlement scheme, the Europeans often driven by the political consequences of the war and the peace settlement. As early as 1928 the annual immigration had risen to 166,783. But the land and the prairies were no longer the sole recipients of the new population; some went direct to the cities, and many simply replaced older settlers who were removing to the cities. A more efficient and less prosperous agriculture was ceasing to be the great absorber of the new Canadian.

With immigration, railway construction was renewed. No more main lines were attempted; there was indeed some elimination of duplication of main lines within the Canadian National system and some reduction of unprofitable competition between the Canadian Pacific and the Canadian National. But new farmlands demanded a considerable increase in branch lines, and public insistence on railway service, competitive if possible, prevented anything like a thoroughgoing rationalization of the lines inherited from the Laurier boom. The greatest change in wheat transport in these years, however, was the beginning of the movement of grain to Vancouver for shipment by the Panama Canal, when the Crowsnest Rates were made to apply to westbound grain and flour in 1926.

The one major railway development projected was the resumption of the Hudson Bay Railway. Construction had been stopped during the war, but northern Saskatchewan and Manitoba began an agitation for its completion in 1921. The project was a purely sectional one and could be advanced only by sectional pressure. The need of both national parties to win western seats led to its being promised by both parties, and after the election of 1926 construction was once more taken in hand. After new surveys had been made, the terminus was changed from Port Nelson to Churchill, and the railway reached that port in 1930. The export of grain began in 1931, but the short shipping season and the lack of inbound cargo resulted in disappointment for the supporters of the railway. The new challenge by the Bay route to that of the St. Lawrence was to remain for many years a slight and ineffectual one.

The advance to the Bay, though intended as a new outlet for the wheat economy, was in fact rather another stage in northern development. The line ran through the mineral belt of northern Manitoba, and its inception had led to mineral discoveries at Flin Flon and Sherridon, which began to be developed in the late twenties. While here again progress was slow, the groundwork had been done for a new phase of growth and for a major alteration in the economy of the prairie provinces. This had begun elsewhere with oil strikes in the Turner Valley of southern Alberta and at Fort Norman on the Mackenzie. Minerals and oil would broaden the prairie economy and some day carry the frontier northward, when means of transport permitted. New means were already being rapidly developed in the sled trains drawn by caterpillar tractors (the "cat-swings") over winter roads, and above all in the development of "bush flying." Daring pilots, and the use of pontoons for summer and skis for winter landing and take-off on the lakes of the Shield, made the airplane a means of exploration, survey and transport which suddenly laid the remoter north open to the prospector and the miner.

The north now began to enter Canadian life as never before; the realm of the fur trader and the explorer was becoming an area of scientific mapping, systematic exploration, and business calculation. The grim inheritance of the arctic explorers began to reveal possibilities undreamt of. Most unfortunately the prophet of this new arctic age and Canadian northern destiny, Vilhjalmur Stefansson, became embroiled in a dispute with former associates on his explorations in the Canadian Arctic. The survivors of the *Karluk* had landed on Wrangel Island off the coast of Siberia, and Stefansson during a rescue operation in 1921 claimed the island for Canada, a claim later withdrawn. In 1922 the publication of his *The Friendly Arctic* brought into the open resentments and doubts which ended his influence on northern affairs at Ottawa. And an attempt by the Hudson's Bay Company to operate a reindeer ranch in Baffin Island under

Stefansson's guidance failed, partly through the insubordination of those in charge, partly because Stefansson's advice was disregarded. Only personal direction might have made a success of this daring venture, and Stefansson was engaged elsewhere. As a result, the national interest in the Arctic which had led to the great expeditions from 1912 to 1922 came to an end, and left a residue of bitterness and distrust which injured northern development for many years.

It was not, then, by expansion of the wheat economy or the far northern frontier that Canada regained prosperity in the mid twenties, but by the growth of the new industries of the nearer north, and of manufacturing. In Quebec, Ontario, and British Columbia, forest industries boomed. The pulp and paper industry, devoted to supplying newsprint to the insatiable American market, made the northern spruce forest a source of new and rapidly increasing wealth. With its growth went a corresponding development of hydro-electric energy. At the same time the mineral strikes of the pre-1914 years developed into the great northern goldfields of Porcupine and Kirkland Lake, while Sudbury's nickel fed an ever growing demand from the new metallurgy. Canada became again, as in the days of the Klondike, one of the world's leading producers of gold, gold won from the hard-rock mines of the Shield. And in British Columbia the exploitation of mineral deposits and of the timber stands of the Pacific slope was rapidly advancing that province from its former role of a distant and picturesque cousin to that of a major and intimate member of the Canadian family. The far west of Alberta and British Columbia began to appear as one of the great development areas, and the relative decline of the western wheat economy, as well as the effect of the Panama Canal in turning freight away from the railways through Winnipeg to ocean shipping, was marked by Vancouver's surpassing Winnipeg in population by 1931.

The growth of manufacturing in the central provinces was, however, the central factor in the revived prosperity. The agriculture of Quebec and Ontario might still greatly exceed that of the west in total value; the old lines of development might still continue, as in the construction of the new Welland Ship Canal, completed in 1927 to a depth of twenty-seven feet. But it was the expansion of old industries and the addition of new, such as the automobile assembly plants at Windsor and Oshawa, that characterized the prosperity of the twenties. The economy of central Canada was now decisively industrial and urban. By 1928 the total net value of Canadian manufacturing was $1,819,046,025, of which $562,581,419 was produced in Quebec and $915,222,879 in Ontario. And Montreal held 818,577 of Quebec's population of 2,874,255 in 1931; Toronto, 631,207 of Ontario's 3,431,684 in the same year. The Progressive revolt of 1921 had been the last attempt of the old agrarian and primary economy to control national policy, and it had failed, and failed permanently. The economy of the great staples which had made Canada, and which still largely sustained it, was being challenged for supremacy by the rise of the manufacturing industry.

The consequences of the political agrarian revolt of 1921, however, troubled the course of Canadian politics until the general election of 1926. The weak and divided parliament elected in 1921 sustained the King administration until 1925, but the ministry was buffeted between the relative conservatism of its supporters, the sectional pressure of the Progressives, and the uncompromising conservatism of the Opposition led by Arthur Meighen. While the retirement of Fielding and Gouin made it possible to bring younger and more liberal men into the Cabinet, no great change in its character resulted for want of men of political ability and, with the exception of Vincent Massey, of personal distinction. The more intellectual and advanced quality of the political and social thought of the Prime Minister himself, and of the Liberal platform of 1919, had to be subordinated to the need to preserve the unity of the nation and to avoid contentious issues. The one measure of genuine liberal quality was the Prime Minister's own, the Industrial Combines Investigation Act. With its emphasis on competition and on the operation of public opinion rather than on regulation, it was liberal but anachronistic in an age in which the old liberal economy was rapidly giving way to one governed by combination, co-operation, and state regulation.

Nor can it be suggested that the Opposition was more aware of the trends of the age. Splendid parliamentarian as he was, Meighen was neither a solid thinker nor an acute gatherer of other men's thought. The Conservative party was caught in the dilemma of its own economic nationalism and its basic imperial sentiment, for which the only reconciliation seemed to be imperial solidarity and imperial preference. But imperial solidarity in any form would continue to keep Quebec Liberal, and imperial preference would expose the industries of central Canada to British competition. From this dilemma Meighen found no escape; nor was he able to exploit the contrary dilemma of the Liberals, which was that their political nationalism, necessary to hold Quebec, weakened the British counterpoise to American influence and so prepared a threat to Canadian nationhood in both its political and its economic aspects.

The one major political change which had occurred by 1925 was the decline of the Progressive movement. The United Grain Growers had withdrawn their financial support of the western Progressives in 1922, and Crerar withdrew from the leadership at the same time. The organization of the Wheat Pools had drawn off the energy and the funds which might have supported farmers' candidates in another election. The farmers' minority government in Ontario had collapsed in 1923 and been replaced by a Conservative administration under Howard Ferguson. Saskatchewan had remained stoutly Liberal under the young and able Charles Dunning. In Alberta the U.F.A. government went on from strength to strength under Premier J. E. Brownlee, and in Manitoba the farmers' government of John Bracken was slowly consolidating itself. In these two provinces the national Progressive candidates would therefore receive help from the provincial régimes, but the result was to stress the difference between the "group government" ideology of the Alberta Progressives and the more conventional outlook of those of Manitoba and Saskatchewan.

Both Liberals and Conservatives might therefore hope to regain some support in the west. It was imperative that the Liberals should, for their concessions to the Progressives on the tariff and freight rates, and their political nationalism, had injured their prospects in Ontario. But it was equally imperative that the Conservatives re-enter the solid Quebec of 1921 if they were to realize the possibility of victory which four years of Liberal weakness had given them. There was, however, scant hope of any gain; and when the election campaign began, Meighen did not venture into the province. No new issue enlivened the election; the parties stoutly threshed the old straw of many previous campaigns, with the tariff and railway rates in all their sectional implications the principal points of controversy.

The electoral results were even more disastrous than those of 1921. The Conservative party had indeed come back from the humiliation of 1921; it outnumbered the Liberals 116–101 in a House of 245, but it had failed to win a majority. Only four Conservatives were elected in Quebec, to sixty Liberals and one Independent. The Liberals were not only defeated; the majority of the English members of the Cabinet, including the Prime Minister himself, had failed to carry their seats. Only twenty-four Progressives had been returned, but these, ironically, held the balance of power far more decisively than the sixty-five of 1921 had done. The four years since 1921 had failed to restore national unity, so far as that was reflected by the national political parties.

Canadian politics now entered on a crisis of nine months' duration. King, without a seat or a majority in the Commons, might have been expected to resign. But neither had Meighen a majority, and the Progressives, if they would support the Liberals rather than the Conservatives, might give King one. They preferred King because of Meighen's uncompromising stand on the protective tariff; and Meighen still had the unrelenting hostility of Quebec to face.

This was shown when, in an endeavour to mollify the French voters and remove their fear that a Conservative government would automatically take Canada into war along with Britain, Meighen in a speech made at Hamilton during a by-election in Bagot, Quebec, explained how the Borden cabinet had considered holding a general election before declaring war in 1914. He now declared that, in his opinion, before Canada went to war, a general election should be held. Quebec, however, was not impressed by this glimpse of Tory democracy, and imperial sentiment in Ontario was greatly angered.

By undertaking to support a list of Progressive measures early in 1926, therefore, King was able to retain office in face of an opponent as embarrassed as himself. Finding a new seat in Prince Albert, he faced Parliament and his ministry was upheld by the House.

King might then have paid at least part of the price of Progressive support and remained in office until a favourable opportunity occurred of going to the country, had not charges been made that serious corruption was present in the Customs service. American prohibition and the temptations of protective tariffs along the international boundary had indeed led to laxity, although its extent was never to be proved nor responsibility for it fixed. But the name of the responsible minister, Jacques Bureau, was involved, and the fact drew attention to the Liberal reliance on support from a province in which political morals were notoriously lax, and from which the only two strong and irreproachable ministers were Ernest Lapointe and Rodolphe Lemieux. When a Special Committee began to uncover the scandal in June, the Progressives, earnest champions of political rectitude and committed only to the support of particular measures, began to talk of joining with the Conservatives in a vote of censure of the administration. King's position in Parliament was becoming impossible by June 1926.

In this situation he approached the Governor General, Lord Byng of Vimy, and advised a dissolution. It was the desperate act of a desperate man, but the alternative was resignation and the exploitation of the scandal by the Conservatives. Moreover, King could argue that Meighen possessed a majority no more than King himself, and that there were recent precedents in the United Kingdom for the grant of a dissolution to a minority government. More important was the fact that by his request King revealed that he viewed the electorate, not Parliament, as the arbiter of the fate of governments and prime ministers. This was the final development in Canadian politics of the principle of plebiscitary sovereignty which Lord Bryce and the reckless Conservatives of the United Kingdom had introduced into British political terminology, and to which even the traditional Laurier and the Conservative Thompson had casually subscribed.

The Governor General, however, demurred at granting a dissolution to a ministry to which a possible alternative existed and therefore a means by which the business of the session might be completed. He urged that it was his duty first to try to find another prime minister who might be supported in Parliament. King then suggested that the Governor General should seek advice on the precedents from the Colonial Office. Byng properly declined to do so, refused the dissolution, and called on Meighen to form a ministry.

Meighen would probably have been well advised to decline, but felt, as a responsible statesman, bound to accept the commission and to attempt to finish the business of the session. He obtained the promise of Progressive support in doing so, but at once encountered the difficulty that, under the law of the day, he and other members of the Cabinet would have to vacate their seats on accepting office, thus reducing the voting power of the party and leaving the government benches leaderless. Meighen met this situation by a legal device faintly reminiscent of the double shuffle of 1858. He himself was sworn of the Privy

Council, thus forfeiting his seat, but his colleagues took office only as acting ministers. As such they were not disqualified from sitting, and it was this "shadow cabinet," as it was promptly dubbed by the furious Liberal opposition and press, that met the House.

Such was the character of the constitutional crisis of 1926. It turned on two points. One was whether the Governor General was justified in refusing King a dissolution in the existing circumstances. There can be little question but that he was. The precedents supported it, all except the most recent, none of which included a pending vote of censure; and the Governor General had found a prime minister who formed a ministry which was supported by the House. The second point was the constitutionality of the acting Meighen cabinet. Its formation had in fact been a legal but not a constitutional proceeding, defensible only – and only defended – as an expedient for winding up the business of the session.

As an expedient, however, it was unfortunate. The Liberal attacks on the constitutionality of the acting ministry detached Progressive votes from the government. King, caution itself on the government benches, showed himself a great parliamentary fighter in opposition, and Lapointe was a formidable companion in attack. While they assailed the ministry, the lonely Meighen sat helpless in the gallery. In a division on the constitutionality of the ministry, the government was defeated by one Progressive vote, cast in inadvertence but ruled as binding by the Speaker. The Governor General then granted Meighen, as he had no choice but to do, the dissolution he had denied to King.

The general election which followed turned not so much on the customs scandal or the constitutional issue, despite its appeal to nationalists, as on the tariff and on Meighen's speech during the Bagot by-election. British sentiment in Ontario had been deeply offended by the latter and Quebec even more alienated by Meighen's attempts to undo the harm it had done. The prospect of a Conservative victory and an undoing of the Liberal tariff-reduction swung western Progressives in Manitoba and Saskatchewan, though not in Alberta, either back to the Liberal party or to alliance with it as Liberal-Progressives. The Conservatives and Meighen, who fought with all his unconvincing brilliance, went down to defeat. The Liberal party won a representation of a hundred and eighteen, which with eleven Liberal Progressives gave it a majority over its opponents, and brought to its leadership new talents in C. A. Dunning, late premier of Saskatchewan, and J. L. Ralston of Nova Scotia. The Conservatives numbered ninety-one. The Progressives were reduced to a splinter group of eight from Alberta, with Miss Agnes Macphail from Ontario to make nine. The election did nothing to resolve the basic divisions of Canadian society, but it did restore a national majority in Parliament drawn from all sections of the country. In a measure, national unity had been regained.

The victory was interpreted by Mackenzie King, once more Prime Minister, as a victory for political nationalism in Canada. And in 1926 the ending of prohibition of appeals in criminal cases to the Judicial Committee of the Privy Council still further irritated Canadian sentiment. It was brought about by the decision of the Judicial Committee in the case of *Nadan* v. *Rex*. The grounds of the decision were that the Canadian act of 1888 prohibiting such appeals was repugnant to the imperial Colonial Laws Validity Act of 1865 and also that it implied an extra-territorial jurisdiction which the Parliament of Canada did not possess. King at once repaired to the Commonwealth Conference of 1926, where the strong lead of Canada, supported by South Africa and the Irish Free State, made explicit and formal the concept of the Commonwealth as a free association of autonomous nations united by a common allegiance to the Crown and a common constitutional heritage. A committee was set up to prepare for the next conference recommendations which would remove the last legal discrepancies between the new status of the Dominions and the remaining vestiges of their legislative subordination to the Parliament of the United Kingdom. The full realization of the implications of the responsible government granted Canada and Nova Scotia in 1848 was at last to be accomplished, and the inevitable goal of independence under the Crown attained.

But it was not yet to be fully attained by Canada. The tradition of provincial rights was still too vigorous, and the wounds to national unity inflicted by the execution of Riel and the cultural conflict which ensued, and by the election of 1917, were still too fresh, for the last step to full nationhood to be taken. That was the amendment of the constitution of Canada by a Canadian process without reference to Westminster. When in 1927, in the sixtieth year of Confederation, a Dominion-Provincial Conference was held, the demands of the Atlantic and western provinces for increased grants from the national treasury to meet their growing responsibilities revealed the need for amendment to bring the powers and responsibilities of the national and provincial governments into balance. But proposals for a Canadian process of amendment were resolutely blocked by the central provinces – by the Liberal premier of Quebec, L. A. Taschereau, and not less resolutely by the Conservative premier of Ontario, Howard Ferguson. The special rights of Quebec were not to be put at the disposition of a national majority, nor did prosperous Ontario feel the disparity between powers and revenues on one hand, and responsibilities on the other, which even in good times was beginning to rack the weaker provinces. And to defend their position the central provinces advanced the theory that Confederation had been a compact among the provinces – a theory to which the language of the Fathers had apparently given support. Full national stature was not to be achieved until national unity had been fully accomplished.

At the time, however, Canada seemed once more to have resumed the confident and vigorous stride of the days before 1914. The Hudson Bay Railway drove forward. The new Welland Ship Canal carried lake freighters down past Niagara. The Diamond Jubilee of Confederation was celebrated with speech and pageantry from sea to sea, in state at Ottawa and with simple ceremony in the villages of the forests and the prairies, the outports and the tank towns. A sense of perils survived informed the national thanksgiving, and little sense of perils to come clouded the occasion.

Some sense of accomplishment was warranted. Not only did the great political structure of Confederation stand after two generations of strain. Within its shelter an articulate national life was expanding. In every field of literature Canadians had found a voice. The poetry of Duncan Campbell Scott and Bliss Carman exhibited an authentic and original beauty, if minor still in key. In Quebec there was for the moment, and uncharacteristically, no outstanding craftsman; the one novel of note, *Maria Chapdelaine*, was by Louis Hémon, a Frenchman. Canadian scholarship had produced in Adam Shortt, H. P. Biggar, O. D. Skelton, John Watson, Thomas Chapais, Lorne Pierce, G. M. Wrong, to mention a few among many, considerable names and durable reputations. In science Sir William Osler still stood for what Canada might send forth, and Frederick Banting and C. H. Best for what might be accomplished in Canadian laboratories. With them may be named William and Charles Saunders, Reginald Buller, and Diamond Jenness. Among journalists J. W. Dafoe towered, carrying his craft to the peak of achievement in Canada, and among pamphleteers Henri Bourassa and J. S. Ewart stood pre-eminent.

In art, the achievement was not less striking. In central Canada the Group of Seven, with a bold impressionism, had brought the Precambrian north into Canadian consciousness and by their paintings made of its barren solitude an imagery of beauty and strength. In British Columbia, Emily Carr, in the loneliness of genius, was performing a similar task in reducing the sombre Pacific forest to human terms. In this pioneering of the spirit the painters achieved the first great conquest by the arts in Canada, in that they made Canadian experience an idiomatic part of universal experience. They alone had broken out from the provincial barriers of colonial existence, but where they had advanced others might follow.

One man indeed did, in the rarest and most universal form of communication, humour. Stephen Leacock made the life of Orillia, Ontario, a focus of laughter to rival Hannibal, Missouri, and sounded that note of satirical hilarity which welled up not only from his own genius but from the sharp, dour, puritanical consciousness of the whole Canadian people, French and English. No one spoke the Canadian idiom more clearly than Leacock, and none did more to make expressive the casual utterance of a people tight-lipped and not yet mature.

Nothing perhaps was more significant of change in the Canadian mind and ethos in these years than the manner in which religion faded out of public life. Since the cultural conflict had closed at the end of the century, religion and politics had largely parted company in English Canada. Even in Quebec the *nationalistes* seemed to become more secular and less clerical. The churches had indeed to face other problems: the pervasion of popular belief by the scientific view of the world and the nature of man, especially in terms of the hypothesis of evolution; the rapid alteration of the social order as the urban and industrial revolution proceeded, with all its effects on the family and its creation of a rootless society; the moral shock of the First World War. Social change and private doubts replaced the old stability and the old convictions.

The one major change in denominational history, in part a response to the growth of the country and the inability of small or declining rural communities to support an indefinite number of churches, was the union in 1925 of the Methodist Church (itself the result of union), the Congregationalist churches, and part of the Presbyterian Church, in the United Church of Canada. While this was no doubt meant in part to balance the numbers and influence of the Roman Catholic communion in Canada, it was undoubtedly most significant of the dying-down of the old denominational differences as these ceased to express differences of class, national origin, or personal conviction. In all these changes, however, the churches remained active organizations, and Canadians a church-supporting people; that they should have done so was perhaps part of the primitive character of the country, of the sense men still had of being opposed by forces greater than themselves.

Canada might, then, continue with business and politics in some confidence that the toil in field and forest had provided not only the necessities of life, but something in the realm of thought and art to return to the human store from which as a pioneer community it had drawn for so many years. So, at least, some Canadians noted with satisfaction at the time. But after 1927 the prosperity of the mid twenties swelled to the great stock-market boom of 1929. Most Canadians, like the rest of the western world, rode that rushing torrent with little thought of where the stream might lead.

Politics receded into the background. James A. Robb as Minister of Finance, and Dunning as his successor in 1929, lowered the tariff as one prosperity budget followed another till for a moment it seemed that the great days of the Laurier boom had been surpassed. The working-out of diplomatic independence went forward; Mr. Vincent Massey became Canadian Minister to Washington in 1927, an event which marked not only Canadian achievement of diplomatic independence but also the acceptance by the United States of Canadian nationhood. A British High Commissioner was appointed to Ottawa in 1928. Mr. Philippe Roy became Minister to France in the same year, and Mr. Herbert Marler to Japan in 1929; the Canadian diplomatic service had been founded.

The one notable political event was the resignation of Arthur Meighen as leader of the Conservative party. A master of flashing phrase and of crisp-cut exposition, Meighen was the victim of his own trenchant clarity. The duel with King had been that of the swordsman with the wielder of the trident and the net, of the gladiator with the *retiarius*. Where Meighen stood, King side-stepped;

where Meighen pledged action, King promised consideration; where Meighen clarified, King obscured. The one challenged opposition, the other offered compromise. And the condition of Canada called for compromise rather than challenge. The public had decided which should dominate their generation, and it is impossible to record the decision without regret for the failure of the great gifts and the gallant spirit which were Meighen's.

The Conservative party, after an interval under the House leadership of Hugh Guthrie, met in convention in Winnipeg in 1927. On the second ballot it elected Richard Bedford Bennett, a New-Brunswick-born Calgary lawyer and an able and eloquent politician, as Meighen's successor. It was noteworthy that two of his rivals, Guthrie being one, were former Liberal-Unionists, and only one a Conservative – the politician's politician, Robert Rogers of Manitoba. To such a dearth of leadership had the party of Macdonald and Borden come. In Bennett, however, it had chosen a leader who was a friend of those other New Brunswick politicians, Bonar Law and Max Aitken, Lord Beaverbrook, who had advocated for years a system of imperial preference, a return to the imperial system which the United Kingdom had discarded for free trade in 1846 and which Joseph Chamberlain had failed to restore in 1906. Now Bennett was to attempt to reconcile the economic nationalism and imperial sentiment of the Canadian Conservative party by seeking to create such a system of imperial preference. And indeed no narrower frame of reference than the British Empire itself would ever have permitted such a reconciliation to take place. Within the limits of Canadian politics it was impossible; and if Bennett failed, the existing basis of Canadian conservatism would be destroyed. The prolonged depression that began in 1929 was to give him his opportunity.

The depression of 1929 was the result of the collapse of the great stock-market boom of 1928 and 1929, which in 1931 to 1933 passed into a collapse of the economic system. The industrial boom of the mid twenties gave rise to a speculative psychosis and an over-extension of credit which led to a wholly unrealistic inflation of the price of stocks. It was actually thought by the enthusiastic that the economy had transcended the process of boom and slump and that the current prosperity was permanent. In fact the industrial boom was already threatened by over-production in relation to the effective demand of the consuming public and by rapidly-increasing technological unemployment. The wage and monetary policies of the day were inadequate for dealing with the problems of effective demand and monetary expansion and contraction. The situation was aggravated by agricultural over-production in America and Europe up to the large harvest of 1928, and thereafter by increasing drought on the western plains of North America. Finally, the credit and foreign-exchange system was burdened by the unproductive transfers of German reparations and of the Allied war debts. Although Canadians contributed to the depression by the policies of their government and their own activities, this catastrophe, like all the crises of Canadian history, had its origins outside Canada. The country was as helpless as a canoe drawn into the current of a rapid.

When therefore the stock-market broke in October 1929, the result was not merely a conventional slump to be liquidated by the classical procedures of bankruptcy and foreclosure. The situation rapidly became one of economic collapse and social and political discontent before which most of the governments of the world fell, some by revolution. The first months of the depression revealed another novel element in Canada, the fact that the family farm was no longer capable as in the past of acting as the absorber of the industrial unemployed. The farm had ceased to be even relatively self-subsistent, and most urban people had lost, if they had ever had, any connection with the land. It was therefore necessary to provide relief and public works on a scale hitherto unknown. In Canada, under the constitution, relief costs were in the first instance the responsibility of the municipalities and in the second that of the provinces. Yet the revenues of the municipalities and the provinces, especially those of economically weaker regions such as the Atlantic provinces and the prairies, were rapidly shown to be wholly inadequate to deal with the unemployment which followed 1929. The basic weakness of the constitution, the increase in the responsibilities of the provinces unaccompanied by a corresponding increase in revenues, was being laid bare. The provinces suddenly had mounting relief costs piled on top of expenditures which were both high in relation to revenue and very difficult to reduce. The increasing number of social services demanded by the Canadian public had been organized and financed by the provinces. The only major contribution the national government made was when J. S. Woodsworth obtained in 1927 an Old Age Pensions Act, half the costs of which the national government met as the provinces individually adopted the measure. But the social services were altering the character of public finance, for they initiated charges on the public treasury which admitted of little reduction in times of falling revenue; they meant in fact that revenues could not be allowed to fall.

The industrial depression was accompanied and aggravated by an agricultural one. That in turn was intensified by severe and prolonged drought. The record wheat crop of 1928 could not be sold off, and a carry-over developed. The Pools were caught, being unable to complete the payments they had undertaken. Wheat prices plummeted, and with them the price of livestock and other farm produce. In central and eastern Canada the old diversity of production and the old thrift kept the farmsteads in being. But the farmer of the prairies, with his dependence on one crop – he had few alternatives – and his high capital requirements and continuing debt, was in the majority of cases hopelessly caught between past commitments and low prices coupled with falling yields. Only state aid could uphold the fragile economy and the local government services of the prairies.

The national Liberal government adopted a negative attitude towards the situation. It was natural for Liberals to do so, for they were perhaps especially disposed to let the conventional processes of a free economy work themselves out. It was natural for any government to suppose in 1930 that the end of the boom was only the preface to a slump which would correct the distortions of the economy; no one yet knew what in fact was in store, a depression so much greater in degree as to be different in kind. Already, however, the public temper was brittle, accustomed as it had insensibly become to government action to deal with a wide range of matters once left to private or municipal disposal. When Prime Minister King, in a rare moment of indiscretion while defending his government's refusal to make direct grants to the provinces for relief, declared that he would not give a single five-cent piece for a Tory government to spend, he was merely expressing in partisan terms the basic constitutional situation. The provinces had the responsibilities and the national government had the revenues to discharge them. The latter could not properly grant funds the expenditure of which it did not control.

The negative attitude of the Liberals was a positive opportunity for the Conservatives. Bennett forthrightly promised national aid to the provinces and increased protection to industries exposed to increased competition. Among these was the dairy industry, just recently afflicted by butter imports from New Zealand. Not less positive was Bennett's approach to the difficulties of Canadian exporters; he would, he said, "blast a way" into world markets. The mood of the country was to give any man with a positive program a chance to try it. As a result, the Conservatives won the general election of 1930 with a representation of a hundred and thirty-eight, including twenty-five from Quebec. Except for nine U.F.A. members from Alberta and Agnes Macphail from Ontario, the Progressives disappeared, and the first effect of the depression was thus to complete that superficial restoration of national unity which the events of 1926 had begun. And the Conservative party had once more, even if in desperate economic circumstances, an opportunity to give the nation a comprehensive and progressive national policy, a policy at once of economic revival and social solidarity.

To this task Prime Minister Bennett brought conviction and great personal powers of decision, but a weak cabinet. His administration was to an extraordinary degree a personal administration. Thus the fortunes of the Conservative party, in a time of crisis, were tied not only to one line of development, a policy of national economic development in a framework of imperial preference, but also to the principles and the capacity of one man. Failure might therefore be not merely failure, but outright collapse.

The intensifying depression Bennett tackled by raising the tariff, by maintaining the value of the Canadian dollar, by making direct grants of half the costs of relief to the provinces, and by launching a program of public works. The gathering collapse of the wheat economy, carrying with it the Pools, he met by appointing in 1930 a government agent, J. I. McFarland, to manage the central selling agency of the Wheat Pools, which he did until 1938. A royal commission considered the distress of the railways and recommended a reduction of branch lines and a pooling of service on certain lines. These measures the government carried out, while resisting pressure to amalgamate the two systems in one. It was a courageous program, but, like all the measures of the time, it was inadequate to deal with the scale of the depression, aggravated as that was by the increasing drought of the unprecedented dry cycle in the prairie provinces.

While awaiting the results of these first measures, the government had to complete the work begun at the Commonwealth Conference of 1926. In 1930 the prime ministers of the Commonwealth agreed to the recommendations of the committee on the operation of Dominion legislation that certain British statutes should be repealed, so far as they applied to the Dominions: the Colonial Laws Validity Act of 1865, the Colonial Courts of Admiralty Act, 1890, and the Merchant Shipping Act of 1894. The parliaments of the Dominions should henceforth have extra-territorial jurisdiction. It was further agreed that only the ministers of the Dominion concerned should advise the King on the appointment of a Governor General and that any change in the royal titles should be made only by agreement of the governments of the Commonwealth. Finally the Parliament of the United Kingdom was to be requested to pass a declaratory act to the effect that its legislative supremacy over the Dominions was at an end. This was done in the Statute of Westminster, 1931.

Bennett, however, after conference with the provinces, had had to request that the Act should contain a section exempting from its operation those sections of the British North America Acts since 1867 which dealt with minority rights and the distribution of powers between the national and the provincial governments. In these matters the amendment of the Canadian constitution was to be only by address to the Parliament of the United Kingdom, and, by convention, only after the unanimous consent of the provinces. This reservation of the amending power, ironical at a time when Canada was assuming legislative independence, failed to detract from the magnitude of the changes completed in the conference of 1930 and the Statute. Henceforth only Canadian ministers would advise the Crown on all Canadian matters; henceforth only the Parliament of Canada could legislate for Canada. This was a further spelling out of that independence under the Crown which had begun with responsible government and had been established in principle at Confederation.

The furtherance of the development of Canadian political nationalism by a Conservative government was carried through without hitch or reserve, in the assurance that the common Crown, common citizenship and constitutional heritage remained. Moreover, it was the ambition of the Prime Minister's life, which the election of 1930 and the adoption of protection by the United Kingdom in 1931 had given him the opportunity to fulfil, to create by Canadian leadership a system of imperial preference that would ensure to Canada an economic destiny separate from that of the United States and at the same time enable the people of the Commonwealth and Empire to realize the potentialities of their enormous territories and unexploited resources. It was a concept as heroic in scope as in its disregard of economic realities and political possibilities. Yet Bennett and the Canadian Conservatives were lured by it as a moth by a light, for in it they might find means to resolve the uneasy contradiction of their imperial sentiment and their national economic policy. And such was Bennett's vigour, such the growing weight of Canada in the Commonwealth, that he induced the reluctant governments of the United Kingdom and the other Dominions to meet in Ottawa in 1932. The result was a formal success and a moral failure. A set of agreements was reached by mutual tariff reductions, but only after hard and recriminatory bargaining which revealed that no member of the Commonwealth – certainly not Canada – would, or could, without serious political risk, make reductions that would create genuinely competitive conditions. Neither could the United Kingdom sacrifice the interest of its European customers in agricultural exports to the British market. The Ottawa Conference demonstrated that the nationalism which had created the Commonwealth was economic as well as political. And while the Agreements were not without value, the substantial failure of the Conference left Canadian Conservatives deprived of half their program, that of imperial economic solidarity, and faced with the need at last to come wholly to terms with the fact of Canadian nationhood.

In 1933 the bottom of the depression was reached. There were 500,000 to 600,000 unemployed men and women in receipt of public relief in Canada. The nightly fires twinkled by the railway yards in the "jungles," the makeshift bivouacs of the wandering workless. The price of wheat sank to its lowest recorded level, thirty-eight cents a bushel at Winnipeg. Drought had turned much of the southern prairies to desert as the wind whipped the topsoil away, and sand dunes lay rippled where once the wheat had swayed. The credit of the weakened provinces was exhausted, their revenues and those of the municipalities reduced to a trickle. Doctors worked without fee, and school-teachers took their pay in kind. Society was reverting to barter and to personal exchange of service. One by one the units of local government, the school districts and municipalities, broke down and were kept functioning only by support from the province. Stage by stage the strain of a disintegrating society was working up to the last remaining fabric of strength in the nation, the national government itself, which remained powerless to remedy the situation except by repeated grants and by further public works. Indeed, the dispersal at Regina by the Mounted Police, on orders from Ottawa, of a march of unemployed from the west to the capital suggested to the embittered unemployed that the national government had no remedy but repression for the evils of the times.

The extent of public suffering was now too great for people to endure the powerlessness of government indefinitely. New political movements began to challenge the ineffectiveness of the old parties and to proclaim the need for radical changes in a society of unexampled productivity and inexplicable poverty. In 1932 the U.F.A. members of Parliament, labour politicians, farmer leaders, trade-union leaders and left-wing intellectuals began the organization of a new party, the Co-operative Commonwealth Federation. The organization of the new movement was completed at Regina in 1933 and its program issued in the Regina Manifesto. The purpose of its founders was to create a popular party with popularly controlled and directed policies which should be national interventionist, if not socialist, in character. It was the historical outgrowth of the farmers' and the labour movements, and of the lack of harmony between the laws and conventions of society and the new industrial order which had grown up in Canada. J. S. Woodsworth, who had lived through and been a part of so much of that historic growth, was elected leader. Canada, it seemed, had produced a left-wing party of principle to challenge the economic liberalism of the Liberals and the lack of social policy in the Conservative party.

At the same time, however, a second movement was beginning which was to appeal to the same discontents and to dispute the role of saviour with the C.C.F. This was the Social Credit movement. The teachings of Major Douglas had won some attention in Alberta in the previous decade, and had spread in that province. In 1932 a high-school principal, William Aberhart, who conducted an evangelical mission by radio and had become a powerful popular influence, took up the idea of Social Credit and began to advocate it as a means of conquering the depression. Under his inspiration Social Credit clubs were organized and spread rapidly. The appeal of Social Credit according to Aberhart was not its economic theory; it was simply that it offered hope to the hopeless and a remedy short of socialism to a people basically conservative and conventional. Moreover, Social Credit was a strictly non-political movement and appealed to a people taught by the U.F.A. and sectional experience to distrust political parties. Little attention was paid to it, however, until 1935 when, in a frenzied campaign, Social Credit candidates defeated both the old U.F.A. government, discredited by scandal and its failure to press legislation for debt reduction, and the new C.C.F. with its promise of socialism.

Even in central Canada, provincial political changes of an unorthodox character occurred. In Ontario in 1933 the Liberals under a new young leader, Mitchell Hepburn, defeated the Conservative government of Premier G. S. Henry, who had succeeded the powerful Howard Ferguson when Ferguson became Canadian High Commissioner in London. Hepburn was a Liberal by profession but in action a reckless and unprincipled demagogue who distinguished himself by his aggressive provincialism, his retroactive legislation, and his flaunted vulgarity. The most significant thing about this potential dictator was his popularity. That Canada's wealthiest and most stable province should have thrown up such a leader revealed how the quality of Canadian democracy had weakened under the strain of depression.

In Quebec the depression produced a movement called the Union Nationale, reminiscent to a degree of the Parti National of 1871, and devoted under the high-minded leadership of the youthful Paul Gouin to cleansing the province of the political corruption of the long-entrenched Taschereau régime. To defeat Taschereau, Gouin combined with the Conservatives under Maurice Duplessis, a reserved, intense, reactionary man who was to make himself one of the most popular and most feared of the political chiefs of his province. Taschereau fell before the combination in 1936, but by that time Gouin had lost the leadership to Duplessis. As a result, what had begun as a reform movement became a narrowly provincial régime devoted to the defence of the rights of Quebec and to the defeat of any radical movement within Quebec.

The discontents and stirrings which gave rise to these provincial and sectional movements did not leave national politics wholly unaffected. The Liberal party, it is true, was not touched either by a sense of need for new ideas or by the demagoguery of Hepburn; its leaders doggedly continued to preach a policy of minimum intervention and a freeing of international trade as the fundamental and only helpful remedies for the depression. But some Conservatives, notably the earnest and volatile H. H. Stevens of Vancouver, Minister of Trade and Commerce, had begun to think that much of the trouble had been caused by practices which had grown up in the world of private business. Stevens had a royal commission known as the Price Spreads Commission appointed in 1934, to go into such matters as price-fixing by manufacturers. The hope was that some relief might be afforded to the small retailer and the consumer, the small people to whom it was essential the Conservative party should appeal if it was to have a future. Because he felt the party was failing to make such an appeal, Stevens in 1935 launched his Reconstruction Party.

In none of these movements was there any great swing to Fascism on the Right or, on the Left, to Communism. The Union Nationale stopped well short of Fascism, as the rise of a Fascist party under Adrien Arcand was to reveal. Quebec did head the general hostility to Communism, and this was to lead to the passage in 1937 of a law giving the Attorney General power to padlock the premises of any organization he declared to be subversive. The measure was aimed at subversion by Leftist elements, as were deportations carried out by the national government. But the resistance to Communism by governmental action went no further. The C.C.F., on the other hand, was ardently and effectively anti-Communist. Since the social misery caused by the depression was so fertile a ground for the growth of Communism, the astonishing thing was that so few Canadians turned to it.

More significant was the intellectual interest shown by young Canadians, for the first time on any considerable scale, in Communism and the other alternatives to the liberal economic system. The feeling that the latter had collapsed, that the remedies attempted by government were unavailing, that the paradox of poverty amid abundant means of production was intolerable, led many of the best minds and most ardent spirits to look into the promises of Communism, and some into those of Fascism. Relatively few were attracted but none were to be unaffected, and a handful were to suffer tragically, in the end, for their quest.

The search for alternatives was set off, however, not only by the final collapse of economic liberalism but also by the failure of the policies of the Bennett government either materially to alleviate the depression or to provide the new measures the new circumstances required. A dynamic policy dealing with fundamentals was needed. The Prime Minister was looking desperately for such a policy. A hint of one was perhaps contained in Stevens's attack on current business practices, but his attempt to appeal to the small business man was in itself reactionary. The government had more constructive achievements to its credit by 1935. One which was greatly to increase the power and efficiency of national policy was the creation of the Bank of Canada as a central bank, crowning and completing the Canadian banking system in 1935. Though its stock was privately held, it was meant to be and became a central agency of national monetary policy. Another was the institution of the Prairie Farm Rehabilitation Act in 1935, an attempt, which was to prove highly successful, to incorporate and put on a permanent administrative basis the experience of the drought areas in order to mitigate the effects of drought in the future. Equally significant was the creation of the Canadian Wheat Board, also in 1935, with the statutory task of disposing of the annual wheat crop. Under the Bennett government, something of the hope of the Pools that a single marketing agency might be able to obtain higher prices was retained. The result was to end from that date the free market in wheat in Canada.

These measures, important as they were for the future, were not directed to dealing with the immediate needs of the country and the issues raised by the depression. The fact was that measures designed to do so would only encounter the constitutional impasse revealed by 1926 – that the national government had the means but not the authority, and the provincial government the authority without adequate means. But the Prime Minister, faced with an election in 1935 and persuaded by his brother-in-law W. D. Herridge, the Canadian minister to Washington, suddenly took the constitutional bull by the horns. He brought before Parliament a "New Deal" program which simply ignored the constitutional limitations on national action in the fields of jurisdiction affected, gambling on the possibility that the Judicial Committee's having ruled in 1930 and 1931 that aeronautics and broadcasting were national subjects might have indicated a new trend in judicial interpretation. The New Deal rested squarely on the assumption that the régime of laissez-faire had ended and that government must take the responsibility of massive and continuous intervention. It was embodied in six acts: the Trade and Industry Commission Act, based on the findings of the Price Spreads Commission; the Minimum Wages Act; the Limitation of Hours of Work Act; the Weekly Rest in Industrial Undertakings Act; the Unemployment Insurance Act, and the Natural Products Marketing Act. By the standards of the times it was a modest enough program, and it did no more than bring Canada into line with the English-speaking world.

The character of the program, however, seemed sweepingly interventionist in Canada, and the sudden conversion of the Conservative party to this principle was greeted with the scepticism that political conversion usually arouses. Nevertheless, the whole was passed by Parliament and the general election followed. The national electorate accepted neither the New Deal nor the genuineness of the Conservative conversion to the principle of state intervention and social solidarity. On the contrary, it held the Bennett administration responsible for the failure of the national government to deal with the depression. It did not turn to the C.C.F., however; only seven members of that party were elected. It turned to the Liberals and Mackenzie King, who had advocated only the conventional remedies of constitutional reform and freer trade, by means of tariff reductions and reciprocity, with a United States once more under Democratic control. The new temper in politics had expressed itself only in the provinces. In national policies Canada had reverted once more to the well-known and unrevised program of the Liberal party and the negative politics of Mackenzie King. Once again a positive and clear-cut man had gone down to defeat, bitter and personal defeat, before the inveterate incoherence of Canadian political opinion, the conservative instincts of the electorate, the fear of central control and positive power, and the perfected political craft of Mackenzie King, now the consummate master of opportunity.

ADDITIONAL READING

DAWSON, R. MACGREGOR *William Lyon Mackenzie King.*
GRAHAM, ROGER *Arthur Meighen, a Biography.*
MCNAUGHT, K. W. *A Prophet in Politics.*
SCOTT, FRANK *Canada Today.*
SMILEY, DONALD V. *The Rowell-Sirois Report,* Book I.
WADE, MASON *The French Canadians, 1760–1945.*
WHEARE, K. C. *The Statute of Westminster.*

CHAPTER 23

The Revival of National Power

1936-1949

The fourth ministry of Mackenzie King was one of unusual ability and experience, and the Liberal party, which had to a large degree absorbed the Progressives and lost little to the new movements, was extraordinarily strong in all sections of the country. Not since 1896 had a Liberal government been so strong or stood so high.

Neither had any Canadian government ever had more expected of it. The low point of the depression had passed in 1933, but the depression in general had not lifted. Prices were still low, business stagnant, agriculture stricken, exports languishing. Only the gold mines of Ontario and Quebec were prosperous, and their output did much to sustain the sagging economy and the credit of the national government. Bennett's orthodox measures of protection and sound money had had little effect, except on balance to aggravate the weight of the depression. Nor had the less conventional methods of the American New Deal succeeded in animating to any great degree the prostrate economy of the United States. Both governments had in effect underwritten the local governments and the national economy; neither had succeeded in restoring prosperity. Times were somewhat better because people had adjusted themselves, to a degree, and the shock of the economic avalanche of 1929–33 had passed. But with the lists of unemployed as long as ever and the relief costs continuing to pile debt on debt, the depression clearly had not ended. It lay like a grey, despondent fog, obscuring all prospects. It made itself felt not only in jobs lost and savings spent, but also in hopes deferred, careers impeded, marriages postponed, children unborn. It made the elderly radical and the young cynical. The "Waste Land" of T. S. Eliot was not of the spirit only; it stood materialized in every listless street and along every dust-scoured country road.

The drought on the prairies had been incredibly prolonged; in 1936 it was to intensify again to the horrors of 1933 and blacken the summer sky as the Saskatchewan fields boiled up in tumult before the insensate wind. In the south, farm after farm was abandoned, the sand piling over the doorways of the empty houses
KC-Q

as people moved to the forest shelter and greater moisture of the north, or left the prairies forever to cross the Rockies into British Columbia. Palliser's Triangle steadily lost its population, and the Report was remembered as though it had been a prophecy. So many people left the southern plains during the drought that between 1931 and 1941 Saskatchewan's population declined from 921,785 to 887,747.

If the new ministry faced a grim situation at home, the outlook abroad was no brighter. Since 1930 Canada had almost ignored the rest of the world. The expansion of its diplomatic service had been halted. No occasion for Canadian initiative abroad occurred, and the main interest of the Bennett government had been in Commonwealth rather than in foreign affairs. The Japanese attack on Manchuria in 1931 indeed aroused and dismayed the supporters of the League of Nations, but the main Canadian concern was with the failure of the United Kingdom and the United States to concert their policies towards Japan. Similarly, Canada viewed with comparative indifference the break-down of the post-Versailles system in the end of reparations and the rise of Hitler. As in Manchuria, no specific Canadian interest was touched, and the issues raised were regarded as matters for the great powers. But the final failure of the Disarmament Conference in 1932 had made some Canadians realize that a drift towards a new war might well be in train.

The Italian attack on Abyssinia in 1935 therefore aroused a keener reaction. Canadian sentiment, except in Quebec, was strongly anti-Italian and in favour of the use of economic sanctions. Even in this, however, there was little thought of Canada's taking action or being involved. When the Canadian representative at Geneva, W. A. Riddell, having been left without instructions, brought in a resolution to strengthen the sanctions already voted, the Liberal government dispatched an abrupt disavowal. Almost alone, Dafoe of the *Winnipeg Free Press* kept up an unpopular campaign, begun in 1931, to have Canada support the League against the aggressions breaking out like prairie fires around the world horizon.

It was the voice of one crying in the wilderness of isolation. Canada in the majority was isolationist, as it had been since 1920; the depression increased the preoccupation with domestic concerns. Canadian nationalists were generally isolationists also, even if only as a means of asserting independence. There was little general support for the League of Nations and the principle of collective security. Those who urged a policy of intervention were often "imperialists," who wished Canada to be explicit and active in support of the United Kingdom. Behind and underlying all such debate was the memory of 1917 and the fierce determination of French Canadians not to be drawn into another "imperialist war." To this isolationist temper Prime Minister King was sympathetic and sensitively responsive.

The Canadian mood was matched and indeed exceeded in the United States.

There isolation was conscious, organized, and fiercely defensive, as the sessions and findings of the Senate Committee on war-time propaganda revealed in 1934, findings which resulted in the Neutrality Acts of 1935 and subsequent years. Yet the very strength of the isolationist sentiment of both countries was a re-action to the recognition that events in Europe and Asia showed the European peace settlement of 1919 at Versailles and the Far Eastern settlement of 1922 at Washington to be on the verge of revision by force. If war were to come, then isolation could not be a mood only; isolationist countries would have to defend themselves. And for Canada the question would be, could Canada indeed be isolationist if the United Kingdom were once more under serious threat? Within a year of 1935 both the United States and Canada were to make a beginning at rearming; rearming as a necessary precaution, for no definite purpose, but none the less rearming in a world whose peace had suddenly become precarious. The world had in fact moved out of post-war into pre-war years.

The Liberal party on its return to power had a free hand and the confidence of the public that it would govern strongly in a time of domestic depression and international menace. It had promised little, but much was expected of it. It had learned little, perhaps, but it remembered much. None of its members betrayed, and none of its actions indicated, any awareness that the world of pre-1914 and even pre-1921 had collapsed in 1931. Seldom can a political party have been more committed to its historic traditions, or more devoted to lost causes. The reasons for this are plain. The failure of the traditional Conservative policies seemed, in the circumstances, to be a vindication of traditional Liberal policies. That both might have been inadequate had yet to be demonstrated. Secondly, as is inevitable in parliamentary government, many of the Cabinet were veterans; men such as T. A. Crerar and Ernest Lapointe, in both of whom also much ex-perience buttressed a massive indolence. Others were men of limited training, such as C. A. Dunning, J. L. Ilsley, and the American-born engineer, C. D. Howe. The Prime Minister himself may have seen as clearly as any man into the character of events, but he had developed a preternatural sense of the limitations on national action in Canada.

It was all too plain, moreover, that the New Deal of Bennett challenged at once the historic trend of the decisions of the Judicial Committee and the con-stitutional sensitivities of the provinces. The Acts were at once referred to the Supreme Court to test their validity, with little doubt of what the result would be. Before there could be bold and novel measures, the constitution must be amended, and the constitution could be amended only by the unanimous con-sent of the provinces. In short, what the provinces would not grant the power to do could not be done in 1935.

The Liberals' policy for bringing about economic recovery was as cautious and conventional as their ideas. It was one of freeing trade from the restrictions which had been imposed by their predecessors. The Ottawa Agreements could not of course be altered until the terms expired; when that with the United Kingdom did so in 1937, it was renewed without substantial change. But tariff reductions were made and advantage was at once taken of the reciprocal trade policy initiated by Cordell Hull in the United States to conclude a trade agreement with that country. What in effect had been sought so long after 1866, and so violently rejected in 1911, was quietly accomplished in 1935 and extended in 1938. The restriction imposed on Canadian trade with the United States by the Fordney-McCumber tariff of 1922 and the Hawley-Smoot tariff of 1932 was ended. The American market steadily replaced the British and European as the principal outlet for the majority of Canadian exports of raw materials and manufactured goods. American goods and capital flowed into Canada in ever-increasing volume. The north-south flow of trade exceeded the east-west, as in the days of the Reciprocity Treaty of 1854. The change arose, however, as much from American need as Canadian, since the vast American economy had to reach out for raw materials, for food, and for markets.

The revival of trade produced by these measures of liberalization came about only slowly. Other measures had to be taken, of a more interventionist nature, to deal with the effects of the depression and the drought. The government purchased a controlling majority of the stock of the Central Bank and made its governor responsible to Parliament for monetary policy. While no practical change of operation followed, the measure was necessitated by the public determination not to allow the vast responsibilities of monetary control to be affected by private interests. The Prairie Farm Rehabilitation Act continued in force and received full support from the Liberal administration. Under the Act the farmers of the west received government aid and direction in adapting tillage practices to drought conditions, in providing waterholes and community pastures for livestock, and in ensuring the supply and distribution of fodder. It was an outstanding example of national aid to a region overwhelmed by natural disabilities which the provinces had not the resources to combat, and a precedent for the national government resuming its historic role in the development of the national economy.

The government also accepted the Wheat Board, simply directing it to follow a policy of selling wheat as the market offered. The attempt of the Pools under the Bennett administration to use the control of supply to enhance the price of wheat had ended. But the free market in wheat, perhaps the most significant factor in the old liberal economy, had also ended. The Board, backed by the credit of the national government, took delivery of the entire crop, made advances against sales, and completed payment as the crop was sold, just as the Wheat Pools had done. The grain-grower had at last achieved stability of wheat prices, even if it was still a depressed stability.

The continuance of the depression and drought was to produce in 1939 yet another addition to the policy of intervention which had created the P.F.R.A.

This was the Prairie Farm Assistance Act, by which farmers in areas proclaimed as drought areas received payments at so much an acre out of a fund formed by an annual levy on the wheat acreage of the prairies.

Nor did state intervention, by a government controlled by Liberals, end there. Radio broadcasting had raised new issues of national policy, for private radio would have become largely a medium for disseminating American advertising and American programs. Following the judicial decision of 1931 which made broadcasting a subject of national jurisdiction, a Canadian Radio Commission had been created in 1932 to regulate broadcasting in Canada and to preserve Canadian control and the Canadian character of the medium. In 1936, Parliament established the Canadian Broadcasting Corporation with the dual function of regulating private broadcasting and of developing Canadian networks in both languages for distribution of programs purchased or produced by the Corporation itself. Thus a national backbone was given to a system which was publicly controlled, and in which public and private broadcasting were integrated.

The same policy, equally interventionist and nationalist, controlled the development of air transport. The Department of National Defence had begun as early as 1933 to develop a line of airfields across Canada, the Trans-Canada Air Route. The Route was not only to serve defence, but to make possible a transcontinental service constituting a base line from which private lines might branch to the north and develop the bush flying which was so rapidly binding northern development into the national life. In 1937 Trans-Canada Air Lines, a Crown corporation, began to operate the service. In both the C.B.C. and T.C.A., the national government had created agencies of national purpose such as the railways had been. In broadcasting, however, so fluid was the medium and so unknown its scope, and in air transport, such was now the strategic significance of all air development, that control of the new agencies was entrusted to public bodies appointed by the government and acting under statute.

These arrangements rested on the two decisions of the Judicial Committee which ran counter to the trend of its decisions over many years. There was no guarantee that that trend would not be resumed, and indeed in 1937 the Committee held five of the Acts of the Bennett New Deal to be invalid. It was therefore most desirable that the powers of the national government should be restored by constitutional amendment, but first it was necessary to reach agreement with the provinces on how the constitution in its national-provincial aspects might be amended, whether by reference to the Parliament of the United Kingdom or by a Canadian process. In the fall of 1935, representatives of the national and provincial governments met in conference to attempt, among other things, to reach agreement on a Canadian process of amendment. The various proposals considered had a common approach in that they made the same classification of the sections of the constitution, grouping them as those which dealt with the religious and educational rights of minorities and the legal and language rights of the French, those which dealt with the distribution of powers between the nation and the provinces, and those which were solely of national concern. For any amendment of the first group, unanimity of the provinces was necessary; for the second, a two-thirds majority of the provinces, with population taken into account, or with such a majority to include Ontario and Quebec; for the third, a simple majority in Parliament. An amending process so cautious and conservative could hardly be criticized, except by ardent nationalists. And indeed all the provinces agreed to the adoption of such a process, except New Brunswick. This last somewhat unexpected and very oddly based opposition, founded as it was on a concept of the character of the provinces as still in effect colonies of the mid-Victorian empire, was enough to render the conference a failure. That line of approach to the problem of national and provincial powers was therefore dropped for the time being.

Once the way of constitutional amendment by Canadian process was closed, there remained only two ways of using national power to strengthen the fabric of the nation. One was to seek amendment at Westminster, and early in 1936 the government moved a joint address requesting that the B.N.A. Act be amended, as the provinces had agreed at the constitutional conference, to enable the provinces to levy certain indirect taxes and the national government to guarantee the debts of the provinces. The Conservative majority in the Senate, however, refused to concur in the admission of the provinces to the field of indirect taxation, and that route was stopped. The other route was to employ the undiminished plenitude of the national taxing power to relieve the financial weakness of the lesser provinces. A study of the financial situation of the prairie provinces by the Bank of Canada in 1936 revealed that they were incapable of maintaining themselves by their own resources. Without national aid their provincial and municipal structures would collapse, as the government of Newfoundland had collapsed and been replaced by a Commission appointed by the United Kingdom in 1934.

When therefore the decisions of the Judicial Committee on the Acts of the Bennett New Deal revealed in 1937 that no help was to be expected from judicial decision, but rather the contrary, a royal commission was appointed to inquire into the financial relations of the national and provincial governments. It was a commission of unusual capacity. The chairman was Newton W. Rowell, an Ontario Liberal who had been a member of the Union Government. Quebec was represented by Joseph Sirois, a distinguished lawyer who succeeded to the chair on the death of Rowell. The Atlantic provinces were represented by R. A. Mackay, a political scientist, the prairies by J. W. Dafoe, and British Columbia by H. F. Angus, economist and political scientist. Even more remarkable was the staff they appointed. Much of the best ability of the developing Civil Service and of the departments of History and Political Economy of Canadian universities was drawn on to make a thorough and penetrating study of the constitutional and especially the financial relations of the national and provincial governments. It was a study far more searching and prolonged than Durham's, and its results were to challenge comparison with his famous report. But three eventful years were to pass before the Commission completed its labours.

Those years were dominated by external events rather than domestic difficulties. Already in 1936 the Commonwealth had undergone a crisis. In 1935, King George V, who had seen the Empire transformed into the Commonwealth and India setting out towards self-government, celebrated the twenty-fifth year of his reign. In that reign the sovereignty of the imperial parliament ended and the Crown emerged as the sole formal link of the Commonwealth. In 1936 the old king, who had reigned with so much dignity and self-discipline, died and was succeeded by Edward VIII. Edward as Prince of Wales had struggled against the Hanoverian authority of his father with all the petulance of a wilful nature. Young, pleasant, and unmarried, he had added to the popularity of the monarchy, especially on his visits to Canada and the other members of the Commonwealth. He might perhaps have reconciled his private taste for the company of the London fast "set" with the ceremonial requirements of the monarchy as the symbol of national unity and dignity, even as Edward VII had done, had he remained unwed or married conventionally. He chose, however, before his coronation, to announce with a curious mixture of frankness and obstinacy that he proposed to marry an American lady who had been twice divorced. The implications of such a marriage Prime Minister Stanley Baldwin and the Archbishop of Canterbury felt, and the prime ministers of the Commonwealth nations agreed, to be quite incompatible with the character of the monarchy. As a result, since Edward refused to change his mind, he was forced to abdicate.

The succession was in no doubt, for he had three brothers, and the next in line, the Duke of York, was widely respected and happily married, with two daughters, the Princess Elizabeth and the Princess Margaret. The crisis consisted both of the shock to the monarchy, although this was much exaggerated, and the possibility of members of the Commonwealth not agreeing on the succession or not acting coincidentally. This fear also proved groundless, but the event revealed how personal, how frail in fact though potent in symbol, the last formal tie of Commonwealth was.

The same year of 1936, however, witnessed in Canada quite another demonstration of how powerful the Crown might be as a symbol of association not only in allegiance, but also in the sharing of the full constitutional and cultural heritage of the Commonwealth. The change in the mode of choosing the King's representative, made in 1931, did not at first affect the character or rank of the personage appointed. Byng had ended his term as Governor General in 1927, and Lord Willingdon succeeded him. Willingdon became Viceroy of India in 1931 and was succeeded by the Earl of Bessborough, on the advice of Prime Minister Bennett, it is true, but after much consultation with the Palace and even some intervention by the Secretary of State for the Colonies. When Bessborough's term ended in 1935, Prime Minister Bennett, by an act of inspiration, recommended the popular Scots writer, John Buchan, to succeed.

Raised to the peerage as Lord Tweedsmuir, Buchan became Governor General late in 1935. The slight, delicate man who left his study to serve Canada and the Commonwealth was clear in mind and strong in purpose. The biographer of one of the abler of his predecessors, the Earl of Minto, Tweedsmuir had a firm grasp of the limits and the opportunities of his office. Government has not only to legislate and administer; it must also educate and inspire, and democratic statesmen may lack the ability or the energy for this aspect of humane rule. To inspire a respect for national purpose and the public service, to instruct by general comment and personal example, are, however, something neither convention nor caution need prevent a Governor General from doing. Indeed, now that the Governor General had become in effect an appointee, subject to the sovereign's demurring, of the Prime Minister, such a role might preserve the office from insignificance and decay. Tweedsmuir, with his knowledge of human nature and politics, his superb historical sense and literary grace, and his extraordinary capacity, while priding himself on his Scots nationality, to identify himself with Canadians of all origins, set himself to touch the national spirit of Canada – like its economy, long depressed. Dufferin had foreshadowed the same concept of the office, but had drowned it in a flood of Irish eloquence and a nervous officiousness. With consummate tact, Tweedsmuir aroused in Canadians a pride in their origins, in the stern, Scottish beauty of their country, in the valour of their past. It was a delicate service, delicately performed, but the effect was profound and lasting, and it was of priceless import, not least in its timing.

Besides the formal link of the Crown, given vitality by the personality of the monarch and the quality of his representatives, the Commonwealth was kept in being by, among other things, the informal and recurrent meetings of the prime ministers. In 1937 the first such conference since 1930 met. Unlike its predecessors, it had no matters of a constitutional nature to discuss. It considered rather the menacing state of Europe following the Italian victory in Abyssinia and the German reoccupation of the Rhineland in 1936 in defiance of the Treaty of Versailles and the Locarno Pact. Little was reported from the conference but it may be inferred that there was agreement on the need to rearm and to prepare to make common cause in the event of a major war in Europe. After the conference, Prime Minister King visited Hitler in Berlin and quietly warned the German leader that he must count on the unity of the British Commonwealth if he pursued a course of aggression. For King believed that if the United Kingdom were involved in a great war, Canada would have to participate, to an extent and by means decided by the Parliament of Canada. His main concern was how to ensure united action by a united nation.

In Canada, however, the prospect of another war created a deep mood of

isolation. This the Prime Minister himself shared and was to voice most eloquently when in 1939 he exclaimed that it seemed "madness" to think that "every
twenty years" Canada must fight a war in Europe. The country was preoccupied
with its economic and the constitutional difficulties. The political nationalism
which had created the Commonwealth was isolationist in spirit, except for a few
nationalists like J. W. Dafoe, who held that an independent Canada should
actively support the League of Nations as the best defence of the independence
of small nations. But the Prime Minister was not one of these; he regarded the
League as simply another commitment, the implementation of which might
strain or destroy national unity. He therefore resolutely diminished Canadian
activity in the League, which in fact the Abyssinian war had mortally wounded.

It was, then, only through the Commonwealth connection that there seemed
to be any danger of involvement in war, and the question arose whether Canada
might declare and maintain neutrality in a war in which the United Kingdom
was a belligerent. In short, was the legal situation still what it had been in 1914,
that when England was at war, Canada was at war? Or in more modern terms,
could the Crown be at war on behalf of the United Kingdom and at peace on
behalf of Canada? This legalistic debate on the "divisibility" or "indivisibility"
of the Crown was one of the many unrealistic issues that bedevilled those bewildered years. The realistic question was whether Canada could in its own
interests afford to see Europe dominated by a power such as National-Socialist
Germany, the policies of which might be expected to be less favourable to
Canada than those of the United Kingdom and of France. More penetrating
was the question whether in fact even the isolationists were prepared to see the
United Kingdom, as the centre of the Commonwealth, threatened with military
defeat, with all that might mean for the Crown and the Commonwealth.

It was with these conflicting and half-defined issues in turmoil that Canada
faced the Munich crisis of September 1938. The mood of the country was more
than ever isolationist. If anything, President F. D. Roosevelt's assurance in his
Kingston speech of August, that the United States would "not stand idly by" if
Canadian soil were threatened with invasion, increased Canadian sympathy
with American isolation. Public opinion ought therefore to have supported the
so-called policy of "appeasement," which was the expression of a similarly
isolationist mood in the United Kingdom. But apart from the more Conservative
papers, which were inclined to support British policy and especially the policy of
a Conservative administration, Canadian opinion – and particularly isolationist
opinion in English Canada – tended to be severely critical of Prime Minister
Neville Chamberlain's policy. The same illogicality, except among the pro-
Germans, was evident in the United States. The meaning of the contradiction
was that Canadian isolationist sentiment in English Canada, as distinct from
French, where isolation rested on a profound distrust of British imperial policy,
was in large part a dislike of the British Conservative party and its desire to

preserve the Commonwealth not only as a free association of independent nations but as an effective diplomatic and military coalition. English Canadian isolation was not, however, like that of French Canada or the United States, either profound or likely to lead to neutrality. In the last analysis, the national development and independence of Canada had arisen from the balance between the United Kingdom and the United States, and the preservation of the United Kingdom and France as powerful and democratic states was a major interest of Canada.

That such was the case Canadians increasingly felt as Hitler's triumph at Munich led on to the seizure of Czechoslovakia and the attack on Poland in 1939. Yet how to prepare for war was a matter of perplexity and embarrassment. The military estimates had risen each year from 1936, and the armed services were being reanimated and strengthened, even if the pace was ludicrously slow in the light of after events. British arms and training continued to be used, and that in itself was a commitment, and a bar to neutrality, as 1914 had revealed. Moreover, there was a great danger that arms might not be available from the United Kingdom, itself inadequately prepared, and even if available perhaps not to be obtained across a blockaded sea. The sure supply lay in the United States; yet, again, American arms would carry with them a measure of American training and an implied commitment. This too could lead to involvement in war, for in 1938 there was the possibility of American forces operating on the Canadian west coast in the event of war between the United States and Japan. But Canadian arms and training were impossible; Canada had always fought in alliance with a great power, and if it fought at all, would do so again. This very fact of military dependence of course inclined the balance towards fighting to maintain the United Kingdom, simply because an alliance with the United States to defend America without a European offset meant absorption to an unpredictable degree into the American power system.

Hitler defied the British ultimatum on September 3, 1939. The Canadian parliament was convened on September 7 and the government introduced a resolution to commit Canada to war with Germany. The debate was brief in a House which had made up its mind that the actions of Germany left no recourse if Europe was not to be dominated by an aggressive and lawless power committed to unlimited conquest. When the vote was taken on September 9, only five members voted nay, the venerable J. S. Woodsworth, a declared and respected pacifist, being one. On September 10 the King declared war on behalf of Canada. Thus, one week after the United Kingdom, Canada was once more at war with Germany. The practical unanimity of the House was, however, the result of more than a determination to resist Hitler. The later and separate declaration of war in Canada's own right, the government's pledge that there would be no resort to conscription, and the declared intention to fight a limited war with the emphasis on supplying war materials rather than men, contributed powerfully to the united action of a nation which had been divided since 1917.

That 1917 was not forgotten in Quebec was revealed two weeks after the declaration of war when Premier Duplessis called a provincial election to protest against the centralization of power in war time and the possible use of conscription. While he did not oppose participation in the war, he did appeal to Quebec to defend its rights and opinions by, as it were, anticipation. The challenge was clear enough and could not be avoided. Lapointe and his three Quebec colleagues in the Cabinet came out in open opposition to Duplessis and campaigned, Lapointe with leonine fury, for the Liberal party and its leader Adélard Godbout against Duplessis and the Union Nationale. They did so in part by pledging that there would be no conscription while they remained in Ottawa. The result was a triumph; the Liberals captured sixty-nine of the eighty-six seats in the legislature. Quebec was decisively committed to the war, provided there were no conscription, and the Liberals' double hold on Quebec afforded the party new strength to resist a growing pressure from English Canada for a "national" – or unionist – government.

The intent of the government, then, was to fight the war along lines suited to Canada's capacity and in proportion to the degree of national unity. That capacity was, moreover, to be carefully husbanded; well-prepared controls of the economy came into effect at once. A Wartime Prices and Trade Board was the first, as it was to become the chief, of many agencies which averted the inflation and the civilian distress of the last years of the war of 1914. One division (raised by volunteering, and consisting of the traditional permanent and militia units) and one squadron of the Royal Canadian Air Force were dispatched to the United Kingdom in 1939. But the emphasis was intended to be put elsewhere. The Navy was to be expanded for convoy duty on the North Atlantic shipping line. Canadian industry, far from bombing attack, was to furnish supplies for the British and French armies. Above all, the wide spaces of Canada and the skill of its airmen were to be used in a great Commonwealth Air Training Plan. The new runways, the long, low huts, the great square hangars, rose rapidly on the prairies, and the peaceful skies began to fill with the brisk little training-planes in which men from all the Commonwealth countries earned their "wings." This was meant to be Canada's principal contribution to the war, as the best use of its resources and as a way of avoiding that demand for infantry masses which had led to the conscription crisis of 1917.

If, however, limited participation in the war was necessary to obtain French support, the limiting of the war effort and the continuation of party government provoked the opposite response in Ontario and elsewhere. Many English Canadians – some "imperialists," some nationalists committed to a war to check aggression – felt that Canada was letting down its allies and its cause. Inspired by memories of the Union Government and by the example of the National Government in the United Kingdom, they demanded the formation of a "national" or "union" government. King resisted these pressures angrily as

"Fascist," for he was convinced that they were directed to the obtaining of advantages for the great financial interests of the country as well as to the introduction of national conscription. But pressures had been developing also within the Liberal party itself, and Premier Hepburn of Ontario, long at odds with the Prime Minister and the national Liberals, made himself their voice. On January 18, 1940, he introduced and carried in the Ontario legislature a vote of censure on the King government for its alleged failure to prosecute the war vigorously. The Prime Minister's reaction was drastic. Parliament met on January 25, only to be dissolved at once. A general election was called for March 26 on the issue of the government's prosecution of the war.

The Prime Minister had actually met to some extent the demand for a "national" government by a strengthening of his cabinet, a process he was to continue until the end of the war. In September he had brought back from private life the able and trusted J. L. Ralston to become Minister of Finance. At the same time the Cabinet had been partly reorganized. Norman Rogers, a politician plucked from academic life, became Minister of Defence, a post in which he made a brilliant beginning.

It was thus a strong administration which faced the electorate on its record. The other parties offered only feeble opposition. Bennett had retired to England and R. B. Hanson served for an interval as House leader. The new leader of the party, R. J. Manion, a former Liberal Unionist and a Roman Catholic from Fort William, was personable but ineffective, and the party lacked not only leadership but both principles and ideas. Parties may survive on instinct, as the Conservative party was to demonstrate; but without ideas they cannot and without principles they ought not to be entrusted with office. Moreover, Manion's seeming endorsement of a national, non-partisan government did little to help the Conservatives. And the C.C.F., though well endowed with both principles and ideas, made little more appeal to the electorate than it had in 1935. It wished to limit the war effort to economic aid. The Social Credit party advocated the conscription of both manpower and wealth. As the result of this fragmentation of the opposition, one hundred and eighty-four Liberals were returned, three more than at dissolution. Mr. King had silenced his critics on both flanks, and the electorate had decided that the war effort was to continue limited.

The character of Canada's war effort, however, was to be settled by events in Europe, not by those in Canada, nor by the memory of 1917. That memory, which had infected Canadian politics for over twenty years, haunted the mind of government, and the Prime Minister was grimly resolved that the strain of war should not develop so as to undo his patient work of national therapy. But the policy of specialized contributions and a limited effort assumed that the armies of Britain and France would be able to contain the forces of Hitler's Third Reich. Poland had gone down quickly in the fall of 1939, but there was little public doubt that the French forces, aided by the British, could hold the Germans until resources could be mustered to break the Reich.

The shattering spring campaign of 1940 swept away that assumption with many another belief. Denmark, Norway, the Netherlands, Belgium, and great France itself went down in two months of "blitzkrieg." The bulk of the British expeditionary force barely escaped, and without its equipment, from Dunkirk. Italy entered the war and the Mediterranean passed from British control. Suddenly the war demanded everything from Canada, even infantry divisions. The tempo and temper of the war effort changed at once from the deliberate build-up of the winter to a series of swift and effective improvisations. Arms were rushed to England, as also from the neutral but deeply friendly United States, to make good the losses of Dunkirk. Planes were bought in the United States to quicken the pace of training for the Air Forces.

Made even more urgent by the tragic death of Norman Rogers in an air crash in early June, a reorganization of the Cabinet was carried out. Ralston became Minister of National Defence, C. G. Power, of Quebec, Minister of National Defence for Air, and J. L. Ilsley, like Ralston a devoted and conscience-driven Nova Scotian, Minister of Finance. It was this strengthened cabinet, working through a central committee or war cabinet set up to administer the war policies of the government, which continued to transform the national war effort. The rate of recruitment was quickened and plans laid for an army of six divisions. The shipyards and munitions factories were driven to full shift production by the unresting energy of C. D. Howe. War industries mushroomed throughout central Canada, and in Quebec a vast hydro-electric development was set going at Shipshaw to smelt aluminium for the thousands of planes necessary to restore the balance in Europe.

With France's divisions gone, every man the countries of the Commonwealth could muster was needed to hold off the Axis and keep alive the hope of victory. The government had already made an inventory of manpower. When the new parliament assembled it considered a bill, the National Resources Mobilization Bill, to authorize compulsory selective service for home defence and civil employment. The administration pledged itself once more that there would be no conscription for service overseas, but declared that the new situation called for compulsory training of Canadian manpower for the defence of Canada. The measure passed, and under the National Resources Mobilization Act the army began to train draftees for home defence.

The transformation of the Canadian war effort from a limited to an all-out one was continued, but even more drastic measures were necessary. The destruction of the Franco-British alliance had altered the world balance of power. Only Russia remained to balance Germany on the continent, and Russia was nominally an ally of Hitler. The one ally whose aid would restore not only the European balance but also European freedom was the United States. To America

Churchill turned in England's desperate need, and received, in Roosevelt's phrase, "all aid short of war." But he had also to pay for some of the aid – fifty old American destroyers, needed to make good those lost at Dunkirk – by leasing naval bases in the British West Indies for a term of ninety-nine years; and two air bases and a naval base in Newfoundland were leased for the same period as a free gift. Thus the destruction of the European balance added to the power of the United States in America and placed American naval power in the mouth of the St. Lawrence. Canadian troops and the R.C.A.F. had already assumed the task of defending Newfoundland; and, while a protocol was added to the agreement stating Canada's special interest in Newfoundland, it was regrettable that the leases were not made terminable on the union of Newfoundland with Canada, which had become a reasonable contingency in the light of the events of 1940.

In this result of Anglo-American action in North America taken without adequate reference to Canadian interests, Canada may have suffered the consequences of Prime Minister King's studied aloofness from the development of special war-time ties with other Commonwealth governments. He denied that any special machinery of consultation was desirable or necessary, and refused to approve the reconstitution of the Imperial War Cabinet of 1917. He did not visit London until August, 1941. He was in consequence, though unfairly, charged with preferring co-operation with the United States to co-operation with Britain. When he did fly to London to consult with the British government on the conduct of the war, he took occasion to remedy the situation in Newfoundland, so far as that could be done, by the addition of the protocol.

The incorporation of Canada into the American defensive system accompanied the American acquisition of the West Indian and Newfoundland bases. Prime Minister King and President Roosevelt met at Ogdensburg in August, 1940, and agreed on the formation of a Permanent Joint Defence Board. A wise and far-sighted measure at the time, it rested on the assumption of the legal equality of the partners and the principle of reciprocal obligation, and was meant to ensure that should the outer defences of America go down entirely, there would at least be co-operation in the defence of the continent itself. A measure in Canada's interest, it none the less left Canada bound to the United States as never before. And when Lend-Lease supplies began to move from the still neutral United States to Britain, Canada abstained from accepting that aid, but sought another arrangement in the Hyde Park Declaration of April 1941. By this agreement Canada was enabled to exchange Canadian war supplies for American, and so conserve its fund of American dollars.

The fall of France and the emergence of the Vichy régime under Marshal Pétain had of course a special meaning for Canada. Many French Canadians were sympathetic towards the neutralist and clerical atmosphere of Vichy and its anti-republican sentiment. For this reason, and as a valuable contact with

German-dominated Europe, Canada, like the United States, maintained relations with Vichy. Unlike the American government, however, the Canadian had much sympathy with the Free French forces of General de Gaulle and accepted their occupation of St. Pierre and Miquelon despite American objection in 1941. The defence alliance with the United States by no means meant the co-ordination of Canadian foreign policy with American.

By the end of 1940 Canada thus found itself in a world transformed, and in a mood which was sharply altering from the puzzled complacency of the first months of the war. The change was produced not only by the shattering events in Europe, but also by a swiftly developing political situation at home. Early in 1940 the Rowell-Sirois Commission had produced its massive report. It recommended that the national government should assume the heavy debts incurred by the provinces for relief during the depression. It also recommended new financial arrangements with provinces. These would provide for a surrender of income, corporation, and succession taxes to the national government, in return for subsidies to the provinces based on population and the cost of providing a minimum national level of governmental and social services. The Report, in brief, recommended that the wealth produced nationally should be taxed nationally and redistributed on a national basis, instead of being taxed in the main by the central provinces for the benefit of the central provinces. Not unnaturally, the governments of those provinces were deeply suspicious of the possible effects of the recommendations. When a conference with the provinces assembled in January 1941, Premier Hepburn of Ontario was loud in his protests and Godbout of Quebec not less hostile. The conference broke up with nothing accomplished.

As a result, the long-attempted strengthening of the framework of national and provincial government had to be postponed indefinitely, and at a time when the additional demands for funds in the new circumstances of an all-out war effort threatened to dry up the provincial sources. Only piecemeal measures could be taken. The national government did assume the relief debts of the provinces. A joint address had already been passed to amend the B.N.A. Act to allow the national government to assume the provision of unemployment relief. This was done and an Unemployment Insurance Fund was begun in 1940. In the budget of 1941 the Minister of Finance offered the provinces annual money grants calculated to compensate for the surrender of income and corporation taxes for the duration of the war, or, as an alternative, the cost of their net debt service, less their succession duty revenues. The provinces, faced with the national government's unlimited power to tax and its war-time support, had little choice but to accept; only Ontario declined. All this was the outcome of the necessities of total war, not of broad-visioned national planning as the Rowell-Sirois Report had intended. Another result, however, was that the national government had command of the tax yield of the growing volume of the national product, and on this basis Ilsley and his advisers achieved a war revenue by taxation and borrowing which not only financed Canada's own war effort but made a major contribution in money and supplies to that of Britain and of Canada's allies other than the United States.

The changes produced in external relations and domestic politics by the military events of 1940 drastically affected the build-up of the armed forces. The 2nd Infantry Division started to reach England in the summer of 1940, and formation of the 1st Canadian Corps was begun. The mobilization of the 3rd and 4th Infantry Divisions was set in train. Two battalions were sent to garrison duties in the British West Indies, relieving British battalions there. In England the Canadian commander, Lieutenant-General A. G. L. McNaughton, had the work of training to complete and the onerous and thankless task of trying to preserve the identity of the Canadian troops when the demands of strategy called for their use as separate divisions in the Commonwealth forces. By the end of 1941 there were about 125,000 men of the Canadian Army in the United Kingdom: three infantry divisions, an armoured division, an army tank brigade, and corps and special troops. At the same time the Royal Canadian Navy grew to a strength of 27,000 men as the corvettes poured from the yards and the convoy duty on the North Atlantic became ever more exacting and important in the face of the rising numbers and improved tactics of the German submarines. The tempo of the Air Training Plan had been greatly increased, and thousands of British and Allied air crew passed through the hands of its instructors, while the number of men and women enlisted in the Royal Canadian Air Force itself grew to 100,000 by the end of 1941.

The manning of the forces and the new war factories while agriculture was kept at full production put an end to unemployment, pulled women into industry and the Services, and justified the resort to selective service in order that the use of the resources of the country might be at once efficient and equitable. But total war created the same demand that the slaughter of the Somme had done, the demand for conscription for overseas service. The situation every reasonable Canadian had hoped might be avoided was developing once more.

The Japanese attack on Pearl Harbor in December 1941, which transformed the war by making it global and bringing the United States into the conflict, increased the feeling that the war effort must be forwarded by conscription for service overseas. The feeling was intensified when Canada suffered the first direct shock of the war as two Canadian battalions, sent to strengthen the garrison of Hong Kong, were compelled after bitter fighting to surrender with the British forces. The Canadian west coast was open to Japanese attack and the United States was now a powerful and influential ally on whose strength the defence of Canada, which had committed so much of its own strength to the European theatre, largely depended. In the construction of the Alaska Highway, and of air-fields in the north and in Labrador to ferry bombers overseas, Canadians worked and served beside the soldiers and airmen of a country which had compulsory service. In consequence the criticism of the Prime Minister – current since the beginning of the war – for continuing party government in war time and refusing to consider a coalition, now became stronger.

The demand for conscription rose so strongly in English Canada that the government, though properly fearful of the effect on Quebec, had to yield. The position of the government in that province was the more delicate in that Lapointe had died in 1941. A successor had been found in Louis Saint-Laurent, who was to achieve an influence in Quebec comparable with Lapointe's, but who was as yet a corporation lawyer turned politician, and untried. The Prime Minister stated his own position clearly enough as being for "conscription if necessary, but not necessarily conscription," a phrase which was not received kindly in those parts of the country where the demand for conscription was strongest. He did, however, say precisely what he intended, that he would try all means, old and new, before he would agree to the precedents of 1917, a coalition government and a conscription election.

Caught between the self-righteous war temper of English Canada and the stubborn and unrealistic determination of Quebec not to be coerced by an English majority, King tried to avoid a collision of the two by a national plebiscite that would release the administration from its pledge not to resort to conscription for overseas service. The result was an affirmative vote of eighty per cent in English Canada and a negative vote of seventy-eight per cent in Quebec. The two nationalities were in complete opposition on the question of conscription for service abroad, and when a bill was introduced to repeal the prohibition of conscription for overseas service in the National Resources Mobilization Act, P. J. A. Cardin felt obliged to resign from the Cabinet in protest. The repeal none the less went through, but no immediate change was made in the use of the draftees. The crisis was muffled for the time being, but heavy losses in the services would awaken it again, and a nasty distinction arose between the volunteers for service overseas and the conscripts for home defence, who were given the pungent nickname of "zombies," a West Indian word for impotent spirits.

Even more disturbing to the student of Canadian history was the illiberal and unjust treatment of the Japanese, and Japanese Canadians, of British Columbia. Some few of these were, no doubt, a danger to national security and properly to be interned. But the war was made an excuse to force the Japanese, whether Canadian or Japanese nationals, to give up their livelihoods and sell their property, preparatory to being removed inland. For this there was no need, and the post-war failure to pay compensation for enforced losses only increased the wrong. The dispersion did actually have the beneficial effect of diminishing anti-Oriental feeling in British Columbia and of further integrating the Japanese Canadians in Canadian society. But benefits achieved through injustice are strictly incidental benefits.

It was thus the temper and the demands of total war, not battle casualties, that had caused the crisis of 1942. Until that year Canadians had suffered few losses except at Hong Kong. There was a steady toll in the fighter and bomber squadrons of the R.A.F., in which a considerable number of Canadians served, in those of the R.C.A.F., and also in the dreary and dangerous convoy duty of the Navy on the North Atlantic route. But the total was not great. And the Canadian divisions in England saw no fighting, only endless battle training. Units of the 1st Division had readied for the campaign in Norway; some had actually crossed to central France, but were withdrawn as France collapsed. In 1942, however, the 2nd Division was chosen for the ill-conceived and ill-fated raid on Dieppe. While there can be no question of the need to try the risks of an assault on the German-held coast of France, or of the lessons learned from the operation, the losses suffered were heavy, and bitter because of futile slaughter on the beaches. One thing only came to Canada from the operation, namely, assurance that the Canadian Army was still of the quality of the old army of 1914–18, which had made the reputation of Canadian troops.

In 1943 the Cabinet overrode McNaughton's desire to keep the Canadian forces entire under his command for the invasion of Europe. While the Cabinet intended that there should be a Canadian army under Canadian command, it thought it important to have Canadian forces co-operate in the conduct of the war and gain experience. McNaughton resigned and returned to Canada. Lieutenant-General H. D. G. Crerar succeeded him. The 1st Division under Major-General Guy Simonds was sent to take part in the invasion of Italy with the Eighth Army of General Bernard Montgomery. The division landed with the Allied assault forces in Sicily and fought its way across the island and over the Strait of Messina. While the bulk of the Eighth Army pressed on to Salerno, the Canadians raced up the instep of Italy towards the Adriatic. In the severe campaign that followed, an Army Tank Brigade and the 5th Armoured Division were added to the 1st Infantry to form a Canadian Corps. On the right wing of the Allied forces it was to fight its way to the north, in a stiff campaign in which it acquitted itself well. Early in 1945 the corps was pulled out to join the Canadian Army in northern Europe.

The First Canadian Army, in England under Crerar, remained in being and was rounded out with British divisions and the Polish division for the opening of the invasion of France in June 1944. It was in the left wing of the assault on the Normandy beaches. The 3rd Infantry Division landed successfully, but as the Canadians fought their way inland by Caen they encountered desperate German resistance. It was an ordeal for troops not battle-hardened, and losses in infantry were heavy, far beyond those anticipated. And when the Americans on the right broke out and encircled the German Seventh Army, the Canadian forces, despite desperate and valorous efforts, failed to close fast the Falaise Gap and ensure the annihilation of the German troops caught by the American columns.

For troops who had been raised in the legend of invincibility, it was a stern lesson in the trials of war.

The experience did nothing to reduce the dash with which the Army next proceeded to clear the Channel Coast and overrun the flying-bomb bases in the Pas de Calais, or the slogging courage with which it cleared the mouth of the Scheldt and opened Antwerp to supply the allied armies fighting up to the Rhine. In the hard fighting in the Rhineland that winter and at the crossing of the Rhine in the early spring, the Army, with the 1st Division reunited, achieved its full stature. Battle-hardened and battle-wise, it had become an army of veterans.

The losses in the Normandy fighting, however, because the role of infantry had been underestimated in warfare which had seemed to turn on the tank and the plane, had revived the latent manpower crisis. The compromise of 1942 had rankled, as all compromise will in times of national strain. The Minister of Defence visited Canadian Army Headquarters, and, like Borden in 1917, returned to Canada determined that the conscripts for home service must be sent overseas to reinforce the infantry. A veteran field officer of the First War, Ralston took the military view of the matter and was prepared to pay the political price. A number of his colleagues agreed with him, and a cabinet crisis developed. The Prime Minister refused to adopt Ralston's view, and informed his Minister of Defence that General McNaughton was confident that the Home Defence men could be persuaded to volunteer in sufficient numbers to meet the need. McNaughton, moreover, was prepared to become Minister of Defence to find the volunteers. At this Ralston left the Cabinet. McNaughton as Minister made his appeal for volunteers. He failed, however, either to win election to the House of Commons or to obtain the recruits. King had to give way, and with bitter misgivings authorized the dispatch overseas, as the National Mobilization Resources Act permitted, of enough conscripts to make good the losses. Then C. G. Power resigned; and many Quebec members opposed the government's act. For a while it seemed that the cleavage of 1917 had occurred again. But King's desperate endeavours and the approaching end of the war prevented the worst. Only some thirteen thousand conscripts had to be sent overseas, and Canada, shaken but not divided, held to its course.

As the Canadian Army drove on to victory in the North German ports, the nation remained united behind it. Victory in Europe, however, was the prelude to further combat in the Pacific. Canada had participated little in the Pacific war. The North-West Staging Route, a line of airfields to Alaska, had served to move aircraft to Alaska and Russia. American troops based at Edmonton had driven the Alaska Highway through the Peace River country and the Rockies. Canadian home defence troops had participated in the reoccupation of Kiska in the Aleutian Islands. That was the sum of Canada's contribution to the Pacific campaign, in consequence of its total commitment to the North Atlantic and Europe. With the end of the war in Europe, Canada undertook to furnish a brigade for the final Pacific operations, but it was to be integrated with American forces when armed with American weapons and trained in American tactics. Japan had surrendered before the brigade was ready for action, but the episode revealed a basic dilemma of Canada's dual commitment to action with the Commonwealth and the American services.

So fundamental was the dilemma, faced even before the war in debates on the choice of arms supply, that it might involve the necessity of a choice between American and Commonwealth ties. Diplomatically there was one way of avoiding the dilemma. That was by membership in a new organization for collective action against threats to the peace, followed by some standardization of armaments between at least the United Kingdom and the United States. As early as 1942, President Roosevelt and Cordell Hull, with the full support of Churchill, had begun an organization of "peace-loving" nations to succeed the League. Prime Minister King was by no means as convinced as the American statesmen, or as liberal opinion in Canada, that a new start could lead to any other result than that which the League had involved – a constant and indefinite commitment to take military action which, when it occurred, might find Canada politically divided. On the other hand, any thought of attempting to turn the remarkable military co-operation of the Commonwealth nations into formal modes of peace-time co-operation, as Lord Halifax, British Ambassador to Washington, suggested in a speech in Toronto in 1944, was as unacceptable to King as it was to a majority of Canadians. Like King at the Commonwealth Conference of 1944, Canadians were glad to express satisfaction with the Commonwealth as it was, but they were suspicious, perhaps unduly and unwisely suspicious, of any attempt to make the Commonwealth a co-ordinated great power. The war had produced in Canada both a stronger sentiment for the Commonwealth as a free association of independent nations and a stronger determination to realize the last implications of national sovereignty.

What, then, was Canada to do? Canada had in the war, as in that of 1914, only one object, the maintenance of the United Kingdom and France as great powers in a Europe of free nations. Unlike the first war, that just completed had no other gains for Canada, such as the realization of national stature in the world. And Canada's major object had been realized only in part. Both the United Kingdom and France had been shaken to their foundations by the defeat of 1940; the old pre-eminence of European power had passed. The world was for the time being dominated by the two extra-European powers of Russia and America. With the European counterbalance no longer effective, Canada was alone in America with the United States, now a tremendous naval and military power, masterful and urgent. The use of atomic bombs to defeat Japan and bring the Second World War to an apocalyptic end had, among many greater results, placed Canada directly between the United States and its late ally and inevitable rival, the Soviet Union.

How intimate the connection with the United States was, and how insidious the Russian danger, was demonstrated with the sharpness and force of an explosion when in 1945 Igor Gouzenko, an official of the Russian Embassy, sought the protection of the Mounted Police and revealed that Canadian citizens and government servants had betrayed secret military information, some of it concerning the atomic bomb, to Russia. This was not only a failure in security, but a betrayal of those of Canada's allies with whom the information was shared. The government reacted drastically. A royal commission was formed to interrogate the suspects before accusation or trial. When this inquisition, shockingly contrary to conventional "due process of law" as known and practised in Canada, was complete, eighteen persons were accused, of whom eight were convicted and imprisoned and one was fined by the courts. The breach of civil liberties was lamentable; the offence of those proved guilty was great; and the extent of Canada's involvement with her allies was revealed. Isolation and neutrality, now legally possible, were actually barren and impossible prospects.

The only way to avoid the fearful possibilities involved in the situation seemed to be to support an effective world organization. King allowed himself to be persuaded by the ardent young men whom the Civil Service of Canada had attracted in the years of depression and war as he himself had been attracted at the beginning of the century. In the Department of External Affairs the chief of these was Lester B. Pearson, an historian by profession, who preserved through his academic training a clipped Canadian accent and the fervour of an evangelical background. Eager, persuasive, dedicated, he turned the defensive Canadianism of his late departmental chief, Skelton, and his minister, King, outward on the world, and brought to Canadian external policy a perhaps not uncharacteristically Canadian union of conscience and common sense in the service of the general good. Behind him was a strong body of liberal and popular thought, the work of many scholars and of the Canadian Institute of International Affairs. The latter was an organization of private discussion groups by which the thoughtful opinion of the country, flowing from public figures like J. W. Dafoe and B. K. Sandwell, from private ones such as E. J. Tarr of Winnipeg and Nik Cavell of Toronto, was clarified and concentrated. From this wide-based thinking came the resolution that Canada should fully support a United Nations in which the major powers would police the peace in the Security Council and in which "middle powers" – a category defined by Canada, and claimed for itself – might find a useful part to play in the General Assembly and above all in the social and economic agencies which, it was hoped, would deal with the causes of war, poverty, disease, and over-population.

The program won general approval and Canada strongly supported the establishment of the United Nations at the San Francisco conference of 1945. Its doing so marked the end of the policy of "no commitment" of Laurier and King, and this fact was underlined by two post-war decisions. One was the reconsideration and confirmation in 1947 of the Permanent Joint Defence Board. Coupled with this was the Visiting Forces, United States of America Act of 1947, which placed American like other visiting forces under Canadian law and thus ended a war-time disregard of Canadian sovereignty by American forces. The other was the separation of the Department of External Affairs from the office of the Prime Minister in 1946 and the appointment of Louis Saint-Laurent as Minister of External Affairs. Saint-Laurent proved to be entirely in accord with the new and active policy formulated by Pearson. Thus, providentially, it was by the lips of a French Canadian that the end of "negative politics" in external affairs was proclaimed, in Saint-Laurent's historic Gray Memorial lecture to the University of Toronto in 1947.

The era of negative politics had ended in domestic affairs also. The change was the result of alteration within the Liberal party itself. There was, in fact, no other way of accomplishing it; the other Canadian parties were ineffectual in national politics. In 1942 the Conservative party had suffered a further change of leadership; R. J. Manion had been defeated in the election of 1940, and Hanson had continued as House leader. Arthur Meighen resumed the leadership, resigned from the Senate, and sought election to the House of Commons. He was defeated in a Toronto by-election by a C.C.F. candidate deliberately supported by the national Liberal party in an extraordinary manifestation of partisanship, to be explained though hardly justified by the Prime Minister's conviction that the union government Meighen and his supporters desired would be "Fascist" in character. When Meighen was thus removed from the formal leadership of the Conservative party, the party met in conference at Winnipeg to choose a leader. There was now general agreement that a western leader was needed to restore Conservative fortunes in the west and balance the weight of Quebec, apparently wedded indefinitely to the Liberal party. The expectation was that Sidney Smith, the able and popular president of the University of Manitoba, and a liberal Conservative born in Nova Scotia and known in Ontario, would be chosen. But Meighen turned the choice to John Bracken, the non-partisan leader since 1922 of the farmers' government in Manitoba. At the same time, at Bracken's insistence, the name of the party was changed to Progressive Conservative. Only time, much thought, much organization, and a fundamental change of character, it was recognized, would restore the fortunes of the Canadian Conservative party.

The outlook for the party was to brighten in Ontario when in 1943 the Conservatives under George A. Drew, already known to the public as a national politician, overthrew the Liberal régime and began a long period of Conservative rule in that province. None of the other parties as yet gave much promise of replacing it as the national Opposition. The C.C.F., it is true, had established itself in British Columbia, Manitoba, and Ontario, where in 1943 it won thirty-four seats. It had then gone on to capture the government of Saskatchewan in 1944.

In the next year it reached its high mark in national politics when it elected twenty-eight members in the general election. But it failed to oust the Conservatives from the place of Opposition to the still victorious Liberals. The Union Nationale of Quebec of course remained a provincial party. Social Credit still remained an Albertan movement, although Social Credit candidates had been elected to other western legislatures and had been sent to the House of Commons from constituencies in Alberta.

Even the Liberals had cause for concern in their decline in the provinces. They still held the three Atlantic provinces, and in Manitoba and British Columbia were the dominant element in coalitions of the old parties. But in Alberta the Social Credit government was still in power despite Aberhart's death, and in 1944 Quebec followed Saskatchewan and Ontario out of the ranks of provincial Liberal governments. In that year Duplessis, making the most of the soreness the plebiscite of 1942 had left, brought his Union Nationale back to power. It was plain that the two-party system, which had seemed to be restored in 1930, had not thrown off the new political growths of the depression with the surge of war-time prosperity. National and provincial politics were steadily parting company. The voters were increasingly independent of party ties; the electorate was volatilized, and Canadian politics, at least in the provinces, were ceasing to be conducted by means of the rivalry and debate of parties and were becoming mass plebiscites on general issues and the choice of leaders. The revolts against the political parties, the rise of the welfare state and the emergence of the bureaucracy of the Civil Service were modifying the old forms of parliamentary government.

In national politics also the same tendency was evident and was reinforced by the fragmentation of the opposition, the strength shown by the C.C.F. in 1943 and 1944, the success of the Liberal party in being all things to all men of the centre of politics, and Prime Minister King's own deep belief in the mandatory character of a general election and the unqualified supremacy of the Prime Minister in government. And to the plebiscitary prime-ministership and the all-providing party were added the enormous war-time growth of the bureaucracy and the adoption of welfare policies by the national government.

Coupled with this drastic development of responsible government as a Caesarean dictatorship of the Prime Minister, with power resting in the electorate rather than in Parliament, went a subtle change in the character of government itself. The depression and the war combined to oust the last remnants of the old limited state in Canada and to create the all-benevolent, all-powerful welfare state. Duplessis' reaction against centralization was not unjustified and the extent to which the national government had become "positive" and centralized was shown in the growth of the national Civil Service. In 1939 there were 46,016 permanent and temporary members; in 1946 there were 120,557, and the growth was to continue.

King, sensing that the requirements of post-war policy made possible the reforms he had urged in his *Industry and Humanity* before he became a party leader, turned to redeem the promise of his far-off, interventionist youth, and the two ideas that governed national policy after 1944 brought to an end his era of negative politics. One was that there should not be a post-war depression such as had followed 1918. The other was that the national government should retain, by exercising it, the authority it had recovered during the war. To realize these two ideas, post-war planning had begun early and was put into effect even before the end of the war. The galaxy of brilliant civil servants furnished by the universities, and particularly by Queen's and Manitoba, were much influenced both by the economic thought of Lord Keynes and by the example of the New Deal. In effect, they proposed to fight an anti-depression campaign and develop welfare policies by monetary means, the magnificent success of the war financing having given them the requisite confidence. It was to this end that a Family Allowance Act was passed in 1944; it would not only help families of low income, it would also maintain purchasing power in the transition from the war to the peace economy. A new National Housing Act, the third, made national funds available on more liberal terms for the dual purpose of providing low-cost housing and stimulating construction. By means of federal grants offered in aid of hospital construction, the provinces were enabled to extend their medical facilities. The many war-time controls were used with surprising effectiveness to ease the transition from a war to a peace economy. The result was, to everyone's surprise, that there was no post-war depression, but instead a prolonged and ever-mounting boom.

The provinces, for their part, had carried on since 1940 with their established sources of income and had abstained from expansion of services and from construction of all kinds as much as possible. The consequence was a pent-up demand for facilities and services of all kinds. The long-delayed rearrangement of financial resources, if not of constitutional powers, had at last to be attempted. If the attempt should result in increased provincial revenues, then again construction of all kinds would be encouraged as war industry ended, social welfare would be increased, and the national government would share the credit with the provinces. In 1947 all the provinces except Quebec and Ontario accepted for a term of three years the proposal of the national government that the provinces agreeing should not collect income, corporation, or succession taxes, and that the national government would pay those provinces annual subsidies at so much a head of population and at a rate varying with the increase or decrease of the national production of wealth. The Tax Agreement did something to offset the provincial taxation of wealth earned nationally, and ensured that all provinces would share according to population in the national output. As a political agreement, it was a major achievement which finally restored to national life a tone and unity it had not known since before 1914.

The national vigour expressed itself in part by carrying further the development of political nationalism. Much of the old spirit was still evident in members of the Liberal government whose thinking had been formed in the 1920's; much in French Canada, where *nationalisme* was still strongly at work not only to preserve the French Catholic culture against English-Canadian encroachment, but also to assert the autonomy of Canadian nationhood and to realize the ideal of a bilingual and bi-cultural nationality. In 1946 a measure of fundamental significance was passed, the Citizenship Act. By this a Canadian citizenship was created, a citizenship to be acquired only by birth or naturalization. It was made primary; Canadian citizenship made one a British subject, but being a British subject did not, with Canadian residence, make one a Canadian citizen. An Englishman or other British subject of the Commonwealth who wished to become a Canadian had, thenceforth, to go through the process of naturalization. Here it would seem national zeal did violence to the spirit of the Commonwealth, created a discrimination where none was needed, and did harm without achieving any corresponding good.

More reasonable, and of great possible benefit to the constitutional development of Canada, was the abolition in 1949 of appeals in civil cases (those in criminal cases had been finally ended in 1931) to the Judicial Committee of the Privy Council. In future the Supreme Court of Canada would conduct the judicial interpretation of the Canadian constitution. While there was much to be said for the maintenance of a great central tribunal in which the common legal and constitutional heritage of the Commonwealth might be kept developing along common lines, long experience had proved that the task was beyond men who had no experience of the communities for which they adjudicated. Much harm had been done the constitutional development of Canada by the constitutional decisions of the Committee, in that they had failed both to understand the essentially national character of the constitution they were interpreting and to realize that the national cabinet and legislature were as sensitive to provincial and minority rights as any provincial administration could be.

To the work of completing national autonomy, that of rounding out the national domain was added in 1949. In that year, eighty-two years after Confederation, Newfoundland joined Canada. Since 1934 it had been governed by the Commission appointed in that year. By careful management, aided by Canadian and American expenditures on airfields and naval bases and the great airports of Gander and Goose, the Commission had been able to restore the finances of the former Dominion. With the return of comparative prosperity, government by the Commission became even more distasteful to the Newfoundlanders, and it became apparent after 1945 that the period of rule by commission must be ended.

Two possible futures faced the Island; return to Dominion status or union with Canada. A third, that of union with the United States, was privately discussed but never became a formal possibility. Newfoundland, jealous of its separate existence, proud of its distinctive history, aware of the discontent of the Atlantic provinces, was reluctant to accept union with Canada. But the generous Canadian terms, which were possible because of the industrial growth of the war years and the financial agreements with the provinces, reinforced by the new national social services, made union more attractive than it had ever been in the past. Finally J. R. Smallwood, a popular, able politician extraordinarily gifted in all the arts of democratic appeal, decided the issue by throwing all the allurement of his vivid personality behind the cause of Confederation.

Canada, for its part, promised all the benefits of the Tax Agreement of 1947 and the social welfare measures, with special payments to meet the exceptional needs of the Island, the assumption of the debt, and the incorporation of the Island's railway into the Canadian National system. In 1948 a referendum was held on the three possibilities: restoration of responsible government, commission government, or union with Canada. Commission government was eliminated, and a second plebiscite followed to decide between responsible government and union. Smallwood's salty, dynamic campaign produced a small but sufficient majority of fifty-two per cent for union. Newfoundland then became the tenth province and the territorial boundaries of Canada stood as the Fathers of Confederation had envisaged them. In Newfoundland there was sadness for the loss of an historic and cherished independence, but the resources of Canada could now be applied to eradicate the ancient poverty of the Island and to aid the development of resources other than the historic fishery of the Banks.

The work of completing national autonomy and the national domain was not finished in these exuberant years; the degree of national unity did not yet admit such a consummation. Parliament had therefore to content itself with taking power in 1949 to amend the national sections of the B.N.A. Acts by Act of Parliament. It thus put itself in the same position with respect to purely national constitutional changes as the provinces were in with respect to their own constitutions. When the fundamental question of amendment of the national-provincial sections of the constitution was taken up in 1950, the continued intransigence of Quebec and Ontario made it impossible to proceed with plans for amendment by a Canadian process. Amendment of national-provincial matters therefore, such as educational, language, and minority rights, continued to be subject to provincial agreement and the concurrence of the Parliament of the United Kingdom. Similarly it proved impossible to reach agreement on a national flag; the development of nationhood had not yet reached a point where one symbol could evoke the same response from all Canadians alike. Until a symbol can unite, its only effect is to divide, and the question was wisely put off until the slow ripening of a common national sentiment should be complete.

It was while the tide of post-war nationalism was flooding towards the crest it was not quite to reach that Prime Minister King, seventy-four years of age and wearied by absolute devotion to the duties imposed by the power he had exercised longer than any other Prime Minister in British history, even Walpole, decided to lay aside that power and retire. The decision to relinquish power was made in the same lonely spirit as he had exercised it. Unmarried, without close friend or confidant, he had added to the loneliness of power a solitude of the spirit which had driven him at last to a secret communion with the world of spirits. This utter loneliness sprang, no doubt, from many sources. One may have been the self-abnegation his political task of restoring national unity had imposed. Himself a man of philosophic training and clear ideas firmly held, his normal approach to politics would have been that of his days in the Civil Service, positive and constructive. But nearly all this side of his nature he had had to deny in order to fulfil the essentially negative task of ensuring that there should be no reopening of the wounds of 1917.

Only in his last years did he allow his young men of the Civil Service and the Cabinet, with what wry paternalism may only be guessed, to attempt by new methods to accomplish the aims of his own frustrated youth. For with King's youth had died, after 1921, his vision of a community adapted to the social structure and urban industry of the twentieth century. His work, on the contrary, proved to be a work of salvage and preservation, not of renovation and creation. No public man, however, may choose his times or what may fall to him to attempt, and King in the end had his reward. Few men by doing so little had accomplished so much. And unlike Macdonald and Laurier, he in some measure entered the promised land. Canada, which had elected but never loved him, owed its stronger national fibre, the greater authority of its national government, its deeper appreciation of its dual culture and its own unique character as a liberal nation-state, to the negative ardour, the cultivated obscurity and the conservative purpose of the rebel's grandson.

ADDITIONAL READING

CANADA *Report of the Royal Commission on Dominion-Provincial Relations.*
IRVING, J. A. *The Philosophy of Social Credit.*
MACPHERSON, C. B. *Democracy in Alberta.*
PICKERSGILL, J. W. *The Mackenzie King Record.* Vol. I, 1939-1944.
SOWARD, F. H., *et al. Canada in World Affairs: The Pre-War Years.*
SPENCER, R. A. *Canada in World Affairs: UN to NATO, 1946-1949.*

CHAPTER 24

The Stresses of Welfare and World Politics

1950-1960

Canada by 1949 had emerged from the immediate post-war years, and entered a decade in which the old issues of national development, the relations of the provincial governments with the national, of English Canada with French, and of Canada with the United States, were to be complicated and even intensified by the rapid growth of the welfare state and the emergence of the United States as a nuclear world power. The growth of the welfare state, initiated by the Liberal party, was meant to buoy up purchasing power and to cushion depression. It was the result of fiscal, not of social policy. But the entry by the national government into the field of welfare not only restored to that government the dynamic of its nation-building days; it also challenged the provinces in the field of social policy. Nowhere was this challenge more resented, or more quickly taken up, than in Quebec. The decade, then, was to see the final settlement of issues, such as the amending of the constitution, delayed and made more difficult by the growing role of government in social welfare and the implication of this growth for national-provincial and French-English relations. In this increase of intimacy between government and society was the source of new strains in the national fabric and of new factors operating to separate French and English Canada. At the same time, the pressure of world politics and the active role of the United States as a world power made national cohesion more important than ever.

Such was the character of problems which faced the national government under the new Prime Minister. When Prime Minister King resigned in 1948, Louis Saint-Laurent had succeeded him and in 1949 had won his first general election. In this simple, courageous man, as fully Canadian as he was French Canadian, the new spirit of the nation found a dignified and lovable symbol. That English Canada should so readily have admired his qualities and taken him to its heart was a clear indication of how far it had advanced towards a full and unreserved acceptance of the duality of Canadian life.

Nor was it less symbolic that one of the new Prime Minister's first major acts should have been the appointment of a royal commission to inquire into the state of the arts, letters, and sciences in Canada. The late Prime Minister had perhaps over-used the great instrument of the commission of inquiry, but only a French prime minister would have employed so formidable an implement of state to take account of the arts, letters and sciences. Such matters English Canadians, whether in private life or public office, were inclined to regard as the concern of the amateur and the academician. But the noble French tradition of state patronage of the arts was nowhere stronger than in Quebec, and this extension into the national life of one of the best aspects of the French spirit was something for which all Canadians might be grateful. Under the chairmanship of Rt. Hon. Vincent Massey, the Commission produced a report of great interest which was to have, still under the Prime Minister's direction, major consequences for the arts and sciences in Canada.

In one other field of national expression a similar success was scored, the appointment of a native Canadian as Governor General, one who took up the tradition of vice-regal duty that Tweedsmuir had begun and carried it to even greater heights of public ceremony. Tweedsmuir had died in office in 1940; had he lived and had his health permitted, his term of office might well have been extended. The appointment of his successor, the Earl of Athlone, was a return to the old tradition of titled figureheads who had little rapport with Canadian life. He in turn was succeeded by Viscount Alexander of Tunis, the brilliant commander under whom Canadian troops had served in Italy. Alexander also performed the duties of the office punctiliously, but without making public ceremony more than a perfunctory ritual. When, however, Vincent Massey, a public servant and a diplomat, a man of taste, and with a sense of history, became the first Canadian to represent the Sovereign, the office awoke to life again as in Tweedsmuir's day, and Canadians were once more persuaded that public life may be humane, that the public service is the highest secular calling, that the dignity and aspiration of a free nation may be expressed in the person, the human concern, and the living voice of a dedicated man.

It was not only in its domestic life that Canada advanced swiftly towards the final realization of its nationhood. The rapid evolution of the Commonwealth, itself so much the product of Canadian experience and purpose, carried Canada forward with it in the post-war years. India, granted a large measure of self-government before 1939, in 1947 claimed and received full self-government and independence as the states of India and Pakistan. Burma and Ceylon also became self-governing. Would the new states choose to remain within the Commonwealth? Would the old members, all of European origin, welcome Asian members? Could the Commonwealth become multi-racial? All these questions, and even one that was new and unforeseen, were quickly and triumphantly answered in the Commonwealth conference of 1948. All but Burma chose to remain; and the secession of Burma, and the final withdrawal of Ireland in 1949, while regretted, only emphasized the entire freedom of the Commonwealth association. All those who chose to enter the Commonwealth were cordially welcomed, even India, which had become a republic. To accommodate India, the King was declared to be Head of the Commonwealth, and that infinitely flexible association elected to combine in its membership nations united by allegiance to the Crown and those united only in a fellowship of common purpose. All this was done in the knowledge that, behind the Asian states, the African colonies were moving rapidly towards autonomy and probable membership in the Commonwealth.

The transformation of the Commonwealth was welcomed in Canada. Its new character, even if it raised many and serious questions, did seem a vindication of the liberal aims and conservative heritage of this free association. But perhaps more deeply interesting was the change in the royal titles which was agreed upon by the Prime Ministers of the Commonwealth in 1952, that the sovereign should henceforth be known as the King of the United Kingdom, Canada, and his other Realms and Territories. Thus the intent of Macdonald and the Fathers of Confederation, unnecessarily disappointed by American protest and British timidity, was realized at last, and Canada became the Kingdom of Canada its history had prepared it to be. When in 1952 George VI died, his daughter Elizabeth was proclaimed in Ottawa as Elizabeth II, Queen of Canada; and when the Queen in 1957 opened Parliament, the new rank of Canada stood revealed in all its historic reality.

The realization of the old destiny occurred, however, in a new order of power in the world, one yet undefined and unresolved. In 1919 the peacemakers had made a settlement and created the League of Nations to revise it as the future might require. The League had failed; and Germany, Italy, and Japan had attempted revision by the ancient methods of aggression and force. In 1945, the victor powers had deliberately refrained from attempting a peace settlement, in the hope that the United Nations might prove a means of creating circumstances more favourable for a settlement than those that could be expected in the years immediately following the war.

This alternative procedure was even more disappointing in its consequences. The Security Council of the United Nations was deadlocked by the Russian use of the "veto" to block actions it feared. Russia, with enormous resources of conventional military power, aimed no doubt to achieve the victory of Communism in the world. Certainly, it was determined to ensure itself against future attack from Europe, but was restrained by the monopoly of atomic power still held by the United States and the United Kingdom. It could not therefore allow the United States to dominate the Security Council, as with its client states the United States dominated the General Assembly. Russia accordingly sought by all means, short of provoking the too terrible retaliation of the atomic bomb, to exploit the position given it by its military victories and by the adherence of the Western allies to the agreement to occupy a partitioned Germany. Only the democratic régime of Eduard Benes in Czechoslovakia and the joint occupation of Berlin kept Russia from possession of the two keys to the domination of central Europe, Prague and Berlin.

That such was the aim of Russian policy Winston Churchill had proclaimed at Fulton, Missouri, in 1947. He was no longer Prime Minister of the United Kingdom after his defeat by the Labour party in the general election of 1945, but he still possessed all the influence of his war-time leadership. The open return to power politics followed quickly. Early in 1948 the United States began the Marshall Plan of financial aid to a Europe devastated by war and riddled with Communism. Assuming the United Kingdom's historic task of supporting the liberal powers of Europe, a task a weakened England could no longer discharge, as the withdrawal from Greece in 1947 had revealed, the United States stood forward as the great power of the free world and began the task of restoring the economic life and the democratic will of the west European and Mediterranean countries.

The Russian reaction was immediate. Moscow first ordered Czechoslovakia not to accept Marshall Aid and then liquidated the Benes régime and installed a pro-Russian government. The Russian occupying forces then cut off access of the Western powers to Berlin on the ground, and the partition of Germany and Europe seemed imminent. The Western powers, however, stood on their right to enter West Berlin and proceeded to supply that city and their forces by an "air-lift." Western resolution defeated the Russian pressure and the blockade was finally lifted.

The extent of Russian purpose and daring had, none the less, been revealed and the need to supplement economic by military aid made imperative. The hope that the "great power" nations of the war might together maintain the peace ended with the Berlin blockade and the Communist victory in China. Peace was not to be kept by "global" action; it might yet be preserved by regional association. The result in the West was the North Atlantic Treaty Organization, by which the United States and the United Kingdom undertook to maintain, in conjunction with the west European powers and the Mediterranean states of Italy, Greece, and Turkey, armed forces in Europe for the defence of the West against Russian pressure. Canada was active and influential in the creation of Nato, and committed ground, air, and naval forces, which might have been used to defend its own empty and now vulnerable north, to the defence of Europe. The psychological and military need to strengthen Europe's will to resist Russian pressure and propaganda explains this strategic decision, the effect of which was to make Canada more than ever dependent on American aid to defend Canada itself. The decision, however, was right, for the continental defence of America extended beyond America, and Canada found in Nato a general alliance which was an insurance against the risks of a merely two-sided alliance with the United States.

Russia, checked in Europe, now turned to Asia. Korea after the defeat of Japan had been partitioned much as Germany had been. American troops occupied Korea south of the 38th parallel of latitude; Russian troops, the territory north of that line. The latter were replaced gradually by Russian-trained and armed North Korean troops. Meantime, American forces also occupied Japan, Okinawa, and Formosa, thus making the Pacific an American sea. The enormous expansion of American power in the Far East – the counterpart of the Russian expansion into Europe – stopped, however, at the coastline of Asia, except in Korea. The long-continued and enormous aid the United States had given to the régime of Chiang Kai-shek vanished fruitlessly in 1949 when the Chinese Communists under Mao Tse-tung drove Chiang from the mainland to a refuge in Formosa. Thus the Far East was partitioned, in a most unstable and threatening manner, between the two Communist powers and the United States; there, as in Europe, the great powers of the new order were ranged menacingly face to face.

Suddenly this delicate and dangerous equilibrium was upset when in June, 1950, North Korean troops crossed the 38th parallel and began to overrun South Korea. The United States at once resisted in aid of the South Korean régime of Syngman Rhee. The fact that the United States was once more at war imposed no obligation on Canada, and Canadian opinion hesitated at the prospect of being drawn into a purely American war in the Pacific. But the United States was fighting in defence of the provisional division of Korea pending a negotiated settlement, and the North Korean attempt to impose a settlement by force was clearly an act of aggression and a threat to world peace. Such was the view taken, with Canada agreeing, by the General Assembly of the United Nations. Taking advantage of temporary withdrawal by Russia, the Security Council ordered action by the members of the United Nations against North Korea. Canada contributed an infantry brigade with artillery, and a naval contingent, to the United Nations forces. By 1952 these forces, largely American and South Korean, had driven from South Korea both the North Koreans and the Chinese Communists who had come to their aid.

One effect of the war was that Canada and the United States were left even more deeply divided than they had been on the question of recognizing the Communist régime as the lawful government of China. The United States, committed to the support of Chiang Kai-shek and embittered by the Chinese rejection of American friendship and influence, proceeded to apply its peculiar doctrine of non-recognition. Canada, in the pragmatic tradition of international law, preferred to recognize a government *de facto* as the government *de jure*, but out of deference to the strong feeling of its great neighbour refrained, with many misgivings, from extending recognition.

The intervention of the Chinese Communists in Korea was, however, a final evidence of what forces were on the move in the world, and the danger was immensely magnified when Russia developed the atomic bomb. The defences of Canada had to be increased and warning of bomber attack across the Arctic against American industrial centres provided by the building of the Pinetree Net across southern Canada. The defence budget, estimated at five billion dollars for a three-year period in 1950, rose to nearly two billion dollars a year, a level at which it was thereafter to continue.

If the external world was under the stress of a new and precarious balance of power and lit by flashes of apocalyptic menace, internally Canada prospered as never before. No depression followed the war. On the contrary, a Canada braced for depression relaxed with a slowly growing delight in the buoyant prosperity of "the affluent society." The measures planned and taken against a post-war slump were surprisingly effective. They were aided by the need to maintain a military, naval, and air-force establishment, considerable in relation to the resources of the country, in order to contribute to the forces of Nato and to the defence of North America. The new principles of monetary policy, applied with dedicated intelligence by the staff of the Bank of Canada and the Ministry of Finance, proved to be effective in preventing either a constriction of credit or an excessive inflation. The task was gigantic, and experimental; success was dependent on too many uncontrollable and elusive factors ever to be taken for granted. For the time being, however, great dangers were surmounted and great hazards turned out to advantage.

As the war-time price and rent controls were piece by piece laid aside, social-service payments and government-supported credit flowed out to maintain the demand of the public for goods and services. Housing construction boomed to meet the needs accumulated by the war and increased by post-war marriages and a flood of immigrants. The activities of a host of Crown corporations, the empire of the forceful C. D. Howe, maintained the production of materials needed for war supply – at the Port Hope refinery of Eldorado Mining and Refining Limited, for example, and the Polymer Corporation plant at Sarnia for making synthetic rubber – or supplied services in which the national interest seemed to call for national control of development, as with Trans-Canada Air Lines and the Canadian Broadcasting Corporation. Not only in days of need but in times of prosperity, the Canadian mixture of governmental and private enterprise in development continued as before. Even when allowance is made for the effect of war-time exigency and the peculiar genius of Howe, it remains true that the Canadian economy, dominated by the need to apply the most highly developed techniques to resources scattered over an enormous and forbidding wilderness, required the alliance of national credit and government support with private capital and enterprise.

All these measures of state intervention, however, would not of themselves have produced the great boom which followed the Second World War and especially the Korean War. The Canadian economy responded to many new

KC R

factors, most of which were developed by private enterprise. Gilbert LaBine's discovery of radioactive ores at Great Bear Lake in 1930 had simply added a Canadian supply of radium to that of the Belgian Congo. But the development of the atomic bomb and the possibility of atomic power created a great and imperative demand for supplies of uranium. Feverish prospecting along the edge of the Shield resulted in many finds, two of them major – one at Beaverlodge Lake in Saskatchewan, one at Elliot Lake in Ontario. Money poured into the new mining industry and the United States contracted to take the full output until 1962. At the same time the oil industry of western Canada suddenly boomed. The dwindling of supplies in the United States had started the great American oil companies prospecting over the world for oil. Western Canada was an area of supply of great strategic interest. In 1947 a strike was made at Leduc near Edmonton, which revealed that Alberta had oil, as well as natural gas, in quantity. The discovery of the Pembina field followed, and strikes were made in southeastern Saskatchewan and south-western Manitoba. Again capital in millions flowed in, mostly American; and the prairie economy, especially that of Alberta, began to undergo a transformation. With these major additions to the Canadian primary economy came many minor but not unimportant ones as the new technology called for rare minerals, hitherto known but little used, such as lithium and the "rare earths."

The secondary economy underwent a no less striking growth. Older industries, such as wood pulp and paper, and steel, grew greatly. New ones arose: the aircraft industry, a heritage of the war; a variety of chemical industries sprung from the war, the new technology, and the increase in oil production; many forms of new fabrication, such as plywoods and plastics. The urban areas of central Canada, particularly the Montreal district and the "Golden Horseshoe" from Toronto around through Hamilton to Niagara, exploded with the multiplication of industry and the growth of population. Industrial Canada reached levels of variety, capitalization and prosperity never dreamt of, and heady in the extreme. Most of this development Canadians financed, but here also there was much American investment by the creation or enlargement of branch plants. Britain and Europe had too little capital to spare from post-war reconstruction, or investment in the countries using sterling currency, to balance the massive American inflow.

The tremendous expansion of Canadian industry was accompanied by a corresponding growth of population. As happened in most of the world, the post-war years saw a great acceleration of the natural increase of population in Canada. The live birth rate rose from 23.5 per thousand in 1941–45 to 28.0 in 1951–55. Earlier marriages and larger families accounted for this, although what accounted for them, other than greater prosperity, remains a mystery. At the same time immigration was resumed and rapidly rose to a scale comparable with that of the reat boom before 1914. In 1950, 73,912 came; in 1956, 164,857. It was an immigration from Britain and Europe; there was none from Ireland and no mass immigration from the United States. Many of the immigrants were refugees from eastern Europe and the new Communist régimes there. The Netherlands, deprived of its Empire and aware of Canada because of the liberation by Canadian troops, sent many people; and over-populated Italy contributed a steadily rising stream.

The main difference, however, between this great influx and that before 1914 was that whereas the latter was preponderantly a movement of European peasants and American farmers to the prairie lands, the new immigration was largely one of middle-class and urban people to the industries and cities of central Canada and British Columbia. These more educated and cultivated immigrants were better suited to the new Canada, and although they were in some ways more difficult to assimilate than the earlier immigrants had been, they made a more immediate contribution to the quality of Canadian life and a more direct impact upon it. The composition of the population was definitely affected by this influx. The old British and French elements declined in their relative proportions; the European element increased. The way was preparing for the third great section of the Canadian population, building up since 1896, to rise to the surface and to assume posts of influence and authority in Canadian life. The increase in variety of course made more imperative and more challenging the process of Canadianization and also the problem of Canadian identity. It was these considerations which had led to the creation in 1949 of a Department of Immigration and Citizenship, with the Indian Affairs Branch under it.

Indian Affairs became part of the Department of Immigration and Citizenship because public opinion and Canadian Indians themselves were demanding a new attitude towards Canada's aboriginal people. Those who were legally Indians under treaty were wards of the Crown, not citizens. Any Indian might by ceasing to "take treaty" become a citizen, but this meant a breach with his people and his culture that most were reluctant to make. Yet it was apparent the treaty system had failed either to prepare the Indian for citizenship or to allow most Indians to lead tolerable lives as Indians. The resources of the reserves under the treaty system were for the most part inadequate, and better medical and educational services after 1945 only increased discontent and augmented the problem by increasing the population. The revision of the Indian Act in 1949 failed to meet the aspirations of the Indians or to reassure public opinion. The truth was that the Indian and the Eskimo faced a crisis of their cultures. The new Canada, the new world order, was making it impossible for them to continue their old way of life. But in the main the Indians were reluctant, as the Eskimoes were not, to surrender their separate being and culture in order to become Canadian citizens. Could they too find a place for themselves in the Canadian mosaic? Would such a place satisfy a people who thought themselves distinct, an independent people within the Canadian nation? There were few more poignant problems in modern Canada, and few more difficult.

That the Canadian economy should have been able to absorb some two million immigrants between 1945 and 1956 was a striking indication of the extent of its expansion. Equally striking was the fact that it was accomplished without opposition from organized labour. Labour indeed had benefited as much from war industry and the post-war expansion as had the economy itself. The organization of unions proceeded rapidly under favourable laws, and recurrent wage increases were negotiated by established procedures in bargaining. The number of strikes was surprisingly small, because both management and labour desired to avoid any check to the prosperity from which both benefited. Some strikes of magnitude there were; the railway strike of 1950, settled only by the intervention of Parliament, and one savage strike of a violence recalling the evil days of 1919, that at the Thetford asbestos mines in Quebec.

In general, however, the times allowed and common sense called for the use of negotiation and the avoidance of the ultimate sanctions of strike and lock-out. Labour and capital were working out a new set of relations from which a common concern for industrial peace and increased efficiency of plant and labour was arising. Labour had arrived as an element of major influence in industry, and had begun to develop a corresponding sense of responsibility. The extent of its growth and the weight of its authority in the community were signalized when in 1956 the Trades and Labour Congress and the Canadian Congress of Labour united in the Canadian Labour Congress under the presidency of Claude Jodoin. The international ties with American unions remained, but Canadian labour was now capable of sustaining an independent role in the national life.

The expansion of industry and labour organization carried further the changes in the Canadian economy which had begun in the late nineteenth century, and they occurred predominantly in central Canada. The growth of the provinces of Alberta and British Columbia was historically almost as remarkable. The oil boom in Alberta shifted the emphasis there from wheat and cattle to oil, gas, and the accompanying industries. Edmonton and Calgary grew rapidly, and the population of the province rose from 796,169 in 1941 to 1,123,116 in 1956. At the same time Edmonton resumed the ambition, which the Klondike gold rush had first stirred, to be the entry to the North. The exciting potentialities of the Athabaska oil sands and of the Mackenzie valley, the gold mining at Yellowknife and the mining of uranium ores at Great Bear, all led to air traffic and investment for prospecting and freighting out of Edmonton.

Even more striking was the rapid development of British Columbia, and, above all, Vancouver. The old staples of the salmon fishery and the lumbering industry continued, and lumbering and paper-making throve especially. Both to these and to new industries attracted by the local market and the great power resources of the mountain rivers, population flowed in a movement corresponding with a similar but vaster movement to the Pacific states south of the border. By 1956 the population had risen to 1,398,464 from 817,861 in 1941, and the gross value of manufactured products to $1,859,368,466 in 1956 as compared with $644,527,898 in 1945. Most outstanding of the new industrial developments was the great hydro-electric plant built at Kitimat on the northern coast for the smelting of bauxite from Jamaica to meet the growing demand for aluminium; and the power of the Columbia and the Peace promised other such developments when the markets warranted. Even the unfinished railway from Vancouver to Prince George, the provincially owned and operated Pacific and Great Eastern, was completed and renovated, an assurance that Vancouver was reaching out to the interior of the province and to the north.

The rise of Alberta and British Columbia accompanied a change as definite, if less marked, in Saskatchewan and Manitoba. Those provinces, and particularly Saskatchewan, remained the area of the old wheat economy. For it the war had meant relief if not revenue; once more wheat was in demand, once more the west fed a world at war, though the fierce struggle of convoy and submarine in the Atlantic enforced a revival of British agriculture. With war came also the ending of the great drought of the thirties. The agriculture of the prairies did not, however, regain its old predominance in the national economy, or its old independence. The Wheat Board continued to operate as a means of the orderly marketing of the wheat staple, which after 1945 became the victim, not of drought and depression, but of the new efficiency of a mechanized and mature agriculture and of a long run of years in which the rains came in season and abundance To the operations of the Wheat Board the new situation added a series of sales agreements from 1946 to 1950 with the United Kingdom, and from 1950 an international agreement in which the producing and consuming countries undertook to supply and accept an agreed amount of wheat at fixed prices. This device stabilized the market in the post-war years, but in 1953 the United Kingdom refused to renew it, and the wheat economy began to founder in its own abundance.

The result, long foreseen, brought a demand for "parity" prices for farm produce. Literally, this was a demand that the government should ensure prices at a level calculated in terms of other prices at a given time. Actually it was a demand that government should intervene to ensure to agriculture profits comparable with those of other industries. In the United States the government complied; in Canada, the government declined to undertake a commitment which might have wrecked the national finances. Once more, therefore, political discontent swelled as the wheat surplus clogged the elevators from the terminals at Fort William and Vancouver to the prairie line elevators, overflowed the farmers' granaries, and piled up in the very fields themselves.

A great measure of prosperity was nevertheless enjoyed in the post-war years even by the wheat farmers, and by those who produced other grains and livestock. And the economy of both provinces was diversified by their oil wells and their mines and a steady growth of industry, especially in Winnipeg but also in Saskatchewan. The old complete dependence on the wheat crop was gone and a modest prosperity based on a more diversified agriculture and a much more diversified general economy stopped the decrease of population in Saskatchewan and led that of both provinces to resume a slow but persistent growth by 1956.

In the Atlantic provinces this story of modest success was repeated, but in even more modest terms. There the end of the war saw the cessation of ship-building and the loss of the war-time shipping from Halifax. The Atlantic region had no northern frontier until Newfoundland brought Labrador with it into Canada. It was rich neither in agricultural land nor, it seemed, in mineral re-sources or water power. The forests and the fisheries were outstanding, but the forests had been cut over, and the fisheries yielded no great profits at the best of times. The coal mines of Cape Breton, some of them far out beneath the sea, were becoming difficult to work, and even the bounties given the steel industry of Sydney barely made it profitable. The provinces were perhaps inclined to overlook this comparative and natural poverty in their resentment against the national tariff and national freight rates. And none of the inquiries into Mari-time grievances had fully faced the task of deciding to what extent the plight of the Atlantic provinces in Confederation was the result of natural poverty and of distance from market, and to what extent the result of national policies. Since 1936, fish had entered the American market more freely under the Trade Agreement; the "better terms" of 1947 far outranged those of 1869 or 1909; the freight-rate reductions of 1927 still operated, if to less effect. Yet the economy continued depressed, and the dynamic endeavours of Premier Smallwood to diversify the industry of Newfoundland with the windfall of Confederation grants, though in a measure successful, soon encountered stubborn difficulties.

It was to face this situation that the provinces formed in 1954 the Atlantic Provinces Economic Council. The purpose of the Council was to consider what measures might be taken by Maritimers on their own to increase the prosperity of the provinces. This was a difficult task to undertake, but the attempt revealed a new spirit. The provinces had at last turned to their chief resource, the quality of their own people, and sought to improve not only the condition of the economy but the spirit in which it was developed. And new prospects soon appeared – the iron ore of Labrador, and the hydro-electric energy and base-metal deposits of New Brunswick. These resources had still to be exploited, but they suggested that the Canadian boom might yet extend to the Atlantic provinces.

Meanwhile, the Tax Agreements – periodically renewed, and increased in Atlantic Provinces Adjustment Grants in 1958 – together with the national social services, diverted some funds at least to the provinces by the sea. For the boom drove the national wealth to unprecedented levels, even when the con-siderable inflation is discounted. The gross national product in 1950 was esti-mated at $18,203,000,000; in 1956, at $30,585,000,000. The volume of retail sales, the torrents of cars on the new highways, the great sections of new housing around every major city, the new business buildings and many-storied apartment blocks, these were the material embodiments of the profits of the new economy. How much confidence it gave to the national mood was shown when in 1953, after years of obstruction by New York and the New England states in the American Senate, the Canadian government announced that it would build the St. Lawrence Seaway alone. The need for more electricity for Ontario industry, as well as the desire to open the St. Lawrence to the ships carrying iron ore from east-central Quebec, prompted the independence of the move. The Canadian initiative and the beginning of construction led to American participation in the great undertaking.

The construction of the Seaway, however, was not only the realization of the old dream of making the Great Lakes an American Mediterranean; it was also a symbol of the overlapping of American and Canadian economic development which had begun with the treaty of partition in 1783 and had grown ever since. Never was the symbol of the common seaway more potent. For the Canadian boom of the mid century had reached the heights it had with the aid of some $9,000,000,000 of American capital. Only some $3,000,000,000 of British and European capital offset this. The American investment was largely spent on American imports; and the properties it had purchased, chiefly in the primary resources of Canada, remained permanently in American ownership and control. As the boom rose to its crest, it became gradually apparent that it was in the main a boom of the same character as that of the first decade of the century. Once more a period of prosperity had resulted in the exploitation of Canadian natural resources by the industries of other countries, and particularly the United States, rather than in the strengthening of Canadian secondary industry. As in defence, Canada had moved economically into an ever closer integration with its great neighbour.

The growth of wealth and population under the stimulus of American investment might well mean absorption into the dynamic life of the United States unless out of the distinctive history and separate political nationality of Canada there grew some expression of a spirit at once authentic and unique. In a society so materially complex and intellectually sophisticated as Canadian urban society had become, the character of art could not be merely national. In literature the old preoccupation with national expression dropped away; Lampman's ideal of a single and universal standard increasingly prevailed. Canadian writers and artists with growing confidence handled Canadian subjects for their own intrinsic interest. Many indeed followed the spirit of the age in regarding art as purely a personal expression to which considerations of nationality were irrelevant. This sophistication was one aspect of the general realization of Canadians that their country in achieving national stature in the twentieth century had in fact begun to try new forms of political association and new modes of civilized interchange. The Canadian identity in future would be what Canadians were and did, not what they might profess. To be Canadian would cease to be an attitude to be maintained, and become a spirit in which to live.

The great question, in short, was no longer whether there would be authentic and devoted artists; in these Canada was rich. The question was rather whether they would find the audience and the patronage which would echo and hearten their work. Canada had never been wanting in people of taste, but their numbers had been small, their influence often less, in a society which had remained a pioneering society throughout its history. The problem was how to achieve a popular patronage of the arts by the diffusion of taste and the creation of an appetite for the strange flavours and strong meat of genuine art.

It was to this question implicitly that the Massey Commission had addressed itself, and the mere fact that the national government had appointed a commission and that the head of the commission, known as a patron of the arts, should become Governor General, had of itself done much to draw attention to the arts as the ultimate achievement of a society. The Canadian Broadcasting Corporation, with its mandate to employ Canadian artists and develop Canadian talent, had done much in radio and television both to encourage artists and to create a public taste. And the work of the Dominion Drama Festivals, Incorporated, the Canadian Authors' Association, the symphony orchestras of the larger cities, the rise of ballet companies in Winnipeg, Toronto, and Montreal, the foundation of the Shakespearean Festival in Stratford, Ontario, and the Vancouver Festival, the building of magnificent auditoria in Alberta and British Columbia, all revealed that the active supporters of the arts were gaining an ever widening audience for their clients. Their work was crowned by the establishment of the Canada Council in 1956 as recommended by the Massey Commission, with an endowment of fifty million dollars from the national government for the encouragement of the arts, letters, and scholarship. It seemed not impossible that in Canada, despite the harshness and puritanism of a frontier society, despite the inveterate provincialism of Canadian life, despite the deliberate degradation of art for the commercial purposes of mass production and mass advertising, despite the pained intolerance of old-fashioned taste, the arts might become popular and part of common life.

The maturing of the arts accompanied a maturing of scholarship. Canadian universities entered on a new period of growth, as more and more students came to them and as more and more was expected of them by a society which now depended on rational control and scientific advance. While all Canadian universities in their founding period had been loyally supported by their churches or their provincial governments, private support in most instances had not been great. It was now apparent that greater financial support must be given if the universities were to meet the demands society was increasingly making upon them. In 1951–52 therefore the national government began to make grants to the universities of each province at so much a head of provincial population. The formula was by no means an equitable one, but it was meant to avoid any appearance of interference with provincial jurisdiction over education. The well-meant endeavour failed in Quebec, in that Premier Duplessis after the first year peremptorily ordered the universities not to accept the grant. The universities in the other provinces, however, were put in a position to raise their standards of teaching and research towards that of British and American universities and to increase the output of scholarly and scientific work.

The same realization of the need for more support and higher standards of achievement suddenly dawned in the field of secondary education. Canadian high schools, to a greater or less degree from province to province, had been adjusting themselves to the fact that most of the adolescent population continued on into high school. To deal with this mass of students at comparatively advanced levels of work, a certain philosophy and approach had become general, though less in eastern, more in western Canada. This was the "progressive" philosophy of John Dewey, interpreted to mean that the primary purpose of schooling was not mastering skills but adjusting to life, a democratic life in which what counted was not personal accomplishment but social acceptability. Canadian schools had indeed been the prime agents of assimilation and personal formation in an immigrant society. But the philosophy could be carried so far as to impair the training of the brighter pupils and even to adumbrate an anti-intellectual and amoral attitude to life. Many thoughtful observers were already dissatisfied with the work of the schools when Hilda Neatby's book *So Little for the Mind* was published, relentlessly criticizing the effects of the progressive philosophy on education. The resulting controversy was wholly salutary. Some reformation of educational standards was begun, not without hope of averting a dangerous lowering of intellectual and moral standards.

In this struggle to save the intellectual integrity of the young, Canadians engaged in a contest that was being fought with equal vigour in the United States. That the contest was in an area so important as that of education suggested how near to one another the two countries had drawn in the twentieth century. They were in fact in all general and popular aspects one society, a society of Canadian as well as American creation, but essentially a North American society of European derivation. Because, however, Canada was in part French, because it possessed its own hard won and slowly elaborated national being, Canadians could not but be concerned with the increasing penetration of home and school, of thought and ideal, by the strident tones, the careful conformity, the insidious and calculated mediocrity of the mass American culture. Was all that was distinctive and cherished in Canadian life, the French culture, the British institutional heritage, the colour and tang contributed by the Icelander, the Ukrainian, the Pole and the Hollander, to be processed and homogenized to soft music and dreamy lighting, packaged and sold in the accents of Madison Avenue to increase the earnings of American stockholders? The Americanization of Canadian life did seem a fate at once as ignoble as it was possible, and more and more Canadians turned to seek with Malcolm Ross the essence of the Canadian identity. But common fears, common dangers and a common prosperity made Americans and Canadians increasingly more aware of what they shared than of what divided them.

During the years of this overwhelming prosperity, politics fell into the background; the discontent which gives an edge to political controversy was absent. Prime Minister Saint-Laurent, gracious and benevolent, passed from triumph to triumph in the general elections of 1949 and 1953. None wished to rock the political boat as the golden tide of prosperity flowed.

In the provinces before 1952 the same political quietude prevailed. The Atlantic provinces all continued under Liberal régimes, including the new one of Premier Smallwood. Quebec continued under Duplessis, who became ever more mediaeval, powerful, and withdrawn as his *mystique* deepened with age and ill health. Only at Laval University, with its faculties imbued with the more liberal spirit of the Dominican Order – and particularly by that of the Dean of the Faculty of Social Sciences, Father Georges Henri Levesque, until his retirement was forced by pressure on the University – was there a source of opposition in the province, other than the Liberal party. In Ontario the Conservative régime identified itself with the extraordinary growth of that province. Manitoba not only kept the successors of the Bracken government in power, first under S. S. Garson, and then under Douglas Campbell, but even seemed incapable of producing an effective Opposition. The C.C.F., weakly led, could not break out from Winnipeg into the rural constituencies. In Saskatchewan, on the other hand, the C.C.F. under T. C. Douglas, a man of integrity and an adroit and charming politician, easily held the great majority of the urban and rural seats. The same placid fortune attended the Social Credit government of Alberta, now become under E. C. Manning a quiet and competent administration of a province which had forgotten the days of debt, drought and depression. Only in British Columbia did the dissolution of a war-time coalition of Conservatives and Liberals against a strengthening C.C.F. create a confused and embittered political scene which invited the entrance of some new alternative to the bickerings of the local parties. In fact a businessman-politician, W. A. C. Bennett, was to leave the Conservative party and head a Social Credit movement in British Columbia, a change of allegiance which brought him in 1952 to the office of Premier in Canada's second Social Credit government.

By this change, British Columbia acquired a characteristic common to Canadian politics east of the Rockies, the extraordinary weakness of the opposition parties. The concurrent development of a dominant cabinet, resting on the Civil Service rather than on the legislature, and of a mass and plebiscitary democracy, speaking through the party leader rather than the party, had resulted in a serious decline of parliamentary government and of the chief feature of that mode of government, the Loyal Opposition, or alternative government. The Canadian voter, it seemed, was more concerned to have a strong administration than to check and criticize government by a vigilant and active opposition never too far removed from the prospect of office.

Nowhere was this more true than at Ottawa. The C.C.F. had fallen from its high-water mark of 1945, although it made up for its deficiency in numbers by the quality of its chief parliamentarians, in particular its leader, M. J. Coldwell and his lieutenant, Stanley Knowles. Social Credit had entered federal politics, but its numbers were few and its leader, Solon Low, not of great ability. Under Bracken's leadership the Conservative party had increased its numbers in 1945 but never came within reach of office. The consequence was a recurrence of that dissatisfaction with the party leadership which had harmed the party so greatly since 1935, and which revealed the belief that elections were now plebiscites to choose leaders rather than contests of principles and parties. Late in 1948, George Drew resigned as Premier of Ontario to become national leader in place of Bracken, who was induced to resign. A western leader had failed; one drawn from central Canada was to try to restore the national fortunes of the Conservative party.

A distinguished airman in World War 1, a bold, handsome, statuesque man, an hereditary Conservative with an ingrained and spontaneous sense of public duty, Drew had been a successful premier of Ontario. He had perhaps been too successful, for he had attracted to himself, as Hepburn had done, much of the distrust in which Ontario's power in the nation was held in the smaller provinces. Drew, moreover, possessed neither magnetism nor intellectual distinction. A valiant and cheerful fighter who animated the Opposition at Ottawa, he failed to catch the national ear or to make the chords of national sentiment vibrate. These things he earnestly wished to do, but it was not in him. Drew did, none the less, by courage and hard work, reanimate the Conservative party. In 1953 the opposition for the first time in years shook the government in debate, on defence production and the scandal of embezzlement and theft at the military camp at Petawawa. But the Conservative gains in the election of that year were few.

The years of prosperity obviously were years of privation for those in the political wilderness. Yet, beneath the surface, vague discontent and flickering uneasiness were stirring and taking form as criticism of government. The American penetration of Canadian life caused the slow realization that Canada had achieved independence only to find itself face to face with the great neighbour which was also a world power. As such the United States had titanic and sobering responsibilities. American opinion still, however, held to the original belief that the American way of life was the goal towards which all creation moved. It retained the same historic disposition to flash from casual friendliness into impatient action, and to elevate the ignored issue of yesterday into the imperative of today. Lester Pearson repeatedly warned that the relations of Canada and the United States would become increasingly difficult. The threat of Russian aerial attack necessitated the building of two more radar warning lines besides the early Pinetree line, across northern Canada. The farthest north of the three, the Distant Early Warning line, was built entirely at American insistence, by American money, and was manned by American personnel. Such action was in accord with the spirit of the alliance, but somehow it left a strong current of feeling that Canada had been overridden and that Canadian sovereignty was threatened. The flood of American investment continued, much of it in forms which admitted of no Canadian participation and much of it managed by Americans who made no attempt to acknowledge Canadian custom or to identify themselves with Canadian sentiments and aspirations. The long record of smooth adjustment of boundary-water matters by Joint Commission ended with a prolonged deadlock over the division of electric power from the development of the Canadian portion of the Columbia River. Thus the anti-Americanism always latent in Canada was building up towards explosion point when early in 1956 the national government undertook to assist a private company to build a gas pipeline from Alberta to central Canada.

While the Liberal government had hoped the project might be carried out by a private company, it did, after the historic fashion of Canadian governments, agree to assist the company formed to build the line. Then two things combined to produce an explosion. One was the fact that the company was American-owned. The other was the insistence of the responsible minister, C. D. Howe, that the bill authorizing the assistance be rushed through Parliament in order that work might begin early that season. Howe had been in office since 1935. He had become the senior minister from Ontario and the second man in the Cabinet. He had rendered the country magnificent service during the war. The industrial war effort was his personal achievement, and in peace he had been to a great extent the creator of the post-war prosperity. Hard-driving, quick and impetuous at work, he was in person genial, good-natured and unassuming. But long success had made him careless of appearances. No politician, he disliked Parliament and was contemptuous of public opinion; not himself arrogant, he seemed arrogant, and did allow, in the Byzantine atmosphere of Ottawa which had grown up in the capital under one-party domination, such dubious practices as the naming of a government vessel after himself.

The result of this Canadian Strafford's attempting to ram a bill through Parliament with the aid of an acquiescent majority, in the interests of a Texan oilman, crystallized the many resentments of Canadians towards the ever-growing penetration of their national life by American capital and American ways – not least, perhaps, Howe's own lack of patience with Parliament and its traditions. The opposition suddenly found it had an issue and that public opinion was behind it. Stoutly it fought the passage of the bill and the ruthless use of closure by a government helpless in the grip of Howe. At one stroke the image of the Liberal party as the infallible guardian of the social welfare and national interest disintegrated as the government seemed to strive to stifle debate in the interests of American investors. Though the government had no such intention, it had been most unwise in yielding to Howe and had grown careless from too much power held much too long. In the Commons the debate became frenzied; and it ended, as the government members voted closure on the second reading, in defiance of the Speaker and the break-up of the sitting in near violence. It was a shameful scene and it was unjust to a gifted Speaker, but it was life after years of torpor.

As such, it should have been a warning to the Liberals that the tide of public opinion was turning against them. But they were not warned. Canada was surging forward; they had averted the extremes of recession and inflation; for every problem but the disposal of the wheat surpluses of the west they had found a solution; they had resisted the corruption of office, and had even reformed the government at least once since 1935. But they did not realize, or, if they realized, were powerless to alter, the fact that the party had ceased to be what it had been since 1935, a party of the centre, jealously holding both sides of the middle line of politics, and had sagged, with a leaden lurch, to the right.

At the same time, the Conservative party faced new difficulties. George Drew had had to retire because of ill health in 1956, and once more that unfortunate if indestructible party was under a new leader. This was John Diefenbaker, yet another westerner. Diefenbaker's chief distinction was a penchant for the cause of civil liberties and a unique ability to get himself elected, from 1940 on, in the long-Liberal-dominated province of Saskatchewan. As such, he was obviously another desperate gamble of a desperate party. He was, moreover, the candidate of the parliamentary party, and in Diefenbaker's election and in the huddling together on a muddled and incoherent platform, the party leaders failed to make contact with the new interest in Conservative principles which was struggling for expression in the country. The old contradiction of imperial sentiment and economic nationalism had in fact dissolved. Empire had been lost in Commonwealth, and imperial preference in Liberal protection and the trade agreements of the post-war period. The natural Conservative concern with the organic life of society might have served at once to discard the outmoded Liberal dogma of "free enterprise" as the sole economic ideal, and to make the coming of the "welfare state" a means to social strength rather than a cause of individual moral debility. Released from its inhibitions, the Canadian Conservative party was free to orientate itself anew. How free, no one seemed to realize.

The Liberal government, as a result, was not warned that there was a new restlessness; the party leaders swept the pipeline debate under the carpet as a regrettable mistake and prepared to win the election of 1957. No one had yet recognized that in fact the government was old, weary, and brittle, and subtly arrogant from the conviction that it was indispensable.

Then upon the clash of the pipeline debate there followed in the fall of 1956 the shock of the Suez crisis. The crisis arose from the seizure by Egypt of the Suez Canal, by treaty an international waterway. Prime Minister Anthony Eden of the United Kingdom, renowned for his adherence to the principle of collective security and his opposition to the policy of appeasement followed in the Munich crisis of 1938, had become convinced that the new leader of Egypt, Colonel Abdel Nasser, was a dictator threatening the peace of the Middle East. Thinking that the United States would not oppose forceful action on which it had not been consulted, and probably knowing through the French government that the government of Israel was preparing to attack Egypt because of border raids, Eden in conjunction with France determined to occupy the Canal Zone to uphold the international rights in the canal and to ensure the movement of oil from the Middle East. That there was much justice in the Anglo-French attitude was clear, but the world was quite unprepared for the sudden resort to force in response to an action which, however illegal, had been peaceful and within the country concerned. When the attack began, therefore, it was promptly denounced by a startled world as an act of aggression, even while Russian troops in a far more aggressive manner were stamping out the rebellion which had flared up against Communist rule in Hungary. The United States in especial denounced the attack on Suez and may have threatened sterner measures. Whatever the facts may prove to be, the main fact for Canada was that, aggression or not, the British action had nearly destroyed the Anglo-American alliance and nearly disrupted the Commonwealth.

It affected the latter because the action seemed to the new members of the Commonwealth a sudden return to the old imperialist habit of the great powers of imposing their will by force. Australia and New Zealand, however reluctantly, were disposed to support the United Kingdom. But India was wild with anger, and in Canada many people felt with Prime Minister Saint-Laurent that the British occupation was an unpardonable reversion to an outmoded imperialism.

Anger, however, was no remedy for the sudden and brutal consequences of Eden's seeming resort to real politik. The Anglo-American alliance as the mainstay of the free world, and the Commonwealth for its value to all its members, must be salvaged from the imminent catastrophe. In a brilliant turn of diplomacy, Lester Pearson, in close touch with Prime Minister Nehru of India, persuaded the United Nations to intervene with an offer to police the zone on condition the British, French, and Israelis withdrew their forces, and that Egypt consented to the intervention. In doing so, he offered the United Kingdom and France a bridge by which they might retreat from their self-appointed task as upholders of international right, to the more defensible ground of action by the United Nations. The conditions were met, and a United Nations Expeditionary

Force, made up in part of Canadian military units, took over the policing of the Canal Zone. To the surprise of all observers, the expedient worked; the canal was peacefully reopened, and Anglo-American relations were repaired by the new British Prime Minister, Harold Macmillan. The Commonwealth had demonstrated an unexpected vigour and an ability to supply leadership other than British.

In English Canada, however, the feeling lingered that the Liberal government had betrayed an anti-British bias which, though not at all to be ascribed to Pearson himself, was deeply resented even while the action of the United Nations was approved. There was now to be added the feeling that the government had failed to be firm enough with the United States in a matter involving the national honour. This was the suicide of Herbert Norman, Canadian Ambassador to Egypt, early in 1957 as a result of repeated persecution by the Security Sub-committee of the United States Senate. The committee had in its first years exposed a number of people disloyal to the United States. Then, lashed by Senator Joseph McCarthy, it had begun a career of persecution of all those of a liberal persuasion who had had any connection with any Communist organization or activity at any time. After the eclipse of Senator McCarthy, the chief purpose of this phase of the committee's work was to procure publicity for its members and to ensure its own continuance. In pursuit of these ends, it did not scruple to concern itself with persons not citizens of the United States. One of these was Herbert Norman, a Canadian born in Japan who had had a career of brilliant scholarship and had become an authority on Japanese history. At Harvard, apparently, he had had, like any intelligent young man in the 1930's, some contact with Communist activities. He had been cleared by his own government, and that should have ended the matter. Three times, however, he was named as a Communist sympathizer before the Senate Sub-committee, in disregard of the impropriety of making such public reference to the officer of a friendly government. Sensitive, over-worked by the Suez crisis, influenced perhaps by his Japanese upbringing, Norman on the third occasion took his own life.

Anger in Canada was instantaneous and deep, as it was also among all thoughtful Americans. Pearson refused to be moved by the wave of resentment which flowed into Ottawa and, perhaps unwisely, declined to recall the Canadian ambassador from Washington. In the upshot, since the American government was powerless to discipline the Sub-committee because of the separation of powers of the American constitution, and was not itself responsible for the behaviour of the Sub-committee, the Canadian government neither received proper satisfaction nor adequately vindicated its ambassador's name, either before the world or to its own public. The memory of this unhappy affair remained both to impair American-Canadian cordiality and to cast doubt on how wisely the Liberal administration had handled this aspect of the ever more intimate and involved relations of Canada with the United States. The latter, it was clear, in view of the constitution of its government, might again disregard Canadian sentiment or sacrifice the reputation of Canadian public servants when sensational publicity or election propaganda required it.

None of these irritations, suspicions, and resentments affected the basic alliance between Canada and the United States, and indeed they stimulated reflective people in both countries to attempt to diminish friction and misunderstanding. American forces stationed in Canada were instructed in Canadian susceptibilities, a joint Congressional and Parliamentary Committee was established, and, contrary to custom, an able career diplomat, Mr. Livingston Merchant, was appointed American Ambassador to Ottawa. In 1957 the two governments agreed to establish the North American Air Defence Command (Norad) which was organized to co-ordinate and, if necessary, commit to instant battle the air forces of the United States and Canada. The commander was American, the second-in-command Canadian. For what would be a matter of sudden national destruction or bare survival, the two North American states, in a striking assertion of interdependence, merged their forces for the common defence. This integration in the continental alliance underlined once more the novel and perilous character of the world in which Canada had become an independent nation.

While none of these things – the pipeline debate, the Suez crisis, the Norman affair – necessarily reflected on the government, yet they all served to alert the Canadian public and to make many critical of a government which had so long basked in a glow of public adulation. The critical disposition might, however unjustly, find an adverse expression in the next election. Moreover, traditional portents of national defeat were multiplying. If the opposition at Ottawa had not revived until 1956, it had been growing in the provinces. The Conservatives had captured New Brunswick in 1952. Social Credit had taken over British Columbia in the same year. Alberta and Saskatchewan remained Social Credit and C.C.F. In Manitoba the Conservative opposition had revived under Dufferin Roblin, and the Campbell government became increasingly Liberal. Ontario and Quebec remained massively anti-Liberal. In 1956 the Conservatives suddenly ended the ancient Liberal régime in Nova Scotia and came to power under Premier R. L. Stanfield. Only the two island provinces and Manitoba remained Liberal. In Canadian history the provinces had traditionally opposed rather than supported Ottawa, and when a majority of them were of a different party than the national government, then that government was in danger if not doomed.

Nevertheless the Liberals did not doubt of victory in the general election of 1957. With a fine exuberance, they appointed a royal commission under Walter L. Gordon, a distinguished Toronto accountant, to study Canada's economic prospects and provide a new program of Liberal legislation. Rarely, if ever, had the great instrument of the royal inquisition been used to shadow forth the future and usurp the prerogative of the fortune-teller, or a party made a more revealing admission of intellectual insolvency. They almost contemptuously declined to promise any additional attempt to deal with the growing wheat surplus or the increasing difficulties of the medium and small farmer as machine and other prices outran the prices his products commanded. They stiffly refused to consider more than a six-dollar increase in the monthly old-age pension; this, they said, with bureaucratic preciseness, was all a prosperous Canada could afford.

Nor, it may be supposed, did the opposition parties have hopes that looked to more than a gain in numbers. Almost at once, however, it became apparent that the Conservative party had found in its leader a campaigner of singular energy and appeal, and that he was finding an audience in a country in which complacency had given way to an angry and confused concern, a concern with farm prices, old-age pensions, Commonwealth relations, relations with the United States, concern over the impatient and smug administration that insisted and continued to insist that all was for the best in the best of all Liberal worlds.

That world collapsed on June 10, 1957. An astounded country heard on radio and saw on television the incredible and pathetic rout of the Liberal government, portrayed in the astonishment and confusion of the Prime Minister who had come once more to thank the electorate for their support. The Conservatives as a matter of electoral strategy had ignored Quebec, and they had carried only half the House, but the Liberal ministers had been decimated as in 1925. Howe, perhaps more than any one man responsible for the debacle, had been defeated in his own seat by a quiet-spoken C.C.F. school-teacher, Douglas Fisher. With Howe went more than half the Cabinet. The smaller parties did not substantially change their numbers, and could not materially affect the composition of the new Parliament.

For a few days it seemed that the Liberal strategy of 1925 might be attempted again. But then Saint-Laurent wisely resigned, and the Liberals, with an ill grace which ill became democratic politicians and revealed how deeply the corruption of power had bitten, resigned and gave way to the first Conservative government since 1935.

The change, for all the extraordinary merits and great achievements of the Liberal régime, had been too long delayed. The new government had not one man with national cabinet experience. It was a government of men surprised by office and unprepared to exercise power. Bonds of affection and common modes of thought had grown up between Liberal ministers and the higher Civil Service, which rendered the new ministers distrustful and made it difficult for the Civil Service to adjust to the new order. Parliamentary government is alternative government, and Canada had nearly abandoned the art. Above all, the new administration was embarrassed by a multitude of reckless promises, hurled wildly at the impregnable Liberal ramparts and now become political commitments difficult to meet, especially as the long boom gave way to a definite recession at the end of 1957.

The new administration was embarrassed, moreover, not only by recent promises, but also by traditional attitudes of the Conservative party. There was the strong desire to give a warmer tone to relations with the Commonwealth, and especially the United Kingdom. There was even the desire to increase the commercial and financial interchanges of the Commonwealth countries, and by so doing to lessen the commitment of the economic future of Canada to trade with the United States and to American investment in Canada. The Prime Minister early gave voice to this hope when he said he would see the proportion of Canadian trade with the United Kingdom increased relative to that with the United States. This statement was reported as being a determination to "divert" fifteen per cent of the trade with the United States to the United Kingdom.

It was to prove difficult in fact to realize this traditional conservative hope that the economic ties of the Commonwealth might be strengthened. The difficulties were cruelly and embarrassingly underlined when the English Chancellor of the Exchequer, Peter Thorneycroft, after a conference on economic affairs of the Commonwealth, blurted out in public that an offer of immediate free trade with Canada had been made by the United Kingdom. Thorneycroft's exposure of the conflict between the government's desire for increased trade with the Commonwealth and the fear of competition felt by certain Canadian industries, notably the textile industry, seemed to be warranted when the Commonwealth Economic Conference, held in Montreal in September 1958 at the earnest wish of the Canadian government, saw no major development in economic relations. It was significant that its one major achievement, the institution of the Commonwealth Fellowships, was in the field of intellectual and scientific co-operation. The ancient Conservative dream, recurrent since the commercial revolution of 1846, of an empire of sentiment which should also be an economic organism, had vanished once more in the bleak light of reality, a light which revealed England faced with the growing success of the European Common Market and Canada faced with a volume of American investment, permanently controlled by American management, which in fact made Canada an economic adjunct to the American market.

A second election, it was clear, must follow soon to give the government a working majority, or to allow the public to change its mind. It came in the early summer of 1958. Saint-Laurent had retired and the Liberal party had elected Lester Pearson to succeed him. The new leader worked earnestly to reorganize his party, but he lacked the lieutenants and the provincial help that were needed. For Manitoba too elected a Conservative government, and all the provinces but Newfoundland had repudiated the Liberal party by 1959. And the national Conservatives, stung by the foolish Liberal taunt that "Tory times were bad times," spared no effort to gain a majority and above all to win seats in Quebec.

There was now hope of doing so, for, while the Duplessis organization stood benevolently by, Quebec Conservatives worked furiously for the national party. Copying the Liberal and American practices of using advertising techniques for political campaigns, the Conservatives stormed the country, led by the fervent oratory of the Prime Minister. The tactics of 1957 were repeated and enlarged; a program of civil liberties ensured by a Bill of Rights, economic expansion, aid to the weaker regions, northern development, and national aspiration were pledged to the electorate. In this emphasis on national development and individual welfare the Conservative party was finding its way back to its central tradition in Canadian history. And it was tradition brought up to date. Diefenbaker had seized and was flourishing the banner of Canadian advance under which the Liberals had marched from 1944 to 1953. It was magnificent campaigning, a resurgence of strength so extraordinary that few paused to note the danger of simply replacing a Liberal-dominated by a Conservative-dominated House of Commons, or stopped to ask whether a Conservative program ought not also to have been concerned with the restoration of vitality to parliamentary government and restraint to public debate.

The result was the greatest electoral victory of Canadian history. The Conservatives carried 210 seats out of 275 and gained a majority in every province but Newfoundland. The Liberals elected only forty-five; the C.C.F., only seven, and lost all their leading men; Social Credit was wiped out. Above all, of Quebec's seventy-five seats, fifty returned Conservative candidates. The government so elected had probably won because the electorate desired to give it a majority and because the Canadian electorate, as always, found a bandwagon irresistible. But four main facts emerged. One was that a great proportion of the Canadian vote had become non-partisan, and that as a result the election of a strong opposition would not be normal in the future. The second was that Diefenbaker's name had broken the hold of the Liberal party on the European-Canadian vote. The third was that for the first time since 1930, and to a degree since 1921, there was a massive shift of support by the great financial interests, *la grande bourgeoisie canadienne*, from the Liberal to the Conservative party. Votes had prevailed in 1957; votes and money swept the country in 1958. The fourth fact, and this was the legacy in some sense of Mackenzie King, was that Quebec, and Canada, had recovered from the trauma of 1917. National unity was never greater than on the morrow of the election of 1958.

The breaking of the long Liberal hold on Quebec was the most significant of the effects of the electoral revolution of 1957 and 1958. For, if it meant, as it seemed to, the end, or the beginning of the end, of the cleavage of 1917, the national defeat of the Liberals foreshadowed the provincial defeat of the Union Nationale. Assuredly, events within Quebec itself were making for change. The Union Nationale, always realistic in political action, was becoming shamelessly as well as inveterately corrupt. French voices were raised in protest, particularly from Laval University; the Dominicans were edging towards another victory in their long rivalry with the Jesuits. Duplessis himself was in ill health; feared and in a measure loved, *le chef* was fading into the shadows, with no one like himself to succeed. When he went, the Union Nationale would face drastic change, for the Union Nationale as it existed was Duplessis.

The end came in September, 1959; the Premier died while visiting a new development in northern Quebec. He was buried in state at Quebec, and an era was entombed with him. For his successor was not a Union Nationale man, although a member of Duplessis's cabinet. Paul Sauvé was a Conservative by long inheritance. Tall, handsome, blond, a war veteran and a sportsman, he was the opposite of his predecessor in appearance and manner. His appointment as premier was like sunrise after dark in both Quebec and national politics. A régime of repression and negative policies had ended; Sauvé by his very presence affirmed that a new era had dawned. At once he made it manifest that great changes would be made, and his simple assertions electrified the province and the country. Never in Canadian history had one man's personality made such a difference in hope and sentiment to the whole nation. When he signified that no more government grants would be made by personal cheque to individuals, and that the Quebec universities would be allowed to accept the national grants, he gave earnest of what the new era would bring, a Quebec not less Quebec, but a Quebec playing a full and a positive part in the life of the nation.

The radiant promise of his premiership, with all it meant to Canada – and perhaps to the Conservative party – ended in a hundred days with Sauvé's sudden death from heart failure in the prime of life and on the threshold of a career of great significance. His death was a national tragedy, and one of immeasurable consequence.

None the less, the forces which had brought Sauvé to the leadership of his province continued to work. The test of Sauvé's career would have been his success or failure in remodelling the Union Nationale. His successor, Antonio Barrette, a likable and well-intentioned man, quite failed to convince the Quebec electorate that he was capable of reforming the régime. It is true that Barrette faced a provincial Liberal party resuscitated and given political integrity by Jean Lesage. Lesage, young, ardent and high-minded, had already made a name in national politics as a member of Saint-Laurent's government, and had gone back to provincial politics to restore Liberal strength in the province. Against hope, he succeeded, and in the provincial election of June, 1960, won a majority in the Quebec Assembly. Lesage had been aided by the growing influence of the Dominicans, and the weakening of the long Jesuit ascendancy, as Laurentian *nationalisme* – the reaction of a rural and clerical society to the growth of an urban and industrial culture – lost its appeal in urban and industrial Quebec. Thus the Union Nationale, condemned for its corruption and also for its rejection of twentieth-century change both within Quebec and in the character of

Canadian nationality, fell not to a reconstituted Conservative party under Sauvé but to a reinvigorated Liberal party under Lesage.

The victory also marked the recovery by the Liberal party of its former stature, for although the Conservatives had renewed their tenure of power in Nova Scotia, the Liberals a month after their victory in Quebec captured power in New Brunswick. It was possible to hope that the long tenures of power in Canada, with their injury to parliamentary democracy, might be giving way to a return to the alternation of governments which, with all its faults, seems the best method to keep politics honest and politicians humble.

The end of the régime of the Union Nationale, however, had yet to make its full impact on the national life. Its negative defence of the provincial rights of Quebec and the privileges of French Canada had been a potent, although by no means the sole, obstacle to the accomplishment of two great national needs, a permanent settlement of the taxing powers and financial resources of the provinces and the nation, and a mode of constitutional amendment within Canada by Canadian process. A third need, scarcely less urgent, was to decide whether the fundamental problem of the Canadian constitution consisted of the relation of provincial rights to national powers, or, as urged by the report in 1956 of the Tremblay Royal Commission of Inquiry on Constitutional Problems, the relations of French and English Canadian cultures within the political nation. Until these things should be done, the country could live from expedient to expedient, from one tax agreement to another.

Yet the Diefenbaker government, despite its extraordinary success in Quebec in 1958, seemed neither to give proper weight to Quebec in national affairs nor to be well informed on what was going forward in that province. The Prime Minister, for example, had brought down his historic Bill of Rights (of such exceptional importance in a land of minorities, as Canada had become) and carried it through a House which approved the intent but questioned the procedure. In what was perhaps his greatest contribution to Canadian history, the Prime Minister refused the Opposition's suggestion that an attempt be made to gain the assent of the provinces and so make the Bill fully binding. He declared the time was not ripe to seek provincial approval, and presumably he feared opposition from Quebec. The government was therefore caught unprepared when, at a preliminary national-provincial conference on the renewal of the tax agreements in 1962, Premier Lesage not only did not, as was assumed, show any of the defensive wariness of Duplessis, but called for a conference to agree on a mode of constitutional amendment in Canada, a conference which he said might lead to the incorporation of the Bill of Rights in the constitutional act itself. Thus Quebec, released from the trauma of 1917 and all that lay behind it, had seized the national initiative, as in the days of Lafontaine and Cartier.

The Prime Minister responded with intuitive quickness to this transforming gesture, and announced the following day that a national-provincial conference would be called to consider ways and means of making the constitution national. Canada at last seemed about to make the final stride to the goal of full nationhood. The increase of state intervention, the rapid growth of the welfare services, the ever augmenting role of government in society, it seemed, would not block the achievement of full national stature, or begin a new separation of the English and French founding stocks of Canada. But when the conference met, late in 1960, no quick agreement followed. Quebec with its historic memory still stood fast on the traditional safeguards, unable to forget its minority position; while Saskatchewan, unable to forget the national power which had sustained it in the drought and depression of the 1930's, maintained the need for a wide area and flexible mode of amendment.

Thus at that moment of time, in Canadian history neither an end nor a beginning, Canada stood poised between the two elements of its destiny, the element of the cultural heritage which kept its two founding stocks, French and English, distinct and separate, and the element of the union sprung from the northern economy which kept it one nation independent in America and involved in a Commonwealth as wide as mankind.

ADDITIONAL READING

COOK, RAMSAY *Canada and the French-Canadian Question.*
EAYRS, JAMES *The Art of the Possible: Government and Foreign Policy in Canada.*
MASSEY, VINCENT *On Being Canadian.*
RUSSELL, PETER H. (ed.) *Nationalism in Canada.*

CHAPTER 25

Old Bottles and New Wine

1960-1968

During the eight years that began in 1960, Canada, so far as a pattern may be seen in events so recent, passed through a transformation at once on the surface and in the depth of its national life. And until 1963 at least, in a sense until 1966, the transformation was to consist more of the failure of old methods, and the erosion of old values and old loyalties, than of the making and acceptance of new affirmations and new commitments. What was old and outmoded had to be consumed in fires of confusion and humiliation before new ideas, new techniques, new men, could rise from the ashes.

It was the sad fate of the Diefenbaker government, so powerful in public support, so well-intentioned, that it should provide the kindling and the fuel for the burning of the old order that had prevailed from the days of Laurier and of Taschereau. Yet the explanation of that fate is to be found not only in the conjuncture of the times, the fact that the old ways of King and of Duplessis would no longer do in Canada. It is to be found also in the character of the Conservative government itself, and in the genuine novelty of the quiet revolution in Quebec.

In the first place, the Cabinet was wholly without previous experience in the administration of government, federal or provincial. The Prime Minister had never held cabinet office before 1957. Almost none had held a senior administrative post before, as had Sidney Smith, Minister of External Affairs, as president of the University of Manitoba and the University of Toronto. None knew the ways, the nuances, the arcana, of government circles in Ottawa. Such was the cost of the failure of alternation in government from 1935 to 1957.

Second, in such circumstances, a cabinet of freshmen was perforce very much dependent on the loyalty and counsel of the senior Civil Service. Those high officials and the members of the administration were both deeply aware of this. Both with the utmost conscientiousness sought to deal wisely with a difficult and delicate situation. Nevertheless, the outcome, in general and with exceptions, was failure. A proper rapport never developed between the Diefenbaker administration and the senior Civil Service.

In the third place, there was the changing character of government, particularly in the relationships of its major parts. The House of Commons had become a body to register decisions of the government and was ceasing to be the effective representation of the country. That function was being increasingly short-circuited by direct expression of opinion through the press, the radio and television, and by the face-to-face appeal of the Prime Minister on television to the public. The rapid increase in the use of the federal-provincial conference had made that extra-constitutional meeting of members of governments at least quasi-constitutional, and in doing so diminished both the representative character and the legislative capacity of Parliament. The cabinet also, as a committee of the House, in the new circumstances of active, positive, continuous government over much of the life of the country, was revealing its peculiar weakness. The Canadian cabinet had always been an essentially representative body, a caucus of provincial political leaders. But ministers were required by the new character of government to be active and able administrators if they were to master their departments. Fewer and fewer were able to do so; partly because their prime role was representative, partly because of the generally mediocre calibre of men drawn into political life, an exacting life with few rewards.

Moreover, the members of the Cabinet, although with distinguished exceptions such as Davie Fulton as Minister of Justice, or Alvin Hamilton as Minister of Northern Resources, were unable to shake off the temper and attitudes of opposition. They were incapable of believing themselves the government. Architects of the greatest electoral victory in Canadian history, they had no confidence in their victory. Given unmatched support as a party, they were unable to obey the most unmistakable of electoral mandates. They could not rid themselves of the uncertainty of over twenty years of party defeat and frustration. Reared in opposition, they remained in opposition still. Nor, with exceptions, were the members of the Cabinet knowing and sophisticated enough to use the ideas and techniques of government available to them in the Civil Service.

There were two immediate reasons for this lack of authority in the Cabinet. First and chief was the temperament and behaviour of the Prime Minister himself. Few men have sought power with such constancy as John Diefenbaker. Few, having won power, have been less happy in exercising it. As the first two years in office revealed, it was not that the Prime Minister was not master of his administration; he indeed dominated his cabinet. It was that he failed to direct it. A man who had fought his way up alone, a trial lawyer by profession, a magnificent election orator, he himself was inexperienced as an administrator. He found it difficult therefore either to delegate power clearly, or to make his cabinet an administrative team. This lack of administrative assurance resulted in distrust between the Prime Minister and his colleagues; the strong ones among them seemed all too likely to be rivals for office. The result was delay, harassment, resentment and confusion in a cabinet of much talent under a Prime Minister of unequalled power.

Alienated from the Civil Service, distrustful of his own cabinet, Diefenbaker moved erratically in increasing loneness, or sought self-justification in the company of favourites, rare members of the Cabinet like David Walker, Minister of Public Works, technicians like his political organizer, Allister Grosart, private persons such as his brother Elmer. As the publicist, Peter Newman, commented regarding Grosart, these were people who were content with influence rather than seekers of power. This "kitchen cabinet" was an aspect of the new mode of government, and was in fact a departure from the cabinet system.

This failure was tragic, and not only for the greatly talented man who caused it; it was tragic also for the country. Diefenbaker had attracted a personal following much beyond party limits, and had aroused a widespread expectation of a more just, more compassionate government in a country adventurously grasping a destiny not dreamed of since the days of Laurier. The creation of a more just society was indeed attempted, in the increasing of old-age pensions, the lowering of taxes, and many similar measures. Something again was done to realize the Prime Minister's "vision" of a greater Canada and to bring the North into the national life, as by the "roads to resources" program. Nor were far-ranging concepts lacking, as in the idea of a national development corporation to ensure Canadian investment in Canada. But the general result was disillusion in the public, and a growing conviction of the incapacity of the government.

The reasons were simple enough. The Conservative party had not prepared itself to govern. Not only did it lack experience; it lacked also a political philosophy and an accepted body of doctrine. Divided between the nineteenth-century liberalism of its right wing and the humanitarian radicalism of its leader, the party had been unable to formulate a distinctive and practical policy for government. In consequence, what ideas the ministry revealed were those of individuals, such as Davie Fulton's on reform of the penitentiary system from one of punishment to one of rehabilitation, or Alvin Hamilton's on the place of the North in Canadian development. What the country received from the Diefenbaker administration was thus not the broad sweep of social reform and national policy it had expected, but instead a new style of politics – the politics of the perpetual canvass, of the political chieftain constantly seeking fortification through contact with the people.

But the times demanded a change of policy, and even of fundamentals. The post-war years had seen the war-time supremacy of the central government prolonged, even intensified, by the joint programs of development, welfare and training thrust on reluctant and perhaps backward provinces. The provinces were kept subdued and compelled to deal with growing difficulties as best they could with limited revenues eked out by the federal grants under the tax-sharing agreement of 1947. Quebec, with its special circumstances, was kept drugged with the negative policies of Duplessis and the old-guard politics of the federal Liberals. But this apathetic state of the provinces could not last. Their needs were too great, the opportunities their distress afforded to the opposition parties too tempting. Diefenbaker himself had won the support of the Frost government of Ontario in 1957 by agreeing to a larger federal grant for that prosperous province. Thus the way opened for a reassertion of that co-ordinate sovereignty of the provinces established in 1896 but masked by national development, depression and war ever since.

How compelling was the need of the provinces for additional revenues was shown year after year by the rising demands for social aid, roads, hospitals, housing and schools, all increased by the surging growth of cities, and all provincial responsibilities. The unremitting pressure of the provinces to obtain a larger share of the federal revenues revealed it even more clearly. This search for additional revenues paralleled the effort of Fulton to obtain an amending process for the British North America Act that would "repatriate" the constitution. Therein lay the possibility of financial demands and constitutional amendment fusing in a quest for greater provincial powers which would alter the basis of the constitution. The federal-provincial conference of 1960 made progress on the amending process, but the fiscal conference of the fall of that year became deadlocked. In 1961 the deadlock was broken by the Prime Minister imposing a formula which increased the grants to the provinces. At the time it could still be hoped that this was only a judicious alteration, but time was to reveal that it was an opening of flood-gates that could not be closed again.

Similarly the development of electric power on the Columbia River opened the way to a victory of a province over national policy. That river rises in British Columbia and flows south into the United States. The development of power on its Canadian section was a provincial matter; the agreement with the United States necessary for the best use of the waters of an international stream was a federal one. An intricate agreement was worked out after much dispute in Canada as to how it affected Canadian interests. On one point, however, there was Canadian agreement, and this was stressed by the principal Canadian negotiator, Davie Fulton. That was that there should be no export of Canadian power, since it had been learned through sad experience with Niagara power that electrical energy once made available for any length of time cannot be withdrawn. The principle was firmly embedded in the draft treaty of 1961. Then Premier Bennett, so far in agreement, demanded that the surplus power be sold to the United States, as he wished the revenue from it, partly for general use, but in especial to develop the energy of the Peace River in the north. In 1962 the Prime Minister forced Fulton to submit to Bennett's demands – one of the greatest examples since the 1880's of a victory of provincial over national interest.

The boldness of Bennett of British Columbia was only the beginning of a disposition of some provinces to set provincial interest before national policy. It was quickly followed by another aggression. In 1958 Canada had obtained, at the International Conference on Maritime Rights, title to the submarine lands running out to the continental shelf. Since no Canadian province exists in international law, the title to the new areas could, it seemed, be only Canadian and national. Yet on the analogy of provincial control of natural resources, Bennett in 1961 laid claim for British Columbia to the shelf off the Pacific shore of Canada. He was to be followed in his claim by the other maritime provinces of Canada – eight out of ten – and most vehemently by Premier Lesage of Quebec. Such claims revealed as clearly the readiness of the provinces to subordinate the nation to the province as they did the seeming inability of the national government to resist. The matter was referred to the Supreme Court, but the impartiality of that body, because it was a federal court, was in turn attacked.

What, then, of the national interest? Part of the answer might lie in the events taking place in the province of Quebec, events of which the claim to off-shore rights was only one example. There the quiet revolution brought to the surface by the Liberal victory in the provincial election of 1960 had proceeded apace. The changes taking place might be quiet – *tranquilles* – but they were, in the context of Quebec, assuredly revolutionary. The revolt was in the first place directed against the régime of the late Premier Duplessis and all its consequences. That régime had been negative, repressive and reactionary. A citizen of the nineteenth century would have likened it to that of the Bourbons of Naples. Clerical, nationalist, corrupt, it strove to keep Quebec as it was, rural in tone and ethic, laissez-faire in economics, and anti-labour in temper, as demonstrated in the use of the provincial police against the strikers at Asbestos in 1949.

Opposition came chiefly from intellectuals, who ranged from Father Georges Henri Lévesque, of the Ecole des Sciences Sociales at Laval, to André Laurendeau of *Le Devoir* and Pierre Elliott Trudeau of *Cité Libre*, a small left-wing periodical of Montreal. Above all, in the minds of its critics, Duplessisism compounded its enormities by a tacit alliance with American and English-Canadian industrial interests in the province. They supplied the election funds that kept Duplessis's Union Nationale unbeatable until 1960; he granted the franchises business sought, and refrained from using the power of the state to make industry and finance serve the needs of the people in working conditions and rewards, in welfare, and in education. It was this alliance that had led Laurendeau to compare Duplessis to a *"roi nègre,"* an African chief who sold his people to exploiters for his own power and enrichment. After the 1960 election, the heritage of Duplessis still cumbered the ground, and much of the work of the revolution was to bury its remains.

The revolution, however, was much more than a revolt against what was reactionary and outmoded in Quebec. It was above all the flowering of a new mentality in the French-Canadian middle class of Quebec. This had been growing, as it were, underground, during Duplessis's régime, although it was apparent enough, and to none more than *le chef* himself. The work of Father Lévesque and Abbé Dion at Laval, the battling of Jean Marchand in the cause of trade unions, the editorials and pamphlets of Laurendeau, Gérard Pelletier, and Trudeau, the French network of the Canadian Broadcasting Corporation, particularly the commentator René Lévesque, had already created the ideas, idiom and aspirations of a new outlook among many French Canadians, especially in the cities of the province. In essence, the new mentality was lay, scientific and reformist. It sought to open to French Canadians, while remaining French and Catholic, the possibilities, the novelties, the promises, of the North American and European civilizations of the twentieth century. It was a new wine that could only break the old bottles of Duplessisism, and of the old rural, clerical Quebec of Louis Hémon and the church.

Less specific, but not less real and powerful, was the awakening of new expectations among all the French people of Quebec. They rejected the limitations of the world their fathers had accepted, aware through television of other ways of life, freer, less demanding, perhaps more satisfying, than their own. They had become impatient of deprivation and restraint, and could no longer accept prohibition of a fuller and richer material life. To the more vehement of their spokesmen, their lot seemed indeed comparable with that of all repressed people, and the nationalist writers and orators hammered at the need for "decolonization." The new expectation was therefore that they would be free, free of the restrictions of their own past, free also of exploitation by an economic order which they neither controlled nor shared.

Perhaps the most important, if most intangible, result of this new mentality and those new expectations was the acceptance at long last of the state, the secular state, as their own and as an instrument of their will. Although political life, both in election and in government, had always been vigorous in Quebec, public opinion had never, despite 170 years of representative government, really accepted the state as the vehicle of the popular will. This was no doubt in part because of the prominence of the church in the public life of Quebec; in part because French-Canadian opinion thought of government as limited in its functions and negative in its attitude towards most of civil life. But at bottom it was the result of the essential passivity of the French Canadian in the history of Canada since the Conquest. He had lived under institutions imposed, or bestowed, on him, not with those of his own making. Now, in 1960, he had taken the government of Quebec as his own, and he expected it to serve him. His new expectations revealed the new attitude; it was exemplified in the vigorous movement of some of the best minds of Quebec into the Civil Service of Quebec to create there a government service as able, as informed, and as dedicated as any in Canada. The quiet revolution had not overthrown the state: it had appropriated it.

With this instrument, the Lesage administration, itself dominated by a new type of politicians in men like René Lévesque, Minister of Natural Resources, and Paul Gérin-Lajoie, Attorney General, could proceed to implement the revolution in specific reforms. The chief of these in 1961 were in social welfare, labour law, fiscal policy, public ownership, and education. Of first note perhaps were the introduction of hospital insurance, the provision of methods of arbitration and conciliation in labour disputes, and the introduction of free and compulsory schooling. In 1962 the electrical industry of Quebec was nationalized, after a provincial election on the issue, as Hydro-Québec. In 1963 the Parent Commission on Education made its first report. It recommended the institution of a ministry of education, to be advised by a superior council of education, the latter a necessity in a system that would remain bilingual and bi-confessional. Debate was prolonged, and it was not until 1964 that Bill 60 creating the ministry and the council was passed. By that date, as the above reforms indicate, Quebec had brought its institutions abreast of those of the other provinces, in itself a revolution.

Far more important, however, was the fact that Quebec had done this in its own way and in its own time. For the essential thing about the quiet revolution was not so much what it did as the spirit which informed it. That was a spirit of strong and confident nationalism – a strong and defiant pride in being French and a resolution to remain French – a spirit which in its heady rush to freedom from a sense of oppression and inferiority recognized few if any limits to its expansion. All-Canadian nationalism, carefully fostered by the Liberal party since Laurier's day, most recently and most fervently expressed by Diefenbaker in its most uncompromising, pan-Canadian form, found itself questioned, indeed challenged, by French-Canadian nationalism.

The latter nationalism now appeared in three forms, one new, one old, one new in its outspokenness. The first was the nationalism of the quiet revolution itself, the assertion of the resolution of the French Canadians of Quebec to be free, equal and self-governing within Quebec and Canada. As interpreted by Premier Lesage, it involved being *maîtres chez nous*, and was something to be realized by a *politique de grandeur*. It meant reform within the province, control and direction of the provincial economy, and a new federalism in Canada. Just what the new federalism was to be was not at first clear, but certainly it was to be one that would admit the aspirations of the new Quebec.

The second form of nationalism was the latest version of the old clerico-nationalism, eloquently expressed since the 1920's by the Abbé Lionel Groulx. That devoted man had created in the *Institut d'histoire* of the Université de Montréal a group of disciples, the strongly nationalist historians Maurice Séguin, Guy Frégault, and Michel Brunet – thinker, writer, speaker. That university indeed, in its school of history and faculty of law, had long been the hotbed of nationalism. It was an intense and fervent nationalism, but still conditioned by its original introversion and thus expressing itself in a negative and sometimes defeatist way. To Frégault, for example, the Conquest seemed the end of the possibility of a free and coherent French society in America.

When nationalism broke free from those historic trammels, it spoke with unmistakable clarity. It became separatism, the intention to set up an independent French state in America by secession from Canada. Urban, leftist, youthful in its spokesmen, the separatist movement was very important, although supported by only a small minority, because it challenged more moderate nationalism.

This whole enormous outburst of vitality was, in the main, to be welcomed by English Canadians if only because it brought English and French Canadians closer to one another in their major purposes and aspirations. Separatism was another matter, if it was to be taken seriously, but English Canadians were too familiar with the verbal fervour of their French compatriots and their own provincial dissidences to do so. The Diefenbaker government understood neither the nature nor the force of the quiet revolution. The Prime Minister himself seemed not to wish to; French nationalism did, after all, question the validity and challenge the reality of his "one Canada." The French ministers from Quebec were either incapable of interpreting the new spirit to their English colleagues, or, if capable, as were Léon Balcer and Noël Dorion, were not listened to with the attention merited by their own weight and the importance of what they had to say. Thus most of the English ministers were left free to assume that the revolution was just another French outburst, which could be left to subside when spent.

Moreover, the weight of western Canadian opinion in the Cabinet gave a particularly unsympathetic cast to governmental thought on Quebec nationalism, with the exception of that of Fulton. The national feeling of the West, and of the prairie provinces in particular, differed from that of the rest of the country. The West thought of Canadian nationality as the result of an assimilative process, although it accepted the mosaic pattern of cultural coloration. In such a process the French Canadian was just another element, to go the way of assimilation with all other elements, including the English. It was this concept that Diefenbaker had expressed with such oratorical passion. But such a view was incompatible with even the milder forms of French nationalism. A strong segment of the Cabinet, including the Prime Minister, was therefore inclined to think it understood French nationalism all too well and was ready flatly to resist its claims.

As with internal matters, so with external. If the Diefenbaker government failed to understand the revolution in Quebec, it failed even more publicly to comprehend and deal with the change in Canada's position in the trading world. The great boom of the first half of the 1950's had been based not only on the war-time expansion of the industries of Canada and the exploitation of resources old and new; it had rested also on the feverish need for these resources by a world devastated by war and undertaking new development, and on foreign investment, largely American, in Canadian resources and industries. By 1956 the post-war recovery was complete, and other resources, often cheaper, had been found. Canada's highly favoured position was undermined, and it had to fall back on its own economic powers to a greater degree. The result was a recession which lasted even longer than did the Diefenbaker administration.

In general, the Diefenbaker policies failed to deal adequately with changing economic circumstances as they revealed themselves. There were, however, some successes; one was the ending of the wheat carry-over, due though that was to the fortunate chance of increased wheat sales to Russia because of short crops, and then, because of famine, to China. The opportunities were exploited by Alvin Hamilton, as Minister of Agriculture, and the result was the consolidation of the Conservative hold on the prairies. Another solid success was that of George Hees, as Minister of Trade and Commerce, in increasing the sale of Canadian manufactures abroad by his insistence on the co-operation of government services and business enterprise. These two achievements alleviated the otherwise lamentable record of the government in economic affairs.

If the government could deal with targets of opportunity well enough, it was less happy in matters requiring deeper and more prolonged thought. This was most clearly revealed in its reaction to the announcement of the government of the United Kingdom, in 1960, that it proposed to seek entry into the European Common Market. It had in reality decided to do so as an attempt to forestall the nationalization of British industry by exposing it to intense competition. To reassure opinion in the United Kingdom and among the other members of the Commonwealth, it undertook to look out for the interests of its Commonwealth associates in making the change. Doubts among the members as to the compatibility of entry to the Common Market and association in the Commonwealth were none the less strong. But the strongest and most vocal opposition came from the government of Canada. Donald Fleming, Finance Minister, observed at the Commonwealth Consultative Conference of 1960 that any losses by Canada as a result of British entry would result in a re-examination of British trade with Canada. In 1961 he and George Hees, at the Commonwealth Economic Conference at Accra, opposed Britain's entry to the European Market in truculent and even threatening terms. This came with peculiar ill grace from men who had failed to increase Canadian imports of British goods and who had been embarrassed by an offer of free trade with Britain. Worse still, it was a failure to realize that the Commonwealth faced trading changes as great as those of 1849, and that the only possible economic offset to American influence in Canada was, not the United Kingdom alone, but Britain and Europe together.

The need of such an offset, of such a multiplying of partners in trade, was steadily underlined by the government's failure to do anything decisive about the twin problems of the increasing American ownership and control of Canadian resources and industries, and of the Canadian dependence, to balance its accounts with the United States, on a continuing inflow of American investment. The Conservative party had voiced its uneasiness at the extent of American investment, and some of its members, particularly the Prime Minister, were pro-Canadian to the point of being anti-American in their attitude. But to do anything really helpful was most difficult. What the government could do, it did. Canadian control of insurance companies was assured by legislation; foreign ownership of oil companies exploring the Arctic Islands was limited to fifty per cent. Equal shares in companies developing energy in Canada had to be available to Canadians.

All this was to set a direction, however, not to achieve a goal. Many Canadians, and especially Conservatives, were inclined to the old view that capital was neutral, and the nationality of ownership therefore unimportant. Economic control need not have political consequences. Yet the American firms were usually branch plants of American parent firms, rather than independent American-owned Canadian companies. Share-holding in American-controlled firms was seldom open to Canadians nor, in many, was high office. Thus much of the Canadian economy, up to eighty per cent of oil resources and up to sixty per cent of some manufacturing industries, was not only American-owned, but American-controlled in the interest of American shareholders and even of the American economy. How direct this might be was shown by the refusal of an American-controlled firm to supply loading equipment needed to speed the wheat sales to China. The Diefenbaker government need not be too severely criticized for failing to deal with a problem no other government has had the wit or courage to tackle, either by laws governing the proportion of foreign ownership allowed in a Canadian firm, as France had done, or by nationalization on the Mexican pattern. It was, however, that government which came face to face with the dependence on American investment.

It did so largely because of its financial policies. The humanitarian impulses of Diefenbaker, and his election promises, resulting in increased old-age pensions and welfare payments, with outlays for development, threw increased charges on the federal revenues. These were already suffering from the slackening of the economy in the recession. Hence the government was driven into deficit financing year after year, until, by 1962, annual interest on the national debt exceeded eight hundred million dollars, or twelve per cent of the government's annual expenditure. And this was happening under a minister of finance who was conservative and orthodox in opinion and who constantly preached the need of balanced budgets, even though governmental financial practice did approve deficit financing in time of recession. Thus, just as political indecision and confusion were dissipating the hopes of the stunning victory of 1958, so unprecedented deficits and debt charges were destroying confidence in the financial soundness of the Diefenbaker government.

All the above elements – economic growth, dependence on the American economy, fiscal soundness – fused in the extraordinary and distressing episode of the dismissal of the Governor of the Bank of Canada, James Coyne. The essential function of the Bank was to regulate the supply of money in the country. In doing so, it created the conditions in which the financial policy of the government operated. While the Bank was autonomous as a Crown corporation, clearly the government, responsible for the economy of the country, had to have the last word if the operations of the Bank and the policy of the government came into conflict. When the Bank pursued a "tight money" policy which offset the inflationary aspects of government financing, the Cabinet had protested, but the Minister accepted the Bank's policy, perhaps because of his own financial orthodoxy. But when, in 1960, Coyne began a series of speeches advocating a policy of national austerity and even protection, with major restrictions on American investment, the conflict became an open and public one. The Minister still declined to intervene, until, ostensibly on the ground that the Governor's pension on retirement had been increased to $25,000 a year, he demanded Coyne's resignation. This Coyne refused, on the grounds that the reasons given threatened the autonomy of all heads of Crown corporations and impugned his own integrity. A bill was therefore brought into Parliament to dismiss the Governor. He asked for a hearing before a Commons Committee, was refused one, but got it in the Senate. Coyne had been appointed by the previous Liberal government, and the Senate still had a Liberal majority. The Senate Committee gave him the vindication sought, and he then submitted his resignation. The episode in itself, though painful, was essentially meaningless. What it did was clinch the conclusion that the Diefenbaker government lacked skill and strength, thereby restoring hope to the Opposition that the triumph of 1958 was not irreversible.

If, however, it was the Coyne affair that placed the administrative weakness
KC-S

of the Diefenbaker government beyond doubt, it was the development of Canadian foreign affairs and defence policy that exposed its greatest failing. For one thing, apart from trade, the Diefenbaker government had no foreign policy of its own. It had uncritically continued that established by the Liberal government after 1945. For doing so, it is not necessarily to be censured; continuity in foreign policy is desirable. But the result was that, by the change of circumstances, the Diefenbaker government had to deal with the ripening of the dilemma inherent in Liberal foreign policy.

That dilemma was that Canada was committed by its policy of strong support for the United Nations to a policy of peace and peace-keeping; and by its membership in Nato and in Norad to one of military defence of Western Europe and North America. The two roles were not necessarily dissimilar, or mutually contradictory. They became so, however, with the development of nuclear tactical weapons and of the inter-continental bomber and missile. The dilemma was indeed apparent in Norad, which the Conservative government had so uncritically accepted. An effective discharge of Canada's responsibilities in both Nato and Norad came to require its acceptance of nuclear weapons. But how could Canada as a universal peacemaker preserve that character if it was to use nuclear arms in its limited alliances? How could the apostle of disarmament carry the nuclear bomb?

Even so, the horns of the dilemma might have been evaded had Sidney Smith not died in 1959, and been succeeded as Minister of External Affairs by Howard Green. Green, an impressively honest and honourable man, amiable and high-minded, had retained a measure of hope in disarmament and the United Nations that recalled the naïveté of the Kellogg-Briand Pact outlawing war. To preach peace, and aid the keeping of it by all means short of war, Green thought a role Canada was imperatively called upon to play. Canada had forgone the use of nuclear arms and urged limitations on their possession by other countries in a long series of conferences. That policy had suffered a set-back in the U-2 incident of 1960, when an American intelligence plane was shot down over Russian territory. But Green persisted in pressing for limitation, and particularly for a ban on nuclear test explosions. The relevance of his policy is shown by the fact that the ban was agreed to in 1961, and that in the same year Britain dropped out of the nuclear arms race and France resolved to continue in it. But there arose in that year also the matter of arming with nuclear bombs the Canadian Air Division in Europe, equipped with planes designed for the purpose. Thus the dilemma became defined, and the Cabinet began to divide into an anti-nuclear faction headed by Green and a pro-nuclear faction headed by Douglas Harkness, Minister of Defence. The Prime Minister on the whole supported Green, but he had to recognize that here was a definite split on policy, with ample argument on both sides. The result was that no decision was taken, despite pressure from the military commanders of Nato and prolonged discussion of the issue in the Canadian press.

The next year, 1962, as the fourth after the general election of 1958, was almost certain to be a year of a general election. Thus the nuclear arms issue had unusual political bearing, as the division in the Cabinet reflected a similar difference in the country. It was bound to be a matter of the keenest concern, and the Opposition of course was certain to insist that it be debated in Parliament and on the hustings. When the Opposition pressed the matter in the House in February, the Prime Minister, in a lengthy but evasive explanation of the government's policy, stated that Nato nuclear policy had been discussed by President Kennedy of the United States and Prime Minister Macmillan of the United Kingdom at a conference at Nassau, the Bahamas, where Diefenbaker had been a post-conference guest. The statement affected relations between the United States and its Nato allies. The State Department therefore felt obliged, in a statement on March 1, to deny flatly the Prime Minister's declaration in order to "set the record straight." So flat a "correction" of a Prime Minister's public statement not only raised questions of the relations of the two governments – the Canadian Ambassador to Washington was called home – but ensured that foreign policy and relations with the United States would be a leading issue in the election.

The Prime Minister advised one early in April, 1962, after Mr. Fleming had brought down his fourth budget, with a deficit forecast of $745,000,000 justified as expansionist. If the government still possessed areas of strength, the Opposition remained weak, negligible in Parliament, attractive only by contrast in the country. The majority of provincial governments remained Conservative; only New Brunswick had been regained by the Liberals in 1960. Moreover, Lester Pearson had proved quite incapable of standing up to Diefenbaker. His inability to do so was partly the result of inexperience in Parliament, still more the result of his long diplomatic training. Used to seeking agreement, he found no joy in contention. But above all, it was probably distaste for the reliance on rhetoric, the satisfaction with effect, the sheer delight in debate, that unnerved Pearson before an opponent he appeared to find incredible.

Yet strength was readily to be found, both in the business community dismayed by four years of fiscal mismanagement and in intellectual circles angered by Diefenbaker's open contempt for the academician and the expert – men like Tom Kent, once editor of the *Winnipeg Free Press*, and Mitchell Sharp, formerly of the Civil Service and now eager to oppose the Prime Minister who had made public use of his confidential report on the economy. In a study conference held at Kingston, the Liberals began to collect the ideas from which an expansive social policy was to be built.

The Opposition, moreover, was to be served, to a degree an opposition seldom is, by the coming home to roost of the government's financial vagaries.

During the late winter there had been much discussion about the Canadian dollar, and warnings of the need for devaluation. The result of this uneasiness was a steady drain on the foreign-exchange reserves as the government strove to maintain the dollar at a high rate of exchange with the American dollar. Finally it gave in to the speculative pressure and fixed the rate at 92½ United States cents. A temporary respite ensued, but doubts persisted and pressure again increased during the election campaign. Scarcely had the election been concluded when a severe austerity program had to be imposed on the country to maintain the devalued dollar.

This background of financial fear blurred the issues of the election: the Diefenbaker record, the Liberal program, the nuclear issue. But the main question was, simply, to what extent had belief in Diefenbaker vanished, and the disillusioned turned to the Liberals? The staggering fact was that they had not done so in sufficient numbers to put the government out of office. The Conservatives lost their majority but elected the largest group, 116 in number. The New Democratic Party – the old C.C.F. reorganized on a wider base – returned nineteen strong from its defeat of 1958. But the Liberals, who had glimpsed victory in the Tory difficulties and dilemmas, were denied it, as perhaps were the Conservatives, by the Créditistes' carrying twenty-six seats in Quebec. (Four Social Crediters were elected in Alberta.) The Liberals as the second group therefore had only a hundred members: a far cry from 1958, but also far from power.

Most notable, however, was the fragmentation and indecision in Canada portrayed by the election returns. Where one man had dominated, no man and no party now had power. The voters were deeply disillusioned – often a condition of Social Credit success. Diefenbaker's four years of government mainly by words had left his "one Canada" divided and nerveless.

The lavish spending had ended in austerity; the indecision on the use or rejection of nuclear arms was to end in the disorganization of the government itself. As the financial crisis had been mainly an international judgement on Canadian financial behaviour, so the resolution of the nuclear dilemma was also to be by international intervention. In early October, 1962, American intelligence learned that Russian air bases for nuclear missiles had been established in Cuba and were about to be armed. Why Russia should have dared to challenge the United States in the sensitive strategic area of the Cuba of Communist Fidel Castro remains a mystery. Perhaps the intent, reflecting the low estimate the Russian Prime Minister, Nikita Krushchev, had formed of the resolution of President Kennedy, was to counter American bases in Turkey. If so, Krushchev had erred, for on October 22, President Kennedy announced that Cuba would be "quarantined" and shipments from Russia stopped on the high seas. The American components of Norad were placed on the alert.

In deciding on these measures, the American President had not consulted the Canadian government, but simply advised it on the eve of operations of what was being done. With the alert, however, Canadian participation was called for by the agreement itself. The Canadian service officers took all possible measures of readiness and sought authority to order the alert. The government, however, refrained from granting the authority. Its reasons remain obscure: distrust of American intelligence, annoyance at not being consulted, unwillingness to take a measure that would have committed Canada to one side and so compromised its role as peacemaker, these remain conjectures. The fact was that American air forces were denied the use of Canadian air space and bases. Not for two days, until October 24, were the Canadian forces put on the alert. By then the Russians had avoided a clash, withdrawing their shipping, and the crisis was nearly over.

The effects were drastic. American-Canadian relations were at their most tense; the division within the Cabinet deepened and hardened; the country itself was embittered, whether by the feeling that it had not behaved well, or that it had nearly been swept into a nuclear war against its will. Thus the nuclear dilemma had been thrust into the forefront of national politics and had to be faced and ended.

On January 3, 1963, the just-retired American commander of the Nato forces, General Lauris Norstad, visited Ottawa. Asked by a reporter whether Canada could discharge its responsibilities to Nato without nuclear arms, he replied that it could not. Again external intervention, again by an American, quickened the debate. The tension within the government was growing intolerable, especially for the Minister of Defence, Douglas Harkness. Not only had he to face the military consequences of the anti-nuclear policy; he also strongly believed it was mistaken. Finally, on February 3, he resigned from the Cabinet.

The resignation of a minister generally respected on an issue so great and so immediate could not but call in question the life of the government itself. Harkness's resignation was merely the one clear act in a dissatisfaction with Diefenbaker's leadership which had been growing since October and by the end of January had become an incipient movement to dislodge him as leader. This, however, was headed off by the Diefenbaker loyalists and resolved in caucus. Only Harkness did the clear and honourable thing; the other dissidents returned to party conformity. But the government could no longer count on the support of some members of the New Democratic Party to give it, with the help of the Social Crediters, the majority it lacked. It therefore became wholly dependent on the Social Credit votes. The leader, Robert Thompson, properly asked terms for his support. These were reasonable, especially his demand for an early budget, and he clearly wanted to keep the government in office. His terms were not accepted, for reasons unknown, and Thompson divided the House on the evening of February 5. The Diefenbaker ministry was overthrown by the vote, the second so defeated since Confederation.

A fall so dramatic for reasons so calamitous – mismanagement, indecision, party revolt and loss of mutual trust – ought to have been the end of Conservative influence in Canadian political life for some time, and of John Diefenbaker conclusively. It was, in fact, almost the beginning of a second career for him, the battle of an unconquerable man to fight his way back to power.

The immediate and main issue of the election campaign was, of course, that of nuclear arms. The leader of the Opposition had already made that explicit by announcing in January his own decision that Canada should accept nuclear warheads for the two Bomarc sites in Canada and for the Air Division in Europe. But behind this was the issue of the government's inefficiency, its muddle, its indecision, its division, what may be called the whole Diefenbaker débâcle despite its considerable successes and its great royal commissions on medical insurance, government efficiency, and taxation. And less tangible, just as pervasive but never definite, was the question of American influence in Canadian politics. American influence in Canadian life of course had never been greater, as British prestige declined and American rose. American influence in economic life was so great as to raise the question of political influence following. Now the nuclear issue seemed to indicate that American political intervention in Canadian affairs, if still veiled, was blunt and direct.

When the House was dissolved, the date of the election was set for June 18. That the government's vast majority would diminish, no one doubted. The long record of mismanagement, with the growing loss of prestige abroad caused by pretentious rhetoric and confused performance, could not but reduce the abnormal majority. Yet the Prime Minister, now a master of television, careless as always of failure, sure as ever of his destiny, remained beyond question the peerless campaigner of his time. He had, after all, created a new kind of politics, immediate, irrational, passionate. Millions would respond again to the torrent of rhetoric, especially the rural, the ethnic and the pensioner voters, always Diefenbaker's peculiar cares, his examples of the "average Canadian." In his zeal, he completed the process of making the holder of the office of Prime Minister the master of all the royal prerogatives. The regal, even Messianic, character assumed by Diefenbaker was such as no Prime Minister had ever imagined.

Diefenbaker did indeed carry his pro-Canadianism to the point of anti-Americanism. But the burden of his desperate and feverish campaign was his prolonged and not unsuccessful defence of the "little man," the "average Canadian," against the wealthy and powerful of the Liberal and business establishments. Defeated in public office, the old electioneer returned to the sources of his strength, the fears, suspicions and resentments of all the subdued and quiet people who felt themselves depressed by the powers of a frightening world. It was splendid humanitarian Toryism, but it was unusual Con-́servatism. It told, however, as did the man's lonely courage.

Perhaps, nevertheless, the main feature of the campaign was the effect of the Diefenbaker style of politics. Gone were the days of stately aloofness in the Prime Minister and the regional and local campaigns that had decided elections. A national party had, in the days of television and Diefenbaker, to campaign nationally and behind one man, a leader. The Liberal Party had no such leader. Pearson was a diplomat and a gentleman long before he was a politician. He would have presided as serenely as Saint-Laurent over the fortunes of a successful party. Except in courage, he quite lacked the means to restore party fortunes in the glare and histrionics of the new politics. He was by nature and breeding wholly incapable of what came to Diefenbaker naturally, public emotion and the impassioned use of the magnificent half-truth. As the campaign waxed, it was inevitable that the Prime Minister should demonstrate in public the ascendancy over his opponent he had already established in Parliament. Here was the main factor among those determining the outcome.

The Liberal party had therefore to turn to the new electioneering to try to overcome the advantage Diefenbaker still had. They studied Theodore H. White's *The Making of the President, 1960*. They turned, as the Conservatives had done with Allister Grosart, to the advertising profession for help. They set up a team of publicity men, headed by Keith Davey. They formed a team of policy-makers and speech-writers, headed by Tom Kent. They employed pollsters to gauge the progress of the campaign. They employed, with the President's knowledge, a former Kennedy aide, an American citizen, to advise them. They foretold their "sixty days of decision." The core of their endeavour was to create an "image" of a leader, benign, wise, infallibly informed and everlastingly concerned.

With a great actor, or a nonentity, they might have succeeded. But the plain decency of Pearson could no more respond to the politics of synthetic charisma than it could imitate the natural flamboyance of Diefenbaker. Pearson came through for what he was, an honest man in unfamiliar circumstances who would do his best. Diefenbaker remained the ever spiralling master of the air. And his colleagues, the men he had never called to his councils, fought their separate battles as best they could, often without their leader's name on their lips.

The result again was that both the main parties were defeated. The Liberals, denied a victory by the solid West of the prairies, elected only 129 members. The Conservative members numbered ninety-five, the New Democrats seventeen, Social Credit twenty-four. The fragmentation of Canada continued, a Liberal Quebec offset by a Tory West.

Because the Liberal party had the largest group, a Pearson government replaced that of Diefenbaker. But no miracle occurred. Never did a slogan back-fire more devastatingly than that of "Sixty days of decision." Three years of incoherence followed. Conservative indecision was succeeded by Liberal ineptitude.

The explanation is to be found in the nature of the new administration itself, in which pride of ancestry conflicted with hope of posterity. In this hybrid of old and new, the old element was the number of former civil servants in the ministry: the Prime Minister himself; Sharp, the Minister of Finance; Pickersgill, the Minister of Transport; Drury, the Minister of Industry. There was also the re-established harmony between the Civil Service and the new government. Ottawa's God was once more in his heaven. But new and incompatible was the brains-trust element marked by the role of Kent as the Prime Minister's special adviser; the unofficial cabinet had been moved from the kitchen to the study. And the Prime Minister himself was personally reluctant to assume the character of a "regal" prime minister, but was forced by circumstances to attempt it.

In its support in the country, the government had the same sharply divided elements of new and old. Business had little choice but to support the Liberals after the Diefenbaker campaign, but business was in a new mood. It demanded the efficient operation of a mixed economy rather than the safeguarding of private enterprise. Coupled with this was the party's success in the urban constituencies in a country increasingly urban in fact and in temper. The essence of urban life was the assured fulfilment of projected expectations; wages and salaries had to be at least stable, preferably steadily increasing, to meet rents, mortgage payments, budget-plan payments. There were fewer and fewer private resources, despite increased saving in non-liquid forms such as pension plans, to meet a failure of expectations. Only government could keep the economy airborne and avoid a crash. The Liberal party was un-doubtedly more in touch with this new necessity than the Conservative, which was no longer really attached to private enterprise as such, though certainly to personal responsibility.

The "old" elements of government support were revealed most clearly in that given by Smallwood's Newfoundland and by Quebec. The Newfoundland members were a solid contingent of good party men, single-mindedly devoted to seeing that the province got the aid it needed; their attitude was as old as Canadian political life. From Quebec, however, the representation consisted of new men like Maurice Lamontagne and Maurice Sauvé, who to some degree stood for the new temper of the province, and the majority who were simply the party-picked and party-returned members, as Quebec representatives had been since Confederation. Even the man who came to lead the Quebec members was "old guard" at bottom, although he was himself able, amiable,

and honest; Guy Favreau. But there was not much place in the old bottle for
the new ferment of the quiet revolution.

Indeed, the "old" predominated in the new government, presented to the
electorate as so novel. Foreign policy, the nuclear issue decided, resumed its
wonted obscurity under Paul Martin. The ideas and symbols of the old King
nationalism were dusted off. In none was this archaism more evident than
in the new Prime Minister, a mediator, a conciliator, not an executive.

The new government plunged at once into its career of failure. Walter L.
Gordon, the Toronto chartered accountant turned thinker and author,
remained a nationalist greatly concerned to reduce American control of the
economy. He was the new Minister of Finance. He brought in a budget calculated to begin that work. It crashed about his ears in what was perhaps the
greatest humiliation a Canadian minister ever had to endure. Not only were
parts of it ill-thought-out; not only did the minister have to confess that he
had employed outside aid – men under oath, it is true, but still not civil
servants; the budget was furiously and openly repudiated by the very business
community that had supported the Liberal return to power, including Eric
Kierans, President of the Montreal Stock Exchange. The budget had to be
remodelled on the floor of the Commons. If this was efficiency, the Opposition
made the most of it. From then on, Diefenbaker dominated the House, lashing
a cowering government with the scorpions of his practised wrath.

The government was prompt in providing further occasions; almost at
once, accusations of scandal befouled it, by no means justly, but for the same
reasons of old-guard carelessness and new men inexperienced. Two ministers
were revealed to have accepted furniture for their Ottawa residences without
immediate payment; a commonplace thing enough, but the supplier was a
supporter of the Liberal party. Both were from Quebec; both were honourable
men. But they had been thoughtless; a pattern was set, and the Government
of Decision was driven back to a harried defence.

This was the beginning of a tragedy as dismal as the failure of the Diefenbaker
government. Again, however, the record of the new government, as that of
the old, was better than it seemed. If in nothing else, it was argued, the Pearson
administration could do better than that of Diefenbaker in understanding
Quebec. Not only had it a large and able representation from Quebec in the
Commons and in the Cabinet; dealing with Quebec was an old Liberal
tradition in which the party had acquired much finesse. In this, its traditional
character would assist it.

The argument was not without force, and perhaps the appointment in 1963
of the Royal Commission on Bilingualism and Biculturalism was the chief
act of the Pearson administration. Jointly chaired by André Laurendeau and
by Davidson Dunton, President of Carleton University and one-time Chairman
of the Canadian Broadcasting Corporation, the commission was representative

of Canadians, English and French, concerned to discover the means of creating a genuine and undoubted equality among Canadians.

Yet few high-minded and courageous acts by a Canadian government have met with more derision, especially in Quebec, and with more critical opposition – especially in English Canada. To the strong French-Canadian nationalist, anything the commission might recommend would be ludicrously late. To the English-Canadian nationalist, any concession to French nationalism would be a betrayal of his concept of Canada, and a division of the country. On the face of it, therefore, the Pearson government itself seemed to be hastening the course of events in Quebec, where the pursuit of a new status continued more vigorously than ever, particularly in the institution of an "Estates-General" by the St. John Baptist Society to discuss and plan the future of French Canada.

That federal policy was in fact precipitating events in Quebec was revealed by the fate of the Canada Pension Plan in 1964. This was a national, contributory pension plan for all Canadians. It was not a measure that a minority government had much difficulty in passing through Parliament, as the plan was not objectionable in principle and was politically impossible to oppose. But opposition came from the provinces and it was considerable. Not only did the provinces have to be assured of the workability of the plan; they opposed the lack of provision for funding the receipts so that the vast pool of money that would accumulate might be used for government finance. And Quebec declined to enter the plan. It proposed to have a plan of its own, the accumulation from which it could use for the realization of the Lesage government's ambition to create a largely self-sustaining provincial economy. Lesage was intransigent in his refusal to enter the national scheme. The Pearson government, faced with both a set-back to its scheme and a flat denial of its ability to deal with Quebec, employed hasty and secret diplomacy to work out a compromise. Quebec was to have its own scheme and control its funds, as the other provinces had to be allowed to do, but "portability" and other national features were to be retained. It was no doubt all that could be done, but English Canada felt that, far from Pearson's having managed Quebec, Quebec had dictated to Canada. Certainly the seal of approval was put on a province "opting out" of a joint federal-provincial undertaking.

The quiet revolution was indeed moving with ever greater force, and the old Liberal controls over Quebec were no longer effective. Premier Lesage, not without a personal predilection for his *politique de grandeur*, had to maintain a pose of truculent nationalism if he were not to lose the support of revolutionary sentiment to his opponents. Whatever he did, he could not afford bland co-operation with Ottawa.

Members of his own administration, moreover, Lévesque and Gérin-Lajoie in particular, would not have allowed him to behave as just another provincial premier. Strong nationalists, themselves convinced that Quebec was not a province like the others, they sought first to exploit the limits of provincial powers under the constitution. It was an exercise for which the legally-trained Gérin-Lajoie was especially fitted. He it was who advanced the argument that in all matters of provincial jurisdiction, such as education, a province – and particularly Quebec – should be able to have its own representation abroad and become an international person to the extent of its jurisdiction. The idea shocked English Canadians. There could be no doubt in view of the Scott decision of 1938 that the national government alone could have representation abroad and an international personality. Yet the federal government in its external policy had given little consideration to matters of provincial jurisdiction, and the various provinces had had international dealings of one kind or another without objection. And Lévesque, ardent, intimate, began to take up the talk of a special status for Quebec, the recognition of its special character as a French-language province to the extent of over eighty per cent of its population, and the bestowal of special powers to accord with that character in a devolution such as had occurred among the members of the old British Empire.

The wild talk was in fact running much further, to consideration of associate status, a dual state of the Austro-Hungarian kind, with "two majorities," one English and one French, like the double majority of the old Canadian Union. The drive of such thought, of course, was really towards the transmutation of the province of Quebec into the nation-state of French Canada. In such heady talk among the students, the idle, the discontented of the middle class, all who felt their future limited by English-Canadian and American cultural pressure and domination of the economy, "separatism" could only flourish, and move towards its logic of secession and independence. A few extremists, influenced by European and Algerian immigrants, and by examples in Africa and Asia, turned to terrorism. One armoury robbed of ammunition, two postboxes filled with home-made bombs, one man killed, one injured, in dismantling these crude weapons, the United States consulate in Montreal bombed, these were the ugly but puny results. French as well as English Canadians were shocked beyond sympathy, and jointly felt the use of terror "un-Canadian."

In such circumstances the conventional Liberal magic was clearly ineffective. The younger Quebec ministers now came forward with an American term to describe a new approach to what they insisted was a matter of federal-provincial relations. That was "co-operative federalism." As a French historian aptly inquired, what kind of federalism could it be that was not co-operative? But what was meant was that the federal government would not plan and then propose to the provinces, but consult them first. This no doubt was wise, but it attempted to ignore the fact that much opinion in Quebec was questioning the federal relationship itself. Only a very loose federal tie would be acceptable in Quebec. What then? Were all federal ties to be loosened accordingly, or was Quebec to be given a special status in the guise of a permissive federal system, as loose or as close as each province might choose? In either event, was this what the majority of Canadian citizens really desired?

If internal affairs were in confusion, external were quiet. In foreign policy the administration enjoyed the unruffled serenity of what had been the image of Liberal administration. That august sphere of policy was once more retired to the arcana of government, about which Paul Martin sometimes spoke to the House with Delphic ambiguity. But the quiet was caused not only by the restoration of control to the expert; there was also a brief lull in the vast convolutions of international politics. The rise of Communist China had ended the Russian domination of the Communist world. The breach between the two Communist super-powers, and the Russian rebuff in Cuba, had resulted in a strengthening of the desire to limit the testing of nuclear arms in 1963, and to nuclear stalemate. At the same time the nuclear dilemma had been ended for Canada; the Bomarc missiles and the Air Division were armed. The outbreak of fighting between Greeks and Turks in Cyprus, and among the factions in the Congo, had given the government in 1964 the opportunity to contribute a Canadian contingent to a peace-keeping force in those countries. Canada was back in its familiar role, apparently without loss of the character it sought as the apostle of peace, armed but pacific. It was in part that role which determined the government to make the armed services one force, commanded, equipped and organized for the conditions of modern warfare and especially for the swift dispatch of forces trained to deal with international emergencies. As the outbreak of hostilities between India and Pakistan in 1965 was to reveal, there was much sense in this line of thought. It rested, however, on the assumption that a mass war effort would not again be necessary. Its implementation would also force an adjustment of service loyalties and might involve a change of service symbols that would encounter a deep and perhaps irrational resistance.

How strong such resistance might become was revealed in 1964 by the controversy over the adoption of a national flag for Canada, for which the Red Ensign had done duty since the 1920's. The matter had long been debated, and there can be little doubt that in principle the great majority of Canadians would have welcomed a national flag. But in the circumstances, when the latent republicanism of elements in the Liberal party was coming into the open, when French nationalists were beginning to advocate a republican form of government at least for Quebec, and when the Liberal party was greatly under Quebec influence and suspected of being too conciliatory to Quebec, the matter was one that could easily be inflamed. It was inflamed in the event because the Prime Minister saw fit to bring the matter up as a personal and party undertaking. That a change of national symbol could be treated as a personal and partisan matter gave the Conservative party a chance to raise a prolonged storm of opposition which raged through the summer of 1964. The matter was forced into a committee of the Commons and changes were made in the design accepted and proposed by the Prime Minister. The outcome, the present flag, could be called the result of national agreement, but in traditional parts of the country the flag was not accepted by older Canadians. The best that can be said is that the controversy purged emotions, and those Canadians who took symbols seriously came to realize that the time had come to revalue all aspects of the national life.

The Opposition had also much to make of the government's failure to obtain the extradition of Hal Banks from the United States. An American labour organizer, Banks had been brought in to rid the Canadian Seamen's Union of Communist influence. This he had done, but his methods were so ruthless and illegal as to provoke a warrant for his arrest on the recommendation of a royal commission of inquiry into the reorganization of the union. Banks evaded arrest so easily as to raise the question of whether there had been official complicity.

The suggestion that the government had allies not given to unfailing observance of the law was only that, until 1964. Then the case of Lucien Rivard, a smuggler of heroin, revealed that the old-guard politicians of Quebec had indeed such allies, and that persons close to the Minister of Justice were in contact with them. To cap the matter, Rivard escaped to the States as easily as Banks had done. The prosecuting genius of Diefenbaker soared on avenging pinions; the government was shamed. It was cleared in a report by Chief Justice Frédéric Dorion of the Quebec Superior Court, but only to its satisfaction when it had insisted on one verbal change in the report. The case itself, however, and that high-handed action, gave the Opposition a chance in 1965 to shake confidence in the government's integrity and to feed a growing appetite for scandal.

For the moment, in that emotion-drunk summer, the observer might well have wondered if the divisions of Canadian life were not widening beyond hope of closing. It was the centennial of the Quebec Conference, and the country was preparing to celebrate the centennial of Confederation in 1967. Part, yet not part, of this celebration was to be the World Exposition at Montreal the same year. To begin the commemoration and mark the historic conference, the Queen was invited to visit Quebec City in October, 1964. The extreme nationalists and the separatists made this the occasion of a demonstration of anti-English feeling; it was indeed a superb opportunity for publicity. In reaction, the Canadian government took the greatest precautions, and the Queen moved with her usual grace through the ancient city between walls of police, and little else. The average French Canadian felt indifferent, or at least not interested enough to risk being caught in a street fight. As a result, the visit was a fiasco. This encouraged the extreme nationalists in Quebec; it deeply angered English Canadians, both nationalists and traditionalists.

Above all, it raised the question of ultimate symbols. Could the monarchy any longer serve as the symbol of one Canada? But could a republic? The answer in 1964 to both questions was, no. One thing, however, was certain. The crypto-republicanism of some Liberals was now open, the creeping republicanism of some elements of Canadian life was now boldly advancing. The presence of republics in the Commonwealth made respectable what was once covert. More important, the change revealed the need of Canadians to make their own decisions.

The more significant feature of this acceleration of change was not that progressive elements in Canadian society welcomed it, but that the conservative elements found no satisfactory mode of opposing it. Blank rejection there was, but it awakened no open response; the classic conservative formula of continuity in change found no convincing spokesman. The Opposition, in consequence, for all that Diefenbaker dominated the Commons, and for all that the party continued to draw its share of the intelligence and integrity in public life, steadily weakened. Not unnaturally the government, unhappy as governments lacking a majority always are, chose to call a general election for November, 1965.

In doing so it stood on its record, considerable in sum, and frankly appealed for a majority – a "mandate" – to continue its program of social reform. It accepted the risk of running on the old distribution despite the fact that a new one, based on the census of 1961 and employing the new method of a statutory commission, had been prepared. Because the latter increased urban representation, it was thought it would favour the Liberals, stronger in the cities while the Conservatives were stronger in the countryside.

As the election approached, the Liberals were heartened by the adherence of three distinguished French Canadians from Quebec, Gérard Pelletier, former editor of La Presse, Jean Marchand, head of the Confederation of National Trade Unions, and Pierre Elliott Trudeau. They had deliberately chosen the Liberals as the best hope of national unity, and they deliberately entered federal politics to oppose the aggression of the provinces agains federal power.

Once more, however, the Liberals, confident in their mastery of advertising electioneering and cheered by the pollsters' repeated predictions of victory, were denied a majority. Diefenbaker campaigned with his old vehemence and much of his old effect, more effective perhaps as an old man indestructible in defeat. And once more the stubborn prairie ranks were unbroken, and as the waves of Liberal victory in the Maritimes and central Canada rolled in they broke on the rockbound conservatism of the West that had made a society it chose to preserve. The Liberals were stopped just short of a majority.

Again the fragmentation of Canada was underlined; again the public had expressed its lack of conviction that any party was worthy of national power. Clearly the internal dissension, the confusion and the mismanagement of the past five years were to continue, and in fact during the next year Canadian political life was to reach its nadir. Not only had the style and courtesies of parliamentary life degenerated to a shameful degree – a continuous process since the pipeline debate of 1956; not only had co-operation, on occasions of national moment, between the head of the administration and the leader of the opposition been lost in the personal feud of Pearson and Diefenbaker; a series of scandals was now to stain the life of Parliament. When one Chartier was killed by a bomb he had intended to throw into the Commons chamber, the distaste for Parliament reached its full. The opposition were much to blame for this unhappy outcome, for they had pushed their prosecution of the government beyond the limits of public need and parliamentary decorum. Bitterly were they and Parliament to pay for their excess when the government replied, quite as irresponsibly, in kind.

The occasion for the dishonouring of the new parliament was the case of George Victor Spencer, a Vancouver postal clerk who had been suspended with loss of pension by administrative order, and without trial, for supplying information to Russian agents. The information was commonplace enough, and so, sadly, was the procedure. But when it became public knowledge late in 1965, public concern was properly aroused. The Minister of Justice, Lucien Cardin, handled the matter in an evasive and bureaucratic manner. When Parliament met, the opposition urged that the government institute an inquiry to ensure that justice had been done, and that the security procedures of the government were indeed tolerable. The government would have been wise to acquiesce, but unfortunately the memory of the Rivard scandal, and the jubilant eagerness of the Conservative opposition once more to question the integrity of a government so badly exposed, made the minister reluctant to agree to an inquiry. What right had the leader of the Opposition to speak on government security in view of the "Monsignor" case? he asked, in public. Finally, however, he was overridden by the Prime Minister himself, and an inquiry was ordered.

But what was the "Monsignor" case? In fact, everyone in the know in Ottawa already knew. Then suddenly the Canadian public knew, through the ingenuity of a Canadian journalist who discovered in Germany the person in question, one Gerda Munsinger. She it was that Cardin in exasperation had referred to in his warning to the Conservatives that there could be tit for tat.

The story that broke was, as news, both shocking and hilarious. Gerda Munsinger was a German immigrant who had had a career in Montreal as model and entertainer. Her contacts were rather surprising; her war-time life in what had become East Germany raised a necessary if formal question of security, if the contacts should be political. During the Diefenbaker régime Mrs. Munsinger did in fact have lunch with one cabinet minister, George Hees; and another, Pierre Sévigny, Associate Minister of Defence, spent a night in her apartment. These contacts were reported by the Mounted Police to the then Minister of Justice, Davie Fulton, who reported the matter to the Prime Minister. The Prime Minister took no overt action. Whatever the risk to the security of Canada and its allies, the shocking thing was the laxness that characterized the whole affair. The public was both angered and wildly amused.

In the heated atmosphere of mutual recrimination that prevailed in the House, these revelations certainly could not be laughed off. As the word of a Minister of Justice had been refused in the Spencer case, so now in the Munsinger affair was that of a former Minister of Justice, and of a former Prime Minister. A judicial inquiry was set up, to refer the matter to the impartiality of the bench. Mr. Justice Wishart Spence of the Supreme Court of Canada agreed to act. It was either a great patriotic sense of duty, or an error in judgement, that led him to consent, because the independence of the bench was impaired by his doing so. His report revealed nothing more than the facts above, and did nothing to cool the temper of the antagonists. But the deepening disgust of the public with the conduct of Parliament made itself felt; all parties decided that the mutual harassment must stop, and Parliament turn back to sober business.

Things, however, would never be quite the same again. Canadians learned that politics was not a game that could be left to politicians. The events of 1965 and 1966 were to lead to greater political sophistication and a greater involvement in politics. The Rivard case, in particular, led to the end of "old guard" politics among Quebec Liberals. The provincial Liberal party, also for reasons of nationalism, became independent of the federal party. The new Liberal leaders, including the three new recruits led by Marchand, insisted on reform. And the Conservative party had to reconsider its attitude of perpetual electioneering and of prosecuting the government like a criminal before a court.

But these changes took time, and one more great controversy in 1966 was to repeat the old established patterns of a government without a majority using weakness as a reason for rigidity, of opposition bordering on obstruction, of appeal to fears of change lest valued traditions and established symbols should suffer. Paul Hellyer, Minister of Defence, had decided to proceed with the long-prepared bill for the integration of the armed forces. He at once became involved in a dispute with senior officers of the Navy, led by Admiral William Landymore, who feared the Navy would be reduced to a simple transport agency of the other arms. The Opposition took up the cry, as did some military critics. Some believed that even the unification of command, let alone the integration of the services, was an administrative error; some that the result would be merely a peace-keeping international force, of little use for the defence of Canada. It was a straight clash of progressive and traditionalist feeling. Hellyer faced down the storm of criticism with Cromwellian firmness, and the bill passed. Canada had taken one more step towards the future, and the wars and battle honours, even the scars of Vimy and Falaise, suddenly seemed as archaic as Agincourt or Lundy's Lane.

Yet the change from the politics of decay and frustration had to be made; to be forced, if necessary. The process began in the Conservative party. If Lester Pearson had failed to win in four elections, John Diefenbaker had failed in three. And there was a growing feeling that the great campaigner, not only because of his age, but because he remained unchanged amid accelerating change, was becoming less and less capable of performing his one great feat of appealing to the electorate. Efforts had been on foot for some time to recondition the party. The election of Dalton Camp as national president in 1963, a "thinkers'" conference at Fredericton in 1964, the holding of a national convention in 1965, the forced acceptance by Diefenbaker of Léon Balcer as Quebec leader in 1965, all were indicative of change; but Diefenbaker had remained his unrepentant self, secure in the support of the parliamentary caucus. Now in a convention in Ottawa late in 1966, Camp forced through, over Diefenbaker's frantic opposition, a resolution to review the leadership of the party within a year, as was to be done in the convention of September, 1967. The break-up of the years of frustration had begun.

It was only a beginning and not noted even as such. The country was to have a year, as it seemed, of recuperation, in fact of euphoria. The economy had recovered. Population, fed by immigration, much of it British, much Italian, had passed the figure of 20,000,000 in 1967. The euphoria was that of material well-being and of a growing sense of accomplishment; accomplishment not necessary national, but still accomplishment. The material well-being was American-derived. It was, in short, as never realized before in Canada or so frankly accepted, that of the affluent society. Both its values and the names of its features were drawn from the United States. Here was an American penetration of Canadian life more serious than American ownership or control of resources and industry. Yet this was the choice Canada had made when it rejected the hair-shirt philosophy of Coyne. Canadians, it seemed, no longer thought it necessary, perhaps did not think it worth while, to pay the costs of a distinct and independent national life. Such had been the theme of George Grant's fierce polemic, *Lament for a Nation*, published in 1965; Canadians, he asserted in a brilliantly reasoned argument, had lost to continentalism their will to be Canadian. Grant embarrassed his countrymen, but did not sway them.

The affluent society, however, expressed itself through the welfare state. And since 1963 the Pearson government had been fumbling its way through many difficulties of circumstance and chance to complete the apparatus of the welfare state. To its Pension Plan it proceeded in 1966 to add a national Medicare plan which would incorporate, replace and make uniform across the country the various provincial schemes for state medical care. And some of its more progressive ministers, notably Allan MacEachen, began to speak of a guaranteed minimum income for all citizens below the poverty line.

Here of course the welfare state revealed the other side of the affluent society, that as the wealth of the well-to-do increased, the poverty of the poor became more apparent. The modern facts had revealed an ancient truth. Above subsistence, wealth and poverty are relative; they are functions one of the other. As wealth increases, even general well-being, poverty must augment; poverty by contrast, at least. How to lop the horns of this dilemma?

Ways to do so were sought. Poverty among Canadians was most apparent and most harmful among Indians, Métis, Eskimos, rural folk in areas of natural poverty, and in the central slums of the great cities. The Indians in particular invited, and got, comparison with the poor of backward or over-populated countries. Yet Canada was neither, and in general Canadians were warmly sympathetic with the plight of the Indian. Improved medical services had first given expression to this concern; the result was a great increase in numbers as mortality fell. Two great contradictions remained. First, what was the Indian to become: a Canadian citizen? or was he to find well-being as an Indian? Second, how was he to be dealt with: through the traditional machinery of missions, treaties, and Indian Affairs, or directly, with the emphasis on self-help? The plight of the Eskimo, his native economy disappearing from his stern environment, was even worse.

Rural poverty, so deep as often to kill the desire for escape, was tackled by the intricate and intelligent machinery of the Agricultural and Rural Development Act, the invention of Alvin Hamilton, skilfully developed by Maurice Sauvé. And after the 1965 election Tom Kent was appointed by the Prime Minister to organize a general "War on Poverty." Even the American Peace Corps was imitated by the creation of the Company of Young Canadians, designed to evade the screen behind which the bureaucrat tends to operate by having devoted people share the poverty they sought to transform.

These schemes, anticipated or duplicated in some manner in most of the provinces, required federal participation because of the great regional disparities in Canada, present from the beginning and now aggravated by affluence and its concomitant poverty. Especially was this so in the Maritimes, symbolized by the increasing difficulties of Dosco, the Cape Breton steel industry, which was finally to be taken over by the province in 1968. The federal government had a clear and definite role as the equalizer of the benefits of affluence and in the deterence of poverty across the country.

This role, however, renewed in another context the struggle with the provinces that had been provoked by the post-war centralization and had ended in the "opting-out" formula insisted on by Quebec, as it sought to substitute its own social planning for that of Ottawa.

The power to administer such schemes was useless without the revenues to pay for them, and the provinces in successive conferences therefore demanded that the federal government yield to them greater and greater percentages of the income and corporation taxes levied by the federal authority. The results could only be an erosion of federal power to the point where it could act neither as equalizer of regional welfare nor as regulator of a national economy. In short, the federal and provincial governments, pushed by the desperate municipal governments of bursting cities and towns, had become positive welfare states with incessant demands upon them, beyond all levels of taxation yet contemplated. The danger was that unless the powers and responsibilities of equally positive states could be sorted out, the provinces, willy-nilly, would end by devouring the corpse of the federal government. Clearly, some new order in federal-provincial relations was needed, quite apart from the increasing demands from Quebec for constitutional reforms peculiar to itself.

How deep the federal-provincial, the national, crisis had become, had been underlined in 1965 by the publication of a preliminary report of the commission on bilingualism and biculturalism. The report declared bluntly "that Canada, without being fully conscious of the fact, is passing through the greatest crisis in its history." It argued that the crisis consisted in the conflict between the determination of French Canadians that they should be able to conduct their lives in French and have a French way of life, and the English-Canadian refusal to acknowledge, or indeed, think desirable, the possibility of such a place for French Canada in Canada outside Quebec. The report was received with reservation and much hostility in both English and French Canada. The commission was, indeed, under a cloud. To French nationalists, it was a subterfuge; at best it could recommend only what would be too little and too late. To "English" Canadians not of British origin it seemed, by stressing the peculiar place of English and French Canadians, to threaten their own equality as Canadian citizens and to make claims for French culture that they might well make for their own. English Canadians of British descent, particularly in Western Canada, were inclined to think the inquiry dangerous as an encouragement to an impracticable French nationalism. And as the commission's inquiries and researches proved very costly, the critics attacked it also as flagrantly expensive. But it had posed squarely the question of whether there was a place for a French Canada in Confederation. And that in turn raised its counter: had English Canada the will to keep Quebec in Confederation, if mutually acceptable arrangements could be found? The question of the possibility of the survival of either English or French Canada alone, few raised.

Canada in crisis was in fact searching the depths of its being. It was, perhaps, facing the consequences of its imperial connection and its growth by evolution within the empire. In that state, allegiance to the Crown had given political unity. But since the Citizenship Act of 1949, political unity lay in a common political citizenship. But what was Canadian citizenship? Canada had not consciously practised assimilation; indeed, it was Canadian custom to recall ethnic origin, and Canadian law to distinguish it, until Diefenbaker insisted on a change. The country had two public languages, one by custom English, one established by law in Quebec and in the federal Parliament and courts. There was no obvious standard to which to assimilate; even in the West, the "mosaic" theory encouraged the preservation of group cultures. The question, then, as presented by the Laurendeau-Dunton commission, was whether a common citizenship was possible in a country committed to diversity.

The instability, however, reached further. One great factor was the acceleration of urban growth, rapid since 1900, but overwhelming since 1950. Nowhere was this more true than in the province of Quebec. Nor was growth alone involved. The old values, associated by tradition with rural life – values religious, personal, habitual – were being rapidly rejected. New styles of living were adopted or sought.

One result was to hasten the growth of a new cosmopolitanism. Canadians, hitherto separated, provincial, traditional, had suddenly become members of a community and citizens of a world in flux. It was a world that was turning from the rational to explore the irrational, that was surrendering three centuries' allegiance to the concept of objective, deterministic cause and effect, the basis of science and invention. It was also a world that, since it could not believe in providence, had to believe in chance. It was, finally, a world of fear and violence. Such accordingly was the world of the television screen, in Canada as elsewhere. The clash of the new world view with established habits of thought gave rise to the greatest of controversies in the Canadian Broadcasting Corporation, that of 1966 over the program called "Seven Days," in which the programmers defied the administrators. Which world was the public corporation to project, the seemly world of tradition, or the world as it was and was becoming?

The new cosmopolitanism, with its challenge to the old nationalism, whether of Canada or of Quebec, was revealed most clearly in the emergence of Canadian thinkers of more than Canadian dimensions. It was revealed also in the new ease in the arts, no longer an effort at culture but an exercise in enjoyment. Canadian artists could now pursue their careers at home or abroad. Even in sport, Canada was becoming cosmopolitan, as the brilliant success of the Pan-American Games in Winnipeg revealed.

The new spirit was of course one result of affluence, not so much wealth itself as the confident use of wealth. It was also the result of the post-war immigration, which had ended the British domination of Canadian life with its sabbatarianism and its puritanism. Even in Quebec, the old Catholic logic came to yield a little to a new pragmatism, the old Jansenist rigour to a fresh humanism. Even in the province committed to nationalism, there were signs that the old preoccupation with national ends, so much on the wane in English Canada, was also beginning to soften.

It was this curious combination of supra-nationalism and superior achievement that marked the celebration of the centennial of Confederation in 1967, and peculiarly the World Exposition – "Expo" – at Montreal. The centennial celebrations were well and widely organized; few Canadians were untouched by them, a remarkable accomplishment in a country so shambling and among a people so infused with self-doubt. They created a sense of something well and purposefully done, and restored much of the national confidence drained by the bitter repudiation of Canadian nationality by the separatists of Quebec, and the ineffectuality of Canadian government. A warm appreciation of the basic goodness of life in Canada spread across the country, as thousands of memorial projects from community waterworks to great art centres testify. It was a great sorrow that Georges Vanier, who had so admirably discharged his duties as Governor General since his appointment in 1959, did not survive to preside at this crowning of a hundred years. He died shortly after his passionate New Year's appeal for continued unity. The appointment of his successor Roland Michener, a distinguished Conservative, placed beyond the claims of party the highest office in Canada under the Crown.

Expo dominated the Centennial. It was principally the work of Jean Drapeau, Mayor of Montreal, and the carrying through of a project many Canadians thought beyond Canadian resources did much to enlighten English Canadians on the capacity of French Canada. It was, moreover, a dramatic assertion of Montreal's new concept of itself as a metropolitan city, no longer only the entry to Canada but also a portal to the world, French in spirit but cosmopolitan in style.

Expo, also, was French in concept and cosmopolitan in expression. Obtained only because Russia declined to have a World Fair, involved in mismanagement, short of funds, lacking a suitable site unless islands were built in the St. Lawrence, it was saved by the financial intervention of the federal government, and the appointment of Pierre Dupuy as commissioner. Still threatened with being late, it was rescued by the organizing genius of a Manitoba engineer, Colonel Edward Churchill. It then moved swiftly to its opening. The theme, Man and His World, seemed to stimulate the participating countries, some sixty in number, to put their best efforts into their pavilions and their exhibits. The total result was an exposition that perhaps excelled

all predecessors, that affected styles and arts, that combined a high sophistication with order, cleanliness, and an easy good humour. Expo was a pleasure
to visit. It was a resounding success after years of failure. It was a joint English-
and French-Canadian effort, and it suggested the possibilities of a new Canada.

Even the humiliation of the Queen's visit to Quebec City in 1964 was
washed away by the brilliance and happiness of her visit to Expo.

Then came a thunder-clap on a sunny day. In midsummer of 1966, the
government of Jean Lesage had narrowly lost a general election, probably
for moving faster than rural Quebec could tolerate. It was brought down by
the Union Nationale under Daniel Johnson, the calm, shrewd, immensely
self-possessed leader who had rebuilt that party. The new Premier was more
intensely nationalist than Lesage, if less demonstratively so, and some members
of his Cabinet were extremist. He began to exploit the relations with France
already begun, and this policy led him to monopolize the visit of President
Charles de Gaulle to Canada and Expo in July 1967. The President began
his visit at Quebec City and the new governor-general, Roland Michener,
played a purely formal part in welcoming him. De Gaulle then led a triumphal
progress to Montreal, where he declaimed the separatist slogan, "Vive le
Québec libre!" Such an insult could only have been calculated. Rebuked
with much finesse by Mayor Drapeau, rebuked with restraint by Prime
Minister Pearson, the President cancelled his visit to Ottawa and returned
to Paris. A *bétise* so gross could only mean that the President of France willed
the victory of separatism and the destruction of Canada. Because it was thought
to be no more than another aberration of the Gaullist *politique de grandeur*,
the Canadian government did no more than repudiate the General's oratory.
But the incident reminded Canadians that the euphoria of the Centennial
could not last, and that at the moment Canada had ceased to be a provincial
country the enduring "Canadian question" of Durham's day could again
become an international one.

The country therefore quickly returned to the issues of English-French
and federal-provincial relations. The former were in fact worsening as Premier
Johnson followed the nationalist tack to take the wind from nationalists more
extreme than he. And René Lévesque, after much soul-searching carried out
in his inimitable way on television, left the Liberal party to found a movement
for a sovereign Quebec. He characteristically thought it the only honest way
out of the English-French dilemma. The provinces, pressed by their municipalities and conscious that with their developed civil services they were at
least as competent to govern as was Ottawa, pressed heavily for more revenues,
Quebec for more powers as well.

Two decisive actions occurred in the fall of 1966. One was the announcement
by the Minister of Finance, Mitchell Sharp, that the federal government
would cease its grants to universities, with a corresponding transfer of taxes

to the provinces. The general direction of federal financial policy, he declared, would be to leave to the provinces as much responsibility as possible for raising the revenues they spent, compatibly with the role of the federal government as equalizer among regions and regulator of the economy. It was a chill wind for the universities and it was a step towards a new federalism of co-ordinate sovereignties with revenues matched to responsibilities. The basic idea was that of the federalism advocated by the more and more influential Pierre Elliott Trudeau.

The second was an extraordinary intervention in the English-French "dialogue," as it was beginning to be called, by Premier John Robarts of Ontario. An earnest, modest man, Robarts had been deeply concerned by the growth of French nationalist animosity to Canadian unity. That unity he was quietly resolved to preserve by any well-considered, fair and honourable means. It was a key decision, since the treatment by Ontario of its French population by educational Regulation 17 in 1913 had been perhaps the principal cause of French nationalist feeling that only in the province of Quebec could French Canadians be French. Robarts therefore arranged a conference, called "Confederation of Tomorrow," which took place at Toronto in November 1967. All provincial premiers, with delegations, attended, but the federal government, thinking a provincial initiative improper, sent only an observer. Well organized and well televised, the conference succeeded both in moderating extremes of opinion and in involving the English-Canadian public in a meaningful discussion of the fundamental issues of Canadian unity. The result was a new hopefulness, not unwarranted even in the instances of Premier Manning of Alberta, chief spokesman of English resistance to French demands, and Premier Johnson, who revealed himself to be not wholly intransigent.

The conference turned out to be a useful prelude to the constitutional conference called by the Prime Minister in Ottawa in February. And in nearly all provinces, concessions of some significance were made in the teaching of French in the public schools. English Canada, in short, showed a surprising readiness to accept the idea of an officially bilingual Canada.

This had been the policy of the federal government in effect since the appointment of the Laurendeau-Dunton commission. Now the Conservative party, hitherto dominated by Diefenbaker's slogan of "One Canada," was swinging over to the concept of English and French "equality" in Canada. The process had begun at the Montmorency Conference in July, 1967. There, Marcel Faribault, who drove with a firm hand a formidable team of talents as leading business man and author, insisted that all matters, including the monarchy, were negotiable, and that the Conservative party to survive in Quebec must be prepared to consider the concept of a Canada of "*deux nations.*" The idea, with *nations* defined as "nations in a sociological sense," was brought to the national convention in September.

That convention was of course primarily concerned to decide the leadership of the party. A strong field of candidates had emerged, of whom Robert Stanfield, successful premier of Nova Scotia and backed by Dalton Camp, and Premier Duff Roblin of Manitoba, despite being a late starter, were the principal contenders. The convention itself was a triumph of organization, of television production, and of the new politics in which the convention was replacing the parliamentary caucus as the chief organ of the party. The public, in short, was immediately involved. After spirited balloting, Stanfield was elected over Roblin, perhaps because of the refusal of Diefenbaker to withdraw. That refusal, however, was based not only on the anguished reluctance of a proud fighter to concede, but also on the old chief's fear and hatred of the two-nations concept. He denounced it with all his unfailing eloquence and it was tabled. But the party was now committed, if not to two nations, certainly to sympathetic negotiation of all issues between English and French, as well as those between the federal and provincial governments of Canada. One major party had altered course, back at least to Macdonald's admonition to "treat [the French] as a nation, and they will behave as a nation," if not to the New Democratic Party's explicit adoption of special status for Quebec.

That 1967 was to be a watershed between the old order declining since 1960 and a new set of undefined but exciting persons and procedures was further confirmed when in December the Prime Minister announced his resignation, to take effect after the constitutional conference that would crown his term of office. The result was a race for the succession, suppressed by the needs of government and Parliament. Appropriate as his decision was, in its abnegation and dignity, to the career and personality of Pearson, it was nevertheless a mistake which placed the contenders for the leadership in an intolerable position. How incompatible was the procedure with the parliamentary system, at least during minority government, appeared when the government, its numbers diminished by the absence of the Prime Minister and several campaigning ministers, was defeated in a vote on third reading of a bill to increase income tax by five per cent. By all tradition, that government ought to have resigned, being defeated on a money bill. It chose not to, on the ground that the tax increase was necessary to maintain the Canadian dollar during the great run on the American dollar. The opposition for that reason did not force the issue; the government survived the crisis, and had a tax increase of three per cent voted. Nevertheless, the action raised again the question of how Parliament was to function when the traditional conventions could be set aside at will. The episode was all too much a part of the mismanagement and the panic adjustments of the past eight years.

Indeed, the first part of 1968 seemed in some respects all too much a continuation of the general character of the sixties. The established directions in foreign policy were not altered. The Egyptian request for the withdrawal of the peace-keeping forces from the Gaza Strip in May 1967 prior to the outbreak of the third Arab-Israeli war, at once complied with, had raised questions as to the validity of the concept of peace-keeping. The event had, however, no effect on policy in the integration of the armed forces. The utility of Nato was increasingly questioned in public, but no change was made. Norad was even more severely attacked, but in the spring of 1968 Canada's commitment was renewed for three years by executive action. Nor did the question of American control of Canadian resources and industries receive an answer. The agreement of 1964 on limited reciprocity in car manufacturing, and the implementation of the tariff reductions agreed on in the "Kennedy round," led, if anywhere, to further integration of a continental economy. The continued efforts of Walter Gordon to ensure Canadian direction of the national economy had resulted in the Watkins Report, a set of reasonable and moderate proposals. But would it join the great body of other distinguished reports on which little or no action had been taken? One of these was the Glassco report on economy and efficiency in government; another was the Carter report, an attempt to make systematic the complex of federal taxation, a sore as well as a difficult subject. It was made doubly so by the rapid increase of municipal and provincial taxation, and by the inflation set going by over-generous wage increases granted the St. Lawrence Seaway workers and the longshoremen of Quebec ports in 1966. The Conservative opposition, the provinces and much public opinion therefore resisted the federal government's scheme for Medicare, even after it had become law and was scheduled to begin on July 1, 1968. Such circumstances continued and intensified the general character of the years since 1957.

This was the background of the constitutional conference of February, 1968. The Prime Minister, playing a role of which his great experience of diplomacy made him the genial master, was at his best. But a new note, first heard in the federal-provincial financial conference, was struck in the proposals of the federal government for constitutional revision. These were made by the Minister of Justice, Pierre Trudeau. They followed the line of thought he had elaborated in his writings over the past decade. First, there should be a Bill of Rights accepted by and binding on all governments, to ensure the civil equality of all Canadian citizens. Then there should be a joint federal-provincial committee to work out a clear pattern of true federalism. What that might be was not defined, but the general trend of Trudeau's thought suggests no considerable formal change was in view, but rather the acceptance as a permanent institution of the quasi-constitutional federal-provincial conference and the continuation of a "co-operative" federalism. Canada would be governed by the diplomatic interaction of its eleven governments in conference assembled, the federal government presiding. There was nothing of special or associate status, nothing of two nations. Johnson of Quebec clashed sharply with the unyielding Trudeau, and the conference was in danger. But the diplomacy of Pearson and the suasion of Robarts saved the situation, and the committee to study constitutional change was approved. The character of the English-French dialogue, however, had been altered. A French-Canadian minister had declared for one Canada, a very federalist one, though resting no doubt on a pluralistic society. And he had already become a candidate for Liberal leader and Prime Minister.

The new note, moreover, was not struck merely to elicit echoes of opinion. It was an inflexible policy, soon to be tested. In March, the French African state of Gabon was host to the representatives of French states in conference on educational and cultural matters. The province of Quebec, ignoring both courtesy and a recent federal act on provincial representation abroad, sent a representative without reference to Ottawa. He was received by Gabon and by the conference as representative of a sovereign state. Ottawa curtly broke off relations with Gabon. Here at last was federal assertion of a federal power violated by a province. But was the issue clear, and could federal authority be vindicated? When the same conference was resumed in Paris, the French government, warned, diluted the provocations of Gabon and the matter passed, but remained unresolved.

Such was the background to the Liberal convention of April, 1968. The number of candidates was considerable, their quality good. All but one, Eric Kierans, were cabinet ministers. But only one was challenging; that was Trudeau. The current story was that he, Marchand and Pelletier had thought it would be well not to have a French-Canadian candidate for the leadership at that time. When they changed their minds, the obvious candidate was Marchand. He declined to run, it was said, because of less than perfect health. Trudeau was then persuaded to yield to the urgings of his friends, mostly English and French intellectuals in Montreal and Toronto. Once he had decided to do so, he transformed the contest to one between the other candidates and himself. They were, for the most part, orthodox, "establishment" Liberals, unhurried radicals, exponents of the conventional wisdom of the Rideau Club, the Liberal segment of the Senate, and the higher echelons of the Civil Service. Trudeau was by background academic, semi-civil-service, semi-socialistic, and a wealthy bohemian, unknown until recently to the public and the party. His ideas were different from those accepted in the conclaves of orthodox politicians and he possessed a steely quality not seen in Liberal politicians since Laurier had put down Tarte.

The convention had therefore to choose between goods all wool and a yard wide, and an exotic, shimmering, exciting fabric of undoubted sheen but unknown wearing quality. It was in fact stampeded by "Trudeaumania" – the mindless adulation poured upon the hapless Trudeau by youngsters who would not vote for years – and the enthusiasm of young workers for the

party, women of all ages, and the Trudeau followers in academic and broadcasting circles. Trudeau won: the McLuhanese sex symbol now challenged
the Freudian father figure in Canadian politics.

All this glamour was unfair to a refined and sensitive person. Trudeau
may have seemed somewhat the playboy, somewhat the ever-available, ever-
charming man. He was, if shy, open to affection and readily responsive. But
his political qualities were far more important, not least the ruthlessness
with which he availed himself of his instant glamour, dissolved Parliament
and went to the country with his assets as a prime minister still untested in
the House. One was his candour, another was his courage. Another was the
clarity, or seeming clarity, of his ideas. Still another was that he was bilingual,
fluent like Laurier in both English and French; unlike Laurier, eloquent in
neither. Quite adventitious, and dangerous, was the appeal he had for some
elements in English Canada because of his readiness to "stand up to Quebec."
Trudeau was himself a Québecois: he was not so much standing up to Quebec
as laying down his opinion in a family row. What the outcome of his federalism
might be for Canada, or for Quebec, he had not made clear, even in his
published essays on the subject.

The two factors of importance, then, in Canadian politics in April 1968
were first the contrast of the new Prime Minister and the leader of the
Opposition, Robert Stanfield, and second the reversal of roles between the
two major parties. Trudeau, unknown, new-style, exciting, dared the electorate
to take a chance on him. This had an almost de-Gaulle-like panache about
it and a suggestion, in its supreme self-confidence, of the Diefenbaker crusade
of 1958. Stanfield, also largely unknown across the country when elected
national leader of his party, had revealed himself as an earnest, conscientious
man, calm, unhurried, devoted and compassionate. Hesitant in speech, slow
to take fire, he was a study in under-emphasis. Thus he won respect, never
aroused enthusiasm. A greater contrast could hardly have been arranged.

Moreover, while the Conservative party had shown itself ready to listen
and discuss with Johnson's Quebec the implications of nationalism for Confederation, the Liberal party, dominated by Trudeau as by no previous leader,
repudiated special or associate status in any form. Since a federal victory for
Trudeau might well be followed by a provincial victory for Johnson, Trudeau
might have to coerce a province. Stanfield on the contrary was certainly
committed to the sunny ways of Robarts and the "Confederation of Tomorrow"
conference. National unity, then, was the prime issue before Canadians as
they prepared to choose between these two men. On other pressing problems
– inflation, taxation troubles, the housing shortage, the instability of the
dollar and the economy – there was no clear line of party division, everyone
being against such ills and no one having any sure cure to propose.

The victor was of course Trudeau. The Conservative campaign was loose-jointed and fumbling; Stanfield generated liking and confidence, but remained wholly unexciting. Trudeau provided a convincing image of the young god who would make all things new. This he did without a concession to anything but the requirements of modern publicity. In the federal, the national, government, power for good or ill would be exercised by a Prime Minister who now centred in himself all authority, with the advice of his personal advisers, the aid of the secretariat of the Privy Council, and such help as might be sought from Cabinet and Parliament.

The Liberals won 153 seats, fifty-six in Quebec; the Conservatives seventy-two, four in Quebec. The New Democrats, with twenty-three, remained the seminal party they had always been. The Créditistes, with fifteen, still declared the poverty of rural Quebec. There was one Independent, the now permanent Speaker.

The composition of Parliament was not new, the electorate was still fragmented. But one major party had a majority, with representation in all parts of the country. New men were in authority, new methods were under trial. The years of frustration were perhaps behind; the years of decision at last at hand. This the future and Prime Minister Trudeau would reveal.

BIBLIOGRAPHY

BERGER, CARL. *The Sense of Power: Studies in the Ideas of Canadian Imperialism, 1867–1914.* Toronto: University of Toronto Press, 1970.

BISHOP, MORRIS. *Champlain: The Life of Fortitude.* New York: Alfred A. Knopf, 1948.

BREBNER, J. B. *The Explorers of North America.* London: A. & C. Black, 1933.

~ *North Atlantic Triangle.* Toronto: Ryerson Press, 1945.

BURT, A. L. *The Old Province of Quebec.* Minneapolis: University of Minnesota Press, 1933.

Canadian Historical Association Annual Reports, from 1920.

CANADIAN HISTORICAL ASSOCIATION. *Historical Booklets* (Ottawa: The Association, c/o Public Archives):

BECK, J. MURRAY. *Joseph Howe: Anti-Confederate.* (No. 17, 1965.)

BONENFANT, J. C. *The French Canadians and the Birth of Confederation.* (No. 10, 1967.)

BRUNET, M. *French Canada and the Early Decades of British Rule.* (No. 13, 1963.)

BURT, A. L. *Guy Carleton, Lord Dorchester, 1724–1808.* Revised version. (No. 5, 1955.)

CORNELL, PAUL. *The Great Coalition.* (No. 8, 1967.)

ECCLES, W. J. *The Government of New France.* (No. 18, 1965.)

FARR, D. M. L. *Great Britain and Confederation.* (No. 1, 1967.)

FRÉGAULT, GUY. *Canadian Society in the French Régime.* (No. 3, 1954.)

GRAHAM, ROGER. *Arthur Meighen.* (No. 16, 1965.)

HAMELIN, JEAN. *First Years of Confederation.* (No. 3, 1967.)

MAC NUTT, W. S. *The Making of the Maritime Provinces, 1713–1784.* (No. 4, 1955.)

~ *The Maritimes and Confederation.* (No. 2, 1967.)

MASTERS, D. C. *Reciprocity, 1846–1911.* (No. 12, 1961.)

MORTON, W. L. *The West and Confederation, 1857–1871.* (No. 9, 1958.)

OUELLET, FERNAND. *Louis-Joseph Papineau: A Divided Soul.* (No. 11, 1960.)

ROBY, YVES. *The United States and Confederation.* (No. 4, 1967.)

ROTHNEY, G. O. *Newfoundland: From International Fishery to Canadian Province.* (No. 10, 1959.)

SOWARD, F. H. *The Department of External Affairs and Canadian Autonomy, 1899–1939.* (No. 7, 1956.)

SWAINSON, D. *Ontario and Confederation.* (No. 5, 1967.)

STACEY, C. P. *The Undefended Border: The Myth and the Reality*. (No. 1, 1953.)

STANLEY, G. F. G. *Louis Riel: Patriot or Rebel?* (No. 2, 1954.)

TRUDEL, MARCEL. *The Seigneurial Régime*. (No. 6, 1960.)

UNDERHILL, F. H. *Canadian Political Parties*. (No. 8, 1957.)

WAITE, P. B. *The Charlottetown Conference*. (No. 6, 1967.)

WHITELAW, W. M. *The Quebec Conference*. (No. 9, 1967.)

Canadian Historical Review, Vols. I–XLVIII.

CARELESS, J. M. S. *Brown of the Globe*. 2 vols. Toronto: Macmillan Company of Canada, 1959 and 1963.

~   *The Union of the Canadas: The Growth of Canadian Institutions, 1841–1857*. Toronto: McClelland and Stewart, 1967.

CLARK, ANDREW HILL. *Acadia: The Geography of Early Nova Scotia to 1760*. Madison, Wisconsin: University of Wisconsin Press, 1968.

CLARK, S. D. *Movements of Political Protest in Canada, 1640–1840*. Toronto: University of Toronto Press, 1959.

COOK, RAMSAY. *Canada and the French-Canadian Question*. Toronto: Macmillan Company of Canada, 1966.

COWAN, HELEN I. *British Emigration to British North America: The First Hundred Years*. Toronto: University of Toronto Press, 1961.

CRAIG, G. M. *Upper Canada: The Formative Years*. Toronto: McClelland and Stewart, 1963.

CREIGHTON, D. G. *The Empire of the St. Lawrence*. Toronto: Macmillan Company of Canada, 1956.

~   *John A. Macdonald: The Young Politician*. Toronto: Macmillan Company of Canada, 1952.

~   *John A. Macdonald: The Old Chieftain*. Toronto: Macmillan Company of Canada, 1955.

~   *The Road to Confederation, 1863–1867*. Toronto: Macmillan Company of Canada, 1964.

~   *Canada's First Century*. Toronto: Macmillan Company of Canada, 1970.

DAFOE, J. W. *Laurier: A Study in Canadian Politics*. Toronto: Thomas Allen, 1922.

DAWSON, R. MAC GREGOR. *Canada in World Affairs: Two Years of War, 1939–1941*. Toronto: Oxford University Press, 1943.

~   *William Lyon Mackenzie King*, Vol. I. Toronto: University of Toronto Press, 1958.

~   *Constitutional Issues in Canada, 1900–1931*. London: Oxford University Press, 1933.

DE KIEWIET, C. W., and UNDERHILL, F. H. *The Dufferin-Carnarvon Correspondence, 1874–1878*. Toronto: Champlain Society, 1955.

DESROSIERS, L. P. *Iroquoisie.* Montreal: L'Institut d'Histoire de l'Amerique Française, 1947.

EASTERBROOK, W. T., and AITKEN, H. G. J. *Canadian Economic History.* Toronto: Macmillan Company of Canada, 1956.

ASTMAN, S. MACK. *Church and State in Early Canada.* Edinburgh: The University Press, 1915.

EAYRS, JAMES. *The Art of the Possible : Government and Foreign Policy in Canada.* Toronto: University of Toronto Press, 1961.

ECCLES, W. J. *Frontenac : The Courtier Governor.* Toronto: McClelland and Stewart, 1959.

~ *Canada under Louis XIV.* Toronto: McCelland and Stewart, 1964.

~ *The Canadian Frontier, 1534-1760.* Toronto: Holt, Rinehart and Winston, 1909.

FRÉGAULT, GUY. *La Civilisation de la Nouvelle-France.* Montreal: Société des Editions Pascal, 1944.

GLAZEBROOK, G. P. DE T. *Canadian External Relations: An Historical Study to 1914.* Toronto: Oxford University Press, 1942.

~ *A History of Transportation in Canada.* Toronto: Ryerson Press, 1938.

~ *Canada at the Paris Peace Conference.* Toronto: Oxford University Press, 1942.

GRAHAM, ROGER. *Arthur Meighen, a Biography.* 3 vols. Toronto: Clarke, Irwin and Company, 1960-1965.

GROULX, LIONEL. *Histoire du Canada français.* 4 vols. Montreal: L'Action Nationale, 1951-1952.

GUNN, GERTRUDE E. *The Political History of Newfoundland, 1832-1864.* Toronto: University of Toronto Press, 1966.

HARRIS, RICHARD COLEBROOK. *The Seigneurial System in Early Canada.* Quebec: Les Presses de l'université Laval, 1966.

HODGETTS, J. E. *Pioneer Public Service, 1841-67.* Toronto: University of Toronto Press, 1955.

HUNT, G. T. *The Wars of the Iroquois.* Madison: University of Wisconsin Press, 1940.

INNIS, H. A. *The Cod Fisheries.* Revised edition. Toronto: University of Toronto Press, 1954.

~ *The Fur Trade in Canada.* Revised edition. Toronto: University of Toronto Press, 1956.

~ *Select Documents in Canadian Economic History, 1497-1783.* Toronto: University of Toronto Press, 1929.

INNIS, H. A. and LOWER, A. R. M. *Select Documents in Canadian Economic History, 1783-1885.* Toronto: University of Toronto Press, 1933.

IRVING, J. A. *The Philosophy of Social Credit.* Toronto: University of Toronto Press, 1959.

JONES, RICHARD. *Community in Crisis: French-Canadian Nationalism in Perspective.* Toronto: McClelland and Stewart, 1967.

KEIRSTEAD, B. S. *Canada in World Affairs, September 1951 to October 1953.* Toronto: Oxford University Press, 1956.

KELLOGG, L. P. *The French Régime in Wisconsin and the Northwest.* Madison: State Historical Society of Wisconsin, 1925.

KENNEDY, W. P. M. *Statutes, Treaties and Documents of the Canadian Constitution, 1713–1929.* Revised edition. Toronto: Oxford University Press, 1930.

KENNEDY, W. P. M. *The Constitution of Canada, 1534–1937.* Second edition. London: Oxford University Press, 1938.

KERR, D. G. G. *Sir Edmund Head: A Scholarly Governor.* Toronto: University of Toronto Press, 1954.

KILBOURN, WILLIAM. *The Firebrand.* Toronto: Clarke, Irwin and Company, 1956.

LANCTOT, GUSTAVE. *A History of Canada.* Vols. I–III (to 1763). Toronto: Clarke, Irwin and Company, 1960–1965.

LOWER, A. R. M. *Canadians in the Making.* Toronto: Longmans, Green and Company, 1958.

~   *The North American Assault on the Canadian Forest.* Toronto: Ryerson Press, 1938.

MAC NUTT, W. S. *Days of Lorne.* Fredericton: Brunswick Press, 1955.

~   *The Atlantic Provinces: The Emergence of Colonial Society.* Toronto: McClelland and Stewart, 1965.

MACPHERSON, C. B. *Democracy in Alberta.* Toronto: University of Toronto Press, 1956.

MANNING, HELEN TAFT. *The Revolt of French Canada: A Chapter in the History of the British Commonwealth.* Toronto: Macmillan Company of Canada, 1972.

MARTIN, CHESTER. *Empire and Commonwealth.* Toronto: Oxford University Press, 1929.

~   *Foundations of Canadian Nationality.* Toronto: University of Toronto Press, 1955.

MASTERS, D. C. *Canada in World Affairs, 1953–1955.* Toronto: Oxford University Press, 1959.

MC INNIS, E. W. *The Unguarded Frontier.* New York: Doubleday, Doran & Company, 1942.

MCNAUGHT, K. W. *A Prophet in Politics.* Toronto: Oxford University Press, 1959.

MOIR, J. S. *Church and State in Canada West.* Toronto: University of Toronto Press, 1959.

MORTON, W. L. *The Progressive Party in Canada*. Toronto: University of Toronto Press, 1950.

~ *Manitoba: A History*. Toronto: University of Toronto Press, 1957.

~ *The Red River Journal of Alexander Begg*. Toronto: Champlain Society, 1956.

~ *The Canadian Identity*. Madison: University of Wisconsin Press, 1961.

~ *The Critical Years: The Union of British North America*, 1857–1873. Toronto: McClelland and Stewart, 1965.

MUNRO, W. B. *The Seigniorial System in Canada*. Cambridge: Harvard University Press, 1907.

NEATBY, HILDA. *Quebec: The Revolutionary Age, 1760–1791*. Toronto: McClelland and Stewart, 1966.

NEW, C. W. *Lord Durham*. London: Oxford University Press, 1929.

NUTE, G. L. *Caesars of the Wilderness*. New York: D. Appleton-Century Company, 1943.

OLESON, T. J. *Early Voyages and Northern Approaches*. Toronto: McClelland and Stewart, 1963.

OUELLET, F. *Histoire économique et sociale du Quebec, 1760–1850*. Montreal: Fides, 1966.

PACEY, DESMOND. *Creative Writing in Canada*. Revised edition. Toronto: Ryerson Press, 1961.

PARK, JULIAN (ed.) *The Culture of Contemporary Canada*. Ithaca: Cornell University Press, 1957.

PATTERSON, II, E. PALMER. *The Canadian Indian: A History since 1500*. Toronto: Collier-Macmillan, 1972.

PICKERSGILL, J. W. *The Mackenzie King Record*. Vol. I, 1939–1944. Toronto: University of Toronto Press, 1960.

RICH, E. E. *History of the Hudson's Bay Company, 1670–1870*. 2 vols. London: Hudson's Bay Record Society, 1958 and 1959.

~ *The Fur Trade and the Northwest, to 1857*. Toronto: McClelland and Stewart, 1967.

ROBIN, MARTIN. *Radical Politics and Canadian Labour, 1880–1930*. Kingston: Industrial Relations Centre, Queen's University, 1968.

SAFARIAN, A. E. *The Canadian Economy in the Great Depression*. Toronto: McClelland and Stewart, 1970.

SAYWELL, J. T. *The Journal of Lady Aberdeen*. Toronto: Champlain Society, 1960.

SHARP, PAUL F. *Whoop-Up Country: the Canadian-American West, 1865–1885*. 2 vols. Minneapolis: University of Minnesota Press, 1955.

SKELTON, O. D. *The Life and Letters of Sir Wilfrid Laurier*. 2 vols. London: Oxford University Press, 1922.

KC–U

562

THE KINGDOM OF CANADA

SOWARD, F. H., PARKINSON, J. F., MACKENZIE, N. A. M., and MAC DERMOT, T. W. *Canada in World Affairs: The Pre-War Years.* London: Oxford University Press, 1941. (Out of print.)

SPENCER, ROBERT A. *Canada in World Affairs: From UN to NATO, 1946–1949.* Toronto: Oxford University Press, 1959.

STANLEY, G. F. G. *The Birth of Western Canada.* Second edition. Toronto: University of Toronto Press, 1960.

~ *Canada's Soldiers.* Revised edition. Toronto: Macmillan Company of Canada, 1960.

~ *New France: The Last Phase, 1744–1760.* Toronto: McClelland and Stewart, 1968.

THOMAS, L. H. *The Struggle for Responsible Government in the North-West Territories, 1870–1897.* Toronto: University of Toronto Press, 1956.

THOMSON, D. C. *Alexander Mackenzie: Clear Grit.* Toronto: Macmillan Company of Canada, 1960.

TROTTER, R. G. *Canadian Federation.* Toronto: J. M. Dent and Sons, 1924.

TRUDEL, M. *L'Influence de Voltaire au Canada.* Montreal: Fides, 1945.

~ *Histoire de la Nouvelle-France.* Vols. I–II. Montreal: Fides, 1963 and 1966.

TUCKER, G. N. *The Canadian Commercial Revolution, 1845–1851.* (Toronto: McClelland and Stewart, 1964), Carleton Library, No. 19.

WADE, MASON. *The French Canadians.* Toronto: Macmillan Company of Canada, 1955.

~ *The French Canadians, 1760–1967,* 1–11. Toronto: Macmillan Company of Canada, 1968.

WAITE, P. B. *The Life and Times of Confederation, 1864–1867.* Toronto: University of Toronto Press, 1961.

~ *Canada, 1874–1896. Arduous Destiny.* Toronto: McClelland and Stewart, 1971.

WALSH, H. H. *The Christian Church in Canada.* Toronto: Ryerson Press, 1956.

WARNER, D. F. *The Idea of Continental Union.* Louisville: University of Kentucky Press, 1960.

WHEARE, K. C. *The Statute of Westminster and Dominion Status.* Fifth edition. London: Oxford University Press, 1953.

WHITELAW, W. M. *The Maritimes and Canada before Confederation.* Toronto: Oxford University Press, 1934.

WILSON, G. E. *The Life of Robert Baldwin.* Toronto: Ryerson Press, 1933.

WINKS, R. W. *Canada and the United States: The Civil War Years.* Baltimore: Johns Hopkins University Press, 1960.

ZASLOW, MORRIS. *The Opening of the Canadian North, 1870–1914.* Toronto: McClelland and Stewart, 1971.

Kings Sovereign over Canada

FRENCH KINGS, 1534–1763

Francis I	(1515)–1547
Henry II	1547–1559
Francis II	1559–1560
Charles IX	1560–1574
Henry III	1574–1589
Henry IV	1589–1610
Louis XIII	1610–1643
Louis XIV	1643–1715
Louis XV	1715–(1774)

BRITISH KINGS, 1763 . . .

George III	(1760)–1820
George IV	1820–1830
William IV	1830–1837
Victoria	1837–1901
Edward VII	1901–1910
George V	1910–1936
Edward VIII	1936
George VI	1936–1952
Elizabeth II	1952 . . .

Governors of Canada since Champlain

(with dates of appointment)

Oct. 15, 1612 (to July 20, 1629) May 23, 1633	Champlain, Samuel de
June 11, 1636	Montmagny, Charles Jacques Huault de
Aug. 20, 1648	Ailleboust de Coulonge, Louis d'
Oct. 14, 1651	Lauzon, Jean de
July 11, 1658	Argenson, Pierre de Voyer, Vicomte d'
Aug. 31, 1661	Avaugour, Pierre Dubois, Baron d'
Sept. 15, 1663	Mézy, Augustin de Saffray, Sieur de
Sept. 12, 1665	Courcelles, Daniel Rémy, Sieur de
Sept. 12, 1672	Frontenac, Louis de Buade, Comte de Palluau et de
Oct. 9, 1682	La Barre, Joseph Antoine Lefebvre de
Aug. 1, 1685	Denonville, Jacques René de Brisay, Marquis de
Oct. 12, 1689	Frontenac, Louis de Buade, Comte de Palluau et de
Sept. 14, 1699	Callières, Louis Hector de
Sept. 17, 1705	Vaudreuil, Philippe de Rigaud, Marquis de
Sept. 2, 1726	Beauharnois, Charles, Marquis de
Aug. 15, 1749	La Jonquière, Jacques Pierre de Taffanel, Marquis de
July, 1752	Duquesne de Menneville, Marquis
July 10, 1755 (to Sept. 8, 1760)	Vaudreuil-Cavagnal, Pierre de Rigaud, Marquis de
Aug. 13, 1764	Murray, James
Oct. 26, 1768	Carleton, Guy
June 27, 1778	Haldimand, Frederick
Oct. 23, 1786	Dorchester, Baron (Guy Carleton)
Apr. 27, 1797	Prescott, Robert
Oct. 24, 1807	Craig, Sir James Henry
July 15, 1812	Prevost, Sir George
July 12, 1816	Sherbrooke, Sir John C.

July 30, 1818	Richmond, Duke of
June 19, 1820	Dalhousie, Earl of
Feb. 4, 1831	Aylmer, Baron
Apr. 2, 1835	Amherst, Earl
Aug. 24, 1835	Gosford, Earl of
May 29, 1838	Durham, Earl of
Jan. 17, 1839	Colborne, Sir John
Oct. 19, 1839	Thomson, Charles Poulett
Feb. 10, 1841	Sydenham, Baron (C. P. Thomson)
Jan. 12, 1842	Bagot, Sir Charles
Mar. 30, 1843	Metcalfe, Sir Charles T.
Apr. 24, 1846	Cathcart, Earl
Jan. 30, 1847	Elgin, Earl of
Dec. 19, 1854	Head, Sir Edmund W.
Nov. 28, 1861	Monck, Viscount
Feb. 2, 1869	Young, Sir John (Lord Lisgar)
June 25, 1872	Dufferin, Earl of
Nov. 25, 1878	Lorne, Marquis of
Oct. 23, 1883	Lansdowne, Marquis of
June 11, 1888	Stanley of Preston, Baron
Sept. 18, 1893	Aberdeen, Earl of
Nov. 12, 1898	Minto, Earl of
Dec. 10, 1904	Grey, Earl
Oct. 13, 1911	Connaught, H.R.H. Duke of
Nov. 11, 1916	Devonshire, Duke of
Aug. 11, 1921	Byng of Vimy, Lord
Oct. 2, 1926	Willingdon of Ratton, Viscount
Apr. 4, 1931	Bessborough, Earl of
Nov. 2, 1935	Tweedsmuir of Elsfield, Lord
June 21, 1940	Athlone, Earl of
Apr. 12, 1946	Alexander of Tunis, Viscount
Feb. 28, 1952	Massey, Vincent
Sept. 15, 1959	Vanier, Georges
Apr. 17, 1967	Michener, Roland

Canadian Prime Ministers since Confederation

(with dates of tenure)

July 1, 1867 – Nov. 5, 1873	Rt. Hon. Sir John Alexander Macdonald
Nov. 7, 1873 – Oct. 16, 1878	Hon. Alexander Mackenzie
Oct. 17, 1878 – June 6, 1891	Rt. Hon. Sir John Alexander Macdonald
June 16, 1891 – Nov. 24, 1892	Hon. Sir John Joseph Caldwell Abbott
Dec. 5, 1892 – Dec. 12, 1894	Rt. Hon. Sir John Sparrow David Thompson
Dec. 21, 1894 – Apr. 27, 1896	Hon. Sir Mackenzie Bowell
May 1, 1896 – July 8, 1896	Hon. Sir Charles Tupper
July 11, 1896 – Oct. 6, 1911	Rt. Hon. Sir Wilfrid Laurier
Oct. 10, 1911 – July 10, 1920	Rt. Hon. Sir Robert Laird Borden
July 10, 1920 – Dec. 29, 1921	Rt. Hon. Arthur Meighen
Dec. 29, 1921 – June 28, 1926	Rt. Hon. William Lyon Mackenzie King
June 29, 1926 – Sept. 25, 1926	Rt. Hon. Arthur Meighen
Sept. 25, 1926 – Aug. 6, 1930	Rt. Hon. William Lyon Mackenzie King
Aug. 7, 1930 – Oct. 23, 1935	Rt. Hon. Richard Bedford Bennett
Oct. 23, 1935 – Nov. 15, 1948	Rt. Hon. William Lyon Mackenzie King
Nov. 15, 1948 – June 21, 1957	Rt. Hon. Louis Stephen St. Laurent
June 21, 1957 – Apr. 17, 1963	Rt. Hon. John George Diefenbaker
Apr. 22, 1963 – Apr. 19, 1968	Rt. Hon. Lester Bowles Pearson
Apr. 20, 1968 . . .	Rt. Hon. Pierre Elliott Trudeau

INDEX

A

Abbott, Sir John Joseph Caldwell, 387
Abenakis, 76; harass New England frontier, 81, 84; and Pemaquid, 86; at war with New England (1702-13), 94-5; to be kept loyal to New France, 103, 109; at war again (1722), 105; guerrilla war with Acadians, 146
Abercromby, General James, 138
Aberdeen, George Gordon, 4th Earl of: Foreign Secretary, 268
Aberdeen, John Campbell Gordon, 7th Earl of: Governor General, 390
Aberhart, William, 461
Abyssinia, Italian attack on, 466
Acadia: colonization, 28-9, 40; Argall's raid, 31; Alexander's claim, 33, 35; population, 50; capture (1654), 51; restoration (1667) 59; dependency of New France, 76; warfare in, 82, 84, 94, 100; surrendered to the English (1713), 102; "ancient limits" of, 102, 105; French pressure on, 126
Acadians: first settlements, 28-9, 40, 50; neutrality, 105; and oath of allegiance, 115; expulsion, 135, 146; survivors, 158
Act of Union (1840), 257; and commercial system, 274
Agricultural and Rural Development Act, 546
Agriculture, Canadian Council of, 411, 422, 432
Aigremont, Clérambault d', and fur-trade posts, 97
Aiguillon, Marie Madeleine de Vignerot, Duchesse d', 39
Aillebousr, Louis d', Governor of New France, 44
Alabama claims, 330, 339, 341
Alaska: Russian possession, 268; neutralized (1854), 302; American purchase, 336; boundary, 395-7
Alaska Highway, building of, 480
Albany, New York: and the fur trade, 64, 66, 95; New York militia at, 82; traders in Montreal, 105
Albany Congress (1754), 175-6, 317
Alberta, Territory of, 372; Province of, 403
Alberta and Great Waterways Railway, 413
Alexander, Sir William, and grant of Acadia (Nova Scotia), 33, 35

Alexander of Tunis, Viscount: Governor General, 493
Algonkians: and fur trade, 23; lack of firearms, 41
Algonkin tribe, 23, 29, 30, 34, 35
Alien and Sedition Act (1794), 191
Allan, Sir Hugh, 345, 350, 356
Allen, Ethan, 163
Allouez, Father Claude, 62
Alverstone, Lord, and Alaska Boundary, 397
American Federation of Labour, 408
American Fur Company, 199
Amherst, General Sir Jeffrey: advance in 1760, 142; his Placard, 145
Ancaster Assizes, 206
Andastes, Iroquois war with, 58, 66, 69
Andros, Sir Edmund, Governor of New York, 79
Anglo-Japanese Treaty (1902), 430
Anglo-Russian Treaty (1825), 396
Angus, H. F., 470
Annand, William, and annexation, 331
Annapolis Royal, 101, 123
Annexation Manifesto (1849), 284
Anse au Foulon, stormed, 141-2
Anti-Confederation League, becomes Annexation League, 332
Anville, Duc d', attempts to recover Louisbourg, 122
Arcand, Adrien, Fascist leader, 462
Archibald, Adams G., 332; Lt.-Gov. of Manitoba, 336; and Riel, 344; and Indian Treaty No. 1, 351
Arctic Archipelago, transfer of, 360; exploration, 416-7
Argall, Samuel, and Port Royal, 31
Argenson, Pierre de Voyer, Comte d', Governor of New France, 51
Arnold, Benedict, invades Canada, 163-5; defeats Burgoyne, 168
Aroostook War, 257
Artaguette, Pierre d', and Chickasaw war, 116
Asbestos strike (1949), 500, 523
Asselin, Olivar, and *Le Devoir*, 407
Assiniboia: Selkirk's colony, 207; restored to Hudson's Bay Co., 219
Assiniboia, Territory of, 372, 403

B

Cartwright, Richard, and free trade, 355, 356; and commercial union, 377; and unrestricted reciprocity, 385; and internationalism, 389
Castors, les (ultramontanes), 371, 422
Cat Indians, attacked by Iroquois, 47; defeated, 63
Cataraqui, 68, 78, 79, 80. See also Fort Frontenac
Cathcart, Charles Murray, Earl, 268, 278
Cauchon, Joseph Edouard, 306
Caughnawaga, Iroquois mission at, 61
Cavell, Nik, 485
Cayley tariff (1858), 311
Cayugas, 79
Céloron de Blainville, 128
Cens et rentes, charge for tenure, 40
Centennial of Confederation, 541, 549
Chamberlain, Joseph, and fisheries commission, 375; Colonial Secretary, 395; and Boer War, 398; and imperial defence, 399
Chambly, a fortified post, 105
Champigny, Jean Bochart de: Intendant, 78; and attack on New York, 81; opposes negotiations with Iroquois, 84; and limiting of up-country trade, 86; and peace with Iroquois, 89
Champlain, Samuel de, 27-8; and fur trade of St. Lawrence, 29; obtains renewal of monopoly, 30; surrenders Quebec, 33; restored as governor, 34; dies, 36
Chanak affair, 441
Chapais, Thomas, historian, 454
Chapleau, Adolphe, and Mercier, 372; and French leadership, 387; refuses to re-enter ministry, 389, 390
Charlevoix, Father Pierre François-Xavier, and Sioux country, 110
Charlottetown Conference, 316
Chaste, Aymar, Sieur de, 27, 28
Château clique, 192
Chateauguay, Canadian victory, 206
Chauveau, P. J. O., Premier of Quebec, 357
Chauvin, Pierre, and monopoly of fur trade, 27-8
Cherry Valley, loyalist raid on, 169
Chesapeake, S. S., captured (1864), 317
Chesapeake, U.S.S., attacked by H.M.S. Leopard, 196
Chickasaws, at war with the French (from 1736), 116
China, Communist, 496, 528, 540
Chipewyans, 83
Chippawa, fighting at, 206
Christian Guardian, Methodist paper, 229; and election of 1844, 244

Christian Island, refuge of Hurons, 46
Churchill, Sir Winston, and the Chanak affair, 441; and planning of United Nations, 484; and Russian threat, 495
Churchill, post at, 83; trade at, 157; capture of, 170
Citizenship Act, 489, 548
Civil Service: 433, 470, 485; growth in war years, 487; adjustment after 1957, 513
Civil Service Act (1920), 433
Civil War, American: and Canadian neutrality, 313
Clarendon-Johnson Treaty, 339
Clark, George Rogers, captures Vincennes 169
Clarke, Sir Alured, Lieutenant-Governor of Lower Canada, 191
Clayton-Bulwer Treaty, abrogation of, 395
Clear Grits: extreme Reformers, 285; increase of, 292
Clergy Reserves, division of, 228; and Committee of 1828, 231; Thomson's Act, 256; imperial Act, 258; and voluntary principle, 288; and reform, 292; abolition, 293, 294, 295
Cobalt (Ont.), mineral discoveries, 394
Coderre, Louis, replaces Monk, 418
Colbert, Jean-Baptiste, 52, 54, 59, 62, 74
Colborne, Sir John, Lieutenant-Governor of Upper Canada, 243; crushes rebellion, 247
Coldwell, M. J., leader of C.C.F., 507
Colonial Advocate, 229
Colonial Conference of 1887, 389; of 1894, 389; of 1902, 399; of 1907, 406-7
Colonial Courts of Admiralty Act, 459
Colonial Laws Validity Act, 453, 459
Coltman, Colonel W. B., and inquiry into Red River troubles, 207
Columbia River power, 508, 522
Columbus, Christopher, 8, 9
Combines, Committee on (1887), 382
Commercial Revolution of 1846, and colonial democracy, 271; effects in Canada, 273; in Atlantic colonies, 276
Commercial Union, policy of, opposed to the National Policy, 347, 376
Commonwealth, beginning of, 424; rapid evolution of, 493; effect of Suez crisis on, 510; and European Common Market, 527-8
Commonwealth Air Training Plan, 475, 480
Commonwealth Conference of 1926, 453; of 1937, 472; of 1944, 484
Commonwealth Economic Conference of 1958, 514
Commonwealth Fellowships, 514
Compagnie des Habitants, 43, 49

D

E

Eastern Townships, and freehold tenure, 192; settled by New Englanders, 199; struggle over settlement, 206; and reforms, 231; and French settlement, 245

Ecclesiastical Chart, attacked by Ryerson, 228-9

Eden, Anthony, and Suez, 510

Edgar, James D., 351-2

Edward VIII, abdication of, 471

Egg Island, wreck of expedition (1711) on, 101

Election of 1844, 267

Election of 1847, 279-80

Election of 1857, 304, 308

Election of 1872, 344

Election of 1887, 373

Election of 1891, 385

Election of 1896, 390

Election of 1911, 412-13

Election of 1917, 427-8

Election of 1921, 435, 437, 439

Election of 1925, 450

Election of 1926, 452

Election of 1930, 458

Election of 1935, 464

Election of 1940, 476

Election of 1957, 509, 512-13

Election of 1958, 514-15

Election of 1962, 531-2

Election of 1963, 535

Election of 1965, 542-3

Election of 1968, 555-6

Elgin, James Bruce, 8th Earl of: career and character, 278; calls Lafontaine to form ministry, 280; and Rebellion Losses Bill, 282; belief in imperial connection and self-government, 284; retirement, 295

Elizabeth II, Queen, opens Parliament (1957), 494; visits Quebec, and Expo, 541, 550

Equal Rights Association, 379-80

Erie Canal, 222, 289

Eries, attacked by Iroquois, 47; defeated, 63

Eskimos, 5; and crisis of culture, 499, 546

Esquimalt, naval station at, 338, 361, 363

European Common Market, 514, 527-8

Ewart, J. S., and Canadian nationalism, 399; pamphleteer, 454

Expeditionary Force, planned, 419; dispatched (1914), 420

'Expo' 1967, 541, 549-50

External Affairs Department, created, 411

F

Fagundes, João Alvares, 13

Falaise Gap, closing of, 482

Falkland, Lord, Lieutenant-Governor of Nova Scotia, 277-8

Fallen Timbers, battle of, 189

Family Allowance Act, 488

Farmers, political action of, 432, 434-5, 449-50

Farmers' Platform, 422, 432

Farmers' Union (Manitoba, 1883), 366, 373

Farrer, Edward, and Commercial Union, 376; and James G. Blaine, 385; and pamphlet on American relations, 386

Fénelon, Abbé François, 68

Fenian Brotherhood, 322

Fenian raids, 323, 330, 341; compensation for, 343, 344; in Manitoba, 344

Ferguson, G. Howard, Premier of Ontario, 449; and constitutional amendment, 453; High Commissioner to United Kingdom, 461

Fergusson Blair, A. J., 315

Fernandez, João, 10

Fielding, W. S., and secession for Nova

Scotia, 364, 373; in Laurier's cabinet, 391; and 1922 budget, 442; and Liberals of Nova Scotia, 445; retirement, 449

Fielding tariff, 391

Filles du roi, immigration of, 60

Fils de la Liberté and Rebellion of 1837, 246-7

Fisheries, 12, 25, 109, 114-15; 148, 157-8, 161, 174, 186, 330, 374-5

Fisheries Award under Treaty of Washington, 354

Fisheries Convention (1818), 211; and reciprocity, 291; in force after reciprocity treaty, 340

Fisheries Treaty of 1887, defeated, 375

Five Nations. See Iroquois

Flag debate, 540-1

Fleming, Donald, 527-8, 531

Fleming, Sandford, 361

Flin Flon ore body, 394

Foley, M. H., in Taché ministry, 315

Forbes, Brigadier John, captures Fort Duquesne, 138

Fort Albany (Ste. Anne), recaptured and held by English, 84, 87; attacked (1711), 101

G

576 INDEX

Ghent, negotiations (1814) at, 206
Giffard, Dr. Robert, 40, 41, 60
Gilbert, Sir Humphrey, and colonization of Newfoundland, 26
"Ginger Group" in Parliament, 443
Gladman, George, 302
Glenelg, Lord: Colonial Secretary, 243; and Robert Baldwin, 244; and reform in Canada, 249
Glengarry Light Infantry, 204
Glenie, James, critic of New Brunswick oligarchy, 189
Globe, Toronto, founded, 292; and annexing of north-west, 302; and constitution on American model, 311; and commercial union, 376, 385
Godbout, Adélard, Quebec Liberal leader, 475; and Rowell-Sirois Report, 479
Gomez, Estevan, expedition of, 13
Gonor, Father Nicolas, and Sioux country, 110
Gordon, Sir Arthur, Lieutenant-Governor of New Brunswick: and Maritime union, 316; confident of Confederation, 320; dismisses Smith ministry, 323
Gordon, Charles W. ("Ralph Connor"), 409
Gordon, Walter L., 512, 537, 553
Gore, Sir Francis, Lieutenant-Governor of Upper Canada, 200
Gosford, Archibald Acheson, Earl of: Governor and Royal Commissioner, 243; set aside, 245; concentrates troops at Montreal, 246; recalled, 249
Gosford Commission Report, 243
Gouin, Sir Lomer, 440, 449
Gouin, Paul, 462
Gourlay, Robert, 219
Gowan, Ogle R., 241
Grain Growers' Associations, begun, 410-11
Grand Trunk Pacific Railway: settlement of strike (1910), 409; building along Skeena R.,

417; collapse, 426; bankruptcy, 433
Grand Trunk Railway: planning, 290; building, 296; financial embarrassment, 300; increasing difficulties, 305, 311-12; hostile to C.P.R., 365; suspect by government, 401; and the north-west, 402; taken over, 433
Grange, the: in Manitoba, 366; and government action, 383; in Ontario, 410
Grant, Cuthbert, and métis at Seven Oaks, 207
Grant, George (*Lament for a Nation*), 545
Granville, George Leveson Gower, Earl: Colonial Secretary, 334, 342
Gray, Robert, discovers Columbia R., 187
Great Northern Railway, 394
Great Western Railway, 289, 290
Green, Howard, 530
Greenland: Norse in, 5; trade, 7; decline of colony, 8
Greenway, Thomas, Premier of Manitoba, 378; and terms on School Question, 389
Grenville, William (later Lord Grenville), 182, 188
Grey, 3rd Earl: colonial reformer (as Lord Howick), 237; Colonial Secretary, 269; believer in colonial self-government, 277, 284; and colonial defence, 288; and Intercolonial Railway, 290
Griffon, La Salle's vessel, 69
Groseilliers, Médard Chouart, Sieur des, and flotilla of 1656, 51; and Hudson Bay, 64
Groulx, Abbé Lionel, 422, 440, 526
Group of Seven, paintings of, 454
Guadeloupe, 147
Guarantee Act of 1849 (railways), 289
Guercheville, Antoinette de Pons, Marquise de, 29
Guibord, Joseph, 357-8
Guigues, Louis, 94
Guthrie, Hugh, Conservative house leader, 456

H

Haldimand, Sir Frederick, Governor of Quebec, 171, 178, 179-80
Haldimand v. *Cochrane*, 180
Haliburton, R. G., 333
Haliburton, Thomas Chandler, 230
Halibut Fisheries Treaty (1923), 441
Halifax, Lord, and Nova Scotia, 127
Halifax, Nova Scotia: founded, 127; political and business centre, 215; naval base

maintained (1870), 342
Hamilton, Alvin, 520, 521, 527, 546
Hamilton, Henry, captured by the Americans, 169; Lieutenant-Governor of Quebec, 180
Hampshire, H.M.S., sunk by *Pélican*, 87
Hanson, R. B., Conservative house leader, 476, 486
Hare, John, expedition of, 13
Harkness, Douglas, 530, 533-4

I

J

M

N

O

P

Q

R

S

T

U

V

Vaillant, Father, and the Senecas, 96
Vancouver, Captain George, 187
Vancouver Festival, 504
Vancouver Island, Colony of, 281; united with British Columbia, 329
Van Horne, Sir William, and building of C.P.R., 362; and movement of troops, 369
Vanier, Georges, Governor General, 549
Vaudreuil, Philippe de Rigaud, Marquis de: commander of militia, 81; Governor of Montreal, 95; Acting Governor of New France, 96; Governor of New France, 100; and defence, 103, 108; and Abenakis, 105
Vaudreuil, Pierre de Rigaud, Marquis de: Governor of Louisiana, 128; Governor of New France, 133; and William Johnson, 134; and Montcalm, 136; saves army, 141; withdraws to France, 155
Verchères, Madeleine de, 85
Vergor, Louis Dupont Du Chambon de, surrenders Beauséjour, 135; surprised by Wolfe at Quebec, 140

Verrazano, Giovanni, 13
Vetch, Samuel, 100-101
Vichy, relations with, 479
Victoria, Queen: Golden Jubilee, 389; Diamond Jubilee, 395
Viger, D. B., 266, 279
Vignau, Nicolas, 30
Villebon, Joseph Robineau, Sieur de, and capture of Port Royal, 84
Villiers, Louis Coulon de, sent against George Washington, 130
Villiers, Nicolas Antoine Coulon de, attacks Annapolis Royal, 123
Vimy Ridge, captured, 422
Vincennes, Canadian village on Mississippi River, 169
Vincent, General John, 205
Visiting Forces (U.S.A.) Act, 486
Voltigeurs, Lower Canada militia, 204
Von Schoultz, Nils, 251
Voyageurs, replacing *coureurs de bois*, 96

W

Waggoner, Joseph, 128
Wakefield, Edward Gibbon, 250
Walkem, G. A., Premier of British Columbia, 352
Walker, Sir Hovenden, 101
Walley, Major John, 82
War of 1812, 202-6, 211
Warren, Commodore (Sir) Peter, and capture of Louisbourg, 122
Wartime Elections Act, 427; and Meighen, 434
Wartime Prices and Trade Board, 475
Washington, George: at Fort Le Boeuf, 130; and Nova Scotia, 166; plans invasion of Canada, 168
Washington Conference, 430
Washington Settlement (1922), 467
Watkin, Edward, and Grand Trunk Railway, 312
Watson, John, philosopher, 410, 454
Wayne, General Anthony, at Fallen Timbers, 189
Webster-Ashburton Treaty, 257, 268
Weekes, William, 200

Welfare state, growth of, 492, 546-7
Welland Canal begun, 222
Welland Ship Canal, 448
Wentworth, Sir John, Governor of Nova Scotia, 189
Westbrook, Andrew, 205
Western posts: retained, 173, 186; surrendered, 188
Western Sea, sought, 110, 113
Westminster Conference, 323
Wheat Board, set up (1917), 423; abolished, 435; re-established, 463; continued, 468, 501
Wheat economy: boom, 393; collapse of prices (1920-21), 435; recovery, 446; depression and drought, 457, 460; surplus, 501, 513
Wheat Pools, 446; and Progressives, 449; and depression, 458-9
Wilkins, Martin, and annexation, 331
Willcocks, Joseph, 200, 206
Willcocks, William, 200, 218
Willingdon, Viscount, Governor General, 471
Willis, Judge John Walpole, 230
Wilmot, Lemuel Allan, 245

PRINTED AND BOUND IN CANADA